Claudia Maienborn, Klaus von Heusinger and Paul Portner (Eds.)
Semantics – Lexical Structures and Adjectives

This volume is part of a larger set of handbooks to Semantics

1　　**Semantics: Foundations, History and Methods**
　　　Klaus von Heusinger, Claudia Maienborn, Paul Portner (eds.)

2　　**Semantics: Lexical Structures and Adjectives**
　　　Claudia Maienborn, Klaus von Heusinger, Paul Portner (eds.)

3　　**Semantics: Theories**
　　　Claudia Maienborn, Klaus von Heusinger, Paul Portner (eds.)

4　　**Semantics: Noun Phrases and Verb Phrases**
　　　Paul Portner, Klaus von Heusinger, Claudia Maienborn (eds.)

5　　**Semantics: Sentence and Information Structure**
　　　Paul Portner, Claudia Maienborn, Klaus von Heusinger (eds.)

6　　**Semantics: Interfaces**
　　　Claudia Maienborn, Klaus von Heusinger, Paul Portner (eds.)

7　　**Semantics: Typology, Diachrony and Processing**
　　　Klaus von Heusinger, Claudia Maienborn, Paul Portner (eds.)

Semantics
Lexical Structures and Adjectives

Edited by
Claudia Maienborn
Klaus von Heusinger
Paul Portner

DE GRUYTER
MOUTON

ISBN 978-3-11-062296-6
e-ISBN (PDF) 978-3-11-062639-1
e-ISBN (EPUB) 978-3-11-062313-0

Library of Congress Cataloging-in-Publication Data
Names: Maienborn, Claudia, editor. | Heusinger, Klaus von, editor. | Portner, Paul, editor.
Title: Semantics - lexical structures and adjectives / edited by Claudia Maienborn, Klaus von Heusinger, Paul Portner.
Description: Berlin ; Boston : De Gruyter, [2019] | Includes bibliographical references.
Identifiers: LCCN 2018041903 (print) | LCCN 2018050149 (ebook) | ISBN 9783110626391 (electronic Portable Document Format (pdf) | ISBN 9783110622966 | ISBN 9783110622966print) | ISBN 9783110626391e-book : | ISBN 9783110623130e-book :
Subjects: LCSH: Semantics. | Lexical grammar. | Grammar, Comparative and general--Adjective.
Classification: LCC P325 (ebook) | LCC P325 .S38137 2019 (print) | DDC 401/.43--dc23
LC record available at https://lccn.loc.gov/2018041903

Bibliographic information published by the Deutsche Nationalbibliothek
The Deutsche Nationalbibliothek lists this publication in the Deutsche Nationalbibliografie; detailed bibliographic data are available in the Internet at http://dnb.dnb.de.

© 2019 Walter de Gruyter GmbH, Berlin/Boston
Cover image: Goettingen / iStock / Getty Images Plus
Typesetting: Integra Software Services Pvt. Ltd.
Printing and binding: CPI books GmbH, Leck

www.degruyter.com

Contents

	Manfred Bierwisch	
1	**Semantic features and primes** —— 1	

	Stefan Engelberg	
2	**Frameworks of lexical decomposition of verbs** —— 47	

	Anthony R. Davis	
3	**Thematic roles** —— 99	

	Beth Levin and Malka Rappaport Hovav	
4	**Lexical Conceptual Structure** —— 126	

	Christiane Fellbaum	
5	**Idioms and collocations** —— 152	

	Ronnie Cann	
6	**Sense relations** —— 172	

	Sebastian Löbner	
7	**Dual oppositions in lexical meaning** —— 201	

	Christopher Kennedy	
8	**Ambiguity and vagueness: An overview** —— 236	

	Markus Egg	
9	**Semantic underspecification** —— 272	

	Henriëtte de Swart	
10	**Mismatches and coercion** —— 321	

	Andrea Tyler and Hiroshi Takahashi	
11	**Metaphors and metonymies** —— 350	

	Violeta Demonte	
12	**Adjectives** —— 381	

Sigrid Beck
13 **Comparison constructions** —— 415

Claudia Maienborn and Martin Schäfer
14 **Adverbs and adverbials** —— 477

Kjell Johan Sæbø
15 **Adverbial clauses** —— 515

Susan Rothstein
16 **Secondary predicates** —— 543

Index —— 569

Manfred Bierwisch
1 Semantic features and primes

1   Introduction —— 1
2   Background assumptions —— 3
3   The form of semantic features —— 5
4   Semantic aspects of morpho-syntactic features —— 13
5   Interpretation of semantic features —— 22
6   Kinds of elements —— 29
7   Primes and universals —— 38
8   References —— 44

Abstract: Semantic features or primes, like phonetic and morpho-syntactic features, are usually considered as basic elements from which the structure of linguistic expressions is built up. Only a small set of semantic features seems to be uncontroversial, however. In this article, semantic primes are considered as basic elements of Semantic Form, the interface level between linguistic expressions and the full range of mental structures representing the content to be expressed. Semantic primes are not just features, but elements of a functor-argument-structure, on which the internal organization of lexical items and their combinatorial properties, including their Thematic Roles, is based. Three types of semantic primes are distinguished: Systematic elements, that are related to morpho-syntactic conditions like tense or causativity; idiosyncratic features, not corresponding to grammatical distinctions, but likely to manifest primitive conceptual conditions like color or taste; and a large range of elements called dossiers, which correspond to hybrid mental configurations, integrating varying modalities, but providing unified conceptual entities. (Idiosyncratic features and dossiers together account for what is sometimes called distinguishers or completers.) A restricted subsystem of semantic primes can reasonably be assumed to be directly fixed by Universal Grammar, while the majority of semantic primes is presumably due to general principles of mental organization and triggered by experience.

1 Introduction

The concept of semantic features, although frequently used in pertinent discussion, is actually in need of clarification with respect to both of its components. The term

---

Manfred Bierwisch, Berlin, Germany

https://doi.org/10.1515/9783110626391-001

feature, referring in ordinary discourse to a prominent or distinctive aspect, quality or characteristic of something, became a technical term in the structural linguistics of the 1930s, primarily in phonology, where it identified the linguistically relevant properties as opposed to other aspects of sound shape. The systematic extension of the concept from phonology to other components of linguistic structure led to a wide variety of terms with similar but not generally identical interpretation, including *component, category, atom, feature value, attribute, primitive element* and a number of others. The qualification *semantic*, which competes with a smaller number of alternatives, *conceptual* being one of them, is not less in need of elucidation though, depending among others on the delimitation of the relevant domains, including syntactic, semantic, conceptual, discourse and pragmatic structure, and the intricate distinction between linguistic and encyclopedic knowledge. In what follows, I will use the term *semantic feature* in the sense of basic component of linguistic meaning, adding amendments and changes, where necessary.

Different approaches and theoretical frameworks of linguistic analysis recognized the need for an overall concept of basic elements in terms of which linguistic phenomena are to be analyzed. Hjelmslev (1938) for instance based his theory of Glossematics on the assumption that linguistic expressions are made up of ultimate, irreducible invariants called *glossemes*. Following the Saussurean view of content and expression as the interdependent planes of linguistic structure, he furthermore distinguished *kenemes* and *pleremes* as the glossemes of the expression and the content plane, respectively. A recent and rather different case in point is the Minimalist Program discussed in Chomsky (1995, 2000), where Universal Grammar is assumed to make available "a set **F** of features (linguistic properties) and operations C_{HL} (the computational procedure for human language) that access **F** to generate expressions", which are pairs ⟨PF, LF⟩ of Phonetic Form and Logical Form, determining the sound shape and the meaning of linguistic expressions.

The general notion of features as primitive components constituting the structure of language must not obscure the fundamental differences between basic elements of the phonetic, morphological, syntactic and semantic aspect of linguistic expressions. On the phonetic side, the nature of distinctive features as properties of segments and perhaps syllables is fairly clear in principle and subject to dispute only with respect to interesting detail. The nature and role of primitive elements on the semantic side however is subject to problems that are unsolved in crucial respects. A number of questions immediately arise:

(1) a. What is the formal character of basic semantic elements?
　　b. Can linguistic meaning be exhaustively reduced to semantic features?
　　c. Is there a fixed set of semantic features?
　　d. What is the origin and interpretation of semantic features?

Any attempt to deal with these questions must obviously rely on general assumptions about the framework which at least makes it possible to formulate the problems.

2 Background assumptions

An indispensable assumption of all approaches concerns the fact that a natural language L provides a sound-meaning correspondence, relating an unlimited range of signals to an equally unlimited range of objects, situations, and conditions the expressions are about. What linguistics is concerned with, however, is neither the set of signals nor the range of things they are about, but rather the invariant patterns on which the production and recognition of signals is based and the distinctions, in terms of which things and situations are experienced, organized or imagined and related to the linguistic expressions. Schematically, these general assumptions can be represented as in (2), where PF and SF (for Phonetic Form and Semantic Form, respectively) indicate the structure of the sound shape and meaning, with A-P (for Articulation and Perception) and C-I (for Conceptualization and Intention) abbreviating the complex mental systems by which linguistic expressions are realized and related to their intended interpretations. Although I will comply with general terminology as far as possible, tension cannot always be avoided. Thus, the Semantic Form SF corresponds in many respects to the Logical Form LF of Chomsky (1986 and subsequent work), to the Conceptual Structure CS of Jackendoff (1984 and later work), and to the Discourse Representation Structure DRS of Kamp and Reyle (1993), to mention just a few comparable approaches. (cf. also article 4 [Semantics: Theories] (Jackendoff) *Conceptual Semantics*, article 5 [Semantics: Theories] (Lang & Maienborn) *Two-level Semantics* and article 11 [Semantics: Theories] (Kamp & Reyle) *Discourse Representation Theory*).

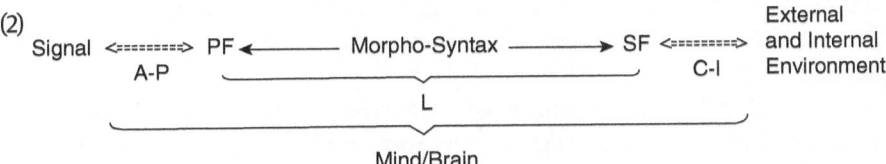

This schema is a simplification in several respects, but it enables us to fix a number of relevant points. First, PF and SF represent the conditions that L imposes on or extracts from extra-linguistic systems. Hence PF and SF are what is often called interfaces, by which language interacts with other mental systems, abridged here as A-P and C-I. Semantic and phonetic features can now be identified as the primitive elements of SF and PF, respectively. Hence their formal and substantive nature is determined by the character and role of these interfaces.

Second, the function of language, to systematically assign meaning to signals, is accomplished by the component indicated here as Morpho-Syntax, which establishes the connection between PF and SF. For obvious reasons, the rules and principles of Morpho-Syntax are the primary concern of all pertinent theories, which in spite of differences that will not be dealt with here agree on the observation that the relation between PF and SF depends on the lexical system LS of L and is organized by rules and principles which make up the Grammar G of L. The content of Morpho-Syntax is relevant in the present context to the extent to which it relies on morphological and syntactic features that relate to features of SF.

Third, according to (2), PF and SF and their primes are abstract in the sense that they do not reflect properties of the signal or the external world directly, but represent the units and configurations in terms of which the mental mechanisms of P-A and C-I perceive or organize external phenomena. Features of PF should according to Halle (1983) most plausibly be construed as instructions for vocal gestures in terms of which speech sounds are articulated and perceived. In a similar vein, features of SF must be construed not as elements of the external reality, but as conditions according to which elements, properties, and situations are experienced or construed. Hence semantic features as components of SF require an essentially mentalistic approach to meaning. This is clearly at variance with various theories of meaning, among them in particular versions of formal or model theoretic semantics like, e.g., Lewis (1972) or Montague (1974), which consider semantics as the relation of linguistic expressions to strictly non-mental, external entities and conditions. It should be emphasized, though, that the mentalistic view underlying (2) does not deny external objects and their properties, corresponding to structures in SF under appropriate conditions. The crucial point is that it is the mental organization of C-I which provides the correspondence to the external reality – if the correspondence actually obtains. Analogous considerations apply, by the way, to PF and its relation to the external signal. For further discussion of these matters and the present position see, e.g., Jackendoff (2002, chapter 10).

It must finally be noted that the symmetrical status of PF and SF suggested in (2) is in need of modification in order to account for the fundamental differences between the two interfaces. While the mechanisms of A-P, which PF has access to, constitute a complex but highly specialized mental system, the range of capacities abbreviated as C-I is not restricted in any comparable way. As a matter of fact, SF has access to the whole range of perceptual modalities, spatial orientation, motor control, conceptual organization, and social interaction, in short: to all aspects of experience. This is not merely a quantitative difference in diversity, size, and complexity of the domains covered, it raises problems for the very status of SF as interface, as we will see. In any case, essential differences concerning the nature of basic elements and their combination in PF and SF have to be recognized.

Two remarks must be added about the items of the lexical system LS. First, whether elements like *killed, left, rose,* or *went* are registered in LS as possibly complex but nevertheless fixed lexical items or are derived by morphological rules of G from the underlying elements *kill, leave, rise, go* plus abstract morphemes for *Person, Number,* and *Tense* is a matter of dispute with different answers in different theories. In any case, regular components like *kill* and *-ed* as well as idiosyncratic conditions holding for *left, rose,* and *went* need to be captured, and it must be acknowledged that the items in question consist of component parts. This is related to, but different from, the question whether basic lexical items like *kill, leave,* or *go* are themselves complex structures. As to PF, the analysis of words into segments and features is obvious, but for SF their decomposition is a matter of debate, to which we will return in more detail, claiming that lexical items are semantically complex in ways that clearly bear on the nature of semantic features.

The second remark concerns the question whether and to what extent rules and principles of G determine the internal structure of lexical items and of the complex expressions made up of them. Elements of LS are stored in long-term memory and thus plausibly assumed to be subject to conditions that differ from those of complex expressions. Surprisingly, though, the character of features and their combination at least seems to be the same within and across lexical items, as we will see.

As to notation, I will adopt the following standard conventions: Features of PF will be enclosed in square brackets like [+ nasal], [– voiced], etc.; morphological and syntactic features are enclosed in square brackets and marked by initial capitals like [+ Past], [– Plural], [+ Nominal], etc.; and semantic features are given in small capitals, like [HUMAN], [MALE], [CAUSE].

3 The form of semantic features

3.1 Features in phonology and morpho-syntax

It is useful to first consider the primitive elements of the phonetic side, where the conditions determining their formal character are fairly clear. PF is based on sequentially organized segments, which represent abstract time slots corresponding to the temporal structure of the phonetic signal. Now features are properties of segments, i.e. one-place predicates specifying articulatory (and perceptual) conditions on temporal units. The predicates either do or do not apply to a given segment, whence basic elements of PF are mostly conceived as binary features. Thus, a feature combination like [+ nasal, + labial, + voiced] would specify a segment by means of the simultaneous articulatory conditions indicated as *nasal, labial,* and *voiced*. Systematic consequences and extensions of these conditions need to be added, such as the difference between presence and absence of a property, marked by the plus- and minus-value of the features leading to the markedness-asymmetry in Chomsky & Halle (1968). Further extensions include relations between features in the feature geometry of Clements (1985), the predictability of unspecified features, the supra-segmental properties of stress and intonation in Halle & Vergnaud (1987), and the arrangement of segmental properties along different tiers, leading to three-dimensional representations, to mention the more obvious extensions of PF.

These extensions, however, do not affect the basic conditions on phonetic features, which can be summarized as follows:

(3) Phonetic features are
   a. binary one-place predicates, represented as [± F];
   b. simultaneous conditions on sequentially connected segments (or syllables);
   c. interpreted as instructions on the mechanisms in A-P.

Some of the considerations supporting distinctive features in phonology have also been applied to syntax and morphology. Thus in Jakobson (1936), Hjelmslev (1938), or Bierwisch (1967) categories like Case, Number, Gender, or Person are characterized in terms of binary features. Similarly, Chomsky (1970) reduced categories like Noun, Verb, Adjective, and their projections Noun Phrase etc. to binary syntactic features. While features of this kind are one-place predicates and thus in line with condition (3a), they clearly don't meet condition (3b): morphological and syntactic features are not conditions on segments of PF connected by sequential ordering, but on lexical and syntactic units, which are related by syntactic conditions like dominance or constituency according to the morpho-syntactic rules of G. The most controversial aspect of morpho-syntactic features is their interpretation analogously to (3c). As these features do not belong to PF or SF directly, but are essentially elements of the mediation between PF and SF, they can only indirectly participate in the interface structures and their interpretation. But they do affect PF as well as SF, although in rather different ways. As to PF, morphological features determine the choice of segments or features by means of inflectional rules like (4), where / – d / abbreviates the features identifying the past tense suffix *d* in cases like *climbed, rolled,* etc.

(4) [+ Past] → / – d /

Actual systems of rules are more complex, taking into account intricate dependencies between different categories, features, and syntactic conditions. For systematic accounts of these matters see e.g., Bierwisch (1967), Halle & Marantz (1993), or Wunderlich (1997a). In any case, morphological or syntactic features are not part of PF, but can only influence its content via particular grammatical rules.

As to SF, it is often assumed that features of morphological categories like tense or number are subject to direct conceptual interpretation, alongside with other semantic elements, and are therefore considered as a particular type of semantic features. This was the position of Jakobson (1936), Hjelmslev (1938), and related work of early structuralism, where in fact no principled distinction between morphological and semantic features was made, supporting the notion of semantic primes as binary features. This view cannot be generally upheld for various reasons, however. To be sure, a feature like [+ Past] has a more stable and motivated relation to the temporal condition attached to it than to its various phonetic realizations e.g., in *rolled, left, went,* or *was,* still there is no reasonable way to treat morphological or syntactic features as elements of SF, as will be discussed in section 4.

3.2 Features and types

Turning to the actual elements of SF, we notice that they differ from the features of PF in crucial respects. To begin with, condition (3a), according to which features are binary one-place predicates, seems to be satisfied by apparently well-established ordinary predicates like [MALE], [ALIVE] or [OPEN]. There are, however, equally well-established elements like [PARENT-OF], [PART-OF], [PERCEIVE], [BEFORE], or [CAUSE], representing relations or functions of a different type, which clearly violate this condition. More generally, SF must be based on an overall system of types integrating the different kinds of properties, relations, and operators. This leads directly to condition (3b), concerning the overall organization of PF in terms of sequentially ordered segments. It should be obvious that SF cannot rely on this sort of organization: it does neither consist of segments, nor does it exhibit linear ordering. Whatever components one might identify in the meaning of e.g., *nobody arrived in time,* or *he needs to know it,* or any other expression, there is no temporal or other sequential ordering among them, neither for the meaning of words nor their components. Although semantic processing in comprehension and production does of course have temporal characteristics, they do not belong to the resulting structure of meaning, in contrast to the linear structure related to phonetic processing. See Bierwisch & Schreuder (1992) for further discussion of this point.

Hence SF is organized according to other conditions, which naturally follow from the type system just mentioned: Elements of SF, including in particular its primitive elements, are connected by the functor-argument relation based on the type-structure of the elements being combined. Notice that this is the minimal assumption to be made, just like the linear organization of PF, with no arbitrary stipulations. We now have the following conditions on semantic features, corresponding to the conditions (3a) and (3b) on the phonetic side:

(5) Semantic elements, including irreducible features, are
 a. members of types determining their combinatorial conditions;
 b. participants of type-based hierarchical functor-argument structures.

These are just two interdependent aspects of the general organization of linguistic meaning, which is, by the way, the counterpart of linear concatenation of segments in PF. There are various notational proposals to make these conditions explicit, usually extending or adapting basic conventions of predicate logic. The following considerations seem to be indispensable in order to meet the requirements in (5). First, each element of SF must belong to some specific type; second, if the element is a functor, its type determines two things: (a) the type of the elements it combines with, and (b) the type the resulting combination belongs to. Thus functor-types must be of the general form $\langle \alpha, \beta \rangle$, where α is the type of the required argument, and β that of the resulting complex. This kind of type-structure was introduced in Ajdukiewicz (1935) in a related but different context, and has since been adapted in various notational ways by Lewis (1972), Cresswell (1973), Montague (1974), to mention just a few; cf. also article 8 [Semantics: Interfaces] (de Hoop) *Type shifting*.

Following standard assumptions, at least two basic types are to be recognized: e (for entity, i.e. objects in the widest sense) and t (for truth-value bearer, roughly propositions or situations). From these basic types, functor types like $\langle e,t \rangle$ and $\langle e,\langle e,t \rangle \rangle$ for one- and two-place predicates, $\langle t,t \rangle$ and $\langle t,\langle t,t \rangle \rangle$ for one- and two-place propositional functions, etc. are built up. To summarize:

(6) Elements of SF belong to types, where
 a. e and t are basic types.
 b. if α and β are types, then $\langle \alpha, \beta \rangle$ is a type.

A crucial point to be added is the possibility of empty slots, i.e. positions to be filled in by way of the syntactic combination of lexical items with the complements they admit or require. Empty slots are plausibly represented as variables, which are assigned to types like elements of SF in general. The kind of resulting structure is illustrated in (6) by an example adapted from Jackendoff (1990: 46), representing the SF of the verb *enter* in three notational variants, indicating the relevant hierarchy of types by a labeled tree (7a), and the corresponding labeled bracketing in (7b) and (7c):

(7) a.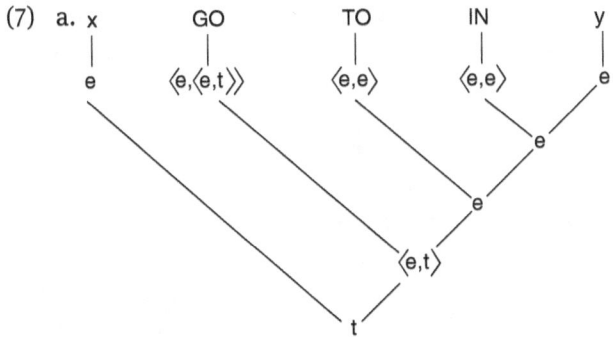

b. $[_t [_e x] [_{(e,t)} [[_{(e,(e,t))} \text{GO}] [_e [_{(e,e)} \text{TO}] [_e [_{(e,e)} \text{IN}] [_e y]]]]]$

c. $[_t [_{(e,t)} [[_{(e,(e,t))} \text{GO}] [_e [_{(e,e)} \text{TO}] [_e[_{(e,e)} \text{IN}] [_e y]]] [_e x]]$

While (7b) simply projects the tree branching of (7a) into the equivalent labeled bracketing, (7c) follows the so-called Polish notation, where functors systematically precede their arguments. This becomes more obvious if the type-indices are dropped, as in: [GO [TO [IN y]]x]. Notice, however, that in all three cases the linear ordering is theoretically irrelevant. What counts is only the functor-argument-relation. For the sake of illustration, GO, TO, and IN are assumed to be primitive constants of SF with more or less obvious interpretation: IN is a function that picks up the interior region of its argument, TO turns its argument into the end of a path, and GO specifies the motion of its "higher" or external argument along the path indicated by its "lower" or internal argument.

Jackendoff's actual treatment of this example is given in (8a), with the equivalent tree representation (8b). In spite of a gross similarity between (7) and (8), a different conception of the combinatorial type system seems to be involved.

(8) (a)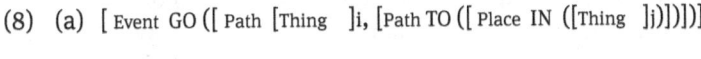

(b)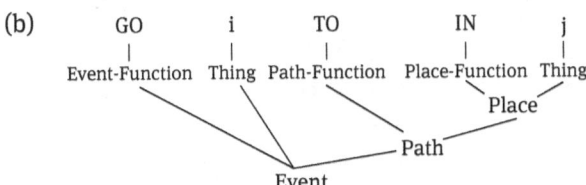

Putting minor notational details aside (such as Jackendoff's notation [X([Y])] to indicate that a component [Y] is the argument of a functor X, or his use of indices i and j instead of variables x and y to identify the relevant slots), the main difference between (7) and (8) consists in the general attachment of substantive content to type nodes in (8), in contrast to the minimal conditions assumed in (7), where types merely determine the combinatorial aspect of their elements. Thus [IN [Y]] in (7) is of the same type e as the variable y, while its counterpart [IN [j]] in (8) is assigned to the type Place, differing from the type Thing of the variable [j]. It is not obvious whether the differences between (7) and (8) have any empirical consequences, after stripping away notational redundancies by which e.g., the functor Path-Function generates a complex of type Path, or the Place-Function a Place without specifying substantial information. With respect to the form of semantic features, however, the two systems can be taken as largely equivalent versions, together with a fair number of further alternatives, including Miller & Johnson-Laird (1976), Kamp & Reyle (1993), and to some extent Dowty (1979), to mention some well-known proposals. Katz (1972) pursues similar goals by means of a somewhat clumsy and mixed notational system.

3.3 SF and argument structure

One of the central consequences emerging from the systems exemplified in (7) and (8) is the account of combinatorial properties of lexical items, especially the selection restrictions they give rise to. Although a systematic survey of these matters would go far beyond the concern for the nature of semantic features, at least the following points must be made. First, as already mentioned, variables like x and y in (7) determine the conditions syntactic complements have to meet semantically, as their SF has to be compatible with the position of the corresponding variables. Second, the position the variables occupy within the hierarchy of a lexical item's SF determines to a large extent the syntactic conditions that the complements in question must meet. What is at issue here is the semantic underpinning of what is usually called the *argument structure* of a lexical item. As Jackendoff (1990: 48) puts it, "argument structure can be thought of as an abbreviation for the part of conceptual structure that is "visible" to syntax." There are various ways in which parts of SF can be made accessible to syntax. Jackendoff (1990) relies on coindexing of semantic slots with syntactic subcategorization, Bierwisch (1996) and Wunderlich (1997b) extend the type system underlying (8) by standard lambda operators, as illustrated in (9) for *open*, where the features [+V(erbal), -N(ominal)] identify the entry's morpho-syntactic categorization, and ACT, CAUSE, BECOME, and OPEN make up its semantic form:

(9) / open / ; [+ V, –N] ;
 λy λx [$_t$ [$_t$ [$_{(e,t)}$ ACT] [$_e$ x]] [$_{(t,t)}$ [$_{(t,(t,t))}$ CAUSE] [$_t$ [$_{(t,t)}$ BECOME] [$_t$ [$_{(e,t)}$ OPEN] [$_e$ y]]]]]

λy and λx mark the argument positions for object and subject, respectively, defining in this way the semantic selection restrictions the complements are subject to. It is worth noting, incidentally, that these operators in some way correspond to the functional categories Agr$_o$ and Agr$_s$ assumed in Chomsky (1995 and related work) to relate the verb to its complements. In spite of relevant similarities, though, there are important differences that can not be pursued here. Representations like (9) also provide a plausible account for the way in which the transitive and intransitive variants of *open* and other "(un)ergative" verbs like *close, change, break* etc. are related: The intransitive version is derived by dropping the causative elements [ACT x] and [CAUSE] and the operator λx, turning λy into the subject position:

(10) / open / ; [+ V, –N] ;   λy [$_t$[$_{(t,t)}$ BECOME] [$_t$[$_{(e,t)}$ OPEN] [$_e$ y]]]

These observations elucidate how syntactic properties of lexical items are routed in configurations of their SF, determining thereby the semantic effect of the syntactic head-complement-construction.

3.4 Extensions

The principles exemplified in (7) to (10) provide the skeleton of SF, determining the form of semantic features, the structure of meaning of lexical items and complex expressions. They do not account for all aspects of linguistically determined meaning, though, but must be augmented with respect to phenomena like shift or continuation of reference, topic-focus-articulation, presupposition, illocutionary force, and discourse relations. To capture these facts, Jackendoff (1990, 2002) enriched semantic representations by distinguishing a referential tier and information structure from the descriptive tier. Similar ideas are pursued in Kamp & Reyle (1993), where a referential "universe of discourse" is distinguished from proper semantic representation, which in Kamp (2001) is furthermore split up into a descriptive and a presuppositional component. Distinctions of this type do not affect the nature of basic semantic components, which they necessarily rely on. Hence we need not go into the details of these extensions. We only mention that components like BECOME involve presuppositions, as observed in Bierwisch (2010), or that the extensively discussed definiteness operator DEF depends on the universe of discourse.

Two further points must be added to this exposition, both of which show up in ordinary nouns like *bottle*, characterized by the following highly provisional lexical entry:

(11) / bottle /; [−V, +N] ; λx [[PHYSICAL x] [ARTIFACT x] [CONTAINER x] [BOTTLE x]]

The first point concerns the role of standard classificatory features like [PHYSICAL] [OBJECT], [ARTIFACT], [FURNITURE], [CONTAINER], etc, which are actually the root of the notion feature, descending from the venerable tradition of analyzing concepts in terms of *genus proximum* and *differentia specifica*. Although natural concepts of objects or any other sort of entities obviously do not comply with orderly hierarchies of classification, the logical relations and the (at least partial) taxonomies that classificatory features give rise to clearly play a fundamental role in conceptual structure and lexical meaning. Entries like (11) indicate how these conditions are reflected in SF: Features like [PERSON], [ARTIFACT], [PHYSICAL] etc. are elements of type ⟨e,t⟩, i.e. properties that classify the argument they apply to. Different conditions that jointly characterize an object x, e.g. as a bottle, must according to the general structure of SF make up an integrated unit of a resulting common type. Intuitively, the four conditions in (11), which are all propositions of type t, are connected by logical conjunction, yielding a complex proposition, again of type t. This can be made explicit by means of an (independently needed) propositional functor & of type ⟨t,⟨t,t⟩⟩, which turns two propositions into simultaneous conditions of one complex proposition. It might be noted that & is asymmetrical, in line with the general definition of functor types in (6b), according to which a functor takes exactly one argument, such that two-place functors combine with their arguments in two hierarchical steps. This is due to the lack of linear order in SF, by which the relation between elements becomes structurally asymmetrical. In case of conjunction, which is generally assumed to be symmetrical with regard to the conjuncts, this asymmetry might to some extent correspond to the specificity of conditions, such that the SF of (11) would come out as (12):

(12) λ x [[PHYSICAL x] [& [ARTIFACT x] [& [CONTAINER x] [& [BOTTLE x]]]]]

Thus [& [CONTAINER x] [& [BOTTLE x]]] is the more specific condition added to the condition [ARTIFACT x]. Whether this is in fact the appropriate way to reflect hierarchical classification must be left open, especially as there are innumerable cases of joint conditions that do not make up hierarchies but reflect properties of cross-classification or just incidental combinations of conditions, differences the asymmetry of & cannot reflect. It might be added that various proposals have been made to formally represent joint conditions within lexical items as well as in standard types of adverbial or adnominal modification like *little, green bottle* or *walk slowly through the garden*.

The second point to be added concerns elements like [BOTTLE], whose status is problematic and characteristic in various respects. On the one hand, standard dictionary definitions of *bottle* like *with a narrow neck, usually made of glass* suggest that [BOTTLE] is a heuristic abbreviation to be replaced by a more systematic analysis, turning it into a complex condition consisting of proper elementary features. On the other hand, any further analysis might run into problems that cannot reasonably be captured in SF. Thus even if the conditions indicated by *narrow neck* could be accounted for by appropriate basic elements, it is unclear whether the features of *neck*, designating the body-part connecting head and shoulders, can be used in *bottle*, without creating a vicious circle, which requires *bottle* to identify the right sort of neck. What is important here is not a matter of particular detail, but a kind of problem which shows up in innumerable places and in fact marks the limits of semantic structure. The issue has been treated in different ways. Laurence & Margolis (1999) appropriately called it "the problem of Completers", dealing with the residue of systematic analysis. It will be taken up below, cf. also article 6 [Semantics: Theories] (Hobbs) *Word meaning and world knowledge*.

Features of PF and SF were compared in §3.2. with respect to form and combination, but not with respect to their interpretation, which for PF according to condition (3c) consists in instructions on mechanisms in A-P. A straightforward counterpart for SF would consider its basic elements as conditions on mechanisms of C-I. This analogy, apparently suggested in schema (1), would be misleading for various reasons, though. The size of the repertoire, the diversity of the involved components of C-I, and the status of SF as interface all raise problems wildly differing from those of PF. The subsequent sections deal with the conditions on interpretation of semantic features in more detail. Distinctions between at least three kinds of basic elements will have to be made, not only because of the ambivalent status of the completers just mentioned.

4 Semantic aspects of morpho-syntactic features

4.1 Interpretability of features and feature instances

The semantic aspect of morphological and syntactic categories is a matter of continuous debate. As already mentioned, morphological features specifying categories like Case, Number, Gender, Tense etc. were considered by Jakobson,

Hjelmslev, and others as grammatical elements with essentially semantic content, independently of the PF-realization assigned to them by rules like (4). We cannot deal here with the interesting results of these approaches in any detail. It must be noted, however, that the insights into conceptual aspects of morphological categories were never incorporated into systematic and coherent semantic representations, their integration was left to common sense understanding – mainly because appropriate frameworks of semantic representation were not available.

To account for conceptual aspects of morpho-syntactic features, two important distinctions must be recognized. First, two different roles of feature instances are to be distinguished, which might be called "dominant" and "subdominant", for lack of better terms. Dominant instances are essentially elements that categorize the expression they belong to, subdominant instances are conditions on participants of various syntactic relations including selection of complements, agreement, and concord. Thus the pronoun *her* is categorized by the dominant features [+Feminine, −Plural, +Accusative], among others, while prepositions like *with* or verbs like *know* specify their selection restriction by subdominant instances of the feature [+Accusative]. Similarly, the proper name *John* is categorized by the dominant features [+N, + 3.Person, −Plural], while the (inflected) verb *knows* has the subdominant features [+ 3.Person, −Plural]. The intricate details of the relevant morpho-syntactic relations and the technicalities of their formal treatment are notoriously complex and cannot be dealt with here. We merely note that different feature instances are decisive in mediating the relation between PF and SF. The crucial point is that subdominant feature instances have no semantic interpretation, neither in selection restrictions nor as conditions in agreement or concord. Thus, in a case like *these boys knew her*, the feature [+Plural] of *boys*, the feature [+Past] in *knew*, and the feature [+ Feminine] in *her* can participate in semantic interpretation, but the feature [+Plural] of *these* or the Number- and Person-features of the verb cannot.

The second distinction to be made concerns the interpretability of dominant feature instances. Three possibilities have to be recognized: First, features that have a constant interpretation, with all dominant instances determining a fixed semantic effect, second, features with a conditional interpretation, subject to different interpretations under different circumstances, and third, features with no interpretation, whether dominant or not. Clear cases of the first type are Tense and Person, whose interpretation is invariant. Gender and Number in many languages are examples of the second type. Thus [+Plural] has a clear conceptual effect in nouns like *boys*, *nails*, *clouds*, or *women*, which it doesn't have in *scissors*, *glasses* or *trousers*, and [+ Feminine] is semantically vacuous in the case of nouns designating ships. The paradigm case of the third type is structural Case. Lack of conceptual content holds even for instances where a clear semantic effect seems to be related to Case-distinctions, such as the contrast between German Dative and Accusative in locative *auf dem Dach* (on the roof) vs. directional *auf das Dach* (onto the roof), because the contrast is actually due to the SF of the preposition, not the dominant Case of its object, as shown in Bierwisch (1997). We will return to abstract Case shortly; see also article 2 [Semantics: Interfaces] (Kiparsky & Tonhauser) *Semantics of inflection*.

This three-way-distinction is realized quite differently in different languages. A particularly intriguing case in point is Gender in German, which has dominant instances in the categorization of all nouns. Now, the feature [+Feminine] corresponds to the concept female in cases like *Frau* (woman) *Schwester* (sister), but has no interpretation in the majority of inanimate nouns like *Zeit* (time), *Brücke* (bridge), *Wut* (rage), many of which inherit the feature [+Feminine] from derivational suffixes like *-t*, *-ung*, *-heit*, as in *Fahr-t* (drive), *Wirk-ung* (effect), *Dummheit* (stupidity), etc. Moreover, some nouns like *Weib* (woman) or *Mädchen* (girl) are categorized as [-Feminine], irrespective of their SF. Even more intricate are [+Feminine]-cases like *Katze* (cat), *Ratte* (rat), which designate either the species (without specified sex) or the female animal. Further complications come with nouns like *Person* (person) with the feature [+ Feminine], which are animate and may or may not be female.

Three conclusions follow from these observations: First, morpho-syntactic features must be distinguished from their possible semantic impact, because these features some-times do, sometimes do not have a conceptual interpretation. Second, the relation between morpho-syntactic features and elements of SF, which mediate the conceptual content, must be determined by conditions comparable to those sketched in (4) relating morphological features to PF, even if the source and the content of the conditions is remarkably different. Third, the relation of morphological features to SF must be conditional, applying to dominant instances depending on sometimes rather special morphological or semantic circumstances.

4.2 The interpretation of morphological features

Morpho-syntactic features are binary conditions of the computational system that accounts for the combinatorial matching of PF and SF. The semantic value corresponding to these features consists of elements of the functor-argument-structure of SF. Hence the conditions that capture this correspondence must correlate elements and configurations of two systems, both of which are subject to their respective principles. (13) illustrates the point for the feature [+Past] occurring, e.g., in *the door opened* indicating that an utterance u of this sentence denotes an event s the time T of which precedes the time T of u, where T is a functor of type ⟨e,e⟩ and BEFORE a relation of type ⟨e,⟨e,t⟩⟩ :

(13)   [+Past] ↔ [T s] [BEFORE [T u]]

This is a simplification which does not reflect the complex details discussed in the huge literature about temporal relations, but (13) should indicate in principle how the feature [+Past], syntactically categorizing the verb (or whatever one's syntactic theory requires), can contribute to meaning. More specifically, most semantic analyses agree that tense information applies to events instantiating in one way or another the propositional condition specified by the verb and its complements. With this proviso, we get (14) as the SF of *the door opened*, if we expand (10) by the event-instantiation expressed by the operator INST of type ⟨t,⟨e,t⟩⟩.

(14)   [[T s [BEFORE [T u]]] & [s [INST [BECOME [OPEN [DEF x [DOOR x]]]]]]]

As [+Past] has a constant interpretation in English, (13) needs no restricting condition: Instances of [+Past] are always subject to (13). It might be considered as a kind of lexical entry for [+Past] which applies to all occurrences of the feature, whether its morpho-phonological realization is regular or idiosyncratic. There are further non-trivial questions related to conditions like (13). One concerns the appropriate choice of the event argument s, which obviously depends on the "scope" of [+Past], i.e. the constituent it categorizes. Another one is the question what (13) means for the interpretation of [−Past], i.e. morphological present tense. One option is to take [−Past] to determine the negation NOT [T s [BEFORE T u]]. A more general strategy would consider [−Past] as the unmarked case, which is semantically unspecified and simply doesn't determine a temporal position of the event s. These issues concerning the conceptual effect of morphological categories are highly controversial and need further clarification.

Conditional interpretation of morphological features is exemplified by [+Plural] in (15), where [COLLECTION] of type ⟨e,t⟩ must be construed as imposing the condition that its argument consists of elements of equal kind, rather than being a set in the sense of set theory, since the denotation of a plural NP like *these students* is of the same type as that of the singular *the student*. See, e.g., Kamp & Reyle (1993) for discussion of these mattes and some consequences.

(15)   [+ Plural] ↔ [COLLECTION x]

Like (13), condition (15) might be construed as a kind of lexical information about the feature [+Plural], which would have the effect that for a *plurale tantum* like *people* the regular collective reading follows from the idiosyncratic categorization by [+Plural]. Now, the conditional character of (15) would have to be captured by lexically blocking nouns like *glasses* or *measles* from the application of (15). Thus *measles* would be marked by two exceptions: idiosyncratic categorization as [+Plural], but at the same time exemption from the feature's interpretation. This again raises the question of interpreting [–Plural], and again, the strategy to leave the unmarked value of the feature [±Plural] without semantic effect seems to be promising, assuming that the default type of reference is just neutral with respect to the condition represented as [COLLECTION]. A revealing illustration of lexical idiosyncrasies is the contrast between German *Ferien* (vacation) and its near synonym *Urlaub*, where *Ferien* is a *plurale tantum* with idiosyncratic singular reading, much like *measles*, while *Urlaub* allows for [+Plur] and [–Plur] with (15) applying in the former case.

Still more complex conditions obtain, as already noted, for the category Gender in German. The two features [± Masculine] and [± Feminine] identify three Genders by two features as follows:

(16) a. Masculine: [+ Masculine] ;   *Mann* (man),   *Löffel* (spoon)
     b. Feminine: [+ Feminine] ;   *Frau* (women),   *Gabel* (fork)
     c. Neuter: [– Masculine,   *Kind* (child),   *Messer* (knife)
                    – Feminine] ;

Only plus values of Gender features are related to semantic conditions, and only for animate nouns. This can be expressed as follows:

(17) a. [+ Masculine] ↔ [MALE x] / [ANIMATE x]
     b. [+ Feminine] ↔ [FEMALE x] / [ANIMATE x]

The correspondence expressed in (17) holds only for cases where the semantic condition [ANIMATE x] is present, hence the Gender features of nouns like *Löffel*, *Gabel* have no semantic impact. According to the strategy that leaves minus-valued features semantically uninterpreted, nouns like *Kind* and *Messer* would both be equally unaffected by (17), while derivational affixes like *-ung*, *-heit*, *-t*, *-schaft* project their inherent Gender-specification even when it is not interpretable by (17). Conditions like (17) and (15) might reasonably be considered as saving lexical redundancy, such that the categorization as [+Masculine] is predictable for nouns like *Vater* (father) the SF of which contains [ANIMATE x & [MALE x]]. Idiosyncratic specifications would then be involved in various cases of blocking (17). Thus *Weib* (woman) is [FEMALE x] in SF, but categorized as [–Masculine, –Feminine]. On the other hand, *Zeuge* (witness) is categorized as [+Masculine], but blocked for (17), although marked as [ANIMATE x]. Similarly *Person* (person) is [+ Feminine], but still not [FEMALE x], as *eine männliche Person* (a male person) is not contradictory.

Finally a short remark is in order about structural or abstract Case, the paradigm case of features devoid of SF-interpretation. Two points have to be made. First, structural Case must be distinguished from semantic or lexical Case, e.g., in Finno-Ugric and Caucasian languages, representing locative and directional relations of the sort expressed by prepositions in Indo-European languages. Semantic Cases like Adessiv, Inessiv, etc. correspond to *in, on, at,* etc. Although the borderline between abstract and semantic Case is not always clear-cut, raising non-trivial questions of detail, the role of abstract Case we are concerned with is clear enough in principle.

There is, of course, a natural temptation to extend successful analyses of semantic Cases to the Case system in general, relying on increasingly abstract characterizations, which are compatible with practically all concrete conditions. Hjelmslev (1935) is an impressive example of an ingenious strategy of this sort; cf. also article 2 [Semantics: Interfaces] (Kiparsky & Tonhauser) *Semantics of inflection.*

Second, the semantic aspect of morphological features must not be confused with their participation in expressions whose semantic structure differs for independent reasons, as already noted with regard to the locative/directive-distinction of the German prepositions *in, an, auf,* etc. The most plausible candidates for possible semantic effects of abstract Case are thematic roles in constructions like *he hit him*, where Nominative and Accusative relate to Agent and Patient. Identity or difference of meaning is not due to semantic features assigned to abstract Case, however, as can be seen from constructions like (18), where the verb *anziehen* (put on, dress) assigns the same role Recipient alternatively by means of Dative, Accusative, Nominative, and Genitive in the four cases in (18a–d), while in (18b) and (18e) the different roles Recipient and Theme are marked by the same Case Accusative.

(18) a. er zieht dem Patienten$_{Dat}$ den Mantel$_{Acc}$ an (he puts the coat on the patient).
 b. er zieht den Patienten$_{Acc}$ an (he dresses the patient).
 c. der Patient$_{Nom}$ wird angezogen (the patient is dressed).
 d. das Anziehen des Patienten$_{Gen}$ (the dressing of the patient).
 e. Er zieht den Mantel$_{Acc}$ an (he puts on the coat).

Hence the roles of complements cannot derive from Case features, but must be determined by the SF of the verb in the way indicated in (9) and (10). The selection restrictions the verb imposes on its complements are inherent lexical conditions of the verb, modulated by passivization in (18c) and nominalization in (18d). See

Wunderlich (1996b) for a discussion of further interactions between grammatical and semantic conditions; cf. also article 7 [Semantics: Interfaces] (Wunderlich) *Operations on argument structure*.

To sum up, morphological features must clearly be distinguished from elements of SF, but may correspond to them by systematic conditions; and they may participate in making semantic distinctions explicit, even if they don't have any semantic purport at all. This point is worth emphasizing in view of considerations like those in Svenonius (2007), who adumbrates conceptual content for morphological features in general, including Gender and abstract Case, not distinguishing instances with and without semantic purport (as in Gender), or semantic purport and the grammatical distinction it depends on (as in structural Case).

4.3 Syntactic categories

While categories like Noun, Verb, Preposition, Determiner, etc. are generally assumed to determine the combinatorial properties of lexical items and complex expressions, the identification of their features is still a matter of debate. Incidentally, the terminology sways between syntactic and lexical categories, depending on whether functional categories like Complementizer, Determiner, Tense, etc. and phrasal categories like NP, VP, DP, etc. are included. For the sake of clarity, I will talk about syntactic categories and their features.

Alternatives of the initial proposal [± Verbal, ± Nominal] generally recognize the determination of argument structure as the major effect of the features in question. One point to be noted is that nouns and adjectives do not have strong argument positions, i.e. they allow their complements to be dropped, in contrast to verbs and prepositions, which normally require their argument positions to be syntactically realized. Hence the feature [+Nominal] could be construed as indicating the argument structure to be weak in this sense. This is more appropriately expressed by an inverse feature like [−Strong Arguments]. Furthermore, verbs and nouns are recognized to require functional heads (roughly Determiner for nouns and Tense and Complementizer for verbs), ultimately supporting the referential properties of their constituents, a condition that does not apply to adjectives and prepositions. This can be expressed by a feature [+Referential], which replaces the earlier feature [Verbal]. A similar proposal is advocated in Wunderlich (1996a). It might be noted that the feature [+Referential] – or whatever counterpart one might prefer – has a direct bearing on the categorization of the functional categories Determiner, Tense, and Complementizer, and the constituents they dominate. These matters go beyond the present topic, though. We would thus get the following still provisional proposal to capture the distinctions just noted:

(19)   Verb   Noun   Adjective   Preposition

	Verb	Noun	Adjective	Preposition
Strong Arg	+	–	–	+
Referential	+	+	–	–

Further systematic effects these features impose on the argument structure and selection restrictions depend on general principles of Universal Grammar and on language-particular morphological categories. Thus in English and German Nominative- and Accusative-complements of verbs must be realized as Genitive-attributes of corresponding nouns, as shown by well-known examples like *John discovered the solution* vs. *John's discovery of the solution*.

On the whole, then, the features in (19) have syntactic consequences and regulate morphological conditions, and don't seem to call for any semantic interpretation. There is, however, a traditional, if not very clear view, according to which syntactic categories have an essentially semantic or conceptual aspect, where nouns, verbs, adjectives, and prepositions denote, roughly speaking, things, events, properties, and relations, respectively. Even Hale & Keyser (1993) adopt within the "Minimalist Program" a notional view of syntactic categories, assuming verbs to have the type "(dynamic) event" e, prepositions the type "interrelation" r, adjectives the type "state" s, with only the type n of nouns left without further specification. There are, however, various kinds of counterexamples such as adjectives denoting relations like *similar* or dynamic aspects of events like *sudden*. Primarily, though, all these conditions are neatly accounted for by the SF and the argument structure of the items in question, as shown by a rough illustration like (20). According to (20a), a transitive verb like *open* denotes an event s which instantiates an activity relating x to y; (20b) shows that the relational noun *father* denotes a person x related to the (syntactically optional) individual y; (20c) indicates that the adjective *open* denotes a property of the entity y, and (20d) sketches the preposition *in*, which denotes a relation locating the entity x in the interior of y.

(20)   a. /open/ $\lambda y \lambda x \lambda s$ [s INST [[ACT x] [CAUSE [BECOME [OPEN y]]]]]
        b. /father/ $\lambda y \lambda x$ [PERSON x [& [MALE x] [& [x [PARENT-OF y]]]]
        c. /open/ λy [OPEN y]
        d. /in/ $\lambda y \lambda x$ [x LOC [INTERIOR y]]

Clearly enough, the relevant sortal or ontological aspects of the items are taken care of without further ado. This is not the whole story, though. Even if the semantic neutrality of the features in (19) might be taken for granted, one is left with the well-known but intriguing asymmetry between nouns and verbs, both marked [+Referential], but subject to different constraints: While nouns have access to practically all sortal or ontological domains, verbs are restricted to events, processes, and states. The asymmetry is highlighted by basic lexical items like (21), which can show up as verbs as well as nouns, but with different semantic consequences:

(21) a. run, walk, jump, rise, sleep, use, ...
      b. bottle, box, shelf, fence, house, saddle, ...

Items like (21a) have essentially the same SF as nouns and verbs, differing only by their morpho-syntactic realization, as in *Eve runs* vs. *Eve's run*. By contrast, items like (21b), occurring as verbs differ semantically from the corresponding noun, as illustrated by *Eve bottles the wine, Max saddles the horse*, etc. In other words, nouns allow for object- as well as event-reference, while verbs cannot refer to objects. Hence items like *run* need only allow for alternative values of the feature [± Strong Arg] to yield nominal or verbal realizations, while nouns like *bottle* with object denotation achieve the necessary event reference only through additional semantic components like CAUSE, BECOME, and LOC. These conditions can be made explicit in various ways. What we are left with in any case is the observation that the event-reference of verbs seems to be constrained by syntactic features. Event reference is used here (as before) in the general sense of eventuality discussed in Bach (1986), including events, processes, states, activities – in short, entities that instantiate propositions and are subject to temporal identification as assumed in (13) above for Tense features.

Two points should be made in this respect: First, the constraint is unidirectional, as verbs require event-reference, but event reference is not restricted to verbs in view of nouns like *decision, event*, etc Second, as it concerns verbs but none of the other categories, it cannot be due to one feature alone, whether (19) or any other choice is adopted. Using the present notation, the constraint could be expressed as follows:

(22) [+ Referential, + Strong Arg] → λ s [s INST [P]]

This condition singles out verbs, as desired, and it determines the relevant notional condition on their referential capacity, if we consider INST as imposing the sortal requirement of eventualities on its first argument. It also has the correct automatic result of fixing the event reference for verbs, which is the basis for the semantic interpretation of Tense, Aspect, and Mood. Something like (22) might, in fact, not only be part of the (perhaps universal) conditions on syntactic features in general and those of verbs in particular, but can also be considered as a redundancy condition on lexical entries, providing verbs with the event instantiation as their general semantic property. If so, the lexical information of entries like (20a) could be reduced to (9), with the event reference being supplied automatically.

5 Interpretation of semantic features

5.1 Conditions on interpretation

Basic elements of SF, including those corresponding to morpho-syntactic features, are eventually related to or interpreted by the structures of C-I. As already mentioned, this interpretation, its conditions, and consequences are analogous to the interpretation of phonetic features in A-P, yet different in fundamental respects. Analogies and differences can be characterized by four major points.

First, phonetic and semantic features alike are primitive elements of the representational systems they belong to, they cannot be reduced to smaller elements. Structural differences of PF cannot be due to distinctions within elements like [–voiced] or [+nasal], just as distinct representations of SF cannot be due to distinctions within components like [ANIMATE], [CAUSE], or [INTERIOR], although acoustic properties of an utterance (say, because of different speakers), or variants of animacy or causation might well be at issue (e.g., due to differences in intentionality). In other words, representations of PF and SF and their correspondence via morpho-syntax cannot affect or depend on internal structures of the primitive elements of PF and SF.

Second, the interpretation of basic elements is nevertheless likely to be complex, and in any case subject to additional, rather different principles and relations. Basically, primitive elements of PF and SF recruit patterns based on different conditions of mental organization for the structural building blocks of language: The correlates of phonetic features in A-P integrate conditions and mechanisms of articulation and auditory perception, whereas correlates of semantic features in C-I involve patterns of various domains of perception, intention, and complex structural dependencies, as shown by cases like [ANIMATE] or [ARTIFACT], combining sensory with abstract, purpose oriented conditions. This is the very gist of positing interface elements, which deal with items of two currencies, so to speak, valid under intra- and extra-linguistic conditions, albeit in different ways.

As the present article necessarily focuses on the interpretation of basic elements, it has to leave aside encroaching conditions involving larger structures, where compositional principles of PF and SF are partially suspended. With respect to PF, overlay-effects can be seen, e.g., in whispering, where suspending [± voiced] has consequences for various other features. With respect to SF, the wide range of metaphor, for instance, is based on more or less systematic shifts within conceptually coherent areas. Projecting, e.g., conditions of animacy into inanimate domains, as is frequently done in talk about computers or other technology, obviously alters the interpretation of features beyond [ANIMATE]. Phenomena of this sort may partially suspend the compositionality of interpretation, still presupposing the base line of compositional matching, though.

Third, PF interacts with one complex but unified domain, viz. production and processing of acoustic signals, and it shares with A-P the linear, time dependent structure as the basic principle of organization. SF on the other hand deals with practically all dimensions of experience, motivating the abstract functor-argument-structure sketched above. It necessarily cannot match the different organizational principles inherent in domains as diverse as visual perception, social relations, emotional values or practical intentions, hence it must be neutral with respect to all of them. In other words, the relation of SF to the diverse subsystems of C-I cannot mean that it shares the specific structure of different domains of interpretation. To mention just one case in point: Color perception, though highly integrated with other aspects of vision, is structured by autonomous principles, which are completely different from the distinctions of color categories and their relations in SF, as discussed in Berlin & Kay (1969) and subsequent work. It follows from these observations that the interpretation of SF must be compatible with conditions obtaining in disparate domains – not only with regard to the compositionality of complex configurations, but also with regard to the nature and content of its primitive elements.

Fourth, while for good reasons PF is assumed to be the interface with both articulation and perception, possibly even granting their integration, it is unclear whether in the same way SF could be the interface integrating all the subsystems and modules of C-I. Notice that this is not the same issue as the fact that two or more systems organized along different principles might well have a common interface. Singing for instance integrates language and music, and visual perception integrates shape and color, which originate from quite different neuronal mechanisms. On the one hand, for reasons of mental economy one would expect language, which forces SF to interface with the whole range of different modules of mental organization anyway, to be the designated representational system unifying the systems of C-I, setting the stage for coherent experience and mental operations like planning, reasoning, orientation. The central system posited in

Fodor (1983) as the global domain the modular input/output systems interface with, might be taken to stipulate this kind of overall interface. On the other hand, there are well-known systems integrating different modules of C-I independently of SF and according to autonomous, different principles of organization. The most extensively studied case in point is spatial orientation, which integrates various modes of perception and locomotion and is fundamental for cognition in general, as it also provides a representational format for various other domains, including patterns of social relation or abstract values, as documented in the vast literature about many aspects of spatial orientation, its neurophysiological basis, its computational realization and psychological representation, including the particular conditions of spatial problem solving. An instructive survey is found in Jackendoff (2002) and the contributions in Bloom et al. (1996), which deal in particular with the representation of space in language; see also article 13 [Semantics: Typology, Diachrony and Processing] (Landau) *Space in semantics and cognition*. Similar considerations hold for other domains, like music, emotion, or plans of action. The question whether SF serves as *the* central instance, providing the common interface that directly integrates the different modules and subsystems of C-I, or whether there are separate interfaces mediating among parts of C-I independently of language must be left open here. In any case, SF and its basic elements must eventually interface with all aspects of experience we can talk about. In other words, color, music, emotions, other people's minds, and theories about everything must all in some way participate in interpreting the basic elements of SF.

5.2 Remarks on Conceptual Structure

One of the major problems originating from these considerations is the difficulty to specify at least tentatively the format of interpretations which elements of SF receive in C-I and its subsystems. To be sure, different branches of psychology and cognitive sciences provide important and elaborate theories for particular mental domains, such as Marr's (1982) seminal theory of vision. But because of their genuine task and orientation, they deal with specific domains within the mental world. Thus they are far from covering the whole range of areas that elements of SF have to deal with, and have little to say about the interpretation of linguistic expressions. Proposals seriously dealing with the question of how extra-linguistic structures correspond to linguistic elements and configurations are largely linguo-centric, i.e. they approach the problem via insights and hypotheses developed and motivated by the analysis of linguistic expressions.

An impressive large scale approach of this sort is Miller & Johnson-Laird (1976), providing an extensive survey of perceptual and conceptual structures that interpret linguistic expressions. The approach systematically distinguishes the "Sensory" Field and representations of the "Perceptual World" it gives rise to from the semantic structure of linguistic expressions, the format of which is very similar to that of SF as discussed here. (23) illustrates elements of the perceptual world, (24) the semantic elements based on them.

(23) a. Cause (e, e')   Event e causes event e'
 b. Event (e) e is an event

(24) a. HAPPEN (S): An event x characterized by S happens at time t if:
  (i) Event$_t$ (x).

 b. CAUSE (S, S'): Something characterized by S causes something S' if:
  (i) HAPPEN (S).
  (ii) HAPPEN (S').
  (iii) Cause ((i),(ii)).

These examples cannot do justice to the general approach, but they correctly show that perceptual and semantic representations have essentially the same format, suggesting that semantic structures and their interpretation are of roughly the same sort and are related by conditions as in (24). (This is surprising in view of the fact that Johnson-Laird (1983) explores the mental structure of spatial representations and the inferences based on them, showing that they are systematically different from the semantic structure of verbal expressions describing the same spatial situations, thus supporting different inferences.) In other words, perceptual interpretation could be (mis)construed as turning the organization of SF into principles of perception, something Miller and Johnson-Laird clearly do not suggest.

In a different but comparable approach, Jackendoff (1984, 2002) assumes representations of the sort illustrated in (8), which he calls Conceptual Structures, to cover semantic representations and much of their perceptual interpretation. Thus, like Miller & Johnson-Laird, he takes the format of semantic representations to be the model of mental systems at large – with one important exception. In Jackendoff (1996, 2002) a system of Spatial Representation SR, which Conceptual Structure CS interfaces with, is explicitly assumed as a system based on separate principles, some of which, like deictic frameworks, identification of axes, or orientation of objects, are made explicit. The systematic interaction of CS and SR, however, is left implicit, except that its roots are fixed by means of hybrid combinations inside lexical items, as indicated by the following entry for *dog*, adapted from Jackendoff (1996: 11).

(25) PF: / dog /
Categorization: [+N, – V, +Count, ...]
CS: [ANIMAL x & [[CARNIVORE x] & [POSSIBLE [PET x]]]]
SR: [3-D model with motion affordances]
Auditory: [sound of barking]

The notion of a 3-D model invoked here is taken from the theory of vision in Marr (1982), extended by a mental representation of motion types Marr's theory does not deal with. The actual model must be construed as the prototype of dogs in the sense of Rosch & Mervis (1975) and related work. Jackendoff's inclusion of auditory information points (without further comment) to the natural condition that the concept of dogs includes the characteristic voice, the mental representation of which requires access to the organization of auditory perception. Besides this purely sensory quality, however, barking is a linguistically classified aspect of dogs (and foxes) and as such belongs to the SF-information of the entry of *dog*.

In general, then, what kind of representations SF must serve as interface for, is anything but obvious and clear. Principles of propositional structure, on which SF is based, are certainly not excluded from mental systems outside of language, but it is more than unlikely that they can all be couched in this format, as it appears to be suggested in Miller & Johnson-Laird (1976), Jackendoff (2002) and (at least implicitly) many others. Spatial reasoning, to mention just one domain, does not rely on descriptions using the principles of predicate logic, as shown in Johnson-Laird (1983).

5.3 The inventory

The diversity of domains SF has to cope with leads to difficulties in identifying the repertoire of its primes – a problem that does not arise in PF, where the repertoire of primes is uncontroversial, at least in principle. For SF, two contrary tendencies can be recognized, which might be called minimal and maximal decomposition. Fodor et al. (1980) defend the view that concepts (which are roughly the meaning of simple lexical items) are essentially basic, unstructured elements. On this account, the inventory of semantic primes (for which the term features ceases to be appropriate) is by and large identical to the repertoire of semantically distinct lexical entries. Although Fodor (1981) admits a certain amount of lexical decomposition, recognizing some undisputable structure within lexical items, for the majority of cases he considers word meanings as primes. As a matter of fact, the problem boils down to the role of Completers, noted above – a point to which we will return.

The opposite view requires the SF of all lexical items to be reducible to one fixed repertoire of basic elements, corresponding to the features of PF. There are various versions of this orientation, but explicit reflections on its feasibility are rare. Jackendoff (2002: 334ff) at least sketches its consequences, even contemplating the possibility of combinatorial principles inside lexical items that differ from lexicon-external combination, a view that is clearly at variance with detailed proposals he pursues elsewhere. On closer inspection, the claims of minimal and maximal decomposition are not really incompatible, though, allowing for intermediate positions with more or less extensive decomposition. As a matter of fact, the contrary perspectives end up, albeit in rather different ways, with the need to account for the nature of irreducible elements. Two points are to be made, however, before these issues will be taken up.

First, with regard to the size of the repertoire, there is no reliable estimate on the market. It is clear that the number of PF-features is on the order of ten or so, but for SF-features the order of magnitude is not even a matter of serious debate. If decomposition is denied, the repertoire of basic elements is on the order of the lexical items, but the decompositional view *per se* does not lead to interesting estimates, either, as there is no direct relation between the number of lexical items and the number of primes. The combinatorial principles of SF would allow for any number of different lexical items on the basis of whatever number of primes is proposed. Hence for standard methodological reasons, parsimonious assumptions should be expected. However, since reasonable assumptions must be empirically motivated, they would have to rely on systematically analyzed, representative sets of lexical items. But so far, available results have not led to any converging guesses. To give at least an idea about possible estimates, the comprehensive analysis of larger domains of linguistic expressions in Miller & Johnson-Laird (1976) can be taken – with all necessary caveats – to deal with remarkably more than a hundred basic elements of the sort illustrated in (24). This repertoire is due to well-motivated considerations of the authors, leading to interesting results with respect to central cognitive domains but with no general implications, except that huge parts of the English vocabulary could not even be touched. One completely different attempt to set up and motivate a general repertoire of basic elements should at least be mentioned: Wierzbicka (1996) has a growing list of 55 primes on the basis of what is called Natural Semantic Meta-language, a rather idiosyncratic framework a more detailed presentation of which would by far exceed the present limits, but cf. article 2 [this volume] (Engelberg) *Frameworks of decomposition*. Among the peculiar assumptions of the approach is the tenet that semantic primes are the meaning of designated, irreducible lexical items, like I, YOU, THIS, NOT, CAN, GOOD, BAD, DO, HAPPEN, WHERE, etc.

Second, as to the content, the repertoire of primes has to respond not only to the richness of the vocabulary of different languages, but first of all to the diversity and nature of the mental domains to be covered. Distinctions must be captured and categorized not only for different perceptual modalities, but also for "higher order", more central domains like social dependencies, goals of action, generating explanations, etc. There is, after all, no simple and unconditional pattern to order sets of primes.

Two perspectives emerge from the contrary views about decomposition. On the one hand, even strong opponents of decomposition grant a certain amount of formal analysis, which requires a limited, not strictly closed core of basic semantic elements. These elements show up in different guises in practically all pertinent approaches. Besides components related to morpho-syntactic features as noted above, there is a small set of primes like CAUSE, BECOME, and a few others that have been treated as direct syntactic elements in different ways. The "light verbs" in Hale & Keyser (1993) and much related work around the Minimalist Program, for instance, are just syntactically realized semantic components. These different perspectives, emphasizing either the semantic or the syntactic role of Logical Form, are the reason for the terminological tensions mentioned at the outset. Three decades earlier, an even stronger syntactification of semantic elements had been proposed in Generative Semantics by McCawley (1968) and subsequent work, also relying on CAUSE, BECOME, NOT, and the like. In spite of deep differences between the alternative frameworks, there are clearly recurring reasons to identify central semantic elements and the structures they give rise to; cf. also article 7 [Semantics: Foundations, History and Methods] (Engelberg) *Lexical decomposition*, article 2 [this volume] (Engelberg) *Frameworks of decomposition*, and article 5 [Semantics: Interfaces] (Harley) *Semantics in Distributed Morphology*.

On the other hand, even if one keeps to the program according to which lexical items are completely decomposed into primitive elements, the problem of idiosyncratic residues, identified as Distinguishers in Katz & Fodor (1963) and Katz (1972) or as Completers in Laurence & Margolis (1999), must be taken seriously. One might consider elements like [BOTTLE] in (11), or taxonomic specifications like [CANINE] for *dog* or [FELINE] for *cat*, or distinguishers like [knight serving under the standard of another knight] in Katz & Fodor (1963) as provisional candidates, to be replaced by more systematic items. But there are different domains where one cannot get rid of elements of this sort for quite principled reasons. Taxonomies of animals, plants, or artifacts are by their very nature based on elements that must be identified by idiosyncratic conditions. For different reasons, distinctions in perceptual dimensions like color, heat, pressure, etc. and other mental domains must be identified by primitive elements. In short, there is a complex variety of possibly systematic sources for Completers, such that an apparently undetermined set of basic elements of this sort must be acknowledged. For two reasons, these elements cannot be considered as a side issue, to be dismissed in view of the more principled, linguistically motivated semantic elements. First, they make up the majority of the inventory of basic semantic elements, which is, moreover, not closed on principled grounds, but open to amendments within systematic limits. Second, they are of remarkably different character with respect to their interpretation and their position within SF and the role of SF as the interface with C-I.

To sum up, the overall repertoire that SF-representations are made up of comprises elements of different kinds. They can reasonably be grouped according to two conditions into (a) elements that are related to language-internal systematic conditions of L as opposed to ones that are not, and (b) elements with homogeneous as opposed to potentially heterogeneous interpretation – an important aspect that will be made explicit below. The emerging kinds of elements can be characterized as follows:

(26)	Systematic Features	Idiosyncratic Features	Dossiers
L-systematic	+	–	–
Homogeneous	+	+	–

The distinctions between these kinds of elements are based on systematic conditions with principled theoretical foundations, although the resulting differences need not always be clear-cut, a usual phenomenon with regard to empirical phenomena. As closer inspection will show, however, the classification reasonably reflects the fact that linguistically entrusted elements exhibit increasingly homogeneous and systematic properties.

6 Kinds of elements

6.1 Systematic semantic features

The distinction between systematic elements and the rest seems reminiscent of that between semantic markers and distinguishers in Katz & Fodor (1963), but it differs fundamentally, both in principle and in empirical detail. There are at least two ways in which semantic primes can be systematic in the sense of bearing on morpho-syntactic distinctions. First, there are elements that participate in the interpretation of morphological and syntactic features as discussed in §4, including both categorization and the various types of selection. These include properties like [FEMALE], [ANIMATE], [PHYSICAL], relations like [BEFORE], [LOCATION], or functions like [SURFACE], [PROXIMATE], [VERTICAL], etc. Second, there are components on which much of the argument structure of expressions, and hence their syntactic behavior depends. Besides well-known and widely discussed elements like [CAUSE], [BECOME], [ACT], also features of relational nouns like [PARENT], [COLOR], [EXTENSION] and others belong to this group. For general reasons, negation, conjunction, possibility, and a number of other connectives and logical operators must be subsumed here, as they are clearly involved in the way in which SF accounts for the logical organization of cognitive structures. It must be noted, however, that logical constants, explored in pertinent theories of logic, are not necessarily identical with their natural counterparts in SF. The functor & assumed in (12), for example, differs from standard conjunction at least by its formal asymmetry. Further differences between logical and linguistic perspectives have been recognized with regard to quantification and modality.

In any case, the interpretation of these elements consists in conceptually basic, integrated conditions, which may or may not be related to particular sensory domains. Causality, for instance, is a fundamental dimension of experience, which lives on integrated perceptual conditions, incorporating information from various domains like change and position, as discussed, e.g., in Miller & Johnson-Laird (1976). More specifically, it is not extracted from, but imposed on perceptual information. Dowty (1979) furthermore shows that the conceptual conditions of causality and change have straightforward external, model-theoretic correlates. Similarly, shape, location, relative size, part-whole-relation, or possession are integrated and often fairly abstract conditions organizing perception and action. For instance, the relation [LOC] or functions like [INTERIOR], [SURFACE], etc. cover conditions of rather different kind, depending on the sortal aspect of their arguments. Thus *a page in the novel, a chapter in the novel, an error in the novel, or a scene in the novel* pick out different aspects by means of the same semantic conditions represented by the features assumed for *in* in (20d). Other and perhaps still more complex and integrated aspects of experience are involved in the recognition of animacy or the identification of male and female sex. Even if some ingredients of these complex patterns can be sorted out and verbalized separately (identifying, e.g., physiological properties or behavioral characteristics), the features are holistic components with no internal structure within SF. This corresponds to the fact that the content of PF-features is sometimes accessible to conscious control and verbalization. The articulatory gestures of features like [voiced] or [labial] for instance may well be reflected on, without their encapsulated character being undercut.

In general, systematic features are to be construed as the stabilized, linguistic reflex of mechanisms involved in organizing and conceptualizing experience. Fundamental conditions of this sort seem to provide a core of possibilities the language faculty can draw on. Which of these options are eventually implemented in a given language obviously depends to some extent on its morphological and lexical regularities.

6.2 Idiosyncratic semantic features

Two factors converge in this kind of features. First, there is the fundamental observation, granted even under a radical denial of lexical decomposition, that the meanings of linguistic expressions respond to distinctions within basic sensory domains, from which more complex concepts are constructed. An extensively debated and explored domain in this respect is color perception. Items like *yellow, green, blue* differ semantically on the basis of perceptual conditions, but with no other linguistic consequences, except common properties of the group as a whole, which is captured by the common, systematic feature [COLOR], while the different chromatic categories are represented by idiosyncratic features like [RED], [GREEN], [BLACK], etc. It might be noted in this respect that color terms – unlike those for size, value, speed, etc. – are adjectives that can also occur as nouns, as shown by *the red of the car* versus **the huge of the car*, due to the component [COLOR] as opposed to the idiosyncratic values [RED], [BLUE], which still are by no means arbitrary, as Berlin & Kay (1969) and subsequent work has shown.

Various other domains categorizing sensory distinctions have attracted different degrees of attention, with limited systematic insight. Intriguing problems arise, e.g., with respect to haptic qualities, concerning texture and plasticity of surfaces or even the perceptual classification of temperature. It might be added that besides perceptual domains, there are biologically determined motor patterns, as in *grasp* or the distinction between *walk* and *run*, which also provide the interpretation of basic elements of SF.

The second factor supporting idiosyncratic features is the obvious need to account for differences of meaning that obviously have no systematic status in morpho-syntax or more general semantic patterns. Whether or not the distinctions between *break, shatter, smash* can be traced back to homogeneous sensory modalities need not be a primary concern, since in any case besides basic modes of perception and motor control, more complex conditions like those involved in the processes denoted by *cough, breath,* or even *sleep, laugh, cry* and *smile* are likely to require semantic features that are motivated by nothing else than the distinctions assigned to them in C-I. These distinctions might well be based on processes that are physiologically or physically complex – they still lead to self-contained features, as long as their interpretation is experientially homogeneous. One easily realizes that lexical knowledge abounds with elements like *shatter, splinter, smash*, and plenty of other sets of items that cannot get along without features of this idiosyncratic kind. They seem to be the paradigm cases demonstrating the need for Distinguishers or Completers.

This is only half of the truth, though, because distinguishing elements like [CANINE], [FELINE] etc. are usually assumed to be equally typical for Completers as are [GREEN] or [SMOOTH] and the like. Characteristic elements identifying the peculiarities of a particular species or a specific artifact are, of course, plausibly considered as Completers or Distinguishers. But they do have an essentially different character, as their interpretation can be heterogeneous for principled reasons, combining information from separate mental modalities. Similar considerations apply to what Pustejovsky (1995) calls the Qualia structure of lexical items, which he supposes to characterize their particular distinctive properties, using the term Qualia, however, in a fairly different sense than the original notion of subjective (usually monomodal) percepts, e.g., in Goodman (1951).

The integration of different types of information acknowledged in these considerations might be a matter of degree, which yields a fuzzy boundary with respect to the kind of elements to be considered next.

6.3 Dossiers

The notion of Dossiers, proposed in Bierwisch (2007), takes up a problem that is present but not made explicit in much of the literature that deals with the phenomena inquestion. The point is illustrated by the entry (25) proposed by Jackendoff for *dog*, the semantically relevant parts of which are repeated here as (27):

(27) CS: [ANIMAL x & [[CARNIVORE x] & [POSSIBLE [PET x]]]]
 SR: [3-D model with motion affordances]
 Auditory: [sound of barking]

The elements in CS (Jackendoff's counterpart of SF) are fairly abstract conceptual conditions, and in fact plausible candidates for systematic features classifying animals. But instead of the distinguisher [CANINE] that would have to identify dogs, we have SR and Auditory information to account for their specificity. Now, SR would either require the domain of 3-D models to be subdivided in prototypes of dogs, cats, horses, spiders, etc. – comparable to the division of the color space by cardinal categories like red, green, yellow, etc. –, clearly at variance with the theory of 3-D representations, or it would leave the information about shape and movement of dogs outside the range of the features of SF. Similar remarks apply to the auditory information. The essential point is, however, that 3-D models (of any kind of object, not just of dogs or animals) are Spatial Representations, which are subject to completely different principles of organization than SF (or CS, for that matter). SR-representations by their very nature preserve three-dimensional relations, allowing for spatial properties and inferences, as discussed in Johnson-Laird (1983) and elsewhere, conditions that SF is incapable to support. Moreover, besides shape, movement, and acoustic characteristics, the distinguishing information about dogs includes a variety of other aspects of behavior, capacities, possible functions, etc. some of which might require propositional specifications that can be represented in the format of SF. In other words, the replacement or interpretation of [CANINE] does not only concern SR and Auditory in (27), but involves a presumably extendible, heterogeneous cluster of conditions, i.e. a dossier of different conditions, which is nevertheless a unified element within SF, as the abbreviation [CANINE] in the SF of *dog* would correctly indicate.

The comments made on the SF of *dog* are easily extended to a large range of lexical items. Take, for the sake of illustration, nouns like *ski* or *bike*, which would be classified by systematic features like [ARTIFACT] and [FOR MOTION], while the more-or-less complex specificities are indicated by dossiers like [SKI], or [BICYCLE], respectively. Again, what is involved are different domains of C-I, indicating e.g., conditions on substance, bits and pieces, and technology, in addition to spatial models, and interpreting integrated elements, which, incidentally, enter into operations of verbalization noted with respect to (21b), such that *ski* and *bike* become verbs denoting movement by means of the specified objects. This in turn shows that dossiers are by no means restricted to the SF of nouns.

Three comments should be made here. First, as noted in (26), dossiers are elements with inhomogeneous interpretation that allow for conditions from different modules of C-I. To the extent to which these conditions may or may not be integrated, the borderline between dossiers and idiosyncratic features gets fuzzy, as noted earlier. With respect to SF, however, they are basic elements, subject to the general type structure and the combinatorial conditions it imposes, as shown by constructions like *we were skiing* or *she biked home*. As a consequence, the Lexical System LS of a given language L must be able to contain a remarkable collection of primitive elements whose idiosyncratic, heterogeneous interpretation is attached to, but not really part of, the lexical entries. In other words, lexical entries are connected to C-I not only by means of the general, systematic primes, but also by means of idiosyncratic files calling up different modules. One might observe that entries like (25) reflect this situation by making the extra-linguistic (e.g. spatial and auditory) information part of the lexical items directly. That way one would avoid ambivalent primes of the sort called Dossier, but the Lexical System would become a hybrid combination of linguistic and other knowledge – which perhaps it is. On that view, dossiers would behave as unified basic elements, a point that will be taken up below. Under the opposite view, dossiers might be construed to a large extent as the meaning of lexical entries without decomposition. And that is in fact what dossiers are – precisely to the extent to which primes resist language-internal decomposition.

Second, for this very reason dossiers are crucial joints for the role of SF as the interface with the different modules of C-I. To the extent to which they include, e.g., 3-D models that allow for spatial characteristics and spatial similarity judgments, dossiers situate the elements they specify in SF with respect to spatial possibilities, whose actual conditions, however, are given by the system of Spatial Representation. Similar considerations apply to auditory or interpersonal information. In general then, insofar as dossiers address different mental subsystems, they directly mediate between language and the different modes of experience.

Third, as already noted, dossiers may integrate propositional information, in particular if they are enriched through individual experience, such that, e.g., the file [FROG] includes conditions of procreation and development or usual habitats besides the characteristic visual and auditory information. Much of this information might be of propositional character, sharing in principle the format of SF. With respect to these components, dossiers are transparent in the sense that on demand their content is available for verbalization. In a way, dossiers might thus be means of sluicing information into the proper lexical representations.

It is worth noting in this respect that Fodor (1981) supports the claim that lexical meanings are basic, indefinable elements by explaining them as a kind of Janus-headed entities, which are logically primitive but may nevertheless depend on and integrate other (basic or complex) elements. The decisive point is that the dependence in question must not be construed as a logical combination of the integrated elements, since this would lead to analyzable complex items, but as something which Fodor calls mental chemistry in the sense of John Stuart Mill (1967), who suggests that by way of mental chemistry simple ideas generate, rather than compose, the complex ones. In other words, the way in which the prerequisites of such a double-faced element are involved is not the kind of combination on which SF is based, but a type of integration by which the mental architecture supports hybrid elements that are primitive in one respect, still recruiting resources that are complex in other respects. This is exactly what Fodor's lexical meanings share with dossiers or completers.

Mill's and Fodor's mental chemistry, the obviously necessary amalgamation of different mental resources and modalities, is a permanent challenge for the cognitive sciences dealing with perception and conceptual organization. The notion of frames introduced, e.g., in Fillmore (1985) and systematically developed in Barsalou (1992, 1999) is one such proposal to relate the meaning of linguistic expressions to the different dimensions of their interpretation, where frames are assumed to integrate and organize the different dimensions of experience; cf. also article 3 [Semantics: Theories] (Gawron) *Frame Semantics*.

In conclusion, in view of the controversial properties of (in)decomposable complex semantic elements it might be unavoidable to recognize ambivalent elements, which are at the same time primitive features of the internal architecture of L and heterogeneous elements at the border of SF.

6.4 Combinatorial effects

The phenomena just noted are related to a number of widely discussed problems. One of them concerns the variation on the basis of the so-called literal meaning, in particular the combinatorial effect that SF-features may exert on their interpretation. (28) is a familiar exemplification of one type of interaction:

(28) a. Tom opened the door.
      b. Sally opened her eyes.
      c. The carpenters opened the wall.
      d. Sam opened his book to page 37.
      e. The surgeon opened the wound.
      f. The chairman opened the meeting.
      g. Bill opened a restaurant.

Searle (1983) remarks about these examples that *open* has the same literal meaning in (28a–e), adumbrating a somewhat different meaning for (28f) and (28g), as incidentally suggested by the German glosses *öffnen* for (28a-e), but *eröffnen* for (28f/g), although he takes it as obvious that the verb is understood differently in all cases. As far as this is correct, the differences are connected to the objects the verb combines with, inducing different acts and processes of opening. If the SF of *open* given in (20a), repeated as (29), represents the invariant meaning of the occurrences in question, then the differences noted by Searle must arise from the feature-interpretation in C-I:

(29) / open / $\lambda y \lambda x \lambda s$ [s INST [[ACT x] [CAUSE [BECOME [OPEN y]]]]]

To sort out the relevant points, we first notice that the different types of transition towards the resulting state of y and their causation by the act of x are intimately related to the nature of the resulting state and the sort of activity that brings it about. In other words, the time course covered by [BECOME] and the act causing the change are different if the eventual state is that of the door, the eye, a book, a bottle, or a meeting. Similarly the character of s instantiating the transition is determined by the nature of x and y and their involvement. Hence [s INST ...] and [CAUSE [BECOME ...]] don't contribute to the variants of interpretation independently of [ACT x] and [OPEN y]. As noted earlier, [BECOME p] moreover involves a presupposition. It requires the preceding state to be [NOT p], which in turn depends on the interpretation of p, i.e. [OPEN y] in the present case. Hence the actual choice in making sense of *open* depends – not surprisingly – on the values of x and y, which are provided by the subject and object of the verb. Now, the subject in all cases at hand has the feature [HUMAN x], allowing for intentional action and thus imposing no relevant differences on the interpretation of x. Variation in the interpretation of [ACT x] is therefore not due to the value of x, but to the interpretation of [OPEN y], which in turn depends on y and the property abbreviated by OPEN. This property is less clear-cut than it appears, however. What it requires is that y does not preclude access, where y is either the container whose interior is at issue, as in *he opened the bottle,* or its boundary or possible barrier, as in *he opened the door,* while in cases like *she opened her eyes* or *he opened the hand* the alternative seems altogether inappropriate. Bowerman (2005) shows that differences of this sort may lead to different lexical items in different languages according to conditions on the specification of y. How these and further variations are to be reflected in SF must be left open here. As a first approximation, [OPEN y] could be replaced by something like [y ALLOW-FOR [ACCESS-TO [INTERIOR]]], leaving undecided how the interior relates to y, i.e. to the container or its boundary. In any case, the interpretation of [OPEN y] depends on how the object of *open*, delivering the value of y, is to be interpreted in C-I in all relevant respects. This in turn modulates the interpretation of [ACT x], fostering the specific activity by which the resulting state can be brought about.

Without going through further details involved in cases similar to (28), it should be clear that the SF-features are not interpreted in isolation, but only with regard to connected scenarios C-I must provide on the basis of experience from different modules. Searle (1983) calls these conditions the "Background" of meaning, without which literal meaning could not be understood. The Background cannot itself be part of the meaning, i.e. of the semantic structure, without leading to an infinite regress, as the background elements would in turn bring in their background. It can be verbalized, however, to the extent to which it is accessible to propositional representation. Roughly the same distinction is made in Bierwisch & Lang (1989), Bierwisch (1996) between Semantic Form and Conceptual Structure; cf. also article 5 [Semantics: Theories] (Lang & Maienborn) *Two-*

level Semantics. A different conclusion with respect to the same phenomena is drawn by Jackendoff (1996, 2002, and related work, cf. article 4 [Semantics: Theories] (Jackendoff) *Conceptual Semantics*), who proposes Conceptual Structure, i.e. the representation of literal meaning, to include spatial as well as any other sensory and motor representation. Carefully comparing various versions to relate semantic, spatial, and other conceptual information, Jackendoff (2002) ends up with the assumption that no principled separation of linguistic meaning from other aspects of meaning is warranted. But besides the fact that there are different types of reasoning based e.g., on spatial and propositional representations, as Jackendoff is well aware, the problem remains whether and how to capture the different interpretations related to the same lexical meaning, as illustrated by cases like (28) and plenty of others, without corresponding differences in Conceptual Structure. In any case, if one does not assume the verb *open* to be indefinitely ambiguous, with equally many different representations in SF (or CS), it is indispensable to have some way to account for the unified literal meaning as opposed to the multitude of its interpretations.

This problem has many facets and consequences, one of which is exemplified by the following contrast:

(30) a. Mary left the institute two hours ago.
b. Mary left the institute two years ago.

Like *open* in (28), *leave* has the same literal meaning in (30a) and (30b), which can roughly be indicated as follows, assuming that [x AT y] provisionally represents the condition that x is in some way connected to y.

(31) / leave / $\lambda y \lambda x \lambda s$ [s INST [[ACT x] [CAUSE [BECOME [NOT [x AT y]]]]]]

Under the preferred interpretation, (30a) denotes a change of place, while (30b) denotes a change of affiliation. The alternatives rely on the interpretation of *institute* as a building or as a social institution. Pustejovsky (1995) calls items of this sort dot-objects. A dot-object connects ontologically heterogeneous conditions by means of a particular type of combination which makes them compatible with alternative qualifications. The entry for *institute* has the feature [BUILDING x] in "dotted" combination (hence the name) with [INSTITUTION x], which are picked up alternatively under appropriate combinatorial conditions, as shown in (32). Whether [BUILDING] and [INSTITUTION] are actually primes or rather configurations of SF built on more basic elements such as [PHYSICAL] and [SOCIAL] etc. can be left open. The point is that they have complementary conditions with incompatible sortal properties.

(32) a. The institute has six floors and an elevator.
　　 b. The institute has three directors and twenty permanent employees.

The cascade of dependencies in (30) turns on the different values for y in (31) – the "dotted" institute –, which induces a different interpretation of the relation AT. This in turn implies a different type of change, caused by different sorts of activity, involving crucially different aspects of the actor Mary, who must either cause a change of her location or of her social relations, participating as a physical or a social, i.e. intentional agent. More generally, the feature [HUMAN x] must be construed as a "dotted" combination tantamount to the very basis of the mind-body-problem. Now, the choice between the physical and the social interpretation is triggered by the time adverbials *two hours ago* vs. *two years ago*, which sets the limits for the event *e*, which in turn affects the interpretation of the time course covered by [CHANGE ...]. The intriguing point is that the contrasting elements *hour* vs. *year* have a fixed temporal interpretation with no dotted properties. Hence they must trigger the relevant cascades via general, extra-linguistic background knowledge.

An intriguing consequence of these observations is the fact that there are clearly violations of the principle of compositionality, according to which the interpretation of a complex expression derives from the interpretation of its constituent parts. Simple and straightforward cases like (31) illustrate the point: The interpretation of *Mary, institute* and *leave* – or rather of the components [PERSON], [ACT], [BUILDING] etc. they contain – depends on background- or context-information not part of SF at all, and definitely outside the SF of the respective constituents. Hence even if SF is not supposed to be systematically separate from conceptual structure and background information, its compositional aspect, following the logic of its type-structure, must be distinguished from differently organized aspects of knowledge.

7 Primes and universals

As noted at the beginning, there are strong and plausible tendencies to consider the primitive elements that make up linguistic expressions as substantive universals, provided by the language faculty, the formal organization of which is characterized by Universal Grammar. In other words, UG is assumed to contain a universal repertoire of basic possibilities, which are activated or triggered by individual experience. Thus individual, ontogenetic processes select the actual distinctions from the general repertoire, which is part of the language capacity as such. This means that the distinctions indicated by features like [tense] or

[round] may or may not appear in the system of PF-features in a given system L, but if the features appear, they just realize options UG provides as one of the prerequisites for the acquisition and use of language.

If these considerations are extended to features of SF, two aspects must be distinguished, which at PF are often considered as essentially one phenomenon, namely features and their interpretation. For articulation this identification is a plausible abbreviation, but it doesn't hold at the conceptual side. For SF, the mental systems that provide the interpretation of linguistic expressions must be conceived as having a rich and to a large extent biologically determined structure of their own, independent of (or in parallel to) the language capacity. Spatial structure is the most obvious, but by no means the only case in point. General conditions of experience such as three-dimensionality of spatial orientation, identification of verticality, dimensions and distinctions of color perception, and many other domains and distinctions may directly correspond to possible features in SF, very much like parameters of articulation correspond to possible features of PF. Candidates in this respect are systematic features like [VERTICAL] or [BEFORE] and their interpretation in C-I, as discussed earlier. Similarly, idiosyncratic features, which correspond to biologically determined conditions of perception, motor control, or emotion might be candidates of this sort. To which extent observations about the role of focal colors or the body-schema and natural patterns of motor activity like walking, grasping, chewing, swallowing, etc. can be considered as options recruited as features of SF, similar to articulatory conditions for features of PF, must be left open. Notice, however, that we are talking about features of SF predetermined by UG, not merely about perceptual or motor correlates in C-I.

In any case, because of the number and diversity of phenomena to be taken into account, there is a problem of principle, which precludes generally extending SF from the notion of universal options predetermined to be triggered by experience. The problem comes from the wide variety of basic elements that must be taken to be available in principle, but cannot be conceived without distinct experience. It primarily concerns dossiers, but also a fair range of idiosyncratic features, and it arises independently of the question whether one believes in decomposition or takes, like Fodor (1981), all concepts or possible word meanings to be innate. It is most easily demonstrated with regard to 3-D models (or visual prototypes) that must belong to many dossiers. We easily identify cats, dogs, birds, chairs, trumpets, trees, flowers, etc. on the basis of limited experience, but it does not make sense to stipulate that the characteristic prototypes are all biologically fixed, ready to be triggered like for instance the prototype of the human face, which is known to unfold along a fixed maturational path. The same holds for the wide variety of auditory patterns (beyond those recruited for features of

PF), by which we distinguish frogs, dogs, nightingales, or flutes and trombones, cars, bikes, and trains. Without adding further aspects and details, it should be obvious that whatever enters the interpretation of these kinds of basic elements, it cannot belong to conditions that are given prior to experience and need only be activated. At the same time, the range of biologically predisposed capacities, by means of which features can be interpreted in C-I and distinguished in SF, is by no means arbitrary, chaotic, and unstructured, but clearly determined by principles organizing experience.

Taken together, these considerations suggest a modified perspective on the nature of primitive elements. Instead of taking features to be generally part of UG, triggered by experience, one might look at UG as affording principles, patterns, or guidelines along which features or primes are constructed or extracted, if experience provides the relevant information. The envisaged distinction between primes and principles is not merely a matter of terminology. It corresponds, metaphorically speaking, to the difference between locations fixed on a map and the principles from which a map indicating the locations would emerge on the basis of exploration. More formally, the difference corresponds to that between the actual set of natural numbers and its construction from the initial element by means of the successor operation. Less metaphorically, the substantial content of the distinction can be explained by analogy with face recognition. Human beings can normally distinguish and recognize a large number of faces on the basis of limited and often short exposure. The resulting knowledge is due to a particular, presumably innate disposition, but it cannot be assumed to result from triggering individual faces that were innately known, just waiting for their eventual activation. In other words, the acquisition of faces depends on incidental, personal information, processed by the biologically determined capacity to identify and recognize faces, a capacity that ontogenetically emerges along a biologically determined schema and a fixed developmental path. With these considerations in mind, UG need not be construed as containing a fixed and finite system of semantic features, but as providing conditions and principles according to which distinctions in C-I can make up elements of SF. The origin and nature of these conditions are twofold, corresponding to the interface character of the emerging elements.

On the one hand the conditions and principles must plausibly be assumed to rely on characteristic structures of the various interpretive domains which are independently given by the modules of C-I. Fundamentals of spatial and temporal orientation, causal explanation, principles of good form, discovered in Gestalt psychology, focal colors, principles of pertinence and possession, or the body schema and its functional determinants are likely candidates. On the other hand, conditions on primes are given by the organization of linguistic expressions, i.e. the format of representations and the principles by which they are built up and mapped onto each other. In this respect, even effects of morpho-syntax come into play through constraints on government, agreement, or selection restrictions, which depend on features at least partially interpreted in C-I, as discussed in § 4. In general, then, a more or less complex configuration of conditions originating from principles and distinctions within C-I serves as a feature of SF just in case this element plays a proper systematic role within the combinatorial structure of linguistic expressions.

Under this perspective, semantic primes would emerge from the interaction of principles of strictly linguistic structure with those of sensory-motor and various other domains of mental organization – just as one should expect from their role as components of an interface level. The effect of this interaction, although resulting from universal principles of linguistic structure and general cognition, is determined (to different degrees) by particular languages and their lexical inventory, as convincingly demonstrated by Bowerman (2000), Slobin et al. (2008) and much related work. This applies already to fairly elementary completers like those indicated by [INTERIOR] in (20d), or [AT] in (31). Thus Bowerman (2005) shows that conditions like containment, (vertical) support, tight fit, or flexibility can make up configurations matched differently by (presumably basic) elements in different languages, marking conditions that children are aware of at the age of 2. (33) is a rather incomplete illustration of distinctions that figure in the resulting situation of actions placing x in/on y.

(33)			English	Dutch	German	Korean
block	→	pan	in	in	in	nehta
book	→	fitted case	in	in	in	kkita
ring	→	finger	on	om	an	kkita
Lego	→	Lego stack	on	op	auf	kkita
cup	→	table	on	op	auf	nohta
hat	→	head	on	op	auf	ssuta
towel	→	hook	on	aan	an	kelta

In a similar vein, joints of distinctions and generalizations are involved in elements like [OPEN] in (20c) and (29), or [ANIMAL] and [PET] in (25), but also [ARTIFACT], [CONTAINER], and [BOTTLE] in (12) and many others. Further complexities along the same lines must be involved in Completers or dossiers specifying concepts like *car, desk, bike, dog, spider, eagle, murky, clever, computer, equation, exaggerate, occupy* and all the rest. In this sense, the majority of lexical items is likely to consist of elements that comprise a basic categorization in terms of systematic features and a dossier indicating its specificity, similarly to proper names, which combine – as argued in Bierwisch (2007) – a categorization of their referent with an individuating dossier. Remember that these specifying conditions are based on cross-modal principles in terms of which experience is organized, integrated by what is metaphorically called mental chemistry, such that dossiers are not in general logically combined necessary and sufficient criteria of classification.

The upshot of these considerations is that primes of SF are clearly determined by UG, as they emerge from principles of the faculty of language and are triggered by conditions of mental organization in general. They are not, however, necessarily elements fixed in UG prior to experience. They are not learned in the sense of inductive learning, but induced or triggered by structures of experience, which linguistic expressions interface with. This may lead, among others, to cross-linguistic differences within the actual repertoire of primes, as suggested in (33). It does not exclude, however, certain core-elements like [CAUSE], [BECOME], [NOT], [LOC] and quite a few others to be explicitly fixed and pre-established in UG, providing the initial foundation to interface linguistic expressions with experience.

This view leads to a less paradoxical reading of Fodor's (1981) claim that lexical concepts must all be innate, including not only *nose* and *triangle*, but also *elephant, electron* or *grandmother*, because they cannot logically be decomposed into basic sensory features. Since Fodor concedes a (very restricted) amount of lexical decomposition, his claim concerns essentially the status of dossiers. Now, these elements can well be considered as innate, if at least the principles by which they originate are innate – either via UG or by conditions of mental organization at large. Under this construal, the specific dossier of e.g., *horse* or *electron* can be genetically determined without being actually represented prior to triggering experience, just as, e.g., the knowledge of all prime numbers could be considered as innate if the successor-operation and multiplication are innate, identifying any prime number on demand, without an infinite set of them being actually represented. As to the general principles of possible concepts, which under this view are the innate aspect of possible entities (analogous to prime numbers fixed by their indivisibility), Fodor assumes a hierarchy of triggering configurations, with a privileged range of Basic-level concepts in the sense of Rosch (1977) as the elements most directly triggered. Their particular status is due to two general conditions, ostensibility and accessibility, both presupposing conceptual configurations to depend on each other along the triggering-hierarchy (or perhaps network). Ostensibility requires a configuration to be triggered by way of ostension or a direct presentation of exemplars, given the elements triggered so far. Accessibility relates to dependence on prior (ontognetic or intellectual) acquisition of other configurations. Thus the basic-level concept *tree* is prior to the superordinate *plant*, but also to the subordinates *oak* or *elm*, etc. Fodor is well aware that ostension and accessibility are plausible, descriptive constraints on the underlying principles, the actual specification of which is still a research program rather than a simple result. What needs to be clarified are at least three problems: First the functional integration of conditions from different domains (the mental chemistry) within complex but unified configurations of CS, second the abstraction or filtering, by which these configurations are matched with proper, basic elements of SF, and third the dependency of clusters or configurations in CS along the triggering hierarchy, which cannot generally be reduced to logical entailment. Some of these dependencies are characteristically reflected within SF by means of ordinary semantic elements and relations, while much of crosslinguistic variation, metaphor and other aspects of reasoning are a matter of essentially extralinguistic principles.

It might finally be added that for quite different reasons a similar orientation seems to be indicated even with respect to features of PF. As pointed out in Bierwisch (2001), if the discoveries about sign language are taken seriously, the language capacity cannot be restricted to articulation by means of the vocal tract. As has been shown by Klima & Bellugi (1979) and subsequent work, sign languages are organized by the same general principles and with the same expressive power as spoken languages. Now, if the faculty of language includes the option of sign languages as a possibility activated under particular conditions, the principles of PF could still be generally valid, using time slots and articulatory properties, but the choice and interpretation of features can no longer be based on elements like [nasal], [voiced], [palatal] etc. Hence even for PF, what UG is likely to provide are principles that create appropriate structural elements from the available input information, rather than a fixed repertoire of articulatory features to be triggered. Logically, of course, UG can be assumed to contain a full set of features for spoken and signed languages, of which normally only those of PF are triggered, but it is not a very plausible scenario.

To sum up, semantic primitives are based on principles of Universal Grammar, even if they do not make up a finite list of fixed elements. UG is assumed to provide the principles that determine both the mapping of an unlimited set of structured signals to an equally infinite array of meanings and the format of representations this mapping requires. These principles specify in particular the formal conditions for possible elements with interpretation provided by different aspects of experience, such as spatial orientation, motor control, social interaction, etc. Although this view does not exclude UG from supporting fixed designated features for certain aspects of linguistic structure, it allows for the repertoire of primitive semantic elements to be extended on demand.

8 References

Ajdukiewicz, Kazimierz 1935. Über die syntaktische Konnexität. *Studia Philosophica* 1, 1–27.
Bach, Emmon 1986. The algebra of events. *Linguistics & Philosophy* 9, 1–16.
Barsalou, Lawrence W. 1992. Frames, concepts, and conceptual fields. In: A. Lehrer & E. Kittay (eds.). *Frames, Fields, and Contrasts*. Hillsdale, NJ: Erlbaum, 21–74.
Barsalou, Lawrence W. 1999. Perceptual symbol systems. *Behavioral and Brain Sciences* 22, 577–660.
Berlin, Brent & Paul Kay 1969. *Basic Color Terms*. Berkeley, CA: University of California Press.
Bierwisch, Manfred 1967. Syntactic features in morphology: General problems of so-called pronominal inflection in German. In: *To Honor Roman Jakobson, vol. I*. The Hague: Mouton, 239–270.
Bierwisch, Manfred 1996. How much space gets into language? In: P. Bloom et al. (eds.). *Language and Space*. Cambridge, MA: The MIT Press, 31–76.
Bierwisch, Manfred 1997. Lexical information from a minimalist point of view. In: C. Wilder, H.-M. Gärtner & M. Bierwisch (eds.). *The Role of Economy Principles in Linguistic Theory*. Berlin: Akademie Verlag, 227–266.
Bierwisch, Manfred 2001. Repertoires of primitive elements – prerequisite or result of acquisition? In: J. Weissenborn & B. Höhle (eds.). *Approaches to Bootstrapping, vol. II*. Amsterdam: Benjamins, 281–307.
Bierwisch, Manfred 2007. Semantic form as interface. In: A. Späth (ed.). *Interfaces and Interface Conditions*. Berlin: de Gruyter, 1–32.
Bierwisch, Manfred 2010. BECOME and its presuppositions. In: R. Bäuerle, U. Reyle & T. E. Zimmermann (eds.). *Presupposition and Discourse*. Bingley: Emerald, Group Publishing, 189–234.
Bierwisch, Manfred & Ewald Lang 1989 (eds.). *Dimensional Adjectives*. Berlin: Springer.
Bierwisch, Manfred & Rob Schreuder 1992. From concepts to lexical items. *Cognition* 42, 23–60.
Bloom, Paul, Mary A. Peterson, Lynn Nadel & Merrill F. Garrett 1996. *Language and Space*. Cambridge, MA: The MIT Press.
Bowerman, Melissa 2000. Where do children's meanings come from? Rethinking the role of cognition in early semantic development. In: P. Nucci, G. Saxe & E. Turiel (eds.). *Culture, Thought, and Development*. Mahwah, NJ: Erlbaum, 199–230.
Bowerman, Melissa 2005. Why can't you 'open' a nut or 'break' a cooked noodle? Learning covert object categories in action word meanings. In: L. Gershkoff-Stowe & D. H. Rakison (eds.). *Building Object Categories in Developmental Time*. Mahwah, NJ: Erlbaum, 209–243.
Chomsky, Noam 1965. *Aspects of the Theory of Syntax*. Cambridge, MA: The MIT Press.
Chomsky, Noam 1970. Remarks on nominalization. In: R. A. Jacobs & P. S. Rosenbaum (eds.). *Readings in English Transformational Grammar*. The Hague: Mouton, 11–61.
Chomsky, Noam 1981. *Lectures on Government and Binding*. Dordrecht: Foris.
Chomsky, Noam 1985. *Knowledge of Language: Its Nature, Origin, and Use*. New York: Praeger.
Chomsky, Noam 1995. *The Minimalist Program*. Cambridge, MA: The MIT Press.
Chomsky, Noam 2000. Minimalist inquiries. In: R. Martin, D. Michaels & J. Uriagereka (eds.). *Step by Step*. Cambridge, MA: The MIT Press, 89–155.
Chomsky, Noam & Morris Halle 1968. *The Sound Pattern of English*. New York: Harper & Row.
Clements, George N. 1985. The geometry of phonological features. *Phonology Yearbook* 2, 225–252.
Cresswell, Max 1973. *Logics and Languages*. London: Methuen.

Dowty, David 1979. *Word Meaning and Montague Grammar*. Dordrecht: Reidel.
Fillmore, Charles J. 1985. Frames and the semantics of understanding. *Quaderni di Semantica* 6, 222–255.
Fodor, Jerry A. 1981. *Representations*. Cambridge, MA: The MIT Press.
Fodor, Jerry A. 1983. *The Modularity of Mind*. Cambridge, MA: The MIT Press.
Fodor, Jerry A., Merrill F. Garrett, Edward Walker & Cornelia Parkes 1980. Against definitions. *Cognition* 8, 263–367.
Goodman, Nelson 1951. *The Structure of Appearance*. Cambridge, MA: Harvard University Press.
Hale, Kenneth & Samuel J. Keyser 1993. Argument structure and the lexical expression of syntactic relations. In: K. Hale & S. J. Keyser (eds.). *The View from Building 20*. Cambridge, MA: The MIT Press, 53–109.
Halle, Morris 1983. On distinctive features and their articulatory implementation. *Natural Language and Linguistic Theory* 1, 91–105.
Halle, Morris & Alec Marantz 1993. Distributed morphology and the pieces of inflection. In: K. Hale & S. J. Keyser (eds.). *The View from Building 20*. Cambridge, MA: The MIT Press, 111–176.
Halle, Morris & Jean-Roger Vergnaud 1987. *An Essay on Stress*. Cambridge, MA: The MIT Press.
Hjelmslev, Louis 1935. *La Catégorie des Cas* I. Aarhus: Universitetsforlaget.
Hjelmslev, Louis 1938. Essai d'une théorie des morphemes. In: *Actes du IVe Congres international de linguists 1936*. Kopenhagen, 140–151. Reprinted in: L. Hjelmslev. *Essais linguistiques*. Copenhague: Nordisk Sprog- og Kulturforlag, 1959, 152–164.
Hjelmslev, Louis 1953. *Prolegomena to a Theory of Language*. Madison, WI: The University of Wisconsin Press.
Jackendoff, Ray 1984. *Semantics and Cognition*. Cambridge, MA: The MIT Press.
Jackendoff, Ray 1990. *Semantic Structures*. Cambridge, MA: The MIT Press.
Jackendoff, Ray 1996. The architecture of the linguistic-spatial interface. In: P. Bloom et al. (eds.). *Language and Space*. Cambridge, MA: The MIT Press, 1–30.
Jackendoff, Ray 2002. *Foundations of Language*. Oxford: Oxford University Press.
Jakobson, Roman 1936. Beitrag zur allgemeinen Kasuslehre. *Travaux du Cercle Linguistique de Prague* 6, 240–288.
Johnson-Laird, Philip N. 1983. *Mental Models: Toward a Cognitive Science of Language, Inference and Consciousness*. Cambridge, MA: Harvard University Press.
Kamp, Hans 2001. The importance of presupposition. In: C. Rohrer, A. Roßdeutscher & H. Kamp (eds.). *Linguistic Form and its Computation*. Stanford, CA: CSLI Publications, 207–254.
Kamp, Hans & Uwe Reyle 1993. *From Discourse to Logic*. Dordrecht: Kluwer.
Katz, Jerrold J. 1972. *Semantic Theory*. New York: Harper & Row.
Katz, Jerrold J. & Jerry A. Fodor 1963. The structure of a semantic theory. *Language* 39, 170–210.
Klima, Edward S. & Ursula Bellugi 1979. *The Signs of Language*. Cambridge, MA: Harvard University Press.
Laurence, Stephen & Eric Margolis 1999. Concepts and cognitive science. In: E. Margolis & S. Laurence (eds.). *Concepts: Core Readings*. Cambridge, MA: The MIT Press, 3–81.
Lewis, David 1972. General semantics. In: D. Davidson & G. Harman (eds.). *Semantics of Natural Language*. Dordrecht: Reidel, 169–218.
Marr, David 1982. *Vision*. San Francisco, CA: Freeman.
McCawley, James D. 1968. Lexical insertion in a transformational grammar without deep structure. In: B. J. Darden, C.-J.N. Bailey & A. Davison (eds.). *Papers from the Regional*

Meeting of the Chicago Linguistic Society (= CLS) 4. Chicago, IL: Chicago Linguistic Society, 71–80.
Mill, John S. 1967. *System of Logic. Collected Works. Vol. III*. Toronto, ON: Toronto University Press.
Miller, George & Philip Johnson-Laird 1976. *Language and Perception*. Cambridge, MA: Harvard University Press.
Montague, Richard 1974. *Formal Philosophy. Selected Papers of Richard Montague*. Edited and with an introduction by Richmond H. Thomason. New Haven, CT: Yale University Press.
Pustejovsky, James 1995. *The Generative Lexicon*. Cambridge, MA: The MIT Press.
Rosch, Eleanor. 1977. Classification of real-world objects: Origins and representations in cognition. In: P. N. Johnson-Laird & P. C. Wason (eds.). *Thinking – Readings in Cognitive Science*. Cambridge: Cambridge University Press, 212–222.
Rosch, Eleanor & Carolin Mervis 1975. Family resemblances: Studies in the internal structure of categories. *Cognitive Psychology* 7, 573–605.
Searle, John R. 1983. *Intentionality*. Cambridge: Cambridge University Press.
Slobin, Dan I., Melissa Bowerman, Penelope Brown, Sonja Eisenbeiß & Bhuvana Narasimhan 2008. Putting things in places: Developmental consequences of linguistic typology. In: J. Bohnemeyer & E. Pederson (eds.). *Event Representation*. Cambridge, MA: Cambridge University Press, 1–28.
Svenonius, Peter 2007. Interpreting uninterpretable features. *Linguistic Analysis* 33, 375–413.
Wierzbicka, Anna 1996. *Semantics: Primes and Universals*. Oxford: Oxford University Press.
Wunderlich, Dieter 1996a. Lexical categories. *Theoretical Linguistics* 22, 1–48.
Wunderlich, Dieter 1996b. Dem Freund die Hand auf die Schulter legen. In: G. Harras & M. Bierwisch (eds.). *Wenn die Semantik arbeitet*. Tübingen: Niemeyer, 331–360.
Wunderlich, Dieter 1997a. A minimalist model of inflectional morphology. In: C. Wilder, H.-M. Gärtner & M. Bierwisch (eds.). *The Role of Economy Principles in Linguistic Theory*. Berlin: Akademie Verlag, 267–298.
Wunderlich, Dieter 1997b. Cause and the structure of verbs. *Linguistic Inquiry* 28, 27–68.

Stefan Engelberg
2 Frameworks of lexical decomposition of verbs

1 Introduction —— 48
2 Generative Semantics —— 49
3 Lexical decomposition in Montague Semantics —— 56
4 Conceptual Semantics —— 60
5 LCS decompositions and the MIT Lexicon Project —— 65
6 Event Structure Theory —— 69
7 Two-level Semantics and Lexical Decompositional Grammar —— 73
8 Natural Semantic Metalanguage —— 79
9 Lexical Relational Structures —— 81
10 Distributed Morphology —— 86
11 Outlook —— 91
12 References —— 92

Abstract: Starting from early approaches within Generative Grammar in the late 1960s, the article describes and discusses the development of different theoretical frameworks of lexical decomposition of verbs. It presents the major subsequent conceptions of lexical decompositions, namely, Dowty's approach to lexical decomposition within Montague Semantics, Jackendoff's Conceptual Semantics, the LCS decompositions emerging from the MIT Lexicon Project, Pustejovsky's Event Structure Theory, Wierzbicka's Natural Semantic Metalanguage, Wunderlich's Lexical Decompositional Grammar, Hale and Kayser's Lexical Relational Structures, and Distributed Morphology. For each of these approaches, (i) it sketches their origins and motivation, (ii) it describes the general structure of decompositions and their location within the theory, (iii) it explores their explanative value for major phenomena of verb semantics and syntax, (iv) and it briefly evaluates the impact of the theory. Referring to discussions in article 7 [Semantics: Foundations, History and Methods] (Engelberg) *Lexical decomposition*, a number of theoretical topics are taken up throughout the paper concerning the interpretation of decompositions, the basic inventory of decompositional predicates, the location of decompositions on the different levels of linguistic representation (syntactic, semantic, conceptual), and the role they play for the interfaces between these levels.

Stefan Engelberg, Mannheim, Germany

https://doi.org/10.1515/9783110626391-002

1 Introduction

The idea that word meanings are complex has been present ever since people have tried to explain and define the meaning of words. When asked the meaning of the verb *persuade*, a competent speaker of the language would probably say something like (1a). This is not far from what semanticists put into a structured lexical decomposition as in (1b):

(1) a. You persuade somebody if you make somebody believe or do something.
 b. *persuade*(x,y,z): x CAUSE (y BELIEVE z)   (after Fillmore 1968a: 377)

However, it was not until the mid-1960s that intuitions about the complexity of verb meanings lead to formal theories of their lexical decomposition. This article will review the history of lexical decomposition of verbs from that time on. For some general discussion of the concept of decomposition and earlier decompositional approaches, cf. article 7 [Semantics: Foundations, History and Methods] (Engelberg) *Lexical decomposition*. The first theoretical framework to systematically develop decompositional representations of verb meanings was Generative Semantics (section 2), where decompositions were representations of syntactic deep structure. Later theories did not locate lexical decompositions on a syntactic level but employed them as representations on a lexical-semantic level as in Dowty's Montague-based approach (section 3) and the decompositional approaches emerging from the MIT Lexicon Project (section 5) or on a conceptual level as in Jackendoff's Conceptual Semantics (section 4). Other lexical approaches were characterized by the integration of decompositions into an Event Structure Theory (section 6), the conception of a comprehensive Natural Semantic Metalanguage (section 7), and the development of a systematic structure-based linking mechanism as in Lexical Decomposition Grammar (section 8). Parallel to these developments, new syntactic approaches to decompositions emerged such as Hale and Kayser's Lexical Relational Structures (section 9) and Distributed Morphology (section 10).

Throughout the paper a number of theoretical topics will be touched upon that are discussed in more detail in article 7 [Semantics: Foundations, History and Methods] (Engelberg) *Lexical decomposition*. Of particular interest will be the questions on which level of linguistic representation (syntactic, semantic, conceptual) decompositions are located, how the interfaces to other levels of linguistic representation are designed, what evidence for the complexity of word meaning is assumed, how decompositions are semantically interpreted, what role the formal structure of decompositions plays in explanations of linguistic phenomena, and what the basic inventory of decompositional predicates is.

In the following sections, the major theoretical approaches involving lexical decompositions will be presented. Each approach will be described in four subsections that (i) sketch the historical development that led to the theory under discussion, (ii) describe the place lexical decompositions take in these theories and their structural characteristics, (iii) present the phenomena that are explained on the basis of decompositions, and (iv) give a short evaluation of the impact of the theory.

2 Generative Semantics

2.1 Origins and motivation

Generative Semantics was a school of syntactic and semantic research that opposed certain established views within the community of Generative Grammar. It was active from the mid-1960s through the mid-1970s. Its major proponents were George Lakoff, James D. McCawley, Paul M. Postal, and John Robert Ross. (For the history of Generative Semantics, cf. Binnick 1972; McCawley 1994.)

At that time, the majority view held within Generative Grammar was that there is a single, basic structural level on which generative rules operate and to which all other structural levels are related by interpretive rules. This particular structural level was syntactic deep structure from which semantic interpretations were derived. It was this view of 'interpretive semantics' that was not shared by the proponents of Generative Semantics.

Although there never was a "standard theory" of Generative Semantics, a number of assumptions can be identified that were wide-spread in the GS-community (cf. Lakoff 1970; McCawley 1968; Binnick 1972): (i) Deep structures are more abstract than Chomsky (1965) assumed. In particular, they are semantic representations of sentences. (ii) Syntactic and semantic representations have the same formal status: They are structured trees. (iii) There is one system of rules that relates semantic representations and surface structures via intermediary representations.

Some more specific assumptions that are important when it comes to lexical decomposition were the following: (iv) In semantic deep structure, lexical items occur as decompositions where the semantic elements of the decomposition are distributed over the structured tree (cf. e.g., Lakoff 1970; McCawley 1968; Postal 1971). (v) Some transformations take place before lexical insertion (prelexical transformations, McCawley 1968). (vi) Semantic deep structure allows only three categories: V (corresponding to predicates), NP (corresponding to arguments), and S (corresponding to propositions). Thus, for example, verbs, adjectives, quantifiers, negation, etc. are all assigned the category V in semantic deep structure (cf. Lakoff 1970: 115ff; Bach 1968; Postal 1971). (vii) Transformations can change syntactic relations: Since *Floyd broke the glass* contains a structure expressing *the glass broke* as part of its semantic deep structure, *the glass* occurs as subject in semantic deep structure and as object in surface structure.

2.2 Structure and location of decompositions

In Generative Semantics, syntactic and semantic structures do not constitute different levels or modules of linguistic theory. They are related by syntactically motivated transformations; that is, although semantic by nature, the lexical decompositions occurring in semantic deep structure and intermediate levels of sentence derivation must be considered as parts of syntactic structure.

In contrast to the "Aspects"-model of Generative Syntax (Chomsky 1965), the terminal constituents of semantic deep structure are semantic and not morphological entities. Particularly interesting for the development of theories of lexical decomposition is the fact that semantic deep structure contained abstract verbs like CAUSE or CHANGE (Fig. 2.1) that were sublexical in the sense that they were part of a lexical decomposition. Moreover, it was assumed that all predicates that appear in semantic deep structure are abstract predicates. A basic abstract predicate like BELIEVE resembles the actual word *believe* in its meaning and its argument-taking properties, but unlike actual words, it is considered to be unambiguous. These abstract entities attach to the terminal nodes in semantic deep structure (cf. Fig. 2.1 and for structures and derivations of this sort Lakoff 1965; McCawley 1968; Binnick 1972).

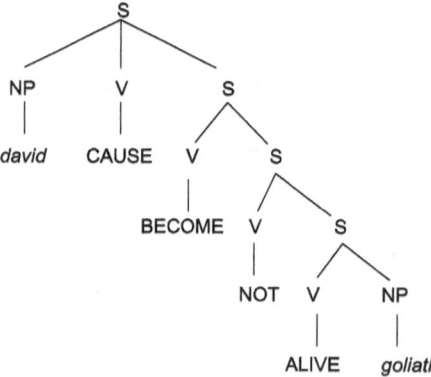

Fig. 2.1: Semantic deep structure *for David killed Goliath*

Abstract predicates can be moved by a transformation called 'predicate raising', a form of Chomsky adjunction that has the effect of fusing abstract predicates into predicate complexes (cf. Fig. 2.2).

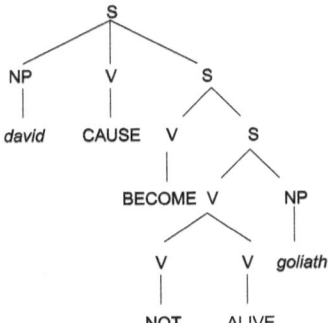

Fig. 2.2: Adjunction of ALIVE to NOT by predicate raising

Performing a series of transformations of predicate raising, the tree in Fig. 2.2 is transformed into the tree in Fig. 2.4 via the tree in Fig. 2.3.

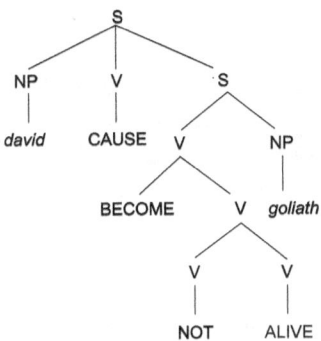

Fig. 2.3: Adjunction of NOT ALIVE to BECOME by predicate raising

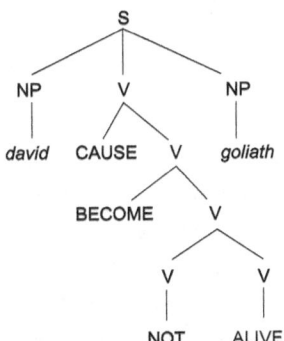

Fig. 2.4: Adjunction of BECOME NOT ALIVE to CAUSE by predicate raising

Finally, the complex of abstract predicates gets replaced by a lexical item. The lexical insertion transformation '[CAUSE[BECOME[NOT[ALIVE]]]] → *kill*' yields the tree in Fig. 2.5.

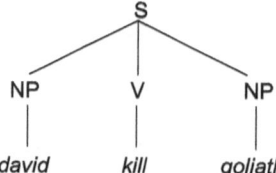

Fig. 2.5: Lexical insertion of *kill*, replacing [CAUSE [BECOME [NOT ALIVE]]]

According to McCawley (1968), predicate raising is optional. If it does not take place, the basic semantic components do not fuse. Thus, *kill* is only one option of expressing the semantic deep structure in Fig. 2.1 besides *cause to die, cause to become dead, cause to become not alive*, etc.

2.3 Linguistic phenomena

Since Generative Semantics considered itself a general theory of syntax and semantics, a large array of phenomena were examined within this school, in particular quantification, auxiliaries, tense, speech acts, etc. (cf. Immler 1974; McCawley 1994; Binnick 1972). In the following, a number of phenomena will be illustrated whose explanation is closely related to lexical decomposition.

(i) Possible words: Predicate raising operates locally. A predicate can only be adjoined to an adjacent higher predicate. For a sentence like (2a), Ross (1972: 109ff) assumes the semantic deep structure in (2b). The local nature of predicate raising predicts that the decompositional structure can be realized as *try to find* or in case of adjunction of FIND to TRY as *look for*. A verb conveying the meaning of 'try-entertain', on the other hand, is universally prohibited since ENTERTAIN cannot adjoin to TRY.

(2) a. Fritz looked for entertainment.
    b. [TRY *fritz* [FIND *fritz* [ENTERTAIN *someone fritz*]]]

(ii) Lexical gaps: Languages have lexical gaps in the sense that not all abstract predicate complexes can be replaced by a lexical item. For example, while the three admitted structures CAUSE BECOME RED (*redden*), BECOME RED (*redden*), and RED (*red*) can be replaced by lexical items, the corresponding structures for *blue* show accidental gaps: CAUSE BECOME BLUE (no lexical item), BECOME BLUE (no lexical item), and BLUE (*blue*) (cf. McCawley 1968). Lexical items missing in English may exist in other languages, for example, French *bleuir*. Since the transformation of predicate raising is restricted in the way described above, Generative Semantics can distinguish between those non-existing lexical items that are ruled out in principle, namely, by the restrictions on predicate raising and those that are just accidentally missing.

(iii) Related sentences: Lexical decompositions allow us to capture identical sentence-internal relations across a number of related sentences. The relation between *Goliath* and NOT ALIVE in the three sentences *David kills Goliath* (cf. Fig. 2.1), *Goliath dies*, and *Goliath is dead* is captured by assigning an identical subtree expressing this relation to the semantic deep structures of all three sentences. Lakoff (1970: 33ff) provides an analysis of the adjective *thick*, the intransitive verb *thicken*, and the transitive verb *thicken* that systematically bridges the syntactic differences between the three items by exploring their semantic relatedness through decompositions.

(iv) Cross-categorical transfer of polysemy: The fact that *the liquid cooled* has two readings ('the liquid became cool' and 'the liquid became cooler') is explained by inserting into the decomposition the adjective from which the verb is derived where the adjective can assume the positive or the comparative form (Lakoff 1970).

(v) Selectional restrictions (cf. e.g., Postal 1971: 204ff): Generative Semantics is capable of stating generalizations over selectional restrictions. The fact that the object of *kill* and the subjects of *die* and *dead* share their selectional restrictions is due to the fact that all three contain the abstract predicate NOT ALIVE in their decomposition (cf. Postal 1971: 204ff).

(vi) Derivational morphology: Terminal nodes in lexical decompositions can be associated with derivational morphemes. McCawley (1968) suggests a treatment of lexical causatives like *redden* in which the causative morpheme *en* is inserted under the node BECOME in the decomposition CAUSE BECOME RED.

(vii) Reference of pronouns: Particular properties of the reference of pronouns are explained by relating pronouns to subtrees within lexical decompositions.

(3) a. Floyd melted the glass though it surprised me that he would do so.
b. Floyd melted the glass though it surprised me that it would do so.

In (3b) in contrast to (3a), the pronoun picks up the decompositional subtree *the-glass* BECOME MELTED within the semantic structure [*Floyd* CAUSE [*the-glass* BECOME MELTED]] (cf. Lakoff 1970; Lakoff & Ross 1972).

(viii) Semantics of adverbials: Adverbials often show scopal ambiguities (cf. Morgan 1969). Sentences like *Rebecca almost killed Jamaal* can have several readings depending on the scope of *almost* (cf. article 7 [Semantics:

Foundations, History and Methods] (Engelberg) *Lexical decomposition*, section 1.2). Assuming the semantic deep structure [DO [*Rebecca* CAUSE [BECOME [*Jamaal* NOT ALIVE]]]], the three readings can be represented by attaching the adverb above to either DO, CAUSE, or NOT ALIVE. Similar analyses have been proposed for adverbs like *again* (Morgan 1969), temporal adverbials (cf. McCawley 1971), and durative adverbials like *for four years* in *the sheriff of Nottingham jailed Robin Hood for four years*, where the adverbial only modifies the resultative substructure indicating that Robin Hood was in jail (Binnick 1968).

2.4 Evaluation

Generative Semantics has considerably widened the domain of phenomena that syntactic and semantic theories have to account for. It stimulated research not only in syntax but particularly in lexical semantics, where structures similar to the lexical decompositions proposed by Generative Semantics are still being used. Yet, Generative Semantics experienced quite vigorous opposition, in particular from formal semantics, psycholinguistics, and, of course, proponents of interpretive semantics within Generative Grammar (e.g., Chomsky 1970). Some of the critical points pertaining to decompositions were the following:

(i) Generative Semantics was criticized for its semantic representations not conforming to standards of formal semantic theories. According to Bartsch & Vennemann (1972: 10ff), the semantic representations of Generative Semantics are not logical forms: The formation rules for semantic deep structures are uninterpreted; operations like argument deletion lead to representations that are not well-formed; and the treatment of quantifiers, negation, and some adverbials as predicates instead of operators is inadequate. Dowty (1972) emphasizes that Generative Semantics lacks a theory of reference.

(ii) While the rules defining deep structure and the number of categories were considerably reduced by Generative Semantics, the analyses were very complex, and semantic deep structure differed extremely from surface structure (Binnick 1972: 14).

(iii) It was never even approximately established how many and what transformations would be necessary to account for all sentential structures of a language (Immler 1974: 121).

(iv) It often remained unclear how the reduction to more primitive predicates should proceed, that is, what criteria allow one to decide whether *dead* is decomposed as NOT ALIVE or *alive* as NOT DEAD (Bartsch & Vennemann 1972: 22) – an objection that also applies to most other approaches to decompositions.

(v) In most cases, a lexical item is not completely equivalent to its decomposition. De Rijk has shown that while *forget* and its presumed decomposition 'cease to know' are alike with respect to presuppositions, there are cases where argument-taking properties and pragmatic behaviour are not interchangeable. If somebody has friends in Chicago who suddenly move to Australia, it is appropriate to say *I have ceased to know where to turn for help in Chicago* but not *I have forgotten where to turn for help in Chicago* (de Rijk, after Morgan 1969: 57ff). More arguments of this sort can be found in Fodor's (1970) famous article *Three Reasons for Not Deriving "Kill" from "Cause to Die"* which McCawley (1994) could partly repudiate by reference to pragmatic principles.

(vi) A lot of the phenomena that Generative Semantics tried to explain by regular transformations on a decomposed semantic structure exhibited lexical idiosyncrasies and were less regular than would be expected under a syntactic approach. Here are some examples. Pronouns are sometimes able to refer to substructures in decompositions. Unlike example (3) above, in sentences with *to kill*, they cannot pick up the corresponding substructure *x* BECOME DEAD (Fodor 1970: 429ff); monomorphemic lexical items often seem to be anaphoric islands:

(4) a. John killed Mary and it surprised me that he did so.
    b. John killed Mary and it surprised me *that she did so.

While *to cool* shows an ambiguity related to the positive and the comparative form of the adjective (cf. section 2.3), *to open* only relates to the positive form of the adjective (Immler 1974: 143f). Sometimes selectional restrictions carry over to related sentences displaying the same decompositional substructure, in other cases they do not. While *the child grew* is possible, a decompositionally related structure does not allow *child* as the corresponding argument of *grow*: **the parents grew the child* (Kandiah 1968). Adverbials give rise to structurally ambiguous sentence meanings, but they usually cannot attach to all predicates in a decomposition (Shibatani 1976: 11; Fodor et al. 1980: 286ff). In particular, Dowty (1979) showed that Generative Semantics overpredicted adverbial scope, quantifier scope, and syntactic interactions with cyclic transformations. He concluded that rules of semantic interpretation of lexical items are different from syntactic transformations (Dowty 1979: 284).

(vii) Furthermore, Generative Semantics was confronted with arguments derived from psycholinguistic evidence (cf. article 7 [Semantics: Foundations, History and Methods] (Engelberg) *Lexical decomposition*, section 3.6).

3 Lexical decomposition in Montague Semantics

3.1 Origins and motivation

The interesting phenomena that emerged from the work of Generative Semanticists, on the one hand, and the criticism of the syntactic treatment of decompositional structures, on the other, led to new approaches to word-internal semantic structure. Dowty's (1972; 1976; 1979) goal was to combine the methods and results of Generative Semantics with Montague's (1973) rigorously formalized framework of syntax and semantics where truth and denotation with respect to a model were considered the central notions of semantics.

Dowty refuted the view that all interesting semantic problems only concern the so-called logical words and compositional semantics. Instead, he assumed that compositional semantics crucially depends on an adequate approach to lexical meaning. While he acknowledged the value of lexical decompositions in that, he considered decompositions as incomplete unless they come with "an account of what meanings really are." Dowty (1979: v, 21) believed that the essential features of Generative Semantics can all be accommodated within Montague Semantics where the logical structures of Generative Semantics will get a model-theoretic interpretation and the weaknesses of the syntactic approaches, in particular overgeneration, can be overcome. In Montague Semantics, sentences are not interpreted directly but are first translated into expressions of intensional logic. These translations are considered the semantic representations that correspond to the logical structure (i.e., the semantic deep structure) of Generative Semantics (Dowty 1979: 22). Two differences between Dowty's approach and classical Generative Semantics have to be noted: Firstly, directionality is inverse. While Generative Semantics maps semantic structures onto syntactic surface structure, syntactic structures are mapped onto semantic representations in Dowty's theory. Secondly, in Generative Semantics but not in Dowty's theory, derivations can have multiple stages (Dowty 1979: 24ff).

3.2 Structure and location of decompositions

Lexical decompositions are used in Dowty (1979) mainly in order to reveal the different logical structures of verbs belonging to the several so-called Vendler classes. Vendler (1957) classified verbs (and verb phrases) into states, activities, accomplishments, and achievements according to their behaviour with respect to the progressive aspect and temporal-aspectual adverbials (cf. also article 9

[Semantics: Noun Phrases and Verb Phrases] (Filip) *Aspectual class and Aktionsart*). Dowty (1979: 52ff) extends the list of phenomena associated with these classes, relates verbs of different classes to decompositional representations as in (5a-c), and also distinguishes further subtypes of these classes as in (5d-f) (cf. Dowty 1979: 123ff).

(5) a. simple statives
$\pi_n(\alpha_1,...,\alpha_n)$
John knows the answer.

b. simple activities
$\text{DO}(\alpha_1, [\pi_n(\alpha_1,...,\alpha_n)])$
John is walking.

c. simple achievements
$\text{BECOME}[\pi_n(\alpha_1,...,\alpha_n)]$
John discovered the solution.

d. non-intentional agentive accomplishments
$[[\text{DO}(\alpha_1, [\pi_n(\alpha_1,...,\alpha_n)])] \text{ CAUSE } [\text{BECOME}[\rho_m(\beta_1,...,\beta_m)]]]$
John broke the window.

e. agentive accomplishments with secondary agent
$[[\text{DO}(\alpha_1, [\pi_n(\alpha_1,...,\alpha_n)])] \text{ CAUSE } [\text{DO}(\beta_1, [\rho_m(\beta_1,...,\beta_m)])]]$
John forced Bill to speak.

f. intentional agentive accomplishments
$\text{DO}(\alpha_1, [\text{DO}(\alpha_1, \pi_n(\alpha_1,...,\alpha_n)) \text{ CAUSE } \phi])$
John murdered Bill.

The different classes are built up out of stative predicates (π_n, ρ_m) and a small set of operators (DO, BECOME, CAUSE). Within an aspect calculus, the operators involved in the decompositions are given model-theoretic interpretations, and the stative predicates are treated as predicate constants. The interpretation of BECOME (6a) is based on von Wright's (1963) logic of change; the semantics of CAUSE (6b) as a bisentential operator (cf. Dowty 1972) is mainly derived from Lewis' (1973) counterfactual analysis of causality, and the less formalized analysis of DO (6c) relates to considerations about will and intentionality in Ross (1972).

(6) a. [BECOME ϕ] is true at I if there is an interval J containing the initial bound of I such that $\neg \phi$ is true at J and there is an interval K containing the final bound of I such that ϕ is true at K (Dowty 1979: 140).

b. [ϕ cause ψ] is true if and only if (i) ϕ is a causal factor for ψ, and (ii) for all other ϕ' such that ϕ' is also a causal factor for ψ, some ¬ϕ-world is as similar or more similar to the actual world than any ¬ϕ'-world is.
ϕ *is a causal factor for* ψ if and only if there is a series of sentences ϕ, $ϕ_1$,..., $ϕ_n$, ψ (for n ≥ 0) such that each member of the series depends causally on the previous member.
ϕ *depends causally on* ψ if and only if ϕ, ψ and ¬ϕ □ → ¬ψ are all true (Dowty 1979: 108f).
c. □[DO(α,ϕ)↔ϕ ∧ UNDER_THE_UNMEDIATED_CONTROL_OF_THE_AGENT_α (ϕ)]
(Dowty 1979: 118)

By integrating lexical decompositions into Montague Semantics, Dowty wants to expand the treatment of the class of entailments that hold between English sentences (Dowty 1979: 31); he aims to show how logical words interact with non-logical words (e.g., words from the domain of tense, aspect, and mood with Vendler classes), and he expects that lexical decompositions help to narrow down the range of possible lexical meanings (Dowty 1979: 34f, 125ff).

With respect to the semantic status of lexical decompositions, Dowty (1976: 209ff) explores two options; namely, that the lexical expression itself is decomposed into a complex predicate, or that it is related to a predicate constant via a meaning postulate (cf. article 7 [Semantics: Foundations, History and Methods] (Engelberg) *Lexical decomposition*, section 3.1). While he mentions cases where a strong equivalence between predicate and decomposition provides evidence for the first option, he also acknowledges that the second option might often be empirically more adequate since it allows the weakening of the relation between predicate and decomposition from a biconditional to a conditional. This would account for the observation that the complex phrase *cause to die* has a wider extension than *kill*.

3.3 Linguistic phenomena

Dowty provides explanations for a wide range of phenomena related to Vendler classes. A few examples are the influence of mass nouns and indefinites on the membership of expressions in Vendler classes (Dowty 1979: 78ff), the interaction of derivational morphology with sublexical structures of meaning (Dowty 1979: 32, 206f, 256ff), explanations of adverbial and quantifier scope (Dowty 1976: 213ff), the imperfective paradox (Dowty 1979: 133), the progressive aspect (Dowty 1979: 145ff), resultative constructions (Dowty 1979: 219ff), and temporal-aspectual adverbials (*for an hour, in an hour*) (Dowty 1979: 332ff).

Dowty also addresses aspectual composition. Since he conceives of Vendler classes in terms of lexical decomposition, he shows that decompositional structures involving CAUSE, BECOME, and DO are not only introduced via semantically complex verbs but also via syntactic and morphological processes. For example, accomplishments that arise when verbs are combined with prepositional phrases get their BECOME operator from the preposition (7a) where the preposition itself can undergo a process that adds an additional CAUSE component (7b) (Dowty 1979: 211f). In (7c), the morphological process forming deadjectival inchoatives is associated with a BECOME proposition (Dowty 1979: 206) that can be expanded with a CAUSE operator in the case of deadjectival causatives (Dowty 1979: 307f).

(7) a. John walks to Chicago.
      walk'($john$) ∧ BECOME be-at'($john, chicago$)

   b. John pushes a rock to the fence.
      ∃x[rock'(x) ∧ ∃y[∀z[fence'(z) ⇔ y = z] ∧ push'($john$, x) CAUSE BECOME beat'(x, y)]]

   c. The soup cooled.
      ∃x[∀y[soup'(y) ⇔ x = y] ∧ BECOME cool'(x)]

3.4 Evaluation

Of the pre-80s work on lexical decomposition, besides the work of Jackendoff (cf. 2.4), it is probably Dowty's "Word Meaning and Montague Grammar" that still exerts the most influence on semantic studies. It has initiated a long period of research dominated by approaches that located lexical decompositions in lexical semantics instead of syntax. It must be considered a major advancement that Dowty was committed to providing formal truth-conditions for operators involved in decompositions. Many of the approaches preceding and following Dowty (1979) lack this degree of explicitness. His account of the compositional nature of many accomplishments, the interaction of aspectual adverbials with Vendler classes, and many other phenomena mentioned in section 3.3 served as a basis for discussion for the approaches to follow. Among the approaches particularly influenced by Dowty (1979) are van Valin's (1993) decompositions within Role and Reference Grammar, Levin and Rappaport Hovav's Lexical Conceptual Structures (cf. section 5), and Pustejovsky's Event Structures (cf. section 6).

4 Conceptual Semantics

4.1 Origins and motivation

Along with lexical decompositions in Generative Semantics, another line of research emerged where semantic arguments of predicates were associated with the roles they played in the events denoted by verbs (Gruber 1965; Fillmore 1968b). Thematic roles like agent, patient, goal, etc. were used to explain how semantic arguments are mapped onto syntactic structures (cf. also article 3 [this volume] (Davis) *Thematic roles*). Early approaches to thematic roles assumed that there is a small set of unanalyzable roles that are semantically stable across the verbal lexicon. Thematic role approaches were confronted with a number of problems concerning the often vague semantic content of roles, their coarse-grained nature as a descriptive tool, the lack of reliable diagnostics for them, and the empirically inadequate syntactic generalizations (cf. the overview in Levin & Rappaport Hovav 2005: 35ff; Dowty 1991: 553ff). As a consequence, thematic role theories developed in different ways by decomposing thematic roles into features (Rozwadowska 1988), by reducing thematic roles to just two generalized macroroles (van Valin 1993) or to proto-roles within a prototype approach based on lexical entailments (Dowty 1991), by combining them with event structure representations (Grimshaw 1990; Reinhart 2002), and, in particular, by conceiving of them as notions derived from lexical decompositions (van Valin 1993). This last approach was pursued by Jackendoff (1972; 1976) and was one of the foundations of a semantic theory that came to be known as Conceptual Semantics, and which, over the years, has approached a large variety of phenomena beyond thematic roles (cf. also article 4 [Semantics: Theories] (Jackendoff) *Conceptual Semantics*).

According to Jackendoff's (1983; 1990; 2002) Conceptual Semantics, meanings are essentially conceptual entities and semantics is "the organization of those thoughts that language can express" (Jackendoff 2002: 123). Meanings are represented on an autonomous level of cognitive representation called "conceptual structure" that is related to syntactic and phonological structure, on the one side, and to non-linguistic cognitive levels like the visual, the auditory, and the motor system, on the other side. Conceptual structure is conceived of as a universal model of the mind's construal of the world (Jackendoff 1983: 18ff). Thus, Conceptual Semantics differs from formal, model-theoretic semantics in locating meanings not in the world but in the mind of speakers and hearers. Therefore, notions like truth and reference do not play the role they play in formal semantics but are relativized to the speaker's conceptualizations of the world (cf. Jackendoff 2002: 294ff). Jackendoff's approach also differs from many others in not assuming a strict division between semantic and encyclopaedic meaning and between grammatically relevant and irrelevant aspects of meaning (Jackendoff 2002: 267ff).

4.2 Structure and location of decompositions

Conceptual structure involves a decomposition of meaning into conceptual primitives (Jackendoff 1983: 57ff). Since Jackendoff (1990: 10f) assumes that there is an indefinitely large number of possible lexical concepts, conceptual primitives must be combined by generative principles to determine the set of lexical concepts. Thus, most lexical concepts are considered to be conceptually complex. Decompositions in Conceptual Semantics differ considerably in content and structure from lexical structure in Generative Semantics and Montague-based approaches to the lexicon. The sentence in (8a) would yield the meaning representation in (8b):

(8) a. John entered the room.
  b. [$_{Event}$ GO ([$_{Thing}$ JOHN], [$_{Path}$ TO ([$_{Place}$ IN ([$_{Thing}$ ROOM])])])]

Each pair of square brackets encloses a conceptual constituent, where the capitalized items denote the conceptual content, which is assigned to a major conceptual category like Thing, Place, Event, State, Path, Amount, etc. (Jackendoff 1983: 52ff). There are a number of possibilities for mapping these basic ontological categories onto functor-argument structures (Jackendoff 1990: 43). For example, the category Event can be elaborated into two-place functions like GO ([Thing], [Path]) or CAUSE ([Thing/Event], [Event]). Furthermore, each syntactic constituent maps into a conceptual constituent, and partly language-specific correspondence rules relate syntactic categories to the particular conceptual categories they can express. In later versions of Conceptual Semantics, these kinds of structures are enriched by referential features and modifiers, and the propositional structure is accompanied by a second tier encoding elements of information structure (cf. Jackendoff 1990: 55f; Culicover & Jackendoff 2005: 154f).

A lexical entry consists of a phonological, syntactic, and conceptual representation. As can be seen in Fig. 2.6, most of the conceptual structure in (8b) is projected from the conceptual structure of the verb that provides a number of open argument slots (Jackendoff 1990: 46).

$$\begin{bmatrix} \text{enter} \\ \text{V} \\ \underline{\quad} <\text{NP}_j> \\ [_{Event} \text{ GO } ([_{Thing}]_i), [_{Path} \text{ TO } ([_{Place} \text{ IN } ([_{Thing}]_j)])]] \end{bmatrix}$$

Fig. 2.6: Lexical entry for *enter*

The conceptual structure is supplemented with a spatial structure that captures finer distinctions between lexical items in a way closely related to non-linguistic cognitive modules (Jackendoff 1990: 32ff; 2002: 345ff).

The same structure can also come about in a compositional way. While *enter* already includes the concept of a particular path (IN), this information is contributed by a preposition in the following example:

(9) a. John ran into the room.
 b. [$_{Event}$ GO ([$_{Thing}$ JOHN]), [$_{Path}$ TO ([$_{Place}$ IN ([$_{Thing}$ ROOM])])]]

The corresponding lexical entries for the verb and the preposition (Fig. 2.7) account for the structure in (9b) (Jackendoff 1990: 45).

$$\begin{bmatrix} \text{run} \\ \text{V} \\ \underline{\quad} \text{<PP}_j\text{>} \\ [_{Event} \text{ GO } ([_{Thing}]_i), [_{Path} \text{ TO }]_j] \end{bmatrix}$$

$$\begin{bmatrix} \text{into} \\ \text{P} \\ \underline{\quad} \text{<NP}_j\text{>} \\ [_{Path} \text{ TO } ([_{Place} \text{ IN } ([_{Thing}]_j)])] \end{bmatrix}$$

Fig. 2.7: Lexical entries for *run* and *into*

An important feature of Jackendoff's (1990: 25ff; 2002: 356ff) decompositions is the use of abstract location and motion predicates in order to represent the meaning of words outside the local domain. For example, a change-of-state verb like *melt* is rendered as 'to go from solid to liquid'. Building on Gruber's (1965) earlier work, Jackendoff thereby relates different classes of verbs by analogy. In Jackendoff (1983: 188), he states that in any semantic field in the domain of events and states "the principle event-, state-, path-, and place-functions are a subset of those used for the analysis of spatial location and motion". To make these analogies work, predicates are related to certain fields that determine the character of the arguments and the sort of inferences. For example, if the two-place function BE(x,y) is supplemented by the field feature *spatial*, it indicates that x is an object and y is its location while the field feature *possession* indicates that x is an object and y the person who owns it. Only the latter one involves inferences about the rights of y to use x (Jackendoff 2002: 359ff).

Jackendoff (2002: 335f) dissociates himself from approaches that compare lexical decompositions with dictionary definitions; the major difference is that the basic elements of decompositions need not be words themselves, just as phonological features as the basic components on phonological elements are not sounds. He also claims that the speaker does not have conscious access to the decompositional structure of lexical items; this can only be revealed by linguistic analysis.

The question of what elements should be used in decompositions is answered to the effect that if the meaning of lexeme A entails the meaning of lexeme B, the decomposition of A includes that of B (Jackendoff 1976). Jackendoff (2002: 336f) admits that it is hard to tell how the lower bound of decomposition can be determined. For example, some approaches consider CAUSE to be a primitive; others conceive of it as a family of concepts related through feature decomposition. In contrast to approaches that are only interested in finding those components that are relevant for the syntax-semantics interface, he argues that from the point of learnability the search for conceptual primitives has to be taken seriously beyond what is needed for the syntax. He takes the stance that it is just a matter of further and more detailed research before the basic components are uncovered.

4.3 Linguistic phenomena

Lexical decompositions within Conceptual Semantics serve much wider purposes than in many other approaches. First of all, they are considered a meaning representation in their own right, that is, not primarily driven by the need to explain linking and other linguistic interface phenomena. Moreover, as part of conceptual structure, they are linked not only to linguistic but also to non-linguistic cognitive domains.

As a semantic theory, Conceptual Semantics has to account for inferences. With respect to decompositions, this is done by postulating inference rules that link decompositional predicates. For example, from any decompositional structure involving GO(x,y,z), we can infer that BE(x,y) holds before the GO event and BE(x,z) after it. This is captured by inference rules as in (10a) that resemble meaning postulates in truth-conditional semantics (Jackendoff 1976: 114). Thus, we can infer from *the train went from Kankakee to Mattoon* that the train was in Kankakee before and in Mattoon after the event. Since other sentences involving a GO-type predicate like *the road reached from Altoona to Johnstown* do not share this inference, the predicates are subtyped to the particular fields *transitional* versus *extensional*. The extensional version of GO is associated with the inference that one part of *x* in GO(x,y,z) is located in *y* and the other in *z* (10b) (Jackendoff 1976: 139):

(10) a. $GO_{Trans}(x,y,z)$ at $t_1 \Rightarrow$ for some times t_2 and t_3 such that $t_2 < t_1 < t_3$, $BE_{Trans}(x,y)$ at t_2 and $BE_{Trans}(x,z)$ at t_3.

b. $GO_{Ext}(x,y,z) \Rightarrow$ for some v and w such that $v \subset x$ and $w \subset x$, $BE_{Ext}(v,y)$ and $BE_{Ext}(w,z)$.

One of Jackendoff's main concerns is the mapping between conceptual and syntactic structure. Part of this mapping is the linking of semantic arguments into syntactic structures. In Conceptual Semantics this is done via thematic roles. Thematic roles are not primitives in Conceptual Semantics but can be defined on the basis of decompositions (Jackendoff 1972; 1987). They "are nothing but particular structural configurations in conceptual structure" (Jackendoff 1990: 47). For example, Jackendoff (1972: 39) identifies the first argument of the CAUSE relation with the agent role. In later versions of his theory, Jackendoff (e.g., 1990: 125ff) expands the conceptual structure of verbs by adding an action tier to the representation. While the original concept of decomposition (the 'thematic tier') is couched in terms of location and motion, thereby rendering thematic roles like theme, goal, or source, the action tier expresses how objects are affected and accounts for roles like actor and patient. Thus, *hit* as in *the car hit the tree* provides a theme (*the car*, the "thing in motion" in the example sentence) and a goal (*the tree*) on the thematic tier, and an actor (*the car*) and a patient (*the tree*) on the action tier. These roles can be derived from the representation in Fig. 2.8 (after Jackendoff 1990: 125ff).

$$\begin{bmatrix} \text{INCH [BE ([CAR], [AT [TREE]])]} \\ \text{Event} \quad \text{AFF ([CAR], [TREE])} \end{bmatrix}$$

Fig. 2.8: Thematic tier and action tier for *the car hit the tree*

The thematic roles derived from the thematic and the action tiers are ordered within a thematic hierarchy. This hierarchy is mapped onto a hierarchy of syntactic functions such that arguments are linked to syntactic functions according to the rank of their thematic role in the thematic hierarchy (Jackendoff 1990: 258, 268f; 2002: 143). Strict subcategorization can largely be dispensed with. However, Jackendoff (1990: 255ff; 2002: 140f) still acknowledges subcategorizational idiosyncrasies.

Among the many other phenomena treated within Conceptual Semantics and related to lexical decompositions are argument structure alternations (Jackendoff 1990: 71ff), aspectual-temporal adverbials and their relation to the boundedness of events (Jackendoff 1990: 27ff), the semantics of causation (Jackendoff 1990: 130ff), and phenomena at the border between adjuncts and arguments (Jackendoff 1990: 155ff).

4.4 Evaluation

Jackendoff's approach to lexical decomposition has been a cornerstone in the development of lexical representations since it covers a wide domain of different classes of lexical items and phenomena associated with these classes. The wide coverage forced Jackendoff to expand the structures admitted in his decompositions. This in turn evoked criticism that his theory lacks sufficient restrictiveness. Furthermore, it has been criticized that the locational approach to decomposition needs to be stretched too far in order to make it convincing that it includes all classes of verbs (Levin 1995: 84). Wunderlich (1996: 171) considers Jackendoff's linking principle problematic since it cannot easily be applied to languages with case systems. In general, Jackendoff's rather heterogeneous set of correspondence rules has attracted criticism because it involves a considerable weakening of the idea of semantic compositionality (cf. article 4 [Semantics: Theories] (Jackendoff) *Conceptual Semantics* for Jackendoff's position).

5 LCS decompositions and the MIT Lexicon Project

5.1 Origins and motivation

An important contribution to the development of decompositional theories of lexical meaning originated in the MIT Lexicon Project in the mid-eighties. Its main proponents are Beth Levin and Malka Rappaport Hovav. Their approach is mainly concerned with the relation between semantic properties of lexical items and their syntactic behaviour. Thus, it aims at "developing a representation of those aspects of the meaning of a lexical item which characterize a native speaker's knowledge of its argument structure and determine the syntactic expression of its arguments" (Levin 1985: 4). The meaning representations were supposed to lead to definitions of semantic classes that show a uniform syntactic behaviour:

> (1) All arguments bearing a particular semantic relation are systematically expressed in certain ways. (2) Predicates fall into classes according to the arguments they select and the syntactic expression of these arguments. (3) Adjuncts are systematically expressed in the same way(s) and their distribution often seems to be limited to semantically coherent classes of predicates. (4) There are regular extended uses of predicates that are correlated with semantic class. (5) Predicates belonging to certain semantic classes display regular alternations in the expression of their arguments.
>
> (Levin 1985: 47)

Proponents of the approach criticized accounts that were solely based on thematic roles, as they were incapable of explaining diathesis alternations (Levin 1985: 49ff; 1995: 76ff). Instead, they proposed decompositions on the basis of Jackendoff's (1972; 1976) conceptual structures, Generative Semantics, earlier work by Carter (1976) and Joshi (1974), and ideas from Hale & Keyser (1987).

5.2 Structure and location of decompositions

The main idea in the early MIT Lexicon Project Working Papers was that two levels of lexical representation have to be distinguished, a lexical-semantic and a lexical-syntactic one (Rappaport, Laughren & Levin 1987, later published as Rappaport, Levin &Laughren 1993; Rappaport & Levin 1988). The lexical-syntactic representation, PAS ("predicate argument structure"), "distinguishes among the arguments of a predicator only according to how they combine with the predicator in a sentence". PAS, which is subject to the projection principle (Rappaport & Levin 1988: 16), expresses whether the role of an NP-argument is assigned (i) by the verb ("direct argument"), (ii) by a different theta role assigner like a preposition ("indirect argument"), or (iii) by the VP via predication ("external argument") (Rappaport, Laughren & Levin 1987: 3). These three modes of assignment are illustrated in the PAS for the verb *put*:

(11) a. *put*, PAS: $x < \underline{y}, P_{loc}\ z>$
      b. *put*, LCS: [x cause [y come to be at z]]

The lexical-semantic basis of PAS is a lexical decomposition, LCS ("Lexical Conceptual Structure") (Rappaport, Laughren & Levin 1987: 8). The main task for an LCS-based approach to lexical semantics is to find the mapping principles between LCS and PAS and between PAS and syntactic structure (Rappaport 1985: 146f).

Not all researchers associated with the MIT Lexicon Project distinguished two levels of representation. Carter (1988) refers directly to argument positions of predicates within decompositions in order to explain linking phenomena. In later work, Levin and Rappaport do not make reference to PAS as a level of representation anymore. The distinction between grammatically relevant and irrelevant lexical information is now reflected in a distinction between primitive predicates that are embedded in semantic templates, which are claimed to be part of Universal Grammar, and predicate constants, which reflect the idiosyncratic part of lexical meaning. The templates pick up distinctions known from Vendler classes (Vendler 1957) and are referred to as event structure representations. For example, (12a) is a template for an activity, and (12b) is a template for a particular kind of accomplishment (Rappaport Hovav & Levin 1998: 108):

(12) a. [x ACT$_{<MANNER>}$]
 b. [[x ACT$_{<MANNER>}$] CAUSE [BECOME [y <STATE>]]]

The templates in (12) illustrate two main characteristics of this approach: templates can embed other templates and constants can function as modifiers of predicates (e.g., <MANNER> with respect to ACT) or as arguments of predicates (e.g., <STATE> with respect to BECOME). The representations are augmented by well-formedness conditions that require that each subevent in a template is represented by a lexical head in syntax and that all participants in lexical structure and all argument XPs in syntax are mapped onto each other. The principle of Template Augmentation makes it possible to build up complex lexical representations from simple ones such that the variants of *sweep* reflected in (13a-13c) are represented by the decompositions in (14a-14c):

(13) a. Phil swept the floor.
 b. Phil swept the floor clean.
 c. Phil swept the crumbs onto the floor.

(14) a. [x ACT$_{<SWEEP>}$ y]
 b. [[x ACT$_{<SWEEP>}$ y] CAUSE [BECOME [y <STATE>]]]
 c. [[x ACT$_{<SWEEP>}$ y] CAUSE [BECOME [z <PLACE>]]]

It is assumed that the nature of the constant can determine the range of templates that can be associated with it (cf. article 4 [this volume] (Levin & Rappaport Hovav) *Lexical Conceptual Structure*).

It should be noticed that the approach based on LCS-type decompositions aims primarily at explaining the regularities of argument realization. Particularly in its later versions, it is not intended to capture different kinds of entailments, aspectual behaviour, or restrictions on adverbial modification. It is assumed that all and only those meaning components that are relevant to grammar can be isolated and represented as LCS templates.

5.3 Linguistic phenomena

Within this approach, most research was focused on argument structure alternations that verbs may undergo.

(15) a. Bill loaded cartons onto the truck.
    b. Bill loaded the truck with cartons.

With respect to alternations as in (15) Rappaport & Levin (1988: 19ff) argued that a lexical meaning representation has to account for (i) the near paraphrase relation between the two variants, (ii) the different linking behaviour of the variants, (iii) and the interpretation of the goal argument in (15b) as completely affected by the action. They argued that a theta role approach could not fulfill these requirements: If the roles for *load* were considered identical for both variants, for example, <agent, locatum, goal>, requirement (i) is met but (ii) and (iii) are not since the different argument realizations cannot follow from identical theta role assignments and the affectedness component in (15b) is not expressed. If the roles for the two variants are considered different, for example, <agent, theme, goal> for (15a) versus <agent, locatum, goal> for (15b), the near paraphrase relation gets lost, and the completeness interpretation of (15b) still needs stipulative interpretation rules.

Within an LCS approach, linking rules make reference not to theta roles but to substructures of decompositions, for example, "When the LCS of a verb includes one of the substructures in [16], link the variable represented by x in either substructure to the direct argument variable in the verb's PAS.

(16) a. ... [x come to be at LOCATION] ...
    b. ... [x come to be in STATE] ..." (Rappaport & Levin 1988: 25)

With respect to *load*, it is assumed that the variant in (17b) with its additional meaning component of completion entails the variant in (17a) giving rise to the following representations:

(17) a. *load*: [x cause [y to come to be at z] /LOAD]
    b. *load*: [[x cause [z to come to be in STATE]] BY MEANS OF [x cause [y to come to be at z]] /LOAD] (Rappaport & Levin 1988: 26)

Assuming that the linking rules apply to the main clause within the decomposition, the two decompositions lead to different PAS representations in which the direct argument is associated with the theme in (18a) and the goal in (18b):

(18) a. *load*: x <$\underline{y}$, P_{loc} z>
    b. *load*: x <$\underline{z}$, P_{with} y>

Thus the three observations, (i) near-paraphrase relation, (ii) different linking behaviour, and (iii) complete affectedness of the theme in one variant, are accounted for.

Among the contemporary studies that proceeded in a similar vein are Hale & Keyser's (1987) work on the middle construction and Guerssel et al.'s (1985) crosslinguistic studies on causative, middle, and conative alternations.

It is particularly noteworthy that Levin and Rappaport have greatly expanded the range of phenomena in the domain of argument structure alternations that a lexical semantic theory has to cover. Their empirical work on verb classes determined by the range of argument structure alternations they allow is documented in Levin (1993): About 80 argument structure alternations in English lead to the definition of almost 200 verb classes. The theoretical work represented by the template approach to LCS focuses on finding the appropriate constraints that guide the extension of verb meanings and explain the variance in argument structure alternations.

5.4 Evaluation

The work of Levin, Rappaport Hovav, and other researchers working with LCS-like structures had a large influence on later work on the syntax-semantics interface. By uncovering the richness of the domain of argument structure alternations, they defined what theories at the lexical syntax-semantic interface have to account for today. Among the work inspired by Levin and Rappaport Hovav's theory are approaches whose goal is to establish linking regularities on more abstract, structural properties of decompositions (e.g., Lexical Decomposition Grammar, cf. section 8) and attempts to integrate elements of lexical decompositions into syntactic structure (cf. section 9).

Levin and Rappaport Hovav's work is also typical of a large amount of lexical semantic research in the 1980s and 90s that has largely given up the semantic rigorousness characteristic of approaches based on formal semantics like Dowty (1979). Less rigorous semantic relations make theories more susceptible to circular argumentations when semantic representations are mapped onto syntactic ones (cf. article 7 [Semantics: Foundations, History and Methods] (Engelberg) *Lexical decomposition*, section 3.5). It has also been questioned whether Levin and Rappaport Hovav's approach allows for a principled account of cross-linguistic variation and universals (Croft 1998: 26; Zubizarreta & Oh 2007: 8).

6 Event Structure Theory

6.1 Origins and motivation

In the late 1980s, two papers approaching verb semantics from a philosophical point of view inspired much research in the domain of aspect and Aktionsart, namely, Vendler's (1957) classification of expressions based on predicational aspect and Davidson's (1967) suggestion to reify events in order to explain adverbial modification. In connection with Dowty's (1979) work on decompositions within Montague semantics, the intensification of research on grammatical aspect, predicational aspect, and Aktionsarten also stimulated event-based research in lexical semantics. In particular, Pustejovsky's (1988; 1991a; 1991b) idea of conceiving of verbs as referring to structured events added a new dimension to decompositional approaches to verb semantics.

6.2 Structure and location of decompositions

According to Pustejovsky (1988; 1991a; 1991b), each verb refers to an event that can consist of subevents of different types, where 'processes' (P) and 'states' (S) are simple types that can combine to yield the complex type 'transition' $[P\ S]_T$ via event composition. A process is conceived of as "a sequence of events identifying the same semantic expression", a state as "a single event, which is evaluated relative to no other event", and a transition as "an event identifying a semantic expression, which is evaluated relative to its opposition" (Pustejovsky 1991a: 56). In addition to this event structure (ES), Pustejovsky assumes a level LCS', where each subevent is related to a decomposition. Out of this, a third level of Lexical Conceptual Structure (LCS) can be derived, which contains a single lexical decomposition. The following examples illustrate how the meaning of sentences is based on these representational levels:

(19) a. Mary ran.
 b. Mary ran to the store.
 c. The door is closed.
 d. The door closed.
 e. John closed the door.

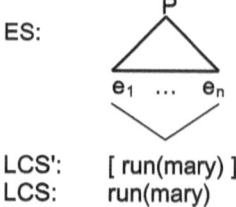

ES:

LCS':   [run(mary)]
LCS: run(mary)

Fig. 2.9: Representation of *Mary ran*

2 Frameworks of lexical decomposition of verbs — 71

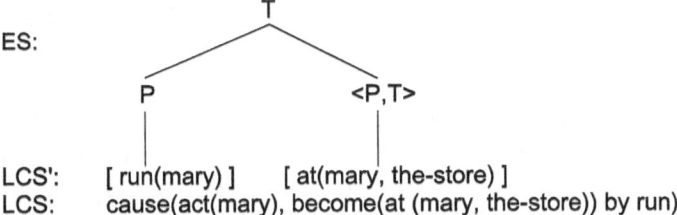

ES:

LCS': [run(mary)]   [at(mary, the-store)]
LCS: cause(act(mary), become(at (mary, the-store)) by run)

Fig. 2.10: Representation of *Mary ran to the store*

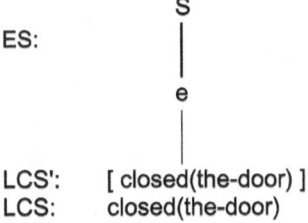

ES:

LCS': [closed(the-door)]
LCS: closed(the-door)

Fig. 2.11: Representation of *the door is closed*

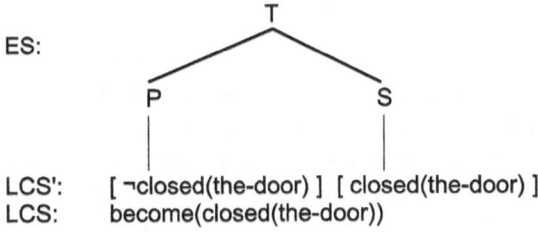

ES:

LCS': [¬closed(the-door)] [closed(the-door)]
LCS: become(closed(the-door))

Fig. 2.12: Representation of *the door closed*

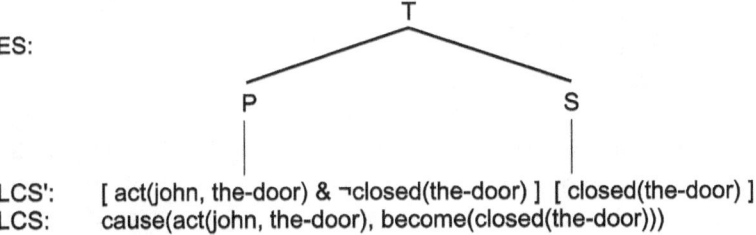

ES:

LCS': [act(john, the-door) & ¬closed(the-door)] [closed(the-door)]
LCS: cause(act(john, the-door), become(closed(the-door)))

Fig. 2.13: Representation of *John closed the door*

In terms of Vendler classes, Fig. 2.9 describes an activity, Fig. 2.11 a state, Figs. 2.10 and 2.13 accomplishments, and Fig. 2.12 an achievement. According to Pustejovsky, achievements and accomplishments have in common that they lead to a result state and are distinguished in that achievements do not involve an act-predicate at LCS'. As in many other decompositional theories (Jackendoff 1972; van Valin 1993), thematic roles are considered epiphenomenal and can be derived from the structured lexical representations (Pustejovsky 1988: 27).

Pustejovsky's event structure theory is part of his attempt to construct a theory of the Generative Lexicon (Pustejovsky 1995) that, besides Event Structure, also comprises Qualia Structure, Argument Structure, and Inheritance Structure (Pustejovsky 1991b, 1995). He criticises contemporary theories for focussing too much on the search for a finite set of semantic primitives:

> Rather than assuming a fixed set of *primitives*, let us assume a fixed number of *generative devices* that can be seen as constructing semantic expressions. Just as a formal language is described in terms of the productions in the grammar rather than its accompanying vocabulary, a semantic language should be defined by the rules generating the structures for expressions rather than the vocabulary of primitives itself.
>
> (Pustejovsky 1991a: 54)

6.3 Linguistic phenomena

The empirical coverage of Pustejovsky's theory is wider than many other decompositional theories: (i) The ambiguity of adverbials as in *Lisa rudely departed* is explained by attaching the adverb either to the whole transition T ('It was rude of Lisa to depart') or to the embedded process P ('Lisa departed in a rude manner') (Pustejovsky 1988: 31f). (ii) The mapping of Vendler classes onto structural event representations allows for a formulation of the restrictions on temporal-aspectual adverbials (*in five minutes, for five minutes*, etc.) (Pustejovsky 1991a: 73). (iii) The linking behaviour of verbs is related to LCS' components; for example, the difference between unaccusatives and unergatives is accounted for by postulating that a participant involved in a predicate opposition (as in Fig. 2.12) is mapped onto the internal argument position in syntax while the agentive participant in an initial subevent (as in Fig. 2.13) is realized as the external argument (Pustejovsky 1991a: 75). Furthermore, on the basis of Event Structure and Qualia Structure, a theory of aspectual coercion is developed (Pustejovsky & Bouillon 1995) as well as an account of lexicalizations of causal relations (Pustejovsky 1995).

6.4 Evaluation

Pustejovsky's concept of event structures has been taken up by many other lexical semanticists. Some theories included event structures as an additional level of representation. Grimshaw (1990) proposed a linking theory that combined a thematic hierarchy and an aspectual hierarchy of arguments based on the involvement of event participants in Pustejovsky-style subevents. In Lexical Decomposition Grammar, event structures were introduced as a level expressing sortal restrictions on events in order to explain the distribution and semantics of adverbials (Wunderlich 1996). It has sometimes been criticised that Pustejovsky's event structures were not fine-grained enough to explain adverbial modification. Consequently, suggestions have been made how to modify and extend event structures (e.g., Wunderlich 1996; cf. also Engelberg 2006).

Apart from those studies and theories that make explicit reference to Pustejovsky's event structures, a number of other approaches emerged in which phasal or mereological properties of events are embedded in lexical semantic representations, among them work by Tenny (1987; 1988), van Voorst (1988), Croft (1998), and some of the syntactic approaches to be discussed in section 9. Even standard lexical decompositions are often conceived of as event descriptions and referred to as 'event structures', for example, the LCS structures in Rappaport Hovav & Levin (1998).

Event structures by themselves can of course not be considered full decompositions that exhaust the meaning of a lexical item. As we have seen above, they are always combined with other lexical information, for example, LCS-style decompositions or thematic role representations. Depending on the kind of representation they are attached to it is not quite clear if they constitute an independent level of representation. In Pustejovsky's approach, event structures are probably by and large derivable from the LCS structures they are linked to.

7 Two-level Semantics and Lexical Decompositional Grammar

7.1 Origins and motivation

Two-level-Semantics originated in the 1980s with Manfred Bierwisch, Ewald Lang and Dieter Wunderlich being its main proponents (Bierwisch 1982; 1989; 1997; Bierwisch & Lang 1989; Wunderlich 1991; 1997a; cf. article 5 [Semantics: Theories] (Lang & Maienborn) *Two-level Semantics*). In particular, Bierwisch's contribution is remarkable for his attempt to define the role of the lexicon within Generative Grammar. Lexical Decomposition Grammar (LDG) emerged out of Two-level Semantics in the early 1990s. LDG has been particularly concerned with the lexical decompositon of verbs and the relation between semantic, conceptual, and syntactic structure. It has been developed by Dieter Wunderlich (1991; 1997a; 1997b; 2000; 2006) and other linguists stemming from the Düsseldorf Institute for General Linguistics (Stiebels 1996; 1998; 2006; Kaufmann 1995a; 1995b; 1995c; Joppen & Wunderlich 1995; Gamerschlag 2005) – with contributions by Paul Kiparsky (cf. article 2 [Semantics: Interfaces] (Kiparsky & Tonhauser) *Semantics of inflection*).

7.2 Structure and location of decompositions

Two-level semantics argues for separating semantic representations (semantic form, SF) that are part of the linguistic system, and conceptual representations that are part of the conceptual system (CS). Only SF is seen as a part of grammar that is integrated into its computational mechanisms while conceptual structure is a level of reasoning that builds on more general mental operations. How the interplay between SF and CS can be spelled out is shown in Maienborn (2003). She argues that spatial PPs can either function as event-external modifiers, locating the event as a whole as in (20a), or as event-internal modifiers, specifying a spatial relation that holds within the event as in (20b). While external event location is semantically straightforward, internal event location is subject to conceptual knowledge. Not only does the local relation expressed in (20b) require world knowledge about spatial relations in bike riding events, it is also reinterpreted as an instrumental relation that is not lexically provided by the verb or the preposition. Furthermore, in sentences like (20c) the external argument of the preposition, the woman's hand or some instrument the woman uses is not even mentioned in the sentence but has to be supplied by conceptual knowledge.

(20) a. Der Bankräuber ist auf der Insel geflohen.
 the bank robber has on the island escaped.
 b. Der Bankräuber ist auf dem Fahrrad geflohen.
 the bank robber has on the bicycle escaped.
 c. Maria zog Paul an den Haaren aus dem Zimmer.
 Maria pulled Paul at the hair out of the room.

Several tests show that event-internal modifiers attach to the edge of V and event external modifiers to the edge of VP. Maienborn (2003: 487) suggests that the two syntactic positions trigger slightly different modification processes at the level of SF. While in both cases the lexical entries entering the semantic composition have the same decompositional representation (21a, b), the process of external modification identifies the external argument of the preposition with the event argument of the verb (21c; λQ applying to the PP, λP to the verb), whereas the process of internal modification turns the external argument of the preposition into a free variable, a so-called SF parameter (variable v in 21d) that is specified as a constituent part (part-of) of what will later be instantiated with the event variable.

(21) a. [$_p$ auf]: λy λx [LOC (x, ON (y))]
  b. [$_v$ fliehen]: λx λe [ESCAPE (e) & THEME (e, x)]
  c. MOD: λQ λP λx [P(x) & Q(x)]
  d. MOD': λQ λP λx [P(x) & PART-OF (x, v) & Q(v)]

The compositional processes yield the representation in (22a) for the sentence (20b), the variable v being uninstantiated. This representation will be enriched at the level of CS which falls back on a large base of shared conceptual knowledge. The utterance meaning is achieved via abduction processes which lead to the most economical explanation that is consistent with what is in the knowledge base. Spelling out the relevant part of the knowledge base, i.e. knowledge about spatial relations, about event types in terms of participants serving particular functions, and about the part-whole organization of physical objects, Maienborn shows how the CS representation for (20b), given in (22b), can be fomally derived (for details cf. Maienborn 2003: 492ff).

(22) a. SF: ∃e [ESCAPE (e) & THEME (e, r) & BANK-ROBBER (r)
     & PART-OF (e, v) & LOC (v, ON (b)) & BIKE (b)]

  b. CS: ∃e [EXTR-MOVE (e) & ESCAPE (e) & THEME (e, r)
     & BANK-ROBBER (r) & INSTR (e, b) & VEHICLE (b)
     & BIKE (b) & SUPPORT (b, r, τ(e)) & LOC (r, ON (b))]

The emergence of Lexical Decomposition Grammar out of Two-level Semantics is particularly interesting for the development of theories of decompositional approaches to verb meaning. LDG locates decompositional representations in semantics and rejects syntactic approaches to decomposition arguing that they have failed to provide logically equivalent paraphrases and an adequate account of scopal properties of adverbials (Wunderlich 1997a: 28f). It assumes four levels of representation: conceptual structure (CS), semantic form (SF), theta structure (TS), and morphological/syntactic structure (MS, in earlier versions of LDG also called phrase structure, PS). SF is a decomposition based on type logic that is related to CS by restrictive lexicalization principles; TS is derived from SF by lambda abstraction and encodes the argument hierarchy. TS in turn is mapped onto MS by linking principles (Wunderlich 1997a: 32; 2000: 249ff). The four levels are illustrated in Fig. 2.14 with respect to the German verb *geben* 'give' in (23).

(23) a. (als) [der Torwart [dem Jungen [den Ball gab]]]
    (when) the goalkeeper the boy the ball gave
  b. [DP$^x_{NOM}$ [DP$^y_{DAT}$ [DP$^z_{ACC}$ *geb*-AGR^x]]]

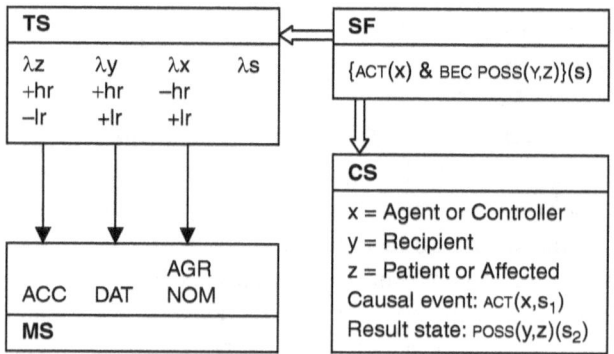

Fig. 2.14: The representational levels of LDG (Wunderlich 2000: 250)

Semantic form does not provide a complete characterization of a word's meaning. It serves to represent those properties of predicate-argument structures that make it possible to account for their grammatical properties (Wunderlich 1996: 170). This level of representation must be finite and not subject to contingent knowledge. In contrast to semantic form, conceptual structures draw on an infinite set of properties and can be subject to contingent knowledge (Wunderlich 1997a: 29). Since SF decompositions consist of hierarchically ordered binary structures - assuming that a & b branches as [a [& b]] – arguments can be ranked according to how deeply they are embedded within this structure. TS in turn preserves the SF hierarchy of arguments in inverse order so that arguments can be discharged by functional application (Wunderlich 1997a: 44). Each argument role in TS is characterized as to whether there is a higher or lower role.

Besides their thematic arguments, nouns and verbs also have referential arguments, which do not undergo linking. Referential arguments are subject to sortal restrictions that are represented as a structured index on the referential argument (Wunderlich 1997a: 34). With verbs, this sortal index consists of an event structure, similar in form to Pustejovsky's event structures but slightly differing with respect to the distinctions expressed (Wunderlich 1996: 175ff).

The relation between the different levels is mediated by a number of principles. For example, ARGUMENT HIERARCHY regulates the inverse hierarchical mapping from SF to TS, and COHERENCE requires that the subevents corresponding to SF predicates be interpreted as contemporaneous or causally related (Kaufmann 1995c). Thus, the causal interpretation of *geben* in (23) is not explicitly given in SF but left to COHERENCE as a general CS principle of interpretation.

7.3 Linguistic phenomena

The main concern of LDG is argument linking, and its basic assumption is that syntactic properties of arguments follow from hierarchical structures within semantic form. Structural linking is based on the assignment of two binary features to the arguments in TS, [± hr] 'there is a / no higher role' and [± lr] 'there is a / no lower role'. The syntactic features are associated with these two binary features, dative with [+ hr, + lr], accusative with [+hr], ergative with [+lr], and nominative/absolutive with [ ] (cf. Fig. 2.14). All and only the structural arguments have to be matched with a structural linker. Besides structural linking, it is taken into account that arguments can be suppressed or realized by oblique markers. This also motivates the distinction between SF and TS (Wunderlich 1997b: 47ff; 2000: 252). The following examples show how structural arguments are matched with structural linkers in nominative-accusative (NA) and absolutive-ergative (AE) languages (Wunderlich 1997a: 49):

(24) a. intransitive verbs: λx
                              [-hr, -lr]
                     NA: nom
                     AE: abs
     b. transitive verbs: λy   λx
                              [+hr, -lr] [-hr, +lr]
                     NA: acc   nom
                     AE: abs   erg
     c. ditransitive verbs: λz   λy   λx
                              [+hr, -lr] [+hr, +lr] [-hr, +lr]
                     NA: acc   dat   nom
                     AE: abs   dat   erg

LDG pursues a strictly lexical account of argument extensions such as possessors, beneficiaries, or arguments introduced by word formation processes or resultative formation. These argument extensions are all handled within SF formation by adding predicates to an existing SF (Stiebels 1996; Wunderlich 2000). Thus, the complex verb in (25a) is represented as the complex SF (25c) on the basis of (25b) and an argument extension principle.

(25) a. Sie erschrieb sich den Pulitzer-Preis.
    she "er"-wrote herself the Pulitzer Prize
    'She won the Pulitzer Prize by her writing.'
  b. *schreib-* 'write': $\lambda y \lambda x \lambda s\ \text{WRITE}(x,y)(s)$
  c. *erschreib*: $\lambda v \lambda u \lambda x \lambda s \exists y\ \{\text{WRITE}(x,y)(s)\ \&\ \text{BECOME POSS}(u,v)\}(s)$

These processes are restricted by two constraints on possible verbs, COHERENCE and CONNEXION, the latter one requiring that each predicate in SF share at least one, possibly implicit, argument with another predicate in SF (Kaufmann 1995c). In (25c), COHERENCE guarantees the causal interpretation, and CONNEXION accounts for the identification of the agent of writing with the possessor of the prize. The resulting SF is then subject to ARGUMENT HIERARCHY and the usual linking principles. As we have seen in (25c), the morphological operation adds semantic content to SF as it does with other operations like resultative formation. In other cases, morphology operates on TS in order to change linking conditions (e.g., passive) (Wunderlich 1997a: 52f).

During the last 20 years, LDG has produced numerous studies on phenomena in a number of typologically diverse languages, dealing with agreement (Wunderlich 1994), word formation of verbs (Wunderlich 1997b; Stiebels 1996; Gamerschlag 2005), locative verbs (Kaufmann 1995a), causatives and resultatives (Wunderlich 1997a; Kaufmann 1995a), dative possessors (Wunderlich 2000), ergative case systems (Joppen & Wunderlich 1995), and nominal linking (Stiebels 2006).

7.4 Evaluation

In contrast to some other decompositional approaches, LDG adheres to a compositional approach to meaning and tries to define its relation to current syntactic theories. In more recent publications (Stiebels 2002; Gamerschlag 2005), LDG has been reformulated within an optimality theoretic framework. Lexical Decomposition Grammar is criticized by Taylor (2000), in particular for its division between semantic and conceptual knowledge. LDG, based on Two-level

Semantics, accounts for the different readings of a lexical item within conceptual structure, leaving lexical entries largely monosemous. Taylor argues that lexical usage is to a large degree conventionalized and that the particular readings a word does or does not have cannot be construed entirely from conceptual knowledge. Bierwisch (2002) presents a number of arguments against the removal of CAUSE from SF decompositions. Further problems, emerging from structural stipulations, are discussed in article 7 [Semantics: Foundations, History and Methods] (Engelberg) *Lexical decomposition*, section 3.5.

8 Natural Semantic Metalanguage

8.1 Origins and motivation

The theory of Natural Semantic Metalanguage (NSM) originated in the early seventies. Its main proponents have been Anna Wierzbicka (1972; 1980; 1985; 1992; 1996) and Cliff Goddard (1998; 2006; 2008a; Goddard & Wierzbicka 2002). NSM theory has been developed as an attempt to construct a semantic metalanguage (i) that is expressive enough to cover all the word meanings in natural languages, (ii) that allows noncircular reductive paraphrases, (iii) that avoids metalinguistic elements that are not part of the natural language it describes, (iv) that is not ethnocentric, and (v) that makes it possible to uncover the universal properties of word meanings (cf. for an overview Goddard 2002a; Durst 2003). In order to achieve this, Wierzbicka suggested that the lexicon of a language can be divided into a small set of indefinable words (semantic primes) and a large set of words that can be defined in terms of these indefinables.

8.2 Structure and location of decompositions

The term Natural Semantic Metalanguage is intended to reflect that the semantic primes used as a metalanguage are actual words of the object language. The indefinables constitute a finite set and, although they are language-specific, each language-specific set "realizes, in its own way, the same universal and innate alphabet of human thought" (Wierzbicka 1992: 209). More precisely, this implies that the set of semantic primes of a particular language and their combinatorial potential have the expressive power of a full natural language and that the sets of semantic primes of all languages are isomorphic to each other. The set of semantic primes consists of 60 or so elements including such words as *you, this, two, good, know, see, word, happen, die, after, near, if, very, kind of,* and *like,* each disambiguated by a canonical context (cf. Goddard 2008b). These primes are claimed to be indefinable and indispensable (cf. Goddard & Wierzbicka 1994b; Wierzbicka 1996; Goddard 2002b; Wierzbicka 2009). Meaning descriptions within NSM theory look like the following (Wierzbicka 1992: 133):

(26) a. (X is *embarrassed*)
    b. X thinks something like this:
       something happened to me now.
       because of this, people here are thinking about me.
       I don't want this.
       because of this, I would want to do something.
       I don't know what I can do.
       I don't want to be here now.
       because of this, X feels something bad.

It is required for the relationship between the defining decomposition and the defined term that they be identical in meaning. This is connected to substitutability; the definiens and the definiendum are supposed to be replaceable by each other without change of meaning (Wierzbicka 1988: 12).

8.3 Linguistic phenomena

More than any other decompositional theory, NSM theory resembles basic lexicographic approaches to meaning, in particular, those traditions of English learner lexicography in which definitions of word meanings are restricted to the non-circular use of a limited "controlled" defining vocabulary (e.g., Summers 1995). Thus, it is not surprising that NSM theory tackles word meanings in many semantic fields that have not been at the centre of attention within other decompositional approaches, for example, pragmatically complex domains like speech act verbs (Wierzbicka 1987). Other investigations focus on the cultural differences reflected in words and their alleged equivalents in other languages, for example, Wierzbicka's (1999) study on emotion words. NSM theory also claims to be able to render the meaning of syntactic constructions and grammatical categories by decompositions. An example is given in (27).

(27) a. *['first person plural exclusive']*
    b. I'm thinking of some people.
       I am one of these people.
       you are not one of these people. (Goddard 1998: 299)

The claim of NSM theory to be particularly apt as a means to detect subtle cross-linguistic differences is reflected in Goddard & Wierzbicka (1994a), where studies on a fairly large number of typologically and genetically diverse languages are presented.

8.4 evaluation

While many of its critics acknowledge that NSM theory has provided many insights into particular lexical phenomena, its basic theoretical assumptions have often been subject to criticism. It has been called into question whether the emphasis on giving dictionary-style explanations of word meanings is identical to uncovering the native speaker's knowledge about word meaning. NSM theory has also been criticized for not putting much effort into providing a foundation for the theory on basic semantics concepts (cf. Riemer 2006: 352). The lack of a theory of truth, reference, and compositionality within NSM theory raised severe doubts about whether it can adequately deal with phenomena like quantification, anaphora, proper names, and presuppositions (Geurts 2003; Matthewson 2003; Barker 2003). This criticism also affects the claim of the theory to be able to cover the semantics of the entire lexicon of a language.

9 Lexical Relational Structures

9.1 Origins and motivation

With the decline of Generative Semantics in the 1970s, lexical approaches to decomposition began to dominate the field. These approaches enriched our understanding of the complexity of lexical meaning as well as the possibility of generalizations across verb classes. Then, in the late 1980s, syntactic developments within the Principles & Parameter framework suggested more complex structures within the VP. The assumption of VP-internal subjects and, in particular, Larson's (1988) theory of VP-shells as layered VP-internal structures suggested the possibility to align certain bits of verb-internal semantic structure with structural positions in layered VPs. With these developments underway, the time was ripe for new syntactic approaches to decomposition (cf. also the summary in Levin & Rappaport Hovav 2005: 131ff).

9.2 Structure and location of decompositions

On the basis of data from binding, quantification, and conjunction with respect to double object constructions, Larson (1988: 381) argues for the SINGLE ARGUMENT HYPOTHESIS, according to which a head can only have one argument. This forces a layered structure with multiple heads within VP. Fig. 2.15 exhibits the structure of *Mary gave a box to Tom* within this VP-shell. The verb moves to the higher V node by head-movement. The mapping of a verb's arguments onto the nodes within the VP-shell is determined by a theta hierarchy 'AGENT > THEME > GOAL > OBLIQUES' such that the lowest role of a verb is assigned to the lowest argument position, the next lowest role to the next lowest argument position, and so on (Larson 1988: 382). Thus, there is a weak correspondence between structural positions and verb semantics in the sense that high argument positions are associated with a comparatively high thematic value. However, structural positions within VP shells are not linked to any stable semantic interpretation.

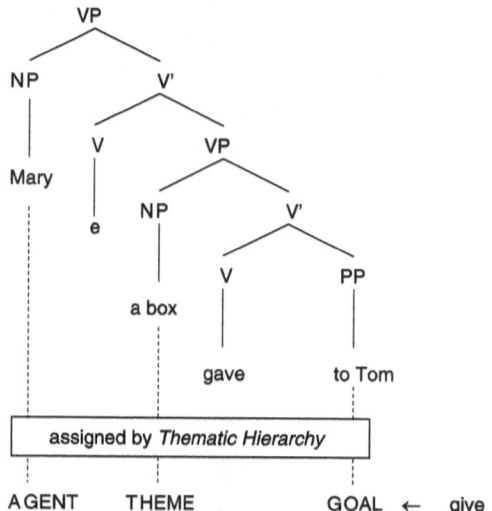

Fig. 2.15: VP-shell and theta role assignment

Larsonian shells inspired research on the syntactic representation of argument structure. Particularly influential was the approach pursued by Hale & Keyser (1993; 1997; 2002). They assume that argument structure is handled within a lexicon component called l-syntax, which is an integral part of syntax as it obeys syntactic principles. The basic assumption is that argument structure, also called "lexical relational structure", is defined in reference to two possible relations between a head and its arguments, namely, the head-complement and the head-specifier relation (Hale & Keyser 1999: 454). Each verb projects an unambiguous structure in l-syntax. In Fig. 2.16, the lexical relational structure of *put* as in *put the books on the shelf* is illustrated.

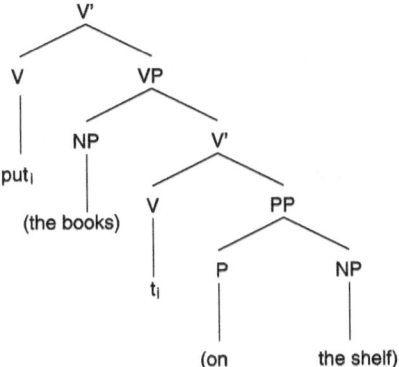

Fig. 2.16: Lexical relational structure of *put* and head movement of the verb

Primary evidence for this approach is taken from verbs that are regarded as denominal. Locational verbs of this sort such as *to shelve*, *to box*, or *to saddle* receive a similar representation as *to put*. The Lexical Relational Structure of *shelve* consists of Larsonian VP-shells with the noun *shelf* as complement of the embedded prepositional head. From there, the noun incorporates into an abstract V head by head movement (cf. Fig. 2.17). (Hale & Keyser 1993: 55ff)

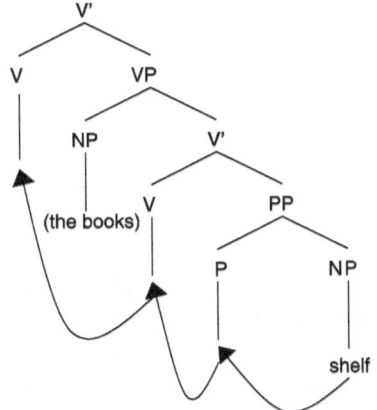

Fig. 2.17: Lexical relational structure of *shelve* and incorporation of the noun

In a similar way, unergative verbs like *sneeze* or *dance* (28b), which are assumed to have a structure parallel to expressions like *make trouble* or *have puppies* (28a), are derived by incorporation of a noun into a V head (Hale & Keyser 1993: 54f).

(28) a. [have $_V$ [puppies $_N$] $_{NP}$] $_{V'}$
     b. [sneeze$_{i\,V}$ [t$_{i\,N}$] $_{NP}$] $_{V'}$

Hale & Kayser (1993: 68) assume that "elementary semantic relations" are "associated" with these syntactic structures: The agent occurs in a Spec position above VP, the theme in a Spec position of a V that takes a PP/AP complement, and so forth. The argument structure of *shelve* is thus related to semantic relations as exhibited in Fig. 2.18.

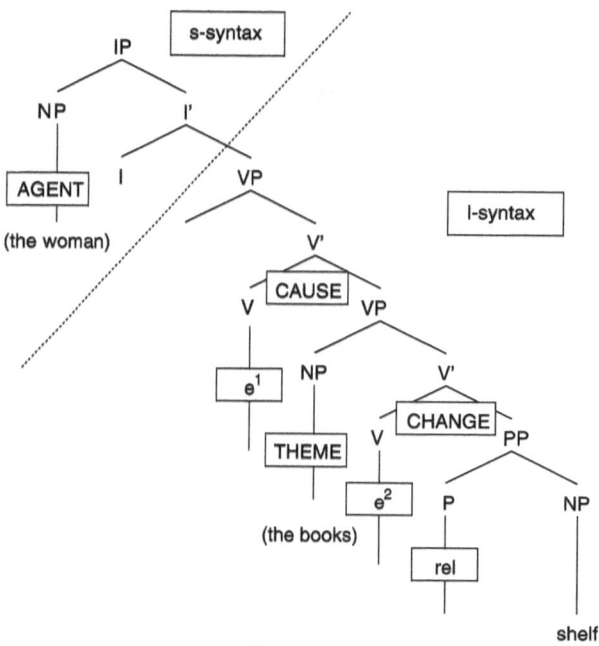

Fig. 2.18: Semantic relations associated with lexical relational structures (after Hale & Keyser 1993: 76ff)

It is important to keep in mind that Hale and Keyser do not claim that argument structures are derived from semantics. On the contrary, they assume that "certain meanings can be assigned to certain structures" in the sense that they are fully determined by l-syntactic configurations (Hale & Keyser 1993: 68; 1999: 463).

Fig. 2.18 also reflects two important points of Hale and Keyser's theory. Firstly, they assume a central distinction between verb classes: Contrary to the early exploration of VP structures as in Fig. 2.17, unergatives and transitives in contrast to unaccusatives are assumed not to have a subject as part of their argument structure; their subjects are assigned in s-syntax (Hale & Keyser 1993: 76ff). Secondly, Hale and Kayser emphasize that their approach explains why the number of theta roles is (allegedly) so small, namely, because there is only a very restricted set of syntactic configurations with which they can be associated.

9.3 Linguistic phenomena

Hale and Keyser's approach aims to explain why certain argument structures are possible while others are not. For example, it is argued that sentences like (29a) are ungrammatical because incorporation of a subject argument violates the Empty Category Principle (Hale & Keyser 1993: 60). The ungrammaticality of (29b) is accounted for by the assumption that unergatives as in (28) do not project a specifier that would allow a transitivity alternation (Hale & Keyser 1999: 455). (29c) is argued to be ungrammatical because the Lexical Relational Structure would have to be parallel to *she gave a church her money*, in which *church* occupies Spec,VP, the "subject" position of the inner VP. Incorporation from this position violates the Empty Category Principle. By the same reasoning, *she flattened the metal* is well-formed, incorporating *flat* from an AP in complement position while (29d) is not since *metal* would have to incorporate from an inner subject position.

(29) a. *It cowed a calf. (with the meaning 'a cow calved' and *it* as expletive)
 b. *An injection calved the cow early.
 c. *She churched the money.
 d. *She metalled flat.

This incorporation approach allows Hale and Keyser to explore the parallels in syntactic behaviour between expressions like *give a laugh* and *laugh* which, besides being near-synonymous, both fail to transitivize, as well as the differences between expressions like *make trouble* and *thicken soups* where only the latter allows middles and inchoatives.

9.4 Evaluation

Hale and Keyser's work has stimulated a growing body of research aiming at a syntactification of notions of thematic roles, decompositional and aspectual structures. Some prominent examples are Mateu (2001), Alexiadou & Anagnostopoulou (2004), Erteschik-Shir & Rapoport (2005; 2007), Zubizarreta & Oh (2007), and Ramchand's (2008) first phase syntax. Some of this work places a strong emphasis on aspectual structure, for example, Ritter & Rosen (1998) and Travis (2000). As Travis (2000: 181f) argues, the new syntactic approaches to decompositions avoid many of the pitfalls of Generative Semantics, which is certainly due to a better understanding of restrictive principles in recent syntactic theories.

However, Hale and Keyser's work has also attracted heavy criticism from proponents of Lexical Conceptual Structure (e.g., Culicover & Jackendoff 2005, Rappaport Hovav & Levin 2005), Two-level Semantics (e.g., Bierwisch 1997; Kiparsky 1997) as well as from anti-decompositionalist positions (e.g., Fodor & Lepore 1999). The analyses themselves raise many questions. For example, it remains unexplained which principles exclude a lexical structure of a putative verb *to church* (29c) along the lines of *she gave the money to the church*, that is, a structure parallel to the one suggested for *to shelve* (cf. also Kiparsky 1997: 481). It has also been observed that the position allegedly vacated by the noun in structures as in Fig. 2.18 can actually show lexical material as in *Joe buttered the toast with rancid butter* (Culicover & Jackendoff 2005: 102). Many other analyses and assumptions have also been under attack, among them assumptions about which verbs are denominal and how their meanings come about (Kiparsky 1997: 485ff; Culicover & Jackendoff 2005: 55) as well as predictions about possible transitivity alternations (Kiparsky 1997: 491). Furthermore, one can of course doubt that the number of different theta roles is as small as Hale and Keyser assume. More empirically oriented approaches to verb semantics come to dramatically different conclusions (cf. Kiparsky 1997: 478 or work on Frame Semantics like Ruppenhofer et al. 2006). Even some problems from Generative Semantics reemerge, such as that expressions like *put on a shelf* and *shelve* are not synonymous, the latter being more specific (Bierwisch 1997: 260). Overgeneralization is not accounted for, either. The fact that there is a verb *to shelve* but no semantically corresponding verb *to basket* points to a location of decomposition in the lexicon (Bierwisch 1997: 232f). Reacting to some of the criticism, Hale & Keyser (2005) later modified some assumptions of their theory; for example, they abandoned the idea of incorporation in favour of a locally operating selection mechanism.

10 Distributed Morphology

10.1 Origins and motivation

Hale & Keyser (1993) and much research inspired by them have attempted to reduce the role of the lexicon in favour of syntactic representations. An even more radical anti-lexicalist approach is pursued by Distributed Morphology (DM), which started out in Halle & Marantz (1993) and since then has been elaborated by a number of DM proponents (Marantz 1997; Harley 2002; Harley & Noyer 1999; 2000; Embick 2004; Embick & Noyer 2007) (cf. also article 5 [Semantics: Interfaces] (Harley) *Semantics in Distributed Morphology*).

10.2 Structure and location of decompositions

According to Distributed Morphology, syntax does not combine words but generates structures by combining morphosyntactic features. Terminal nodes, so-called "morphemes", are bundles of these morphosyntactic features. DM distinguishes f-nodes from l-nodes. F-nodes correspond to what is traditionally known as functional, closed-class categories; their insertion at spell-out is deterministic. L-nodes correspond to lexical, open-class categories; their insertion is not deterministic. Vocabulary items are only inserted at spell-out. These vocabulary items are minimally specified in that they only consist of a phonological string and some information where this string can be inserted (cf. Fig. 2.19).

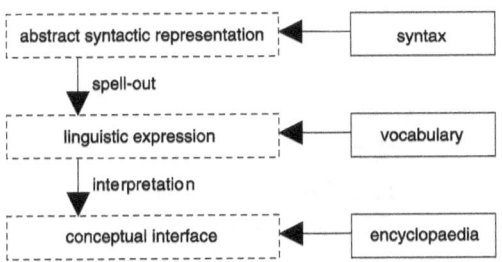

Fig. 2.19: The architecture of distributional morphology cf. Harley & Noyer 2000: 352; Embick & Noyer 2007)

Neither a syntactic category nor any kind of argument structure representation is included in vocabulary entries as can be seen in example (30a) from Harley & Noyer (1999: 3). The distribution information in the vocabulary item replaces what is usually done by theta-roles and selection. In addition to the Vocabulary, there is a component called Encyclopaedia where vocabulary items are linked to those aspects of meaning that are not completely predictable from morphosyntactic structure (30b).

(30)   a. Vocabulary item: /dog/: [Root] [+count] [+animate] ...
       b. Encyclopaedia item: dog: four legs, canine, pet, sometimes bites etc... chases balls, in environment "let sleeping ___s lie", refers to discourse entity who is better left alone...

While the formal information in vocabulary items in part determines grammatical well-formedness, the encyclopaedic information guides the appropriate use of expressions. For example, the oddness of (31a) is attributed to encyclopaedic knowledge. The sentence is pragmatically anomalous but interpretable: It could refer to some unusual telepathic transportation event. (31b), on the other hand, is considered ungrammatical because *put* is not properly licensed and, therefore, uninterpretable under any circumstances (Harley & Noyer 2000: 354).

(31) a. Chris thought the book to Mary.
 b. *James put yesterday.

Part of speech is reflected in DM by the constellation in which a root morpheme occurs. For example, a root is a noun if its nearest c-commanding f-node is a determiner and a verb if its nearest c-commanding f-nodes are *v*, aspect, and tense. Not only are lexical entries more reduced than in approaches based on Hale & Keyser (1993), there is also no particular part of syntax corresponding to l-syntax (cf. for this overview Harley & Noyer 1999, 2000; Embick & Noyer 2007).

10.3 Linguistic phenomena

Distributed Morphology has been applied to all kinds of phenomena in the domain of inflectional and derivational morphology. Some work has also been done with respect to the argument structure of verbs and nominalizations. One of the main topics in this area is the explanation of the range of possible argument structure alternations. A typical set of data is given in (32) and (33) (taken from Harley & Noyer 2000: 362).

(32) a. John grows tomatoes.
 b. Tomatoes grow.
 c. The insects destroyed the crop.
 d. *The crops destroyed.

(33) a. the growth of the tomatoes.
 b. the tomatoes' growth.
 c. *John's growth of the tomatoes.
 d. the crop's destruction.
 e. the insects' destruction of the crop.

It has to be explained why *grow*, but not *destroy*, has an intransitive variant and why *destruction*, but not *growth*, allows the realization of the causer argument in Spec, DP (for the following, cf. Harley & Noyer 2000: 356ff). Syntactic structures are based on VP-shells. For each node in these structures, there is a set of possible items that can fill this position (with LP corresponding approximately to VP):

(34)   node   possible filling
     a.   Spec,*v*P   DP, ∅
     b.   *v* head   HAPPEN/BECOME, CAUSE, BE
     c.   Spec,LP   DP, ∅
     d.   L head   l-node
     e.   Comp,LP   DP, ∅

Picking from this menu, a number of different syntactic configurations can be created:

(35)

	Spec,*v*P	v	Spec,LP	L	Comp,LP	(example)
a.	DP	CAUSE	∅	l	DP	*grow* (tr.)
b.	∅	BECOME	∅	l	DP	*grow* (itr.)
c.	DP	CAUSE	∅	l	DP	*destroy*
d.	DP	CAUSE	DP	l	DP	*give*
e.	∅	BECOME	∅	l	DP	*arrive*
f.	∅	BE	DP	l	DP	*know*

The items filling the *v* head are the only ones conceived of as having selectional properties: CAUSE, but not BECOME or BE, selects an external argument. The grammaticality of the configurations in (35) is also determined by the licensing environment specified in the Vocabulary (cf. Fig. 2.20).

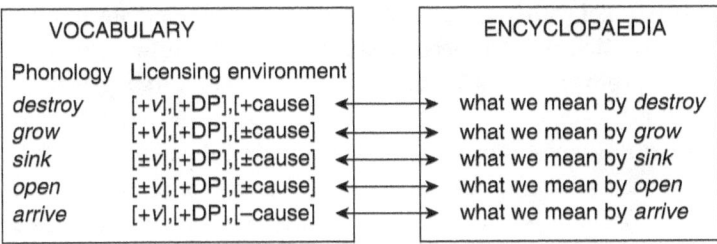

Fig. 2.20: Vocabulary and encyclopaedic entries of verbs (after Harley & Noyer 2000: 361)

Thus, the transitive and intransitive uses of the roots in (32a) through (32c) are reflected in the syntactic structures in (36), where CAUSE and BECOME are realized as zero morphemes (cf. article 5 [Semantics: Interfaces] (Harley) *Semantics in Distributed Morphology*) and the LP head is assumed to denote a resulting state:

(36) a. [$_{vP}$ [DP John] [$_{v'}$ CAUSE [$_{LP}$ grown [$_{DP}$ tomatoes]]]]
 b. [$_{v'}$ BECOME [$_{LP}$ grown [$_{DP}$ tomatoes]]]
 c. [$_{vP}$ [DP the insects] [$_{v'}$ CAUSE [$_{LP}$ destroyed [$_{DP}$ the crop]]]]

The fact that *destroy* does not allow an intransitive variant is due to the fact that its licensing environment requires embedding under CAUSE while *grow* is underspecified in this respect. The explanation for the nominalization data in (33) relies on the assumption that Spec,DP is not as semantically loaded as Spec,vP. It is further assumed that by encyclopaedic knowledge *destroy* always requires external causation while *grow* refers inherently to an internally caused spontaneous activity, which is optionally facilitated by some agent. Since CAUSE is only implied with *destroy* but not with *grow*, only the causer of *destroy* can be interpreted in a semantically underspecified Spec,DP position. The fact that some verbs like *explode* behave partly like *grow*, in allowing the transitive-intransitive alternation, and partly like *destroy*, in allowing the realization of the causer in nominalizations, is explained by the assumption that the events denoted by such roots can occur spontaneously (internal causation) but can also be directly brought about by some agent (external causation) (cf. also Marantz 1997). In summary, the phenomena in (32) are traced back to syntactic regularities, those in (33) to encyclopaedic, that is, pragmatic conditions.

10.4 Evaluation

While some other approaches to argument structure share a number of assumptions with DM – for example, they also operate on category-neutral roots (e.g., Borer 2005; Arad 2002) – of course the radical theses of Distributed Morphology have also drawn some criticism. It has been doubted that all the differences in the syntactic behaviour of verbs can be accounted for with a syntax-free lexicon (cf. e.g., Ramchand 2008).

Cross-linguistic differences might also pose some problems. For example, it is assumed that verbs allowing the unaccusative-transitive alternation are distinguished on the basis of encyclopaedic semantic knowledge from those that do not (Embick 2004: 139). The causative variant of the showcase example *grow* in (32a) is grammatically licensed and pragmatically acceptable because of encyclopaedic knowledge. However, it is not clear why German *wachsen* 'grow' does not have a causative variant. The alternation would be expected since *wachsen* does not seem to differ from *grow* in its encyclopaedic properties. Moreover, many other verbs like *to dry* 'trocknen' (37) demonstrate that German does not show any kind of structural aversion to alternations of this sort.

(37) a. Der Salat trocknet / wächst.
'The lettuce dries / grows.'

b. Peter trocknet Salat / *wächst Salat.
'Peter dries lettuce / grows lettuce.'

The way the line is drawn between grammatical and pragmatic (un)acceptability also poses some problems. If the use of *put* with only one argument is considered ungrammatical, then how can similar uses of three-place verbs like German *stellen* 'put (in upright position)' and *geben* 'give' be explained (38)?

(38) a. Er gibt. 'He deals (in a card game).'
b. Sie stellt. 'She plays a volleyball such that somebody can smash it.'

Since they are ruled out by grammar, encyclopaedic knowledge cannot save these examples by assigning them an idiomatic meaning. Thus, it might turn out that sometimes argument-structure flexibility is not as general as DM's encyclopaedia suggests, and grammatical restrictions are not as strict as syntax and DM's vocabulary predict.

11 Outlook

The overview has shown that stances on lexical decomposition still differ widely, in particular with respect to the questions of where to locate lexical decompositions, how to interpret them, and how to justify them. It has to be noted that most work on lexical decompositions has not been accompanied by extensive empirical research. With the rise of new methods in the domain of corpus analysis, grammaticality judgements, and psycholinguistics (cf. article 7 [Semantics: Foundations, History and Methods] (Engelberg) *Lexical decomposition*, section 3.6), the empirical basis for further decompositional theories will alter dramatically. It remains to be seen how theories of the sort presented here will cope with the empirical turn in contemporary linguistics.

12 References

Alexiadou, Artemis & Elena Anagnostopoulou 2004. Voice morphology in the causative-inchoative alternation: Evidence for a non-unified structural analysis of unaccustives. In: A. Alexiadou, E. Anagnostopoulou & M. Everaert (eds.). *The Unaccusativity Puzzle. Explorations of the Syntax-Lexicon Interface*. Oxford: Oxford University Press, 114–136.

Arad, Maya 2002. Universal features and language-particular morphemes. In: A. Alexiadou (ed.). *Theoretical Approaches to Universals*. Amsterdam: Benjamins, 15–29.

Bach, Emmon 1968. Nouns and noun phrases. In: E. Bach & R. T. Harms (eds.). *Universals in Linguistic Theory*. New York: Holt, Rinehart & Winston, 90–122.

Barker, Chris 2003. Paraphrase is not enough. *Theoretical Linguistics* 29, 201–209.

Bartsch, Renate & Theo Vennemann 1972. *Semantic Structures. A Study in the Relation between Semantics and Syntax*. Frankfurt/M.: Athenäum.

Bierwisch, Manfred 1982. Formal and lexical semantics. *Linguistische Berichte* 30, 3–17.

Bierwisch, Manfred 1989. Event nominalizations: Proposals and problems. In: W. Motsch (ed.). *Wortstruktur und Satzstruktur*. Berlin: Akademie Verlag, 1–73.

Bierwisch, Manfred 1997. Lexical information from a minimalist point of view. In: C. Wilder, H.-M. Gärtner & M. Bierwisch (eds.). *The Role of Economy Principles in Linguistic Theory*. Berlin: Akademie Verlag, 227–266.

Bierwisch, Manfred 2002. A case for CAUSE. In: I. Kaufmann & B. Stiebels (eds.). *More than Words: A Festschrift for Dieter Wunderlich*. Berlin: Akademie Verlag, 327–353.

Bierwisch, Manfred & Ewald Lang (eds.) 1989. *Dimensional Adjectives. Grammatical Structure and Conceptual Interpretation*. Berlin: Springer.

Binnick, Robert I. 1968. On the nature of the 'lexical item'. In: B. J. Darden, C.-J. N. Bailey & A. Davison (eds.). *Papers from the Fourth Regional Meeting of the Chicago Linguistic Society* (= *CLS*). Chicago, IL: Chicago Linguistic Society, 1–13.

Binnick, Robert J. 1972. Zur Entwicklung der generativen Semantik. In: W. Abraham & R. J. Binnick (eds.). *Generative Semantik*. Frankfurt/M.: Athenäum, 1–48.

Borer, Hagit 2005. *Structuring Sense, vol. 2: The Normal Course of Events*. Oxford: Oxford University Press.

Carter, Richard J. 1976. Some constraints on possible words. *Semantikos* 1, 27–66.

Carter, Richard 1988. Arguing for semantic representations. In: B. Levin & C. Tenny (eds.). *On Linking: Papers by Richard Carter*. Lexicon Project Working Papers 25. Cambridge, MA: Center for Cognitive Science, MIT, 139–166.

Chomsky, Noam 1965. *Aspects of the Theory of Syntax*. Cambridge, MA: The MIT Press.

Chomsky, Noam 1970. Some empirical issues in the theory of transformational grammar. In: P. S. Peters (ed.). *Goals of Linguistic Theory*. Englewood Cliffs, NJ: Prentice Hall, 63–130.

Croft, William 1998. Event structure in argument linking. In: M. Butt & W. Geuder (eds.). *The Projection of Arguments: Lexical Compositional Factors*. Stanford, CA: CSLI Publications, 21–63.

Culicover, Peter W. & Ray Jackendoff 2005. *Simpler Syntax*. Oxford: Oxford University Press.

Davidson, Donald 1967. The logical form of action sentences. In: N. Rescher (ed.). *The Logic of Decision and Action*. Pittsburgh, PA: University of Pittsburgh Press, 81–95.

Dowty, David R. 1972. *Studies in the Logic of Verb Aspect and Time Reference in English*. Ph.D. dissertation. University of Texas, Austin, TX.

Dowty, David R. 1976. Montague Grammar and the lexical decomposition of causative verbs. In: B. Partee (ed.). *Montague Grammar*. New York: Academic Press, 201–246.

Dowty, David R. 1979. *Word Meaning and Montague Grammar. The Semantics of Verbs and Times in Generative Semantics and in Montague's PTQ.* Dordrecht: Reidel.
Dowty, David R. 1991. Thematic proto-roles and argument selection. *Language* 67, 547–619.
Durst, Uwe 2003. The Natural Semantic Metalanguage approach to linguistic meaning. *Theoretical Linguistics* 29, 157–200.
Embick, David 2004. Unaccusative syntax and verbal alternations. In: A. Alexiadou, E. Anagnostopoulou & M. Everaert (eds.). *The Unaccusativity Puzzle. Explorations of the Syntax-Lexicon Interface.* Oxford: Oxford University Press, 137–158.
Embick, David & Rolf Noyer 2007. Distributed Morphology and the syntax/morphology interface. In: G. Ramchand & C. Reiss (eds.). *The Oxford Handbook of Linguistic Interfaces.* Oxford: Oxford University Press, 289–324.
Engelberg, Stefan 2006. A theory of lexical event structures and its cognitive motivation. In: D. Wunderlich (ed.). *Advances in the Theory of the Lexicon.* Berlin: de Gruyter, 235–285.
Erteschik-Shir, Nomi & Tova Rapoport 2005. Path predicates. In: N. Erteschik-Shir & T. Rapoport (eds.). *The Syntax of Aspect. Deriving Thematic and Aspectual Interpretation.* Oxford: Oxford University Press, 65–86.
Erteschik-Shir, Nomi & Tova Rapoport 2007. Projecting argument structure. The grammar of hitting and breaking revisited. In: E. Reuland, T. Bhattacharya & G. Spathas (eds.). *Argument Structure.* Amsterdam: Benjamins, 17–35.
Fillmore, Charles J. 1968a. Lexical entries for verbs. *Foundations of Language* 4, 373–393.
Fillmore, Charles J. 1968b. The case for case. In: E. Bach & R. T. Harms (eds.). *Universals in Linguistic Theory.* New York: Holt, Rinehart & Winston, 1–88.
Fodor, Jerry A. 1970. Three reasons for not deriving 'kill' from 'cause to die'. *Linguistic Inquiry* 1, 429–438.
Fodor, Jerry A., Merrill F. Garrett, Edword C. T. Walker & Cornelia H. Parkes 1980. Against definitions. *Cognition* 8, 263–367.
Fodor, Jerry & A. & Ernie Lepore 1999. Impossible words? *Linguistic Inquiry* 30, 445–453.
Gamerschlag, Thomas 2005. *Komposition und Argumentstruktur komplexer Verben. Eine lexikalische Analyse von Verb-Verb-Komposita und Serialverbkonstruktionen.* Berlin: Akademie Verlag.
Geurts, Bart 2003. Semantics as lexicography. *Theoretical Linguistics* 29, 223–226.
Goddard, Cliff 1998. *Semantic Analysis. A Practical Introduction.* Oxford: Oxford University Press.
Goddard, Cliff 2002a. Lexical decomposition II: Conceptual axiology. In: A. D. Cruse et al. (eds.). *Lexikologie – Lexicology. Ein internationales Handbuch zur Natur und Struktur von Wörtern und Wortschätzen – An International Handbook on the Nature and Structure of Words and Vocabularies*, (HSK 21.1). Berlin: de Gruyter, 256–268.
Goddard, Cliff 2002b. The search for the shared semantic core of all languages. In: C. Goddard & A. Wierzbicka (eds.). *Meaning and Universal Grammar, vol. 1: Theory and Empirical Finding.* Amsterdam: Benjamins, 5–40.
Goddard, Cliff 2006. Ethnopragmatics: A new paradigm. In: C. Goddard (ed.). *Ethnopragmatics. Understanding Discourse in Cultural Context.* Berlin: de Guyter, 1–30.
Goddard, Cliff 2008a. Natural Semantic Metalanguage: The state of the art. In: C. Goddard (ed.). *Cross-Linguistic Semantics.* Amsterdam: Benjamins, 1–34.
Goddard, Cliff 2008b. Towards a systematic table of semantic elements. In: C. Goddard (ed.). *Cross-Linguistic Semantics.* Amsterdam: Benjamins, 59–81.

Goddard, Cliff, & Anna Wierzbicka (eds.) 1994a. *Semantic and Lexical Universals – Theory and Empirical Findings*. Amsterdam: Benjamins.

Goddard, Cliff & Anna Wierzbicka 1994b. Introducing lexical primitives. In: C. Goddard & A. Wierzbicka (eds.). *Semantic and Lexical Universals – Theory and Empirical Findings*. Amsterdam: Benjamins, 31–54.

Goddard, Cliff & Anna Wierzbicka 2002. Semantic primes and universal grammar. In: C. Goddard & A. Wierzbicka (eds.). *Meaning and Universal Grammar, vol. 1: Theory and Empirical Findings*. Amsterdam: Benjamins, 41–85.

Grimshaw, Jane 1990. *Argument Structure*. Cambridge, MA: The MIT Press.

Gruber, Jeffrey S. 1965. *Studies in Lexical Relations*. Ph.D. dissertation. MIT, Cambridge, MA.

Guerssel, Mohamed, Kenneth Hale, Mary Laughren, Beth Levin & Josie White Eagle 1985. A cross-linguistic study of transitivity alternations. In: W. H. Eilfort, P. D. Kroeber & K. L. Peterson (eds.). *Papers from the Parasession on Causatives and Agentivity at the 21st Regional Meeting of the Chicago Linguistic Society (= CLS), April 1985*. Chicago, IL: Chicago Linguistic Society, 48–63.

Hale, Ken & Samuel Jay Keyser 1987. *A View from the Middle*. Lexicon Project Working Papers 10. Cambridge, MA: Center for Cognitive Science, MIT.

Hale, Ken & Samuel Jay Keyser 1993. On argument structure and the syntactic expression of lexical relations. In: K. Hale & S. J. Keyser (eds.). *The View from Building 20. Essays in Linguistics in Honor of Sylvain Bromberger*. Cambridge, MA: The MIT Press, 53–109.

Hale, Ken & Samuel Jay Keyser 1997. On the complex nature of simple predicators. In: A. Alsina, J. Bresnan & P. Sells (eds.). *Complex Predicates*. Stanford, CA: CSLI Publications, 29–65.

Hale, Ken & Samuel Jay Keyser 1999. A response to Fodor and Lepore, "Impossible words?" *Linguistic Inquiry* 30, 453–466.

Hale, Ken & Samuel Jay Keyser 2002. *Prolegomenon to a Theory of Argument Structure*. Cambridge, MA: The MIT Press.

Hale, Ken & Samuel Jay Keyser 2005. Aspect and the syntax of argument structure. In: N. Erteschik-Shir & T. Rapoport (eds.). *The Syntax of Aspect. Deriving Thematic and Aspectual Interpretation*. Oxford: Oxford University Press, 11–41.

Halle, Morris & Alec Marantz 1993. Distributed Morphology and the pieces of inflection. In: K. Hale & S. J. Keyser (eds.). *The View from Building 20. Essays in Honor of Sylvain Bomberger*. Cambridge, MA: The MIT Press, 111–176.

Harley, Heidi 2002. Possession and the double object construction. In: P. Pica & J. Rooryck (eds.). *Linguistic Variation Yearbook, vol. 2*. Amsterdam: Benjamins, 31–70.

Harley, Heidi & Rolf Noyer 1999. Distributed Morphology. *GLOT International* 4, 3–9.

Harley, Heidi & Rolf Noyer 2000. Formal versus encyclopedic properties of vocabulary: Evidence from nominalizations. In: B. Peeters (ed.). *The Lexicon-Encyclopedia Interface*. Amsterdam: Elsevier, 349–375.

Immler, Manfred 1974. *Generative Syntax – Generative Semantik*. München: Fink.

Jackendoff, Ray 1972. *Semantic Interpretation in Generative Grammar*. Cambridge, MA: The MIT Press.

Jackendoff, Ray 1976. Toward an explanatory semantic representation. *Linguistic Inquiry* 7, 89–150.

Jackendoff, Ray 1983. *Semantics and Cognition*. Cambridge, MA: The MIT Press.

Jackendoff, Ray 1987. Relations in linguistic theory. *Linguistic Inquiry* 18, 369–411.

Jackendoff, Ray 1990. *Semantic Structures*. Cambridge, MA: The MIT Press.

Jackendoff, Ray 2002. *Foundations of Language. Brain, Meaning, Grammar, Evolution*. Oxford: Oxford University Press.
Joppen, Sandra & Dieter Wunderlich 1995. Argument linking in Basque. *Lingua* 97, 123–169.
Joshi, Aravind 1974. Factorization of verbs. In: C. H. Heidrich (ed.). *Semantics and Communication*. Amsterdam: North-Holland, 251–283.
Kandiah, Thiru 1968. Transformational Grammar and the layering of structure in Tamil. *Journal of Linguistics* 4, 217–254.
Kaufmann, Ingrid 1995a. *Konzeptuelle Grundlagen semantischer Dekompositionsstrukturen. Die Kombinatorik lokaler Verben und prädikativer Komplemente*. Tübingen: Niemeyer.
Kaufmann, Ingrid 1995b. O- and D-predicates: A semantic approach to the unaccusative-unergative distinction. *Journal of Semantics* 12, 377–427.
Kaufmann, Ingrid 1995c. What is an (im-)possible verb? Restrictions on semantic form and their consequences for argument structure. *Folia Linguistica* 29, 67–103.
Kiparsky, Paul 1997. Remarks on denominal verbs. In: A. Alsina, J. Bresnan & P. Sells (eds.). *Complex Predicates*. Stanford, CA: CSLI Publications, 473–499.
Lakoff, George 1965. *Irregularity in Syntax*. Ph.D. dissertation. Indiana University, Bloomington, IN. Reprinted: New York: Holt, Rinehart & Winston, 1970.
Lakoff, George & John Robert Ross 1972. A note on anaphoric islands and causatives. *Linguistic Inquiry* 3, 121–125.
Larson, Richard K. 1988. On the double object construction. *Linguistic Inquiry* 19, 335–391.
Levin, Beth 1985. Lexical semantics in review: An introduction. In: B. Levin (ed.). *Lexical Semantics in Review*. Cambridge, MA: The MIT Press, 1–62.
Levin, Beth 1993. *English Verb Classes and Alternations. A Preliminary Investigation*. Chicago, IL: The University of Chicago Press.
Levin, Beth 1995. Approaches to lexical semantic representation. In: D. E. Walker, A. Zampolli & N. Calzolari (eds.). *Automating the Lexicon: Research and Practice in a Multilingual Environment*. Oxford: Oxford University Press, 53–91.
Levin, Beth & Malka Rappaport Hovav 2005. *Argument Realization*. Cambridge: Cambridge University Press.
Lewis, David 1973. Causation. *The Journal of Philosophy* 70, 556–567.
Maienborn, Claudia 2003. Event-internal modifiers: Semantic underspecification and conceptual interpretation. In: E. Lang, C. Maienborn & C. Fabricius-Hansen (eds.). *Modifying Adjuncts*. Berlin: Mouton de Gruyter, 475–509.
Marantz, Alec 1997. No escape from syntax: Don't try morphological analysis in the privacy of your own lexicon. In: A. Dimitriadis, L. Siegel, C. Surek-Clark & A. Williams (eds.). *Proceedings of the 21st Annual Penn Linguistics Colloquium*. Philadelphia, PA: University of Pennsylvania Press, 201–225.
Mateu, Jaume 2001. Unselected objects. In: N. Dehé & A. Wanner (eds.). *Structural Aspects of Semantically Complex Verbs*. Frankfurt/M.: Lang, 83–104.
Matthewson, Lisa 2003. Is the meta-language really natural? *Theoretical Linguistics* 29, 263–274.
McCawley, James D. 1968. Lexical insertion in a Transformational Grammar without deep structure. In: B. J. Darden, C.-J. N. Bailey & A. Davison (eds.). *Papers from the Fourth Regional Meeting of the Chicago Linguistic Society*. Chicago, IL: Chicago Linguistics Society, 71–80.
McCawley, James D. 1971. Prelexical syntax. In: R. J. O'Brien (ed.). *Report of the 22nd Annual Round Table Meeting on Linguistics and Language Studies*. Washington, DC: Georgetown University Press, 19–33.

McCawley, James D. 1994. Generative Semantics. In: R. E. Asher & J. M. Y. Simpson (ed.). *The Encyclopedia of Language and Linguistics*. Oxford: Pergamon, 1398–1403.
Montague, Richard 1973. The proper treatment of quantification in ordinary English. In: J. Hintikka, J. M. E. Moravcsik & P. Suppes (eds.). *Approaches to Natural Language. Proceedings of the 1970 Stanford Workshop on Grammar and Semantics*. Dordrecht: Reidel, 221–242.
Morgan, Jerry L. 1969. On arguing about semantics. *Papers in Linguistics* 1, 49–70.
Postal, Paul M. 1971. On the surface verb 'remind'. In: C. J. Fillmore & D. T. Langendoen (eds.). *Studies in Linguistic Semantics*. New York: Holt, Rinehart & Winston, 180–270.
Pustejovsky, James 1988. The geometry of events. In: C. Tenny (ed.). *Studies in Generative Approaches to Aspect*. Cambridge, MA: The MIT Press, 19–39.
Pustejovsky, James 1991a. The syntax of event structure. *Cognition* 41, 47–81.
Pustejovsky, James 1991b. The generative lexicon. *Computational Linguistics* 17, 409–441.
Pustejovsky, James 1995. *The Generative Lexicon*. Cambridge, MA: The MIT Press.
Pustejovsky, James & Pierrette Bouillon 1995. Aspectual coercion and logical polysemy. *Journal of Semantics* 12, 133–162.
Ramchand, Gillian C. 2008. *Verb Meaning and the Lexicon. A First-Phase Syntax*. Cambridge: Cambridge University Press.
Rappaport, Malka 1985. Review of Joshi's "Factorization of verbs". In: B. Levin (ed.). *Lexical Semantics in Review*. Cambridge, MA: The MIT Press, 137–148.
Rappaport, Malka, Mary Laughren & Beth Levin 1987. *Levels of Lexical Representation*. Lexicon Project Working Papers 20. Cambridge, MA: MIT.
Rappaport, Malka & Beth Levin 1988. What to do with θ-roles. In: W. Wilkins (ed.). *Syntax and Semantics 21: Thematic Relations*. New York: Academic Press, 7–36.
Rappaport, Malka, Beth Levin & Mary Laughren 1993. Levels of lexical representation. In: J. Pustejovsky (ed.). *Semantics and the Lexicon*. Dordrecht: Kluwer, 37–54.
Rappaport Hovav, Malka & Beth Levin 1998. Building verb meanings. In: M. Butt & W. Geuder (eds.). *The Projection of Arguments: Lexical Compositional Factors*. Stanford, CA: CSLI Publications, 97–134.
Rappaport Hovav, Malka & Beth Levin 2005. Change-of-state verbs: Implications for theories of argument projection. In: N. Erteschik-Shir & T. Rapoport (eds.). *The Syntax of Aspect. Deriving Thematic and Aspectual Interpretation*. Oxford: Oxford University Press, 274–286.
Reinhart, Tanya 2002. The theta system – an overview. *Theoretical Linguistics* 28, 229–290.
Riemer, Nick 2006. Reductive paraphrase and meaning: A critique of Wierzbickian semantics. *Linguistics & Philosophy* 29, 347–379.
Ritter, Elizabeth & Sara Thomas Rosen 1998. Delimiting events in syntax. In: M. Butt & W. Geuder (eds.). *The Projection of Arguments: Lexical Compositional Factors*. Stanford, CA: CSLI Publications, 135–164.
Ross, John Robert 1972. Act. In: D. Davidson & G. Harman (eds.). *Semantics of Natural Language*. Dordrecht: Reidel, 70–126.
Rozwadowska, Bozena 1988. Thematic restrictions on derived nominals. In: W. Wilkins (ed.). *Syntax and Semantics 21: Thematic Relations*. New York: Academic Press, 147–165.
Ruppenhofer, Josef, Michael Ellsworth, Miriam R. L. Petruck, Christopher R. Johnson & Jan Scheffczyk 2006. *Frame Net II: Extended Theory and Practice*, http://framenet.icsi.berkeley.edu/index.php?option=com_wrapper&Itemid=126. December 30, 2006.
Shibatani, Masayoshi 1976. The grammar of causative constructions: A conspectus. In: M. Shibatani (ed.). *The Grammar of Causative Constructions*. New York: Academic Press, 1–40.

Stiebels, Barbara 1996. *Lexikalische Argumente und Adjunkte. Zum semantischen Beitrag von verbalen Präfixen und Partikeln.* Berlin: Akademie Verlag.
Stiebels, Barbara 1998. Complex denominal verbs in German and the morphology-semantics interface. In: G. Booij & J. van Marle (eds.). *Yearbook of Morphology 1997.* Dordrecht: Kluwer, 265–302.
Stiebels, Barbara 2002. *Typologie des Argumentlinkings. Ökonomie und Expressivität.* Berlin: Akademie Verlag.
Stiebels, Barbara 2006. From rags to riches. Nominal linking in contrast to verbal linking. In: D. Wunderlich (ed.). *Advances in the Theory of the Lexicon.* Berlin: de Gruyter, 167–234.
Summers, Della (Med.) 1995. *Longman Dictionary of Contemporary English.* München: Langenscheidt-Longman.
Taylor, John R. 2000. The network model and the two-level model in comparison. In: B. Peeters (ed.). *The Lexicon-Encyclopedia Interface.* Amsterdam: Elsevier, 115–141.
Tenny, Carol 1987. *Grammaticalizing Aspect and Affectedness.* Ph.D. dissertation. MIT, Cambridge, MA.
Tenny, Carol 1988. The aspectual interface hypothesis: The connection between syntax and lexical semantics. In: C. Tenny (ed.). *Studies in Generative Approaches to Aspect.* Cambridge, MA: The MIT Press, 1–18.
Travis, Lisa 2000. Event structure in syntax. In: C. Tenny (ed.). *Events as Grammatical Objects. The Converging Perspectives of Lexical Semantics and Syntax.* Stanford, CA: CSLI Publications, 145–185.
van Valin, Robert D. Jr. 1993. A synopsis of Role and Reference Grammar. In: R. D. van Valin (ed.). *Advances in Role and Reference Grammar.* Amsterdam: Benjamins, 1–164.
Vendler, Zeno 1957. Verbs and times. *The Philosophical Review* LXVI, 143–160.
van Voorst, Jan 1988. *Event Structure.* Amsterdam: Benjamins.
Wierzbicka, Anna 1972. *Semantic Primitives.* Frankfurt/M.: Athenäum.
Wierzbicka, Anna 1980. *Lingua Mentalis. The Semantics of Natural Language.* Sydney: Academic Press.
Wierzbicka, Anna 1985. *Lexicography and Conceptual Analysis.* Ann Arbor, MI: Karoma.
Wierzbicka, Anna 1987. *English Speech Act Verbs. A Semantic Dictionary.* Sydney: Academic Press.
Wierzbicka, Anna 1988. *The Semantics of Grammar.* Amsterdam: Benjamins.
Wierzbicka, Anna 1992. *Semantics, Culture, and Cognition. Universal Human Concepts in Culture-Specific Configurations.* Oxford: Oxford University Press.
Wierzbicka, Anna 1996. *Semantics. Primes and Universals.* Oxford: Oxford University Press.
Wierzbicka, Anna 1999. *Emotions across Languages and Cultures.* Cambridge: Cambridge University Press.
Wierzbicka, Anna 2009. The theory of the mental lexicon. In: S. Kempgen et al. (eds.). *Die slavischen Sprachen – The Slavic Languages. Ein internationales Handbuch zu ihrer Geschichte, ihrer Struktur und ihrer Erforschung – An International Handbook of their History, their Structure and their Investigation.* (HSK 32.1). Berlin: de Gruyter, 848–863.
von Wright, George Henrik 1963. *Norm and Action.* London: Routledge & Kegan Paul.
Wunderlich, Dieter 1991. How do prepositional phrases fit into compositional syntax and semantics? *Linguistics* 25, 283–331.
Wunderlich, Dieter 1994. Towards a lexicon-based theory of agreement. *Theoretical Linguistics* 20, 1–35.

Wunderlich, Dieter 1996. Models of lexical decomposition. In: E. Weigand & F. Hundsnurscher (eds.). *Lexical Structures and Language Use. Proceedings of the International Conference on Lexicology and Lexical Semantics, Münster, September 13–15, 1994. Vol. 1: Plenary Lectures and Session Papers.* Tübingen: Niemeyer, 169–183.

Wunderlich, Dieter 1997a. CAUSE and the structure of verbs. *Linguistic Inquiry* 28, 27–68.

Wunderlich, Dieter 1997b. Argument extension by lexical adjunction. *Journal of Semantics* 14, 95–142.

Wunderlich, Dieter 2000. Predicate composition and argument extension as general options – a study in the interface of semantic and conceptual structure. In: B. Stiebels & D. Wunderlich (eds.). *Lexicon in Focus.* Berlin: Akademie Verlag, 247–270.

Wunderlich, Dieter 2006. Towards a structural typology of verb classes. In: D. Wunderlich (ed.). *Advances in the Theory of the Lexicon.* Berlin: de Gruyter, 57–166.

Zubizarreta, Maria Luisa & Eunjeong Oh 2007. *On the Syntactic Composition of Manner and Motion.* Cambridge, MA: The MIT Press.

Anthony R. Davis
3 Thematic roles

1 Introduction —— 99
2 Historical and terminological remarks —— 100
3 The nature of thematic roles —— 101
4 Thematic role systems —— 109
5 Concluding remarks —— 121
6 References —— 122

Abstract: Thematic roles provide one way of relating situations to their participants. Thematic roles have been widely invoked both within lexical semantics and in the syntax-semantics interface, in accounts of a wide range of phenomena, most notably the mapping between semantic and syntactic arguments (argument realization). This article addresses two sets of issues. The first concerns the nature of thematic roles in semantic theories: what are thematic roles, are they specific to individual predicates or more general, how do they figure in semantic representations, and what interactions do they have with event and object individuation and with the semantics of plurality and aspect? The second concerns properties of systems of thematic roles: what is the inventory of thematic roles, and what relationships, such as an ordering of roles in a thematic hierarchy, or the consistency of roles across semantic domains posited by the thematic relations hypothesis, exist among roles? Various applications of thematic roles will be noted throughout these two sections, in some cases briefly mentioning alternative accounts that do not rely on them. The conclusion notes some skepticism about the necessity for thematic roles in linguistic theory.

1 Introduction

Thematic roles provide one way of relating situations to their participants. Somewhat informally, we can paraphrase this by saying that participant x plays role R in situation e. Still more informally, the linguistic expression denoting the participant is said to play that role.

Thematic roles have been widely invoked both within lexical semantics and in the syntax-semantics interface, in accounts of a wide range of phenomena,

---

Anthony R. Davis, Washington, DC, USA

https://doi.org/10.1515/9783110626391-003

including the mapping between semantic and syntactic arguments (*argument realization*), controller choice of infinitival complements and anaphors, constraints on relativization, constraints on morphological or syntactic phenomena such as passivization, determinants of telicity and distributivity, patterns of idiom frequencies, and generalizations about the lexicon and lexical acquisition. Automatic role labeling is now an active area of investigation in computational linguistics as well (Marquez et al. 2008).

After a brief terminological discussion, this article addresses two sets of issues. The first concerns the nature of thematic roles in semantic theories: what are thematic roles, are they specific to individual predicates or more general, how do they figure in semantic representations, and what interactions do they have with event and object individuation and with the semantics of plurality and aspect? The second concerns properties of systems of thematic roles: what is the inventory of thematic roles, and what relationships, such as an ordering of roles in a *thematic hierarchy*, or the consistency of roles across semantic domains posited by the *thematic relations hypothesis*, exist among roles? Various applications of thematic roles will be noted throughout these two sections, in some cases briefly mentioning alternative accounts that do not rely on them. The conclusion notes some skepticism about the necessity for thematic roles in linguistic theory.

2 Historical and terminological remarks

Pāṇini's *kārakas* are frequently noted as forerunners of thematic roles in modern linguistics. Gruber (1965) and Fillmore (1968) are widely credited with initiating the discourse on thematic roles within generative grammar and research relating to thematic roles has blossomed since the 1980s in conjunction with growing interest in the lexicon and in semantics. A variety of terms appear in the literature to refer to essentially the same notion of thematic role: *thematic relation*, *theta-role*, *(deep) case role*, and *participant role*. A distinction between "broad", general roles and "narrow", predicate-specific roles is worth noting as well. General roles (also termed *absolute roles* (Schein 2002) or *thematic role types* (Dowty 1989)) apply to a wide range of predicates or events; they include the well-known *Agent, Patient, Theme, Goal,* and so on. Predicate-specific roles (also termed *relativized* (Schein 2002), *individual thematic roles* (Dowty 1989), or "relation-specific roles") apply only to a specific event, situation, or predicate type; such roles as *Devourer* or *Explainer* are examples. There need not be a sharp distinction between broad and narrow roles; indeed, roles of various degrees of specificity, situated in a subsumption hierarchy, can be posited. In this article the term *thematic role* will cover both broad and narrow roles, though some authors restrict its use to broad roles.

3 The nature of thematic roles

Thematic roles have been formally defined as relations, functions, and sets of entailments or properties. As Rappaport & Levin (1988: 17) state: "Theta-roles are inherently relational notions; they label relations of arguments to predicators and therefore have no existence independent of predicators." Within model-theoretic semantics, an informal definition like the one that begins this article needs to be made explicit in several respects. First, what are the entities to be related? Are thematic roles present in the semantic representations of verbs and other predicators (i.e., lexical items that take arguments), or added compositionally? Are they best viewed as relations or as more complex constructs such as sets of entailments, bundles of features, or merely epiphenomena defined in terms of other linguistic representations that need not be reified at all?

3.1 Defining thematic roles in model-theoretic semantics

Attempts to characterize thematic roles explicitly within model-theoretic semantics begin with works such as Chierchia (1984) and Carlson (1984). Both Chierchia and Carlson treat thematic roles as relations between an event and a participant in it. Dowty (1989: 80) provides the following version of Chierchia's formulation. Events are regarded as tuples of individuals, and thematic roles are therefore defined thus:

(1) A θ-role θ is a partial function from the set of events into the set of individuals such that for any event k, if $\theta(k)$ is defined, then $\theta(k) \in k$.

For example, given (2a), an event tuple in which ^kill' is the intension of the verb *kill* and x is the killer of y, the functions *Agent* and *Patient* yield the values in (2b) and (2c:)

(2) a. $\langle$^kill', $x, y\rangle$
    b. Agent($\langle$^kill', $x, y\rangle$) = x
    c. Patient ($\langle$^kill', $x, y\rangle$) = y

This shows how thematic roles can be defined within an *ordered argument system* for representing event types. The roles are distinguished by the order of arguments of the predicate, though there is no expectation that the same roles appear in the same order for all predicates (some predicates may not have an *Agent* role at all, for example). Another representation, extending Davidson's (1967) insights on the representation of events, is the *neo-Davidsonian* one, in which thematic roles appear explicitly as relations between events and participants; see article 8 [Semantics: Theories] (Maienborn) *Event semantics*. The roles are labeled, but not ordered with respect to one another. In one form of such a representation, the equivalent of (2) would be (3):

(3) ∃e [killing(e) & Agent(e, x) & Patient(e, y)]

Here, thematic roles are binary predicates, taking an eventuality (event or state) as first argument and a participant in that eventuality as second argument. For a discussion of other possibilities for the type of the first argument; see Bayer (1997: 24–28). Furthermore, as Bayer (1997: 5) notes, there are two options for indexing arguments in a neo-Davidsonian representation: lexical and compositional. In the former, used, e.g., in Landman (2000), the lexical entry for a verb includes the thematic roles that connect the verb and its arguments. This is also effectively the analysis implicit in structured lexical semantic representations outside model-theoretic semantics, such as Jackendoff (1987, 1990), Rappaport & Levin (1988), Foley & van Valin (1984), and van Valin (2004). But it is also possible to pursue a compositional approach, in which the lexical entry contains only the event type, with thematic roles linking the arguments through some other process, as does Krifka (1992, 1998), who integrates the thematic role assignments of the verb's arguments through its subcategorization. Bayer (1997: 127–132) points out some difficulties with Krifka's system, including coordination of VPs that assign different roles to a shared NP.

A position intermediate between the lexical and compositional views is advocated by Kratzer (1996), who claims that what has been regarded as a verb's external argument is in fact not an argument at all, although its remaining arguments are present in its lexical entry. Thus the representation of *kill* in (3) would lack the clause Agent(e, x), this role being assigned by a VoiceP (or "little v") above VP. This, Kratzer argues, accounts for subject/object asymmetries in idiom frequencies and the lack of a true overt agent argument in gerunds. Svenonius (2007) extends Kratzer's analysis to adpositions. However, Wechsler (2005) casts doubt on Kratzer's prediction of idiom asymmetries and notes that some mechanism must still select which role is external to the verb's lexical entry, particularly in cases where there is more than one agentive participant, such as a commercial transaction involving both a buyer and a seller.

Characterizing a thematic role as a partial function leaves open the question of how to determine the function's domain and range; that is, what events is a role defined for, and which participant does the role pick out? In practice, this problem of determining which roles are appropriate for a predicate plagues every system of broad thematic roles, but it is less serious for roles defined on individual predicates. Dowty (1989: 76) defines the latter in terms of a set of entailments, as in (4):

(4) Given an *n*-place predicate δ and a particular argument x_i, the *individual thematic role* ⟨δ, *i*⟩ is the set of all properties α such that the entailment $\Box[\delta(x_1, ... x_i, ... x_n) \rightarrow \alpha(x_i)]$ holds.

What counts as a "property" must be specified, of course. And as Bayer (1997: 119–120) points out, nothing in this kind of definition tells us which of these properties are important for, say, argument realization. Formulating such cross-lexicon generalizations demands properties or relations that are shared across predicates. Dowty defines cross-predicate roles, or *thematic role types*, as he terms them, as "the intersection of all the individual thematic roles" (Dowty 1989: 77). Therefore, as stated by Dowty (1991: 552): "From the semantic point of view, the most general notion of thematic role (type) is A SET OF ENTAILMENTS OF A GROUP OF PREDICATES WITH RESPECT TO ONE OF THE ARGUMENTS OF EACH. (Thus a thematic role type is a kind of second-order property, a property of multiplace predicates indexed by their argument positions.)." Thematic role types are numerous; however, he argues, linguists will generally be interested in identifying a fairly small set of these that play some vital role in linguistic theory.

This definition of thematic role types imposes no restrictions on whether an argument can bear multiple roles to a predicate, whether roles can share entailments in their defining sets and thus overlap or subsume one another, whether two arguments of a predicate can bear the same role (though this is ruled out by the functional requirement in (1)), and whether every argument must be assigned a role. These constraints, if desired, must be independently specified (Dowty 1989: 78–79) As the discussion of thematic role systems below indicates, various models answer these questions differently. Whether suitable entailments for linguistically significant broad thematic roles can be found at all is a further issue that leads Rappaport & Levin (1988, 2005), Dowty (1991), Wechsler (1995), Croft (1991, 1998), and many others to doubt the utility of positing such roles at all.

Finally, note that definitions such as (1) and (4) above, or Dowty's thematic role types, make no reference to morphological, lexical, or syntactic notions. Thus they are agnostic as to which morphemes, words, or constituents have thematic roles associated with them; that depends on the semantics assigned to these linguistic entities and whether roles are defined only for event types or over a broader range of situation types. Verbs are the prototypical bearers of thematic roles, but nominalizations are typically viewed as role-bearing, and other nouns, adjectives, and adpositions (Gawron 1983, Wechsler 1995, Sevenonius 2007), as predicators denoting event or situation types, will have roles associated with them, too.

3.2 Thematic role uniqueness

Many researchers invoking thematic roles have explicitly or implicitly adopted a criterion of *thematic role uniqueness*. Informally, this means that only one participant in a situation bears a given role. Carlson (1984: 271) states this constraint at a lexical level: "one of the more fundamental constraints is that of 'thematic uniqueness' – that no verb seems to be able to assign the same thematic role to two or more of its arguments." This echoes the θ-criterion of Chomsky (1981), discussed below. Parsons (1990: 74) defines thematic uniqueness with respect to events and their participants: "No event stands in one of these relations to more than one thing." Note that successfully connecting the lexical-level constraint and the event-level constraints requires the Davidsonian assumption that there is a single event variable in the semantic representation of a predicator, as Carlson (1998: 40) points out. In some models of lexical representation (e.g., Jackendoff's lexical decomposition analyses and related work), this is not the case, as various subevents are represented, each of which can have a set of roles associated with it.

The motivations for role uniqueness are varied. One is that it simplifies accounts of mapping from thematic roles to syntactic arguments of predicators (which are also typically regarded as unique). It is implicit in hypotheses such as the Universal Alignment Hypothesis (Rosen 1984) and the Uniformity of Theta Assignment Hypothesis (Baker 1988, 1997), described in greater detail in the section on argument realization below. Role uniqueness also provides a tool to distinguish situations – if two different individuals appear to bear the same role, then there must be two distinct situations involved (Landman 2000: 39). A further motivation, emphasized in the work of Krifka (1992, 1998), is that role uniqueness and related conditions are crucial in accounting for the semantics of events in which a participant is incrementally consumed, created, or traversed.

Role uniqueness does not apply straightforwardly to all types of situations. Krifka (1998: 209) points out that a simple definition of uniqueness – "it should not be the case that one and the same event has different participants" – is "problematic for *see* and *touch*." If one sees or touches an orange, for example, then one also typically sees or touches the peel of the orange. But the orange and its peel are distinct; thus the seeing or touching event appears to have multiple entities bearing the same role.

A corollary of role uniqueness is *exhaustivity*, the requirement that whatever bears a given thematic role to a situation is the only thing bearing that role. Thus if some group is designated as the Agent of an event, then there can be no larger group that is also the Agent of that same event. Exhaustivity is equivalent to role uniqueness under the condition that only one role may be assigned to an individual; as Schein (2002: 272) notes, however, if thematic roles are allowed to be "complex" – that is, multiple roles can be assigned conjunctively to individuals, then exhaustivity is a weaker constraint than uniqueness.

3.3 How fine-grained should thematic roles be?

As noted in the introduction, thematic roles in the broad sense are frequently postulated as crucial mechanisms in accounts of phenomena at the syntax-semantics interface, such as argument realization, anaphoric binding, and controller choice. For thematic roles to serve many of these uses, they must be sufficiently broad, in the sense noted above, that they can be used in stating generalizations covering classes of lexical items or constructions. To be useful in this sense, therefore, a thematic role should be definable over a broad class of situation types. Bach (1989: 111) articulates this view: "Thematic roles seem to represent generalizations that we make across different kinds of happenings in the world about the participation of individuals in the eventualities that the various sentences are about." Schein (2002: 265) notes that if "syntactic positions [of arguments given their thematic roles] are predictable, we can explain the course of acquisition and our understanding of novel verbs and of familiar verbs in novel contexts."

Within model-theoretic semantics, two types of critiques have been directed at the plausibility of broad thematic roles. One is based on the difficulty of formulating definitional criteria for such roles, arguing that after years of effort, no rigorous definitions have emerged. The other critique examines the logical implications of positing such roles, bringing out difficulties for semantic representations relying on broad thematic roles given basic assumptions, such as role uniqueness.

It is clear that the *Runner* role of *run* and the *Jogger* role of *jog* share significant entailments (legs in motion, body capable of moving along a path, and so on). Indeed, to maintain that these two roles are distinct merely because there are two distinct verbs *run* and *jog* in English seemingly determines a semantic issue on the basis of a language-particular lexical accident. But no attempt to provide necessary, sufficient, and comprehensive criteria for classifying most or all of the roles of individual predicates into a few broad roles has yet to meet with consensus. This problem has been noted by numerous researchers; see, for example, Dowty (1991: 553–555), Croft (1991: 155–158), Wechsler (1995: 9–11), and Levin & Rappaport Hovav (2005: 38–41) for discussion. *Theme* in particular is notoriously defined in vague and differing ways, but it is not an isolated case; many partially overlapping criteria for *Agenthood* have been proposed, including volitionality, causal involvement, and control or initiation of an event; see Kiparsky (1997: 476) for a remark on cross-linguistic variation in this regard and Wechsler (2005: 187–193) for a proposal on how to represent various kinds of agentive involvement.

Moreover, there are arguments against the possibility of broad roles even for situations that seemingly semantically quite close, in cases where two predicators would appear to denote the same situation type. The classic case of this, examined from various perspectives by numerous authors, involves the verbs *buy* and *sell*. As Parsons (1990: 84) argues, given the two descriptions of a commercial transaction in (5):

(5) a. Kim bought a tricycle from Sheehan.
 b. Sheehan sold a tricycle to Kim.

and the assumptions that "Kim is the *Agent* of the buying, and Sheehan is the *Agent* of the selling", then to "insist that the buying and the selling are one and the same event, differently described" entails that "Kim sold a tricycle to Kim, and Sheehan bought a tricycle from Sheehan." Parsons concludes that the two sentences must therefore describe different, though "intimately related", events; see article 3 [Semantics: Theories] (Gawron) *Frame Semantics*. Landman (2000: 31–33) and Schein (2002) make similar arguments; the import of which is that one must either individuate fine-grained event types or distinguish thematic roles in a fine-grained fashion.

Schein (2002) suggests, as a possible alternative to fine-grained event distinctions, a ternary view of thematic roles, in which the third argument is essentially an index to the predicate, as in (6), rather than the dyadic thematic roles in, e.g., (3):

(6) Agent($e, x, kill'$)

The *Agent* role of *kill* is thereby distinguished from the *Agent* of *murder*, *throw*, *explain*, and so on. This strategy, applied to *buy* and *sell*, blocks the invalid inference above. However, this would allow the valid inference from one sentence in (5) to the other only if we separately ensure that the *Agent* of *buy* corresponds to the *Recipient* of *sell*, and vice versa. Moreover, other problems remain even under this relativized view of thematic roles, in particular concerning symmetric predicates, the involvement of parts of individuals or of groups of individuals in events, whether they are to be assigned thematic roles, and whether faulty inferences would result if they are.

Assuming role uniqueness (or exhaustivity), and drawing a distinction between an individual car and the group of individuals constituting its parts, one is seemingly forced to conclude that (7a) and (7b) describe different events (Carlson 1984, Schein 2002). The issue is even plainer in (8), as the skin of an apple is not the same as the entire apple.

(7) a. I weighed the Volvo.
    b. I weighed (all) the parts of the Volvo.

(8) a. Kim washed the apple.
    b. Kim washed the skin of the apple.

Similar problems arise with symmetric predicators such as *face* or *border*, as illustrated in (9) (based on Schein 2002) and (10).

(9) a. The Carnegie Deli faces Carnegie Hall.
    b. Carnegie Hall faces the Carnegie Deli.

(10) a. Rwanda borders Burundi.
     b. Burundi borders Rwanda.

If two distinct roles are ascribed to the arguments in these sentences, and the mapping of roles to syntactic positions is consistent, then the two sentences in each pair must describe distinct situations.

Schein remarks that the strategy of employing fine-grained roles indexed to a predicator fails for cases like (7) through (10), since the verb in each pair is the same. Noting that fine-grained events seem to be required regardless of the availability of fine-grained roles, Schein (2002) addresses these issues by introducing additional machinery into semantic representations, including fine-grained scenes as perspectives on events, to preserve absolute (broad) thematic roles. Each sentence in (9) or (10) involves a different scene, even though the situation described by the two sentences is the same. "In short, scenes are fine-grained, events are coarser, and sentences rely on (thematic) relations to scenes to convey what they have to say about events." (Schein 2002: 279). Similarly, the difficulties posed by (7) and (8) are dealt with through "a notion of resolution to distinguish a scene fine-grained enough to resolve the Volvo's parts from one which only resolves the whole Volvo." (Schein 2002: 279).

3.4 Thematic roles and plurality

Researchers with an interest in the semantics of plurals have studied the interaction of plurality and thematic roles. Although Carlson (1984: 275) claims that "it appears to be necessary to countenance groups or sets as being able to play thematic roles", he does not explore the issues in depth. Landman (2000: 167), contrasting collective and distributive uses of plural subjects, argues that "distributive predication is not an instance of thematic predication." Thus, in the distributive reading of a sentence like *The boys sing.*, the semantic properties of Agents hold only of the individual boys, so "no thematic implication concerning the sum of the boys itself follows." For "on the distributive interpretation, not a single property that you might want to single out as part of agenthood is predicated of the denotation of *the boys*" (Landman 2000: 169). Therefore, Landman argues, "the subject *the boys* does not fill a thematic role" of *sing*, but rather a "non-thematic role" that is derived from the role that *sing* assigns to an individual subject. He then develops a theory of plural roles, derived from singular roles (which are defined only on atomic events), as follows (Landman 2000: 184), where E is the domain of events (both singular and plural):

(11) If e is an event in E, and for every atomic part a of e, thematic role R is defined for a, then plural role *R is defined for e, and maps e onto the sum of the R-values of the atomic parts of e.

Thus *R subsumes R (if e is itself atomic then R is defined for e). Although Landman does not directly address the issue, his treatment of distributive readings and plural roles seems to imply that a role-based theory of argument realization – indeed, any theory of argument realization based on entailments of singular arguments – must be modified to extend to distributive plural readings.

3.5 Thematic roles and aspectual phenomena

Krifka (1992, 1998) explores the ways in which entailments associated with participants can account for aspectual phenomena. In particular, he aims to make precise the notions of incremental theme and of the relationships of incremental participants to events and subevents, formalizing properties similar to some of the proto-role properties of Dowty (1991). Krifka (1998: 211–212) defines some of these properties as follows, where ⊕ denotes a mereological sum of objects or events, ≤ denotes a part or subevent relation, and ∃x means that there exists a unique entity x of which the property following x holds:

(12) a. A role θ shows *uniqueness of participants*, UP(θ), iff:
$\theta(x, e)$ & $\theta(y, e) \rightarrow x = y$
b. A role θ is *cumulative*, CUM(θ), iff:
$\theta(x, e)$ & $\theta(y, e') \rightarrow \theta(x \oplus_P y, e \oplus_E e')$
c. A role θ shows *uniqueness of events*, UE(θ), iff:
$\theta(x, e)$ & $y \leq_P x \rightarrow \exists! e'[e' \leq_E e$ & $\theta(y, e')]$
d. A role θ shows *uniqueness of objects*, UO(θ), iff:
$\theta(x, e)$ & $e' \leq_E e \rightarrow \exists! y[y \leq_P x$ & $\theta(y, e')]$

The first of these is a statement of role uniqueness, and the second is a weak property that holds of a broad range of participant roles, which somewhat resembles Landman's definition of plural roles in (11). The remaining two are ingredients of *incremental* participant roles, including those borne by entities gradually consumed or created in an event. Krifka's analysis treats thematic roles as the interface between aspectual characteristics of events, such as telicity, and the mereological structure of entities (parts and plurals). In the case of event types with incremental roles, the role's properties establish a homomorphism between parts of the participant and subevents of the event. Slightly different properties are required for a parallel analysis of objects in motion and the paths they traverse.

4 Thematic role systems

This section examines some proposed systems of thematic roles; that is, inventories of roles and relationships among them, if any. One simple version of such a system is an unorganized set of broad roles, such as *Agent, Instrument, Experiencer, Theme, Patient*, etc., each assumed to be atomic, primitive, and independent of one another. In other systems, roles may be treated as non-atomic, being defined either in terms of more basic features, as derived from positional criteria within structured semantic representations, or situated within a hierarchy of roles and subroles (for example, the *Location* role might have *Source* and *Goal* subroles). Dependencies among roles are also posited; it is reasonable to claim that predicates allowing an *Instrument* role should also then require an *Agent* role, or that *Source* or *Goal* are meaningless without a *Theme* in motion from one to the other. Another type of dependency among roles is a *thematic hierarchy*, a global ordering of roles in terms of their prominence, as reflected in, for instance, argument realization or anaphoric binding phenomena. These applications of thematic roles at the syntax-semantic interface are examined at the end of this section.

4.1 Lists of primitive thematic roles

Fillmore (1968) was one of the earliest in the generative tradition to present a system of thematic roles (which he terms "deep cases"). This foreshadows the hypotheses of later researchers about argument realization, such as the Universal Alignment Hypothesis (Perlmutter & Postal 1984, Rosen 1984), and the Uniformity of Theta Assignment Hypothesis (Baker 1988, 1997), discussed in the section on argument realization below. Fillmore's cases are intended as an account of argument realization at deep structure, and are, at least implicitly, ranked. A version of role uniqueness is also assumed, and roles are treated as atomic and independent of one another.

A simple use of thematic roles that employs a similar conception of them is to ensure a one-to-one mapping from semantic roles of a predicate to its syntactic arguments. This is exemplified by the θ-criterion, a statement of thematic uniqueness formulated by Chomsky (1981: 36), some version of which is assumed in most syntactic research in Government and Binding, Principles and Parameters, early Lexical-Functional Grammar, and related frameworks.

(13) Each argument bears one and only one θ-role, and each θ-role is assigned to one and only one argument.

This use of thematic roles as "OK marks", in Carlson's (1984) words, makes no commitments as to the semantic content of θ-roles, nor to the ultimate syntactic effects. As Ladusaw & Dowty (1988: 62) remark, "the θ-criterion and θ-roles are a principally diacritic theory: what is crucial in their use in the core of GB is whether an argument is assigned a θ-role or not, which limits possible structures and thereby constrains the applications of rules." The θ-criterion as stated above is typically understood to apply to coreference chains; thus "each chain is assigned a θ-role." and "the θ-criterion must be reformulated in the obvious way in terms of chains and their members.." (Chomsky 1982: 5–6).

Other researchers have continued along the lines suggested by Fillmore (1968), furnishing each lexical item with a list of labeled thematic roles. These representations are typically abstracted away from the issue of whether roles should be represented in a Davidsonian fashion; an example would look like (14), where the verb *cut* is represented as requiring the two roles *Agent* and *Patient* and allowing an optional *Instrument*:

(14) *cut* (Agent, Patient, (Instrument))

This is one version of the "θ-grid" in the GB/P&P framework. Although the representation in (14) uses broad roles, the granularity of roles is an independent issue. For an extensive discussion of such models, see chapter 2 of Levin & Rappaport Hovav (2005). They note several problems with thematic list approaches: difficulties in determining which role to assign "symmetric" predicates like *face* and *border* with two arguments seemingly bearing the same role, "the assumption that semantic roles are taken to be discrete and unanalyzable" Levin & Rappaport Hovav (2005: 42) rather than exhibiting relations and dependencies amongst themselves, and the failure to account for restrictions on the range of possible case frames (Davis & Koenig 2000: 59–60).

An additional feature of some thematic list representations is the designation of one argument as the external argument. Belletti & Rizzi (1988: 344), for example, annotate this external argument, if present, by italicizing it, as in (15a), as opposed to (15b) (where lexically specified case determines argument realization, and there is no external argument).

(15) a. *temere* ('fear') (*Experiencer*, Theme)
      b. *preocupare* ('worry') (Experiencer, Theme)

This leaves open the question of how the external argument is to be selected; Belletti & Rizzi address this issue only in passing, suggesting the possibility that a thematic hierarchy is involved.

4.2 Thematic hierarchies

It is not an accident that thematic list representations, though ostensibly consisting of unordered roles, typically list the *Agent* role first if it is present. Apart from the intuitive sense of *Agents* being the most "prominent", the widespread use of thematic role lists in argument realization leads naturally to a ranking of thematic roles in a *thematic hierarchy*, in which prominence on the hierarchy corresponds to syntactic prominence, whether configurationally or in terms of grammatical functions.

As Levin & Rappaport Hovav (2005: chapters 5 and 6) make clear, there are several distinct bases on which a thematic hierarchy might be motivated, independently of its usefulness in argument realization: prominence in lexical semantic representations (Jackendoff 1987, 1990), event structure, especially causal structure (Croft 1991, Wunderlich 1997), and topicality or salience (Fillmore 1977). However, many authors motivate a hierarchy primarily by argument realization, adopting some version of a correspondence principle to ensure that the thematic roles defined for a predicate are mapped to syntactic positions (or grammatical functions) in prominence order.

The canonical thematic hierarchy is a total ordering of all the thematic roles in a theory's inventory (many hierarchies do not distinguish an ordering among *Source*, *Goal*, and *Location*, however). While numerous variants have been proposed – Levin & Rappaport Hovav (2005: 162–163) list over a dozen – they agree on ranking *Agent/Actor* topmost, *Theme* and/or *Patient* near the bottom, and *Instrument* between them. As with any model invoking broad thematic roles, thematic hierarchy approaches face the difficulty of defining the roles they use, and addressing the classification of roles of individual verbs that do not fit well. A thematic hierarchy of fine-grained roles would face the twin drawbacks of a large number of possible orderings and a lack of evidence for establishing a relative ranking of many roles.

Some researchers emphasize that the sole function of the thematic hierarchy is to order the roles; the role labels themselves are invisible to syntax and morphology, which have access only to the ordered list of arguments. Thus Grimshaw (1990: 10) states that though she will "use thematic role labels to identify arguments ... the theory gives no status to this information." Williams (1994) advocates a similar view of the visibility of roles at the syntactic level. Wunderlich (1997) develops an approach that is similar in this regard, where depth of embedding in a lexical semantic structure determines the prominence of semantic arguments.

It is worth noting that these kinds of rankings can be achieved by means other than a thematic hierarchy, or even thematic roles altogether. Rappaport & Levin's (1988) predicate argument structures consist of an ordered list of argument variables derived from lexical conceptual structures like those in (17) below, but again no role information is present. Fillmore (1977) provides a saliency hierarchy of criteria for ascertaining the relative rank of two arguments; these include active elements outranking inactive ones, causal arguments outranking noncausal ones, and changed arguments outranking unchanged ones. Gawron (1983) also makes use of this system in his model of argument realization. Wechsler (1995) similarly relies on entailments between pairs of participants, such as one having a notion of the other, to determine a partial ordering amongst arguments. Dowty's (1991) widely-cited system of comparing numbers of proto-agent and proto-patient entailments is a related though distinct approach, discussed in greater detail below. Finally, Grimshaw (1990) posits an aspectual hierarchy in addition to a thematic hierarchy, on which causers outrank other elements. Li (1995) likewise argues for a causation-based hierarchy independent of a thematic hierarchy, based on argument realization in Mandarin Chinese resultative compounds. Primus (1999, 2006) presents a system of two role hierarchies, corresponding to involvement and causal dependency. "Morphosyntactic linking , i.e., case in the broader sense, corresponds primarily to the degree and kind of involvement ... while structural linking responds to semantic dependency" (Primus 2006: 54). These multiple-hierarchy systems bear an affinity to systems that assign multiple roles to participants and to the structured semantic representations of Jackendoff, discussed in the following section.

4.3 Multiple role assignment

Thematic role lists and hierarchies generally assume some principle of thematic uniqueness. However, there are various arguments for assigning multiple roles to a single argument of a predicator, as well as cases where it is hard to distinguish the roles of two arguments. Symmetric predicates such as those in (9) and (10) exemplify the latter situation. As for the former, Jackendoff (1987: 381–382) suggests *buy*, *sell*, and *chase* as verbs with arguments bearing more than one role, and any language with morphologically productive causative verbs furnishes examples such as 'cause to laugh', in which the laugher exhibits both *Agent* and *Patient* characteristics. Williams (1994) argues that the subject of a small clause construction like *John arrived sad.* is best analyzed as bearing two roles, one from each predicate. Broadwell (1988: 123) offers another type of evidence for multiple role assignment in Choctaw (a Muskogean language of the southeastern U.S.). Some verbs have suppletive forms for certain persons and numbers, and "1 [= subject] agreement is tied to the θ-roles Agent, Effector, Experiencer, and Source/Goal. Since the Choctaw verb 'arrive' triggers 1 agreement, its subject must bear one of these θ-roles. But I have also argued that suppletion is tied to the Theme, and so the subject must bear the role Theme." Similarly, one auxiliary is selected if the subject is a *Theme*, another otherwise, and *arrive* in Choctaw selects the *Theme*-subject auxiliary.

Cases like these have led many researchers to pursue representations in which roles are derived, not primitive. Defining roles in terms of features, or positions in lexical representations based on semantic decomposition, can more readily accommodate those predicators that appear to violate role uniqueness within a system of broad thematic roles.

4.4 Structural and featural analyses of thematic roles

Many researchers, perhaps dissatisfied with the seemingly arbitrary set of descriptions of the meanings of thematic roles such as *Agent, Patient, Goal*, and, notoriously, *Theme*, have sought organizing principles that would characterize the range of broad thematic roles. These efforts can be loosely divided into two, somewhat overlapping types. The first might be called *structural* or *relational*, situating roles within structures typically representing lexical entries, including properties of the event type they denote. The second approach is *featural*, analyzing roles in terms of another set of more fundamental features that provides some structure for the set of possible roles. Both approaches are compatible with viewing thematic roles as sets of entailments. Under the structural approach, the entailments are associated with positions in a lexical or event structure, while under the featural approach, the entailments can be regarded as features. Both approaches are also compatible with thematic hierarchies or other prominence schemes. However, a notion of prominence within event structures can do the work of a thematic hierarchy in argument selection within a structural approach, and prominence relations between features can do the same within a featural approach.

While Fillmore's cases are presented as an unstructured list, Gruber (1965) and Jackendoff (1983) develop a model in which the relationships between entities in motion and location situations provide an inventory of roles: *Theme, Source, Goal*, and *Location*. Through analogy, these extend to a wide range of semantic domains, as phrased by Jackendoff (1983: 188):

(16) Thematic Relations Hypothesis
In any semantic field of [EVENTS] and [STATES], the principal event-, state-, path-, and place-functions are a subset of those used for the analysis of spatial location and motion. Fields differ in only three possible ways:
a. what sorts of entities may appear as theme;
b. what sorts of entities may appear as reference objects;
c. what kind of relation assumes the role played by location in the field of spatial expressions.

This illustrates one form of lexical decomposition (see article 2 [this volume] (Engelberg) *Frameworks of decomposition*) allowing thematic roles to be defined in terms of their positions within the structures representing the semantics of lexical items. Such an approach is compatible with the entailment-based treatments of thematic roles discussed above, but developing a model-theoretic interpretation of these structures that would facilitate this has not been a priority for those advocating this kind of analysis. However, lexical decomposition does reflect the internal complexity of natural language predicators. For example, causative verbs are plausibly analyzed as denoting two situation types standing in a causal relationship to one another, and transactional verbs such as *buy*, *sell*, and *rent* as denoting two oppositely-directed transfers. The Lexical Conceptual Structures of Rappaport & Levin (1988) (see article 4 [this volume] (Levin & Rappaport Hovav) *Lexical Conceptual Structure*) illustrate decomposition into multiple subevents of the two alternants of "spray/load" verbs; the LCS for the *Theme*-object alternant is shown in (17a) and that of the *Location*-object alternant in (17b), in which the LCS of the former is embedded as a substructure:

(17) a. [x cause [y to come to be at z]]
　　 b. [x cause [z to come to be in STATE]
　　　　　BY MEANS OF [x cause [y to come to be at z]]]

As noted above, in such representations, thematic roles are not primitive, but derived notions. And because LCSs – or their counterparts in other models – can be embedded as in (17b), there may be multiple occurrences of the same role type within the representation of a single predicate. A causative or transactional verb can then be regarded as having two *Agents*, one in each subevent. Furthermore, participants in more than one subevent can accordingly be assigned more than one role; thus the buyer and seller in a transaction are at once *Agents* and *Recipients* (or *Goals*). This leads to a view of thematic roles that departs from the formulations of role uniqueness developed within an analysis of predicators as denoting a unitary, undecomposed event, though uniqueness can still be postulated for each subevent in a decompositional representation. It also can capture some of the dependencies among roles; for example Jackendoff (1987: 398–402) analyzes the *Instrument* role in terms of conceptual structures representing intermediate causation, and this role exists only in relation to others in the chain of causation.

　　Croft (1991, 1998) has taken causation as the fundamental framework for defining relationships between participants in events, with the roles more closely matching the *Agent*, *Patient*, and *Instrument* of Fillmore (1968). The causal ordering is plainly correlated with the ordering of roles found in thematic hierarchies and with the Actor-Undergoer cline of Role and Reference Grammar (Foley & van Valin 1984, van Valin 2004), which orders thematic roles according to positions in a structure intended to represent causal and aspectual characteristics of situations. In Jackendoff (1987, 1990) the causal and the motion/location models are combined in representations of event structures, some quite detailed and elaborate. Thematic roles within these systems are also derived notions, defined in terms of positions within these event representations. As the systems become more elaborate, one crucial issue is: how can we tell what the correct representation should be? Both types of systems exploit metaphorical extensions of space, motion, and causation to other, more abstract domains, and it is often unclear what the "correct" application of the metaphors should be. The implication for thematic roles defined within such systems is that their semantic foundations are not always sound.

Notable featural analyses of thematic roles include Ostler (1979), whose system uses eight binary features that characterize 48 roles. His features are further specifications of the four generalized roles: *Theme, Source, Goal,* and *Path* from the Thematic Role Hypothesis, and include some that resemble entailments (*volitional*) and some that specify a semantic domain (*positional, cognitive*). Somers (1987) puts forward similar systems, again based on four broad roles that appear in various semantic domains, and Sowa (2000), takes this as a point of departure for a hierarchy of role types within a knowledge representation system. Sowa decomposes the four types of Somers into two pairs of roles characterized by features or entailments: *Source* ("present at the beginning of the process") and *Goal* ("present at the end of the process"), and *Determinant* ("determines the direction of the process") and *Immanent* ("present throughout the process", but "does not actively control what happens"). Sowa argues that this system allows for useful underspecification; in *the dog broke the window*, the dog might be involved volitionally or nonvolitionally as initiator, or used as an instrument by some other initiator, but *Source* covers all of these possibilities. This illustrates another characteristic of Sowa's system; he envisions an indefinitely large number of roles, of varying degrees of specificity, but all are subtypes of one of these four. In this kind of system, the set of features will also grow indefinitely, so that it is more naturally viewed as a hierarchy of roles induced from the hierarchy of event types, at least below the most general roles. Similar ideas have been pursued in Lehmann (1996) and the Framenet project (http://framenet.icsi.berkeley.edu); see article 3 [Semantics: Theories] (Gawron) *Frame Semantics*.

Rozwadowska (1988) pursues a somewhat different analysis, with three binary features: ±*sentient*, ±*cause*, and ±*change*, intended to characterize broad thematic roles. This system permits natural classes of roles to be defined, which Rozwadowska argues are useful in describing restrictions on the interpretation of English and Polish specifiers of nominalizations. For example, the distinction between *the movie's shock of the audience*, vs. *the audience's shock at the movie* is accounted for by a requirement that the specifier's role not be *Neutral*; that is, not have negative values of all three features. Thus either an *Agent* or an *Experiencer* NP (both marked as +*change*) can appear in specifier position, but not a *Neutral* one.

Featural analyses of thematic roles are close in spirit to entailment-based frameworks that dispense with reified roles altogether. If the features can be defined with sufficient clarity and consistency, then a natural question to ask is whether the work assigned to thematic roles can be accomplished simply by direct reference to these definitions of participant properties. The most notable exponent of this approach is Dowty (1991), with the two sets of proto-Agent and proto-Patient entailments. Wechsler (1995) is similar in spirit but employs entailments as a means of partially ordering a predicator's arguments. Davis & Koenig (2000) and Davis (2001) combine elements of these with a limited amount of lexical decomposition. While these authors eschew the term "thematic role" for their characterizations of a predicate's arguments, such definitions do conform to Dowty's (1989) definition of thematic role types noted above, though they do not impose any thematic uniqueness requirements.

4.5 Thematic roles and argument realization

Argument realization, the means by which semantic roles of predicates are realized as syntactic arguments of verbs, nominalizations, or other predicators, has been a consistent focus of linguists seeking to demonstrate the utility of thematic roles. This section examines some approaches to argument realization, and the following one briefly notes other syntactic and morphological phenomena that thematic roles have been claimed to play a role in.

Levin & Rappaport Hovav (2005) provide an extensive discussion of diverse approaches to argument realization, including those in which thematic roles play a crucial part. Such accounts can involve a fixed, "absolute" rule, such as "map the *Agent* to the subject (or external argument)" or relative rules, which establish a correspondence between an ordering (possibly partial) among a predicate's semantic roles and an ordering among grammatical relations or configurationally-defined syntactic positions. The role ordering may correspond to a global ordering of roles, such as a thematic hierarchy, or be derived from relative depth of semantic roles or from relationships, such as entailments, holding among sets of roles. One example is the Universal Alignment Hypothesis developed within Relational Grammar; the version here is from Rosen (1984: 40):

(18) There exists some set of universal principles on the basis of which, given the semantic representation of a clause, one can predict which initial grammatical relation each nominal bears.

Another widely employed principle of this type is the Uniformity of Theta Assignment Hypothesis (UTAH), in Baker (1988: 46), which assumes a structural conception of thematic roles:

(19) Identical thematic relationships between items are represented by identical structural relationships between those items at the level of D-structure.

Baker (1997) examines a relativized version of this principle, under which the ordering of a predicator's roles, according to the thematic hierarchy, must correspond to their relative depth in D-structure.

In Lexical Mapping Theory (Bresnan & Kanerva 1989, Bresnan & Moshi 1990, Alsina 1992), the correspondence is more complex, because grammatical relations are decomposed into features, which in turn interface with the thematic hierarchy. A role's realization is thus underspecified in some cases until default assignments fill in the remaining feature. For example, an *Agent* receives an intrinsic classification of −O(bjective), and the highest of a predicate's roles is assigned the feature −R(estricted) by default, with the result that *Agents* are by default realized as subjects.

These general principles typically run afoul of the complexities of argument realization, including cross-linguistic and within-language variation among predicators and diathesis alternations. A very brief mention of some of the difficulties follows. First, to avoid an account that is essentially stipulative, the inventory of roles cannot be too large or too specific; once again this leads to the problem of assigning roles to the large range of verbs whose arguments appear to fit poorly in any of the roles. Second, cross-linguistic variation in realization patterns poses problems for principles like (18) and (19) that claim universally consistent mapping; some languages permit a wide range of ditransitive constructions, for example, while others entirely lack them (Gerdts 1992). Third, there are some cases where argument realization appears to involve information outside what would normally be ascribed to lexical semantic representations; some semantically similar verbs require different subcategorizations (*wish for* vs. *desire*, *look at* vs. *watch*, *appeal to* vs. *please*) or display differing diathesis alternations (*hide* and *dress* permit an intransitive alternant with reflexive meaning, while *conceal* and *clothe* are only transitive) (Jackendoff 1987: 405–406, Davis 2001: 171–173). Fourth, there are apparent cases of the same roles being mapped differently, as in the Italian verbs *temere* and *preocupare* in (15) above; these cases prove problematic particularly for a model with a thematic hierarchy and a role list for each predicate.

These difficulties have been addressed in large degree through entailment-based models described in the following section, and through models that employ more elaborate semantic decomposition that what is assumed by principles such as (18) and (19) (Jackendoff 1987, 1990, Alsina 1992, Croft 1991, 1998).

4.6 Lexical entailments as alternatives to thematic roles

Dowty (1991) is an influential proposal for argument realization avoiding reified thematic roles in semantic representations. The central idea is that subject and object selection relies on a set of *proto-role entailments*, grouped into two sets, proto-agent properties and proto-patient properties, as follows (Dowty 1991: 572):

(20) Contributing properties for the Agent Proto-Role.
   a. volitional involvement in the event or state.
   b. sentience. (and/or perception)
   c. causing an event or change of state in another participant.
   d. movement. (relative to the position of another participant)
   e. exists independently of the event named by the verb.

(21) Contributing properties for the Patient Proto-Role.
   a. undergoes change of state.
   b. incremental theme.
   c. causally affected by another participant.
   d. stationary relative to the movement of another participant.
   e. does not exist independently of the event, or not at all.

Each of these properties may or may not be entailed of a participant in a given type of event or state. Dowty's Argument Selection Principle, in (22), characterizes how transitive verbs may realize their semantic arguments (Dowty 1991: 576):

(22) In predicates with grammatical subject and object, the argument for which the predicate entails the greatest number of Proto-Agent properties will be lexicalized as the subject of the predicate; the argument having the greatest number of Proto-Patient properties will be lexicalized as the direct object.

This numerical comparison across semantic roles accounts well for the range of attested transitive verbs in English, but fares less well with other kinds of data (Primus 1999, Davis & Koenig 2000, Davis 2001, Levin & Rappaport Hovav 2005). In the Finnish causative example in (23), for example (Davis 2001: 69), the subject argument bears fewer proto-agent entailments than the direct object.

(23) Uutinen   puhu-tt-i   nais-i-a   pitkään.
      news-item talk-CAUS-PAST   woman-PL-PART   long-ILL
      'The news made the women talk for a long time.'

Causation appears to override the other entailments in (23) and similar cases. In addition, (22) makes no prediction regarding predicators other than transitive verbs, but their argument realization is not unconstrained; as with transitive verbs, a causally affecting argument or an argument bearing a larger number of proto-agent entailments is realized as the subject of verbs such as English *prevail (on)*, *rely (on)*, *hope (for)*, *apply (to)*, and many more.

Wechsler (1995) presents a model of argument realization that resembles Dowty's in eschewing thematic roles and hierarchies in favor of a few relational entailments amongst participants in a situation, such as whether one participant necessarily has a notion of another, or is part of another. Davis & Koenig (2000) and Davis (2001) borrow elements of Dowty's and Wechsler's work but posit reified "proto-role attributes" in semantic representations reflecting the flow of causation in response to the difficulties noted above.

4.7 Other applications of thematic roles in syntax and morphology

Thematic roles and thematic hierarchies have been invoked in accounts of various other syntactic phenomena, and the following provides only a sample.

Some accounts of anaphoric binding make explicit reference to thematic roles, as opposed to structural prominence in lexical semantic representations. Typically, such accounts involve a condition that the antecedent of an anaphor must outrank it on the thematic hierarchy. Wilkins (1988) is one example of this approach. Williams (1994) advocates recasting the principles of binding theory in terms of role lists defined on predicators (including many nouns and adjectives). This allows for "implicit", syntactically unrealized arguments to participate in binding conditions. For example, the contrast between *admiration of him* (admirer and admiree must be distinct) and *admiration of himself* (admirer and admiree must be identical) suggests that even arguments that are not necessarily syntactically realized play a crucial role in binding. Thematic role labels, however, play no part in this system; rather, the arguments of a predicator are simply in an ordered list, as in the argument structures of Rappaport & Levin (1988) and Grimshaw (1990), though ordering on the list might be determined by a thematic hierarchy. And Jackendoff (1987) suggests that indexing argument positions within semantically decomposed lexical representations can address these binding facts, without reference to thematic hierarchies.

Everaert & Anagnostopoulou (1997) argue that local anaphors in Modern Greek display a dependence on the thematic hierarchy; as a *Goal* or *Experiencer* antecedent can bind a *Theme*, for example, but not the reverse. This holds even when the lower thematic role is realized as the subject, resulting in a subject anaphor.

Nishigauchi (1984) argues for thematic role-based effect in controller selection for infinitival complements and purpose clauses, a view defended by Jones (1988). For example, the controller of a purpose clause is said to be a *Goal*. Ladusaw & Dowty (1988) counter that the data is better handled by verbal entailments and by general principles of world knowledge about human action and responsibility.

Donohue (1996) presents data on relativization in Tukang Besi (an Austronesian language of Indonesia) that suggest a distinct relativization strategy for *Instruments*, regardless of their grammatical relation.

Mithun (1984) proposes an account of noun incorporation in which *Patient* is preferred over other roles for incorporation, though in some languages arguments bearing other roles (*Instrument* or *Location*) may incorporate as well. But alternatives based on underlying syntactic structure (Baker 1988) and depth of embedding in lexical semantic representations (Kiparsky 1997) have also been advanced. Evans (1997) examines noun-incorporation in Mayali (a non-Pama-Nyungan language of northern Australia) and finds a thematic-role based account inadequate to deal with the range of incor-porated nominals. He instead suggests that constraints based on animacy and prototypicality in the denoted event are crucial in selecting the incorporating argument.

5 Concluding remarks

Dowty (1989: 108–109) contrasts two positions on the utility of (broad) thematic roles. Those advocating that thematic roles are crucially involved in lexical, morphological, and syntactic phenomena have consequently tried to define thematic roles and develop thematic role systems. But, even 20 years later, the position Dowty states in (24) can also be defended:

(24) Thematic roles per se have no priviledged [sic] status in the conditioning of syntactic processes by lexical meaning, except insofar as certain semantic distinctions happen to occur more frequently than others among natural languages.

Given the range of alternative accounts of argument realization, lexical acquisition, and other phenomena for which the "traditional", broad thematic roles have sometimes been considered necessary, and the additional devices required even in those approaches that do employ them, it is unclear how much is gained by introducing them as reified elements of linguistic theory. There do appear to be some niche cases of phenomena that depend on such notions, some of which are noted above, and there are stronger motivations for entailment-based approaches to argument realization, diathesis alternations, aspect, and complement control. Such entailments can certainly be viewed as thematic roles, some even as roles in a broad sense that apply to a large class of predicates. But the overall picture is not one that lends support to the "traditional" notion of a small inventory of broad roles, with each of a predicate's arguments uniquely assigned one of them.

Fine-grained roles serve a somewhat different function in model-theoretic semantics, one not dependent on the properties of a thematic role system but on the use of roles in individuating events and how they are related to their participants. But in this realm, too, they do not come without costs; as Landman and Schein have argued, dyadic thematic roles, coupled with principles of role uniqueness, lead both to unwelcome inferences that can be blocked only with additional mechanisms and to requiring events that are intuitively too fine-grained. These difficulties arise in connection with symmetric predicators, transactional verbs, and other complex event types that may warrant a more elaborated treatment than thematic roles defined on a unitary predicate can offer.

The author gratefully acknowledges detailed comments on this article from Cleo Condoravdi and from the editors.

6 References

Alsina, Alex 1992. On the argument structure of causatives. *Linguistic Inquiry* 23, 517–555.
Bach, Emmon 1989. *Informal Lectures on Formal Semantics*. Albany, NY: State University of New York Press.
Baker, Mark C. 1988. *Incorporation. A Theory of Grammatical Function Changing*. Chicago, IL: The University of Chicago Press.

Baker, Mark C. 1997. Thematic roles and syntactic structure. In: L. Haegeman (ed.). *Elements of Grammar*. Dordrecht: Kluwer, 73–137.
Bayer, Samuel L. 1997. *Confessions of a Lapsed Neo-Davidsonian. Events and Arguments in Compositional Semantics*. New York: Garland.
Belletti, Adriana & Luigi Rizzi 1988. Psych-verbs and θ-Theory. *Natural Language and Linguistic Theory* 6, 291–352.
Bresnan, Joan & Jonni Kanerva 1989. Locative inversion in Chichewa. A case study of factorization in grammar. *Linguistic Inquiry* 20, 1–50.
Bresnan, Joan & Lioba Moshi 1990. Object asymmetries in comparative Bantu syntax. *Linguistic Inquiry* 21, 147–185.
Broadwell, George A. 1988. Multiple θ-role assignment in Choctaw. In: W. Wilkins (ed.). *Syntax and Semantics 21: Thematic Relations*. New York: Academic Press, 113–127.
Carlson, Greg 1984. On the role of thematic roles in linguistic theory. *Linguistics* 22, 259–279.
Carlson, Greg 1998. Thematic roles and the individuation of events. In: S. Rothstein (ed.). *Events and Grammar*. Dordrecht: Kluwer, 35–51.
Chierchia, Gennaro 1984. *Topics in the Syntax and Semantics of Infinitives and Gerunds*. Ph.D. dissertation. University of Massachusetts, Amherst, MA.
Chomsky, Noam 1981. *Lectures on Government and Binding*. Dordrecht: Foris.
Chomsky, Noam 1982. *Some Concepts and Consequences of the Theory of Government and Binding*. Cambridge, MA: The MIT Press.
Croft, William 1991. *Syntactic Categories and Grammatical Relations: The Cognitive Organization of Information*. Chicago, IL: The University of Chicago Press.
Croft, William 1998. Event structure in argument linking. In: M. Butt & W. Geuder (eds.). *The Projection of Arguments. Lexical and Compositional Factors*. Stanford, CA: CSLI Publications, 21–63.
Davidson, Donald 1967. The logical form of action sentences. In: N. Rescher (ed.). *The Logic of decision and Action*. Pittsburgh, PA: University of Pittsburgh Press, 81–95.
Davis, Anthony R. 2001. *Linking by Types in the Hierarchical Lexicon*. Stanford, CA: CSLI Publications.
Davis, Anthony R. & Jean-Pierre Koenig 2000. Linking as constraints on word classes in a hierarchical lexicon. *Language* 76, 56–91.
Donohue, Mark 1996. Relative clauses in Tukang Besi. Grammatical functions and thematic roles. *Linguistic Analysis* 26, 159–173.
Dowty, David 1989. On the semantic content of the notion of 'thematic role'. In: G. Chierchia, B. Partee & R. Turner (eds.). *Properties, Types, and Meaning, vol. 2. Semantic Issues*. Dordrecht: Kluwer, 69–129.
Dowty, David 1991. Thematic proto-roles and argument selection. *Language* 67, 547–619.
Everaert, Martin & Elena Anagnostopoulou 1997. Thematic hierarchies and Binding Theory. Evidence from Greek. In: F. Gorblin, D. Godard & J.-M. Marandin (eds.). *Empirical Issues in Formal Syntax and Semantics. Selected Papers from the Colloque de Syntaxe et de Sémantique de Paris (CSSP 1995)*. Bern: Lang, 43–59.
Evans, Nick 1997. Role or cast. In: A. Alsina, J. Bresnan & P. Sells (eds.). *Complex Predicates*. Stanford, CA: CSLI Publications, 397–430.
Fillmore, Charles J. 1968. The case for case. In: E. Bach & R. T. Harms (eds.). *Universals of Linguistic Theory*. New York: Holt, Rinehart & Winston, 1–88.
Fillmore, Charles J. 1977. Topics in lexical semantics. In: R. W. Cole (ed.). *Current Issues in Linguistic Theory*. Bloomington, IN: Indiana University Press, 76–138.

Foley, William A. & Robert D. van Valin, Jr. 1984. *Functional Syntax and Universal Grammar*. Cambridge: Cambridge University Press.
Gawron, Jean Mark 1983. *Lexical Representations and the Semantics of Complementation*. Ph.D. dissertation. University of California, Berkeley, CA.
Gerdts, Donna B. 1992. Morphologically-mediated relational profiles. In: L. A. Buszard-Welcher, L. Wee & W. Weigel (eds.). *Proceedings of the 18th Annual Meeting of the Berkeley Linguistics Society (=BLS)*. Berkeley, CA: Berkeley Linguistic Society, 322–337.
Grimshaw, Jane 1990. *Argument Structure*. Cambridge, MA: The MIT Press.
Gruber, Jeffrey S. 1965. *Studies in Lexical Relations*. Ph.D. dissertation. MIT, Cambridge, MA.
Jackendoff, Ray 1983. *Semantics and Cognition*. Cambridge, MA: The MIT Press.
Jackendoff, Ray 1987. The Status of thematic relations in linguistic theory. *Linguistic Inquiry* 18, 369–411.
Jackendoff, Ray 1990. *Semantic Structures*. Cambridge, MA: The MIT Press.
Jones, Charles 1988. Thematic relations in control. In: W. Wilkins (ed.). *Syntax and Semantics 21: Thematic Relations*. New York: Academic Press, 75–89.
Kiparsky, Paul 1997. Remarks on denominal verbs. In: A. Alsina, J. Bresnan & P. Sells (eds.). *Complex Predicates*. Stanford, CA: CSLI Publications, 473–499.
Kratzer, Angelika 1996. Severing the external argument from its verb. In: J. Rooryck & L. Zaring (eds.). *Phrase Structure and the Lexicon*. Dordrecht: Kluwer, 109–137.
Krifka, Manfred 1992. Thematic relations as links between nominal reference and temporal constitution. In: I. A. Sag & A. Szabolcsi (eds.). *Lexical Matters*. Stanford, CA: CSLI Publications, 29–53.
Krifka, Manfred 1998. The origins of telicity. In: S. Rothstein (ed.). *Events and Grammar*. Dordrecht: Kluwer, 197–235.
Ladusaw, William A. & David R. Dowty 1988. Towards a nongrammatical account of thematic roles. In: W. Wilkins (ed.). *Syntax and Semantics 21: Thematic Relations*. New York: Academic Press, 61–73.
Landman, Fred 2000. *Events and Plurality. The Jerusalem Lectures*. Dordrecht: Kluwer.
Lehmann, Fritz 1996. Big posets of participatings and thematic roles. In: P. W. Eklund, G. Ellis & G. Mann (eds.). *Proceedings of the 4th International Conference on Conceptual Structures. Knowledge Representation as Interlingua*. Berlin: Springer, 50–74.
Levin, Beth & Malka Rappaport Hovav 2005. *Argument Realization*. Cambridge: Cambridge University Press.
Li, Yafei 1995. The thematic hierarchy and causativity. *Natural Language and Linguistic Theory* 13, 255–282.
Màrquez, Lluís et al. 2008. Semantic role labeling. An introduction to the special issue. *Computational Linguistics* 34, 145–159.
Mithun, Marianne 1984. The evolution of noun incorporation. *Language* 60, 847–894.
Nishigauchi, Taisuke 1984. Control and the thematic domain. *Language* 60, 215–250.
Ostler, Nicholas 1979. *Case Linking. A Theory of Case and Verb Diathesis Applied to Classical Sanskrit*. Ph.D. dissertation. MIT, Cambridge, MA.
Parsons, Terence 1990. *Events in the Semantics of English. A Study in Subatomic Semantics*. Cambridge, MA: The MIT Press.
Perlmutter, David M. & Paul Postal. 1984. The I-advancement exclusiveness law. In: D.M. Perlmutter & C. Rosen (eds.). *Studies in Relational Grammar, vol. 2*. Chicago, IL: The University of Chicago Press, 81–125.

Primus, Beatrice 1999. *Cases and Thematic Roles. Ergative, Accusative and Active.* Tübingen: Niemeyer.
Primus, Beatrice 2006. Mismatches in semantic-role hierarchies and the dimensions of Role Semantics. In: I. Bornkessel et al. (eds.). *Semantic Role Universals and Argument Linking. Theoretical, Typological, and Psycholinguistic Perspectives.* Berlin: Mouton de Gruyter, 53–88.
Rappaport, Malka & Beth Levin 1988. What to do with θ-roles. In: W. Wilkins (ed.). *Syntax and Semantics 21: Thematic Relations.* New York: Academic Press, 7–36.
Rosen, Carol 1984. The interface between semantic roles and initial grammatical relations. In: D.M. Perlmutter & C. Rosen. (eds.). *Studies in Relational Grammar, vol. 2.* Chicago, IL: The University of Chicago Press, 38–77.
Rozwadowska, Bożena 1988. Thematic restrictions on derived nominals. In: W. Wilkins (ed.). *Syntax and Semantics 21: Thematic Relations.* New York: Academic Press, 147–165
Schein, Barry 2002. Events and the semantic content of thematic relations. In: G. Preyer & G. Peter (eds.). *Logical Form and Language.* Oxford: Oxford University Press, 263–344.
Somers, Harold L. 1987. *Valency and Case in Computational Linguistics.* Edinburgh: Edinburgh University Press.
Sowa, John F. 2000. *Knowledge Representation. Logical, Philosophical, and Computational Foundations.* Pacific Grove, CA: Brooks Cole Publishing Co.
Svenonius, Peter 2007. Adpositions, particles and the arguments they introduce. In: E. Reuland, T. Bhattacharya & G. Spathas (eds.). *Argument Structure.* Amsterdam: Benjamins, 63–103.
van Valin, Robert D., Jr. 2004. Semantic macroroles in Role and Reference Grammar. In: R. Kailuweit & M. Hummel (eds.). *Semantische Rollen.* Tübingen: Narr, 62–82.
Wechsler, Stephen 1995. *The Semantic Basis of Argument Structure.* Stanford, CA: CSLI Publications.
Wechsler, Stephen 2005. What is right and wrong about little *v*. In: M. Vulchanova & T. A. Åfarli (eds.). *Grammar and Beyond. Essays in Honour of Lars Hellan.* Oslo: Novus Press, 179–195.
Wilkins, Wendy 1988. Thematic structure and reflexivization. In: W. Wilkins (ed.). *Syntax and Semantics 21: Thematic Relations.* New York: Academic Press, 191–213.
Williams, Edwin 1994. *Thematic Structure in Syntax.* Cambridge, MA: The MIT Press.
Wunderlich, Dieter 1997. CAUSE and the structure of verbs. *Linguistic Inquiry* 28, 27–68.

Beth Levin and Malka Rappaport Hovav
4 Lexical Conceptual Structure

1   Introduction —— 126
2   The introduction of LCSs into linguistic theory —— 127
3   Components of LCSs —— 131
4   Choosing primitive predicates —— 135
5   Subeventual analysis —— 139
6   LCSs and syntax —— 141
7   Conclusion —— 145
8   References —— 146

Abstract: The term "lexical conceptual structure" was introduced in the 1980s to refer to a structured lexical representation of verb meaning designed to capture those meaning components which determine grammatical behavior, particularly with respect to argument realization. Although the term is no longer much used, representations of verb meaning which share many of the properties of LCSs are still proposed in theories which maintain many of the aims and assumptions associated with the original work on LCSs. As LCSs and the representations that are their descendants take the form of predicate decompositions, the article reviews criteria for positing the primitive predicates that make up LCSs. Following an overview of the original work on LCS, the article traces the developments in the representation of verb meaning that characterize the descendants of the early LCSs. The more recent work exploits the distinction between root and event structure implicit in even the earliest LCS in the determination of grammatical behavior. This work also capitalizes on the assumption that predicate decompositions incorporate a subeventual analysis which defines hierarchical relations among arguments, allowing argument realization rules to be formulated in terms of the geometry of the decomposition.

1 Introduction

Lexical Conceptual Structure (LCS) is a term that was used in the 1980s and 1990s to refer to a structured lexical representation of verb meaning. Although the term

Beth Levin, Stanford, CA, USA
Malka Rappaport Hovav, Jerusalem, Israel

https://doi.org/10.1515/9783110626391-004

"LCS" is no longer widely used, structured representations of verb meaning which share many of the properties of LCSs are still often proposed, in theories which maintain many of the aims and assumptions associated with those originally involving an LCS. These descendants of the original LCSs go by various names, including lexical relational structures (Hale & Keyser 1992, 1993), event structures (Rappaport Hovav & Levin 1998, Levin & Rappaport Hovav 2005), semantic structures (Pinker 1989), L-syntax (Mateu 2001a, Travis 2000), l-structure (Zubizarreta & Oh 2007) and first phase syntax (Ramchand 2008); representations called Semantic Forms (Wunderlich 1997a, 1997b) and Semantic Representations (Van Valin 1993, 2005, Van Valin & LaPolla 1997) are also close in spirit to LCSs. Here we provide an overview of work that uses a construct called LCS, and we then trace the developments which have taken place in the representation of verb meaning in descendants of this work. We stress, however, that we are not presenting a single coherent or unified theory, but rather a synthetic perspective on a collection of related theories.

2 The introduction of LCSs into linguistic theory

In the early 1980s, the idea emerged that major facets of the syntax of a sentence are projected from the lexical properties of the words in it (e.g. Chomsky 1981, Farmer 1984, Pesetsky 1982, Stowell 1981; see Fillmore 1968 for an earlier proposal of this sort), and over the course of that decade its consequences were explored. Much of this work assumes that verbs are associated with predicate-argument structures (e.g. Bresnan 1982, Grimshaw 1990), often called theta-grids (Stowell 1981, Williams 1981). The central idea is that the syntactic structure that a verb appears in is projected from its predicate-argument structure, which indicates the number of syntactic arguments a verb has, and some information about how the arguments are projected onto syntax, for example, as internal or external arguments (Marantz 1984, Williams 1981). One insight arising from the closer scrutiny of the relationship between the lexical properties of verbs and the syntactic environments in which they appear is that a great many verbs display a range of what have been called argument – or diathesis – alternations, in which the same verb appears with more than one set of morphosyntactic realization options for its arguments, as in the causative and dative alternations, in (1) and (2), respectively.

(1)   a. Pat dried the clothes.
      b. The clothes dried.

(2) a. Pat sold the rare book to Terry.
    b. Pat sold Terry the rare book.

Some argument alternations seem to involve two alternate realizations of the same set of arguments (e.g. the dative alternation), while others seem to involve real changes in the meaning of the verb (e.g. the causative alternation) (Levin & Rappaport Hovav 1998). Researchers who developed theories of LCS assumed that in addition to a verb's argument structure, it is possible to isolate a small set of recurring meaning components which determine the range of argument alternations a particular verb can participate in. These meaning components are embodied in the primitive predicates of predicate decompositions such as LCSs. Thus, LCSs are used both to represent systematic alternations in a verb's meaning and to define the set of verbs which undergo alternate mappings to syntax, as we now illustrate.

A case study which illustrates this line of investigation is presented by Guerssel et al. (1985). Their study attempts to isolate those facets of meaning which determine a verb's participation in several transitivity alternations in four languages: Berber, English, Warlpiri, and Winnebago. Guerssel et al. compare the behavior of verbs corresponding to English *break* (as a representative of the class of change of state verbs) and *cut* (as a representative of the class of motion-contact-effect verbs) in several alternations, including the causative and conative alternations in these languages (cf. Fillmore 1970). They suggest that participation in the causative alternation is contingent on the LCS of a verb containing a constituent of the form '[come to be STATE]' (represented via the predicate BECOME or CHANGE in some other work), while participation in the conative alternation requires an LCS with components of contact and effect.

The LCSs suggested for the intransitive and transitive uses of *break*, which together make up the causative alternation, are given in (3), and the LCSs for the transitive and intransitive uses of *cut*, which together make up the conative alternation, illustrated in (4), are presented in (5).

(3) a. *break*: y come to be BROKEN (Guerssel et al. 1985: 54, ex. (19))
    b. *break*: x cause (y come to be BROKEN) (Guerssel et al. 1985: 55, ex. (21))

(4) a. I cut the rope around his wrists.
    b. I cut at the rope around his wrists.

(5) a. *cut*: x produce CUT in y, by sharp edge coming into contact with y
       (Guerssel et al. 1985: 51, ex. (11))

b. *cut* Conative LCS: x causes sharp edge to move along path toward y, in order to produce CUT on y, by sharp edge coming into contact with y (Guerssel et al. 1985: 59, ex. (34))

We cite semantic representations in the forms given in the source, even though this leads to inconsistencies in notation; where we formulate representations for the purposes of this article, we adopt the representations used by Rappaport Hovav & Levin (1998) and subsequent work. Although the LCSs for *cut* in (5) include semantic notions not usually encountered in predicate decompositions, central to them are the notions 'move' and 'produce', which have more common analogues: GO and the combination of CAUSE and BECOME, respectively.

The verb *cut* does not have an intransitive noncausative use, as in (6), since its LCS does not have an isolatable constituent of the form '[come to be in STATE]', while the verb *break* lacks a conative variant, as in (7), because its LCS does not include a contact component. Finally, verbs like *touch*, whose meaning does not involve a change of state and simply involves contact with no necessary effect, display neither alternation, as in (8).

(6) *The bread cut.

(7) *We broke at the box.

(8) a. We touched the wall.
    b. *The wall touched.
    c. *We touched at the wall.

For other studies along these lines, see Hale & Keyser (1987), Laughren (1988), and Rappaport, Levin & Laughren (1988).

Clearly, the noncausative and causative uses of a verb satisfy different truth conditions, as do the conative and nonconative uses of a verb. As we have just illustrated, LCSs can capture these modulations in the meaning of a verb which, in turn, have an effect on the way a verb's arguments are morphosyntactically realized. As we discuss in sections 5 and 6, subsequent work tries to derive a verb's argument realization properties in a principled way from the structure of its LCS.

However, as mentioned above, verbs with certain LCSs may also simply allow more than one syntactic realization of their arguments without any change in meaning. Rappaport Hovav & Levin (2008) argue that this possibility is instantiated by the English dative alternation as manifested by verbs that inherently lexicalize caused possession such as *give*, *rent*, and *sell*. They propose that these verbs have a single LCS representing the causation of possession, as in (9), but differ from each other with respect to the specific type of possession involved. The verb *give* lexicalizes nothing more than caused possession, while other verbs add further details about the event: it involves the exchange of money for *sell* and is temporary and contractual for *rent*.

(9) Caused possession LCS: [x CAUSE [y HAVE z]]

According to Rappaport Hovav & Levin (2008), the dative alternation arises with these verbs because the caused possession LCS has two syntactic realizations. (See Harley 2003 and Goldberg 1995 for an alternative view which takes the dative alternation to be a consequence of attributing both caused motion and caused possession LCSs to all alternating verbs; Rappaport Hovav & Levin only attribute both LCSs to verbs such as *send* and *throw*, which are not inherently caused possession verbs.)

As these case studies illustrate, the predicate decompositions that fall under the rubric "LCS" are primarily designed to capture those facets of meaning which determine grammatical facets of behavior, including argument alternations. This motivation sets LCSs apart from other predicate decompositions, which are primarily posited on the basis of other forms of evidence, such as the ability to capture various entailment relations between sets of sentences containing morphologically related words and the ability to account for interactions between event types and various tense operators and temporal adverbials; cf. article 2 [this volume] (Engelberg) *Frameworks of decomposition*. To give one example, it has been suggested that verbs which pass tests for telicity all have a state predicate in their predicate decomposition (Dowty 1979, Parsons 1990). Nevertheless, LCS representations share many of the properties of other predicate decompositions used as explications of lexical meaning, including those proposed by Dowty (1979), Jackendoff (1976, 1983, 1990), and more recently in Role and Reference Grammar, especially in Van Valin & LaPolla (1997), based in large part on the work of generative semanticists such as Lakoff (1968, 1970), McCawley (1968, 1971), and Ross (1972). These similarities, of course, raise the question of whether the same representation can be the basis for capturing both kinds of generalizations.

LCSs, however, are not intended to provide an exhaustive representation of a verb's meaning, as mentioned above. Positing an LCS presupposes that it is possible to distinguish those facets of meaning that are grammatically relevant from those which are not; this assumption is not uncontroversial, see, for example, the debate between Taylor (1996) and Jackendoff (1996a). In addition, the methodology and aims of this form of "componential" analysis of verb meaning differs in fundamental ways from the type of componential analysis proposed by the structuralists (e.g. Nida 1975). For the structuralists, meaning components were isolatable insofar as they were implicated in semantic contrasts within a lexical field (e.g. "adult" to distinguish *parent* from *child*); the aim of a componential analysis, then, was to provide a feature analysis of the words in a particular semantic field that distinguishes every word in that field from every other. In contrast, the goal of the work assuming LCS is not to provide an exhaustive semantic analysis, but rather to isolate only those facets of meaning which recur in significant classes of verbs and determine key facets of the linguistic behavior of verbs. This approach makes the crucial assumption that verbs may be different in significant respects, while still having almost identical LCSs; for example, *freeze* and *melt* denote "inverse" changes of state, yet they would both share the LCS of change of state verbs.

Although all these works assume the value of positing predicate decompositions (thus differing radically from the work of Fodor & Lepore 1999), the nature of the predicate decomposition and its place in grammar and syntactic structure vary quite radically from theory to theory. Here we review the work which takes the structured lexical representation to be a specifically linguistic representation and, thus, to be distinct from a general conceptual structure which interfaces with other cognitive domains. Furthermore, this work assumes that the information encoded in LCSs is a small subset of the information encoded in a fully articulated explication of lexical meaning. In this respect, this work is different from the work of Jackendoff (1983, 1990), who assumes that there is a single conceptual representation, used for linguistic and nonlinguistic purposes; cf. article 4 [Semantics: Theories] (Jackendoff) *Conceptual Semantics*.

3 Components of LCSs

Since verbs individuate and name events, LCS-style representations are taken to specify the limited inventory of basic event types made available by language for describing happenings in the world. Thus, our use of the term "event" includes all situation types, including states, similar to the notion of "eventuality" in some work on event semantics (Bach 1986). For this reason, such representations are often currently referred to as "event structures". In this section, we provide an overview of the representations of the lexical meaning of verbs which are collectively called event structures and identify the properties which are common to the various instantiations of these representations. In section 6, we review theories which differ in terms of how these representations are related to syntactic structures.

All theories of event structure, either implicitly or explicitly, recognize a distinction between the primitive predicates which define the range of event types available and a component which represents what is idiosyncratic in a verb's meaning. For example, all noncausative verbs of change of state have a predicate decomposition including a predicate representing the notion of change of state, as in (10); however, these verbs differ from one another with respect to an attribute of an entity whose value is specified as changing: the attribute relevant to *cool* involves temperature, while that relevant to *widen* involves a dimension. One way to represent these components of meaning is to allow the predicate representing the change to take an argument which represents the attribute, and this argument position can then be associated with distinct attributes. This idea is instantiated in the representations for the three change of state verbs in (11) by indicating the attribute relevant to each verb in capital italics placed within angle brackets.

(10) [BECOME [y <*RES-STATE*>]]

(11) a. *dry*: [BECOME [y <*DRY*>]]
 b. *widen*: [BECOME [y <*WIDE*>]]
 c. *dim*: [BECOME [y <*DIM*>]]

As this example shows, LCSs are constructed so that common substructures in the representations of verb meanings can be taken to define grammatically relevant classes of verbs, such as those associated with particular argument alternations. Thus, the structure in (10), which is shared by all change of state verbs, can then be associated with displaying the causative alternation. Being associated with this LCS substructure is a necessary, but not sufficient, condition for participating in the causative alternation, since only some change of state verbs alternate in English. The precise conditions for licensing the alternation require further investigation, as does the question of why languages vary somewhat in their alternating verbs; see Alexiadou, Anagnostopoulou & Schäfer (2006), Doron (2003), Haspelmath (1993), Koontz-Garboden (2007), and Levin & Rappaport Hovav (2005) for discussion.

The idiosyncratic component of a verb's meaning has received several names, including "constant", "root", and even "verb". We use the term "root" (Pesetsky 1995) in the remainder of this article, although we stress that it should be kept distinct from the notion of root used in morphology (e.g. Aronoff 1993). Roots may be integrated into LCSs in two ways: a root may fill an argument position of a primitive predicate, as in the change of state example (10), or it may serve as a modifier of a predicate, as with various types of activity verbs, as in (12) and (13). (Modifier status is indicated by subscripting the root to the predicate being modified.)

(12) Casey ran.
 [x ACT$_{<RUN>}$]

(13) Tracy wiped the table.
 [x ACT$_{<WIPE>}$ y]

Although early work on the structured representation of verb meaning paid little attention to the nature and contribution of the root (the exception being Grimshaw 2005), more recent work has taken seriously the idea that the elements of meaning lexicalized in the root determine the range of event structures that a root can be associated with (e.g. Erteschik-Shir & Rapoport 2004, 2005, Harley 2005, Ramchand 2008, Rappaport Hovav 2008, Rappaport Hovav & Levin 1998, Zubizarreta & Oh 2007).

Thus, Rappaport Hovav & Levin (1998) propose that roots are of different ontological types, with the type determining the associated event structures. Two of the major ontological types of roots are manner and result (Levin & Rappaport Hovav 1991, 1995, Rappaport Hovav & Levin 2010; see also Talmy 1975, 1985, 2000). These two types of roots are best introduced through an examination of verbs apparently in the same semantic field which differ as to the nature of their root: the causative change of state verb *clean*, for example, has a result root that specifies a state that often results from some activity, as in (14), while the verb *scrub* has a manner root that specifies an activity, as in (15); in this and many other instances, the activity is one conventionally carried out to achieve a particular result. With *scrub* the result is "cleanness", which explains the intuition of relatedness between the manner verb *scrub* and the result verb *clean*.

(14) [[x ACT$_{<MANNER>}$] CAUSE [BECOME [y <CLEAN>]]]

(15) [x ACT$_{<SCRUB>}$]

Result verbs specify the bringing about of a result state – a state that is the result of some sort of activity; it is this state which is lexicalized in the root. Thus, the verbs *clean* and *empty* describe two different result states that are often brought about by removing material from a place; neither verb is specific about how the relevant result state comes about. Result verbs denote externally caused eventualities in the sense of Levin & Rappaport Hovav (1995). Thus, while a cave can be empty without having been emptied, something usually becomes empty as a result of some causing event. Result verbs, then, are associated with a causative change of state LCS; see also Hale & Keyser (2002) and Koontz-Garboden (2007) and for slightly different views Alexiadou, Anagnostopoulou & Schäfer (2006) and Doron (2003).

A manner root is associated with an activity LCS; such roots describe actions, which are identified by some sort of means, manner, or instrument. Thus, the manner verbs *scrub* and *wipe* both describe actions that involve making contact with a surface, but differ in the way the hand or some implement is moved against the surface and the degree of force and intensity of this movement. Often such activities are characterized by the instrument used in performing them and the verbs themselves take their names from the instruments. Again among verbs describing making contact with a surface, there are the verbs *rake* and *shovel*, which involve different instruments, designed for different purposes and, thus, manipulated in somewhat different ways. Despite the differences in the way the instruments are used, linguistically all these verbs have a basic activity LCS. In fact, all instrument verbs have this LCS even though there is apparent diversity among them: Thus, the verb *sponge* might be used in the description of removing events (e.g. *Tyler sponged the stain off the fabric*) and the verb *whisk* in the description of adding events (e.g. *Cameron whisked the sugar into the eggs*), while the verbs *rake* and *shovel* might be used for either (e.g. *Kelly shoveled the snow into the truck, Kelly shoveled the snow off the drive*). According to Rappaport Hovav & Levin (1998), this diversity has a unified source: English allows the LCSs of all activity verbs to be "augmented" by the addition of a result state, giving rise to causative LCSs, such as those involved in the description of adding and removing events, via a process they call Template Augmentation. This process resembles Wunderlich's (1997a, 2000) notion of argument extension; cf. article 7 [Semantics: Interfaces] (Wunderlich) *Operations on argument structure*; see also Rothstein (2003) and Ramchand (2008). Whether an augmented instrument verb receives an adding or removing interpretation depends on whether the instrument involved is typically used to add or remove stuff.

In recent work, Rappaport Hovav & Levin (2010) suggest an independent characterization of manner and result roots by appealing to the notions of scalar and nonscalar change – notions which have their origins in Dowty (1979, 1991) and McClure (1994), as well as the considerable work on the role of scales in determining telicity (e.g. Beavers 2008, Borer 2005, Hay, Kennedy & Levin 1999, Jackendoff 1996b, Kennedy & Levin 2008, Krifka 1998, Ramchand 1997, Tenny 1994). As dynamic verbs, manner and result verbs all involve change, though crucially not the same type of change: result roots specify scalar changes, while manner roots do not. Verbs denoting events of scalar change in one argument lexically entail a scale: a set of degrees – points or intervals indicating measurement values – ordered on a particular dimension representing an attribute of an argument (e.g. height, temperature, cost) (Bartsch & Vennemann 1972, Kennedy 1999, 2001); the degrees indicate the possible values of this attribute. A scalar change in an entity involves a change in the value of the relevant attribute in a particular direction along the associated scale. The change of state verb *widen* is associated with a scale of increasing values on a dimension of width; and a widening event necessarily involves an entity showing an increase in the value along this dimension. A nonscalar change is any change that cannot be characterized in terms of a scale; such changes are typically complex, involving a combination of many changes at once. They are characteristic of manner verbs. For example, the verb *sweep* involves a specific movement of a broom against a surface that is repeated an indefinite number of times. See Rappaport Hovav (2008) for extensive illustration of the grammatical reflexes of the scalar/nonscalar change distinction.

As this section makes clear, roots indirectly influence argument realization as their ontological type determines their association with particular event structures. We leave open the question of whether roots can more directly influence argument realization. For example, the LCS proposed for *cut* in (5) includes elements of meaning which are normally associated with the root since "contact" or a similar concept has not figured among proposals for the set of primitive predicates constituting an LCS. Yet, this element of meaning is implicated by Guerssel et al. in the conative alternation. (In contrast, the notion "effect" more or less reduces to a change of state of some type.)

4 Choosing primitive predicates

LCSs share with other forms of predicate decomposition the properties that are said to make such representations an improvement over lists of semantic roles, whether Fillmore's (1968) cases or Gruber (1965/1976) and Jackendoff's (1972) thematic relations, as structured representations of verb meaning. There is considerable discussion of the problems with providing independent, necessary and sufficient definitions of semantic roles (see e.g. Dowty 1991 and article 3 this volume (Davis) *Thematic roles*), and one suggestion for dealing with this problem is the suggestion first found in Jackendoff (1972) that semantic roles can be identified with particular open positions in predicate decompositions. For example, the semantic role "agent" might be identified with the first argument of a primitive predicate CAUSE. There is a perception that the set of primitive predicates used in a verb's LCS or event structure is better motivated than the set of semantic role labels for its arguments, and for this reason predicate decompositions might appear to be superior to a list of semantic role labels as a structured representation of a verb's meaning. However, there is surprisingly little discussion of the explicit criteria for positing a particular primitive predicate, although see the discussion in Carter (1978), Jackendoff (1983: 203–204), and Joshi (1974).

The primitive predicates which surface repeatedly in studies using LCSs or other forms of predicate decomposition are ACT or DO, BE, BECOME or CHANGE, CAUSE, and GO, although the predicates HAVE, MOVE, STAY, and, more recently, RESULT are also proposed. Jackendoff (1990) posits a significantly greater number of predicates than in his previous work, introducing the predicates CONFIGURE, EXTEND, EXCHANGE, FORM, INCH(OATIVE), ORIENT, and REACT. Article 6 [Semantics: Theories] (Hobbs) *Word meaning and world knowledge* discusses how some of these predicates may be grounded in an axiomatic semantics.

Once predicates begin to proliferate, theories of predicate decomposition face many of the well-known problems facing theories of semantic roles (cf. Dowty 1991). The question is whether it is possible to identify a small, comprehensive, universal, and well-motivated set of predicates accepted by all. It is worthwhile, therefore, to scrutinize the motivation for proposing a predicate in the first place and to try to make explicit when the introduction of a new predicate is justified.

In positing a set of predicates, researchers have tried to identify recurring elements of verb meaning that figure in generalizations holding across the set of verbs within (and, ultimately, across) languages. Often these generalizations involve common entailments or common grammatical properties. Wilks (1987) sets out general desiderata for a set of primitive predicates that are implicit in other work. For instance, the set of predicates should be finite in size and each predicate in the set should indeed be "primitive" in that it should not be reducible to other predicates in the set, nor should it even be partially definable in terms of another predicate. Thus, in positing a new predicate, it is important to consider its effect on the overall set of predicates. Wilks also proposes that the set of predicates should be able to exhaustively describe and distinguish the verbs of each language, but LCS-style representations, by adopting the root–event structure distinction, simply require that the set of primitives should be able to describe all the grammatically relevant event types. It is the role of the root to distinguish between specific verbs of the same event type, and there is a general, but implicit assumption that the roots themselves cannot be reduced to a set of primitive elements. As Wilks (1987: 760) concludes, the ultimate justification for a set of primitive is in their "special organizing role in a language system". We now briefly present several case studies chosen to illustrate the type of reasoning used in positing a predicate.

One way of arriving at a set of primitive predicates is to adopt a hypothesis that circumscribes the basic inventory of event types, while allowing for all events to be analyzed in terms of these types. This approach is showcased in the work of Jackendoff (1972, 1976, 1983, 1987, 1990), who develops ideas proposed by Gruber (1965/1976). Jackendoff adopts the localist hypothesis: motion and location events are basic and all other events should be construed as such events. There is one basic type of motion event, represented by the primitive predicate GO, which takes as arguments a theme and a path (e.g. *The cart went from the farm to the market*). There are two basic types of locational events, represented by the predicate BE (for stative events) and STAY (for non-stative events); these predicates also take a theme and a location as arguments (e.g. *The coat was/stayed in the closet*). In addition, Jackendoff introduces the predicates CAUSE and LET, which are used to form complex events taking as arguments a causer and a motion or location event.

Events that are not obviously events of motion or location are construed in terms of some abstract form of motion or location. For example, with events of possession, possessums can be taken as themes and possessors as locations in an abstract possessional "field" or domain. The verb *give* is analyzed as describing a causative motion event in the possessional field in which a possessum is transferred from one possessor to another. Physical and mental states and changes of state can be seen as involving an entity being "located" in a state or "moving" from one state to a second state in an identificational field; the verb *break*, for instance, describes an entity moving from a state of being whole to a state of being broken. Generalizing, correspondences are set up between the components of motion and location events and the components of other event domains or "semantic fields" in Jackendoff's terms; this is what Jackendoff (1983: 188) calls the Thematic Relations Hypothesis; see article 4 [Semantics: Theories] (Jackendoff) *Conceptual Semantics*. In general on this view, predicates are most strongly motivated when they figure prominently in lexical organization and in cross-field generalizations.

This kind of cross-field organization can be illustrated in a number of ways. First, many English verbs have uses based on the same predicate in more than one field (Jackendoff 1983: 203–204). Thus, the predicate STAY receives support from the English verb *keep*, whose meaning presumably involves the predicates CAUSE and STAY, combined in a representation as in (16), because it shows uses involving the three fields just introduced.

(16) [CAUSE (x, (STAY y, z))]

(17) a. Terry kept the bike in the shed. (Positional)
 b. Terry kept the bike basket. (Possessional)
 c. Terry kept the bike clean. (Identificational)

Without the notion of semantic field, there would be no reason to expect English to have verbs which can be used to describe events which on the surface seem quite different from each another, as in (17). Second, rules of inference hold of shared predicates across fields (Jackendoff 1976). One example is that "if an event is caused, it takes place" (Jackendoff 1976: 110), so that the entailment *The bike stayed in the shed* can be derived from (17a), the entailment *The bike basket stayed with Terry* can be derived from (17b), and the entailment *The bike stayed clean* can be derived from (17c). This supports the use of the predicate CAUSE across fields. Finally, predicates are justified when they explain cross-field generalizations in the use of prepositions. The use of the allative preposition *to* is taken to support the analysis of *give* as a causative verb of motion.

These very considerations lead Carter (1978: 70–74) to argue against the primitive predicate STAY. Carter points out that few English words have meanings that include the notion captured by STAY, yet if STAY were to number among the primitive predicates, such words would be expected to be quite prevalent. So, while the primitives CAUSE and BECOME are motivated because languages often contain a multitude of lexical items differentiated by just these predicates (e.g. the various uses of *cool* in *The cook cooled the cake*, *The cake cooled*, *The cake was cool*), there is no minimal pair differentiated by the existence of STAY, for example, the verb *cool* cannot also mean 'stay cool'. Carter also notes that if NOT is included in the set of predicates, then the predicate STAY becomes superfluous, as it could be replaced by NOT plus CHANGE, a predicate which is roughly an analogue to Jackendoff's GO. Carter further notes that as a result simpler statements of certain inference rules and other generalizations might be possible.

However, the primitive predicates which serve best as the basis for cross-field generalizations are not necessarily the ones that emerge from efforts to account for argument alternations–the efforts that lead to LCS-style representations and their descendants. This point can be illustrated by examining another predicate whose existence has been controversial, HAVE. Jackendoff posits a possessional field that is modeled on the locational field: being possessed is taken to be similar to being at a location – existing at that location (see also Lyons 1967, 1968: 391–395). This approach receives support since many entailments involving location also apply to possession, such as the entailment described for STAY. Furthermore, in some languages, including Hindi-Urdu, the same verb is used in basic locational and possessive sentences, suggesting that possession can be reduced to location (though the facts are often more complicated than they appear on the surface; see Harley 2003). Nevertheless, Pinker (1989: 189–190) and Tham (2004: 62–63, 74–85, 100–104) argue that an independent predicate HAVE is necessary; see also Harley (2003). Pinker points out that in terms of the expression of its arguments, it is *belong* and not *have* which resembles locational predicates. The verb *belong* takes the possessum, which would be analyzed as a theme (i.e. located entity), as its subject and the possessor, which would be analyzed as a location, as an oblique. Its argument realization, then, parallels that of a locational predicate; compare (18a) and (18b). In contrast, *have* takes the possessor as subject and the possessum as object, as in (19), so its arguments show the reverse syntactic prominence relations – a "marked" argument realization, which would need an explanation, on the localist analysis.

(18) a. One of the books belongs to me.
    b. One of the books is on the table.

(19) I have one of the books.

Pinker points out that an analysis which takes *have* to be a marked possessive predicate is incompatible with the observations that it is a high-frequency verb, which is acquired early and unproblematically by children. Tham (2004: 100–104) further points out that it is *belong* that is actually the "marked" verb from other perspectives: it imposes a referentiality condition on its possessum and it is used in a restricted set of information structure contexts – all restrictions that *have* does not share. Taking all these observations together, Tham concludes that *have* shows the unmarked realization of arguments for possessive predicates, while *belong* shows a marked realization of arguments. Thus, she argues that the semantic prominence relations in unmarked possessive and locative sentences are quite different and, therefore, warrant positing a predicate HAVE.

5 Subeventual analysis

One way in which more recent work on event structure departs from earlier work on LCSs is that it begins to use the structure of the semantic representation itself, rather than reference to particular predicates in this representation, in formulating generalizations about argument realization. In so doing, this work capitalizes on the assumption, present in some form since the generative semantics era, that predicate decompositions may have a subeventual analysis. Thus, it recognizes a distinction between two types of event structures: simple event structures and complex event structures, which themselves are constituted of simple event structures. The prototypical complex event structure is a causative event structure, in which an entity or event causes another event, though Ramchand (2008) takes some causative events to be constituted of three subevents, an initiating event, a process, and a result.

Beginning with the work of the generative semanticists, the positing of a complex event structure was supported using evidence from scope ambiguities involving various adverbial phrases (McCawley 1968, 1971, Morgan 1969, von Stechow 1995, 1996). Specifically, a complex event structure may afford certain adverbials, such as *again*, more scope-taking options than a simple event structure, and thus adverbials may show interpretations in sentences denoting complex events that are unavailable in those denoting simple events. Thus, (20) shows both so-called "restitutive" and "repetitive" readings, while (21) has only a "repetitive" reading.

(20) Dale closed the door again.

Repetitive: the action of closing the door was performed before.

Restitutive: the door was previously in the state of being closed, but there is no presupposition that someone had previously closed the door.

(21) John kicked the door again.

Repetitive: the action of kicking the door was performed before.

The availability of two readings in (20) and one reading in (21) is explained by attributing a complex event structure to (20) and a simple event structure to (21).

A recent line of research argues that the architecture of event structure also matters to argument realization, thus motivating complex event structures based on argument realization considerations. This idea is proposed by Grimshaw & Vikner (1993), who appeal to it to explain certain restrictions on the passivization of verbs of creation (though the pattern of acceptability that they are trying to explain turns out to have been mischaracterized; see Macfarland 1995). This idea is further exploited by Rappaport Hovav & Levin (1998) and Levin & Rappaport Hovav (1999) to explain a variety of facts related to objecthood.

In this work, the notion of event complexity gains explanatory power via the assumption that there must be an argument in the syntax for each subevent in an event structure (Rappaport Hovav & Levin 1998, 2001; see also Grimshaw & Vikner 1993 and van Hout 1996 for similar conditions). Given this assumption, a verb with a simple event structure may be transitive or intransitive, while a verb with a complex event structure, say a causative verb, must necessarily be transitive. Rappaport Hovav & Levin (1998) attribute the necessary transitivity of *break* and *melt*, which contrasts with the "optional" transitivity of *sweep* and *wipe*, to this constraint; the former, as causative verbs, have a complex event structure.

(22) a. *Blair broke/melted.
b. Blair wiped and swept.

Levin & Rappaport Hovav (1999) use the same assumption to explain why a resultative based on an unergative verb can only predicate its result state of the subject via a "fake" reflexive object.

(23) My neighbor talked *(herself) hoarse.

Resultatives have a complex, causative event structure, so there must be a syntactically realized argument representing the argument of the result state subevent; in (23) it is a reflexive pronoun as it is the subject which ends up in the result state. Levin (1999) uses the same idea to explain why agent-act-on-patient verbs are transitive across languages, while other two-argument verbs vary in their transitivity: only the former are required to be transitive. As in other work on LCSs and event structure, the use of subeventual structure is motivated by argument realization considerations.

Pustejovsky (1995) and van Hout (1996) propose an alternative perspective on event complexity: they take telic events, rather than causative events, to be complex events. Since most causative events are telic events, the two views of event complexity assign complex event structures in many of the same instances. A major difference is in the treatment of telic uses of manner of motion verbs such as *Terry ran to the library* and telic uses of consumption verbs such as *Kerry ate the peach*; these are considered complex predicates on the telicity approach, but not on the causative approach. See Levin (2000) for some discussion.

The subeventual analysis also defines hierarchical relations among arguments, allowing rules of argument realization to be formulated in terms of the geometry of the LCS. We now discuss advantages of such a formulation over direct reference to semantic roles.

6 LCSs and syntax

LCSs, as predicate decompositions, include the embedding of constituents, giving rise to a hierarchical structure. This hierarchical structure, which includes the subeventual structure discussed in section 5, allows a notion of semantic prominence to be defined, which mirrors the notion of syntactic prominence. For instance, Wunderlich (1997a, 1997b, 2006) introduces a notion of a-command defined over predicate decompositions, which is an analogue of syntactic c-command. By taking advantage of the hierarchical structure of LCSs, it becomes possible to formulate argument realization rules in terms of the geometry of LCSs and, more importantly, to posit natural constraints on the nature of the mapping between LCS and syntax. As discussed at length in Levin & Rappaport Hovav (2005: chapter 5), many researchers assume that the mapping between lexical semantics and syntax obeys a constraint of prominence preservation: relations of semantic prominence in a semantic representation are preserved in the corresponding syntactic representation, so that prominence in the syntax reflects prominence in semantics (Bouchard 1995). This idea is implicit in the many studies that use a thematic hierarchy – a ranking of semantic roles – to guide the semantics-syntax mapping and explain various other facets of grammatical behavior; however, most work adopting a thematic hierarchy does not provide independent motivation for the posited role ranking. Predicate decompositions can provide some substance to the notion of a thematic hierarchy by correlating the position of a role in the hierarchy with the position of the argument bearing that role in a predicate decomposition (Baker 1997, Croft 1998, Kiparsky 1997, Wunderlich 1997a, 1997b, 2000). (There are other ways to ground the thematic hierarchy; see article 3 [this volume] (Davis) *Thematic roles*.)

Researchers such as Bouchard (1995), Kiparsky (1997), and Wunderlich (1997a, 1997b) assume that predicate decompositions constitute a lexical semantic representation, but many other researchers now assume that predicate decompositions are syntactic representations, built from syntactic primitives and constrained by principles of syntax. This move obviates the need for prominence preservation in the semantics-syntax mapping since the lexical semantic representation and the syntactic representation are one. The idea that predicate decompositions motivated by semantic considerations are remarkably similar to syntactic structures, and thus should be taken to be syntactic structures has previously been made explicit in the generative semantics literature (e.g. Morgan 1969). Hale & Keyser were the first to articulate this position in the context of current syntactic theory; their LCS-style syntactic structures are called "lexical relational structures" in some of their work (1992, 1993, 1997). The proposal that predicate decompositions should be syntactically instantiated has gained currency recently and is defended or assumed in a range of work, including Erteschik-Shir & Rapoport (2004), Mateu (2001a, 2001b), Travis (2000), and Zubizaretta & Oh (2007), who all build directly on Hale & Keyser's work, as well as Alexiadou, Anagnostopoulou & Schäfer (2006), Harley (2003, 2005), Pylkkänen (2008), and Ramchand (2008), who calls the "lexical" part of syntax "first phase syntax". We now review the types of arguments adduced in support of this view.

Hale & Keyser (1993) claim that their approach explains why there are few semantic role types (although this claim is not entirely uncontroversial; see Dowty 1991 and Kiparsky 1997). For them, the argument structure of a verb is syntactically defined and represented. Furthermore, individual lexical categories (V, in particular) are constrained so as to project syntactic structures using just the syntactic notions of specifier and complement. These syntactic structures are associated with coarse-grained semantic notions, often corresponding to the predicates typical in standard predicate decompositions; the positions in these structures correspond to semantic roles, just as the argument positions in a standard predicate decomposition are said to correspond to semantic roles; see section 4. For example, the patient of a change of state verb is the specifier of a verbal projection in which a verb takes an adjective complement (i.e. the N position in '[$_v$ N [$_v$ V A]]'). Since the number of possible structural relations in syntax is limited, the number of expressible semantic roles is also limited. Furthermore, Hale & Keyser suggest that the nature of these syntactic representations of argument structure also provide insight into Baker's (1988: 46, 1997) Uniformity of Theta Role Assignment, which requires that identical semantic relationships between items be represented by identical structural relations between those items at d-structure. On Hale & Keyser's approach, this principle must follow since semantic roles are defined over a hierarchical syntactic structure, with a particular role always having the same instantiation. These ideas are developed further in Ramchand (2008), who assumes a slightly more articulated lexical syntactic structure than Hale & Keyser do.

Hale & Keyser provide support for their proposal that verb meanings have internal syntactic structure from the syntax of denominal verbs. They observe that certain impossible types of denominal verbs parallel impossible types of noun-incorporation. In particular, they argue that just as there is no noun incorporation of either agents or recipients in languages with noun-incorporation (Baker 1988: 453–454, fn. 13, 1996: 291–295), so there is no productive denominal verb formation where the base noun is interpreted as an agent or a recipient (e.g. *I churched the money, where church$_N$ is understood as a recipient; *It cowed a calf, where cow$_N$ is understood as the agent). However, denominal verbs are productively formed from nouns analyzed as patients (e.g. I buttered the pan) and containers or locations (e.g. I bottled the wine). Hale & Keyser argue that the possible denominal verb types follow on the assumption that these putative verbs are derived from syntactic structures in which the base noun occupies a position which reflects its semantic role. This point is illustrated using their representations for the verbs *paint* and *shelve* given in (24) and (25), respectively, which are presented in the linearized form given in Wechsler (2006: 651, ex. (17)–(18)) rather than in Hale & Keyser's (1993) tree representations.

(24) a. We painted the house.
 b. We [$_{v'}$ V1 [$_{vp}$ house [$_{v'}$ V2 [$_{pp}$ P$_{with}$ paint]]]]

(25) a. We shelved the books.
 b. We [$_{v'}$ V1 [$_{vp}$ books [$_{v'}$ V2 [$_{pp}$ P$_{on}$ shelf]]]]

The verbs *paint* and *shelf* are derived through the movement of the base noun – the verb's root – into the empty V1 position in the structures in (b), after first merging it with the preposition P$_{with}$ or P$_{on}$ and then with V2. Hale & Keyser argue that the movement of the root is subject to a general constraint on the movement of heads (Baker 1988, Travis 1984). Likewise, putative verbs such as *bush* or *house*, used in sentences such as **I bushed a trim* (with the intended interpretation 'I gave the bush a trim') or **I housed a coat of paint* (with the intended interpretation 'I gave the house a coat of paint') are also excluded by the same constraint.

Hale & Keyser's approach is sharply criticized by Kiparsky (1997). He points out that the syntax alone will not prevent the derivation of sentences such as **I bushed some fertilizer* from a putative source corresponding to *I put some fertilizer on the bush* (cf. the source for *I bottled the wine* or *I corralled the horse*). The association of a particular root with a specific lexical syntactic structure is governed by conceptual principles such as "If an action refers to a thing, it involves a canonical use of the thing" (Kiparsky 1997: 482). Such principles ensure that *bush* will not be inserted into a structure as a location, since unlike a bottle, its canonical use is not as a container or place.

Denominal verbs in English, although they do not involve any explicit verb-forming morphology, have been said, then, to parallel constructions in other languages which do involve overt morphological or syntactic derivation (e.g. noun incorporation), and this parallel has been taken to support the syntactic derivation of these words. Comparable arguments can be made in other areas of the English lexicon. For example, in most languages of the world, manner of motion verbs cannot on their own license a directional phrase, though in English all manner of motion verbs can. Specifically, sentences parallel to the English *Tracy ambled into the room* are derived through a variety of morphosyntactic means in other languages, including the use of directional suffixes or applicative morphemes on manner of motion verbs and the combination of manner and directed motion verbs in compounds or serial verb constructions (Schaefer 1985, Slobin 2004, Talmy 1991). Japanese, for example, must compound a manner of motion verb with a directed motion verb in order to express manner of motion to a goal, as the contrast in (26) shows.

(26) a. ?John-wa   kishi-e   oyoida.
       John-TOP   shore-to   swam.
       'John swam to the shore.' (intended; Yoneyama 1986: 1, ex. (1b))

     b. John-wa   kishi-e   oyoide-itta.
       John-TOP   shore-to   swimming-went.
       'John swam to the shore.' (Yoneyama 1986: 2, ex. (3b))

The association of manner of motion roots with a direction motion event type is accomplished in theories such as Rappaport Hovav & Levin (1998, 2001) and Levin & Rappaport Hovav (1999) by processes which augment the event structure associated with the manner of motion verbs. But such theories never make explicit exactly where the derivation of these extended structures takes place. Ramchand (2008) and Zubizarreta & Oh (2007) argue that since these processes are productive and their outputs are to a large extent compositional, they should be assigned to the "generative computational" module of the grammar, namely, syntax. Finally, as Ramchand explicitly argues, this syntacticized approach suggests that languages that might appear quite different, are in fact, underlyingly quite similar, once lexical syntactic structures are considered.

Finally, we comment on the relation between structured event representations and the lexical entries of verbs. Recognizing that many roots in English can appear as words belonging to several lexical categories and that verbs themselves can be associated with various event structures, Borer (2005) articulates a radically nonlexical position: she proposes that roots are category neutral. That is, there is no association specified in the lexicon between roots and the event structures they appear with. Erteschik-Shir & Rapoport (2004, 2005), Levin & Rappaport Hovav (2005), Ramchand (2008), and Rappaport Hovav & Levin (2005) all point out that even in English the flexibility of this association is still limited by the semantics of the root. Ramchand includes in the lexical entries of verbs the parts of the event structure that a verbal root can be associated with, while Levin & Rappaport Hovav make use of "canonical realization rules", which pair roots with event structures based on their ontological types, as discussed in section 3.

7 Conclusion

LCSs are a form of predicate decomposition intended to capture those facets of verb meaning which determine grammatical behavior, particularly in the realm of argument realization. Research on LCSs and the structured representations that are their descendants has contributed to our understanding of the nature of verb meaning and the relation between verb syntax and semantics. This research has shown the importance of semantic representations that distinguish between root and event structure, as well as the importance of the architecture of the event structure to the determination of grammatical behavior. Furthermore, such developments have led some researchers to propose that representations of verb meaning should be syntactically instantiated.

This research was supported by Israel Science Foundation Grants 806–03 and 379–07 to Rappaport Hovav. We thank Scott Grimm, Marie-Catherine de Marneffe, and Tanya Nikitina for comments on an earlier draft.

8 References

Alexiadou, Artemis, Elena Anagnostopoulou & Florian Schäfer 2006. The properties of anti-causatives crosslinguistically. In: M. Frascarelli (ed.). *Phases of Interpretation*. Berlin: Mouton de Gruyter, 187–211.
Aronoff, Mark 1993. *Morphology by Itself. Stems and Inflectional Classes*. Cambridge, MA: The MIT Press.
Bach, Emmon 1986. The algebra of events. *Linguistics & Philosophy* 9, 5–16.
Baker, Mark C. 1988. *Incorporation. A Theory of Grammatical Function Changing*. Chicago, IL: The University of Chicago Press.
Baker, Mark C. 1996. *The Polysynthesis Parameter*. New York: Oxford University Press.
Baker, Mark C. 1997. Thematic roles and syntactic structure. In: L. Haegeman (ed.). *Elements of Grammar. Handbook of Generative Syntax*. Dordrecht: Kluwer, 73–137.
Bartsch, Renate & Theo Vennemann 1972. The grammar of relative adjectives and comparison. *Linguistische Berichte* 20, 19–32.
Beavers, John 2008. Scalar complexity and the structure of events. In: J. Dölling & T. Heyde-Zybatow (eds.). *Event Structures in Linguistic Form and Interpretation*. Berlin: de Gruyter, 245–265.
Borer, Hagit 2005. *Structuring Sense, vol. 2: The Normal Course of Events*. Oxford: Oxford University Press.
Bouchard, Denis 1995. *The Semantics of Syntax. A Minimalist Approach to Grammar*. Chicago, IL: The University of Chicago Press.
Bresnan, Joan 1982. The passive in lexical theory. In: J. Bresnan (ed.). *The Mental Representation of Grammatical Relations*. Cambridge, MA: The MIT Press, 3–86.
Carter, Richard J. 1978. Arguing for semantic representations. *Recherches Linguistiques de Vincennes* 5–6, 61–92.
Chomsky, Noam 1981. *Lectures on Government and Binding*. Dordrecht: Foris.
Croft, William 1998. Event structure in argument linking. In: M. Butt & W. Geuder (eds.). *The Projection of Arguments. Lexical and Compositional Factors*. Stanford, CA: CSLI Publications, 21–63.
Doron, Edit 2003. Agency and voice. The semantics of the Semitic templates. *Natural Language Semantics* 11, 1–67.
Dowty, David R. 1979. *Word Meaning and Montague Grammar. The Semantics of Verbs and Times in Generative Semantics and in Montague's PTQ*. Dordrecht: Reidel.
Dowty, David R. 1991. Thematic proto-roles and argument selection. *Language* 67, 547–619.
Erteschik-Shir, Nomi & Tova R. Rapoport 2004. Bare aspect. A theory of syntactic projection. In: J. Guéron & J. Lecarme (eds.). *The Syntax of Time*. Cambridge, MA: The MIT Press, 217–234.
Erteschik-Shir, Nomi & Tova R. Rapoport 2005. Path predicates. In: N. Erteschik-Shir & T. Rapoport (eds.). *The Syntax of Aspect. Deriving Thematic and Aspectual Interpretation*. Oxford: Oxford University Press, 65–86.
Farmer, Ann K. 1984. *Modularity in Syntax. A Study of Japanese and English*. Cambridge, MA: The MIT Press.
Fillmore, Charles J. 1968. The case for case. In: E. Bach & R. T. Harms (eds.). *Universals in Linguistic Theory*. New York: Holt, Rinehart & Winston, 1–88.
Fillmore, Charles J. 1970. The grammar of hitting and breaking. In: R. A. Jacobs & P. S. Rosenbaum (eds.). *Readings in English Transformational Grammar*. Waltham, MA: Ginn, 120–133.

Fodor, Jerry & Ernest Lepore 1999. Impossible words? *Linguistic Inquiry* 30, 445–453.
Goldberg, Adele E. 1995. *Constructions. A Construction Grammar Approach to Argument Structure*. Chicago, IL: The University of Chicago Press.
Grimshaw, Jane 1990. *Argument Structure*. Cambridge, MA: The MIT Press.
Grimshaw, Jane 2005. *Words and Structure*. Stanford, CA: CSLI Publications.
Grimshaw, Jane & Sten Vikner 1993. Obligatory adjuncts and the structure of events. In: E. Reuland & W. Abraham (eds.). *Knowledge and Language, vol. 2: Lexical and Conceptual Structure*. Dordrecht: Kluwer, 143–155.
Gruber, Jeffrey S. 1965/1976. *Studies in Lexical Relations*. Ph.D. dissertation. MIT, Cambridge, MA. Reprinted in: J. S. Gruber. *Lexical Structures in Syntax and Semantics*. Amsterdam: North-Holland, 1976, 1–210.
Guerssel, Mohamed et al. 1985. A cross-linguistic study of transitivity alternations. In: W. H. Eilfort, P. D. Kroeber & K. L. Peterson (eds.). *Papers from the Parasession on Causatives and Agentivity*. Chicago, IL: Chicago Linguistic Society, 48–63.
Hale, Kenneth L. & Samuel J. Keyser 1987. *A View from the Middle*. Lexicon Project Working Papers 10. Cambridge, MA: Center for Cognitive Science, MIT.
Hale, Kenneth L. & Samuel J. Keyser 1992. The syntactic character of thematic structure. In: I. M. Roca (ed.). *Thematic Structure. Its Role in Grammar*. Berlin: Foris, 107–143.
Hale, Kenneth L. & Samuel J. Keyser 1993. On argument structure and the lexical expression of syntactic relations. In: K. L. Hale & S. J. Keyser (eds.). *The View from Building 20. Essays in Linguistics in Honor of Sylvain Bromberger*. Cambridge, MA: The MIT Press, 53–109.
Hale, Kenneth L. & Samuel J. Keyser 1997. On the complex nature of simple predicators. In: A. Alsina, J. Bresnan & P. Sells (eds.). *Complex Predicates*. Stanford, CA: CSLI Publications, 29–65.
Hale, Kenneth L. & Samuel J. Keyser 2002. *Prolegomenon to a Theory of Argument Structure*. Cambridge, MA: The MIT Press.
Harley, Heidi 2003. Possession and the double object construction. In: P. Pica & J. Rooryck (eds.). *Linguistic Variation Yearbook, vol. 2*. Amsterdam: Benjamins, 31–70.
Harley, Heidi 2005. How do verbs get their names? Denominal verbs, manner incorporation and the ontology of verb roots in English. In: N. Erteschik-Shir & T. Rapoport (eds.). *The Syntax of Aspect. Deriving Thematic and Aspectual Interpretation*. Oxford: Oxford University Press, 42–64.
Haspelmath, Martin 1993. More on the typology of inchoative/causative verb alternations. In: B. Comrie & M. Polinsky (eds.). *Causatives and Transitivity*. Amsterdam: Benjamins, 87–120.
Hay, Jennifer, Christopher Kennedy & Beth Levin 1999. Scalar structure underlies telicity in 'degree achievements'. In: T. Matthews & D. Strolovich (eds.). *Proceedings of Semantics and Linguistic Theory (=SALT) IX*. Ithaca, NY: Cornell University, 127–144.
van Hout, Angeliek 1996. *Event Semantics of Verb Frame Alternations. A Case Study of Dutch and Its Acquisition*. Ph.D. dissertation. Katholieke Universiteit Brabant, Tilburg.
Jackendoff, Ray S. 1972. *Semantic Interpretation in Generative Grammar*. Cambridge, MA: The MIT Press.
Jackendoff, Ray S. 1976. Toward an explanatory semantic representation. *Linguistic Inquiry* 7, 89–150.
Jackendoff, Ray S. 1983. *Semantics and Cognition*. Cambridge, MA: The MIT Press.
Jackendoff, Ray S. 1987. The status of thematic relations in linguistic theory. *Linguistic Inquiry* 18, 369–411.

Jackendoff, Ray S. 1990. *Semantic Structures*. Cambridge, MA: The MIT Press.
Jackendoff, Ray S. 1996a. Conceptual semantics and cognitive linguistics. *Cognitive Linguistics* 7, 93–129.
Jackendoff, Ray S. 1996b. The proper treatment of measuring out, telicity, and perhaps even quantification in English. *Natural Language and Linguistic Theory* 14, 305–354.
Joshi, Aravind 1974. Factorization of verbs. In: C. H. Heidrich (ed.). *Semantics and Communication*. Amsterdam: North-Holland, 251–283.
Kennedy, Christopher 1999. *Projecting the Adjective. The Syntax and Semantics of Gradability and Comparison*. New York: Garland.
Kennedy, Christopher 2001. Polar opposition and the ontology of 'degrees'. *Linguistics & Philosophy* 24, 33–70.
Kennedy, Christopher & Beth Levin 2008. Measure of change. The adjectival core of degree achievements. In: L. McNally & C. Kennedy (eds.). *Adjectives and Adverbs. Syntax, Semantics, and Discourse*. Oxford: Oxford University Press, 156–182.
Kiparsky, Paul 1997. Remarks on denominal verbs. In: A. Alsina, J. Bresnan & P. Sells (eds.). *Complex Predicates*. Stanford, CA: CSLI Publications, 473–499.
Koontz-Garboden, Andrew 2007. *States, Changes of State, and the Monotonicity Hypothesis*. Ph.D. dissertation. Stanford University, Stanford, CA.
Krifka, Manfred 1998. The origins of telicity. In: S. Rothstein (ed.). *Events and Grammar*. Dordrecht: Kluwer, 197–235.
Lakoff, George 1968. Some verbs of change and causation. In: S. Kuno (ed.). *Mathematical Linguistics and Automatic Translation*. Report NSF-20. Cambridge, MA: Aiken Computation Laboratory, Harvard University.
Lakoff, George 1970. *Irregularity in Syntax*. New York: Holt, Rinehart & Winston.
Laughren, Mary 1988. Towards a lexical representation of Warlpiri verbs. In: W. Wilkins (ed.). *Syntax and Semantics 21: Thematic Relations*. New York: Academic Press, 215–242.
Levin, Beth 1999. Objecthood. An event structure perspective. In: S. Billings, J. Boyle & A. Griffith (eds.). *Proceedings of the Chicago Linguistic Society (=CLS) 35, Part 1: Papers from the Main Session*. Chicago, IL: Chicago Linguistic Society, 223–247.
Levin, Beth 2000. Aspect, lexical semantic representation, and argument expression. In: L. J. Conathan et al. (eds.). *Proceedings of the 26th Annual Meeting of the Berkeley Linguistics Society (=BLS). General Session and Parasession on Aspect*. Berkeley, CA: Berkeley Linguistics Society, 413–429.
Levin, Beth & Malka Rappaport Hovav 1991. Wiping the slate clean. A lexical semantic exploration. *Cognition* 41, 123–151.
Levin, Beth & Malka Rappaport Hovav 1995. *Unaccusativity. At the Syntax-Lexical Semantics Interface*. Cambridge, MA: The MIT Press.
Levin, Beth & Malka Rappaport Hovav 1998. Morphology and lexical semantics. In: A. Spencer & A. Zwicky (eds.). *The Handbook of Morphology*. Oxford: Blackwell, 248–271.
Levin, Beth & Malka Rappaport Hovav 1999. Two structures for compositionally derived events. In: T. Matthews & D. Strolovich (eds.). *Proceedings of Semantics and Linguistic Theory (=SALT) IX*. Ithaca, NY: Cornell University, 199–223.
Levin, Beth & Malka Rappaport Hovav 2005. *Argument Realization*. Cambridge: Cambridge University Press.
Lyons, John 1967. A note on possessive, existential and locative sentences. *Foundations of Language* 3, 390–396.

Lyons, John 1968. *Introduction to Theoretical Linguistics*. Cambridge: Cambridge University Press.
Macfarland, Talke 1995. *Cognate Objects and the Argument/Adjunct Distinction in English*. Ph.D. dissertation. Northwestern University, Evanston, IL.
Marantz, Alec P. 1984. *On the Nature of Grammatical Relations*. Cambridge, MA: The MIT Press.
Mateu, Jaume 2001a. Small clause results revisited. In: N. Zhang (ed.). *Syntax of Predication*. ZAS Papers in Linguistics 26. Berlin: Zentrum für Allgemeine Sprachwissenschaft.
Mateu, Jaume 2001b. Unselected objects. In: N. Dehé & A. Wanner (eds.). *Structural Aspects of Semantically Complex Verbs*. Frankfurt/M.: Lang, 83–104.
McCawley, James D. 1968. Lexical insertion in a transformational grammar without deep structure. In: B. J. Darden, C.-J. N. Bailey & A. Davison (eds.). *Papers from the Fourth Regional Meeting of the Chicago Linguistic Society (=CLS)*. Chicago, IL: Chicago Linguistic Society, 71–80.
McCawley, James D. 1971. Prelexical syntax. In: R. J. O'Brien (ed.). *Report of the 22nd Annual Roundtable Meeting on Linguistics and Language Studies*. Washington, DC: Georgetown University Press, 19–33.
McClure, William T. 1994. *Syntactic Projections of the Semantics of Aspect*. Ph.D. dissertation. Cornell University, Ithaca, NY.
Morgan, Jerry L. 1969. On arguing about semantics. *Papers in Linguistics* 1, 49–70.
Nida, Eugene A. 1975. *Componential Analysis of Meaning. An Introduction to Semantic Structures*. The Hague: Mouton.
Parsons, Terence 1990. *Events in the Semantics of English*. Cambridge, MA: The MIT Press.
Pesetsky, David M. 1982. *Paths and Categories*. Ph.D. dissertation. MIT, Cambridge, MA.
Pesetsky, David M. 1995. *Zero Syntax. Experiencers and Cascades*. Cambridge, MA: The MIT Press.
Pinker, Steven 1989. *Learnability and Cognition. The Acquisition of Argument Structure*. Cambridge, MA: The MIT Press.
Pustejovsky, James 1995. *The Generative Lexicon*. Cambridge, MA: The MIT Press.
Pylkkänen, Liina 2008. *Introducing Arguments*. Cambridge, MA: The MIT Press.
Ramchand, Gillian C. 1997. *Aspect and Predication. The Semantics of Argument Structure*. Oxford: Clarendon Press.
Ramchand, Gillian C. 2008. *Verb Meaning and the Lexicon. A First-Phase Syntax*. Cambridge: Cambridge University Press.
Rappaport Hovav, Malka 2008. Lexicalized meaning and the internal temporal structure of events. In: S. Rothstein (ed.). *Theoretical and Crosslinguistic Approaches to the Semantics of Aspect*. Amsterdam: Benjamins, 13–42.
Rappaport Hovav, Malka & Beth Levin 1998. Building verb meanings. In: M. Butt & W. Geuder (eds.). *The Projection of Arguments. Lexical and Compositional Factors*. Stanford, CA: CSLI Publications, 97–134.
Rappaport Hovav, Malka & Beth Levin 2001. An event structure account of English resultatives. *Language* 77, 766–797.
Rappaport Hovav, Malka & Beth Levin 2005. Change of state verbs. Implications for theories of argument projection. In: N. Erteschik-Shir & T. Rapoport (eds.). *The Syntax of Aspect. Deriving Thematic and Aspectual Interpretation*. Oxford: Oxford University Press, 276–286.
Rappaport Hovav, Malka & Beth Levin 2008. The English dative alternation. The case for verb sensitivity. *Journal of Linguistics* 44, 129–167.

Rappaport Hovav, Malka & Beth Levin 2010. Reflections on manner/result complementarity. In: E. Doron, M. Rappaport Hovav & I. Sichel (eds.). *Syntax, Lexical Semantics, and Event Structure*. Oxford: Oxford University Press 5, 21–38.

Rappaport, Malka, Beth Levin & Mary Laughren 1988. Niveaux de représentation lexicale. *Lexique* 7, 13–32. English translation in: J. Pustejovsky (ed.). *Semantics and the Lexicon*. Dordrecht: Kluwer, 1993, 37–54.

Ross, John Robert 1972. Act. In: D. Davidson & G. Harman (eds.). *Semantics of Natural Language*. Dordrecht: Reidel, 70–126.

Rothstein, Susan 2003. *Structuring Events. A Study in the Semantics of Aspect*. Oxford: Blackwell.

Schaefer, Ronald P. (1985) Motion in Tswana and its characteristic lexicalization. *Studies in African Linguistics* 16, 57–87.

Slobin, Dan I. 2004. The many ways to search for a frog. Linguistic typology and the expression of motion events. In: S. Strömqvist & L. Verhoeven (eds.). *Relating Events in Narrative, vol. 2: Typological and Contextual Perspectives*. Mahwah, NJ: Erlbaum, 219–257.

von Stechow, Arnim 1995. Lexical decomposition in syntax. In: U. Egli et al. (eds.). *Lexical Knowledge in the Organization of Language*. Amsterdam: Benjamins, 81–118.

von Stechow, Arnim 1996. The different readings of *wieder*. A structural account. *Journal of Semantics* 13, 87–138.

Stowell, Timothy 1981. *Origins of Phrase Structure*. Ph.D. dissertation. MIT, Cambridge, MA.

Talmy, Leonard 1975. Semantics and syntax of motion. In: J. P. Kimball (ed.). *Syntax and Semantics 4*. New York: Academic Press, 181–238.

Talmy, Leonard 1985. Lexicalization patterns. Semantic structure in lexical forms. In: T. Shopen (ed.). *Language Typology and Syntactic Description, vol. 3: Grammatical Categories and the Lexicon*. Cambridge: Cambridge University Press, 57–149.

Talmy, Leonard 1991. Path to realization. A typology of event conflation. In: L. A. Sutton, C. Johnson & R. Shields (eds.). *Proceedings of the 17th Annual Meeting of the Berkeley Linguistics Society (=BLS). General Session and Parasession*. Berkeley, CA: Berkeley Linguistics Society, 480–519.

Talmy, Leonard 2000. *Toward a Cognitive Semantics, vol. 2: Typology and Process in Concept Structuring*. Cambridge, MA: The MIT Press.

Taylor, John R. 1996. On running and jogging. *Cognitive Linguistics* 7, 21–34.

Tenny, Carol L. 1994. *Aspectual Roles and the Syntax-Semantics Interface*. Dordrecht: Kluwer.

Tham, Shiao Wei 2004. *Representing Possessive Predication. Semantic Dimensions and Pragmatic Bases*. Ph.D. dissertation. Stanford University, Stanford, CA.

Travis, Lisa D. 1984. *Parameters and Effects of Word Order Variation*. Ph.D. dissertation. MIT, Cambridge, MA.

Travis, Lisa D. 2000. The l-syntax/s-syntax boundary. Evidence from Austronesian. In: I. Paul, V. Phillips & L. Travis (eds.). *Formal Issues In Austronesian Linguistics*. Dordrecht: Kluwer, 167–194.

Van Valin, Robert D. 1993. A synopsis of Role and Reference grammar. In: R. D. van Valin (ed.). *Advances in Role and Reference Grammar*. Amsterdam: Benjamins, 1–164.

Van Valin, Robert D. 2005. *Exploring the Syntax-Semantics Interface*. Cambridge: Cambridge University Press.

Van Valin, Robert D. & Randy J. LaPolla 1997. *Syntax. Structure, Meaning, and Function*. Cambridge: Cambridge University Press.

Wechsler, Stephen 2006. Thematic structure. In: K. Brown (ed.). *Encyclopedia of Language and Linguistics*. 2nd edn. Amsterdam: Elsevier, 645–653. 1st edn. 1994.
Wilks, Yorick 1987. Primitives. In: S. C. Shapiro (ed.). *Encyclopedia of Artificial Intelligence*. New York: Wiley, 759–761.
Williams, Edwin 1981. Argument structure and morphology. *The Linguistic Review* 1, 81–114.
Wunderlich, Dieter 1997a. Argument extension by lexical adjunction. *Journal of Semantics* 14, 95–142.
Wunderlich, Dieter 1997b. CAUSE and the structure of verbs. *Linguistic Inquiry* 28, 27–68.
Wunderlich, Dieter 2000. Predicate composition and argument extension as general options. A study in the interface of semantic and conceptual structure. In: B. Stiebels & D. Wunderlich (eds.). *Lexicon in Focus*. Berlin: Akademie Verlag, 247–270.
Wunderlich, Dieter 2006. Argument hierarchy and other factors determining argument realization. In: I. Bornkessel et al. (eds.). *Semantic Role Universals and Argument Linking. Theoretical, Typological, and Psycholinguistic Perspectives*. Berlin: Mouton de Gruyter, 15–52.
Yoneyama, Mitsuaki 1986. Motion verbs in conceptual semantics. *Bulletin of the Faculty of Humanities* 22. Tokyo: Seikei University, 1–15.
Zubizarreta, Maria Luisa & Eunjeong Oh 2007. *On the Syntactic Composition of Manner and Motion*. Cambridge, MA: The MIT Press.

Christiane Fellbaum
5 Idioms and collocations

1. Introduction: Collocation, collocations and idioms —— 152
2. Lexical properties of idioms —— 156
3. Compositionality —— 157
4. How frozen are idioms? —— 159
5. Syntactic flexibility —— 160
6. Morphosyntax —— 161
7. Idioms as constructions —— 164
8. Diachronic changes —— 165
9. Idioms in the lexicon —— 166
10. Idioms in the mental lexicon —— 166
11. Summary and conclusion —— 168
12. References —— 169

Abstract: Idioms constitute a subclass of multi-word units that exhibit strong collocational preferences and whose meanings are at least partially non-compositional. Drawing on English and German corpus data, we discuss a number of lexical, syntactic, morphological and semantic properties of Verb Phrase idioms that distinguish them from freely composed phrases. The classic view of idioms as "long words" admits of little or no variation of a canonical form. Fixedness is thought to reflect semantic non-compositionality: the non-availability of semantic interpretation for some or all idiom constituents and the impossibility to parse syntactically ill-formed idioms block regular grammatical operations. However, corpus data testify to a wide range of discourse-sensitive flexibility and variation, weakening the categorical distinction between idioms and freely composed phrases. We cite data indicating that idioms are subject to the same diachronic developments as simple lexemes. Finally, we give a brief overview of psycholinguistic research into the processing of idioms and attempts to determine their representation in the mental lexicon.

1 Introduction: Collocation, collocations and idioms

Words in text and speech do not co-occur freely but follow rules and patterns. We draw an initial three-fold distinction for recurrent lexical co-occurrences:

Christiane Fellbaum, Princeton, NJ, USA

https://doi.org/10.1515/9783110626391-005

collocation, patterns of words found in close neighborhood, and *collocations* and *idioms*, multi-word units with lexical status that are often distinguished in terms of their fixedness and semantic non-compositionality. The remainder of the paper will focus on idioms, in particular verb phrase idioms. We describe their syntactic, morphosyntactic and lexical properties with respect to frozenness and variation. The data examined here show a sliding scale of fixedness and a concomitant range of semantic compositionality. We next consider the diachronic behavior of idioms, which does not seem to differ from that of simple lexemes. Finally, several theories concerning the mental representation of idioms are discussed.

1.1 Collocation: A statistical property of language

Collocation, the co-occurrence patterns of words observed in spoken and written language, is constrained by syntactic (grammatical), semantic, and lexical properties of words. At each level, linguists have attempted to formulate rules and constraints for co-occurrence.

The syntactic constraints on lexical co-occurrence are specific to a word but constrained by its syntactic class membership. For example, the adjective *prone*, unlike *hungry* and *tired*, subcategorizes for a Prepositional Phrase headed by *to*; moreover, *hungry* and *tired*, but not *prone*, can occur pre-nominally. Firth (1957) called the syntactic constraints on a word's selection of neighboring words "colligation".

Firth moreover recognized that words display collocational properties beyond those imposed by syntax. He coined the term "collocation" for the "habitual or customary places" of a word. Firth's statement that "you can recognize a word by the company it keeps" has been given scientific validation by corpus studies establishing lexical profiles for words, which reflect their regular attraction to other words. Co-occurrence properties of individual lexical items can be expressed quantitatively (Halliday 1966, Sinclair 1991, Stubbs 2001, Krenn 2000, Evert 2005, inter alia).

Church & Hanks (1990), and Church et al. (1991) proposed Mutual Information as a measure of the tendency of word forms to select or deselect one another in a context. Mutual Information compares the probability of two lexemes' co-occurrence with the probability that they occur alone and that their co-occurrence is merely chance.

Mutual Information is a powerful tool for measuring the degree of fixedness, and thus lexical status, of word groups. Highly fixed expressions that have been identified statistically are candidates for inclusion in the lexicon, regardless of their semantic transparency. Fixed expressions are also likely to be stored as units in speakers' mental lexicons, and retrieved as units rather than composed anew each time. Psycholinguists are aware of people's tendency to chunk (Miller 1956).

Statistical analyses can also quantify the flexibility of fixed expressions, which are rarely complelety frozen (see sections 3 and 4). Fazly & Stevenson (2006) propose a method for the automatic discovery of the set of syntactic variations that VP idioms can undergo and that should be included in their lexical representation. Fazly & Stevenson further incorporate this information into statistical measures that effectively predict the idiomaticity level of a given expression. Others have measured the distributional similarity between the expression and its constituents (McCarthy, Keller & Carroll 2003, Baldwin et al. 2003).

The collocational properties of a language are perhaps best revealed in the errors committed by learners and non-native speakers. A fluent speaker may have sufficient command of the language to find the words that express the intended concept. However, only considerable competence allows him to select that word from among several near-synonyms that is favored by its neighbors; the subtlety of lexical preference appears unmotivated and arbitrary.

1.2 Collocations: Phrasal lexical items

We distinguish collocation, the linguistic and statistically measurable phenomenon of co-occurrence, from collocations, specific instances of collocation that have lexical status. Collocations like *beach house, eat up,* and *blood-red* are mappings of word forms and word meanings, much like simple lexemes such as *house* and *eat* and *red*. Collocations are "pre-fabricated" combinations of simple lexemes.

Jackendoff (1997) collected multi-word units (MWUs) from the popular U.S. television show "Wheel of Fortune" and showed the high frequency of collocations and phrases, both in terms of types and tokens. He estimates that MWUs constitute at least half the entire lexicon; Cowie (1998) reports the percentage of verb phrase idioms and collocations in news stories and feature articles to be around forty percent. Such figures make it clear that MWUs constitute a significant part of the lexicon and collocating is a pervasive aspect of linguistic behavior.

Collocations include a wide range of MWUs. A syntax-based typology (e.g., Moon 1998) distinguishes sentential proverbs (*the early bird gets the worm*), routine formulae (*thanks a lot*), and adjective phrases expressing similes (*sharp as a whistle*). Frames or constructions (Fillmore, Kay & O'Connor 1988) consist of closed-class words with slots for open-class words, such as *what's X doing y?* and *the X-er the Y-er*; these frames carry meaning independent of the particular lexemes that fill the open slots. A large class of collocations are support (or "light") verb constructions, where a noun collocates with a specific verbal head such as *make a decision* and *take a photograph* (Storrer 2007).

Under a semantically-based classification, phrasal lexemes form a continuous scale of fixedness and semantic transparency. Following Moon (1998), we say that collocations are decomposable multi-word units that often follow the paradigmatic patterns of free language. For example, a number of German verb phrase collocations show the causative/inchoative/stative alternation pattern, e.g., *in Rage bringen/kommen/sein* (make/become/be enraged).

1.3 Idioms

Idioms like *hit the ceiling*, *lose one's head*, and *when the cows come home*, constitute another class of MWUs with lexical status. They differ from the kinds of collocations discussed in the previous section in several respects.

To begin with, the lexical make-up of idioms is usually unpredictable and often highly idiosyncratic, violating the usual rules of selectional restrictions. Examples are English *rain cats and dogs* and *talk turkey*, and German *unter dem Pantoffel stehen* (lit., 'stand under the slipper', be dominated). Some idioms have a possible literal (non-idiomatic) interpretation, such as *drag one's feet* and *not move a finger*.

Certain idioms are syntactically ill-formed, such as English *trip the light fantastic* and German *an jemandem einen Narren gefressen haben* (lit. 'have eaten a fool on/at somebody', be infatuated with somebody), or *Bauklötze staunen* (lit. 'be astonished toy blocks', be very astonished), which violate the verb's subcategorization properties. Others, like *by and large*, do not constitute syntactic categories.

Perhaps the most characteristic feature ascribed to idioms is their semantic non-compositionality. Because the meaning of idioms is not made up by the meanings of their constituents (or only to a limited extent), their meanings are considered largely opaque. A common argument says that if the components of idioms are semantically non-transparent to speakers, they are not available for the kinds of grammatical operations found in free, literal, language. As a result, idioms are often considered fixed, "frozen" expressions, or "long words" (Swinney & Cutler 1979, Bobrow & Bell 1973).

We will consider each of these properties attributed to idioms, focusing largely on verb phrase (VP) idioms with a verbal head that select for at least one noun phrase or prepositional phrase complement. Such idioms have generated much discussion, focused mostly on putative constraints on their syntactic frozenness. VP idioms were also found to be the most frequent type of MWUs in the British Hector Corpus (Moon 1998).

2 Lexical properties of idioms

Idioms are perhaps most recognizable by their lexical make-up. Selectional restrictions are frequently violated, and the idiom constituents tend not to be semantically related to words in the surrounding context, thus signaling the need for a non-literal interpretation.

But there are many syntactically and semantically well-formed strings that are polysemous between an idiomatic and a literal, compositional meaning, such as *play first fiddle* and *fall off the wagon*. Here, context determines which meaning is likely the intended one. Of course, the ambiguity between literal and idiomatic reading is related to the plausibility of the literal reading. Thus, *pull yourself up by your bootstraps*, *give/lend somebody a hand*, and German *mit der Kirche ums Dorf fahren* (lit. 'drive with the church around the village', deal with an issue in an overly complicated or laborious manner) denote highly implausible events in their literal readings.

2.1 Polarity

Many idioms are negative polarity items: *not have a leg to stand on, not give somebody the time of day, not lift a finger, be neither fish nor fowl, no love lost, not give a damn/hoot/shit*. Without the negation, the idiomatic reading is lost; in specific contexts, it may be preserved in the presence of a marked stress pattern. Corpus data show that many idioms do not require a fixed negation component but can occur in other negative environments (questions, conditionals, etc.), just like their non-idiomatic counterparts (Söhn 2006, Sailer & Richter 2002, Stantcheva 2006 for German).

Idioms as negative polarity items occur crosslinguistically, and negative polarity may be one universal hallmark of idiomatic language.

2.2 Idiom-specific lexemes

Many idioms contain lexemes that do not occur outside their idiomatic contexts. Examples are English *thinking cap* (in *put on one's thinking cap*), *humble pie* (in *eat humble pie*), and German *Hungertuch* (*am Hungertuch nagen*; lit. 'gnaw at the hunger-cloth', be destitute). Similarly, the noun *Schlafittchen* in the idiom *am Schlafittchen packen*, (lit. 'grab someone by the wing', confront or catch somebody), is an obsolete word referring to "wing" and its meaning is opaque to contemporary speakers.

Other idiom components have meaning outside their idiomatic context but may occur rarely in free language (*gift horse* in *don't look a gift horse in the mouth*), cf. article 4 [Semantics: Interfaces] (Olsen) *Semantics of compounds*.

2.3 Non-referential pronouns

Another lexical peculiarity of many English idioms is the obligatory presence of a non-referential *it*: *have it coming, give it a shot, lose it, have it in for somebody*, etc. These pronouns are a fixed component of the idioms and no number or gender variation can occur without loss of the idiomatic reading. They do not carry meaning, though they may have referred at an earlier stage before the idiom became fixed. Substituting a context-appropriate noun does not seem felicitous, either: *have the punishment coming, give the problem a shot* etc. seem odd at best. (A somewhat similar phenomenon are a number of German idioms containing *eins, einen* (lit. 'one'): *sich eins lachen, einen draufmachen*, 'have a good laugh/have a night on the town.')

3 Compositionality

Idioms are often referred to as non-compositional, i.e., their meaning is not composed of the meanings of their constituents, as is the case in freely composed language. In fact, idioms vary with respect to the degree of non-compositionality. One way to measure the extent to which an idiom violates the compositional norms of the language is to examine and measure statistically the collocational properties of its constituents. The verb *fressen* (eat like an animal) co-occurs with nouns that fill the roles of the eating and the eaten entities; among the latter *Narr* ("fool") will stand out as not belonging into the class of entities included in the verb's selectional preferences; a thesaurus or WordNet (Fellbaum 1998) could firm up this intuition.

In highly opaque idioms, none of the constituents can be mapped onto a referent, as is the case with *and jemandem einen Narren gefressen haben* and the much-cited *kick the bucket*. The literal equivalents of these verbs do not select for arguments that the idiom constituents could be mapped to in a one-to-one fashion so as to allow a "translation".

An idiom's lexeme becomes obsolete outside its idiomatic use, with the result that meaning becomes opaque. For example, *Fittiche* in the idiom *unter die Fittiche nehmen* seems not to be interpreted as "wings" by some contemporary speakers, as attested by corpus examples like *unter der/seiner Fittiche*, where the morphology shows that the speaker analyzed the noun as a feminine singular rather than the plural and possibly it assigned a new meaning.

Lexical substitutions and adjectival modifications show that speakers often assign a meaning to one or more constituents of an idiom (see section *Lexical variation*), though such variations from the "canonical forms" tend to be idiosyncratic and are often specific to the discourse in which they are found.

Many idioms are partially decomposable; they may contain one or more lexemes with a conventional meaning or a metaphor.

3.1 Metaphors

Many idioms contain metaphors, and the notion of metaphor is closely linked to idioms; cf. article 11 [this volume] (Tyler & Takahashi) *Metaphors and metonymies*. We use the term here to denote a single lexeme (most often a noun or noun phrase) with a figurative meaning. For example, *jungle* is often used as a metaphor for a complex, messy, competitive, and perhaps dangerous situation; this use of *jungle* derives from its literal meaning, "impenetrable forest" and preserves some of the salient properties or the original concept (Glucksberg 2001). A metaphor like *jungle* may become conventionalized and be readily interpreted in the appropriate contexts as referring to a competitive situation. Thus, the expression *it's a jungle out here* is readily understandable due to the interpretability of the noun. Idioms that contain conventional or transparent metaphors are thus at least partly compositional.

Many idioms arguably contain metaphors, though their use is bound to a particular idioms. For example, *nettle* in *grasp the nettle* and *bull* in *take the bull by the horns* can be readily interpreted as referring to specific entities in the context where the idioms are used. But such metaphors do not work outside the idioms; *this assignment involves numerous nettles/bulls* would be difficult to interpret, despite the fact that *nettle* and *bull* seem like appropriate expressions referring to a difficult problem or a challenge, respectively, and could thus be considered "motivated".

Arguments have been made for a cognitive, culturally-embedded basis of metaphors and idioms containing metaphors that shapes their semantic structure and makes motivation possible (Lakoff & Johnson 1980, Lakoff 1987, Gibbs & Steen 1999, Dobrovol'skij 2004, inter alia). Indeed, certain conceptual metaphors are cross-linguistically highly prevalent and productive. For example, the "time is money" metaphor is reflected in the many possession verbs (*have, give, take, buy, cost*) that take *time* as an argument.

However, Burger (2007) points out that not all idioms are metaphorical and that not all metaphorical idioms can be traced back to general conceptual metaphors. For example, in the idiom *pull strings*, *strings* does not encode an established metaphor that is readily understandable outside the idiom and that is exploited in related idioms. Indeed, a broad claim to the universality and cultural independence of metaphor seems untenable. The English idiom *pull strings* structurally and lexically resembles the German idiom *die Drähte ziehen* (lit.: 'pull the wires'), but the German idiom does not mean "to use one's influence to one's favor", but rather "to mastermind".

Testing the conceptual metaphor hypothesis, Keysar & Bly (1995) asked speakers guess the meanings of unfamiliar idioms involving such salient concepts as "high" and "up", which many cognitivists claim to be universally associated with increased quality and quantity. Subjects could not guess the meanings of many of the phrases, casting doubt on the power and absolute universality of conceptual metaphors.

4 How frozen are idioms?

A core property associated with idioms is lexical, morphosyntactic, and syntactic fixedness, which is said to be a direct consequence of semantic opacity. Many grammatical frameworks, beginning with early Transformational-Generative Grammar, explicitly classify idioms as "long words" that are exempt from regular and productive rules, much like strong verbs.

Lexicographic resources implicitly reinforce the view of idioms as fixed strings by listing idioms in morphologically unmarked citation forms, or lemmata, usually based of the lexicographer's intuition. And experimental psycholinguists studying idiom processing commonly use only such citation forms.

The few much-cited classic examples, including *kick the bucket* and *trip the light fantastic*, served well to exemplify the properties ascribed in a wholesale fashion to all idioms.

But soon linguists began to note that not all idioms were alike. Fraser (1970) distinguished several degrees of syntactic frozenness among idioms. Where a mapping can be made from the idiom's constituents to those of its literal counterpart, syntactic flexibility is possible; simply put, the degree of semantic opacity is reflected in the degree of syntactic frozenness.

Echoing Weinreich (1969), Fraser states that there is no idiom that is completely free. In particular, he rules out focusing operations like clefting and topicalization, as these are conditional on the focused constituent bearing a meaning. Citing constructed data, Cruse (2004) also categorically rules out cleft constructions for idioms.

Syntactic and lexical frozenness is commonly ascribed to the semantic non-compositionality of idioms. Indeed, it seems reasonable to assume that semantically unanalyzable strings cannot be subject to regular grammatical processes as syntactic variations typically serve to (de-)focus or modify particular constituents; when these carry no meanings, such operations are unmotivated.

But corpus studies show that a "standard", fixed form cannot be determined for many idioms, at least not on a quantitative basis. Speakers use many idioms in ways that deviate from that given in dictionary in more than one way; some idioms exhibit the same degree of freedom as freely composed strings.

We rely in this article on corpus examples to illustrate idiom variations. The English data come from Moon's (1998) extensive analysis of the Hector Corpus. The German data are based on the in-depth analysis of 1,000 German idioms in a one billion word corpus of German (Fellbaum 2006, 2007b). We are not aware of similar large-scale corpus analyses in other languages and therefore the data in this article will be somewhat biased towards English and German.

5 Syntactic flexibility

As a wider range of idioms were considered, linguists realized that syntactic flexibility was not an exception. The influential paper by Nunberg, Sag & Wasow (1994) argued for the systematic relation between semantic compositionality and flexibility.

Both Abeillé (1995), who based her analysis on a number of French idioms, and Dobrovol'skij (1999) situate idioms on a continuum of flexibility that interacts with semantic transparency. But while it seems true that constituents that are assigned a meaning by speakers are open to grammatical operations as well as modification and even lexical substitution, semantic transparency is not a requirement for variation.

We consider as an example the German idiom *kein Blatt vor den Mund nehmen* (lit. 'take no leaf/sheet in front of one's mouth', be outspoken, speak one's mind). *Blatt* (leaf, sheet) has no obvious referent. Yet numerous attested corpus examples are found where *Blatt* is passivized, topicalized, relativized and pronominalized; moreover, this idiom need not always appear as a Negative Polarity Item:

(1) Bei BMW wird kein Blatt vor den Mund genommen.

(2) Ein Blatt habe er nie vor den Mund genommen.

(3) Das Blatt, das Eva vor ihr erregendes Geheimnis gehalten, ich nähme es nicht einmal vor den Mund.

(4) Ein Regierungssprecher ist ein Mann, der sich 100 Blätter vor den Mund nimmt.

Even "cran-morphemes", i.e., words that do not usually occur outside the idiom, can behave like free lexemes. For example, *Fettnäpfchen* rarely occurs outside the idiom *ins Fettnäpfchen treten* (lit. 'step into the little grease pot', commit a social gaffe), and no meaning can be attached to it by a contemporary speaker that would map to the meaning of a constituent in the literal equivalent. Yet the corpus shows numerous uses of this idiom where the noun is relativied, topicalized, quantified, and modified.

(5) Das Fettnäpfchen, in das die Frau ihres jüngsten Sohnes gestiegen ist, ist aber auch riesig.

(6) Ins Fettnäpfchen trete ich bestimmt mal und das ist gut so.

(7) Silvio Berlusconi: Ein Mann, viele Fettnäpfchen.

(8) Immer trat der New Yorker ins bereitstehende Fettnäpfchen.

Syntactic variation is probably due to speakers' ad-hoc assignment of meanings of idiom components. Adjectival modification and lexical variations in particular indicate that the semantic interpretation of inherently opaque constituents are dependent on the particular context in which the idiom is embedded.

For more examples and discussion see Moon (1998) and Fellbaum (2006, 2007b).

6 Morphosyntax

The apparent fixedness of many idioms extends beyond constituent order and lexical selection to their morphosyntactic make-up.

6.1 Modality, tense, aspect

The idiomatic reading of many strings requires a specific modality, tense, or aspect. Thus *horses wouldn't get (NP) to (VP)* is at best odd without the conditional: *horses don't get (NP) to (VP)*. Similarly, the meaning of *I couldn't care less* is not preserved in *I could care less*. Interestingly, the negation in the idiom is often omitted even when the speaker does not intend a change of polarity, as in *I could care less*; perhaps speakers are uneasy about the double negation in such cases but do not decompose the idiom to realize that a single negation changes the meaning. Another English idiom requiring a specific modal is *will not/won't hear of it*.

The German idioms *in den Tuschkasten gefallen sein* (lit. 'have fallen into the paint box', be overly made up) and *nicht auf den Kopf gefallen sein* (lit. 'not have fallen on one's head', be rather intelligent) denote states and cannot be interpreted as idioms in any tense other than the perfect (Fellbaum 2007a).

6.2 Determiner and number

The noun in many VP idioms is preceded by a definite determiner even though it lacks definiteness and, frequently, reference: *kick the bucket, fall off the wagon, buy the farm*. The determiner here may be a relic from the time when transparent phrases became lexicalized as idioms.

A regular and frequent grammatical process in German is the contraction of the determiner with a preceding preposition. Thus, the idiom *jemanden hinters Licht führen* (lit. 'lead someone behind the light', deceive someone), occurs most frequently with *hinter* (behind) and *das* (the) contracted to *hinters*.

Eisenberg (1999, inter alia) assert that the figurative reading of many German idioms precludes a change in the noun's determiner. This hypothesis seems appealing: if the noun phrase is semantically opaque, the choice of determiner does not follow the usual rules of grammar and is therefore arbitrary. As speakers cannot interpret the noun, the determiner is not subject to grammatical processes. Decontraction in cases like *hinters Licht führen* is thus ruled out by Eisenberg, as is contraction in cases where the idiom's citation form found in dictionaries shows the preposition separated from the determiner.

However, Firenze (2007) cites numerous corpus examples of idioms with decontraction. In some cases, the decontraction is conditioned by the insertion of lexical material such as adjectives between the preposition and the determiner or number variation of the noun; in other cases, contracted and decontracted forms alternate freely.

Such data show that the NP is subject to the regular grammatical processes of free language, even when its meaning is not transparent: *Licht* in the idiom has no referent, like *wool* in the corresponding English idiom *pull the wool over someone's eyes*.

Corpus data also show number variations for the nouns. For example, in *den Bock zum Gärtner machen* (lit. 'make the buck the gardener', put an incompetent person in charge), both nouns occur predominantly in the singular. But we find examples with plural nouns, *Böcke zu Gärtnern machen*, where the speaker refers to several specific incompetent persons.

6.3 Lexical variation

Variation is frequently attested for the nominal, verbal, and adjectival components of VP idioms. In most cases, this variation is context-dependent, and shows conscious playfulness on the part of the speaker or writer.

Fellbaum & Stathi (2006) discuss three principal cases of lexical variation: paradigmatic variation, adjectival modification, and compounding. In each case, the variation plays on the literal interpretation of the varied component. Paradigmatic substitution has occurred in the case where verb in *jemandem die Leviten lesen* (lit., 'read the Levitus to someone', read someone the riot act) has been replaced by *quaken* (croak like a frog) and *brüllen* (scream). An adjective has been added to the noun in an economics text in *die marktwirtschaftlichen Leviten lesen*, 'read the market-economical riot act.' An example for compounding is *er nimmt kein Notenblatt vor den Mund* where the idiom *kein Blatt vor den Mund nehmen* (lit. 'take no leaf/sheet in front of one's mouth', meaning be outspoken) occurs in the context of musical performance and *Blatt* becomes *Notenblatt*, 'sheet of music.'

Besides morphological and syntactic variation, corpus data show that speakers vary the lexical form of many idioms. Moon's (1998) observation that lexical variation is often humorous is confirmed by the German corpus data, as is Moon's finding that such variation is found most frequently in journalism. (See also Kjellmer 1991 for examples of playful lexical variations in collocations, such as *not exactly my cup of tequila*.)

Ad-hoc lexical variation is dependent on the particular discourse and must play on the literal reading of the substituted constituent rather than on a metaphoric one. That is, *spill the secret* would be hard to interpret, whereas *rock the submarine* would be interpretable in the appropriate context, as *submarine* invokes the paradigmatically related boat.

Moon (1998) discusses another kind of lexical variation, called idiom schemas, exemplified by the group of idioms *hit the deck/sack/hay*. Idiom schemas correspond to Nunberg, Sag & Wasow's (1994) idiom families, such as *don't give a hoot/damn/shit*. The variation is limited, and each variant is lexicalized rather than ad-hoc. But in other cases, lexical variation is highly productive. An example is the German idiom *hier tanzt der Bär* (lit. 'here dances the bear', this is where the action is), which has spawned a family of new expressions with the same meaning, including *hier steppt der Bär* (lit. 'the bear does a step dance here') and even *hier rappt der Hummer* (lit. 'the lobster raps here') and *hier boxt der Papst* (lit., 'the Pope is boxing here'). There are clear constraints on the lexical variations in terms of semantic sets, unlike in cases like *don't give a hoot/damn/shit*; this may account for the productivity of the "bear" idiom.

6.4 Semantic reanalysis

Motivation is undoubtedly a strong factor in the variability of idioms; if speakers can assign meaning to a component, even if only in a specific context, the component is available for modification and syntactic operations.

Corpus examples with lexical and syntactic variations suggest that speakers attribute meaning to idiom components that are opaque to contemporary speakers and remotivate them. Gehweiler (2007) discusses the German idiom *in die Röhre schauen* (lit. 'look into the pipe', go empty-handed), which originates in the language of hunters and referred to dogs peering into foxholes. The meaning of noun here is opaque to contemporary speakers, but the idiom has aquired more recent, additional senses where the noun is re-interpreted.

7 Idioms as constructions

Fillmore, Kay & O'Connor (1988) discuss the idiomaticity of syntact constructions like *the X-er the Y-er*, which carry meaning independent of the lexical items that fill the slots; cf. article 9 [Semantics: Interfaces] (Kay & Michaelis) *Constructional meaning*.

Among VP idioms with a more regular phrase structure, some require the suppression of an argument for the idiomatic reading, resulting in a violation of the verb's subcategorization properties. For example, *werfen* ('throw') in the German idiom *das Handtuch werfen*, lit. 'throw the towel' does not co-occur with a Location (Goal) argument, which is required in the verb's non-idiomatic use.

Other idioms require the presence of an argument that is optional in the literal language; this is the case for many ditransitive German VP idioms, including *jemandem ein Bein stellen*, lit., 'place a leg for someone', 'trip someone up' and *jemandem eine Szene machen*, lit. 'make a scene for someone', cause a scene that embarrasses someone in German. Here, the additional indirect object (indicated by the placeholder *someone*) is most often an entity that is negatively affected by the event, a Maleficiary. Whereas in free language use, ditransitive constructions often denote the transfer of a Theme from a Source to a Goal or Recipient, this is rarely the case for ditransitive idioms (Moon 1998, Fellbaum 2007c). Instead, such idioms exemplify Green's (1974) "symbolic action", events intended by the Agent to have a specific effect on a Beneficiary, or, more often, a Maleficiary. Ditransitives that do not denote the transfer of an entity are highly restricted in the literal language (Green 1974); it is interesting that so many idioms denoting an event with a negatively affected entity are expressed with a ditransitive construction.

Structurally defined classes of idioms can be accounted for under Goldberg's (1995) Construction Grammar, where syntactic configurations carry meaning independent of lexical material; however, Goldberg (1995) and Goldberg & Jackendoff (2004) consider syntactically well-formed and lexically productive structures such as resultatives rather than idioms. The identification of classes of grammatically marked idioms points to idiom-specific syntactic configurations or frames that carry meaning.

8 Diachronic changes

The origins of specific idioms is a subject of much speculation and folk etyomology. Among the idioms with an indisputable history are those found in the Bible (e.g., *throw pearls before the swine, fall from grace, give up the ghost* from the King James Bible). These tend to be found in many of the languages into which the Bible was translated. Many other idioms originate in specific domains: *pull one's punches, go the distance* (boxing), *have an ace up your sleeve, let the chips fall where they may* (gambling), and *fall on one's sword, bite the bullet* (warfare).

Idioms are subject to the same diachronic processes that have been observed for lexemes with literal interpretation. Longitudinal corpus studies by Gehweiler, Höser & Kramer (2007) shows how German VP idioms undergo extension, merging, and semantic splitting and may develop new, homonymic readings.

Idioms may also change their usage over time. Thus, the German idiom *unter dem Pantoffel stehen* (lit., 'stand underneath somebody's slipper', be under someone's thumb) used to refer to domestic situations where a husband is dominated by his wife. But corpus data from the past few decades show that this idiom is extended to not only to female spouses but also to other social relations, such as employees in a workplace dominated by a boss (Fellbaum 2005).

Idioms change their phrase structure over time. Kwasniak (2006) examines cases where a sentential idiom turns into a VP idiom when a fixed component becomes a "free" constituent that is no longer part of the idiom.

9 Idioms in the lexicon

As form-meaning pairs, idioms belong in the lexicon. A dual nature – semantic simplicity but structural complexity – is often ascribed to them. But the question arises as to why natural languages show complex encoding for concepts whose semantics are as straightforward as those of simple lexemes.

It has often been observed that many idioms express concepts already covered by simple lexemes but with added connotational nuances or restrictions to specific contexts and social situations; classic examples are the many idioms meaning to "die", ranging from disrespectful to euphemistic. But many – perhaps most – idioms, including *cut one's teeth on, live from hand to mouth, have eyes for, lend a hand, lose one's head* are neutral with respect to register. Similar idioms are found across languages, for example idioms expressing a range of judgments of physical appearance, mental ability, and social aptitude.

Subtle register differences alone do not seem to warrant the structural and lexical extravagance of idioms, the constraints on their use, and the added burden on language acquisition and processing.

An examination of how English VP idioms fit into the structure of the lexicon reveals that many lack non-idiomatic synonyms and express meanings not covered by simple lexemes, arguably filling "lexical gaps". Moreover, many idioms appear not to fit the regular lexicalization patterns of English. A typology of idioms based on semantic criteria is suggested in (Fellbaum 2002, 2007a). It includes idioms expressing negations of events or states (*miss the bus, fall through the cracks, go begging*) and idioms expressing several events linked by a Boolean operator (*fish or cut bair, have one's cake and eat it*). Such structurally and semantically complex idioms can be found across languages. One function of idioms may be to encode pre-packaged complex messages that cannot be expressed by simple words and whose salience makes them candidates for lexical encoding.

10 Idioms in the mental lexicon

How are idioms represented in the mental lexicon and speakers' grammar? On the one hand, they are more or less fixed MWUs – long words – that speakers produce and recognize as such, which suggests that they are represented exactly like simple lexemes. On the other hand, attested idiom use shows a wide range of syntactic, morphological, and especially lexical variation, indicating that speakers access the internal structure of idioms and subject them to all the grammatical processes found in literal language. To determine whether idioms are represented and processed as unanalyzable units or as of potentially (and often partially) decomposable strings, psycholinguistic experiments have investigated both the production and the comprehension of idioms. The materials used in virtually all experiments are constructed and not based on corpus examples, yet the findings and the hypothesis based on the results are fully compatible with naturally occurring data.

Comprehension time studies show that familiar idioms like *kick the bucket* are processed faster in their idiomatic meaning ('die') that in a literal one (kicking a pail). Glucksberg (2001) asserts that the literal meaning may be inhibited by the figurative meaning of a string, though both may be accessed. However, the timing experiments argue against a processing model where the idiomatic reading kicks in only after a literal one has failed.

Cutting & Bock (1997), based on a number of experiments involving idiom production, propose a "hybrid" theory of idiom representation. They argue for the existence of a lexical concept node for each idiom; at the same time, idioms are syntactically and semantically analyzed during production, independent of the idioms' degree of compositionality.

This "hybrid account" is also supported by Sprenger, Levelt & Kempen (2006), who show that idioms can be primed with lexemes that are semantically related to constituents of the idioms. Sprenger, Levelt & Kempen propose the notion of a "superlemma" as a conceptual unit whose lexemes are bound both to their idiomatic use and their use in the free language.

The Superlemma theory is compatible with the Configuration Hypothesis that Cacciari & Tabossi (1988) formulated on the basis of idiom comprehension experiments. The Configuration Theory maintains that speakers activate the literal meanings of words in a phrase and recognize the idiomatic meaning of a polysemous string only when they recognize an idiom-specific configuration of lexems or encounter a "key" lexeme. One such key in many idioms may be the definite article (*kick the bucket, fall off the wagon, buy the farm*) which suggests that a referent for the noun has been previously introduced into the discourse; when no matching antecedent can be found, another interpretation of the string must be attempted (Fellbaum 1993). The keyhypothesis is compatible with Cutting & Bock's proposal concerning idioms' representation in the mental lexicon.

Kuiper (2004) analyzed a collection of slips of the tongue for idioms, comprising 1,000 errors. He proposes a taxonomy of sources for the errors from all levels of grammar. Kuiper's analysis of the data shows that idioms are not simply stored as frozen long words, consistent with the superlemma theory of idiom representation.

10.1 Idioms in natural language processing

If one inputs an idiom into a machine translation engine (such as Babelfish or Google translate), it does not – in many cases – return a corresponding idiom or an adequate non-idiomatic translation in the target language. This is one indication that the recognition and processing especially of non-compositional idioms are still a challenge. One reason is that lexical resources that many NLP applications rely on do not include many idioms and fixed collocations. When idioms are listed in computational lexicons, it is often in a fixed form; idioms exhibiting morphosyntactic flexibility and lexical variations make automatic recognition very challenging. A more promising approach than lexical look-up is to search for the co-occurrence of the components of an idiom within a specific window, regardless of syntactic configuration and morphological categories. Lexical variation can be accounted for by searching for words that are semantically similar, as reflected in a thesaurus.

Another difficulty for the automatic processing of idioms is polysemy. Many idioms are "plausible" and have a literal reading (*keep the ball rolling, make a dent in, not move a finger*). To distinguish the literal and the idiomatic readings, a system would have to perform a semantic analysis of the wider context, a task similar to that performed by human when disambiguating between literal and idiomatic meanings.

11 Summary and conclusion

A prevailing view in linguistics represents idioms as "long words", largely non-compositional multi-word units with little or no room for deviation from a canonical form; any morphosyntactic flexibility is often thought to be directly related to semantic transparency. Corpus investigations show, first, that idioms are subject to far more variation than the traditional view would allow, and, second, that speakers use idioms in creative ways even in the absence of full semantic interpretation. The boundary between compositional and non-compositional strings appears to be soft, as speakers assign ad-hoc, discourse-specific meanings to idiom constituents that are opaque outside of certain contexts.

Psycholinguistic experiments, too, indicate that idiomatic and non-idiomatic language is not strictly separated in our mental lexicon and grammar.

Perhaps the most important function of many idioms, which may account for their universality and ubiquity, is that they provide convenient, pre-fabricated, conventionalized encodings of often complex messages.

12 References

Abeillé, Anne 1995. The flexibility of French idioms. A representation with lexicalized tree adjoining grammar. In: M. Everaert et al. (eds.). *Idioms. Structural and Psychological Perspectives*. Hillsdale, NJ: Erlbaum, 15–42.

Baldwin, Timothy, Colin Bannard, Takaaki Tanaka & Dominic Widdows 2003. An empirical model of multiword expression decomposability. In: *Proceedings of the ACL-03 Workshop on Multiword Expressions. Analysis, Acquisition and Treatment*. Stroudsburg, PA: ACL, 89–96.

Bobrow, Daniel & Susan Bell 1973. On catching on to idiomatic expressions. *Memory & Cognition* 1, 343–346.

Burger, Harald 2007. *Phraseologie. Eine Einführung am Beispiel des Deutschen*. 3rd edn. Berlin: Erich Schmidt. 1st edn. 1998.

Cacciari, Cristina & Patrizia Tabossi 1988. The comprehension of idioms. *Journal of Memory and Language* 27, 668–683.

Church, Kenneth W. & Patrick Hanks 1990. Word association norms, mutual information, and lexicography. *Computational Linguistics* 16, 22–29.

Church, Kenneth W., William Gale, Patrick Hanks & Donald Hindle 1991. Using statistics in lexical analysis. In: U. Zernik (ed.). *Lexical Acquisition. Exploiting On-Line Resources to Build a Lexicon*. Hillsdale, NJ: Erlbaum, 115–164.

Cowie, Anthony P. 1998. *Phraseology. Theory, Analysis, and Applications*. Oxford: Oxford University Press.

Cruse, D. Alan 2004. *Meaning in Language. An Introduction to Semantics and Pragmatics*. 2nd edn. Oxford: Oxford University Press. 1st edn. 2000.

Cutting, J. Cooper & Kathryn Bock 1997. That's the way the cookie bounces. Syntactic and semantic components of experimentally elicited idiom blends. *Memory & Cognition* 25, 57–71.

Dobrovol'skij, Dmitrij 1999. Haben transformationelle Defekte der Idiomstruktur semantische Ursachen? In: N. Fernandez Bravo, I. Behr & C. Rozier (eds.). *Phraseme und typisierende Rede*. Tübingen: Stauffenburg, 25–37.

Dobrovol'skij, Dmitrij 2004. Lexical semantics and combinatorial profile. A corpus-based approach. In: G. Williams & S. Vesser (eds.). *Euralex 11*. Lorient: Université de Bretagne Sud, 787–796.

Eisenberg, Peter 1999. *Grundriss der deutschen Grammatik, Vol. 2: Der Satz*. Stuttgart: Metzler.

Evert, Stefan 2005. *The Statistics of Word Cooccurrences. Word Pairs and Collocations*. Doctoral dissertation. University of Stuttgart.

Fazly, Afsaneh & Suzanne Stevenson 2006. Automatically constructing a lexicon of verb phrase idiomatic combinations. In: *Proceedings of the European Chapter of the Association for Computational Linguistics (EACL)* 11. Stroudsburg, PA: ACL, 337–344.

Fellbaum, Christiane 1993. The determiner in English idioms. In: C. Cacciari & P. Tabossi (eds.). *Idioms. Processing, Structure, and Interpretation*. Hillsdale, NJ: Erlbaum, 271–295.

Fellbaum, Christiane 1998. *WordNet. An Electronic Lexical Database*. Cambridge, MA: The MIT Press.

Fellbaum, Christiane 2002. VP idioms in the lexicon. Topics for research using a very large corpus. In: S. Busemann (ed.). *Proceedings of Konferenz zur Verarbeitung natürlicher Sprache (= KONVENS)* 6. Kaiserslautern: DFKI, 7–11.

Fellbaum, Christiane 2005. Unter dem Pantoffel stehen. *Circular der Berlin-Brandenburgischen Akademie der Wissenschaften* 31, 18.

Fellbaum, Christiane (ed.) 2006. *Corpus-Based Studies of German Idioms and Light Verbs*. Special issue of the *Journal of Lexicography* 19.
Fellbaum, Christiane 2007a. The ontological loneliness of idioms. In: A. Schalley & D. Zaefferer (eds.). *Ontolinguistics. How Ontological Status Shapes the Linguistic Coding of Concepts*. Berlin: Mouton de Gruyter, 419–434.
Fellbaum, Christiane (ed.) 2007b. *Idioms and Collocations. Corpus-Based Linguistic and Lexicographic Studies*. London: Continuum.
Fellbaum, Christiane 2007c. Argument selection and alternations in VP idioms. In: Ch. Fellbaum (ed.). *Idioms and Collocations. Corpus-Based Linguistic and Lexicographic Studies*. London: Continuum, 188–202.
Fellbaum, Christiane & Ekaterini Stathi 2006. Idiome in der Grammatik und im Kontext. Wer brüllt hier die Leviten? In: K. Proost & E. Winkler (eds.). *Von Intentionalität zur Bedeutung konventionalisierter Zeichen. Festschrift für Gisela Harras zum 65. Geburtstag*. Tübingen: Narr, 125–146.
Fillmore, Charles, Paul Kay & Mary O'Connor 1988. Regularity and idiomaticity in grammatical constructions. *Language* 64, 501–538.
Firenze, Anna 2007. 'You fool her' doesn't mean (that) 'you conduct her behind the light'. (Dis)agglutination of the determiner in German idioms. In: Ch. Fellbaum (ed.). *Idioms and Collocations. Corpus-Based Linguistic and Lexicographic Studies*. London: Continuum, 152–163.
Firth, John R. 1957. A Synopsis of Linguistic Theory 1930–1955. In: *Studies in Linguistic Analysis*. Oxford: Blackwell, 1–32.
Fraser, Bruce 1970. Idioms within a transformational grammar. *Foundations of Language* 6, 22–42.
Gehweiler, Elke 2007. How do homonymic idioms arise? In: M. Nenonen & S. Niemi (eds.). *Proceedings of Collocations and Idioms* 1. Joensuu: Joensuu University Press.
Gehweiler, Elke, Iris Höser & Undine Kramer 2007. Types of changes in idioms. Some surprising results of corpus research. In: Ch. Fellbaum (ed.). *Idioms and Collocations. Corpus-Based Linguistic and Lexicographic Studies*. London: Continuum, 109–137.
Gibbs, Ray & Gerard J. Steen (eds.) 1999. *Metaphor in Cognitive Linguistics*. Amsterdam: Benjamins.
Glucksberg, Sam 2001. *Understanding Figurative Language. From metaphors to Idioms*. New York: Oxford University Press.
Goldberg, Adele 1995. *Constructions. A Construction Grammar Approach to Argument Structure*. Chicago, IL: The University of Chicago Press.
Goldberg, Adele & Ray Jackendoff 2004. The English resultative as a family of constructions. *Language* 80, 532–568.
Green, Georgia M. 1974. *Semantics and Syntactic Regularity*. Bloomington, IN: Indiana University Press.
Halliday, Michael 1966. Lexis as a linguistic level. In: C. E. Bazell et al. (eds.). *In Memory of J.R. Firth*. London: Longman, 148–162.
Jackendoff, Ray 1997. Twistin' the night away. *Language* 73, 534–559.
Keysar, Boaz & Bridget Bly 1995. Intuitions of the transparency of idioms. Can one keep a secret by spilling the beans? *Journal of Memory and Language* 34, 89–109.
Kjellmer, Göran 1991. A mint of phrases. In: K. Aijmer & B. Altenberg (eds.). *English Corpus Linguistics. Studies in Honor of Jan Svartvik*. London: Longman, 111–127.
Krenn, Brigitte 2000. *The Usual Suspects. Data-Oriented Models for Identification and Representation of Lexical Collocations*. Doctoral dissertation. University of Saarbrücken.

Kuiper, Konrad 2004. Slipping on superlemmas. In: A. Häcki-Buhofer & H. Burger (eds.). *Phraseology in Motion, vol. 1.* Baltmannsweiler: Schneider, 371–379.

Kwasniak, Renata 2006. Wer hat nun den Salat? Now who's got the mess? Reflections on phraseological derivation. From sentential to verb phrase idiom. *International Journal of Lexicography* 19, 459–478.

Lakoff, George 1987. *Women, Fire, and Dangerous Things. What Categories Reveal about the Mind.* Chicago, IL: The University of Chicago Press.

Lakoff, George & Mark Johnson 1980. *Metaphors We Live By.* Chicago, IL: The University of Chicago Press.

McCarthy, Diana, Bill Keller & John Carroll 2003. Detecting a continuum of compositionality in phrasal verbs. In: *Proceedings of the ACL-03 Workshop on Multiword Expressions. Analysis, Acquisition and Treatment.* Stroudsburg, PA: ACL, 73–80.

Miller, George A. 1956. The magical number seven, plus or minus two. Some limits on our capacity for processing information. *Psychological Review* 63, 81–97.

Moon, Rosamund 1998. *Fixed Expressions and Idioms in English. A Corpus-Based Approach.* Oxford: Clarendon Press.

Nunberg, Geoffrey, Ivan Sag & Thomas Wasow 1994. Idioms. *Language* 70, 491–538.

Sailer, Manfred & Frank Richter 2002. Not for love or money. Collocations! In: G. Jäger et al. (eds.). *Proceedings of Formal Grammar 7.* Stanford, CA: CSLI Publications, 149–160.

Sinclair, John 1991. *Corpus, Concordance, Collocation.* Oxford: Oxford University Press.

Söhn, Jan-Philipp 2006. On idiom parts and their contexts. *Linguistik Online* 27, 11–28.

Sprenger, Simone A., William J. M. Levelt & Gerard A. M. Kempen 2006. Lexical access during the production of idiomatic phrases. *Journal of Memory and Language* 54, 161–184.

Stantcheva, Diana 2006. The many faces of negation. German VP idioms with a negative component. *International Journal of Lexicography* 19, 397–418.

Storrer, Angelika 2007. Corpus-based investigations on German support verb constructions. In: Ch. Fellbaum (ed.). *Idioms and Collocations. Corpus-Based Linguistic and Lexicographic Studies.* London: Continuum, 164–187.

Stubbs, Michael 2001. *Words and Phrases. Corpus Studies of Lexical Semantics.* Oxford: Blackwell.

Swinney, Douglas & Anne Cutler 1979. The access and processing of idiomatic expressions. *Journal of Verbal Learning and Verbal Behavior* 18, 523–534.

Weinreich, Uriel 1969. Problems in the analysis of idioms. In: J. Puhvel (ed.). *Substance and Structure of Language.* Berkeley, CA: University of California Press, 23–81.

Ronnie Cann
6 Sense relations

1 Introduction —— 172
2 The basic sense relations —— 173
3 Sense relations and word meaning —— 190
4 Conclusion —— 198
5 References —— 199

Abstract: This article explores the definition and interpretation of the traditional paradigmatic sense relations such as hyponymy, synonymy, meronymy, antonymy, and syntagmatic relations such as selectional restrictions. A descriptive and critical overview of the relations is provided in section 1 and in section 2 the relation between sense relations and different theories of word meaning is briefly reviewed. The discussion covers early to mid twentieth century structuralist approaches to lexical meaning, with its concomitant view of the lexicon as being structured into semantic fields, leading to more recent work on decompositional approaches to word meaning. The latter are contrasted with atomic views of lexical meaning and the capturing of semantic relations through the use of meaning postulates.

1 Introduction

Naive discussions of meaning in natural languages almost invariably centre around the meanings of content words, rather than the meanings of grammatical words or phrases and sentences, as is normal in academic approaches to the semantics of natural languages. Indeed, at first sight, it might seem to be impossible to construct a theory of meaning of sentences without first uncovering the complexity of meaning relations that hold between the words of a language that make them up. So, it might be argued, to know the meaning of the sentence *Matthew rears horses* we need also to at least know the meaning of *Matthew rears animals* or *Matthew breeds horses*, since horses are a kind of animal and rearing tends to imply breeding. It is in this context that the notion of *sense relations*, the meaning relations between words (and expressions) of a language, could be seen as fundamental to the success of the semantic enterprise. Indeed, the study of sense relations has a long tradition in the western grammatical and philosophical

Ronnie Cann, Edinburgh, United Kingdom

traditions, going back at least to Aristotle with discussions of relevant phenomena appearing throughout the medieval and later literature. However, the systematisation and taxonomic classification of the system of sense relations was only taken up in the structuralist movements of the twentieth century, particularly in Europe following the swift developments in structuralist linguistics after de Saussure. This movement towards systematic analyses of word sense was then taken up in the latter part of that century and the early part of the twenty-first century in formal modelling of the sense relations and, in particular, the development of computational models of these for the purposes of natural language processing.

The notion of 'sense' in this context may be variously interpreted, but is usually interpreted in contrast to the notion of *reference* (or, equivalently, *denotation* or *extension*). The latter expresses the idea that one aspect of word meaning is the relation between words and the things that they can be used properly to talk about. Thus, the reference/denotation of *cat* is the set of all cats (that are, have been and will be); that of *run* (on one theoretical approach), the set of all past, present and future events of running (or, on another view, the set of all things that ever have, are or will engage in the activity we conventionally refer to in English as *running*). Sense, on the other hand, abstracts away from the things themselves to the property that allows us to pick them out. The sense of *cat* is thus the property that allows us to identify on any occasion an object of which it can truthfully be said *that is a cat* – 'catness' (however that might be construed, cognitively in terms of some notion of concept, see for instance Jackendoff 2002 or model-theoretically in terms of denotations at different indices, see Montague 1973). Sense relations are thus relations between the properties that words express, rather than between the things they can be used to talk about (although, as becomes clear very quickly, it is often very difficult to separate the two notions).

Whether or not the study of sense relations can provide a solid basis for the development of semantic theories (and there are good reasons for assuming they cannot, see for example Kilgarriff 1997), nevertheless the elaboration and discussion of such meaning relations can shed light on the nature of the problems we confront in providing such theories, not least in helping to illuminate features of meaning that are truly amenable to semantic analysis and those that remain mysterious.

2 The basic sense relations

There are two basic types of sense relation. The most commonly presented in introductory texts are the *paradigmatic* relations that hold between words of the same general category or type and that are characterised in terms of contrast and hierarchy. Typically, a paradigmatic relation holds between words (or word-forms) when there is choice between them. So given the string *John bought a*, it is possible to substitute any noun that denotes something that can be bought: *suit, T-shirt, cauliflower, vegetable, house, ...* Between some of these words there is more to the choice between them than just the fact they are nouns denoting commodities. So, for example, if *John bought a suit* is true then it follows that *John bought a pair of trousers* is also true by virtue of the fact that pairs of trousers are parts of suits and if *John bought a cauliflower* is true then *John bought a vegetable* is also true, this time by virtue of the fact that cauliflowers are vegetables.

The second type of sense relations are *syntagmatic* which hold between words according to their ability to co-occur meaningfully with each other in sentences. Typically syntagmatic sense relations hold between words of different syntactic categories or (possibly) semantic types such as verbs and nouns or adverbs and prepositional phrases. In general, the closer the syntactic relation between two words such as between a head word and its semantic arguments or between a modifier and a head, the more likely it is that one word will impose conditions on the semantic properties the other is required to show. For example, in the discussion in the previous paragraph, the things that one can (non-metaphorically) buy are limited to concrete objects that are typically acceptable commodities in the relevant culture: in a culture without slavery adding *boy* to the string would be highly marked. As we shall see below, there is a sense in which these two dimensions, of paradigm and syntagm, cannot be kept entirely apart, but it is useful to begin the discussion as if they do not share interdependencies.

Of the paradigmatic sense relations there are three basic ones that can be defined between lexemes, involving sense inclusion, sense exclusion and identity of sense. Within these three groups, a number of different types of relation can be identified and, in addition, to these other sorts of sense relations, such as part-whole, have been identified and discussed in the literature. As with most taxonomic endeavours, researchers may be 'lumpers', preferring as few primary distinctions as possible, and 'splitters' who consider possibly small differences in classificatory properties as sufficient to identify a different class. With respect to sense relations, the problem of when to define an additional distinction within the taxonomy gives rise to questions about the relationship between knowledge of the world and knowledge of a word: where does one end and the other begin (see article 6 [Semantics: Theories] (Hobbs) *Word meaning and world knowledge*). In this article, I shall deal with only those relations that are sufficiently robust as to have become standard within lexical semantics: antonymy, hyponymy, synonymy and meronymy. In general, finer points of detail will be ignored and the discussion will be confined to the primary, and generally accepted, sense relations, beginning with hyponymy.

2.1 Hyponymy

Hyponymy involves specific instantiations of a more general concept such as holds between *horse* and *animal* or *vermilion* and *red* or *buy* and *get*. In each case, one word provides a more specific type of concept than is displayed by the other. The more specific word is called a *hyponym* and the more general word is the *superordinate* which may also be referred to as a *hyperonym* or *hypernym*, although the latter is dispreferred as in non-rhotic dialects of English it is homophonic with hyponym. Where the words being classified according to this relation are nouns, one can test for hyponymy by replacing X and Y in the frame 'X is a kind of Y' and seeing if the result makes sense. So we have '(A) horse is a kind of animal' but not '(An) animal is a kind of horse' and so on. A very precise definition of the relation is not entirely straightforward, however. One obvious approach is to have recourse to class inclusion, so that the set of things denoted by a hyponym is a subset of the set of things denoted by the superordinate. So the class of buying events is a subset of the class of getting events. This works fine for words that describe concrete entities or events, but becomes metaphysically more challenging when abstract words like *thought emotion*, *belief*, *understand*, *think* etc. are considered. More importantly there are words that may be said to have sense but no denotation such as *phoenix, hobbit, light sabre* and so on. As such expressions do not pick out anything in the real word they can be said to denote only the empty set and yet, obviously, there are properties that such entities would possess if they existed that would enable us to tell them apart. A better definition of hyponymy therefore is to forego the obvious and intuitive reliance on class membership and define the relation in terms of sense inclusion rather than class inclusion: the sense of the superordinate being included in the sense of the hyponym. So a daffodil has the sense of flower included in it and more besides. If we replace 'sense', as something we are trying to define, with the (perhaps) more neutral term 'property', then we have:

(1) *Hyponymy*: X is a hyponym of Y if it is the case that if anything is such that it has the property expressed by X then it also has the property expressed by Y.

Notice that this characterisation in terms of a universally quantified implication statement, does not require there to be actually be anything that has a particular property, merely that if such a thing existed it would have that property. So *unicorn* may still be considered a hyponym of *animal*, because if such things did exist, they would partake of 'animalness'.

Furthermore, in general if X and Y are hyponyms of Z they are called *co-hyponyms*, where two words can be defined as co-hyponyms just in case they share the same superordinate term and one is not a hyponym of the other.

Co-hyponyms are generally incompatible in sense, unless they are synonymous (see below section 2.3). For example, *horse, cat, bird, sheep*, etc. are all co-hyponyms of *mammal* and all mutually incompatible with each other: **That sheep is a horse*. Hyponymy is a transitive relation so that if X is a hyponym of Y and Y is a hyponym of Z then X is a hyponym of Z: *foal* is a hyponym of *horse*, *horse* is a hyponym of *animal*, and so *foal* is a hyponym of *animal*. Note that because of this transitivity, *foal* is treated as a co-hyponym of, and so incompatible with, not only *filly* and *stallion*, but also *sheep, lamb* and *bull*, etc. This sort of property indicates how hyponymy imposes partial hierarchical structure on a vocabulary. Such hierarchies may define a taxonomy of (say) natural kinds as in Fig. 6.1. Complete hierarchies are not common, however. Often in trying to define *semantic fields* of this sort, the researcher discovers that there may be gaps in the system where some expected superordinate term is missing. For example, in the lexical field defined by *move* we have hyponyms like *swim, fly, roll* and then a whole group of verbs involving movement using legs such as *run, walk, hop, jump, skip, crawl*, etc. There is, however, no word in English to express the concept that classifies the latter group together. Such gaps abound in any attempt to construct a fully hierarchical lexicon based on hyponymy. Some of these gaps may be explicable through socio-cultural norms (for example, gaps in kinship terms in all languages), but many are simply random: languages do not require all hierarchical terms to be lexicalised. That is not to say, however, that languages cannot express such apparently superordinate concepts. As above, we can provide the concept required as superordinate by modifying its apparent superordinate to give *move using legs*. Indeed, Lyons (1977) argues that hyponymy can in general be defined in terms of predicate modification of a superordinate. Thus, *swim* is *move through fluid*, *mare* is *female horse*, *lamb* is *immature sheep* and so on. This move pushes a paradigmatic relation onto some prior syntagmatic basis:

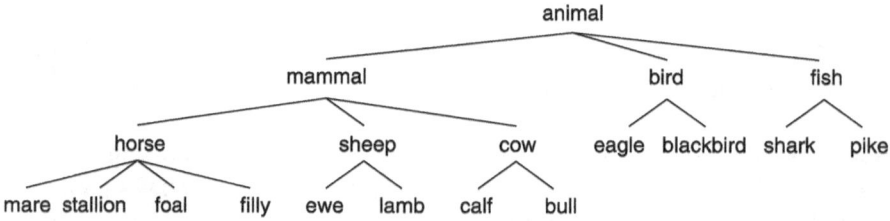

Fig. 6.1: Hyponyms of *animal*

> Hyponymy is a paradigmatic relation of sense which rests upon the encapsulation in the hyponym of some syntagmatic modification of the sense of the superordinate relation.
> Lyons (1977: 294)

Such a definition does not work completely. For example, it makes no sense at the level of natural kinds (is *horse* to be defined as *equine animal*?) and there are other apparent syntagmatic definitions that are problematic in that precise definitions are not obvious (*saunter* is exactly what kind of *walk*?). Such considerations, of course, reflect the vagueness of the concepts that words express out of context and so we might expect any such absolute definition of hyponymy to fail.

Hyponymy strictly speaking is definable only between words of the same (syntactic) category, but some groups of apparent co-hyponyms seem to be related to a word of some other category. This seems particularly true of predicate-denoting expressions like adjectives which often seem to relate to (abstract) nouns as superordinates rather than some other adjective. For example, *round, square, tetrahedral*, etc. all seem to be 'quasi-hyponyms' of the noun *shape* and *hot, warm, cool, cold* relate to *temperature*.

Finally, the hierarchies induced by hyponymy may be cross-cutting. So the *animal* field also relates to fields involving maturity (*adult, young*) or sex (*male, female*) and perhaps other domains. This entails that certain words may be hyponyms of more than one superordinate, depending on different dimensions of relatedness. As we shall see below, such multiple dependencies have given rise to a number of theoretical approaches to word meaning that try to account directly for sense relations in terms of primitive sense components or inheritance of properties in some hierarchical arrangement of conceptual or other properties.

2.2 Synonymy

Synonymy between two words involves sameness of sense and two words may be defined as synonyms if they are mutually hyponymous. For example, *sofa* and *settee* are both hyponyms of *furniture* and both mutually entailing since if *Bill is sitting on a settee* is true, then it is true that *Bill is sitting on a sofa*, and vice versa. This way of viewing synonymy defines it as occurring between two words just in case they are mutually intersubstitutable in any sentence without changing the meaning (or truth conditions) of those sentences. So *violin* and *fiddle* both denote the same sort of musical instrument so that *Joan plays the violin* and *Joan plays the fiddle* both have the same truth conditions (are both true or false in all the same circumstances). Synonyms are beloved of lexicographers and thesauri contain lists of putative synonyms. However, true or absolute synonyms are very rarely attested and there is a significant influence of context on the acceptability of apparent synonyms. Take an example from

Roget's thesaurus at random, 726, for *combatant* in which some of the synonyms presented are:

(2) disputant, controversialist, litigant, belligerent; competitor, rival; fighter, assailant, agressor, champion; swashbuckler, duellist, bully, fighting-man, boxer, gladiator, ...

Even putting to one side the dated expressions, it would be difficult to construct a single context in which all these words could be substituted for each other without altering the meaning or giving rise to pragmatic awkwardness. Context is the key for acceptability of synonym construal. Even the clear synonymy of *fiddle = violin* mentioned above shows differences in acceptability in different contexts: if Joan typically plays violin in a symphony orchestra or as soloist in classical concerti, then someone might object that she does not play the fiddle, where that term may be taken to imply the playing of more popular styles of music. Even the *sofa = settee* example might be argued to show some differences, for example in terms of the register of the word or possibly in terms of possible differences in the objects the words pick out. It would appear, in fact, that humans typically don't entertain full synonymy and when presented with particular synonyms in context will try and provide explanations of (possibly imaginary) differences. Such an effect would be explicable in terms of some pragmatic theory such as Relevance Theory (Sperber & Wilson 1986/1995) in which the use of different expressions in the same contexts is expected to give rise to different inferential effects.

A more general approach to synonymy allows there to be degrees of synonymy where this may be considered to involve degrees of semantic overlap and it is this sort of synonymy that is typically assumed by lexicographers in the construction of dictionaries. *Kill* and *murder* are strongly but not absolutely synonymous, differing perhaps in terms of intentionality of the killer/murderer and also the sorts of objects such expressions may take (one may kill a cockroach but does not thereby murder it). Of course, there are conditions on the degree of semantic similarity that we consider to be definitional of synonymy. In the first place, it should in general be the case that the denial of one synonym implicitly denies the other. *Mary is not truthful* seems correctly to implicitly deny the truth of *Mary is honest* and *Joan didn't hit the dog* implies that she didn't beat it. Such implications may only go one way and that is often the case with near synonyms. The second condition on the amount of semantic overlap that induces near synonymy is that the terms should not be contrastive. Thus, *labrador* and *corgi* have a large amount of semantic overlap in that they express breeds of dog, but there is an inherent contrast between these terms and so they cannot in general be intersubstitutable in any context and maintain the truth of the sentence. Near-synonyms are often used to explain a word already used: *John was dismissed, sacked in fact*. But if the terms contrast in meaning in some way then the resulting expression is usually nonsensical: *#John bought a corgi, a labrador, in fact*, where # indicates pragmatic markedness.

The felicity of the use of particular words is strongly dependent on context. The reasons for this have to do with the ways in which synonyms may differ. At the very least two synonymous terms may differ in style or register. So, for example, *baby* and *neonate* both refer to newborn humans, but while *the neonate was born three weeks premature* means the same as *the baby was born three weeks premature*, *What a beautiful neonate!* is distinctly peculiar. Some synonyms differ in terms of stylistic markedness. *Conceal* and *hide*, for example, are not always felicitously intersubstitutable. *John hid the silver in the garden* and *John concealed the silver in the garden* seem strongly synonymous, but *John concealed Mary's gloves in the cupboard* does not have the same air of normality about it as *John hid Mary's gloves in the cupboard*. Other aspects of stylistic variation involve expressiveness or slang. So while *gob* and *mouth* mean the same, the former is appropriately used in very informal contexts only or for its shock value. Swear words in general often have acceptable counterparts and euphemism and dysphemism thus provides a fertile ground for synonyms: *lavatory = bathroom = toilet = bog = crapper*, etc.; *fuck = screw = sleep with*, and so on. Less obvious differences in expressiveness come about through the use of synonyms that indicate familiarity with the object being referred to such as the variants of kinship terms: *mother = mum = mummy = ma*. Regional and dialectal variations of a language may also give rise to synonyms that may or may not co-occur in the language at large: *valley = dale = glen* or *autumn = fall*. Sociolinguistic variation thus plays a very large part in the existence of near synonymy in a language.

2.3 Antonymy

The third primary paradigmatic sense relation involves oppositeness in meaning, often called *antonymy* (although Lyons 1977 restricts the use of this term to gradable opposites) and is defined informally in terms of contrast, such that if 'A is X' then 'A is not Y'. So, standardly, if *John is tall* is true then *John is not small* is also true. Unlike hyponymy, there are a number of ways in which the senses of words contrast. The basic distinction is typically made between gradable and ungradable opposites. Typically expressed by adjectives in English and other Western European languages, gradable antonyms form instances of contraries and implicitly or explicitly invoke a field over which the grading takes place, i.e. a standard of comparison. Assuming, for example, that John is human, then human size provides the scale against which *John is tall* is measured. In this way, John's being tall for a human does not mean that he is tall when compared to buildings. Note that the implicit scale has to be the same scale invoked for any antonym: *John is tall* contrasts with *John is not small for a human*, not *John is not small for a building*. Other examples of gradable antonyms are easy to identify: *cold/hot*, *good/bad*, *old/young* and so on.

(3) *Gradable antonymy*: Gradable antonyms form instances of contraries and implicitly or explicitly invoke a field over which the grading takes place, i.e. a standard of comparison.

Non-gradable antonyms are, as the name suggests, absolutes and divide up the domain of discourse into discrete classes. Hence, not only does the positive of one antonym imply the negation of the other, but the negation of one implies the positive of the other. Such non-gradable antonyms are also called complementaries and include pairs such as *male/female, man/woman, dead/alive*.

(4) *Complementaries* (or binary antonyms) are all non-gradable and the sense of one entails the negation of the other and the negation of one sense entails the positive sense of the other.

Notice that there is, in fact, a syntagmatic restriction that is crucial to this definition. It has to be the case that the property expressed by some word is meaningfully predicable of the object to which it is applied. So, while *that person is male* implies that *that person is not female* and *that person is not female* implies that *that person is male*, *that rock is not female* does not imply that *that rock is male*. Rocks are things that do not have sexual distinctions. Notice further that binary antonyms are quite easily coerced into being gradable, in which case the complementarity of the concepts disappears. So we can say of someone that they are not very alive without committing ourselves to the belief that they are very dead.

Amongst complementaries, some pairs of antonyms may be classed as *privative* in that one member expresses a positive property that the other negates. These include pairs such as *animate/inanimate*. Others are termed *equipollent* when both properties express a positive concept such as *male/female*. Such a distinction is not always easy to make: is the relation *dead/alive* equipollent or privative?

Some relational antonyms differ in the perspective from which a relation is viewed: in other words, according to the order of their arguments. Pairs such as *husband/wife, parent/child* are of this sort and are called converses.

(5) *Converses*: involve relational terms where the argument positions involved with one lexeme are reversed with another and vice versa.

So if *Mary is John's wife* then *John is Mary's husband*. In general, the normal antonymic relation stands, provided that the relation expressed is strictly asymmetric: *Mary is Hilary's child* implies *Mary is not Hilary's parent*. Converses may involve triadic predicates as well, such as *buy/sell*, although it is only the agent and the goal that are reversed in such cases. If *Mary buys a horse from Bill* then it must be the case that *Bill sells a horse to Mary*. Note that the relations between the two converses here are not parallel: the agent subject of *buy* is related to the goal object of *sell* whereas the agent subject of *sell* is related to the source object of *buy*. This may indicate that the converse relation, in this case at least, resides in the actual situations described by sentences containing these verbs rather than necessarily inherently being part of the meanings of the verbs themselves.

So far, we have seen antonyms that are involved in binary contrasts such as *die/live*, *good/bad* and so on, and the relation of antonymy is typically said only to refer to such binary contrasts. But contrast of sense is not *per se* restricted to binary contrasts. For example, co-hyponyms all have the basic oppositeness property of exclusion. So, if something is a cow, it is not a sheep, dog, lion or any other type of animal and equally for all other co-hyponyms that are not synonyms. It is this exclusion of sense that makes *corgi* and *labrador* non-synonymous despite the large semantic overlap in their semantic properties (as breeds of dogs). Lyons (1977) calls such a non-binary relation 'incompatibility'. Some contrastive gradable antonyms form *scales* where there is an increase (decrease) of some characteristic property from one extreme of the scale to another. With respect to the property heat or temperature we have the scale {*freezing, cold, cool, lukewarm, warm, hot, boiling*}. These adjectives may be considered to be quasi-hyponyms of the noun *heat* and all partake of the oppositeness relation. Interestingly (at least for this scale), related points on the scale act like (gradable) antonyms: *freezing/boiling, cold/hot, cool/warm*. There are other types of incompatible relations such as *ranks* (e.g. {*private (soldier), corporal, sergeant, staff sergeant, warrant officer, lieutenant, major, . . .*}) and *cycles* (e.g. {*monday, tuesday, wednesday, thursday, friday, saturday, sunday*}).

Finally on this topic, it is necessary again to point out the context-sensitivity of antonymy. Although within the colour domain *red* has no obvious antonym, in particular contexts it does. So with respect to wine, the antonym of *red* is *white* and in the context of traffic signals, its opposite is green. Without a context, the obvious antonym to *dry* is *wet*, but again within the context of wine, its antonym is *sweet*, in the context of skin it is *soft* and for food *moist* (examples taken from Murphy 2003). This contextual dependence is problematic for the definition of antonymy just over words (rather than concepts), unless it is assumed that the lexicon is massively *homonymous* (see below). (See also article 7 [this volume] (Löbner) *Dual oppositions*.)

2.4 Part-whole relations

The final widely recognised paradigmatic sense relation is that involving 'part-of' relations or *meronymies*.

(6) *Meronymy*: If X is part-of Y or Y has X then X is a *meronym* of Y and Y is a *holonym* of X.

Thus, *toe* is a meronym of *foot* and *foot* is a meronym of *leg*, which in turn is a meronym of *body*. Notice that there is some similarities between meronymy and hyponymy in that a (normal) hand includes fingers and *finger* somehow includes the idea of *hand*, but, of course, they are not the same things and so do not always take part in the same entailment relations as hyponyms and superordinates. So while *Mary hurt her finger* (sort of) entails *Mary hurt her hand*, just as *Mary hurt her lamb* entails *Mary hurt an animal*, *Mary saw her finger* does not entail *Mary saw her hand*, unlike *Mary saw her lamb* does entail *Mary saw an animal*. Hence, although meronymy is like hyponymy in that the part-whole relations define hierarchical distinctions in the vocabulary, it is crucially different in that meronyms and holonyms define different types of object that may not share any semantic properties at all: a finger is not a kind of hand, but it does share properties with hands such as being covered in skin and being made of flesh and bone; but a wheel shares very little with one of its holonyms *car*, beyond being a manufactured object. Indeed, appropriate entailment relations between sentences containing meronyms and their corresponding holonyms are not easily stated and, while the definition given above is a reasonable approximation, it is not unproblematic. Cruse (1986) attempts to restrict the meronymy relation just to those connections between words that allow both the 'X is part of Y' and 'Y has X' paraphrases. He points out that the 'has a' relation does not always involve a 'part of' one, at least between the two words: *a wife has a husband* but not *#a husband is part of a wife*. On the other hand, the reverse may also not hold: *stress is part of the job* does not mean that *the job has stress*, at least not in the sense of possession.

However, even if one accepts that both paraphrases must hold of a meronymic pair, there remain certain problems. As an example, the pair of sentences *a husband is part of a marriage* and *a marriage has a husband* seems to be reasonably acceptable, it is not obvious that *marriage* is strictly a holonym of *husband*. It may be, therefore, that it is necessary to restrict the relation to words that denote things of the same general type: concrete or abstract, which will induce different 'part of' relations depending on the way some word is construed. So, *a chapter is part of a book = Books have chapters* if book is taken to be the abstract construal of structure, but not if it is taken to be the concrete object. Furthermore, it might be necessary to invoke notions like 'discreteness' in order to constrain the relation. For example, *flesh* is part of a *hand* and *hands* have *flesh*, but are these words thereby in a meronymic relationship? Flesh is a substance and so not individuated and if meronymy requires parts and wholes to be discretely identifiable, then the relationship would not hold of these terms. Again we come to the problem of world-knowledge, which tells us that fingers are prototypically parts of hands, versus word-knowledge: is it the case that the meaning of 'finger' necessarily contains the information that it forms part of a hand and thus that some aspect of the meaning of 'hand' is contained in the meaning of 'finger'? If that were the case, how do we account for the lack of any such inference in extensions of the word to cover (e.g.) emerging shoots of plants (cf. *finger of asparagus*)? (See article 6 [Semantics: Theories] (Hobbs) *Word meaning and world knowledge*.)

This short paragraph does not do justice to the extensive discussions of meronymy, but it should be clear that it is by far the most problematic of the paradigmatic relations to pin down, a situation that has led some scholars to reject its existence as a different type of sense relation altogether. (See further Croft & Cruse 2004: 159–163, Murphy 2003: 216–235.)

2.5 Syntagmatic relations

Syntagmatic relations between words appear to be less amenable to the sort of taxonomies associated with paradigmatic relations. However, there is no doubt that some words 'go naturally' with each other, beyond what may be determined by general syntactic rules of combination. At one extreme, there are fixed idioms where the words must combine to yield a specific meaning. Hence we have idiomatic expressions in English meaning 'die' such as *kick the bucket* (a reference to death by hanging) or *pass away* or *pass over (to the other side)* (references to religious beliefs) and so on. There are certain words also that only have a very limited ability to appear with others such as is the case with *addled* which can only apply to *eggs* or *brains*. Other collocational possibilities may be much freer, although none are constrained solely by syntactic category. For example, *hit* is a typical transitive verb in English that takes a noun phrase as object. However, it further constrains which noun phrases it acceptably collocates with by requiring the thing denoted by that noun phrase to have concrete substance. Beyond that, collocational properties are fairly free; see article 5 [this volume] (Fellbaum) *Idioms and collocations*:

(7) The plane hit water/a building/#the idea.

That words do have semantic collocational properties can be seen by examining strings of words that are 'grammatical' (however defined) but make no sense. An extreme example of this is Chomsky (1965)'s ubiquitous *colorless green ideas sleep furiously* in which the syntactic combination of the words is licit (as an example of a subject noun phrase containing modifiers and a verb phrase containing an intransitive verb and an adverb) but no information is expressed because of the semantic anomalies that result from this particular combination. There are various sources of anomaly. In the first place, there may be problems resulting from what Cruse (2000) calls *collocational preferences*. Where such preferences are violated, various degrees of anomaly can arise, ranging from marginally odd through to the incomprehensible. For example, the sentence *my pansies have passed away* is peculiar because *pass away* is typically predicated of a human (or pet) not flowers. However, the synonymous sentence, *my pansies have died*, involves no such peculiarity since the verb *die* is predicable of anything which is capable of life such as plants and animals. A worse clash of meaning thus derives from the collocation of an inanimate subject and any verb or idiom meaning 'die'. *My bed has died* is thus worse than *my pansies have passed away*, although notice that metaphorical interpretations can be (and often are) attributed to such strings. For example, one could interpret *my bed has died* as indicating that the bed has collapsed or is otherwise broken and such metaphorical extensions are common. Compare the use of *die* collocated with words such as *computer, car, phone*, etc. Notice further in this context that the antonym of *die* is not *live* but *go* or *run*. It is only when too many clashes occur that metaphorical interpretation breaks down and no information at all can be derived from a string of words. Consider again *colorless green ideas sleep furiously*. Parts of this sentence are less anomalous than the whole and we can assign (by whatever means) some interpretation to them:

(8) a. *Green ideas*: 'environmentally friendly ideas' or 'young, untried ideas' (both via the characteristic property of young plant shoots);
 b. *Colorless ideas*: 'uninteresting ideas' (via lacklustre, dull);
 c. *Colorless green ideas*: 'uninteresting ideas about the environment' or 'uninteresting untried ideas' (via associated negative connotations of things without colour);
 d. *Ideas sleep*: 'ideas are not currently active' (via inactivity associated with sleeping);
 e. *Green parrots sleep furiously*: 'parrots determinedly asleep (?)' or 'parrots restlessly asleep'.

But in putting all the words together, the effort involved in resolving all the contradictions just gets beyond any possible effect on the context by the information content of the final proposition. The more contradictions that need to be resolved in processing some sentence the greater the amount of computation required to infer a non-contradictory proposition from it and the less information the inferred proposition will convey. A sentence may be said to be truly anomalous if there is no relevant proposition that can be deduced from it by pragmatic means.

A second type of clash involving collocational preferences is induced when words are combined into phrases but add no new information to the string. Cruse calls this *pleonasm* and exemplifies it with examples such as *John kicked the ball with his foot* (Cruse 2000: 223). Since kicking involves contact with something by a foot the string final prepositional phrase adds nothing new and the sentence is odd (even though context may allow the apparent tautology to be acceptable). Similar oddities arise with collocations such as *female mother* or *human author*. Note that pleonasm does not always give rise to feelings of oddity. For example, *pregnant female* does not seems as peculiar as *#female mother*, even although the concept of 'female' is included in 'pregnant'. This observation is indicative of the fact that certain elements in strings of words have a privileged status. For example, it appears that pleonastic anomaly is worse in situations in which a semantic head, a noun or verb that determines the semantic properties of its satellites, which does not always coincide with what may be identified as the syntactic head of a construction, appears with a modifier (or sometimes complement, but not always) whose meaning is contained within that of the head: *bovine mammal* is better than *#mammalian cow* (what other sort of cow could there be?). Pleonastic anomaly can usually be obviated by substituting a hyponym for one expression or a superordinate of the other since this will give rise to informativity with respect to the combination of words: *female parent, He struck the ball with his foot* and so on.

Collocational preferences are often discussed with respect to the constraints imposed by verbs or nouns on their arguments and sometimes these constraints have been incorporated into syntactic theories. In Chomsky (1965), for example, the subcategorisation of verbs was defined not just in terms of the syntactic categories of their argument but also their semantic selectional properties. A verb like *kick* imposes a restriction on its direct object that it is concrete (in non-metaphorical uses) and on its subject that it is something with legs like an animal, whereas verbs like *think* require abstract objects and human subjects. Subsequent research into the semantic properties of arguments led to the postulation of participant (or case or thematic) roles which verbs 'assign' to their arguments with the effect that certain roles constrained the semantic preferences of the verb to certain sorts of subjects and objects. A verb like *fear*, therefore, assigns to its subject the role of *experiencer*, thus limiting acceptable collocations to things that are able to fear such as humans and other animals. Some roles such as *experiencer, agent, recipient*, etc. are more tightly constrained by certain semantic properties, such as animacy, volition, and mobility than others such as *theme, patient* (Dowty 1991).

We have seen that paradigmatic relations cannot always be separated from concepts of syntagmatic relatedness. So Lyons' attempts to define hyponymy in terms of the modification of a superordinate while the basic relation of antonymy holds only if the word being modified denotes something that can be appropriately predicated of the relevant properties. Given that meanings are constructed in natural languages by putting words together, it would be unsurprising if syntagmatic relations are, in some sense, primary and that paradigmatic relations are principally determined by collocational properties between words. Indeed the primacy of syntagmatic relations is supported by psycholinguistic and acquisition studies. It is reported in Murphy (2003), for example, that in word association experiments, children under 7 tend to provide responses that reflect collocational patterns rather than paradigmatic ones. So to a word like *black* the response of young children is more likely to give rise to responses such as *bird* or *board* rather than the antonym *white*. Older children and adults, on the other hand, tend to give paradigmatic responses. There is, furthermore, some evidence that knowledge of paradigmatic relations is associated with metalinguistic awareness: that is, awareness of the properties of, and interactions between, those words.

The primacy of syntagmatic relations over paradigmatic relations seems further to be borne out by corpus and computational studies of collocation and lexis. For example, there are many approaches to the automatic disambiguation of *homonyms*, identical word forms that have different meanings (see below), that rely on syntagmatic context to determine which sense is the most likely on a particular occasion of the use of some word. Such studies also rely on corpus work from which collocational probabilities between expressions are calculated. In this regard, it is interesting also to consider experimental research in computational linguistics which attempts to induce automatic recognition of synonyms and hyponyms in texts. Erk (2009) reports research which uses vector spaces to define representations of words meanings where such spaces are defined in terms of collocations between words in corpora. Without going into any detail here, she reports that (near) synonyms can be identified in this manner to a high degree of accuracy, but that hyponymic relations cannot be identified easily without such information being directly encoded, but that the use of vector spaces allows such encoding to be done and to yield good results. Although this is not her point, Erk's results are interesting with respect to the possible relation between syntagmatic and paradigmatic sense relations. Synonymy may be defined not just semantically as involving sameness of sense, but syntactically as allowing substitution in the all the same linguistic contexts (an idealisation, of course, given the rarity of full synonymy, but probabilistic techniques may be used to get a definition of degree of similarity between the contexts in which two words can appear). Hence, we might expect that defining vector spaces in terms of collocational possibilities in texts will yield a high degree of comparability between synonyms. But hyponymy cannot be defined easily in syntactic terms, as hyponyms and their superordinates will not necessarily collocate in the same way (for example, *four-legged animal* is more likely than *four-legged dog* while *Collie dog* is fine but #*Collie animal* is marginal at best). Thus, just taking collocation into account, even in a sophisticated manner, will fail to identify words in hyponymous relations. This implies that paradigmatic sense relations are 'higher order' or 'metalexical' relations that do not emerge directly from syntagmatic ones.

I leave this matter to one side from now on, because, despite the strong possibility that syntagmatic relations are cognitively primary, it remains the case that the study of paradigmatic relations remains the focus of studies of lexical semantics.

2.6 Homonymy and polysemy

Although not sense relations of the same sort as those reviewed above in that they do not structure the lexicon in systematic ways, *homonymy* and *polysemy* have nevertheless an important place in considerations of word meaning and have played an important part in the development of theories of lexical semantics since the last two decades of the twentieth century. Homonymy involves formal identity between words with distinct meanings (i.e. interpretations with distinct extensions and senses) which Weinreich (1963) calls "contrastive ambiguity". Such formal identity may involve the way a word is spoken (*homophony* 'same sound') such as *bank, line, taxi, can, lead (noun)/led (verb)* and/or orthography *bank, line, putting*, in which case it is referred to as *homography* 'same writing'. It is often the case that the term *homonymy* is reserved only for those words that are both homophones and homographs, but equally often the term is used for either relation. Homonymy may be full or partial: in the former case, every form of the lexeme is identical for both senses such as holds for the noun *punch* (the drink or the action) or it may be partial in which only some forms of the lexeme are identical for both senses, such as between the verb *punch* and its corresponding noun. Homonymy leads to the sort of ambiguity that is easily resolved in discourse context, whether locally through syntactic disambiguation (9a), the context provided within a sentence (9b) or from the topic of conversation (9c).

(9) a. His illness isn't terminal.
 b. My terminal keeps cutting out on me.
 c. I've just been through Heathrow Airport. The new terminal is rubbish.

In general, there is very little to say about homonymy. It is random and generally only tolerated when the meanings of the homonyms are sufficiently semantically differentiated as to be easily disambiguated.

Of more interest is polysemy in which a word has a range of meanings in different local contexts but in which the meaning differences are taken to be related in some way. While homonymy may be said to involve true ambiguity, polysemy involves some notion of vagueness or underspecification with respect to the meanings a polyseme has in different contexts (see article 8 [this volume] (Kennedy) *Ambiguity and vagueness*). The classic example of a polysemous word is *mouth* which can denote the mouth of a human or animal or various other types of opening, such as bottle, and more remotely of river. Unlike homonymy no notion of contrast in sense is involved and polysemes are considered to have an apparently unique basic meaning that is modified in context. The word *bank* is both a homonym and a polyseme in its meaning of 'financial establishment' between its interpretation as the institution (*The bank raised its interest rates yesterday*) and its physical manifestation (*The bank is next to the school*). One of the things that differentiates polysemy from homonymy is that the different senses of polysemes are not 'suppressed' in context (as with homonyms) but one aspect of sense is foregrounded or highlighted. Other senses are available in the discourse and can be picked up by other words in the discourse:

(10) a. Mary tried to jump through the window (aperture), but it was closed (aperture/physical object) and she broke it (physical object).
  b. *Mary walked along the bank of the river. It had just put up interest rates yet again.

Polysemy may involve a number of different properties: change of syntactic category (11); variation in valency (12); and subcategorisation properties (13).

(11) a. Rambo picked up the hammer (noun).
  b. Rambo hammered (verb) the nail into the tree.

(12) a. The candle melted.
  b. The heat melted the candle.

(13) a. Rambo forgot that he had buried the cat. (clausal complement - factive interpretation)
  b. Rambo forgot to bury the cat. (infinitival complement - non-factive interpretation)

Some polysemy may be hidden and extensive, as often with gradable adjectives where the adjective often picks out some typical property associated with the head noun that it modifies which may vary considerably from noun to noun, as with the adjective *good* in (15), where the interpretation varies considerably according to the semantics of the head noun and contrasting strongly with other adjectives like *big*, as illustrated in (14). Note that one might characterise the meaning of this adjective in terms of an underspecified semantics such as that given in (15e).

(14) *big car/big computer/big nose*: 'big for N'

(15) a. *good meal*: 'tasty, enjoyable, pleasant'
   b. *good knife*: 'sharp, easy to handle'
   c. *good car*: 'reliable, comfortable, fast'
   d. *good typist*: 'accurate, quick, reliable'
   e. *good N*: 'positive evaluation of some property associated with N'

There are also many common alternations in polysemy that one may refer to as *constructional (or logical) polysemy* since they are regular and result from the semantic properties of what is denoted.

(16) a. Figure/Ground: *window, door, room*
   b. Count/Mass: *lamb, beer*
   c. Container/Contained: *bottle, glass*
   d. Product/Producer: *book, Kleenex*
   e. Plant/Food: *apple, spinach*
   f. Process/Result: *examination, merger*

Such alternations depend to a large degree on the perspective that is taken with respect to the objects denoted. So a window may be viewed in terms of an aperture (e.g. when it is open) or in terms of what it is made of (glass, plastic in some sort of frame) while other nouns can be viewed in terms of their physical or functional characteristics, and so on.

Polysemy is not exceptional but rather the norm for word interpretation in context. Arguably every content word is polysemous and may have its meaning extended in context, systematically or unsystematically. The sense extensions of *mouth*, for example, are clear examples of unsystematic metaphorical uses of the word, unsystematic because the metaphor cannot be extended to just any sort of opening: *?#mouth of a flask, #mouth of a motorway, ?#mouth of a stream, #mouth of a pothole*. Of course, any of these collocations could become accepted, but it tends to be the case that until a particular collocation has become commonplace, the phrase will be interpreted as involving real metaphor rather than the use of a polysemous word. Unsystematic polysemy, therefore, may have a diachronic dimension with true (but not extreme) metaphorical uses becoming interpreted as polysemy once established within a language. It is also possible for diachronically homonymous terms to be interpreted as polysemes at some later stage. This has happened with the word *ear* where the two senses (of a head and of corn) derive from different words in Old English (*ēare* and *ēar*, respectively).

More systematic types of metaphorical extension have been noted above, but may also result from *metonymy*: the use of a word in a non-literal way, often based on a partwhole or 'connected to' relationships. This may happen with respect to names of composers or authors where the use of the name may refer to the person or to what they have produced. (17) may be interpreted as Mary liking the man or the music (and indeed listening to or playing the latter).

(17) Mary likes Beethoven.

Ad hoc types of metonymy may simply extend the concept of some word to some aspect of a situation that is loosely related to, but contextually determined by, what the word actually means. *John has new wheels* may be variously interpreted as John having a new car or, if he was known to be paraplegic, as him having a new wheelchair. A more extreme, but classic, example is one like (18) in which the actual meaning of the food *lasagna* is extended to the person who ordered it. (Such examples are also known as 'ham sandwich' cases after the examples found in Nunberg 1995).

(18) The lasagna is getting impatient.

Obviously context is paramount here. In a classroom or on a farm, the example would be unlikely to make any sense, whereas in a restaurant where the situation necessarily involves a relation between customers and food, a metonymic relation can be easily constructed. Some metonymic creations may become established within a linguistic community and thus become less context-dependent. For example, the word *suit(s)* may refer not only to the garment of clothing but also to people who wear them and thus the word gets associated with types of people who do jobs that involve the wearing of suits, such as business people.

3 Sense relations and word meaning

As indicated in the discussion above, the benefit of studying sense relations appears to be that it gives us an insight into word meaning generally. For this reason, such relations have often provided the basis for different theories of lexical semantics.

3.1 Lexical fields and componential analysis

One of the earliest modern attempts to provide a theory of word meaning using sense relations is associated with European structuralists, developing out of the work of de Saussure in the first part of the twentieth century. Often associated with theories of componential analysis (see below), lexical field theory gave rise to a number of vying approaches to lexical meaning, but which all share the hypothesis that the meanings (or senses) of words derive from their relations to other words within some thematic/conceptual domain defining a semantic or lexical field. In particular, it is assumed that hierarchical and contrastive relations between words sharing a conceptual domain is sufficient to define the meaning of those words. Early theorists such as Trier (1934) or Porzig (1934) were especially interested in the way such fields develop over time with words shifting with respect to the part of a conceptual field that they cover as other words come into or leave that space. For Trier, the essential properties of a lexical field are that:

(i) the meaning of an individual word is dependent upon the meaning of all the other words in the same conceptual domain;
(ii) a lexical field has no gaps so that the field covers some connected conceptual space (or reflects some coherent aspect of the world);
(iii) if a word undergoes a change in meaning, then the whole structure of the lexical field also changes.

One of the obvious weaknesses of such an approach is that the identification of a conceptual domain cannot be identified independently of the meaning of the expressions themselves and so appears somewhat circular. Indeed, such research presented little more than descriptions of diachronic semantic changes as there was little or no predictive power in determining what changes are and are not possible within lexical fields, nor what lexical gaps are tolerated and what not. Indeed, it seems reasonable to suppose that no such theory could exist, given the randomness that the lexical development of contentive words displays and so there is no reason to suppose that sense relations play any part in determining such change. (See Ullman 1957, Geckeler 1971, Coseriu & Geckeler 1981, for detailed discussions of field theories at different periods of the twentieth century.)

Although it is clear that 'systems of interrelated senses' (Lyons 1977: 252) exist within languages, it is not clear that they can usefully form the basis for explicating word meaning. The most serious criticism of lexical field theory as more than a descriptive tool is that it has unfortunate implications for how humans could ever know the meaning of a word: if a word's meaning is determined by its relation to other words in its lexical field, then to know that meaning someone has to know all the words associated with that lexical field. For example, to know the meaning of *tulip*, it would not be enough to know that it is a hyponym of *(plant) bulb* and a co-hyponym of *daffodil, crocus, anemone, lily, dahlia* but also to *trillium, erythronium, bulbinella, disia, brunsvigia* and so on. But only a botanist specialising in bulbous plants is likely to know anything like the complete list of names, and even then this is unlikely. Of course, one might say that individuals might have a shallower or deeper knowledge of some lexical field, but the problem persists, if one is trying to characterise the nature of word meaning within a language rather than within individuals. And it means that the structure of a lexical field and thus the meaning of a word will necessarily change with any and every apparent change in knowledge. But it is far from clear that the meaning of *tulip* would be affected if, for example, botanists decided that that a disia is not bulbous but rhizomatous, and thus does not after all form part of the particular lexical field of plants that have bulbs as storage organs. It is obvious that someone can be said to know the meaning of *tulip* independently of whether they have any knowledge of any other bulb or even flowering plant.

Field theory came to be associated in the nineteen-sixties with another theory of word meaning in which sense relations played a central part. This is the theory of *componential analysis* which was adapted by Katz & Fodor (1963) for linguistic meaning from similar approaches in anthropology. In this theory, the meaning of a word is decomposed into semantic components, often conceived as features of some sort. Such features are taken to be cognitively real semantic primitives which combine to define the meanings of words in a way that automatically predicts their paradigmatic sense relations with other words. For example, one might decompose the two meanings of *dog* as consisting of the primitive features [CANINE] and [CANINE, MALE, ADULT]. Since the latter contains the semantic structure of the former, it is directly determined to be a hyponym. Assuming that *bitch* has the componential analysis [CANINE, FEMALE, ADULT], the hyponym meaning of *dog* is easily identified as an antonym of *bitch* as they differ one just one semantic feature. So the theory provides a direct way of accounting for sense relations: synonymy involves identity of features; hyponymy involves extension of features; and antonymy involves difference in one feature. Although actively pursued in the nineteen sixties and seventies, the approach fell out of favour in mainstream linguistics for a number of reasons. From an ideological perspective, the theory became associated with the Generative Semantics movement which attempted to derive surface syntax from deep semantic meaning components. When this movement was discredited, the logically distinct semantic theory of componential analysis was mainly rejected too. More significantly, however, the theory came in for heavy criticism. In the first place, there is the problem of how primitives are to be identified, particularly if the assumption is that the set of primitives is universal. Although more recent work has attempted to give this aspect of decompositional theories as a whole a more empirically motivated foundation (Wierzbicka 1996), nevertheless there appears to be some randomness to the choice of primitives and the way they are said to operate within particular languages. Additionally, the theory has problems with things like natural kinds: what distinguishes [CANINE] from the meaning of *dog* or [EQUINE] from *horse*? And does each animal (or plant) species have to be distinguished in this way? If so, then the theory achieves very little beyond adding information about sex and age to the basic concepts described by *dog* and *horse*. Using Latinate terms to indicate sense components for natural kinds simply obscures the fact that the central meanings of these expressions are not decomposable. An associated problem is that features were often treated as binary so that, for example, *puppy* might be analysed as [CANINE,-ADULT]. Likewise, instead of MALE/FEMALE one might have ±MALE or [-ALIVE] for *dead*. The problem here is obvious: how does one choose a non-arbitrary property as the unmarked one? ±FEMALE and ±DEAD are just as valid as primitive features, as the reverse, reflecting the fact that *male/female* and *dead/alive* are equipollent antonyms (see section 2.3). Furthermore, restriction to binary values excludes the inclusion of relational concepts that are necessary for any analysis of meaning in general. Overall, then, while componential analysis does provide a means of predicting sense relations, it does so at the expense of a considerable amount of arbitrariness.

3.2 Lexical decomposition

Although the structuralist concept of lexical fields is one that did not develop in the way that its proponents might have expected, nevertheless it reinforced the view that words are semantically related and that this relatedness can be identified and used to structure a vocabulary. It is this concept of a structured lexicon that persists in mainstream linguistics. In the same way, lexical decompositional analyses have developed in rather different ways than were envisaged at the time that componential semantic analysis was developed. See article 2 [this volume] (Engelberg) *Frameworks of decomposition*.

Decomposition of lexical meaning appears in Montague (1973), one of the earliest attempts to provide a formal analysis of a fragment of a natural language as one of two different mechanisms for specifying the interpretations of words. Certain expressions with a logical interpretation, like *be* and *necessarily*, are decomposed, not into cognitive primitives, but into complex logical expressions, reflecting their truth-conditional content. For example, *necessarily* receives the logical translation $\lambda p[\Box px]$, where the abstracted variable, p, ranges over propositions and the decomposition has the effect of equating the semantics of the adverb with that of the logical necessity operator, $\Box$. Montague restricted decomposition of this sort to those grammatical expressions whose truth conditional meaning can be given a purely logical characterisation. In a detailed analysis of word meaning within Montague Semantics, however, Dowty (1979) argued that certain entailments associated with content expressions are constant in the same way as those associated with grammatical expressions and he extended the decompositional approach to analyse such words in order to capture such apparently independent entailments.

Dowty's exposition is concerned primarily with inferences from verbs (and more complex predicates) that involve tense and modality. By adopting three operators *DO, BECOME* and *CAUSE*, he is able to decompose the meanings of a range of different types of verbs, including activities, accomplishments, inchoatives and causatives, to account for the entailments that can be drawn from sentences containing them. For example, he provides decomposition rules for de-adjectival inchoative and causative verbs in English that modify the predicative interpretation of base adjectives in English. Dowty uses the propositional operator BECOME for inchoative interpretations of (e.g.) *cool*: $\lambda x\ [BECOME\ cool'(x)]$ where *cool* is the semantic representation of the meaning of the predicative adjective and the semantics of *BECOME* ensures that the resulting predicate is true of some individual just in case it is now cool but just previously was not cool. The causative interpretation of the verb involves the *CAUSE* operator in addition: $\lambda y\ \lambda x\ [x\ CAUSE\ BECOME\ cool'(y)]$ which guarantees the entailment between (e.g.) *Mary cooled the wine* and *Mary caused the wine to become cool*. Dowty also gives more complex (and less obviously logical) decompositions for other content expressions, such as *kill* which may be interpreted as x causes y to become not alive.

The quasi-logical decompositions suggested by Dowty have been taken up in theories such as Role and Reference Grammar (van Valin & LaPolla 1997) but primarily for accounting for syntagmatic relations such as argument realisation, rather than for accounting for paradigmatic sense relations. The same is not quite true for other decompositional theories of semantics such as that put forward in the Generative Lexicon Theory of Pustejovsky (1995). Pustejovsky presents a theory designed specifically to account for structured polysemous relations such as those given in (11–13) utilising a complex internal structure for word meanings that goes a long way further than that put forward by Katz & Fodor (1963). In particular, words are associated with a number of different 'structures' that may be more or less complex. These include: argument structure which gives the number and semantic type of logical arguments; event structure specifying the type of event of the lexeme; and lexical inheritance structure, essentially hyponymous

relations (which can be of a more general type showing the hierarchical structure of the lexicon). The most powerful and controversial structure proposed is the qualia structure. *Qualia* is a Latin term meaning 'of whatever sort' and is used for the Greek *aitiai* 'blame', 'responsibility' or 'cause' to link the current theory with Aristotle's modes of explanation. Essentially the qualia structure gives semantic properties of a number of different sorts concerning the basic sense properties, prototypicality properties and encyclopaedic information of certain sorts. This provides an explicit model for how meaning shifts and polyvalency phenomena interact. The qualia structure provides the structural template over which semantic combinatorial devices, such as co-composition, type coercion and subselection, may apply to alter the meaning of a lexical item. Pustejovsky (1991: 417) defines qualia structure as:
– The relation between [a word's denotation] and its constituent parts
– That which distinguishes it within a larger domain (its physical characteristics)
– Its purpose and function
– Whatever brings it about

Such information is used in interpreting sentences such as those in (19)

(19) a. Bill uses the train to get to work.
 b. This car uses diesel fuel.

The verb *use* is semantically underspecified and the factors that allow us to determine which sense is appropriate for any instance of the verb are the qualia structures for each phrase in the construction and a rich mode of composition, which is able to take advantage of this information. For example, in (19a) it is the function of trains to take people to places, so *use* here may be interpreted as 'catches', 'takes' or 'rides on'. Analogously, cars contain engines and engines require fuel to work, so the verb in (19b) can be interpreted as 'runs on', 'requires', etc. Using these mechanisms Pustejovsky provides analyses of complex lexical phenomena, including coercion, polysemy and both paradigmatic and syntagmatic sense relations.

Without going into detail, Pustejovskys fundamental hypothesis is that the lexicon is generative and compositional, with complex meanings deriving from less complex ones in structured ways, so that the lexical representations of words should contain only as much information as they need to express a basic concept that allows as wide a range of combinatorial properties as possible. Additionally, lexical information is hierarchically structured with rules specifying how phrasal representations can be built up from lexical ones as words are combined. A view which contrasts strongly with that discussed in the next section. See article 2 [this volume] (Engelberg) *Frameworks of decomposition*.

3.3 Meaning postulates and semantic atomism

In addition to decomposition for logico-grammatical word meaning, Montague (1973) also adopted a second approach to accounting for the meaning of basic expressions, one that relates the denotations of words (analogously, concepts) to each other via logical postulates. *Meaning Postulates* were introduced in Carnap (1956) and consist of universally quantified conditional or bi-conditional statements in the logical metalanguage which constrain the denotations of the constant that appears in the antecedent. For example, Montague provides an example that relates the denotations of the verb *seek* and the phrase *try to find*. (20) states (simplified from Montague) that for every instance of x seeking y there is an instance of x trying find y:

(20)   □∀x∀y[seek'(x, y) ↔ try-to (x,^ find'(x, y)]

Note that the semantics of *seek*, on this approach, does not contain the content of *try to find*, as in the decompositional approach. The necessity operator, □, ensures that the relation holds in all admissible models, i.e. in all states-of-affairs that we can talk about using the object language. This raises the bi-conditional statement to the status of a logical truth (an axiom) which ensures that on every occasion in which it is true to say of someone that she is seeking something then it is also true to say that she is trying to find that something (and vice versa). Meaning postulates provide a powerful tool for encoding detailed information about non-logical entailments associated with particular lexemes (or their translation counterparts). Note that within formal, model-theoretic, semantics such postulates act, not as constraints on the meaning of words, but their denotations. In other words, they reflect world knowledge, how situations are, not how word meanings relate to each other. While it is possible to use meaning postulates to capture word meanings within model-theoretic semantics, this requires a full intensional logic and the postulation of 'impossible worlds', to allow fine-grained differentiations between worlds in which certain postulates do not hold. (See Cann 1993 for an attempt at this and a critique of the notion of impossible worlds in Fox & Lappin 2005, cf. also article 7 [Semantics: Theories] (Zimmermann) *Model-theoretic semantics*).

A theory that utilises meaning postulates treats the meaning of words as atomic with their semantic relations specified directly. So, although traditional sense relations, both paradigmatic and syntagmatic, can easily be reconstructed in the system (see Cann 1993 for an attempt at this) they do not follow from the semantics of the words themselves. For advocates of this theory, this is taken as an advantage. In the first place, it allows for conditional, as opposed to bi-conditional, relations, as necessary in a decompositional approach. So while we might want to say that an act of killing involves an act of causing something to die, the reverse may not hold. If *kill* is decomposed as *x CAUSE (BECOME(¬alive'(y)))*, then this fact cannot be captured. A second advantage of atomicity is that even if a word's meaning can be decomposed to a large extent, there is nevertheless often a 'residue of meaning' which cannot be decomposed into other elements. This is exactly what the feature CANINE is in the simple componential analysis given above: it is the core meaning of *dog/bitch* that cannot be further decomposed. In decomposition, therefore, one needs both some form of atomic concept and the decomposed elements whereas in atomic approaches word meanings are individual concepts (or denotations), not further decomposed. What relations they have with the meanings of other words is a matter of the world (or of experience of the world) not of the meanings of the words themselves. Fodor & Lepore (1998) argue extensively against decompositionality, in particular against Pustejovsky's notion of the generative lexicon, in a way similar to the criticism made against field theories above. They argue that while it might be that a dog (necessarily) denotes an animal, knowing that dogs are animals is not necessary for knowing what dog means. Given the non-necessity of knowing these inferences for knowing the meaning of the word means that they (including interlexical relations) should not be imposed on lexical entries, because these relations are not part of the linguistic meaning.

Criticisms can be made of atomicity and the use of meaning postulates (see Pustejovsky 1998 for a rebuttal of Fodor & Lepore's views). In particular, since meaning postulates are capable of defining any type of semantic relation, traditional sense relations form just arbitrary and unpredictable parts of the postulate system, impossible to generalise over. Nevertheless it is possible to define theories in which words have atomic meanings, but the paradigmatic sense relations are used to organise the lexicon. Such a one is WordNet developed by George A. Miller (1995) to provide a lexical database of English organised by grouping words together that are cognitive synonyms (a synset), each of which expresses a distinct concept with different concepts associated with a word being found in different synsets (much like a thesaurus). These synsets then are related to each other by lexical and conceptual properties, including the basic paradigmatic sense relations. Although it remains true that the sense relations are stated independently of the semantics of the words themselves, nonetheless it is possible to claim that using them as an organisational principle of the lexicon provides them with a primitive status with respect to human cognitive abilities. WordNet was set up to reflect the apparent way that humans process expressions in a language and so using the sense relations as an organisational principle is tantamount to claiming that they are the basis for the organisation of the human lexicon, even if the grouping of specific words into synsets and the relations defined between them is not determined directly by the meanings of the words themselves. (See article 16 [Semantics: Typology, Diachrony and Processing] (Frank & Padó) *Semantics in computational lexicons*).

A more damning criticism of the atomic approach is that context-dependent polysemy is impossible because each meaning (whether treated as a concept or a denotation) is in principle independent of every other meaning. A consequence of this, as Pustejovsky points out, is that every polysemous interpretation of a word has to be listed separately and the interpretation of a word in context is a matter of selecting the right concept/denotation a priori. It cannot be computed from aspects of the meaning of a word with those of other words with which it appears. For example, the meanings of gradable adjectives such as *good* in (15) will need different concepts associated with each collocation that are in principle independent of each other. Given that new collocations between words are made all the time and under the assumption that the number of slightly new senses that result are potentially infinite in number, this is a problem for storage given the finite resources of the human brain. A further consequence is that, without some means of computing new senses, the independent concepts cannot be learned and so must be innate. While Fodor (1998) has suggested the possibility of the consequence being true, this is an extremely controversial and unpopular hypothesis that is not likely to help our understanding of the nature of word meaning.

4 Conclusion

In the above discussion, I have not been able to more than scratch the surface of the debates over the sense relations and their place in theories of word meaning. I have not discussed the important contributions of decompositionalists such as Jackendoff, or the problem of analyticity (Quine 1960), or the current debate between contextualists and semantic minimalists (Cappelen & Lepore 2005, Wedgwood 2007). Neither have I gone into any detail about the variations and extensions of sense relations themselves, such as is often found in Cognitive Linguistics (e.g. Croft & Cruse 2004). And much more besides. Are there any conclusions that we can currently draw? Clearly, sense relations are good descriptive devices helping with the compilation of dictionaries and thesauri, as well as the development of large scale databases of words for use in various applications beyond the confines of linguistics, psychology and philosophy. It would, however, appear that the relation between sense relations and word meaning itself remains problematic. Given the overriding context dependence of the latter, it is possible that pragmatics will provide explanations of observed phenomena better than explicitly semantic approaches (see for example, Blutner 2002, Murphy 2003, Wilson & Carston 2006). Furthermore, the evidence from psycholinguistic and developmental studies, as well as the collocational sensitivity of sense, indicates that syntagmatic relations may be cognitively primary and that paradigmatic relations may be learned, either explicitly or through experience as part of the development of inferential capability, rather than as being a central part of the semantics of words themselves. (See articles 4 [this volume] (Levin & Rappaport Hovav) *Lexical Conceptual Structure,* 1 [Semantics: Theories] (Talmy) *Cognitive Semantics,* 4 [Semantics: Theories] (Jackendoff) *Conceptual Semantics.*)

5 References

Blutner, Reinhard 2002. Lexical semantics and pragmatics. In: F. Hamm & T. E. Zimmermann (eds.). *Linguistische Berichte Sonderheft 10. Semantics,* 27–58.
Cann, Ronnie 1993. *Formal Semantics. An Introduction.* Cambridge: Cambridge University Press.
Cappelen, Herman & Ernest Lepore 2005. *Insensitive Semantics. A Defense of Semantic Minimalism and Speech Act Pluralism.* Malden, MA: Blackwell.
Carnap, Rudolf 1956. *Meaning and Necessity. A Study in Semantics and Modal Logic.* 2nd edn. Chicago, IL: The University of Chicago Press. 1st edn. 1947.
Chomsky, Noam 1965. *Aspects of the Theory of Syntax.* Cambridge, MA: The MIT Press.
Coseriu, Eugenio & Horst Geckeler 1981. *Trends in Structural Semantics.* Tübingen: Narr.
Croft, William & D. Alan Cruse 2004. *Cognitive Linguistics.* Cambridge: Cambridge University Press.
Cruse, D. Alan 1986. *Lexical Semantics.* Cambridge: Cambridge University Press.
Cruse, D. Alan 2000. *Meaning in Language. An Introduction to Semantics and Pragmatics.* Oxford: Oxford University Press.
Dowty, David R. 1979. *Word Meaning and Montague Grammar. The Semantics of Verbs and Times in Generative Semantics and in Montague's PTQ.* Dordrecht: Reidel.
Dowty, David R. 1991. Thematic proto-roles and argument selection. *Language* 67, 547–619.
Erk, Katrin 2009. Supporting inferences in semantics space. Representing words as regions. In: H. Bunt, O. Petukhova & S. Wubben (eds.). *Proceedings of the Eighth International Conference on Computational Semantics (= IWCS).* Tilburg: Tilburg University, 104–115.
Fodor, Jerry A. 1998. *Concepts. Where Cognitive Science Went Wrong.* Oxford: Clarendon Press.
Fodor, Jerry A. & Ernest Lepore 1998. The emptiness of the lexicon. Reflections on James Pustejovsky's 'The generative lexicon'. *Linguistic Inquiry* 29, 269–288.
Fox, Chris & Shalom Lappin 2005. *Foundations of Intensional Semantics.* Malden, MA: Blackwell.
Geckeler, Horst 1971. *Strukturelle Semantik und Wortfeldtheorie.* München: Fink.
Jackendoff, Ray 2002. *Foundations of Language. Brain, Meaning, Grammar, Evolution.* Oxford: Oxford University Press.
Katz, Jerrold J. & Jerry A. Fodor 1963. The structure of a semantic theory. *Language* 39, 170–210.
Kilgarriff, Adam 1997. I don't believe in word senses. *Computers and the Humanities* 31, 91–113.

Lyons, John 1977. *Semantics*. Cambridge: Cambridge University Press.
Miller, George A. 1995. WordNet. A lexical database for English. *Communications of the ACM* 38, 39–41.
Montague, Richard 1973. The proper treatment of quantification in ordinary English. In: J. Hintikka, J. M. E. Moravcsik & P. Suppes (eds.). *Approaches to Natural Language*. Dordrecht: Reidel, 221–242. Reprinted in: R. Thomason (ed.). *Formal Philosophy. Selected Papers of Richard Montague*. New Haven, CT: Yale University Press, 1974, 247–270.
Murphy, Lynne 2003. *Semantic Relations and the Lexicon*. Cambridge: Cambridge University Press.
Nunberg, Geoffrey 1995. Transfers of meaning. *Journal of Semantics* 12, 109–132.
Porzig, Walter 1934. Wesenhafte Bedeutungsbeziehungen. *Beiträge zur Deutschen Sprache und Lite-ratur* 58, 70–97.
Pustejovsky, James 1991. The generative lexicon. *Computational Linguistics* 17, 409–441.
Pustejovsky, James 1995. *The Generative Lexicon*. Cambridge, MA: The MIT Press.
Pustejovsky, James 1998. Generativity and explanation in semantics. A reply to Fodor and Lepore. *Linguistic Inquiry* 29, 289–311.
Quine, Willard van Orman 1960. *Word and Object*. Cambridge, MA: The MIT Press.
Sperber, Dan & Deirdre Wilson 1986/1995. *Relevance. Communication and Cognition*. Oxford: Blackwell. 2nd edn. (with postface) 1995.
Trier, Jost 1934. Das sprachliche Feld. Eine Auseinandersetzung. *Neue Jahrbücher für Wissenschaft und Jugendbildung* 10, 428–449. Reprinted in: L. Antal (ed.). *Aspekte der Semantik. Zu ihrer Theorie und Geschichte 1662–1970*. Frankfurt/M.: Athenäum, 1972, 77–104.
Ullman, Stephen 1957. *The Principles of Semantics*. 2nd edn. Glasgow: Jackson. 1st edn. 1951.
van Valin, Robert D. & Randy J. LaPolla 1997. *Syntax. Structure, Meaning, and Function*. Cambridge: Cambridge University Press.
Wedgwood, Daniel 2007. Shared assumptions. Semantic minimalism and relevance theory. *Journal of Linguistics* 43, 647–681.
Weinreich, Uriel 1963. On the semantic structure of language. In: J. H. Greenberg (ed.). *Universals of Language*. Cambridge, MA: The MIT Press, 142–216.
Wierzbicka, Anna 1996. *Semantics. Primes and Universals*. Oxford: Oxford University Press.
Wilson, Deirdre & Robyn Carston 2006. Metaphor, relevance and the 'emergent property' issue. *Mind & Language* 21, 404–433.

Sebastian Löbner
7 Dual oppositions in lexical meaning

1 Preliminaries —— 201
2 Duality —— 210
3 Examples of duality groups —— 216
4 Semantic aspects of duality groups —— 223
5 Phase quantification —— 228
6 Conclusion —— 233
7 References —— 234

Abstract: Starting from well-known examples, a notion of duality is presented that overcomes the shortcomings of the traditional definition in terms of internal and external negation. Rather duality is defined as a logical relation in terms of equivalence and contradiction. Based on the definition, the notion of duality groups, or squares, is introduced along with examples from quantification, modality, aspectual modification and scalar predication (adjectives). The groups exhibit remarkable asymmetries as to the lexicalization of their four potential members. The lexical gaps become coherent if the members of duality groups are consistently assigned to four types, corresponding e.g. to *some*, *all*, *no*, and *not all*. Among these types, the first two are usually lexicalized, the third is only rarely and the fourth almost never. Using the example of the German *schon* ("already") group, scalar adjectives and standard quantifiers, the notion of phase quantification is introduced as a general pattern of second-order predication which subsumes quantifiers as well as aspectual particles and scalar adjectives. Four interrelated types of phase quantifiers form a duality group. According to elementary monotonicity criteria the four types rank on a scale of markedness that accounts for the lexical distribution within the duality groups.

1 Preliminaries

Duality of lexical expressions is a fundamental logical relation. However, unlike others such as antonymy it enjoys much less attention. Duality relates *all* and *some*, *must* and *can*, *possible* and *necessary*, *already* and *still*, *become* and *stay*. Implicitly, it is even involved in ordinary antonymy such as between *big* and *small*.

Sebastian Löbner, Düsseldorf, Germany

https://doi.org/10.1515/9783110626391-007

Traditionally duality is defined in terms of inner and outer negation: two operators are dual iff the outer negation of one is equivalent to the inner negation of the other; alternatively two operators are dual iff one is equivalent to the simultaneous inner and outer negation of the other. For example, *some* is equivalent to *not all not*. Duality, in fact, is a misnomer. Given the possibility of inner and outer negation, there are always four cases involved with duality: a given operator, its outer negation, its inner negation and its dual, i.e. inner plus outer negation. Gottschalk (1953) therefore proposed to replace the term *duality* by *quaternality*.

In this article, a couple of representative examples are introduced before we proceed to a formal definition of duality. The general definition is not as trivial as it might appear at first sight. Inner and outer negations are not always available for dual operators at the syntactic level whence it is necessary to base the definition on a semantic notion of negation. Following the formal definition of duality, a closer look is taken at a variety of complete duality groups of four, their general structure and their relationship to the so-called Square of Oppositions of Aristotle's.

Duality groups of four exhibit striking asymmetries: of the four possible cases, two are almost always lexicalized, while the third is occasionally and the fourth almost never. (If the latter two are not lexicalized they are expressed by using explicit negation with one of the other two cases.) Criteria will be offered for assigning the members of a group to four types defined in terms of monotonicity and "tolerance".

A general conceptual format is described that allows the analysis of dual operators as instances of the general pattern of "phase quantification". This is a pattern of second-order predication; a phase quantifier predicates about a given first-order predication that there is, or is not, a transition on some scale between the predication being false and being true, i.e. a switch in truth-value. Four possibilities arise out of this setting: (i) there is a transition from false to true, (ii) there is no transition from false to true, (iii) there is a transition from true to false; (iv) there is no transition from true to false. These four possibilities of phase quantification form a duality group of four. It can be argued that all known duality groups semantically are instances of this general scheme.

1.1 First examples

1.1.1 Examples from logic

Probably the best-known cases of duality are the quantifiers in standard predicate logic, $\exists$ and $\forall$. The quantifiers are attached a variable and combined with a sentence (formula, proposition), to yield a quantified sentence.

(1) a. ∀x P   for every x P
    b. ∃x P   for at least one x P

Duality of the two quantifiers is stated in the logical equivalences in (2):

(2) a. ∃x P   ≡   ¬∀x ¬P
    b. ∀x P   ≡   ¬∃x ¬P
    c. ¬∃x P   ≡   ∀x ¬P
    d. ¬∀x P   ≡   ∃x ¬P

Duality can be paraphrased in terms of EXTERNAL NEGATION and INTERNAL NEGATION (cf. article 2 [Semantics: Sentence and Information Structure] (Herburger) *Negation*). External negation is the negation of the whole statement, as in the left formula in (2c,d) and in the right formula in (2a,b). Internal negation concerns the part of the formula following the quantifier, i.e. the "scope" of the quantifier (cf. article 1 [Semantics: Sentence and Information Structure] (Szabolcsi) *Scope and binding*). For example, according to (2c) the external negation of existential quantification is logically equivalent to the internal negation of universal quantification, and vice versa in (2d). If both sides in (2c) and (2d) are negated and double negation is eliminated, one obtains (2a) and (2b), respectively. In fact the four equivalences in (2) are mutually equivalent: they all state that universal and existential quantification are duals.

Dual operators are not necessarily operators on sentences. It is only required that at least one of their operands can undergo negation ("internal negation"), and that the result of combining the operator with its operand(s) can be negated, too ("external negation").

Another case of duality is constituted by conjunction ∧ and disjunction ∨; duality of the two connectives is expressed by De Morgan's Laws, for example:

(3) ¬(A ∧ B) ≡ (¬A ∨ ¬B)

These dual operators are two-place connectives, operating on two sentences, and internal negation is applied to both operands.

1.1.2 First examples from natural language

The duality relationship between ∃ and ∀ is analogously found with their natural language equivalents *some* and *every*. Note that sentences with *some* NPs as subject are properly negated by replacing *some* with *no* (cf. Löbner 2000: §1 for the proper negation of English sentences):

(4) a. **some** *tomatoes are green* ≡ **not every** *tomato is* **not** *green*
    b. **every** *tomato is green* ≡ **no** *tomato is* **not** *green*
    c. **no** *tomato is green* ≡ **every** *tomato is* **not** *green*
    d. **not every** *tomato is green* ≡ **some** *tomatoes are* **not** *green*

The operand of the quantificational subject NP is its 'nuclear' scope, the VP.

Modal verbs are another field where duality relations are of central importance. Modal verbs combine with infinitives. A duality equivalence for epistemic *must* and *can* is stated in (5):

(5) *he* **must** *have lied* ≡ *he* **cannot** *have told the truth*

Aspectual particles such as *already* and *still* are among the most thoroughly studied cases of dual operators. Their duality can be demonstrated by pairs of questions and negative answers as in (6). Let us assume that *on* and *off* are logically complementary, i.e. equivalent to the negations of each other:

(6) a. *Is the light* **already** *on? – No, the light is* **still** *off.*
    b. *Is the light* **still** *on? – No, the light is* **already** *off.*

1.2 Towards a general notion of duality

The relationship of duality is based on logical equivalence. Duality therefore constitutes a logical relation. In model-theoretic semantics (cf. article 7 [Semantics: Theories] (Zimmermann) *Model-theoretic semantics*), meaning is equated with truth conditions; therefore logical relations are considered sense relations (cf. article 6 [this volume] (Cann) *Sense relations*). However, in richer accounts of meaning that assume a conceptual basis for meanings, logical equivalence does not necessarily amount to equal meanings (cf. Löbner 2013, 2015: §§7.6, 13.5). It could therefore not be inferred from equivalences such as in (4) to (6) that the meanings of the pairs of dual expressions match in a particular way. All one can say is that their meanings are such that they result in these equivalences.

In addition, expressions which exhibit duality relations are rather abstract in meaning and, as a rule, can all be used in various constructions and meanings. In general, the duality relationship only obtains when the two expressions are used in particular constructions and/or in particular meanings. For example, the dual of German *schon* "already" is *noch* "still" in cases like the one in (6), but in other uses the dual of *schon* is *erst* (temporal "only"); *noch* on the other hand has uses where it does not possess a dual altogether (cf. Löbner 1989 for detailed discussion).

The duality relation crucially involves external negation of the whole complex of operator with operands, and internal operand negation. The duality relationship may concern one operand (out of possibly more) as in the case of the quantifiers, modal verbs or aspectual particles, or more than one (witness conjunction and disjunction). In order to permit internal negation, the operands have to be of sentence type or else of some type of predicate expression. For external negation, the result of combining dual operators with their operands must itself be eligible for negation.

A first definition of duality, in accordance with semantic tradition, would be:

(7) Let q and q' be two operators that fulfil the following conditions:
   a. they can be applied to the same domain of operands.
   b. the operands can be negated. (internal negation)
   c. the results of applying the operators to appropriate operands can be negated. (external negation)
   Then q and q' are DUALS iff external negation of one is equivalent to internal negation of the other.

This definition, however, is in need of modification. First, "negation" must not be taken in a syntactic sense as it usually is. If it were, English *already* and *still* would not be candidates for duality, as they allow neither external nor internal syntactic negation. This is shown in Löbner (1999: 89f) for internal negation; as to external negation, *already* and *still* can only be negated by replacing them with *not yet* and *no more/not anymore*, respectively. The term 'negation' in (7) has therefore to be replaced by a proper logical notion.

A second inadequacy is hidden in the apparently harmless condition (a): dual operators need not be defined for the same domain of operands. For example, *already* and *still* have different domains: *already* presupposes that the state expressed did not obtain before, while *still* presupposes that it may not obtain later. Therefore, (8a) and (8b) are semantically odd if we assume that one cannot be not young before being young, or not old after being old:

(8) a. *She's already young.*
    b. *She's still old.*

These inadequacies of the traditional definition will be taken care of below.

1.3 Predicates, equivalence, and negation

1.3.1 Predicates and predicate expressions

For proper semantic considerations, it is very important to carefully distinguish between the levels of expression and of meaning, respectively. Unfortunately there is a terminological tradition that conflates these two levels when talking of "predicates", "arguments", "operators", "operands", "quantifiers" etc.: these terms are very often used both for certain types of expressions and for their meanings. In order to avoid this type of confusion, the following terminological distinctions will be observed in this article: A "predicate" is a meaning; what a meaning is depends on semantic theory (cf. article 1 [Semantics: Foundations, History and Methods] (Maienborn, von Heusinger & Portner) *Meaning in linguistics*). In a model-theoretic approach, a predicate would be a function that assigns truth values to one or more arguments; in a cognitive approach, a predicate can be considered a concept that assigns truth values to arguments. For example, the meaning of *has lied* would be a predicate (function or concept) which in a given context (or possible world) assigns the truth value TRUE to everyone who has lied and FALSE to those who told the truth. Expressions, lexical or complex, with predicate meanings will be called PREDICATE EXPRESSIONS. ARGUMENTS which a predicate is applied to are neither expressions nor meanings; they are objects in the world (or universe of discourse); such objects may or may not be denoted by linguistic expressions; if they are, let us call these expressions ARGUMENT TERMS. (For a more comprehensive discussion of these distinctions see Löbner 2013, 2015: §5.2) Sometimes, arguments of predicate expressions are not explicitly specified by means of an argument term. For example, sentences are usually considered as predicating about a time argument, the time of reference (cf. article 13 [Semantics: Noun Phrases and Verb Phrases] (Ogihara) *Tense*), but very often, the time of reference is not specified by an explicit expression such as *yesterday*. The terms OPERATOR, OPERAND and QUANTIFIER will all be used for certain types of expressions.

If the traditional definition of duality given in (7) is inadequate, it is basically because it attempts to define duality at the level of expressions. Rather it has to be defined at the level of meanings because it is a logical relation and logical relations between expressions originate from their meanings.

1.3.2 The operands of dual operators

The first prerequisite for an adequate definition of duality is a precise semantic characterization of the operands of dual operators ("d-operators", for short). Since the operands must be eligible for negation, their meanings have to be predicates, i.e. something that assigns a truth-value to arguments. Negation ultimately operates on truth-values; its effect on a predicate is the conversion of the truth value it assigns. Predicate expressions range from lexical expressions such as verbs, nouns and adjectives to complex expressions like VPs, NPs, APs or whole sentences. In (4), the dual operators are the subject NPs *some tomatoes* and *every tomato*; their operands are the VPs *is/are green* and their respective negations *is/are not green*; they express predications about the tomatoes referred to. In (5), the operands of the dual modal verbs are the infinitives *have lied* and *have told the truth*; they express predications about the referent of the subject NP *he*; in (6), the operands of *already* and *still* are the remainders of the sentence: *the light is on/off*; in this case, these sentences are taken as predicates about the reference time implicitly referred to.

Predicates are never universally applicable, but only in a specific DOMAIN of cases. For a predicate P, its domain D(P) is the set of those tuples of arguments the predicate assigns a truth value to. The notion of domain carries over to predicate expressions: their domain is the domain of the predicate that constitutes their meaning.

In the following, PRESUPPOSITIONS (cf. article 14 [Semantics: Interfaces] (Beaver & Geurts) *Presupposition*) of a sentence or other predicate expression are understood as conditions that simply restrict the domain of the predicate that is its meaning. For example, the sentence *Is the light already on* in (6) presupposes (among other conditions) (p1) that there is a uniquely determined referent of the NP *the light* (cf. article 2 [Semantics: Noun Phrases and Verb Phrases] (Heim) *Definiteness and indefiniteness*) and (p2) that this light was not on before. The predication expressed by the sentence about the time of reference is thus restricted to those times when (p1) and (p2) are fulfilled, i.e. those times where there is a unique light which was not on before. In general, a predicate expression p will yield a truth-value for a given tuple of arguments if and only if the presuppositions of p are fulfilled. This classical Fregean view of presuppositions is adequate here, as we are dealing with the logical level exclusively. It follows from this notion of presupposition that predicate expressions which are defined for the same domain of arguments necessarily carry identical presuppositions. In particular that is the case if two predicate expressions are logically equivalent:

Definition 1: logical equivalence

Let p and p' be predicate expressions with identical domains. p and p' are LOGICALLY EQUIVALENT – $\mathbf{p} \equiv \mathbf{p}'$ – iff for every argument tuple in their common domain, p and p' yield identical truth values.

1.3.3 The negation relation

The crucial relation of logical contradiction can be defined analogously. It will be called 'neg', the 'neg(ation) relation'. Expressions in this relationship, too, have identical presuppositions.

> **Definition 2: negation relation**
> Let p and p' be predicate expressions with identical domains. p and p' are NEG-OPPOSITES, or NEGATIVES, of each other – **p neg p'** – iff for every argument tuple out of their common domain, p and p' yield opposite truth values.

Note that this is a semantic definition of negation, as it is defined in terms of predicates, i.e. at the level of meaning. The tests of duality require the construction of pairs of neg-opposites, or NEG-PAIRS for short. This means to come up with means of negation at the level of expressions, i.e. with lexical or grammatical means of converting the meanings of predicate expressions.

For sentences, an obvious way of constructing a negative is the application (or de-application) of grammatical negation ('g-negation', in the following). In English, g-negation takes up different forms depending on the structure of the sentence (cf. Löbner 2000: §1 for more detail). The normal form is g-negation by VP negation, with *do* auxiliarization in the case of non-auxiliary verbs. If the VP is within the scope of a higher-order operator such as a focus particle or a quantifying expression, either the higher-order operator is subject to g-negation or it is substituted by its neg-opposite. Such higher-order operators include many instances of duality. English *all, every, always, everywhere, can* and others can be directly negated, while *some, sometimes, somewhere, must, always, still* etc. are replaced for g-negation by *no, never, nowhere, need not, not yet* and *no more*, respectively.

For the construction of neg-pairs of predicate expressions other than sentences, sometimes g-negation can be used, e.g. for VPs. In other cases, lexical inversion may be available, i.e. the replacement of a predicate expression by a lexical neg-opposite such as *on/off, to leave/to stay, member/non-member*. Lexical inversion is not a systematic means of constructing neg-pairs because it is contingent on what the lexicon provides. But it is a valuable instrument for duality tests.

1.4 Second-order predicates and subnegation

1.4.1 D-operators

D-operators must be eligible to negation and therefore predicate expressions themselves; as we saw, at least one of their operand(s) must, again, be a predicate expression. For example, the auxiliary *must* in (5) is a predicate expression that takes another predicate expression *have lied* as its operand. In this sense, the d-operators are second-order predicate expressions, i.e. predicate expressions that predicate about predicates. D-operators may have additional predicate or non-predicate arguments. For an operator q and its operand p let 'q(p)' denote the morpho-syntactic combination of q and p, whatever its form. In terms of the types of Formal Semantics, the simplest types of d-operators would be (t,t) (sentential operators) and ((α,t),t) (quantifiers); a frequent type, represented by focus particles, is (((α,t),α),t) (cf. article 7 [Semantics: Theories] (Zimmermann) *Model-theoretic semantics* for logical types).

1.4.2 Negation and subnegation

When the definition of the neg-relation is applied to d-operators, it captures external negation. The case of internal negation is taken care of by the 'subneg(ation) relation'. Two operators are subneg-opposites if, loosely speaking, they yield the same truth values for neg-opposite operands.

Definition 3: subnegation opposites

Let q and q' be operators with a predicate type argument. Let the predicate domains of q and q' be such that q yields a truth value for a predicate expression p iff q' yields a truth value for the neg-opposites of p.

q and q' are SUBNEG(ATION) OPPOSITES, or SUBNEGATIVES, of each other – **q** SUBNEG **q'** – iff

> for any predicate expressions p and p' eligible as operands of q and q', respectively:
> if p neg p' then q(p) ≡ q'(p').

(For operators with more than one predicate argument, such as conjunction and disjunction, the definition would have to be modified in an obvious way.)

If two d-operators are subnegatives, their domains need not be identical. The definition only requires that if q is defined for p, any subnegative q' is defined for the negatives of p. If the predicate domain of q contains negatives for every predicate it contains, then q and q' have the same domain. Such are the domains of the logical quantifiers, but that does not hold for pairs of operators with different presuppositions, e.g. *already* and *still* (cf. §5.1).

An example of subnegatives is the pair *always/never*:

(9) *Max **always** is late* ≡ *Max **never** is on time*

To be late and *to be on time* are neg-opposites, here in the scope of *always* and *never*, respectively. The two quantificational adverbials have the same domain, whence the domain condition in Definition 3 is fulfilled.

2 Duality

2.1 General definition

Definition 3 above paths the way for the proper definition of duality:

Definition 4: dual opposites

Let q and q' be operators with a predicate type argument. Let the predicate domains of q and q' be such that q yields a truth value for a predicate expression p iff q' yields a truth value for the neg-opposites of p.

q and q' are DUAL (OPPOSITE)S of each other – **q** DUAL **q'** – iff:

> for any predicate expressions p and p' eligible as operands of q and q', respectively:

   if p neg p' then q(p) neg q'(p').

The problem with condition (a) in the traditional definition in (7) is taken care of by the domain condition here; and any mention of grammatical negation is replaced by relating to the logical relation neg. If q and q' and an operand p can all be subjected to g-negation NEG, duality of q and q' amounts to the equivalence of NEGq(p) and q'(NEGp).

2.2 Duality groups

Any case of duality involves, in fact, not only two dual expressions, but also the negatives and subnegatives of the dual operators. In total, these are four cases, not more. First, a dual of a dual is equivalent to the operator itself; the analogue holds for negation and subnegation. Therefore, if q is a d-operator and N, S, D are any morpho-syntactic operations to the effect of creating a negative, subnegative or dual of q, respectively, we observe:

(10) a. NNq ≡ q
     b. SSq ≡ q
     c. DDq ≡ q

Furthermore, the joint application of any two operations N, S or D amounts to the third:

(11) a. NSq ≡ SNq ≡ Dq
     b. NDq ≡ DNq ≡ Sq
     c. DSq ≡ SDq ≡ Nq

For the logical quantifiers, these laws can be read off the equivalences in (3); as for natural language, consider the following illustration for *already* and *still*. Let p be *the light is on*; and let us accept that *the light is off* is its negative, Np. Let q be *already*. q(p) is thus (12a). The subnegation of q(p), Sq(p), is gained by replacing p with Np in (12b). The negation of *already* is expressed by replacing it with *not yet* (12c). The dual of *already* is *still* (12d).

(12) a. q(p)   the light is already on   = already(the light is on)
     b. Sq(p) = q(Np) =   the light is already off = already(the light is off)
     c. Nq(p)   the light is not yet on   = not yet(the light is on)
     d. Dq(p)   the light is still on   = still(the light is on)

The combination of S and N (the order does not matter) yields (13a), the application of Nq to Np; this is obviously equivalent to Dq. NDq(p) would be the negation of the dual of *already*(p), i.e. the negation of *the light is still on*; this is accomplished by replacing *still* with *not anymore*: *the light isn't on anymore*, which in turn is equivalent to *the light is already off*, i.e. Sq (13b). Finally, the combination of dual and subnegation is yielded by replacing *already* by its dual *still* and p by its negative. This is equivalent to applying the negative of *already*, i.e. *not yet* to p (13c):

(13) a. NSq(p) = Nq(Np) =   the light is not yet off   ≡ the light is still on
     b. NDq(p) = N still p = the light isn't on anymore   ≡ the light is already off
     c. DSq(p) = still Np = the light is still off   ≡ the light not yet on

Due to the equivalences in (10) and (11), with any d-operator q, the operations N, S and D yield a group of exactly four cases: q, Nq, Sq, Dq – provided Nq, Sq and Dq each differ from q (see §2.3 for reduced groups of two members). Each of the four cases may be expressible in different, logically equivalent ways. Thus what is called a "case" here, is basically a set of logically equivalent expressions. According to (10) and (11), any further application of the operations N, S and D just yields one of these four cases: the group is closed under these operations. Within such a group, no element is logically privileged: instead of defining the group in terms of q and its correlates Nq, Sq and Dq, we might, for example, just as well start from Sq and take its correlates NSq = Dq, SSq = q, and DSq = Nq.

> **Definition 5: duality group**
> A DUALITY GROUP is a group of up to four operators in the mutual relations neg, subneg and dual that contains at least a pair of dual operators.

Duality groups can be graphically represented as a square of the structure depicted in Fig. 7.1.

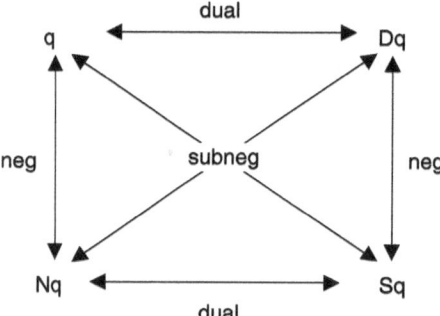

Fig. 7.1: Duality square

Although the underlying groups of four operators related by neg, subneg and dual are perfectly symmetrical, duality groups in natural, and even in formal, languages are almost always deficient, in that not all operators are lexicalized. This issue will be taken up in §§3, 4 and 5 below.

2.3 Reduced duality groups and self-duality

For the sake of completeness, we will briefly mention cases of reduced (not deficient) duality groups. The duality square may collapse into a constellation of two, or even one case, if the operations N, D, or S are of no effect on the truth conditions, i.e. if Nq, Dq or Sq are equivalent to q itself. Neutralization of N contradicts the Law of Contradiction: if $q \equiv Nq$, and q were true for any predicate operand p, it would at the same time be false. Therefore, the domain of q must be empty. This might occur if q is an expression with contradictory presuppositions, whence the operator is never put to work. For such an "idle" operator, negatives, subnegatives and duals are necessarily idle, too. Hence the whole duality group collapses into one case.

Neutralization of S results in equivalence of N and D, since in this case Dq ≡ NSq ≡ Nq. One such example is the quantifier *some, but not all*: if a predication p is true in some but not all cases, its negation, too, is true in some, but not all cases. Quantificational expressions, nominal or adverbial, meaning "exactly half of" represent another case: if a predication is true of exactly half of its domain, its opposite is true of the other half: the quantification itself logically amounts to the subnegation of the quantification.

(14) a. q   half of the students failed
      b. Sq   half of the students didn't fail

When S is neutralized, the duality square melts down to q/Sq neg/dual Nq/Dq.

More interesting is the case of D neutralization. If Dq ≡ q, q is its own dual, i.e. SELF-DUAL. For self-dual operators, N and S are equivalent. The domain of self-dual operators is generally closed under neg: since Nq ≡ Sq, q is defined for p iff it is defined for Np. The square reduces to q/Dq neg/subneg Nq/Sq. The phenomenon of self-duality encompasses a heterogeneous set of examples.

POLARITY. The simplest example is g-negation NEG: N NEG(p) ≡ NNp ≡ p and S NEG(p) ≡ NEG(Np) ≡ NNp ≡ p. Similarly, if there were a means of expressing just positive polarity, say POS, this would be self-dual, too, since POS(Np) ≡ Np ≡ N POS(p).

ARGUMENT INSERTION. Let D be a domain of a first-order predicate p and u an element of D. Let I_u be the operation of supplying p with u as its argument. Then I_u applied to p yields the truth value that p yields for u: $I_u(p) = p(u)$. If we apply I_u to a neg-opposite of p (subnegation), we obtain the opposite truth value, and so we do if we negate the application of I_u to p (negation). I_u is exerted, for example, when a definite NP is combined as an argument term with a predicate expression. This point is of importance for the discussion of NP semantics. It can be argued that all definite NPs are essentially individual terms; when combined with a predicate expression, they have the effect of I_u for their referent u. See Löbner (2000: §2) for an extensive discussion along this line. It is for that reason that (15b) and (15c) are logically equivalent:

(15) p "is on", p' "is off", u "the light"
      a. $I_u(p)$ = p(u)   the light is on
      b. $SI_u(p)$ = $I_u(p')$ the light is off
      c. $NI_u(p)$ =   the light is not on

"MORE THAN HALF". If the scale of quantification is discrete, and the total number of cases is odd, "more than half" is self-dual, too. Under these circumstances, external negation "not more than half" amounts to "less than half".

(16) a. q   *more than half of the seven dwarfs carry a shovel*
     b. Nq   *not more than half of the seven dwarfs carry a shovel*
     c. Sq   *more than half of the seven dwarfs don't carry a shovel*

NEG-RAISING VERBS. So-called neg-raising verbs (NR verbs), such as "want", "believe", "hope", can be used with N to express S, as in (17). If this is not regarded as a displacement of negation, as the term 'neg-raising' suggests, but in fact as resulting from equivalence of N and S for these verbs, neg-raising is tantamount to self-duality:

(17) *I don't want you to leave* ≡ *I want you not to leave*

The question as to which verbs are candidates for the neg-raising phenomenon is, as far as I know, not finally settled (see Horn (1978) for a comprehensive discussion, also Horn (1989: §5.2)). The fact that NR verbs are self-dual allows, however, a certain general characterization. The condition of self-duality has the consequence that if v is true for p, it is false for Np, and if v is false for p, it is true for Np. Thus NR verbs express propositional attitudes that in their domain "make up their mind" for any proposition as to whether the attitude holds for the proposition or its negation. For example, NR *want* applies only to such propositions the subject has either a positive or a negative preference for. The claim of self-duality is tantamount to the presupposition that this holds for any possible operand. Thereby the domains of NR verbs are restricted to such pairs of p and Np to which the attitude either positively or negatively obtains.

Among the modal verbs, those meaning "want to" like German *wollen* do not partake in the duality groups listed below. I propose that these modal verbs are NR verbs, whence their duality groups collapse to a group of two [q/Dq, Nq/Sq], e.g. [*wollen, wollen* NEG].

THE GENERIC OPERATOR. In mainstream accounts of characterizing (i-generic) sentences (cf. Krifka et al. 1995, also article 8 [Semantics: Noun Phrases and Verb Phrases] (Carlson) *Genericity*) it is commonly assumed that their meanings involve a covert genericity operator GEN. For example, *men are dumb* would be analyzed as (18a):

(18) a. GEN[x](x is a man; x is dumb]

According to this analysis, the meaning of the negative sentence *men are not dumb* would yield the GEN analysis (18b), with the negation within the scope of GEN:

(18) b. GEN[x](x is a man; ¬ x is dumb]

The sentence *men are not dumb* is the regular grammatical negation of *men are dumb*, whence it should also be analysed as (18c), i.e. as external negation w.r.t. to GEN:

(18) c. ¬GEN[x](x is a man; x is dumb]

It follows immediately that GEN is self-dual. This fact has not been recognized in the literature on generics. In fact, it invalidates all available accounts of the semantics of GEN which all agree in analyzing GEN as some variant of universal quantification. Universal quantification, however, is not self-dual, as internal and external negation clearly yield different results (see Löbner 2000: §4.2 for elaborate discussion).

HOMOGENEOUS QUANTIFICATION. Ordinary restricted quantification may happen to be self-dual if the predicate quantified yields the same truth-value for all elements of the domain of quantification, i.e. if it is either true of all cases or false of all cases. (As a special case, this condition obtains if the domain of quantification contains just one element u; both ∃ and ∀ are then equivalent to self-dual I_u.) The "homogeneous quantifier" ∃∀ (cf. Löbner 1989: 179, and Löbner 1990: 27ff for more discussion) is a two-place operator which takes one formula for the restriction and a second formula for the predication quantified. It will be used in §5.2.

Definition 6: homogeneous quantification

For arbitrary predicate logic sentences b and p,

∃∀x(b : p) =$_{df}$ ∃x(b ∧ p) if [∃x(b ∧ p)] = [∀x(b → p)], otherwise undefined.

The colon in '∃∀x(b : p)' cannot be replaced by any logical connective; [A] represents the truth value of A. According to the definition, ∃∀x(b : p) presupposes that ∃x(b ∧ p) and ∀x(b → p) are either both true or both false. The presupposition makes sure that the truth of p in the domain defined by b is an all-or-nothing-matter: if p is true for at least one "b", it is true for all, and if it is false for at least one "b", it is false for all, whence it cannot be true for some. ∃∀x(b : p) can be read essentially as "the b's are p". (See Löbner 2000: §2.6 for the all-or-nothing-character of distributive predications with definite plural arguments.) ∃∀x(b : p) is self-dual: the b's are not-p iff the b's are not p. (A simple proof is given in Löbner 1990: 207f.)

(19) ¬ ∃∀x(b : p) ≡ ∃∀x(b : ¬p)

As a general trait of self-dual operators we may fix the following. Applying to a domain of predicates that necessarily is closed under negation, they cut the domain into two symmetric halves of mutually negative predicates: for every neg-pair of operands, they "make up their mind", i.e. they are true of one member of the pair and false of the other.

3 Examples of duality groups

3.1 Duality tests

The first thing to observe when testing for duality relations is the fact that they are highly sensitive to the constructions in which a d-operator can be used. Strictly speaking, duality relations are defined for more or less specific constructions. For example, there are different duality groups for German *schon* with stative IP focus, with focus on a scalar, time-dependent predicate, with focus on a temporal frame adverbial and others (Löbner 1989). Similarly, the duality groupings of modal verbs differ for epistemic vs. deontic uses. Many operators belong to duality groups only in certain constructions, but not when used in others. For example, German *werden* ("become") is the dual of *bleiben* ("stay") in the copula uses. As was pointed out by Schlücker (2008), there are, however, several uses of *werden* where it is not the dual match of *bleiben*, often because *bleiben* cannot even be used in certain constructions for *werden*.

For a given construction, the duality test involves the use of subneg-opposites for the operands and of neg-opposites for the whole. Often, even if available, g-negation is a problematic tool due to potential scope ambiguities and ambivalence between neg and subneg readings. For example, VP negation in sentences with universal quantifier subjects has ambiguous scope, unlike, of course, scopeless lexical inversion:

(20) *every light wasn't on*
   subneg reading: ≡ *every light was off* (lexical inversion *on* vs. *off*)
   neg reading: ≡ *not every light was on*

Similarly, for modal verbs g-negation sometimes yields a neg reading, sometimes a subneg reading:

(21) a. *she may not stay* (epistemic use) ≡ *she may leave*
      b. *she may not stay* (deontic use) ≡ *she must leave,* not *she may leave*

Apart from these problems, g-negation may not be available, either for the operands or for the operators. For forming subnegatives it is generally recommended to use lexical inversion. Although not generally available, there are usually some cases of lexical neg-opposites in the domain of the operator which can be employed for tests. Since the operators can be assumed to operate in a logically uniform way on their operands, the findings on such cases can be generalized to the whole domain.

If g-negation is not available at the d-operator level, pairs of questions and negative answers can be used. The negative answer has to be carefully formed as to exactly match the question. This is secured if any denial of the question entails that answer, i.e. if that answer is the weakest denial possible. As mentioned above, *already* and *noch* are operators that bar both internal and external g-negation. The duality relations can be proved by using lexical inversion for the assessment of subneg (22), and the negative-answer test plus lexical inversion for duality (23).

(22) a. *the lights are **already** off* ≡ *the lights are **not** on **anymore***
 b. *the lights are **still** off* ≡ *the lights are **not yet** on*

(23) a. *Are the lights **already** on? – No.* ≡ *the lights are **still** off*
 b. *Are the lights **still** on? – No.* ≡ *the lights are **already** off*

3.2 Duality groups

3.2.1 Quantifiers

One group of instances of dual operators is constituted by various expressions of quantification. Different sets of quantifiers are used for quantifying over individuals, portions, times, places, and other types of cases. Assessing the duality relationships within the respective groups involves the distinction between count and mass reference, collective and distributive predication and generic or particular quantification (cf: Löbner 2000: §3, §4 for these distinctions). The groups include nominal and adverbial quantifiers.

In the following (see Tab. 7.1), duality groups will be represented in the form '[operator, dual, negative, subnegative]' with non-lexical members in parentheses, '–' indicates a case that cannot be expressed. Throughout, the existential quantifier is chosen as the first member of each group. The additions 'pl' and 'sg' indicate the use with plural or singular, respectively.

All these cases in Tab. 7.1 are obvious instances of existential and universal quantification and their negations. In no group the subnegative is lexicalized. The *partly* groups exhibit a peculiar gap for the negative. The conjunctions *and*

and *or* can be subsumed under quantification, as they serve to express that all or some of the conjuncts are true.

The case of negated conjunction needs careful intonation; its status is certainly marginal; one would prefer to say, e.g. *Mary and Paul are not both sick.*

Tab. 7.1: Duality Groups of Quantifiers

type of quantification	q	dual	negative	subnegative
particular or generic nominal distributive q.	*some* pl	*every* sg	*no* sg	(NEG *every*)
particular or generic nominal collective q.	*some* pl	*all* pl	*no* pl	(NEG *all*)
particular nominal distributive q.	*some* pl	*each* sg	*no* sg	(??NEG *each*)
particular nominal q. over two cases	*either* sg	*both* pl	*neither* sg	(NEG *both*)
particular or generic nominal mass q.	*some* sg	*all* sg	*no* sg	(NEG *all*)
particular or generic adverbial count q.	*partly*	*all*	–	(NEG *all*)
particular or generic adverbial mass q.	*partly*	*all* or *entirely*	–	(NEG *all*) or (NEG *entirely*)
adverbial q. over times, adverbial generic q. over cases	*sometimes*	*always*	*never*	(NEG *always*)
adverbial q. over places	*somewhere*	*everywhere*	*nowhere*	(NEG *everywhere*)
truth conditional connectives	*or*	*and*	*neither ... nor*	(NEG *and*)

3.2.2 Deontic modality

From the point of view of modal logic, modalities such as possibility and necessity, too, are instances of quantification. Necessity corresponds to truth, or givenness, in all cases out of a given set of alternatives, while possibility means truth in some such cases. The expressions of modality include grammatical forms such as causatives, potentials, imperatives etc. as well as modal verbs, adverbs, adjectives, verbs, and nouns. (For a survey of modality, and mood, see Palmer 2001; also article 11 [Semantics: Noun Phrases and Verb Phrases] (Portner) *Verbal mood*, article 14 [Semantics: Noun Phrases and Verb Phrases] (Hacquard) *Modality*.)

Modal verbs such as those in English and other Germanic languages express various kinds of modality, among them deontic and epistemic. The composition of duality groups out of the same pool of verbs differs for different modalities. Although duality relations constitute basic semantic data for modal verbs, they are hardly taken into account in the literature (e.g. Palmer 2001 or Huddleston & Pullum 2002 do not mention duality relations.).

In the groups of modal verbs, *may* can often be replaced by *can*. The second group of modal verbs differs in that they have *shall* as the dual of *may* instead of *must*. Since the meanings of *must* and *shall* are not logically equivalent – they express different variants of deontic modality – *may* and *need* in the two duality groups have different meanings, too, since they are interrelated to *shall* and *must* by logical equivalence relations within their respective duality groups. Thus, the assessment of duality relations may serve as a means of distinguishing meaning variants of the expressions involved.

The vocabulary for the adjective group is rich, comprising several near-synonyms for denoting necessity (*obligatory, mandatory, imperative* etc.) or possibility (*permitted, allowed, admissible* and others). Strictly speaking, each adjective potentially spans a duality group of its own. Again the vocabulary of the subneg type is the most restricted one.

Tab. 7.2: Duality Groups of Deontic Expressions

type of expression	q	dual	negative	subnegative
modal verbs (deontic modality)	*may/can*	*must*	(*must* NEG) (*may* NEG)	(*need* NEG)
modal verbs (2)	*may*	*shall*	(*shall* NEG)	(*need* NEG)
adjectives	*possible*	*necessary*	*impossible*	*unnecessary*
German causative deontic verbs	*ermöglichen* "render possible"	*erzwingen* "force"	*verhindern* "prevent"	*erübrigen* "render unnecessary"
imperative	imperative of permission	imperative of request	(NEG imperative)	–
causative	causative of permission	causative of causation	(NEG causative)	–
verbs of deontic and causal modality	*accept allow let/admit*	*demand request let/make/force*	*refuse forbid prevent*	(*demand* NEG) (*request* NEG) (*force* NEG)

The imperative form has two uses, the prototypical one of request, or command, and a permissive use, corresponding to the first cell of the respective duality group. The negation of the imperative, however, only has the neg-reading of prohibition. The case of permitting not to do something cannot be expressed by a simple imperative and negation. Similarly, grammatical causative forms such as in Japanese tend to have a weak (permissive) reading and a strong reading (of causation), while their negation inevitably expresses prevention, i.e. causing not to. The same holds for English *let* and German *lassen*.

3.2.3 Epistemic modality

In the groups of modal verbs in epistemic use, g-negation of *may* yields a subnegative, unlike the neg-reading of the same form in the deontic group. *Can*, however, yields a neg-reading with negation. Thus, the duality groups exhibit remarkable inconsistencies such as the near-equivalence of *may* and *can* along with a clear difference of their respective g-negations, or the equivalence of the g-negations of non-equivalent *may* and *must*.

Tab. 7.3: Duality Groups of Epistemic Expressions

type of expression	q	dual	negative	subnegative
modal verbs (1)	*can*	*must*	*can* NEG	*need* NEG
modal verbs (2)	*may*	*must*	*can* NEG	*may* NEG
epistemic adjectives	*possible*	*certain*	*impossible*	*questionable*
adverbs	*possibly*	*certainly*	*in no case*	–
verbs of attitude	*hold possible*	*believe*	*exclude*	*doubt*
adjectives for logical properties	*satisfiable*	*tautological*	*contradictory unsatisfiable*	(NEG *tautological*)
verbs for logical relations	*be compatible with*	*entail*	*exclude*	(NEG *entail*)

Logical necessity and possibility can be considered a variant of epistemic modality. Here the correspondence to quantification is obvious, as these properties and relations are defined in terms of existential and universal quantification over models (or worlds, or contexts).

3.2.4 Aspectual operators

Aspectual operators deal with transitions in time between opposite phases, or equivalently, with beginning, ending and continuation. Duality groups are defined by verbs such as *begin*, *become* and by focus particles such as *already* and *still*. The

German particle *schon* will be analyzed in §5.1 in more detail, as a paradigm case of 'phase quantification'. The particles of the *nur noch* group have no immediate equivalents in English. See Löbner (1999: §5.3) for semantic explanations.

Tab. 7.4: Duality Groups of Aspectual Expressions

type of expression	q	dual	negative	subnegative
verbs of beginning etc.	*begin* *become*	*continue* *stay*	*end* (*become* NEG)	(NEG *begin*) (NEG *stay*)
German aspectual particles with stative operands (1)	*schon* "already"	*noch* "still"	(*noch* NEG) "NEG yet"	(NEG *mehr*) "NEG more"
German aspectual particles with focus on a specification of time	*schon* "already"	*erst* "only"	(*noch* NEG) "NEG yet"	(NEG *erst*) "NEG still"
German aspectual particles with stative operands (2)	*endlich* "finally"	*noch immer* "STILL"	*noch immer* NEG "STILL NEG"	(*endlich* NEG *mehr*) "finally NEG more"
German aspectual particles with scalar stative operands (3)	*nur noch*	*noch*	(NEG *nur noch*)	(NEG *mehr*)

3.2.5 More focus particles, conjunctions

More focus particles such as *only, even, also* are candidates for duality relations. A duality account of German *nur* ("only", "just") is proposed in Löbner (1990: §9). In some of the uses of *only* analyzed there, it functions as the dual of *auch* ("also"). An analysis of *auch*, however, is not offered there. König (1991a, 1991b) proposed to consider causal *because* and concessive *although* duals, due to the intuition that '*although p, not q*' means something like '*not (because p, q)*'. However, Iten (2005) argues convincingly against that view.

3.2.6 Scalar adjectives

Löbner (1990: §8) offers a detailed account of scalar adjectives analysing them as dual operators on an implicit predication of markedness. The analysis will be briefly sketched in §5.1. According to this view, pairs of antonyms, together with their negations, form duality groups such as [*long, short,* (NEG *long*), (NEG *short*)].

Independently of this analysis, certain functions of scalar adjectives exhibit logical relations that are similar to the duality relations. Consider the logical relationships between positive with *enough* and *too* with positive, as well as between equative and comparative:

(24) a. *x is not too short* ≡ *x is long enough*
 x is too long ≡ *x is not short enough*
 b. *x is not as long as y* ≡ *x is shorter than y*
 x is as long as y ≡ *x is not shorter than y*

The negation of *too* with positive is equivalent to the positive of the antonym with *enough*, and the negation of the equative is equivalent to the comparative of the antonym. Antonymy essentially means reversal of the underlying common scale. Thus the equivalences in (24) represent instances of a "duality" relation that is based on negation and scale reversal, another self-inverse operation, instead of being based on negation and subnegation. In view of such data, the notion of duality might be generalized as to capture analogous logical relations based on two self-inverse operations.

3.3 Asymmetries within duality groups

The duality groups considered here exhibit remarkable asymmetries. Let us refer to the first element of a duality group as type 1, its dual as type 2, its negative as type 3 and its subnegative as type 4. The first thing to observe is the fact that there are always lexical or grammatical means of directly expressing type 1 and type 2, sometimes type 3 and almost never type 4. This tendency has long been observed for the quantifier groups (see Horn 1972 for an early account, Döhmann 1974a,b for cross-linguistic data, and Horn 2012 for a comprehensive recent survey). In addition to the lexical gaps, there is a considerable bias of negation towards type 3, even if the negated operand is type 2. Types 3 and 4 are not only less frequently lexicalized; if they are, the respective expressions are often derived from type 1 and 2, if historically, by negative affixes, cf. *n-either*, *n-ever*, *n-or*, *im-possible*. The converse never occurs. Thus, type 4 appears to be heavily marked: on a scale of markedness we obtain 1, 2 < 3 < 4.

A closer comparison of type 1 and type 2 shows that type 2 is marked vs. type 1, too. As for nominal existential quantification, languages are somehow at pain when it comes to an expression of neutral existential quantification. This might at a first glance appear to indicate markedness of existential vs. universal quantification. However, nominal existential quantification can be considered practically "built into" mere predication under the most frequent mode of particular (non-generic) predication: particular predication entails reference, which in turn entails existence. Thus, existential quantification is so unmarked that it is even the default case not in need of overt expression. A second point of preference compared to universal quantification is the degree of elaboration of existential quantification by more specific operators such as numerals and other quantity specifications.

For the modal types, this argumentation does not apply. What distinguishes type 1 from type 2 in these cases, is the fact that irregular negation, i.e. subneg readings of g-negation only occurs with type 2 operators; in this respect, epistemic *may* constitutes an exception.

The aspectual groups will be discussed later. So much may, however, be stated. In all languages there are very many verbs that incorporate type 1 'become' or 'begin' as opposed to very few verbs that would incorporate type 2 'continue' or 'stay' or type 3 'stop', and apparently no verbs incorporating 'not begin'.

These observations that result in a scale of markedness of type 1 < type 2 < type 3 < type 4 are tendencies. In individual groups, type 2 may be unmarked vs. type 1. Conjunction is unmarked vs. disjunction, and so is the command use of the imperative opposed to the permission use.

Of course, the tendencies are contingent on which element is chosen as the first of the group. They emerge only if the members of the duality groups are assigned the types they are. Given the perfect internal symmetry of duality groups, the type assignment might seem arbitrary — unless it can be motivated independently. What is needed, therefore, is independent criteria for the assignment of the four types. These will be introduced in §4.2 and §5.3.

4 Semantic aspects of duality groups

4.1 Duality and the Square of Opposition

The quantificational and modal duality groups (Tab. 7.1, 7.2, 7.3) can be arranged in a second type of logical constellation, the ancient Square of Opposition (SqO), established by the logical relations of entailment, contradiction contrariety and subcontrariety. The four relations are essentially entailment relations (cf. Löbner 2013, 2015: §7 for an introduction). They are defined for arbitrary, not necessarily second-order, predicates. The relation of contradictoriness is just neg.

> **Definition 7: entailment relations for predicate expressions**
>
> Let p and p' be arbitrary predicate expressions with the same domain D.
>
> (i) p ENTAILS p' iff for every a in D, if p is true for a, then p' is true for a.
> (ii) p and p' are CONTRARIES iff p entails Np'.
> (iii) p and p' are SUBCONTRARIES iff Np entails p'.

The traditional SqO has four vertices, A, I, E, O corresponding to ∀, ∃, ¬∃ and ¬∀, or type 1, 2, 3, 4, respectively, although in a different arrangement than in Fig. 7.1:

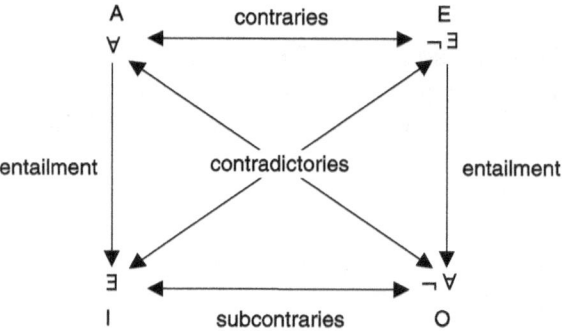

Fig. 7.2: Square of Oppositions

The duality square and the SqO depict different, in fact independent logical relations. Unlike the duality square, the SqO is asymmetric in the vertical dimension: the entailment relations are unilateral, and the relation between A and E is different from the one between I and O. The relations in the SqO are basically second-order relations (between first-order predicates), while the duality relations dual and subneg are third-order relations (between second-order predicates).

The entailment relations can be established between arbitrary first-order predicate expressions; the duality relations would then simply be unavailable due to the lack of predicate-type arguments. For example, any pair of contrary first-order predicate expressions such as *frog* and *dog* together with their negations span a SqO with, say, A = *dog*, E = *frog*, I = N *frog*, O = N *dog*. There are also SqO's of second-order operators which are not duality groups. For example, let A be *more than one* and E *no* with their respective negations O *not more than one/at most one* and I *some/at least one*. The SqO relations obtain, but A and I, i.e. *more than one* and *some* are not duals: the dual of *more than one* is *not more than one not*, i.e. *at most one not*. This is clearly not equivalent with *some*.

On the other hand, there are duality groups which do not constitute SqO's, for example the *schon* group. An SqO arrangement of this group would have *schon* and *noch nicht*, and *noch* and *nicht mehr*, as diagonally opposite vertices. However, in this group duals have different presuppositions, in fact this holds for all horizontal or vertical pairs of vertices. Therefore, since the respective relations of entailment, contrariety and subcontrariety require identical presuppositions, none of these obtains. In Löbner (1990: 210) an artificial example is constructed which shows that the duality relations do not entail the SqO relations even if all four operators share the same domain. There may be universal constraints for natural language which exclude such cases.

4.2 Criteria for the distinction among the four types

4.2.1 Monotonicity: types 1 and 2 vs. types 3 and 4

The most salient difference among the four types is that between types 1 and 2 and types 3 and 4: types 1 and 2 are positive, types 3 and 4 negative. The difference can be captured by the criterion of monotonicity. Barwise & Cooper (1981) first introduced this property for quantifiers; see also article 4 [Semantics: Noun Phrases and Verb Phrases] (Keenan) *Quantifiers*.

Definition 8: monotonicity

a. An operator q is UPWARD MONOTONE – MON↑– if for any operands p and p' if p entails p' then q(p) entails q(p').
b. An operator q is DOWNWARD MONOTONE – MON↓ – if for any operands p and p' if p entails p' then q(p') entails q(p).

All type 1 and type 2 operators of the groups listed are mon↑ while the type 3 and type 4 operators are mon↓. Negation inverses entailment: if p entails p' then Np' entails Np. Hence, both N and S inverse the direction of monotonicity. To see this, consider (25):

(25) *have a coke* entails *have a drink*, therefore
    a. *every* is mon↑: *every student had a coke* entails *every student had a drink*
    b. *no* is mon↓: *no student had a drink* entails *no student had a coke*

Downward monotonicity is a general trait of semantically negative expressions (cf. Löbner 2000: §1.3). It is generally marked vs. upward monotonicity. Mon↓ operators, including most prominently g-negation itself, license negative polarity items (cf. article 3 [Semantics: Sentence and Information Structure] (Giannakidou) *Polarity items*) and are thus specially restricted. Negative utterances in general are heavily marked pragmatically since they require special context conditions (Givón 1975).

4.2.2 Tolerance: types 1 and 4 vs. types 2 and 3

Intuitively, types 1 and 4 are weak as opposed to the strong types 2 and 3. The weak types make weaker claims. For example, one positive or negative case is enough to verify existential or negated universal quantification, respectively, whereas for the verification of universal and negated existential quantification the whole domain of quantification has to be checked. This distinction can be captured by the property of (in)consistency, or (in)tolerance:

Definition 9: tolerance and intolerance

a. An operator q is TOLERANT iff
   for some neg-pair p and Np of operands, q is true for both p and Np.

b. An operator q is INTOLERANT iff it is not tolerant.

Intolerant operators are "strong", tolerant ones "weak".

(26) a. intolerant *every*: *every light is off* excludes *every light is on*
     b. tolerant *some*: *some lights are on* is compatible with *some lights are off*

An operator q is intolerant iff for all operands p, if q(p) is true then q(Np) is false, i.e. Nq(Np) is true. Hence an operator is intolerant iff it entails its dual. Unless q is self-dual, it is different from its dual, hence only one of two different duals can entail its dual. Therefore, of two different dual operators one is intolerant and the other tolerant, or both are tolerant. In the quantificational and modal groups, type 2 generally entails type 1, whence type 2 is intolerant and type 1 tolerant. Since negation inverses entailment, type 3 entails type 4 if type 2 entails type 1. Thus in these groups, type 4 is tolerant, and type 3 intolerant. The criterion of (in)tolerance cannot be applied to the aspectual groups in Tab. 7.4. This gap will be taken care of in §5.3.

As a result, for those groups that enter the SqO (the quantificational and modal groups), the four types can be distinguished as follows.

Tab. 7.5: Type Distinctions in Duality Squares and the Square of Opposition

	type 1 / I	type 2 / A	type 3 / E	type 4 / O
	mon↑	mon↑	mon↓	intolerant
	tolerant	intolerant	mon↓	tolerant

Horn (2012: 14) directly connects (in)tolerance to the asymmetries of g-negation w.r.t. types 3 and 4. He states that 'intolerant q may lexically incorporate S, but tends not to lexicalize N; conversely, tolerant q may lexically incorporate N, but bars lexicalization of S' (the quotations are modified as to fit the terminology and notation used here). Since intolerant operators are of type 2 and tolerant ones of type 1, the two incorporations of N and S, respectively, lead to type 3.

The logical relations in the SqO can all be derived from the fact that ∀ entails ∃. They are logically equivalent to ∀ being intolerant which, in turn, is equivalent to each of the (in)tolerance values of the other three quantifiers. The monotonicity properties cannot be derived from the SqO relations. They are inherent to the semantics of universal and existential quantification.

4.3 Explanations of the asymmetries

There is considerable discussion as to the reasons for the gaps observed in the SqO groups. Horn (1972) and Horn (2012) suggest that type 4 is a conversational implicature of type 1 and hence in no need of extra lexicalization: *some* implicates *not all*, since if it were in fact *all*, one would have chosen to say so. This being so, type 4 is not altogether superfluous; some contexts genuinely require the expression of type 4; for example, only *not all*, but not *some*, can be used with normal intonation as a refusal of *all*.

Löbner (1990: §5.7) proposes a speculative explanation in terms of possible differences in cognitive cost. The argument is as follows. Assume that the relative unmarkedness of type 1 indicates that type 1 is cognitively basic and that the other types are cognitively implemented as type 1 plus some cognitive equivalents of N, S, or D. If the duality group is built up as [q, Dq, Nq, DNq], this would explain the scale of markedness, if one assumes that application of D is less costly than application of N, and simultaneous application of both is naturally even more costly than either alone. Since we are accustomed to think of D as composed of S and N, this might appear implausible; however, an analysis is offered (see §5.2), where, indeed, D is simple (essentially presupposition negation) and S the combined effect of N and D.

Jaspers (2005) discusses the asymmetries within the SqO, in particular the missing lexicalization of type 4 / O, in more breadth and depth than any account before. He, too, takes type 1 as basic, "pivotal" in his terminology, and types 2 and types 3 as derived from type 1 by two different elementary relations, one of them N. The fourth type, he argues, does not exist at all (although it can be expressed compositionally). His explanation is therefore basically congruent with the one in Löbner (1990), although the argument is based not on speculations about cognitive effort, but on a reflection on the character of human logic. For details of a comparison between the two approaches see Jaspers (2005: §2.2.5.2 and §4).

5 Phase quantification

In Löbner (1987, 1989, 1990) a theory of "phase quantification" was developed which was first designed to provide uniform analyses of the various *schon* groups in a way that captures the duality relationships. The theory later turned out to be also applicable to "only" (German *nur*), scalar adjectives and, in fact, universal and existential quantification in a procedural approach. To the extent that the quantificational and modal groups are all derivative of universal and existential quantification, this theory can be considered a candidate for the analysis of all known cases of duality groups, including all cases of quantification. It is for that reason that, somewhat misleadingly, the notion 'phase quantifier' was introduced. The theory will be introduced in a nutshell here. The reader is referred to the publications mentioned for a more elaborate introduction.

Phase quantification is about some first-order predication p; the truth value of p depends on the location of its argument on some scale; for example, p may be true of t only if t is located beyond some critical point on the scale. For a given predicate p and a relevant scale, there are four possible phase quantifications:

(27) (i) p is true of t, but false for some cases lower on the scale.
(ii) p is true of t as it is for the cases lower on the scale.
(iii) p is false of t as it is for the cases lower on the scale.
(iv) p is false of t, but true of some cases lower on the scale.

Alternatively, the four cases can be put in terms of transitions.

(28) (i) up to t on the scale, there is a transition from false to true w.r.t. p.
(ii) up to t on the scale, there is no transition from true to false w.r.t. p.
(iii) up to t on the scale, there is no transition from false to true w.r.t. p.
(iv) up to t on the scale, there is a transition from false to true w.r.t. p.

5.1 Instances of phase quantifications

Schon. In the uses of the *schon* group considered here, the particles are associated with the natural focus of a stative sentence p, i.e. of imperfective, perfect or prospective aspect (for the aspectual distinctions see Comrie 1976, Löbner 2013, 2015: §6.3. Other uses of *schon* and *noch* are discussed in Löbner (1989, 1999). Such sentences predicate over an evaluation time t_e. Consequently, p can be considered a one-place predicate over times. Due to this function of *p*, type 1, 2, 3, 4 are therefore referred to as $schon(t_e, p)$, $noch(t_e, p)$, $noch\ nicht(t_e, p)$ and $nicht\ mehr(t_e, p)$. The operators are about possible transitions in time between p being true and p being false. $schon(t_e, p)$ and $noch\ nicht(t_e, p)$ share the presupposition that before t_e there was a period of p being false, i.e. Np. $schon(t_e, p)$ states that this period is over and at t_e, p is true; $noch\ nicht(t_e, p)$ negates this: the Np-period is not over, p still is false at t_e. The other pair, $noch(t_e, p)$ and $nicht\ mehr(t_e, p)$ has the presupposition that there was a period of p before. According to $noch(t_e, p)$ this period at t_e still continues; $nicht\ mehr(t_e, p)$ states that it is over, whence p is false at t_e.

Tab. 7.6: Presuppositions and Assertions of the schon Group

operator	relation to *schon*	presupposition: previous state	assertion: state at t_e
$schon(t_e, p)$		not-p	p
$noch(t_e, p)$	dual	p	p
$noch\ nicht(t_e, p)$	neg	not-p	not-p
$nicht\ mehr(t_e, p)$	subneg	p	not-p

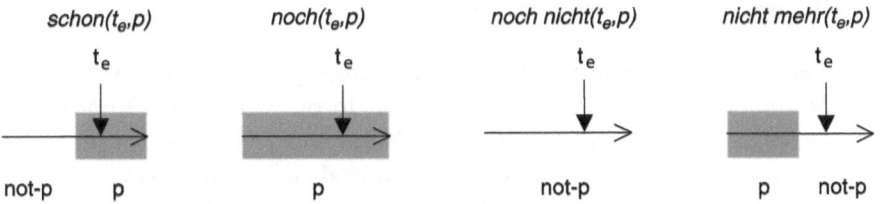

Fig. 7.3: Phase diagrams for *schon, noch, noch nicht* and *nicht mehr*

Types 2, 3, and 4 can be directly analyzed as generated from type 1 by application of N and D, where D is just negation of the presupposition.

Mittwoch (1993) and van der Auwera (1993) questioned the presuppositions of the *schon* group. Their criticism, however, is essentially due to a confusion of types of uses (each use potentially comes with different presuppositions), or of presuppositions and conversational implicatures. Löbner (1999) offers an elaborate discussion, and refutation, of these arguments.

Scalar adjectives. Scalar adjectives frequently come in pairs of logically contrary antonyms such as *long/short, old/young, expensive/cheap*. They relate to a scale that is based on some ordering. They encode a dimension for their argument such as size, length, age or price, and rank its degree on the respective scale. Pairs of antonyms consist of a positive element +A and a negative element −A (see Bierwisch 1989 for an elaborate general discussion). +A states for its argument that it occupies a high degree on the scale, a degree that is marked against lower degrees. −A states that the degree is low, i.e. marked against higher degrees. The respective negations predicate an unmarked degree on the scale as opposed to marked higher degrees (NEG +A), or marked lower degrees (NEG −A). The criteria of markedness are context dependent and need not be discussed here.

Similar to the meanings of the *schon* group, +A can be seen as predicating of an argument t that on the given scale it is placed above a critical point where unmarkedness changes into markedness, and analogously for the other three cases. In the diagrams in Fig. 7.4, unmarkedness is denoted by 0 and markedness by 1, as (un)markedness coincides with the truth value that +A and −A assign to their argument.

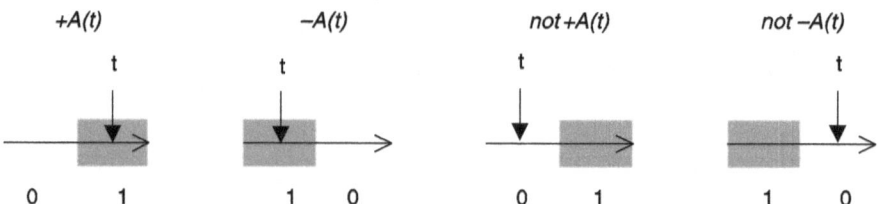

Fig. 7.4: Phase diagrams for scalar adjectives

Other uses of scalar adjectives such as comparative, equative, positive with degree specification, *enough* or *too* can be analyzed analogously (Löbner 1990: §8).

Existential and universal quantification. In order to determine the truth value of quantification restricted to some domain b and about a predicate expressed by p, the elements of b have to be checked in some arbitrary order as to whether p is true or false for them. Existential quantification can be regarded as involving a checking procedure which starts with the outcome 0 and switches to 1 as soon as a positive case of p is encountered in b. Universal quantification would start from the outcome 1 and switch to 0 if a negative case is encountered. This can be roughly depicted as in Fig. 7.5. In the diagrams, b marks the point where the domain of quantification is checked completely. It may be assumed without loss of generality that b is ordered in such a way that there is at most one change of polarity within the enumeration of the total domain.

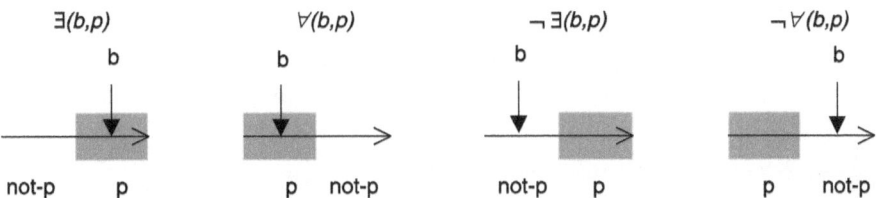

Fig. 7.5: Phase diagrams for logical quantifiers

5.2 The general format of phase quantification

The examples mentioned can all be considered instances of the general format of phase quantification which can be defined as follows. We first need the notion of an 'admissible α-interval'. This is a section of the underlying scale with at most one positive and one negative subsection in terms of p, where α is the truth value of p for the first subsection. An admissible interval may or may not contain a switch of polarity, and this is what phase quantification is all about.

> **Definition 10: admissible α-intervals in terms of <, p and t**
>
> Let p be a predicate expression with domain D, < a partial ordering in D, t∈D and α = 0 or 1. The set of admissible α-intervals in terms of <, p and t – AI(α, <, p, t) – is the set of all subsets of D which
>
> (i) are linearly ordered by <
> (ii) contain t and some t' < t,
> (iii) start with a phase of [p] = α
> (iv) contain at most one transition between p and not-p below t.

Phase quantification in general is then defined as follows:

> **Definition 11: phase quantification**
>
> Given the conditions of Definition 10,
>
> PQ(α, <, p, t) ≡$_{df}$ ∃∀ I (I ∈ AI(α, <, p, t) : p(t))

The formula reads: For the admissible α-intervals in terms of <, p and t, p is true of t.

With this definition, four phase quantifiers can be defined which form a duality group of the respective four types:

(29) a. $PQ1(<, p, t) \equiv_{df}$ $PQ(0, <, p, t)$

b. $PQ2(<, p, t) \equiv_{df}$ $PQ(1, <, p, t)$ = D PQ1(<, p, t)

c. $PQ3(<, p, t) \equiv_{df}$ ¬PQ(0, <, p, t) = N PQ1(<, p, t)

d. $PQ4(<, p, t) \equiv_{df}$ ¬PQ(1, <, p, t) = N D PQ1(<, p, t)

Dual formation D reverses the initial truth value with respect to p, i.e. the truth value of p the admissible interval starts with. D corresponds to presupposition reversal in the case of the *schon* group. Thus the group is built up by N and D, in accordance with the hypothesis proposed in §4.3. The duality relations can now be formally proved, making use of the fact that the homogeneous quantifier is self-dual. For the details of applying the general format to the *schon* group, scalar adjectives, and logical quantifiers, the reader is referred to Löbner (1990: §7, 8, 10).

5.3 The four types revisited

The four types can be distinguished by the criterion of monotonicity w.r.t. p, or p-monotonicity for short: PQ1 and PQ2 are p-mon↑ and PQ3 and PQ4 are p-mon↓. A second monotonicity criterion, t-monotonicity, concerns the dependence of the truth value of the whole on the position of t. PQ1 and PQ4 are true for t if t is beyond the transition point on the scale, hence PQ1 and PQ4, if true for t, are true for all t' > t within the admissible intervals (t-mon↑) because a further change is impossible. Conversely, PQ2 and PQ3, if true for t, are true for all t' < t within those intervals (t-mon↓). For adjectives this means, e.g., that if t is 'long' or 'not short', so are all t' longer than t, while if t is 'short' or 'not long', all t' shorter than t are, too. For quantifiers, the criterion coincides with tolerance (t-mon↑) and intolerance. Similar to tolerance, PQ1 and PQ4, which are true when t is in the second phase, allow for both p and not-p below t. A third monotonicity criterion, s[cale]-monotonicity, concerns the truth value of p at the beginning of the admissible intervals: if α is 0, then p(t) entails p(t') for all t' > t (s-mon↑ for PQ1 and PQ3) because t is beyond the transition point; if the intervals start with [p] = 1, p(t) entails p(t') for all t' < t (s-mon↓ for PQ2 and PQ4) because any transition point would be above t. S-monotonicity groups together operators with their negatives, i.e. pairs with identical presuppositions.

Tab. 7.7: Monotonicity Properties for Phase Quantifiers

type	instances			p-monotonicity	t-monotonicity	s-monotonicity
PQ1	schon	long	some	p-mon↑ positive	t-mon↑ (tolerant)	s-mon↑ (neg. presupp.)
PQ2	noch	short	all	p-mon↑ positive	t-mon↓ (intolerant)	s-mon↓ (pos. presupp.)
PQ3	noch nicht	not long	no	p-mon↓ negative	t-mon↓ (intolerant)	s-mon↑ (neg. presupp.)
PQ4	nicht mehr	not short	not all	p-mon↓ negative	t-mon↑ (tolerant)	s-mon↓ (pos. presupp.)

The three monotonicity properties change with the application of N (p-mon), S (t-mon) and D (s-mon), respectively. PQ1 is basic, ↑ changes to ↓ with application of the respective type-changing operations. The ↓ cases can generally be regarded marked (Löbner 1990: §7). Let us assume that PQ2, PQ3 and PQ4 are derived from PQ1 by N and D as indicated in (29). Then the relevant markedness features are p-monotonicity and s-monotonicity: type 2 is s-mon↓, type 3 p-mon↓, type 4 both s-mon↓ and p-mon↓. If we further assume that p-mon↓ outweighs s-mon↓, we obtain the observed scale of markedness: PQ1 < PQ2 < PQ3 < PQ4.

6 Conclusion

The article offered a general definition of duality as a logical relation between second-order operators. (In the case of dimensional adjectives, the operator type is first-order; their duality rests on an implicit first-order predicate of markedness.) The duality relation gives rise to squares of up to four expressions related in terms of the logical relations of negation, subnegation and duality. Such squares are to be distinguished from the traditional Aristotelian Square of Opposition, even if the duality relationships and the Aristotelian oppositions obtain within the same group of four.

It was shown that the known cases can be considered instances of phase quantification, a pattern of second-order predication which deals with transitions of the argument predicate between truth and falsity on some scale the truth-value depends on. This analysis offers a hypothetical explanation for the fact that duality squares are lexicalized in a clearly asymmetric manner.

7 References

van der Auwera, Johan 1993. *Already* and *still*: Beyond duality. *Linguistics & Philosophy* 16, 613–653.
Barwise, Jon & Robin Cooper 1981. Generalized quantifiers and natural language. *Linguistics & Philosophy* 4, 159–219.
Bierwisch, Manfred 1989. The semantics of gradation. In: M. Bierwisch & E. Lang (eds.). *Dimensional Adjectives. Grammatical Structure and Conceptual Interpretation*. Berlin: Springer, 71–262.
Comrie, Bernard 1976. *Aspect*. Cambridge: Cambridge University Press.
Döhmann, Karl 1974a. Die sprachliche Darstellung logischer Funktoren. In: A. Menne & G. Frey (eds.). *Logik und Sprache*. Bern: Francke, 28–56.
Döhmann, Karl 1974b. Die sprachliche Darstellung der Modalfunktoren. In: A. Menne & G. Frey (eds.). *Logik und Sprache*. Bern: Francke, 57–91.
Döhmann, Karl 1974c. Die sprachliche Darstellung der Quantifikatoren. In: A. Menne & G. Frey (eds.). *Logik und Sprache*. Bern: Francke, 92–118.
Givón, Talmy 1975. Negation in language; pragmatics, function, ontology. *Working Papers on Language Universals 18*. Stanford, CA: Stanford University, 1–39.
Gottschalk, Walter H. 1953. The Theory of Quaternality. *Journal of Symbolic Logic* 18, 193–196.
Horn, Laurence 1972. *On the Semantic Properties of Logical Operators in English*. Ph.D. dissertation. UCLA, Los Angeles, CA. Reprinted: Bloomington, IN: Indiana University Linguistics Club, 1976.
Horn, Laurence 1978. Remarks on neg-raising. In: P. Cole (ed.). *Syntax and Semantics 9: Pragmatics*. New York: Academic Press, 129–210.
Horn, Laurence 1989. *A Natural History of Negation*. Chicago, IL: The University of Chicago Press.
Horn, Laurence 2012. Histoire d'*O: Lexical pragmatics and the geometry of opposition. In: J. Y. Béziau and G. Payette (eds.). *The Square of Opposition: A General Framework for Cognition*. Bern: Lang, 393–426.
Huddleston, Rodney & Geoffrey K. Pullum 2002. *The Cambridge Grammar of the English Language*. Cambridge: Cambridge University Press.
Iten, Corinne 2005. *Linguistic Meaning, Truth Conditions and Relevance. The Case of Concessives*. Houndmills: Palgrave Macmillan.
Jaspers, Dany 2005. *Operators in the Lexicon: On the Negative Logic of Natural Language*. Ph.D. dissertation. University of Leiden. Utrecht: Landelijke Onderzoekschool Taalwetenschap (=LOT).
König, Ekkehard 1991a. Concessive relations as the dual of causal relations. In: D. Zaefferer (ed.). *Semantic Universals and Universal Semantics*. Dordrecht: Foris, 190–209.
König, Ekkehard 1991b. *The Meaning of Focus Particles in German*. London: Routledge.
Krifka, Manfred, Francis J. Pelletier, Gregory N. Carlson, Alice ter Meulen, Godehard Link & Gennaro Chierchia 1995. Genericity: An introduction. In: G. N. Carlson & F. J. Pelletier (eds.). *The Generic Book*. Chicago, IL: The University of Chicago Press, 1–124.
Löbner, Sebastian 1987. Quantification as a major module of natural language semantics. In: J. A. G. Groenendijk, M. J. B. Stokhof & D. de Jongh (eds.). *Studies in Discourse Representation Theory and the Theory of Generalized Quantifiers*. Dordrecht: Foris, 53–85.
Löbner, Sebastian 1989. German *schon – erst – noch*: An integrated analysis. *Linguistics & Philosophy* 12, 167–212.

Löbner, Sebastian 1990. *Wahr neben Falsch. Duale Operatoren als die Quantoren natürlicher Sprache*. Tübingen: Niemeyer.
Löbner, Sebastian 1999. Why German *schon* and *noch* are still duals: A reply to van der Auwera. *Linguistics & Philosophy* 22, 45–107.
Löbner, Sebastian 2000. Polarity in natural language: Predication, quantification and negation in particular and characterizing sentences. *Linguistics & Philosophy* 23, 213–308.
Löbner, Sebastian 2013. *Understanding Semantics*. 2nd edition. London, New York: Routledge.
Löbner, Sebastian 2015. *Semantik. Eine Einführung*. 2. Aufl. Berlin: De Gruyter (German version of Löbner 2013).
Mittwoch, Anita 1993. The relationship between *schon/already* and *noch/still*: A reply to Löbner. *Natural Language Semantics* 2, 71–82.
Palmer, Frank R. 2001. *Mood and Modality*. Cambridge: Cambridge University Press.
Schlücker, Barbara 2008. Warum *nicht bleiben* nicht *werden* ist: Ein Plädoyer gegen die Dualität von *werden* und *bleiben*. *Linguistische Berichte* 215, 345–371.

Christopher Kennedy
8 Ambiguity and vagueness: An overview

1   Interpretive uncertainty —— 236
2   Ambiguity —— 240
3   Vagueness —— 252
4   Conclusion —— 268
5   References —— 268

Abstract: Ambiguity and vagueness are two varieties of interpretive uncertainty which are often discussed together, but are distinct both in their essential features and in their significance for semantic theory and the philosophy of language. Ambiguity involves uncertainty about mappings between levels of representation with different structural characteristics, while vagueness involves uncertainty about the actual meanings of particular terms. This article examines ambiguity and vagueness in turn, providing a detailed picture of their empirical characteristics and the diagnostics for identifying them, and explaining their significance for theories of meaning. Although this article continues the tradition of discussing ambiguity and vagueness together, one of its goals is to emphasize the ways that these phenomena are distinct in their empirical properties, in the factors that give rise to them, and in the analytical tools that can be brought to bear on them.

1 Interpretive uncertainty

Most linguistic utterances display "interpretive uncertainty", in the sense that the mapping from an utterance to a meaning (Grice's 1957 "meaning$_{NN}$") appears (at least from the external perspective of a hearer or addressee) to be one-to-many rather than one-to-one. Whether the relation between utterances and meanings really is one-to-many is an open question, which has both semantic and philosophical significance, as I will outline below. What is clear, though, is that particular strings of phonemes, letters or manual signs used to make utterances are, more often than not, capable of conveying distinct meanings.

As a first step, it is important to identify which kinds of interpretive uncertainty (viewed as empirical phenomena) are of theoretical interest. Consider for example (1a-b), which manifest several different kinds of uncertainty.

Christopher Kennedy, Chicago, IL, USA

https://doi.org/10.1515/9783110626391-008

(1) a. Sterling's cousin is funny.
    b. Julian's brother is heavy.

One kind concerns the kinds of individuals that the English noun phrases *Sterling's cousin* and *Julian's brother* can be used to pick out: the former is compatible with Sterling's cousin being male or female and the latter is compatible with Julian's brother being older or younger than him. However, this sort of uncertainty merely reflects the fact that *cousin* and *brother* are INDETERMINATE with respect to sex and age, respectively: both terms have conditions of application that specify certain kinds of familial relationships, and *brother*, unlike *cousin*, also imposes conditions on the sex of the individuals it applies to, but beyond these constraints these terms do not discriminate between objects as a matter of meaning. (Indeterminacy is also sometimes referred to as "generality"; see Zwicky & Sadock 1975, 1984; Gillon 1990, 2004.)

That this is so can be seen from the fact that distinctions of this sort do not affect judgments of truth or falsity. For example, assuming that the antecedents of the conditionals in (2a–b) specify the minimal difference between the actual world and the counter-factual worlds under consideration, the fact that (2a) is false and (2b) is true shows that a change in sex, unlike a change in familial relationships, does not affect the truth of the application of *cousin*.

(2) Lily is Sterling's cousin....
    a. ...but if she were a boy, she wouldn't be Sterling's cousin anymore.
    b. ...but if her mother weren't Sterling's father's sister, she wouldn't be Sterling's cousin anymore.

Likewise, the hypothetical change in age in (3a) doesn't affect the truth of the application of *brother*, though the change in sex in (3b) now does make a difference.

(3) Sterling is Julian's brother...
    a. ...but if their ages were reversed, he wouldn't be Julian's brother anymore.
    b. ...but if he were a girl, he wouldn't be Julian's brother anymore.

Indeterminacy reflects the fact that the meaning of a word or phrase typically does not involve an exhaustive specification of the features of whatever falls under its extension; some features are left open, resulting in the sort of flexibility of application we see above. This is not to say that such features couldn't be specified: many languages contain cousin terms that do make distinctions based on sex (either through grammatical gender, as in Italian *cugino* 'cousin$_{masc}$' vs. *cugina* 'cousin$_{fem}$', or lexically, as in Norwegian *fetter* 'male cousin' vs. *kusine* 'female cousin'), and some contain male sibling terms that specify age (such as Mandarin *gēge* 'older brother' vs. *dìdi* 'younger brother'). Whether a particular distinction is indeterminate or not is thus somewhat arbitrary and language specific, and while it might be interesting to determine if there are cultural or historical explanations for the presence/absence of such distinctions in particular languages, the existence of indeterminacy in any single language is typically not a fact of particular significance for its semantic analysis.

A second type of uncertainty manifested by (1a) and (1b) is of much greater importance for semantic analysis, however, as it involves variability in the truth or satisfaction conditions that a particular bit of an utterance introduces into the meaning calculation. This kind of uncertainty is AMBIGUITY, which manifests itself as variation in truth conditions: one and the same utterance token can be judged true of one situation and false of another, or the other way around, depending on how it is interpreted. In (1a) and (1b), we see ambiguity in the different ways of understanding the contributions of *funny* and *heavy* to the truth conditions. (1a) can be construed either as a claim that Sterling's cousin has an ability to make people laugh ("funny ha-ha") or that she tends to display odd or unusual behavior ("funny strange"). Similarly, (1b) can be used to convey the information that Julian's brother has a relatively high degree of weight, or that he is somehow serious, ponderous, or full of gravitas. That these pairs of interpretations involve distinct truth conditions is shown by the fact that we can use the same term (or, more accurately, the same bits of phonology) to say something that is true and something that is false of the same state of affairs, as in (4) (Zwicky & Sadock 1975).

(4) Sterling's cousin used to make people laugh with everything she did, though she was never in any way strange or unusual. She was funny without being funny. Lately, however, she has started behaving oddly, and has lost much of her sense of humor. Now she's funny but not very funny.

Both examples also manifest an ambiguity in the nature of the relation that holds between the genitive-marked nominal in the possessive construction and the denotation of the whole possessive DP; cf. article 6 [Semantics: Noun Phrases and Verb Phrases] (Barker) *Possessives and relational nouns*. While the most salient relations are the familial ones expressed by the respective head nouns (*cousin of* and *brother of*), it is possible to understand these sentences as establishing different relations. For example, if Julian is one of several tutors working with a family of underachieving brothers, we could use (1b) as a way of saying something about the brother who has been assigned to Julian, without in any way implying that Julian himself stands in the *brother of* relation to anyone. (He could be an only child.)

Even after we settle on a particular set of conditions of application for the ambiguous terms in (1a) and (1b) (e.g. that we mean "funny ha-ha" by *funny* or are using *heavy* to describe an object's weight), a third type of uncertainty remains about precisely what properties these terms ascribe to the objects to which they are applied, and possibly about whether these terms can even be applied in the first place. This is VAGUENESS, and is of still greater significance for semantic theory, as it raises fundamental questions about the nature of meaning, about deduction and reasoning, and about knowledge of language.

Consider, an utterance of (1b) in a context in which we know that *heavy* is being used to characterize Julian's brother's weight. If we take the person who utters this sentence to be speaking truthfully, we may conclude that Julian's brother's weight is above some threshold. However, any conclusions about how heavy he is will depend on a range of other contextual factors, such as his age, his height, information about the individuals under discussion, the goals of the discussion, the interests of the discourse participants, and so forth, and even then will be rough at best. For example, if we know that Julian's brother is a 4-year old, and that we're talking about the children in his preschool class, we can conclude from an utterance of (1b) that his weight is somewhere above some threshold, but it would be extremely odd to follow up such an utterance by saying something like (5).

(5) Well, since that means he is at least 17.5 kg, we need to make sure that he is one of the carriers in the piggy-back race, rather than one of the riders.

(5) is odd because it presumes a specific cut-off point separating the heavy things from the non-heavy things (17.5 kg), but the kind of uncertainty involved in vagueness is precisely uncertainty about where the cut off is.

This can be further illustrated by a new context. Imagine that we are in a situation in which the relevant contextual factors are clear: Julian's brother is a 4-year old, we're talking about the children in his class, and we want to decide who should be the anchor on the tug-of-war team. In addition, we also know that Julian's brother weighs exactly 15.2 kg. Even with these details spelled out – in particular, even with our knowledge of Julian's brother's actual weight – we might still be uncertain as to whether (1b) is true: Julian's brother is a BORDERLINE CASE for truthful application of the predicate.

Borderline cases and uncertainty about the boundaries of a vague predicate's extension raise significant challenges for semantic theory. If we don't (and possibly can't) know exactly how much weight is required to put an object in the extension of *heavy* (in a particular context of use), even when we are aware of all of the potentially relevant facts, can we truly say that we know the meaning of the term? Do we have only incomplete knowledge of its meaning? If our language contained only a few predicates like *heavy*, we might be able to set them aside as interesting but ultimately insignificant puzzles. Vagueness is pervasive in natural language, however, showing up in all grammatical categories and across lexical fields, so understanding the principles underlying this type of uncertainty is of fundamental importance for semantic theory.

In the rest of this article, I will take a closer look at ambiguity and vagueness in turn, providing a more detailed picture of their empirical characteristics and the diagnostics for identifying them, and explaining their significance for theories of meaning. Although this article follows in a long tradition of discussing ambiguity and vagueness together, a goal of the article is to make it clear that these phenomena are distinct in their empirical properties, in the factors that give rise to them, and in the analytical tools that can be brought to bear on them. However, both present important challenges for semantics and philosophy of language, and in particular, for a compositional, truth conditional theory of meaning.

2 Ambiguity

2.1 Varieties of ambiguity

Ambiguity is associated with utterance chunks corresponding to all levels of linguistic analysis, from phonemes to discourses, and is characterized by the association of a single orthographic or phonological string with more than one meaning. Ambiguity can have significant consequences, for example if the wording of a legal document is such that it allows for interpretations that support distinct judgments. But it can also be employed for humorous effect, as in the following examples from the 1980s British comedy series *A Bit of Fry and Laurie* (created by Stephen Fry and Hugh Laurie).

(6) FRY: You have a daughter, I believe.
     LAURIE: Yeah, Henrietta.
     FRY: Did he? I'm sorry to hear that. That must've hurt.

(6) illustrates a case of PHONOLOGICAL AMBIGUITY, playing on the British comedians' pronunciations of the name *Henrietta* and the sentence *Henry ate her*. (7) makes use of the LEXICAL AMBIGUITY between the name *Nancy* and the British slang term *nancy*, which means weak or effeminate when used as an adjective.

(7) FRY: Something I've always been meaning to ask you: How did you manage to keep Nancy for so long?
LAURIE: I've never been nancy, John.

Sometimes the humor is unintended, as in the classified advertisement in (8) (Pinker 1994: 102).

(8) FOR SALE: Mixing bowl set designed to please a cook with round bottom for efficient beating.

This example illustrates a case of STRUCTURAL AMBIGUITY: whether the cook or the mixing bowl set has a round bottom (and whether the round bottom supports efficient beating of eggs, flour, etc. or efficient beating of the cook) depends on the structural relationships among the constituents of the sentence, in particular whether *with a round bottom* is parsed as a syntactic modifier of the nominal headed by *mixing bowl set* or the one headed by *cook*.

SCOPE AMBIGUITY is illustrated by (9), which can have either the interpretation in (9a) or the one in (9b), depending on whether the quantifier *every chef* is understood as taking scope above or below negation.

(9) Every chef wasn't a madman.
    a. No chef was a madman.
    b. Not every chef was a madman.

This example is actually part of a larger chunk of discourse in which it becomes clear that the intended interpretation is (9b):

(10) Every chef wasn't a madman. Most weren't, in fact. But many were and are, and the very best chefs, I knew, as I wrote my book at what my chef, Chef Pardus, would call production speed, were a little twisted in the dark spaces of their brain. (From Michael Ruhlman, *Soul of a Chef*, 133)

But the sentence could also be used to make the stronger claim paraphrased in (9a), indicating a real truth conditional distinction. Scope ambiguities involving quantifiers and other logical expressions (negation, other quantifiers, modals, intensional verbs, and so forth) have played a significant role in linguistic theory, since different methods of accounting for them involve different assumptions about the syntax-semantics interface (cf. article 6 [Semantics: Foundations, History and Methods] (Pagin & Westerståhl) *Compositionality*, article 1 [Semantics: Sentence and Information Structure] (Szabolcsi) *Scope and binding*, and article 6 [Semantics: Interfaces] (von Stechow) *Syntax and semantics*), a point I will come back to in more detail below.

2.2 Testing for ambiguity

Zwicky & Sadock (1975) provide comprehensive discussion of several different tests for ambiguity, some of which distinguish particular types of ambiguity from each other; here I will focus on the two tests that are most commonly employed in semantic argumentation. The first and most straightforward test is what Zwicky and Sadock call the TEST OF CONTRADICTION, which involves determining whether the same string of words or phonemes (modulo the addition/subtraction of negation) can be used to simultaneously affirm and deny a particular state of affairs. We saw this test illustrated with *funny* in (4) above; the fact that (11) is read as a true contradiction shows that a merely indeterminate term like *cousin* does not allow for this.

(11) Lily's mother is Sterling's father's sister. Since Lily is a girl, she is Sterling's cousin but not his cousin.

A second important test involves IDENTITY OF SENSE ANAPHORA, such as ellipsis, anaphoric *too*, pronominalization and so forth. As pointed out by Lakoff (1970), such relations impose a parallelism constraint that requires an anaphoric term and its antecedent to have the same meaning (cf. article 9 [Semantics: Sentence and Information Structure] (Reich) *Ellipsis*, for a discussion of parallelism in ellipsis), which has the effect of reducing the interpretation space of an ambiguous expression. For example, consider (12), which can have either of the truth-conditionally distinct interpretations paraphrased in (12a) and (12b), depending on whether the subject *the fish* is associated with the agent or theme argument of the verb *eat*.

(12) The fish is ready to eat.
    a. The fish is ready to eat a meal.
    b. The fish is ready to be eaten.

When (12) is the antecedent in an identity of sense anaphora construction, as in (13a–b), the resulting structure remains two-ways ambiguous; it does not become four-ways ambiguous: if the fish is ready to do some eating, then the chicken is too; if the fish is ready to be eaten, then the chicken is too.

(13) a. The fish is ready to eat, and the chicken is ready to eat too.
    b. The fish is ready to eat, but the chicken isn't.

That is, these sentences do not have understandings in which the fish is an agent and the chicken is a theme, or vice-versa.

This fact can be exploited to demonstrate ambiguity by constructing test examples in such a way that one of the expressions in the identity of sense relation is compatible only with one interpretation of the ambiguous term or structure. For example, since potatoes are not plausible agents of an eating event, the second conjunct of (14a) disambiguates the first conjunct towards the interpretation in (14b). In contrast, (14c) is somewhat odd, because children are typically taken to be agents of eating events, rather than themes, but the context of a meal promotes the theme- rather than agent-based interpretation of the first conjunct, creating a conflict. This conflict is even stronger in (14c), which strongly implies either agentive potatoes or partially-cooked children, giving the whole sentence a certain dark humour.

(14) a. The fish is ready to eat, but the potatoes are not.
  b. ?The fish is ready to eat, but the children are not.
  c. ??The potatoes are ready to eat, but the children are not.

Part of the humorous effect of (14c) is based on the fact that a sensible interpretation of the sentence necessitates a violation of the default parallelism of sense imposed by ellipsis, a parallism that would not be required if there weren't two senses to begin with. The use of such violations for rhetorical effect is referred to as SYLLEPSIS, or sometimes by the more general term ZEUGMA.

2.3 Ambiguity and semantic theory

Ambiguity has played a central role in the development of semantic theory by providing crucial data for both building and evaluating theories of lexical representation and semantic composition. Cases of ambiguity are often "analytical choice points" which can lead to very different conclusions depending on how the initial ambiguity is evaluated. For example, whether scope ambiguities are taken to be structural (reflecting different Logical Forms), lexical (reflecting optional senses, possibly derived via type-shifting), or compositional (reflecting indeterminacy in the application of composition rules) has consequences for the overall architecture of a theory of the syntax-semantics interface, as noted above.

Consider also the ambiguity of adjectival modification structures such as (15) (first discussed in detail by Bolinger 1967; see also Siegel 1976; McConnell-Ginet 1982; Cinque 1993; Larson 1998 and article 12 [this volume] (Demonte) *Adjectives*), which is ambiguous between the "intersective" reading paraphrased in (15a) and the "nonintersective" one paraphrased in (15b).

(15) Olga is a beautiful dancer.
   a. Olga is a dancer who is beautiful.
   b. Olga is a dancer who dances beautifully.

Siegel (1976) takes this to be a case of lexical ambiguity (in the adjective *beautiful*), and builds a theory of adjective meaning on top of this assumption. In contrast, Larson (1998) argues that the adjectives themselves are unambiguous, and shows how the different interpretations can be accommodated by hypothesizing that nouns (like verbs) introduce a Davidsonian event variable, and that the adjective can take either the noun's individual variable or its event variable as an argument. (The first option derives the interpretation in (15a); the second derives the one in (15b).)

In addition to playing an important methodological role in semantic theory, ambiguity has also been presented as a challenge for foundational assumptions of semantic theory. For example, Parsons (1973) develops an argument which aims to show that the existence of ambiguity in natural language provides a challenge for the hypothesis that sentence meaning involves truth conditions (see Saka 2007 for a more recent version of this argument). The challenge goes like this. Assume that a sentence S contains an ambiguous term whose different senses give rise to distinct truth conditions p and q (as in the case of (15)), such that (16a–b) hold.

(16) a. S is true if and only if p.
   b. S is true if and only if q.
   c. p if and only if q.

But (16a–b) mutually entail (16c), which is obviously incorrect, so one of our assumptions must be wrong; according to Parsons, the problematic assumption is the one that the meaning of S can be stated in terms of Tarskian truth definitions like (16a–b). In other words, the presence of ambiguity in natural language shows that sentence meaning is not truth conditional. Note that this argument extends to any theory in which truth conditions are a part of sentence meaning, as in mainstream semantic theory for example, where truth conditions are joined by presuppositions, implicatures, expressive meaning, context change potential and possibly other kinds of information. Even if we adopt this richer view of sentence meaning, it is still the case that truth conditions constitute both an analytical and methodological foundation, playing crucial roles in the way that we go about building hypotheses about semantic competence and constructing the data that we use to test them. Parson's challenge based on ambiguity is therefore an important one.

This sketch of the challenge is not quite complete, however, because it omits the crucial fact that an argument based on (16a–c) has weight only relative to specific assumptions about the grammatical principles that regulate the mapping between sound (or manual gestures or orthography, depending on the modality of communication) and meaning. (16) hides the fact that S is a syntactic object (something Parsons accepts), and as such needs to be mapped both to a meaning of the appropriate type via a finite set of recursively defined composition rules, and to a (modality-dependent) pronunciation. The fact that a particular pronunciation may be consistent with more than one meaning is a problem for a truth conditional view of meaning only if the mapping principles necessarily relate that pronunciation to a single syntactic object, which must then (somehow) be mapped onto distinct sets of truth conditions, giving us the situation in (16). If, on the other hand, the mapping principles allow for the possibility of relating the pronunciation to distinct syntactic objects, we end up with S in (16a) and S' in (16b), and the problem disappears.

Parsons acknowledges this in her discussion of lexical ambiguity when she says that "it may be that 'bank' (financial institution) and 'bank' (wall of a river channel) can be distinguished on the basis of a good syntax", and Saka (2007) does the same, but both are skeptical that the full range of ambiguity phenomena can be handled in this way. In order to make the skeptical case, however, one would need to address actual proposals about these relations within linguistic theory, and show that none provide a coherent basis for handling the challenge of uncertainty. While it is not possible to address all plausible linguistic analyses of these phenomena, a quick look at a few reasonably well-established approaches to them suggests that current linguistic theory can take us fairly far in meeting the challenge presented by ambiguity for truth conditional theories of meaning.

Let's begin with lexical and structural ambiguity. The latter is straightforward: the fact that syntactic representations (or well-formedness derivations/proofs, if we are working in a theory that eschews levels of representation) have hierarchical structure but phonological representations have only linear structure ensures that two structurally distinct representations may have the same pronunciation. This is the case in (17a–b), which are both pronounced /a b c/, assuming that syntactic precedence relations determine linear order of pronunciation.

(17) a.   b.

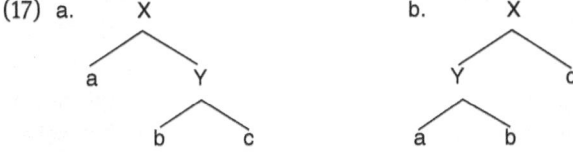

If we further assume a (conservative) set of composition rules whereby the denotation of any constituent α is a function of the denotations of its immediate subconstituents (its daughters), we end up with structural ambiguity: (17a) and (17b) can have different interpretations but the same pronunciations.

In fact, lexical ambiguity (homonymy) is handled in essentially the same way – in terms of representational properties that are obscured in the mapping to phonology – a point made by Gillon (1990). This fact is often obscured by a convenient notational shortcut, however: the use of orthographic units (written words) to represent terminal nodes in a syntactic representation. Because of this convention, a representation like (18) gives the impression that the first occurrence of *bank* and the second occurrence are the same objects.

(18)

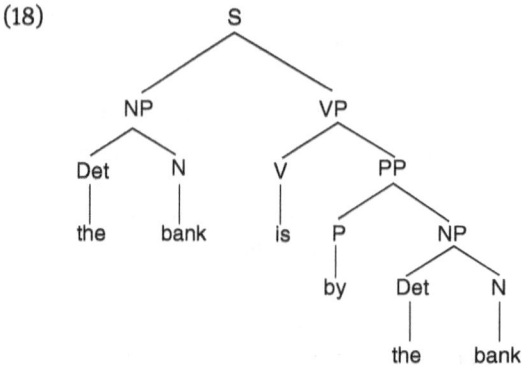

But this impression is incorrect. In fact, in most theories of syntax all nodes in a syntactic representation have the same basic formal properties: they are structured bundles of features. In particular, a syntactic object σ is at least a triple of the form $\langle P, S, D \rangle$ (depending on the theory, they may have more features), where P is a set of phonological features (the pronunciation of σ), S is a set of morphosyntactic features (category, case, number, etc.), and D is a set of semantic features: whatever is used to characterize denotations in the context of a broader theory of compositional interpretation. The exact properties of these features vary across framework and assumptions, but the overall architecture is the same. Crucially, nothing forbids a language from containing objects – either simple or complex – that have the same phonological features but distinct semantic (or syntactic) features. Such objects sound the same, but are formally distinct, and their use in syntactic structures that are otherwise identical entails that those structures are distinct syntactic objects, which may in turn be mapped onto distinct meanings. Some researchers, such as Gillon (1990), attempt to capture this fact through the use of indices ($bank_1$ vs. $bank_2$), though the indices themselves have no theoretical significance. They are merely notational devices that let us distinguish an object of the form ⟨P, S, D⟩ from one of the form ⟨P, S, D'⟩ without having to write much more than what is specified by P.

Polysemy is a harder problem; cf. article 6 [this volume] (Cann) *Sense relations* for additional discussion. The most bare-bones way of handling it is to bite the bullet and assume that polysemy has the same representational status as homonymy: polysemous terms involve syntactic objects that have identical phonological features but distinct semantic features, and so are formally distinct. This view is completely consistent with a broader theory of lexical organization that explains why e.g. (19a-b) are related in a way that (20a–b) are not.

(19) a. ⟨/run/, V, *manner of locomotion*⟩
     b. ⟨/run/, V, *compete for elected office*⟩

(20) a. ⟨/bank/, N, *financial institution*⟩
     b. ⟨/bank/, N, *wall of a river channel*⟩

However, there is a wide body of work in lexical semantics that has attempted to more directly capture the differences between polysemy and homonymy, typically in terms of semantic underspecification (see e.g. Pinkal 1999; this strategy can also be applied to representations larger than words, as explained in article 9 [this volume] (Egg) *Semantic underspecification*). On this view, a polysemous term may have disjunctive or incomplete semantic features, but in the course of putting together a syntactic representation a particular option must be selected, possibly via interactions with the semantic features of other terms. For example, Pustejovsky (1995) shows how the various senses of the verb *enjoy* in (21) are typically determined by semantic properties of its nominal argument, and develops a generative grammar of lexical semantic feature composition to account for these patterns.

(21) a. enjoy a martini. (*enjoy drinking it*)
     b. enjoy a cigarette. (*enjoy smoking it*)
     c. enjoy a recording of Britten's opera *Billy Budd*. (*enjoy listening to it*)
     d. enjoy a debate. (*enjoy participating in it or enjoy debating*)

Whether Pustejovsky's specific analysis is ultimately the best way of accounting for these facts remains to be determined (it could be the case that they involve coercion of the sort discussed below; see Pylkkänen & McElree 2006 for recent work on this); what is important for the current discussion is that it is the type of analysis that needs to be addressed in order to make the case that polysemy is a problem for truth conditional semantics, since it provides exactly the sort of representational basis for distinguishing sentences that involve distinct senses of polysemous terms, as well as empirical arguments for the representational status of that distinction.

Saka (2007) extends Parsons' argument by pointing to various sorts of "coercion" phenomena, such as deferred reference, metonymy, metaphor, type/token alternations, and so forth, which are not so clearly amenable to the type of representational analysis posited above for ambiguity and polysemy (cf. article 10 [this volume] (de Swart) *Mismatches and coercion* and article 11 [this volume] (Tyler & Takahashi) *Metaphors and metonymies*). For example, there is no reason to assume that the syntactic object pronounced *ham sandwich* in (22a) is a different lexical item (or is composed of different lexical items) from the one in (22b).

(22) a. This is the ham sandwich. (waitress holding up a ham sandwich)
     b. I am the ham sandwich. (raising my hand and beckoning to the waitress)

In fact, as both Nunberg (1995) and Ward (2004) argue, there is good reason to believe that the basic meaning of *ham sandwich* is preserved, since it can be straightforwardly targeted by discourse anaphora, as in (23).

(23) The ham sandwich seems to be enjoying it. (it = the ham sandwich)

This is particularly striking, considering that access to part of a meaning (which we might take deferred reference to involve, since *the ham sandwich* in (23) is actually being used to pick out an individual distinct from the sandwich) is generally bad. (24), for example, does not readily permit an interpretation in which *it* refers only to the ham, not to the whole sandwich (Postal 1969; Ward, Sproat & McKoon 1991).

(24) The ham sandwich didn't go down well because it was two years old.

However, even these facts can be accommodated by assuming with Ward and Nunberg that the relevant readings are derived by mapping the denotation of *ham sandwich* (or the verb, in Ward's case) to a new one of the right sort; formally, we can implement this by positing a type-shifting rule that maps properties to properties. The broader motivation for type-shifting rules as part of the compositional interpretation system is very well established (e.g., to account for the fact that the conjunction *and* can combine with categories of any type without having to posit a large set of lexical entries; see Partee & Rooth 1983 and article 8 [Semantics: Interfaces] (de Hoop) *Type shifting*). What is relevant for the current discussion is that they map meanings into new meanings, providing just the representational distinction we need to ensure that deferred reference can be handled by a truth conditional semantics. For example, if (25a) is the basic representation of *ham sandwich*, (25b) is the type-shifted representation, where f is a context-sensitive function mapping properties into properties.

(25) a. ⟨ham sandwich, *NP, ham sandwich*⟩
b. ⟨ham sandwich, *NP, f (ham sandwich)*⟩

This analysis explains why discourse anaphora is possible – the core meaning is still part of the representation – and also has no problem with examples like (26), where the shifted version of the nominal provides a "regular" restriction for the quantifier *every* in the usual way.

(26) a. Every ham sandwich is enjoying his meal.
b. for all x such that x is a f(ham sandwich), x is enjoying x's meal, f a contextually salient function from ham sandwiches to individuals. (the *eater-of* function)

Referential ambiguity does not pose a particular challenge, since it can be handled straightforwardly either by assuming a semantics with variables and assignment functions and a syntax in which syntactic features distinguish one variable from another (here indices do have theoretical significance; Heim & Kratzer 1998 provides a good overview of such a system), or by assuming a semantics without variables and letting sentences that contain anaphoric terms denote incomplete propositions (as in Jacobson 1999, 2000). On this latter view, sentences with anaphoric terms aren't actually assigned truth conditions, and two uses of e.g. *He is from Chicago* that are "about" different individuals will in fact have identical meanings: they denote a function from individuals to truth values that is true of an individual if it is from Chicago. So this sort of analysis bypasses the problem of interpretive uncertainty completely by denying that fixing the reference of pronouns is part of semantics.

In each of the cases discussed above, the key to responding to Parsons' challenge was to demonstrate that standard (or at least reasonable) assumptions about lexico-syntactic representation and composition support the view that observed variability in truth-conditions has a representational basis: in each case, the mappings from representations to meanings are one-to-one, but the mappings from representations (and meanings) to pronunciations are sometimes many-to-one. But what if standard assumptions fail to support such a view? In such a case, Parsons' challenge would reemerge, unless a representational distinction can be demonstrated.

One of the strongest cases of this sort comes from the work of Charles Travis, who discusses a particular form of truth conditional variability associated with color terms (see e.g., Travis 1985, 1994, 1997). The following passage illustrates the phenomenon:

> A story. Pia's Japanese maple is full of russet leaves. Believing that green is the colour of leaves, she paints them. Returning, she reports, 'That's better. The leaves are green now.' She speaks truth. A botanist friend then phones, seeking green leaves for a study of green-leaf chemistry. 'The leaves (on my tree) are green,' Pia says. 'You can have those.' But now Pia speaks falsehood. (Travis 1997: 89)

This scenario appears to show that distinct utterances of the words in (27), said in order to describe the same scenario (the relation between the leaves and a particular color), can be associated with distinct truth values.

(27) The leaves are green.

Following the line of reasoning initially advanced by Parsons, Travis concludes from this example that sentence meaning is not truth conditional; that instead, the semantic value of a sentence at most imposes some necessary conditions under which it may be true (as well as conditions under which it may be used), but those conditions need not be sufficient, and the content of the sentence does not define a function from contexts to truth.

Travis' skeptical conclusion is challenged by Kennedy & McNally (2010), however, who ask us to consider a modified version of the story of Pia and her leaves. Now she has a pile of painted leaves of varying shades of green (pile A) as well as a pile of naturally green leaves, also of varying shades (pile B). Pia's artist friend walks in and asks if she can have some green leaves for a project. Pia invites her to sort through the piles and take whichever leaves she wants. In sorting through the piles, the artist might utter any of the sentences in (28) in reference either to leaves from pile A or to leaves from pile B, as appropriate based on the way that they manifest green: the particular combination of hue, saturation, and brightness, extent of color, and so forth.

(28) a. These leaves are green.
　　 b. These leaves are greener than those.
　　 c. These leaves aren't as green as those.
　　 d. These leaves are less green than those.
　　 e. These leaves are not green enough.
　　 f. These leaves are too green.
　　 g. These leaves are completely green.

h. These leaves are perfectly green.
  i. These leaves are pretty/really green.
  j. These leaves are not so green.

What is important to observe is that for the artist, who is interested in the colors of the leaves in her composition, any of these sentences would in principle be felicitous. Furthermore, (28a) is true of all of the leaves – both the painted ones and the natural ones – provided they are "green enough". The only issue is how green they are, or maybe how much of each of them is green; why they are green (i.e. because they are naturally or artificially so) is irrelevant.

The situation is different for the botanist. She is perfectly justified in continuing to reject (the words in) (28a) as a false description of the painted leaves, while accepting it as true of the natural leaves. However, if these are her judgments about (28a), then none of the examples in (28b-i) are acceptable as descriptions of any of the leaves. That is, she cannot point to pile B (the naturally green leaves) and utter (28a) with the intended meaning (that the leaves are naturally green), and then strengthen or reiterate her point by pointing to pile A and uttering (28e) or (28j). Similarly, there is no way for her to use (28b) to justify her selection of the naturally green leaves over the painted ones, or (28c-d) to justify rejection of the latter, strictly on the basis of their biological properties. In short, once she starts using sentences that involve some notion of degree or comparison, the painted/natural distinction is out of the picture; all that is relevant is the relative degree of color.

What these facts show is that there is a semantic difference between occurrences of *green* that are used to distinguish between objects on the basis of *why* they are green (e.g., chlorophyll vs. paint) and instances that are used to distinguish between objects on the basis of *how* they are green (depth of hue, proximity to a prototype, extent of color, etc.). Each of (28b-j) involves the combination of the color adjective with a different element from the set of English degree morphemes, all of which require the adjective they combine with to be gradable. The fact that (28b-j) are acceptable when (28a) is true of both sorts of leaves shows that on this use, it is gradable; the fact that (28b-j) are unacceptable when (28a) is true only of the naturally green leaves (in a context in which both piles contain objects with the same range of objective color features) shows that, on this use, it is nongradable.

The gradable/nongradable distinction is a matter of meaning, typically cashed out as a distinction of semantic type (see Kennedy 1999 for discussion, and article 12 [this volume] (Demonte) *Adjectives*). It follows, then, that the two utterances of *green* in Travis' story about Pia and her painted leaves involve utterances of distinct terms with distinct meanings, and therefore the sentences in which they are uttered are distinct sentences which may have distinct conditions for truth. This example therefore poses no more of a challenge for truth conditional semantics than other cases of lexical ambiguity. It does, however, highlight the importance of a detailed and comprehensive linguistic analysis, since it shows that some cases of lexical ambiguity are revealed only through a close examination of the distribution and interpretation of the terms of interest in a variety of syntactic and morphological contexts.

3 Vagueness

3.1 The challenge of vagueness

It is generally accepted that the locus of vagueness in sentences like (29) is the predicate headed by the gradable adjective *expensive*: this sentence is vague because, intuitively, what it means to count as expensive is unclear.

(29) The coffee in Rome is expensive.

Sentences like (29) have three distinguishing characteristics, which have been the focus of much work on vagueness in semantics and the philosophy of language. The first is contextual variability in truth conditions: (29) could be judged true if asserted as part of a conversation about the cost of living in Rome vs. Naples (*In Rome, even the coffee is expensive!*), for example, but false in a discussion of the cost of living in Chicago vs. Rome (*The rents are high in Rome, but at least the coffee is not expensive!*). This kind of variability is of course not restricted to vague predicates – for example, the relational noun *citizen* introduces variability because it has an implicit argument (*citizen of x*) but it is not vague – though all vague predicates appear to display it.

The second feature of vagueness is the existence of borderline cases. For any context, in addition to the sets of objects that a predicate like *is expensive* is clearly true of and clearly false of, there is typically a third set of objects for which it is difficult or impossible to make these judgments. Just as it is easy to imagine contexts in which (29) is clearly true and contexts in which it is clearly false, it is also easy to imagine a context in which such a decision cannot be so easily made. Consider, for example, a visit to a coffee shop to buy a pound of coffee. The Mud Blend at $1.50/pound is clearly not expensive, and the Organic Kona at $20/pound is clearly expensive, but what about the Swell Start Blend at $9.25/pound? A natural response is "I'm not sure"; this is the essence of being a borderline case.

Finally, vague predicates give rise to the Sorites Paradox, illustrated in (30).

(30) *The Sorites Paradox.*
P1. A $5 cup of coffee is expensive. (for a cup of coffee)
P2. Any cup of coffee that costs 1 cent less than an expensive one is expensive. (for a cup of coffee)
C. Therefore, any free cup of coffee is expensive

The structure of the argument appears to be valid, and the premises appear to be true, but the conclusion is without a doubt false. Evidently, the problem lies somewhere in the inductive second premise; what is hard is figuring out exactly what goes wrong. And even if we do, we also need to explain both why it is so hard to detect the flaw and why we are so willing to accept it as valid in the first place.

These points are made forcefully by Fara (2000), who succinctly characterizes the challenges faced by any explanatorily adequate account of vagueness in the form of the following three questions:

(31) a. *The Semantic Question.*
If the inductive premise of a Sorites argument is false, then is its classical negation – the SHARP BOUNDARIES CLAIM that there is an adjacent pair in a sorites sequence such that one has the property named by the vague predicate and the other doesn't – true?
(i) If yes, how is this compatible with borderline cases?
(ii) If no, what revision of classical logic and semantics must be made to accommodate this fact?

b. *The Epistemological Question.*
If the inductive premise is false, why are we unable to say which of its instances fail, even in the presence of (what we think is) complete knowledge of the facts relevant to judgments about the predicate?

c. *The Psychological Question.*
If the inductive premise is false, why are we so inclined to accept it in the first place? What makes vague predicates tolerant in the relevant way? Why do they seem "boundaryless"?

These questions provide a set of evaluation criteria for theories of vagueness: one theory can be preferred over another to the extent that it provides satisfactory answers to these questions. Of particular importance is answering the Epistemological and Psychological Questions: it is fairly straightforward to construct a theory that answers the Semantic Question, but many such theories fail to say anything about the other two, and so fail as explanatory theories of vagueness.

In particular, this is the case with most linguistic analyses of the class of vague predicates most commonly discussed by semanticists: gradable adjectives like *expensive*. A fruitful and rich line of research, primarily on comparatives, superlatives and other complex expressions of quantity and degree, analyzes the meaning of gradable adjectives as relations between objects and degrees (see e.g., Seuren 1973; Cresswell 1977; von Stechow 1984; Heim 2000; Bierwisch 1989; Schwarzschild & Wilkinson 2002; Kennedy 1999, 2001; Kennedy & McNally 2005; Rotstein & Winter 2004; and see article 13 [this volume] (Beck) *Comparison constructions*). The adjective *expensive*, on this view, denotes the relation in (32), which is true of an object x and a degree (of cost) d just in case the cost of x is at least as great as d.

(32) $[[expensive]] = \lambda d \lambda x.\text{COST}(x) \geq d$

When it comes to analyzing the positive (unmarked) form of a gradable predicate, which is what we see in examples like (29) and on which a Sorites argument is based (i.e., the vague form), the usual strategy is to hypothesize that the degree argument is saturated by a contextually determined STANDARD OF COMPARISON, which represents the "cut off point" between the positive and negative extensions of the predicate, possibly relativized to a COMPARISON CLASS of objects deemed somehow similar to the target of predication. (For discussion of standards of comparison and comparison classes, see Wheeler 1972; Rips & Turnbull 1980; Klein 1980; Ludlow 1989; Bierwisch 1989; Kamp & Partee 1995; Fara 2000; Kennedy 2007.) The standard of comparison is usually treated as a free variable over degrees whose value is determined by a special assignment function (see Barker 2002 for an explicit statement of this idea), though it is sometimes linked to a particular value, such as the average degree to which the objects in the comparison class manifest the relevant gradable property (as in e.g., Bartsch & Vennemann 1972).

This type of approach clearly provides an explanation for the truth conditional variability of vague predicates. (29) is true just in case the cost of the coffee in Rome exceeds the value of the standard of comparison, whatever that is, and false if it is exceeded by the standard. Since different contexts of utterance will invoke different standards (e.g., one based on the price of coffee in Italian cities vs. one based on the price of coffee in Rome and Chicago), the truth of (29) may shift. For the very same reason, this approach provides a partial answer to Fara's Semantic Question: characterizing the meaning of (the positive form of) *expensive* in terms of a relation between two degrees amounts to accepting the sharp boundaries claim, since the truth or falsity of a sentence like (29) is simply a function of the relation between these two degrees.

This looks like a good result at first: the Sorites Paradox disappears, because the second premise is guaranteed to be false. However, we have no obvious account for our judgments about borderline cases, and certainly no explanation for why we might have thought the second premise to be true. That is, we have no answers to the borderline case subpart of the Semantic Question, nor do we have answers to the Epistemological or Psychological Questions. We might appeal to some sort of indeterminacy in, or incomplete knowledge of, the assignment function involved in fixing standards of comparison in order to gain some traction on the Epistemological Question and the status of borderline cases, but this move will not help us with the Psychological Question. If knowing the meaning of a vague predicate means knowing that it requires its argument to have a degree of a scalar property whose value exceeds a standard that gets *fixed by the context*, then all other things being equal, we ought to be willing to reject the inductive premise of the Sorites Paradox. We should know that at some point along the line this relation must fail to hold, even if we don't know exactly where it is.

This is not to say that something like the traditional linguistic analysis of gradable predicates couldn't be augmented or supplemented with some other principles that would allow for an answer to all of Fara's questions. Such principles could be semantic, but they could also be pragmatic or even cognitive; the analyses I will discuss in more detail below are differentiated roughly along these lines. The importance of taking this extra step must be emphasized, however. Semantic theories (such as the approach to gradable predicates outlined above) are typically designed in such a way that lexical and compositional meaning together result in expressions that support clear judgments of truth or falsity, possibly in a context dependent way, given a certain set of facts. The Epistemological and Psychological Questions highlight the fact that even when a set of crucial facts is known – the actual distribution of costs of coffee in various cities, for example, or even just the knowledge that there is a distribution of costs – judgments of truth and falsity can remain unclear (with borderline cases) or can even be wrong (the inductive premise of the Sorites, if the sharp boundaries claim is in fact correct). But this then calls into question the initial step of characterizing meanings in terms of truth functions: if we want to maintain this aspect of semantic theory, then we need to have answers to all three questions about vagueness.

Before moving to a discussion of particular approaches to vagueness, I also want to point out that vagueness is by no means restricted to gradable adjectives, even though the majority of examples discussed in both the linguistic and philosophical literature involve expressions from this class. Using the three characteristics of truth conditional variability, borderline cases, and the Sorites Paradox as a guide, we can find vague terms in all grammatical classes: nouns (like *heap*, which gives the Sorites Paradox its name), verbs (such as *like*, or more significantly, *know*), determiners (such as *many* and *few*), prepositions (such as *near*) and even locative adverbials, as in the Fry and Laurie dialogue in (33).

(33) FRY: There are six million people out there....
    LAURIE: Really? What do they want?

Here the humor of Laurie's response comes from the vagueness of *out there*: whether it extends to cover a broad region beyond the location of utterance (Fry's intention) or whether it picks out a more local region (Laurie's understanding). Vagueness is thus pervasive, and its implications for the analysis of linguistic meaning extend to all parts of the lexicon.

3.2 Approaches to vagueness

It is impossible to summarize all analysis of vagueness in the literature, so I will focus here on an overview of four major approaches, based on supervaluations, epistemic uncertainty, contextualism, and interest relativity. For a larger survey of approaches, see Williamson (1994); Keefe & Smith (1997); and Fara & Williamson (2002).

3.2.1 Supervaluations

Let's return to one of the fundamental properties of vague predicates: the existence of borderline cases. (34a) is clearly true; (34b) is clearly false; (34c) is (at least potentially) borderline.

(34) a. Mercury is close to the sun.
    b. Pluto is close to the sun.
    c. The earth is close to the sun.

However, even if we are uncertain about the truth of (34c), we seem to have clear intuitions about (35a-b): the first is a logical truth, and the second is a contradiction.

(35) a. The earth is or isn't close to the sun.
    b. The earth is and isn't close to the sun.

This is not particularly surprising, as these sentences are instances of (36a-b):

(36) a. $p \vee \neg p$
 b. $p \wedge \neg p$

As noted by Fine (1975), these judgments show that logical relations (such as the Law of the Excluded Middle in (36a)) can hold between sentences which do not themselves have clear truth values in a particular context of utterance. Fine accepts the position that sentences involving borderline cases, such as (34c), can fail to have truth values in particular contexts (this is what it means to be a borderline case), and accounts for judgments like (35a) by basing truth valuations for propositions built out of logical connectives not on facts about specific contexts of evaluation, but rather on a space of interpretations in which all "gaps" in truth values have been filled. In other words, the truth of examples like (35a-b) is based on SUPERVALUATIONS (van Fraassen 1968, 1969) rather than simple valuations.

The crucial components of Fine's theory are stated in (37)–(39); a similar set of proposals (and a more comprehensive linguistic analysis) can be found in Kamp (1975) and especially Klein (1980).

(37) *Specification space*
A partially ordered set of points corresponding to different ways of specifying the predicates in the language; at each point, every proposition is assigned true, false or nothing according to an "intuitive" valuation. This valuation must obey certain crucial constraints, such as Fine's *Penumbral Connections* which ensure e.g., that if x is taller than y, it can never be the case that *x is tall* is false while *y is tall* is true (cf. the *Consistency Postulate* of Klein 1980).

(38) *Completability*
Any point can be extended to a point at which every proposition is assigned a truth value, subject to the following constraints:
a. FIDELITY: Truth values at complete points are 1 or 0.
b. STABILITY: Definite truth values are preserved under extension.

(39) *Supertruth*
A proposition is supertrue (or superfalse) at a partial specification iff it is true (false) at all complete extensions.

According to this approach, the reason that we have clear intuitions about (35a) and (35b) is because for any ways of making things more precise, we're always going to end up with a situation where the former holds for any proposition and the latter fails to hold, regardless of whether the proposition has a truth value at the beginning. In particular, given (38), (35a) is supertrue and (35b) is superfalse.

This theory provides an answer to Fara's Semantic Question about vagueness. According to this theory, any complete and admissible specification will entail a sharp boundary between the things that a vague predicate is true and false of. This renders inductive statements like the second premise of (40) superfalse, even when the argument as a whole is evaluated relative to a valuation that does not assign truth values to some propositions of the form *x is heavy*, i.e., one that allows for borderline cases.

(40) a. A 100 kilogram stone is heavy.
b. Any stone that weighs 1 gram less than a heavy one is heavy.
c. #A 1 gram stone is heavy.

The supervaluationist account thus gives up bivalence (the position that all propositions are either true or false relative to particular assignments of semantic values), but still manages to retain important generalizations from classical logic (such as the Law of the Excluded Middle) and assign a definitive value of FALSE to the inductive premise of the Sorites through the concept of supertruth.

However, although supervaluation accounts address the semantic question, on their own they have little to say about the Epistemological and Psychological Questions, as pointed out by Fara (2000). Fine (1975) attempts to answer the former by arguing that the extension boundaries for vague predicates are both arbitrary and infinitely variable. We are unable to identify a cutoff point, according to Fine, because it could in principle be in an infinite number of different places, if we allow an infinite domain (though it must always respect "admissibility"). There need be no determinate fact about where it is; and in particular, there need be no *linguistic* fact (one rooted in our knowledge of meaning) about where it is.

A number of objections can be raised to Fine's response to the Epistemological Question. (For example, it is is not clear that the boundaries for a vague predicate are entirely arbitrary: intuitively, an object counts as *expensive* or *heavy* only if it has an appropriately "high" degree of the relevant property.) But even if it is accepted, the Psychological Question still remains unanswered. If knowing the meaning of the universal statement in (40b) means knowing that it invokes supertruth, and if knowing the meaning of a vague predicate means knowing how it could be made precise (as claimed in Fine 1975: 277), then it is unclear why we are unwilling to assign a judgment of false when we are confronted with such statements.

Finally, supervaluationist accounts have been criticized for not even providing a satisfactory answer to the Semantic Question. The problem is that even though a supervaluation analysis predicts the existence of borderline cases by allowing for incomplete models, in any particular incomplete model, the boundary between the things that a vague predicate is definitely true of and those things for which it is indeterminate is crisp. But our judgments about "borderline borderlines" are no more clear than our judgments about "central borderlines", suggesting that the boundaries aren't so crisp after all. If we now need to invoke some other mechanism to explain such cases of HIGHER ORDER VAGUENESS, then we can legitimately ask whether supervaluations provide the right starting point for the core cases.

3.2.2 Epistemic uncertainty

The epistemic analysis of vagueness, developed most extensively in the work of Timothy Williamson (1992, 1994, 1997), starts from the assumption that vague predicates (and in fact all predicates in language) sharply define a positive and negative extension: there are no extension gaps, and there is no denial of bivalence, as in supervaluation accounts. Vagueness arises because the exact boundaries of these sets are not known; in fact, they are *unknowable*. Vagueness thus reflects an underlying ignorance about a fundamental feature of meaning: the precise factors that determine the extension of a predicate.

It should be clear that this approach provides a straightforward answer to the first part of the Semantic Question: It begins from an assumption of sharp boundaries, so the second premise of the Sorites is false. In order to see how it handles borderline cases and the Epistemological and Psychological Questions, we need to take a closer look at its answer to the core question of why we are ignorant about extension boundaries. Why can't we figure out what the sharp boundaries of a vague predicate are, and in so doing eliminate borderline cases and identify where the second premise of the Sorites Paradox fails?

Williamson's response comes in several parts. First, he assumes that meaning supervenes on use; as such, a difference in meaning entails a difference in use, but not vice-versa. Second, he points out that the meanings of some terms may be stabilized by natural divisions (cf. Putnam's 1975 distinction between H_2O and XYZ), while the meanings of others (the vague ones) cannot be so stabilized: a slight shift in our disposition to say that the earth is close to the sun would slightly shift the meaning of *close to the sun*. The boundary is sharp, but not fixed. But this in turn means that an object around the borderline of a vague predicate *P* could easily have been (or not been) *P* had the facts (in particular, the linguistic facts) been slightly different – different in ways that are too complex for us to fully catalogue, let alone compute. Given this instability, we can never really know about a borderline case whether it is or is not P.

This last point leads to the principle in (41), which is another way of saying that vague knowledge requires a margin for error.

(41) *The Margin for Error Principle*

> For a given way of measuring differences in measurements relevant to the application of property P, there will be a small but non-zero constant c such that if x and y differ in those measurements by less than c and x is known to be P, then y is known to be P.

The upshot of this reasoning is that it is impossible to know whether x *is* P is true or false when x and y differ by less than c. That's why we fail to reject the second premise of the Sorites, and also why "big" changes make a difference. (If we replace *1 cent* with *1 dollar* in (30), or *1 gram* with *10 kilograms* in (40), the paradox disappears.)

There are a number of challenges to this account, most of which focus on the central hypothesis that we can be ignorant about core aspects of meaning and still somehow manage to have knowledge of meaning at all. Williamson (1992) lists these challenges and provides responses to them; here I focus on the question of whether this theory is adequate as an account of vagueness. According to Fara (2000), it is not, because although it addresses the Semantic and Epistemological Questions, it does not address the Psychological one. In particular, there is no account of why we don't have the following reaction to the inductive premise: "That's false! I don't know where the shift from P to $\neg P$ is, so there are cases that I'm not willing to make a decision about, but I know it's in there somewhere, so the premise must be false."

Williamson (1997) suggests the answer has to do with the relation between imagination and experience. The argument runs as follows:

(42) i. It is impossible to gain information through imagination that cannot be gained through experience.
 ii. It is impossible to recognize the experience of the boundary transition in a sorites sequence because the transition lacks a distinctive appearance.
 iii. Therefore, it is impossible to imagine the transition.

This failure of imagination then makes it impossible to reject the inductive premise, since doing so precisely requires imagination of the crucial boundary transition. However, according to Fara, this response doesn't help us with the trickier question of why we *believe* of every pair in a sorites sequence that the boundary is NOT there. In order to answer the psychological question, she says, we need an account that is more directly *psychological*.

We will examine two such accounts in the next section, but before moving to this discussion, I want to point out a more purely empirical problem for the epistemic analysis of vagueness, which comes from the phenomenon of CRISP JUDGMENTS, discussed in Kennedy (2007). For an illustration of the phenomenon, consider a context in which we are deciding who should review various papers for a semantics journal. Our two reviewers are Professors Jones and Smith. We are considering pairs of papers, which are similar in content but distinguished by their length, as described in (43).

(43) SCENARIO A: a 15-page paper and a 25-page paper
SCENARIO B: a 25-page paper and a 40-page paper
SCENARIO C: a 24-page paper and a 25-page paper

In scenarios A and B, we could felicitously use (44) to issue instructions about which reviewer should get which paper.

(44) Let Jones review the long paper and let Smith review the short one.

In each scenario, *the long paper* refers to the longer of the two papers and *the short paper* refers to the shorter of the two. Focusing on the former case (the latter is the same), the existence and uniqueness presuppositions of the definite description require that there be one and only one object in each scenario that satisfies the predicate *long* (since both satisfy *paper*); this means that a length of 25 pages counts as long in scenario A but does not count as long in scenario B. That this is so is not surprising given what we already know about the context-dependence of standards of comparison: in this kind of example, the presuppositions of the definite determiner cause us to accommodate a standard that makes *long* uniquely true of one of a pair of objects of different lengths.

What is surprising is that (44) cannot be felicitously used in scenario C, where the length difference between the two papers is small; here only a variant using the comparative form of the adjective (*longer*) is acceptable (the comparative form is also acceptable in scenarios A and B, of course):

(45) Let Jones review the longer paper and let Smith review the shorter one.

The contrast between (44) and (45) in scenario C is important because it shows that even under pressure from the presuppositions of the definite determiner, we cannot accommodate a standard of comparison for *long* that makes it true of a 25-page paper and false of a 24-page paper: we cannot use the positive form of the adjective to make what Kennedy (2007) calls "crisp judgments" to distinguish between a pair of objects that differ in length by only a small degree. This kind of judgment is precisely analogous to the kind of judgment that would be involved in rejecting the inductive premise of the Sorites, but there is a crucial difference: in this case, we know exactly where the cutoff point for *long* would have to be, namely somewhere between 24 and 25 pages in length. The epistemic account of vagueness provides no account of this fact (nor does an unaugmented supervaluationist account, since it too needs to allow for contextual shifting of standards of comparison). If the impossibility of crisp judgments in examples like these involving definite descriptions and our judgments about the second premise of the Sorites Paradox are instances of the same basic phenomenon, then the failure of the epistemic account of vagueness to explain the former raises questions about its applicability to the latter.

3.2.3 Contextualism and interest relativity

Raffman (1996) observes three facts about vague predicates and Sorites sequences. First, as we have already discussed, vague predicates have context dependent extensions. Second, when presented with a sorites sequence based on a vague predicate P, a competent speaker will at some point stop (or start, depending on direction) judging P to be true of objects in the sequence. Third, even if we fix the (external) context, the shift can vary from speaker to speaker and from run to run. This is also a part of competence with P.

These observations lead Raffman (1994, 1996) to a different perspective on the problem of vagueness: reconciling tolerance (insensitivity to marginal changes) with categorization (the difference between being red and orange, tall and not tall, etc.). She frames the question in the following way: how can we simultaneously explain the fact that a competent speaker seems to be able to apply incompatible predicates (e.g., *red* vs. *orange*; *tall* vs. *not tall*) to marginally different (adjacent) items in the sequence and the fact that people are unwilling to reject the inductive premise of the Paradox?

Her answer involves recognizing the fact that evaluation of a sorites sequence triggers a context shift, which in turn triggers a shift in the extension of the predicate in such a way as to ensure that incompatible predicates are never applied to adjacent pairs, and to make (what looks like) a sequence of inductive premises all true. (For similar approaches, see Kamp 1981; Bosch 1983; Soames 1999.) This gives the illusion of validity, but since there is an extension shift, the predicate at the end of the series is not the same as the one at the beginning, so the argument is invalid.

There are three pieces to her account. The first comes from work in cognitive psychology, which distinguishes between two kinds of judgments involved in a sorites sequence. The first is categorization, which involves judgments of similarity to a prototype/standard; the second is discrimination, which involves judgments of sameness/difference between pairs. Singular judgments about items involve categorization, and it is relative to such judgments that a cutoff point is established. Discrimination, on the other hand, doesn't care where cutoff points fall, but it imposes a different kind of constraint: adjacent pairs must be categorized in the same way (Tversky & Kahneman 1974).

At first glance, it appears that the categorization/discrimination distinction just restates the problem of vagueness in different terms: if for any run of a sorites sequence, a competent speaker will at some point make a category shift, how do we reconcile such shifts with the fact that we resist discrimination between adjacent pairs? Note that the problem is not the fact that a speaker might eventually say of an object o_i in a sorites sequence based on P that it is not P, even if she judged o_{i+1} to be P, because this is a singular judgment about o_i. The problem is that given the pair $\langle o_i, o_{i+1} \rangle$, the speaker will refuse to treat them differently. This is what underlies judgments about the inductive premise of the Sorites Paradox and possibly the crisp judgment effects discussed above as well, though this is less clear (see below).

The second part of Raffman's proposal is designed to address this problem, by positing that a category shift necessarily involves a change in perspective such that the new category instantaneously absorbs the preceding objects in the sequence. Such BACKWARDS SPREAD is the result of entering a new psychological state, a Gestalt shift that triggers a move from one 'category anchor' or prototype to another, e.g., from the influence of the *red* anchor to the influence of the *orange* one. This gives rise to the apparent boundlessness of vague predicates: a shift in category triggers a shift in the border away from the edge, giving the impression that it never was there in the first place.

And in fact, as far as the semantics is concerned, when it comes to making judgments about pairs of objects, it never is. This is the third part of the analysis, which makes crucial appeal to the context dependence of vague predicates. Raffman proposes that the meaning of a vague predicate P is determined by two contextual factors. The EXTERNAL CONTEXT includes discourse factors that fix domain, comparison class, dimension, etc. of P. The INTERNAL CONTEXT includes the properties of an individual's psychological state that determine dispositions to make judgments of P relative to some external context. Crucially, a category shift causes a change in internal context e.g., (from a state in which the *red* anchor dominates to one in which the *orange* anchor does), which in turn results in a change in the extension of the predicate in the way described above, resulting in backwards spread.

Taken together, these assumptions provide answers to each of Fara's questions. The answer to the Semantic Question is clearly positive, since the commitment to category shifts involves a commitment to the position that a vague predicate can be true of one member of an adjacent pair in a sorites sequence o_i and false of o_{i+1}. The reason we cannot say which $\langle o_i, o_{i+1}\rangle$ has this property, however, is that the act of judging o_i to be not P (or P) causes a shift in contextual meaning of P to P', which, given backwards spread, treats o_i and o_{i+1} the same. This answer to the Epistemological Question also underlies the answer to the Psychological Question: even though the inductive premise of the Sorites Paradox is false for any fixed meaning of a vague predicate, we think that it is true because it is possible to construct a sequence of true statements that look like (instantiations of) the inductive premise, but which in fact do not represent valid reasoning because they involve different contextual valuations of the vague predicate. For example, if we are considering a sequence of 100 color patches $\{p_1, p_2, \ldots p_{100}\}$ ranging from 'pure' red to 'pure' orange, such that a category shift occurs upon encountering patch p_{47}, the successive conditional statements in (46a) and (46c) work out to be true thanks to backwards spread (because their subconstituents are both true and both false in their contexts of evaluation, respectively), even though *red* means something different in each case.

(46) a. If p_{45} is red, then p_{46} is red.
$p_{45}, p_{46} \in [[red]]^c$
TRUE → TRUE ⊨ TRUE

b. SHIFT at p_{47}: change from context c to context c'

c. If p_{46} is red, then p_{47} is red.
$p_{46}, p_{47} \notin [[red]]^{c'}$
FALSE → FALSE ⊨TRUE

A variant of the contextualist analysis is provided by Fara (2000). Like the contextualist, Fara assumes that there is a fixed point (a 'standard') in any context that distinguishes the objects that a vague predicate is true of from those which it is false of, And like the contextualist, Fara's analysis entails that adjacent elements in a sorites sequence are always treated in the same way, an effect that she describes in terms of the constraint in (47).

(47) *Similarity Constraint.*
Whatever standard is in use for a vague expression, anything that is saliently similar, in the relevant respect, to something that meets the standard itself meets the standard; anything saliently similar to something that fails to meet the standard itself fails to meet the standard.

With (47) in hand, Fara provides answers to the Epistemological and Psychological Questions that are also quite similar to those provided in a contextualist analysis. We are unable to pinpoint the boundary between objects that a vague predicate is true and false of because in evaluating the predicate for any adjacent pair of objects in a sorites sequence, we raise the similarity of the pair relative to the property that generates the sequence to salience, thereby rendering it true (or false) of both of the objects we are considering. Since this further entails that any instance of the universal premise of the Sorites Paradox (expressed as a conditional statement of the sort we saw in (46)) is true, it is no surprise that we are unwilling to judge the universal premise false.

Where Fara's account crucially differs from the contextualist approach is in the way that the Similarity Constraint is derived. In a Raffman-style contextualist account, (47) is a consequence of backward spread, which reflects a change in the content of a vague predicate at the moment of category shift. In contrast, the content of a vague predicate remains constant in Fara's account, but its extension can shift in a way that derives the Similarity Constraint. Specifically, Fara argues that vague predicates denote INTEREST RELATIVE properties, of the following sort: for any vague scalar predicate *P*, an object falls in its the positive extension of *P* just in case it has a degree of the scalar concept that *P* encodes that is *significant* given our interests (see also Boguslawski 1975). Interest relativity allows for shifts in the extension of a vague predicate without a corresponding shift in its content: whether an object counts as red or not might change as the interests of the individual evaluating the predicate changes, but the denotation of the predicate is the fixed property of having a significant degree of redness.

This proposal derives the Similarity Constraint in the following way. Among our interests is a standing interest in efficiency, which has the consequence that whenever two objects are saliently similar with respect to a vague scalar predicate and they are being actively considered, the cost of discriminating between them typically outweighs the benefit. As a result, they count as 'the same for present purposes', and one will have a degree of the relevant property that is significant relative to an evaluator's interests if and only if the other does. This result is the key to understanding how Fara reconciles her 'sharp boundaries' answer to the Semantic Question with the apparent 'shiftiness' entailed by her answer to the Epistemological and Psychological Questions. In any context, there is a pair of objects in a sorites sequence o_i

and o_{i+1} such that the predicate on which the sequence is based is true of one and false of the other. However, any attempt to evaluate the predicate for this particular pair will render them saliently similar, which, given interest relativity, will cause the extension of the predicate to shift in a way that ensures that they are evaluated in the same way. In Fara's words: "the boundary between the possessors and the lackers in a sorites series is not sharp in the sense that we can never bring it into focus; any attempt to bring it into focus causes it to shift somewhere else." (Fara 2000: 75–76)

One of the reasons that the contextualist and interest relative analyses provide compelling answers to the Psychological Question is that they are inherently psychological: the former in the role that psychological state plays in fixing context sensitive denotations; the latter in the role played by interest relativity. Moreover, in providing an explanation for judgments about pairs of objects, these analyses can support an explanation of the 'crisp judgment' effects discussed in the previous section, provided they can be linked to a semantics that appropriately distinguishes the positive and comparative forms of a scalar predicate. However, the very aspects of these analyses that are central to their successes also raise fundamental problems that question their ultimate status as comprehensive accounts of vagueness, according to Stanley (2003).

Focusing first on the contextualist analysis, Stanley claims that it makes incorrect predictions about versions of the Sorites that involve sequential conditionals and ellipsis. Stanley takes the contextualist to be committed to a view in which vague predicates are a type of indexical expression. Indexicals, he observes, have the property of remaining invariant under ellipsis: (48b), for example, cannot be used to convey the information expressed by (48a).

(48) a. Kim voted for that$_A$ candidate because Lee voted for that$_B$ candidate.
 b. Kim voted for that$_A$ candidate because Lee did ~~vote for that$_B$ candidate~~.

Given this, Stanley argues that if the contextualist account of vagueness entails that vague predicates are indexicals, then our judgments about sequences of conditionals like (46) (keeping the context the same) should change when the predicates are elided. Specifically, since ellipsis requires indexical identity, it must be the case that the elided occurrences of *red* in (49) be assigned the same valuation as their antecedents, i.e. that $[[red]]^c = [[red]]^{c'}$.

(49) a. If p_{45} is red, then p_{46} is red too.
 $p_{45}, p_{46} \in [[red]]^c$
 TRUE → TRUE |= TRUE

 b. shift at p_{47}: change from context c to context c'

c. If p_{46} is ~~red~~, then p_{47} is ~~red~~ too.
p_{46}, ∈ $[[red]]^{c'}$; $p_{47} \notin [[red]]^{c'}$
TRUE → FALSE |= FALSE

But this is either in conflict with backwards spread, in which case ellipsis should be impossible, or it entails that (49c) should be judged false while (49a) is judged true. Neither of these predictions are borne out: the judgments about (49) are in all relevant respects identical to those about (46). Raffman (2005) responds to this criticism by rejecting the view that the contextualist account necessarily treats vague predicates as indexicals, and suggests that the kind of 'shiftability' of vague predicates under ellipsis that is necessary to make the account work is analogous to what we see with comparison classes in examples like (50a), which has the meaning paraphrased in (50b) (Klein 1980).

(50) a. That elephant is large and that flea is too.
b. That elephant is large for an elephant and that flea is large for a flea.

This is probably not the best analogy, however: accounts of comparison class shift in examples like (50a) rely crucially on the presence of a binding relation between the subject and a component of the meaning of the predicate (see e.g., Ludlow 1989; Kennedy 2007), subsuming such cases under a general analysis of 'sloppy identity' in ellipsis. If a binding relation of this sort were at work in (49), the prediction would be that the predicate in the consequent of (49a) and the antecedent of (49b) should be valued in exactly the same way (since the subjects are the same), which, all else being equal, would result in exactly the problematic judgments about the truth and falsity of the two conditionals that Stanley discusses. In the absence of an alternative contextualist account of how vague predicates should behave in ellipsis, then, Stanley's objection remains in force.

This objection does not present a problem for Fara's analysis, which assumes that vague predicates have fixed denotations. However, the crucial hypothesis that these denotations are interest relative comes with its own problems, according to Stanley. In particular, he argues that this position leads to the implication that the meaning of a vague predicate is always relativized to some agent, namely the entity relative to whom significance is assessed. But this implication is inconsistent with the fact that we can have beliefs about the truth or falsity of a sentence like (51) without having beliefs about any agent relative to whom Mt. Everest's height is supposed to be significant.

(51) Mt. Everest is tall.

Moreover, the truth of the proposition conveyed by an utterance of (51) by a particular individual can remain constant even in hypothetical worlds in which that individual doesn't exist, something that would seem to be impossible if the truth of proposition has something to do with the utterer's interests. Fara (2008) rejects Stanley's criticism on the grounds that it presumes that an "agent of interest" is a constituent of the proposition expressed by (51), something that is not the case given her particular assumptions about the compositional semantics of the vague scalar predicates she focuses on, which builds on the decompositional syntax and semantics of Kennedy (1999, 2007) (see also Bartsch & Venneman 1972). However, to the extent that her analysis creates entailments about the existence of individuals with the relevant interests, it is not clear that Stanley's criticisms can be so easily set aside.

4 Conclusion

Ambiguity and vagueness are two forms of interpretive uncertainty, and as such, are often discussed in tandem. They are fundamentally different in their essential features, however, and in their significance for semantic theory and the philosophy of language. Ambiguity is essentially a "mapping problem", and while there are significant analytical questions about how (and at what level) to best capture different varieties of ambiguity, the phenomenon per se does not represent a significant challenge to current conceptions of semantics. Vagueness, on the other hand, raises deeper questions about knowledge of meaning. The major approaches to vagueness that I have outlined here, all of which come from work in philosophy of language, provide different answers to these questions, but none is without its own set of challenges. Given this, as well as the fact that this phenomenon has seen relatively little in the way of close analysis by linguists, vagueness has the potential to be an important and rich domain of research for semantic theory.

5 References

Barker, Chris 2002. The dynamics of vagueness. *Linguistics & Philosophy* 25, 1–36.
Bartsch, Renate & Theo Vennemann 1972. The grammar of relative adjectives and comparison. *Linguistische Berichte* 20, 19–32.
Bierwisch, Manfred 1989. The semantics of gradation. In: M. Bierwisch & E. Lang (eds.). *Dimensional Adjectives. Grammatical Structure and Conceptual Interpretation*. Berlin: Springer, 71–261.

Bogusławski, Andrzej 1975. Measures are measures. In defence of the diversity of comparatives and positives. *Linguistische Berichte* 36, 1– 9.
Bolinger, Dwight 1967. Adjectives in English. Attribution and predication. *Lingua* 18, 1–34.
Bosch, Peter 1983. 'Vagueness' is context-dependence. A solution to the Sorites Paradox. In: T. Ballmer & M. Pinkal (eds.). *Approaching Vagueness*. Amsterdam: North-Holland, 189–210.
Cinque, Guglielmo 1993. On the evidence for partial N movement in the Romance DP. *University of Venice Working Papers in Linguistics* 3(2), 21–40.
Cresswell, Max J. 1976. The semantics of degree. In: B. Partee (ed.). *Montague Grammar*. New York: Academic Press, 261–292.
Fara, Delia Graff 2000. Shifting sands. An interest-relative theory of vagueness. *Philosophical Topics* 28, 45–81. Originally published under the name "Delia Graff".
Fara, Delia Graff 2008. Profiling interest relativity. *Analysis* 68, 326–335.
Fara, Delia Graff & Timothy Williamson (eds.) 2002. *Vagueness*. Burlington, VT: Ashgate. Originally published under the name "Delia Graff".
Fine, Kit 1975. Vagueness, truth and logic. *Synthese* 30, 265–300.
van Fraassen, Bas C. 1968. Presupposition, implication, and self-reference. *Journal of Philosophy* 65, 136–152.
van Fraassen, Bas C. 1969. Presuppositions, supervaluations, and free logic. In: K. Lambert (ed.). *The Logical Way of Doing Things*. New Haven, CT: Yale University Press, 69–91.
Gillon, Brendan S. 1990. Ambiguity, generality, and indeterminacy. Tests and definitions. *Synthese* 85, 391–416.
Gillon, Brendan S. 2004. Ambiguity, indeterminacy, deixis, and vagueness. Evidence and theory. In: S. Davis & B. Gillon (eds.). *Semantics. A Reader*. Oxford: Oxford University Press, 157–187.
Grice, H. Paul 1957. Meaning. *The Philosophical Review* 66, 377–388.
Heim, Irene 2000. Degree operators and scope. In: B. Jackson & T. Matthews (eds.). *Proceedings of Semantics and Linguistic Theory (= SALT) X*. Ithaca, NY: Cornell University, 40–64.
Heim, Irene & Angelika Kratzer 1998. *Semantics in Generative Grammar*. Oxford: Blackwell.
Jacobson, Pauline 1999. Towards a variable-free semantics. *Linguistics & Philosophy* 22, 117–184.
Jacobson, Pauline 2000. Paycheck pronouns, Bach-Peters sentences, and variable-free semantics. *Natural Language Semantics* 8, 77–155.
Kamp, Hans 1975. Two theories of adjectives. In: E. Keenan (ed.). *Formal Semantics of Natural Language*. Cambridge: Cambridge University Press, 123–155.
Kamp, Hans 1981. The paradox of the heap. In: U. Mönnich (ed.). *Aspects of Philosophical Logic*. Dordrecht: Reidel, 225–277.
Kamp, Hans & Barbara H. Partee 1995. Prototype theory and compositionality. *Cognition* 57, 129–191.
Keefe, Rosanna & Peter Smith (eds.) 1997. *Vagueness. A Reader*. Cambridge, MA: The MIT Press.
Kennedy, Christopher 1999. *Projecting the Adjective. The Syntax and Semantics of Gradability and Comparison*. New York: Garland.
Kennedy, Christopher 2001. Polar opposition and the ontology of 'degrees'. *Linguistics & Philosophy* 24, 33–70.
Kennedy, Christopher 2007. Vagueness and grammar. The semantics of relative and absolute gradable adjectives. *Linguistics & Philosophy* 30, 1–45.

Kennedy, Christopher & Louise McNally 2005. Scale structure and the semantic typology of gradable predicates. *Language* 81, 345–381.
Kennedy, Christopher & Louise McNally 2010. Color, context and compositionality. *Synthese* 174, 79–98.
Klein, Ewan 1980. A semantics for positive and comparative adjectives. *Linguistics & Philosophy* 4, 1–45.
Lakoff, George 1970. A note on vagueness and ambiguity. *Linguistic Inquiry* 1, 357–359.
Larson, Richard 1998. Events and modification in nominals. In: D. Strolovich & A. Lawson (eds.). *Proceedings of Semantics and Linguistic Theory (=SALT) VIII*. Ithaca, NY: Cornell University, 145–168.
Ludlow, Peter 1989. Implicit comparison classes. *Linguistics & Philosophy* 12, 519–533.
McConnell-Ginet, Sally 1982. Adverbs and logical form. A linguistically realistic theory. *Language* 58, 144–184.
Nunberg, Geoffrey 1995. Transfers of meaning. *Journal of Semantics* 12, 109–132.
Parsons, Kathryn 1973. Ambiguity and the truth condition. *Noûs* 7, 379–394.
Partee, Barbara H. & Mats Rooth 1983. Generalized conjunction and type ambiguity. In: R. Bäuerle, Ch. Schwarze & A. von Stechow (eds.). *Meaning, Use, and Interpretation of Language*. Berlin: Mouton de Gruyter, 361–383.
Pinkal, Manfred 1999. On semantic underspecification. In: H. Bunt & R. Muskens (eds.). *Computing Meaning, vol. 1*. Dordrecht: Kluwer, 33–55.
Pinker, Steven 1994. *The Language Instinct. How the Mind Creates Language*. New York: Morrow.
Postal, Paul 1969. Anaphoric islands. In: R. Binnick et al. (eds.). *Papers from the Fifth Regional Meeting of the Chicago Linguistic Society (=CLS)*. Chicago, IL: Chicago Linguistic Society, 205–239.
Pustejovsky, James 1995. *The Generative Lexicon*. Cambridge, MA: The MIT Press.
Putnam, Hilary 1975. The meaning of 'meaning'. In: K. Gunderson (ed.). *Language, Mind and Knowledge*. Minneapolis, MN: University of Minnesota Press, 131–193.
Pylkkänen, Liina & Brian McElree 2006. The syntax-semantics interface. On-line composition of sentence meaning. In: M. Traxler & M. A. Gernsbacher (eds.). *The Handbook of Psycholinguistics*. 2nd edn. New York: Elsevier, 539–580. 1st edn. 1994.
Raffman, Diana 1994. Vagueness without paradox. *The Philosophical Review* 103, 41–74.
Raffman, Diana 1996. Vagueness and context relativity. *Philosophical Studies* 81, 175–192.
Raffman, Diana 2005. How to understand contextualism about vagueness. Reply to Stanley. *Analysis* 65, 244–248.
Rips, Lance J. & William Turnbull 1980. How big is big? Relative and absolute properties in memory. *Cognition* 8, 145–174.
Rotstein, Carmen & Yoad Winter 2004. Total adjectives vs. partial adjectives. Scale structure and higher-order modifiers. *Natural Language Semantics* 12, 259–288.
Saka, Paul 2007. *How to Think about Meaning*. Dordrecht: Springer.
Schwarzschild, Roger & Karina Wilkinson 2002. Quantifiers in comparatives. A semantics of degree based on intervals. *Natural Language Semantics* 10, 1–41.
Seuren, Pieter A. M. 1973. The comparative. In: F. Kiefer & N. Ruwet (eds.). *Generative Grammar in Europe*. Dordrecht: Reidel, 528–564.
Siegel, Muffy E. A. 1976. *Capturing the Adjective*. Ph.D. dissertation. University of Massachusetts, Amherst, MA.
Soames, Scott 1999. *Understanding Truth*. Oxford: Oxford University Press.
Stanley, Jason 2003. Context, interest relativity, and the Sorites. *Analysis* 63, 269–280.

von Stechow, Arnim 1984. Comparing semantic theories of comparison. *Journal of Semantics* 3, 1–77.
Travis, Charles 1985. On what is strictly speaking true. *Canadian Journal of Philosophy* 15, 187–229.
Travis, Charles 1994. On constraints of generality. *Proceedings of the Aristotelian Society* 94, 165–188.
Travis, Charles 1997. Pragmatics. In: B. Hale & C. Wright (eds.). *A Companion to the Philosophy of Language*. Oxford: Blackwell, 87–107.
Tversky, Amos & Daniel Kahneman 1974. Judgment under uncertainty. Heuristics and biases. *Science* 185(4157), 1124–1131.
Ward, Gregory 2004. Equatives and deferred reference. *Language* 80, 262–289.
Ward, Gregory, Richard Sproat & Gail McKoon 1991. A pragmatic analysis of so-called anaphoric islands. *Language* 67, 439–474.
Wheeler, Samuel 1972. Attributives and their modifiers. *Noûs* 6, 310–334.
Williamson, Timothy 1992. Vagueness and ignorance. *Proceedings of the Aristotelian Society. Supplementary Volume* 66, 145–162.
Williamson, Timothy 1994. *Vagueness*. London: Routledge.
Williamson, Timothy 1997. Imagination, stipulation and vagueness. *Philosophical Issues* 8, 215–228.
Zwicky, Arnold & Jerrold Sadock 1975. Ambiguity tests and how to fail them. In: J. P. Kimball (ed.). *Syntax and Semantics*. 4. New York: Academic Press, 1–36.
Zwicky, Arnold & Jerrold Sadock 1984. A reply to Martin on ambiguity. *Journal of Semantics* 3, 249–256.

Markus Egg
9 Semantic underspecification

1 Introduction —— 272
2 The domain of semantic underspecification —— 273
3 Approaches to semantic underspecification —— 283
4 Motivation —— 299
5 Semantic underspecification and the syntax-semantics interface —— 307
6 Further processing of underspecified representations —— 309
7 References —— 314

Abstract: This article reviews semantic underspecification, which has emerged over the last three decades as a technique to capture several readings of an ambiguous expression in one single representation by deliberately omitting the differences between the readings in the semantic descriptions. After classifying the kinds of ambiguity to which underspecification can be applied, important properties of underspecification formalisms will be discussed that can be used to distinguish subgroups of these formalisms. The remainder of the article then presents various motivations for the use of underspecification, and expounds the derivation and further processing of underspecified semantic representations.

1 Introduction

Underspecification is defined as the deliberate omission of information from linguistic descriptions to capture several alternative realisations of a linguistic phenomenon in one single representation.

Underspecification emerged in phonology (see Steriade 1995 or Harris 2007 for an overview), where it was used e.g. for values of features that need not be specified because they can be predicted independently, e.g., by redundancy rules or by phonological processes. The price for this simplification, however, are additional layers or stages in phonological processes/representations, which resurfaces in most approaches that use underspecification in semantics.

In the 1980's, underspecification was adopted in semantics. Here the relevant linguistic phenomenon is *meaning*, thus, underspecified representations are intended to capture whole sets of different meanings in one representation. Since

Markus Egg, Berlin, Germany

https://doi.org/10.1515/9783110626391-009

this applies only to sets of meanings that correspond to the readings of a linguistic expression, semantic underspecification emerges as a technique for the treatment of *ambiguity*. (Strictly speaking, underspecification could be applied to *semantic indefiniteness* in general, which also encompasses vagueness, see Pinkal 1995 and article 8 [this volume] (Kennedy) *Ambiguity and vagueness*. But since underspecification focusses almost exclusively on ambiguity, vagueness will be neglected.)

While underspecification is not restricted to expressions with systematically related sets of readings (as opposed to homonyms), it is in practice applied to such expressions only. The bulk of the work in semantic underspecification focusses on scope ambiguity.

In natural language processing, underspecification is endorsed to keep semantic representations of ambiguous expressions tractable and to avoid unnecessary disambiguation steps; a completely new use of underspecification emerged in *hybrid processing*, where it provides a common format for the results of deep and shallow processing.

Underspecification is used also in syntax and discourse analysis to obtain compact representations whenever several structures can be assigned to a specific sentence (Marcus, Hindle & Fleck 1983; Rambow, Weir & Shanker 2001; Muskens 2001) or discourse, respectively (Asher & Fernando 1999; Duchier & Gardent 2001; Schilder 2002; Egg & Redeker 2008; Regneri, Egg & Koller 2008).

This article gives an overview over underspecification techniques in semantics. First the range of phenomena in semantics to which underspecification (formalisms) can be applied is sketched in section 2. Section 3 outlines important properties of underspecification formalisms which distinguish different subgroups of these formalisms. Various motivations for using underspecification in semantics are next outlined in section 4.

The remaining two sections focus on the derivation of underspecified semantic representations by a suitable syntax-semantics interface (section 5) and on the further processing of these representations (section 6).

2 The domain of semantic underspecification

Before introducing semantic underspecification in greater detail, ambiguous expressions that are in principle amenable to a treatment in terms of semantic underspecification will be classified according to two criteria. These criteria compare the readings of these expressions from a semantic and a syntactic point of view, respectively, and are called *semantic* and *syntactic homogeneity*:
- Do the readings all comprise the *same semantic material*?
- Is it possible to give a *single syntactic analysis* for all the readings?

These criteria will classify ambiguity in four classes (see also article 8 [this volume] (Kennedy) *Ambiguity and vagueness),* which only partially coincides with the taxonomy in Bunt (2007). In the descriptions of these classes, I will also outline how they compare to Bunt's classes.

2.1 Semantically and syntactically homogeneous ambiguities

The main focus of attention in underspecification approaches to ambiguity is on ambiguous expressions that fulfil the two homogeneity conditions. Classic representatives of this group are quantifier scope ambiguities. (The word *quantifier* refers to DP meanings (sets of properties), except in expressions such as 'universal quantifier', see article 4 [Semantics: Noun Phrases and Verb Phrases] (Keenan) *Quantifiers.*)

Consider e.g. the well-worn (1) with the simplistic syntactic analysis (2) and its two readings (3a) 'for every woman, her own man' ($\forall > \exists$; '>' indicates scope of its left argument over the right one) and (3b) 'one man for all women' ($\exists > \forall$). Here and in (21) below, unary branching nodes are omitted. I ignore the discussion of whether indefinite quantifiers indeed introduce scope (see Kratzer 1998), my argumentation does not depend on this issue.

(1) Every woman loves a man.

(2)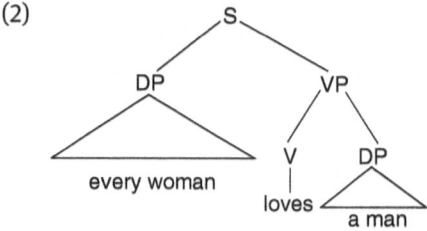

The arrangement of the formulae in (3) highlights the fact that they consist of the same three parts (roughly coinciding with the semantic contributions of the verb and its two arguments), and that the relation of loving as introduced by the verb always gets lowest scope. The only difference between the formulae is the ordering of the semantic contributions of the arguments of the verb.

(3) a. $\forall x.\mathbf{woman}'(x) \rightarrow$
$\exists y.\mathbf{man}'(y) \wedge$
$\mathbf{love}'(x,y)$

b. $\exists y.\mathbf{man}'(y) \wedge$
$\forall x.\mathbf{woman}'(x) \rightarrow$
$\mathbf{love}'(x,y)$

Since quantifier scope ambiguity is the prototypical domain for the application of underspecification, involved cases of quantifier scope ambiguity are handled in advanced underspecification formalisms. Some of these cases have developed into benchmark cases for underspecification formalisms, e.g., (4)–(6):

(4) Every researcher of a company saw most samples.

(5) [Every man]$_i$ read a book he$_i$ liked.

(6) Every linguist attended a conference, and every computer scientist did, too.

The subject in (4) exhibits *nested quantification*, where one quantifier-introducing DP comprises another one. (4) is challenging because the number of its readings is less than the number of the possible permutations of its quantifiers (3! = 6). The scope ordering that is ruled out in any case is ∀ > **most'** > ∃ (Hobbs & Shieber 1987). (See section 3.1. for further discussion of this example.)

In (5), the anaphoric dependency of *a book he liked* on *every man* restricts the quantifier scope ambiguity in that the DP with the anaphor must be in the scope of its antecedent (Reyle 1993).

In (6), quantifier scope is ambiguous, but must be the same in both sentences (i.e., if *every linguist* outscopes *a conference*, *every computer scientist* does, too), which yields two readings. In a third reading, *a conference* receives scope over everything else, i.e., both linguists and computer scientists attending the same conference (Hirschbühler 1982; Crouch 1995; Dalrymple, Shieber & Pereira 1991; Shieber, Pereira & Dalrymple 1996; Egg, Koller & Niehren 2001).

Other scope-bearing items can also enter into scope ambiguity, e.g., negation and modal expressions, as in (7) and (8):

(7) Everyone didn't come. (∀ > ¬ or ¬ > ∀)

(8) A unicorn seems to be in the garden. (∃ > *seem* or *seem* > ∃)

Such cases can also be captured by underspecification. For instance, Minimal Recursion Semantics (Copestake et al. 2005) describes them by underspecifying the scope of the quantifiers and fixing the other scope-bearing items scopally.

But cases of scope ambiguity without quantifiers show that underspecifying quantifier scope only is not general enough. For instance, cases of *'neg raising'* (Sailer 2006) like in (9) have a reading denying that John believes that Peter will come, and one attributing to John the belief that Peter will not come:

(9) John doesn't think Peter will come.

Sailer analyses these cases as a scope ambiguity between the matrix verb and the negation (whose syntactic position is invariably in the matrix clause).

Other such examples involve coordinated DPs, like in (10), (11), or (12) (Hurum 1988; Babko-Malaya 2004; Chaves 2005b):

(10) I want to marry Peggy or Sue.

(11) Every man and every woman solved a puzzle.

(12) Every lawyer and his secretary met.

(10) shows that in coordinated DPs scope ambiguity can arise between the conjunction and other scope-bearing material, here, *want*, even if there are no scope-bearing DPs. (10) is ambiguous in that the conjunction may have scope over *want* (I either have the wish to marry Peggy or the wish to marry Sue), or vice versa (my wish is to marry either Peggy or Sue).

(11) has two readings, every man and every woman solving their own (possibly different) puzzle, or one puzzle being solved by every man and every woman. (There are no intermediate readings in which the indefinite DP intervenes scopally between the conjoined DPs.)

Finally, (12) has a reading in which every lawyer meets his own secretary, and one in which all the lawyers with their secretaries meet together. This example can be analysed in terms of a scope ambiguity between the operator G that forms groups out of individuals (assuming that only such groups can be the argument of a predicate like *meet*) and the conjoined DPs (Chaves 2005b). If G has narrow scope with respect to the DPs, every lawyer and his secretary form a specific group that meet (13a), if the DPs end up in G's restriction (indicated by brackets in (13)), there is one big meeting group consisting of all lawyers and their secretaries (13b).

(13) a. $\forall x.\textbf{lawyer}'(x) \to \exists y.\textbf{secr\_of}\,'(y, x) \wedge \exists Z.[x \in Z \wedge y \in Z] \wedge \textbf{meet}'(Z)$
      b. $\exists Z.[\forall x.\textbf{lawyer}'(x) \to \exists y.\textbf{secr\_of}\,'(y, x) \wedge x \in Z \wedge y \in Z] \wedge \textbf{meet}'(Z)$

Another group of scope ambiguities involves scope below the word level:

(14) beautiful dancer

(15) John's former car

(16) John almost died

In (14), the adjective may pertain to the noun as a whole or to the stem only, which yields two readings that can roughly be glossed as 'beautiful person characterised by dancing' and 'person characterised by beautiful dancing', respectively (Larson 1998). This can be modelled as scope ambiguity between the adjective and the nominal affix -*er* (Egg 2004). (15) as discussed in Larson & Cho (2003) is a case of scope ambiguity between the possessive relation introduced by the Anglo-Saxon genitive *'s* and the adjective *former*, which yields the readings 'car formerly in the possession of John' or 'ex-car in the possession of John' (Egg 2007). Finally, the readings of (16), viz., 'John was close to undergoing a change from being alive to being dead' (i.e., in the end, nothing happened to him) and 'John underwent a change from being alive to being close to death' (i.e., something did happen) can be modelled as scope ambiguity between a change-of state operator like BECOME and the adverbial (Rapp & von Stechow 1999; Egg 2007).

The cases of semantically and syntactically homogeneous ambiguity discussed so far have readings that not only comprise the same semantic building blocks, each reading has in addition exactly one instance of each of these building blocks. This was highlighted e.g. for (1) in the representation of its readings in (3), where each semantic building block appears on a different line.

However, the definition of semantically and syntactically homogeneous ambiguity includes also cases where the readings consist of the same building blocks, but differ in that some of the readings exhibit more than one instance of specific building blocks.

This kind of semantically and syntactically homogeneous ambiguity shows up in the ellipsis in (17). Its two readings 'John wanted to greet everyone that Bill greeted' and 'John wanted to greet everyone that Bill wanted to greet' differ in that there is one instance of the semantic contribution of the matrix verb *want* in the first reading, but two instances in the second reading (Sag 1976):

(17) John wanted to greet everyone that Bill did.

This is due to the fact that the pro-form *did* is interpreted in terms of a suitable preceding VP (its antecedent), and that there are two such suitable VPs in (17), viz., *wanted to greet everyone that Bill did* and *greet everyone that Bill did*. ((17) is a case of *antecedent-contained deletion*, see Shieber, Pereira & Dalrymple 1996 and Egg, Koller & Niehren 2001 for underspecified accounts of this phenomenon; see also article 9 [Semantics: Sentence and Information Structure] (Reich) *Ellipsis.)*

Another example of this kind of semantically and syntactically homogeneous ambiguity is the Afrikaans example (18) (Sailer 2004). Both the inflected form of the matrix verb *wou* 'wanted' and the auxiliary *het* in the subordinate clause introduce a past tense operator. But these examples have three readings:

(18) Jan wou gebel het.
 Jan want.PAST called have
 'Jan wanted to call/Jan wants to have called/Jan wanted to have called.'

The readings can be analysed (in the order given in (18)) as (19a-c): That is, the readings comprise one or two instances of the past tense operator:

(19) a. PAST(**want'**(j,ˆ (**call'**(j))))
 b. **want'**(j,ˆ PAST(**call'**(j)))
 c. PAST(**want'**(j,ˆ PAST(**call'**(j))))

Finally, the criterion 'syntactically and semantically homogeneous' as defined in this subsection will be compared to similar classes of ambiguity from the literature. Syntactic and semantic homogeneity is sometimes referred to as *structural ambiguity*. But this term is itself ambiguous in that it is sometimes used in the broader sense of 'semantically homogeneous' (i.e., syntactically homogeneous or not). But then it would also encompass the group of semantically but not syntactically homogeneous ambiguities discussed in the next subsection.

The group of semantically and syntactically homogeneous ambiguities coincides by and large with Bunt's (2007) 'structural semantic ambiguity' class, excepting ambiguous compounds like *math problem* and the collective/distributive ambiguity of quantifiers, both of which are syntactically but not semantically homogeneous: Different readings of a compound each instantiate an unspecific semantic relation between the components in a unique way. Similarly, distributive and quantitative readings of a quantifier are distinguished in the semantics by the presence or absence of a distributive or collective operator, e.g., Link's (1983) distributive D-operator (see article 7 [Semantics: Noun Phrases and Verb Phrases] (Lasersohn) *Mass nouns and plurals*).

2.2 Semantically but not syntactically homogeneous ambiguities

The second kind of ambiguity is semantically but not syntactically homogeneous. The ambiguity has a syntactic basis in that the same *syntactic* material is arranged in different ways. Consequently, the meanings of the resulting syntactic structures all consist of the same semantic material (though differently ordered, depending on the respective syntactic structure), but no common syntactic structure can be postulated for the different interpretations.

The notorious modifier attachment ambiguities as in (20) are a prime example of this kind of ambiguity:

(20) Max strangled the man with the tie.

There is no common phrase marker for the two readings of (20). In the reading that the man is wearing the tie, the constituent *the tie* is part of a DP (or NP) *the man with the tie*. In the other reading, in which the tie is the instrument of Max' deed, *the tie* enters a verbal projection (as the syntactic sister of *strangled the man*) as a constituent of its own:

(21) a. 'tie worn by victim' b. 'tie as instrument of crime'

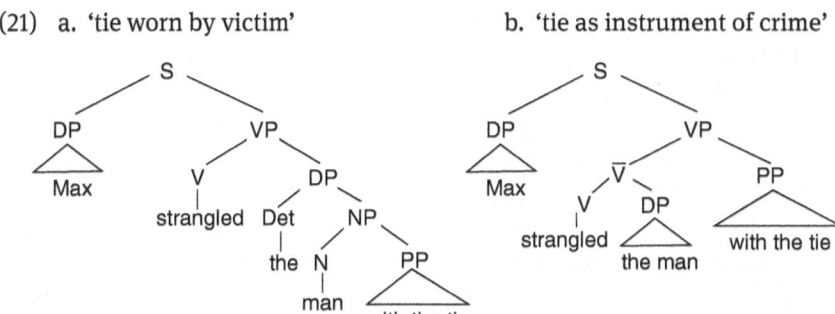

There is an intuitive 1:1 relation between the two phrase markers in (21) and the two readings of (20). None of the phrase markers would be suitable as the syntactic analysis for *both* readings.

Semantically but not syntactically homogeneous ambiguity is usually not described in terms of semantic underspecification in the same fashion as semantically and syntactically homogeneous ambiguity; exceptions include Muskens (2001), Pinkal (1996), or Richter & Sailer (1996).

In Bunt's classification, the group of semantically but not syntactically homogeneous ambiguites are called 'syntactic ambiguity'.

2.3 Syntactically but not semantically homogeneous ambiguities

The third kind of ambiguity is instantiated by expressions whose readings share a single syntactic analysis but do not comprise the same semantic material.

These expressions can be classified in four subgroups. Members of the first subgroup comprise *lexically* ambiguous words, whose ambiguity is inherited by the whole expression. For instance, the ambiguity of the noun *Schule* 'school' (with readings like 'building', 'institution', 'staff and pupils', or 'lessons') makes expressions like *die Schule begutachten* 'evaluate (the) school' ambiguous, too. Polysemy belongs to this group but homonymy does not: Different readings of polysemous words belong to the same lexeme and do not differ syntactically. In contrast, homonymous items are syntactically different lexemes.

Underspecified accounts of polysemy model the semantics of a polysemous item in terms of a core meaning common to all readings. This was worked out in *Two-level Semantics* (Bierwisch 1983; Bierwisch & Lang 1987; Bierwisch 1988), which distinguished a semantic level (where the core meanings reside) and relegated the specification of the individual readings to a conceptual level (see articles 1 [this volume] (Bierwisch) *Semantic features and primes* and 5 [Semantics: Theories] (Lang & Maienborn) *Two-level Semantics*). In the case of *Schule* 'school', the ambiguity can be captured in terms of a core meaning S 'related to processes of teaching and learning'. This meaning is then fully specified on the conceptual level in terms of operators that map S onto an intersection of S with properties like 'building', 'institution' etc.

Underspecification formalisms covering polysemy include the semantic representation language in the PHLIQA question-answering system (Bronnenberg et al. 1979), Poesio's (1996) Lexically Underspecified Language, and Cimiano & Reyle's (2005) version of Muskens' (2001) Logical Description Grammar.

Lexical ambiguities were also spotted in sentences with quantifiers that have *collective* and *distributive* readings (Alshawi 1992; Frank & Reyle 1995; Chaves 2005a). For instance, in (22), the lawyers can act together or individually:

(22) The lawyers hired a secretary.

The distributive reading differs from the collective one in that there is a quantification over the set of lawyers whose scope is the property of hiring a secretary (instead of having this property apply to an entity consisting of all lawyers together). The collective reading lacks this quantification, which makes expressions like (22) semantically heterogeneous.

The proposed analyses of such expressions locate the ambiguity differently. The Core Language Engine account (Alshawi 1992) and the Underspecified DRT (UDRT) account of Frank & Reyle (1995) suggest an underspecification of the DP semantics (they refer to DPs as NPs) that can be specified to a collective or a distributive interpretation.

Chaves (2005a) notes that mixed readings like in (23) are wrongly ruled out if the ambiguity is attributed to the DP semantics.

(23) The hikers met in the train station and then left.

His UDRT analysis places the ambiguity in the verb semantics in the form of an underspecified operator, which can be instantiated as universal quantification in the spirit of Link's (1983) account of distributive readings.

Lexically based ambiguity also includes compounds like *math problem*. Their semantics comprises an unspecified relation between their components, which can be specified differently (e.g., for *math problem*, 'problem from the domain of mathematics' or 'problem with understanding mathematics').

Referential ambiguity is the second subgroup of syntactically but not semantically homogeneous expressions, because there are different interpretations of a deictic expression, which is eventually responsible for the ambiguity. For a discussion of referential ambiguity and its underspecified representation, see e.g. Asher & Lascarides (2003) and Poesio et al. (2006).

Some cases of referential ambiguity are due to ellipses where the antecedents comprise anaphors, e.g., the antecedent VP *walks his dog* in (24):

(24) John walks his dog and Max does, too.

The interpretation of *does* in terms of *walks his dog* comprises an anaphor, too. This anaphor can refer to the same antecedent as the one in *walks his dog* ('strict' reading, Max walks John's dog), or to its own subject DP in analogy to the way in which the anaphor in *John walks his dog* refers ('sloppy' reading, Max walks his own dog). For an extended discussion of this phenomenon, see Gawron & Peters (1990).

The third kind of syntactically but not semantically homogeneous ambiguity where underspecification has been proposed is *missing information* (Pinkal 1999). In this case, parts of a message could not be decoded due to problems in production, transmission, or reception. These messages can be interpreted in different ways (depending on how the missing information is filled in), while the syntactic representation remains constant.

The fourth subgroup is *reinterpretation* (metonymy and aspectual coercion), if it is modelled in terms of underspecified operators that are inserted during semantic construction (Hobbs et al. 1993; Dölling 1995; Pulman 1997; de Swart 1998; Egg 2005). Such operators will avoid impending clashes for semantic construction by being inserted between otherwise (mostly) incompatible semantic material during the construction process. (See articles 10 [this volume] (de Swart) *Mismatches and coercion* and 11 [this volume] (Tyler & Takahashi) *Metaphors and metonymies*.)

This strategy can introduce ambiguity, e.g., in (25). Here a coercion operator is inserted between *play the Moonlight Sonata* and its modifier *for some time*, which cannot be combined directly; this operator can be specified to a progressive or an iterative operator (i.e., she played part of the sonata, or she played the sonata repetitively):

(25) Amélie played the Moonlight Sonata for some time.

The readings of such expressions have a common syntactic analysis, but, due to the different specification of the underspecified reinterpretation operator, they no longer comprise the same semantic material.

Syntactically but not semantically homogeneous ambiguities (together with vagueness) encompass Bunt's (2007) classes 'lexical ambiguity' (except homonymy), 'semantic imprecision', and 'missing information' with the exception of ellipsis: In ellipsis (as opposed to incomplete utterances), the missing parts in the target sentences are recoverable from the preceding discourse (possibly in more than one way), while no such possibility is available for incomplete utterances (e.g., for the utterance *Bill?* in the sense of *Where are you, Bill?*).

2.4 Neither syntactically nor semantically homogeneous ambiguities

The group of ambiguous expressions that are neither syntactically nor semantically homogeneous consists of homonyms. Homonymy has not been a prime target of underspecification, because there is not enough common ground between the readings that would support a sufficiently distinctive underspecified representation (which would differ from the representation of other lexical items). Consider e.g., *jumper* in its textile and its electrical engineering sense: 'concrete object' as common denominator of the readings would fail to distinguish *jumper* from a similarly underspecified representation of the homonym *pen* ('writing instrument' or 'enclosure for animals'). This group does not show up in Bunt's (2007) taxonomy.

2.5 The focus of underspecified approaches to ambiguity

While underspecification can in principle be applied to all four groups of ambiguity, most of the work on underspecification focusses on semantically and syntactically homogeneous ambiguity.

I see two reasons for this: First, it is more attractive to apply underspecification to semantically homogeneous (than to semantically heterogeneous) ambiguity: Suitable underspecified representations of a semantically homogeneous ambiguous expression can delimit the range of readings of the expression and specify them fully without disjunctively enumerating them (for a worked out example, see (40) below).

No such delimitation and specification are possible in the case of semantically heterogeneous ambiguity: Here semantic representations must restrict themselves to specifying the parts of the readings that are common to all of them and leave open those parts that distinguish the specific readings. Further knowledge sources are then needed to define the possible instantiations of these parts (which eventually delimits the set of readings and fully specifies them).

Second, syntactically heterogeneous ambiguity seems to be considered less of an issue for the syntax-semantics interface, because each reading is motivated by a syntactic structure of its own. Underspecified presentations of these readings would cancel out the differences between the readings in spite of their independent syntactic motivation. Syntactically homogeneous ambiguity has no such syntactic motivation, which makes it a much greater challenge for the syntax-semantics interface (see section 4.1).

I will follow this trend in underspecification research and focus on syntactically and semantically homogeneous ambiguities in the remainder of this article.

3 Approaches to semantic underspecification

This section offers a general description of underspecification formalisms. It will outline general properties that characterise these formalisms and distinguish subgroups of them (see also article 14 [Semantics: Typology, Diachrony and Processing] (Pinkal & Koller) *Semantics in computational linguistics).*

I will first show that underspecification formalisms handle ambiguity by either *describing* it or by providing an algorithm for the *derivation* of the different readings of an ambiguous expression. Then I will point out that these formalisms may but need not distinguish different *levels of representation*, and implement *compositionality* in different ways. Finally, underspecification formalisms also differ with respect to their *compactness* (how efficiently can they delimit and specify the set of readings of an ambiguous expression) and their *expressivity* (can they also do this for arbitrary subsets of this set of readings).

3.1 Describing ambiguity

Underspecification is implemented in semantics in two different ways: The readings of an ambiguous expression can either be *described* or *derived*. This distinction shows up also in Robaldo (2007), who uses the terms 'constraint-based' and 'enumerative'. An obsolete version of Glue Language Semantics (Shieber, Pereira & Dalrymple 1996) mixed both approaches to handle ellipses like (17).

The first way of implementing semantic underspecification is to describe the meaning of an ambiguous expression directly. The set of semantic representations for its readings is characterised in terms of *partial information*. This characterisation by itself delimits the range of readings of the ambiguous expression and specifies them. That is, the way in which fully specified representations for the readings are derived from the underspecified representation does not contribute to the delimitation.

This strategy is based on the fact that there are two ways of describing a set: a list of its elements or a property that characterises all the and only the elements of the set. In the second way, a set of semantic representations is delimited by describing the common ground between the representations only. Since the description deliberately leaves out everything that distinguishes the elements of the set, it can only be partial.

Most underspecification formalisms that follow this strategy distinguish an object level (semantic representations) and a meta-level (descriptions of these representations). The formalisms define the expressions of the meta-level and their relation to the described object-level representations.

3.1.1 A simple example

As an illustration, reconsider (26) [= (1)] and its readings (27a-b) [= (3a-b)]:

(26) Every woman loves a man.

(27) a. $\forall x.\textbf{woman}'(x) \rightarrow \exists y.\textbf{man}'(y) \wedge \textbf{love}'(x,y)$
 b. $\exists y.\textbf{man}'(y) \wedge \forall x.\textbf{woman}'(x) \rightarrow \textbf{love}'(x,y)$

A description of the common ground in (27) can look like this:

(28) $\forall x. \textbf{woman}'(x) \rightarrow \square \quad \exists y. \textbf{man}'(y) \wedge \square$

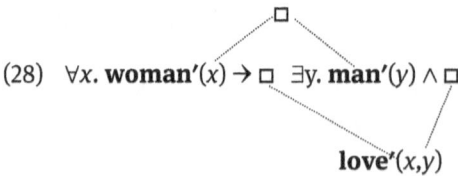

$\textbf{love}'(x,y)$

In (28), we distinguish four *fragments* of semantic representations (here, λ-terms) which may comprise *holes* (parts of fragments that are not yet determined, indicated by '□'). Then there is a relation R between holes and fragments (depicted as dotted lines), if R holds for a hole h and a fragment F, F must be part of the material that determines h.

R determines a partial scope ordering between fragments: A fragment F_1 has scope over another fragment F_2 iff F_1 comprises a hole h such that $R(h, F_2)$ or $R(h,F_3)$, where F_3 is a third fragment that has scope over F_2 (cf. e.g. the definition of 'qeq relations' in Copestake et al. 2005). Furthermore, we assume that variable binding operators in a fragment F bind occurrences of the respective variables in all fragments outscoped by F (ignoring the so-called variable capturing problem, see Egg, Koller & Niehren 2001) and that the description explicates all the fragments of the described object-level representations.

The description (28) can then be read as follows: The fragment at the top consists of a hole only, i.e., we do not yet know what the described representations look like. However, since the relation R relates this hole and the right and the left fragment, they are both part of these representations – only the order is open. Finally, the holes in both the right and the left fragment are related to the bottom fragment in terms of R, i.e., the bottom fragment is in the scope of either quantifier. The only semantic representations compatible with this description are (27a-b).

To derive the described readings from such a constraint (its *solutions*), the relation R between holes and fragments is monotonically strengthened until all the holes are related to a fragment, and all the fragments except the one at the top are identified with a hole (this is called 'plugging' in Bos 2004).

In (28), one can strengthen R by adding the pair consisting of the hole in the left fragment and the right fragment. Here the relation between the hole in the universal fragment and the bottom fragment in (28) is omitted.

(29)   □
         ┊
    $\forall x.$ **woman**$'(x) \to$ □
                                    ┊
              $\exists y.$ **man**$'(y) \wedge$ □
                                                ┊
                         love$'(x, y)$

Identifying the hole-fragment pairs in R in (29) then yields (27a), one of the solutions of (28). The other solution (27b) can be derived by first adding to R the pair consisting of the hole in the right fragment and the left fragment.

Underspecification formalisms that implement scope in this way comprise Underspecified Discourse Representation Theory (UDRT; Reyle 1993; Reyle 1996; Frank & Reyle 1995), Minimal Recursion Semantics (MRS; Copestake et al. 2005), the Constraint Language for Lambda Structures (CLLS; Egg, Koller & Niehren 2001), the language of Dominance Constraints (DC; subsumed by CLLS; Althaus et al. 2001), Hole Semantics (HS; Bos 1996; Bos 2004; Kallmeyer & Romero 2008), and Logical Description Grammar (Muskens 2001).

Koller, Niehren & Thater (2003) show that expressions of HS can be translated into expressions of DC and vice versa; Fuchss et al. (2004) describe how to translate MRS expressions into DC expressions. Player (2004) claims that this is due to the fact that UDRT, MRS, CLLS, and HS are the same 'modulo cosmetic differences', however, his comparison does not pertain to CLLS but to the language of dominance constraints.

Scope relations like the one between a quantifying DP and the verb it is an argument of can also be expressed in terms of suitable variables. This is implemented e.g. in the Underspecied Semantic Description Language (USDL; Pinkal 1996, Niehren, Pinkal & Ruhrberg 1997; Egg & Kohlhase 1997 present a dynamic version of this language). In USDL, the constraints for (26) are expressed by the equations in (30):

(30) a. $X_0 = C_1(\textbf{every\_woman}@L_{x_1}(C_2(\textbf{love}@x_2@x_1)))$
b. $X_0 = C_3(\textbf{a\_man}@L_{x_2}(C_4(\textbf{love}@x_2@x_1)))$

Here **'every_woman'** and **'a_man'** stand for the the two quantifiers in the semantics of (26), '@' denotes explicit functional application in the metalanguage, and 'L_x', λ-abstraction over x.

These equations can now be solved by an algorithm like the one in Huet (1975). For instance, for the ∀∃-reading of (26), the variables would be resolved as in (31a-c). This yields (31d), whose right hand side corresponds to (27a):

(31) a. $C_1 = C_4 = \lambda P.P$
b. $C_2 = \lambda P.\textbf{a\_man}@L_{x_2}(P)$
c. $C_3 = \lambda P.\textbf{every\_woman}@L_{x_1}(P)$
d. $X_0 = \textbf{every\_woman}@L_{x_1}(\textbf{a\_man}@L_{x_2}(\textbf{love}@x_2@x_1))$

Another way to express such scope relations is used in the version of the Quasi-Logical Form (QLF) in Alshawi & Crouch (1992), viz., list-valued metavariables in semantic representations whose specification indicates quantifier scope. Consider e.g. the (simplified) representation for (26) in (32a), which comprises an underspecified scoping list (the variable _s before the colon). Here the meanings of *every woman* and *a man* are represented as complex terms; such terms comprise term indices (+m and +w) and the restrictions of the quantifiers (man and woman, respectively). Specifying this underspecified reading to the reading with wide scope for the universal quantifier then consists in instantiating the variable _s to the list [+w,+m] in (32b), which corresponds to (27a):

(32) a. _s: love(term(+w,...,woman,...), term(+m,...,man,...))
     b. [+w,+m]: love (term (+w,...,woman,...), term (+m,...,man,...))

Even though QLF representations seem to differ radically from the ones that use dominance constraints, Lev (2005) shows how to translate them into expressions of Hole Semantics, which is based on dominance relations.

Finally, I will show how Glue Language Semantics (GLS; Dalrymple et al. 1997; Crouch & van Genabith 1999; Dalrymple 2001) handles scope ambiguity. Each lexical item introduces so-called *meaning constructors* that relate syntactic constituents (I abstract away from details of the interface here) and semantic representations. For instance, for the proper name *John*, the constructor is '$DP \leadsto$ **john**'', which states that the DP *John* has the meaning **john**' ('$\leadsto$' relates syntactic constituents and their meanings).

Such statements can be arguments of *linear logic* connectives like the conjunction ⊗ and the implication ⊸ , e.g., the meaning constructor for *love*:

(33) $\forall X, Y. DP_{subj} \leadsto X \otimes DP_{obj} \leadsto Y \multimap S \leadsto love'(X, Y)$

In prose: Whenever the subject interpretation in a sentence S is X and the object interpretation is Y, then the S meaning is **love'**(X, Y). That is these constructors specify how the meanings of smaller constituents determine the meaning of a larger constituent.

The implication ⊸ is resource-sensitive: '$A \multimap B$' can be paraphrased as 'use a resource A to derive (or produce) B'. The resource is 'consumed' in this process, i.e., no longer available for further derivations. Thus, from A and $A \multimap B$ one can deduce B, but no longer A. For (33), this means that after deriving the S meaning the two DP interpretations are no longer available for further processes of semantic construction (consumed).

The syntax-semantics interface collects these meaning constructors during the construction of the syntactic structure of an expression. For ambiguous expressions such as (26), the resulting collection is an underspecified representation of its different readings. Representations for the readings of the expression can then be derived from this collection by linear-logic deduction.

In the following, the presentation is simplified in that DP-internal semantic construction is omitted and only the DP constructors are given:

(34) a. $\forall H, P.(\forall x.DP \leadsto x \multimap H \leadsto_t (x)) \multimap H \leadsto$ **every'(woman'**, P)
 b. $\forall G, R.(\forall y.DP \leadsto y \multimap G \leadsto_t (y)) \multimap G \leadsto$ **a'(man'**,R)

The semantics of *every woman* in (34a) can be paraphrased as follows: Look for a resource of the kind 'use a resource that a DP semantics is x, to build the truth-valued (subscript t of $\leadsto$) meaning $P(x)$ of another constituent H'. Then consume this resource and assume that the semantics of H is **every'(woman'**,P); here **every'** abbreviates the usual interpretation of *every*. The representation for *a man* works analogously.

With these constructors for the verb and its arguments, the semantic representation of (26) in GLS is (35d), the conjunction of the constructors of the verb and its arguments. Note that semantic construction has identified the DPs that are mentioned in the three constructors:

(35) a. $\forall H, P.(\forall x.DP_{subj} \leadsto x \multimap H \leadsto_t P(x)) \multimap H \leadsto$ **every'(woman'**, P)
 b. $\forall G, R.(\forall y.DP_{obj} \leadsto y \multimap G \leadsto_t R(y)) \multimap G \leadsto$ **a'(man'**,R)
 c. $\forall X, Y. DP_{subj} \leadsto X \otimes DP_{obj} \leadsto Y \multimap S \leadsto$ **love'**(X, Y)
 d. (35a)⊗(35b)⊗(35c)

From such conjunctions of constructors, fully specified readings can be derived. For (26), the scope ambiguity is modelled in GLS in that two different semantic representations for the sentence can be derived from (35d).

Either derivation starts with choosing one of the two possible specifications of the verb meaning in (35c), which determine the order in which the argument interpretations are consumed:

(36) a. $\forall X.DP_{subj} \leadsto X \multimap (\forall Y.DP_{obj} \leadsto Y \multimap S \leadsto$ **love'**(X, Y))
 b. $\forall Y. DP_{obj} \leadsto Y \multimap (\forall X. DP_{subj} \leadsto X \multimap S \leadsto$ **love'**(X, Y))

I will now illustrate the derivation of the reading of ∀∃-reading of (26). The next step uses the general derivation rule (37) and the instantiations in (38):

(37) from $A \multimap B$ and $B \multimap C$ one can deduct $A \multimap C$

(38) $G \mapsto S$, $Y \mapsto y$, and $R \mapsto \lambda y.$**love'**(X, y))

From specification (36a) and the object semantics (35b) we then obtain (39a), this goes then together with the subject semantics (35a) to yield (39b), a notational variant of (27a):

(39)   a. $\forall X.DP_{subj} \rightsquigarrow X \multimap S \rightsquigarrow \mathbf{a'}(\mathbf{man'}, \lambda y.\mathbf{love'}(X, y))$
      b. $\mathbf{every'}(\mathbf{woman'}, \lambda x.\mathbf{a'}(\mathbf{man'}, \lambda y.\mathbf{love'}(x, y)))$

The derivation for the other reading of (26) chooses the other specification (36b) of the verb meaning and works analogously.

3.1.2 A more involved example

After this expository account of the way that the simple ambiguity of (26) is captured in various underspecification formalisms, reconsider the more involved nested quantification in (40) [= (4)], whose constraint is given in (41).

(40)   Every researcher of a company saw most samples.

(41)

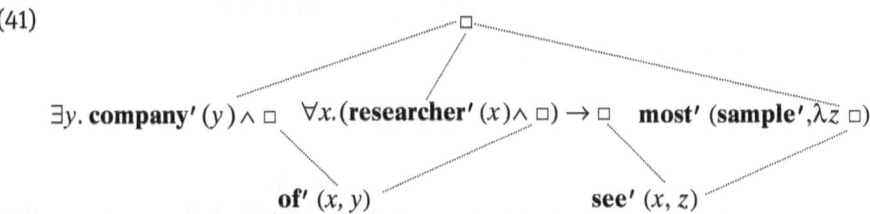

As expounded in section 2.1, not all scope relations of the quantifiers are possible in (40). I assume that (40) has exactly five readings, there is no reading with the scope ordering $\forall > \mathbf{most'} > \exists$. (41) is a suitable underspecified representation of (40) in that it has exactly its five readings as solutions.

As a first step of disambiguation, we can order the existential and the universal fragment. Giving the former narrow scope yields (42):

(42)

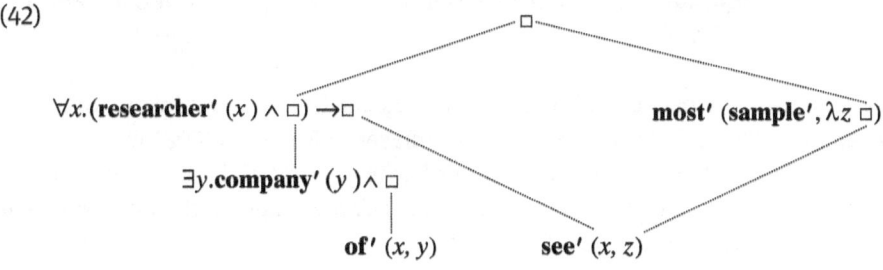

But once the existential fragment is outscoped by the universal fragment, it can no longer interact scopally with the *most* - and the *see*-fragment, because it is part of the *restriction* of the universal quantifier. That is, there are two readings to be derived from (42), with the *most*-fragment scoping below or above the universal fragment. This rules out a reading in which *most* scopes below the universal, but above the existential quantifier:

(43) a. $\forall x.(\textbf{researcher}'(x) \land \exists y.\textbf{company}'(y) \land \textbf{of}'(x,y)) \rightarrow \textbf{most}'(\textbf{sample}', \lambda z.\textbf{see}'(x, z))$
 b. $\textbf{most}'(\textbf{sample}', \lambda z \forall x.(\textbf{researcher}'(x) \land \exists y.\textbf{company}'(y) \land \textbf{of}'(x,y)) \rightarrow \textbf{see}'(x,z))$

The second way of fixing the scope of the existential w.r.t. the universal quantifier in (41) gives us (44):

(44)

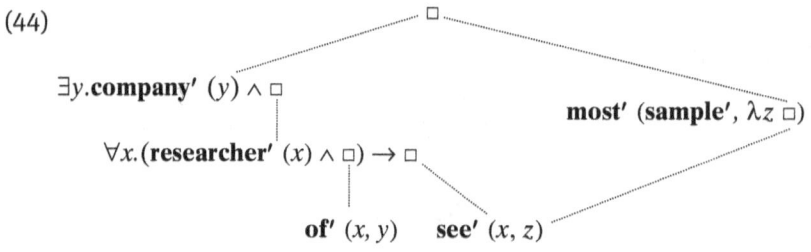

This constraint describes the three readings in (45), whose difference is whether the *most*-fragment takes scope over, between, or below the other two quantifiers. In sum, constraint (41) encompasses the five desired interpretations.

(45) a. $\textbf{most}'(\textbf{sample}', \lambda z \exists y.\textbf{company}'(y) \land \forall x.(\textbf{researcher}'(x) \land \textbf{of}'(x,y)) \rightarrow \textbf{see}'(x,z))$
 b. $\exists y.\textbf{company}'(y) \land \textbf{most}'(\textbf{sample}', \lambda z \forall x.(\textbf{researcher}'(x) \land \textbf{of}'(x,y)) \rightarrow \textbf{see}'(x,z))$
 c. $\exists y.\textbf{company}'(y) \land \forall x.(\textbf{researcher}'(x) \land \textbf{of}'(x,y)) \rightarrow \textbf{most}'(\textbf{sample}', \lambda z.\textbf{see}'(x, z))$

While most approaches follow Hobbs & Shieber in assuming five readings for examples like (40), Park (1995) and Kallmeyer & Romero (2008) claim that in cases of nested quantification no quantifier may interfere between those introduced by the embedding and the embedded DP, regardless of their ordering. For (40), this would block the reading (45b).

But even (40) is a comparatively simple case of nested quantification. Appropriate underspecification formalisms must be able to handle nested quantification in general and to cope with the fact that there are always less readings than the factorial of the number of the involved DPs, since some scoping options are ruled out. For instance, simple sentences consisting of a transitive verb with two arguments that together comprise n quantifying DPs have $C(n)$ readings, where $C(n)$ is the Catalan number of n ($C(n)$) $\frac{(2n)!}{(n+1)!n!}$). For instance, example (46) has 5 nested quantifiers and thus $C(5) = 42$ readings (Hobbs & Shieber 1987):

(46) Some representative of every department in most companies saw a few samples of each product.

Nested quantification highlights the two main characteristics of this approach to semantic underspecification: Underspecified expressions (typically, of a meta-level formalism) *describe* a set of semantic representations to delimit the range of this set and to fully specify its elements. The derivation of solutions from such expressions does thus not add information in that it restricts the number of solutions in any way.

3.2 Deriving ambiguity

The second approach to semantic underspecification derives rather than describes object-level semantic representations on the basis of an initial representation. Consider e.g. the initial semantic representation of (26) in the formalism of Schubert & Pelletier (1982), which closely resembles its syntactic structure:

(47) **love**′(⟨forall x **woman**′(x)⟩, ⟨exists y **man**′(y)⟩)

(47) renders the semantics of DPs as *terms*, i.e., scope-bearing expressions whose scope has not been determined yet. Terms are triples of a quantifier, a bound variable, and a restriction.

The set of fully specified representations encompassed by such a representation is then determined by a resolution algorithm. The algorithm 'discharges' terms, i.e., integrates them into the rest of the representation, which determines their scope. (Formally, a term is replaced by its variable, then quantifier, variable, and restriction are prefixed to the resulting expression.) For instance, to obtain the representation (27a) for the '∀∃'-reading of (26) the existential term is discharged first, which yields (48):

(48) $\exists y.\mathbf{man}'(y) \wedge \mathbf{love}'(\langle \text{forall } x \, \mathbf{woman}'(x) \rangle, y)$

Discharging the remaining term then yields (27a); to derive (27b) from (47), one would discharge the universal term first. Such an approach is adopted e.g. in the Core Language Engine version of Moran (1988) and Alshawi (1992).

Hobbs & Shieber (1987) show that a rather involved resolution algorithm is needed to prevent overgeneration in more complicated cases of scope ambiguity, in particular, for nested quantification. Initial representations for nested quantification comprise nested terms, e.g., the representation (49) for (40):

(49) $\mathbf{see}'(\langle \text{forall } x \, \mathbf{researcher}'(x) \wedge \mathbf{of}'(x, \langle \text{exists } y \, \mathbf{company}'(y) \rangle) \rangle, \langle \text{most } z \, \mathbf{sample}'(z) \rangle)$

Here the restriction on the resolution is that the inner term may never be discharged before the outer one, which in the case of (40) rules out the unwanted 6th possible permutation of the quantifiers. Otherwise, this permutation could be generated by discharging the terms in the order '∃, **most**, ∀'. Such resolution algorithms lend themselves to a straightforward integration of *preference rules* such as '*each* outscopes other determiners', see section 6.4.

Other ways of handling nested quantification by restricting resolution algorithms for underspecified representations have been discussed in the literature. First, one could block *vacuous binding* (even though vacuous binding does not make formulae ill-formed), i.e., requesting an appropriate bound variable in the scope of every quantifier. In Hobbs & Shieber's (1987) terms, the step from (51), the initial representation for (50), to (52) is blocked, because the discharged quantifier fails to bind an occurence of a variable *y* in its scope (the only occurrence of *y* in its scope is inside a term, hence not accessible for binding). Thus, the unwanted solution (53) cannot be generated:

(50) Every researcher of a company came.

(51) $\mathbf{come}'(\langle \text{forall } x \, \mathbf{researcher}'(x) \wedge \mathbf{of}'(x, \langle \text{exists } y \, \mathbf{company}'(y) \rangle) \rangle)$

(52) $\exists y.\mathbf{company}'(y) \wedge \mathbf{come}'(\langle \text{forall } x \, \mathbf{researcher}'(x) \wedge \mathbf{of}'(x,y) \rangle)$

(53) $\forall x.(\mathbf{researcher}'(x) \wedge \mathbf{of}'(x,y)) \rightarrow \exists y. \mathbf{company}'(y) \wedge \mathbf{come}'(x)$

But Keller (1988) shows that this strategy is not general enough: If there is a second instance of the variable that is not inside a term, as in the representation (55) for (54), the analogous step from (55) to (56) cannot be blocked, even though it would eventually lead to structure (57) where the variable y within the restriction of the universal quantifier is not bound:

(54) Every sister of [a boy]$_i$ hates him$_i$.

(55) **hate'**(⟨forall x **sister-of'**(x, ⟨exists y **boy'**(y)⟩)⟩,y)

(56) ∃y.**boy'**(y) ∧ **hate'**(⟨forall x **sister-of'**(x, y)⟩, y)

(57) ∀x.**sister-of'**(x, y) → ∃y.**boy'**(y) ∧ **hate'**(x,y)

A second way of handling nested quantification (Nerbonne 1993) is restricting the solutions of underspecified representations to *closed formulae* (without free variables), although free variables do not make formulae ill-formed.

This approach can handle problems with sentences like (54), but is inefficient in that resolution steps must be performed before the result can be checked against the closedness requirement. It also calls for an (otherwise redundant) bookkeeping of free variables and bars the possibility of modelling the semantic contribution of non-anaphoric pronouns in terms of free variables.

Another way of deriving scope ambiguities is instantiated by Hendriks' (1993) *Flexible Montague Grammar* and Sailer's (2000) *Lexicalized Flexible Ty2*. Here scope ambiguity is put down to the polysemous nature of specific constituents (in particular, verbs and their arguments), which have an (in principle unlimited yet systematically related) set of interpretations. This ambiguity is then inherited by expressions that these constituents are part of, but this does not influence the constituent structure of the expression, because all readings of these constituents have the same syntactic category.

Every lexical entry gets a maximally simple interpretation, which can be changed by general rules such as *Argument Raising* (AR). For instance, *love* would be introduced as a relation between two individuals, and twofold application of AR derives the λ-terms in (58), relations between properties of properties, whose difference is due to the different order of applying AR to the arguments:

(58) a. λYλX.X(λx.Y(λy.**love'**(x,y)))
      b. λYλX.Y(λy.X(λx.**love'**(x,y)))

Applying these λ-terms to the semantic representations of *a man* and *every woman* (in this order, which follows the syntactic structure in (2)) then derives the two semantic representations in (27).

Another formalism of this group is Ambiguous Predicate Logic (APL; Jaspars & van Eijck 1996). It describes scope underspecification in terms of so-called *formulae*, in which *contexts* (structured lists of scope-bearing operators) can be prefixed to expressions of predicate logic (or other formulae).

For instance, (59a) indicates that the existential quantifier has wide scope over the universal one, since they form one list element together, whereas negation, as another element of the same list, can take any scope w.r.t. the two quantifiers (wide, intermediate, or narrow). In contrast, (59b) leaves the scope of the existential quantifier and negation open, and states that the universal quantifier can have scope over or below (not between) the other operators.

(59) a. $(\exists x \Box \forall y \Box, \neg \Box) Rxy$
 b. $((\exists x \Box, \neg \Box) \Box, \forall y \Box) Rxy$

Explicit rewrite rules serve to derive the set of solutions from these formulae. In a formula $C(\alpha)$, one can either take any simple list element from the context C and apply it to α, or take the last part of a complex list element, e.g., $\forall y \Box$ from $\exists x \Box \forall y \Box$ in (59a). This would map (59a) onto (60a), which can then be rewritten as (60c) with the intermediate step (60b):

(60) a. $(\exists x \Box, \neg \Box) \forall y.Rxy$
 b. $(\exists x \Box) \neg \forall y.Rxy$
 c. $\exists x. \neg \forall y.Rxy$

In sum, the underspecification formalisms expounded in this subsection give initial underspecified representations for ambiguous expressions that do not by themselves delimit the range of intended representations fully. This delimitation is the joint effect of the initial representations and the resolution algorithm.

The difference between underspecification formalisms describing the readings of an ambiguous expression and those that derive the readings is thus not the existence of suitable algorithms to enumerate the readings (see section 6 for such algorithms for descriptive underspecification formalisms), but the question of whether such an algorithm is essential in determining the set of solutions.

3.3 Levels of representation

In the previous sections, underspecification formalisms were introduced as distinguishing a meta and an object level of representation. This holds good for the majority of such formalisms, but in other ones both the underspecified and the fully specified representations are expressions of the same kind (what Cimiano & Reyle 2005 call 'representational' as opposed to 'descriptive' approaches).

UDRT (Reyle 1993, 1996) belongs to the second group. It separates information on the ingredients of a semantic representation (DRS fragments, see article 11 [Semantics: Theories] (Kamp & Reyle) *Discourse Representation Theory)* from information on the way that these fragments are combined. Consider e.g. (61) and its representation in (62):

(61) Everybody didn't pay attention.

(62) $\langle l_T : \langle l_1 : [x \mid human(x)] \Rightarrow [\ ], l_2: [\neg [\ ]], l_3: [x\ pay\ attention] \rangle, ORD \rangle$

In prose: The whole structure (represented by the label l_T) consists of a set of labelled DRS fragments (for the semantic contributions of DP, negation, and VP, respectively) that are ordered in a way indicated by a relation ORD.

For an underspecified representation of the two readings of (61), the scope relations between l_1 and l_2 are left open in ORD:

(63) ORD = $\langle l_T \geq l_1, l_T \geq l_2, scope(l_1) \geq l_3, scope(l_2) \geq l_3 \rangle$.

Here '≥' means 'has scope over', and *scope* maps a DRS fragment onto the empty DRS box it contains. Fully specified representations for the readings of (61) can then also be expressed in terms of (62). In these cases, ORD comprises in addition to the items in (63) a relation to determine the scope between universal quantifier and negation, e.g., $scope(l_1) \geq l_2$ for the reading with wide scope of the universal quantifier.

Another instance of such a 'monostratal' underspecification formalism is the (revised) Quasi-Logical Form (QLF) of Alshawi & Crouch (1992), which uses list-valued meta-variables in semantic representations whose specification indicates quantifier scope. See the representation for (26) in (32a).

Kempson & Cormack (1981) also assume a single level of semantic representation (higher-order predicate logic) for quantifier scope ambiguities.

3.4 Compositionality

Another distinction between underspecification formalisms centres upon the notion of *resource:* In most underspecification formalisms, the elements of a constraint show up at least once in all its solutions, in fact, exactly once, except in special cases like ellipses. For instance, in UDRT constraints and their solutions share the same set of DRS fragments, in CLLS (Egg, Koller & Niehren 2001) the relation between constraints and their solutions is defined as an assignment function from node variables (in constraints) to nodes (in the solutions), and in Glue Language Semantics this resource-sensitivity is explicitly encoded in the representations (expressions of linear logic).

Due to this resource-sensitivity, every solution of an underspecified semantic representation of a linguistic expression preserves the semantic contributions of the parts of the expression. If different parts happen to introduce identical semantic material, then each instance must show up in each solution. For instance, any solution to a constraint for (64a) must comprise two universal quantifiers. The contributions of the two DPs may not be conflated in solutions, which rules out that (64a) and (64b) could share a reading 'for every person x: x likes x'.

(64) a. Everyone likes everyone.
b. Everyone likes himself.

While this strategy seems natural in that the difference between (64a) and (64b) need not be stipulated by additional mechanisms, there are cases where different instances of the same semantic material seem to merge in the solutions.

Reconsider e.g. the case of Afrikaans past tense marking (65) [= (18)] in Sailer (2004). This example has two tense markers and three readings. Sailer points out that the two instances of the past tense marker seem to merge in the first and the second reading of (65):

(65) Jan wou gebel het.
Jan want.PAST called have.
'Jan wanted to call/Jan wants to have called/Jan wanted to have called'.

A direct formalisation of this intuition is possible if one relates fragments in terms of *subexpressionhood,* as in the underspecified analyses in the LRS framework (Richter & Sailer 2006; Kallmeyer & Richter 2006). If constraints introduce identical fragments as subexpressions of a larger fragment, these fragments can but need not coincide in the solutions of the constraints.

For the readings of (18), the constraint (simplified) is (66a):

(66) a. $\langle [\text{PAST}(\gamma)]_\beta, [\text{PAST}(\zeta)]_\varepsilon, [\textbf{want}'(j, \hat{}\eta)]_\theta, [\textbf{call}'(j)]_\iota, \beta \triangleleft \alpha, \varepsilon \triangleleft \delta, \theta \triangleleft \delta, \iota \triangleleft \zeta,$
$i \triangleleft \eta, \iota \triangleleft \eta \rangle$
b. $\text{PAST}(\textbf{want}'(j, \hat{} (\textbf{call}'(j))))$

In prose: The two PAST- and the *want*-fragments are subexpressions of (relation '$\triangleleft$') the whole expression (as represented by the variables α or δ), while the *call*-fragment is a subexpression of the arguments of the PAST operators and the intensionalised second argument of *want*. This constraint describes all three semantic representations in (19); e.g., to derive (66b) [= (19a)], the following equations are needed: $\alpha = \delta = \beta = \varepsilon$, $\gamma = \zeta = \theta$, and $\eta = \iota$. The crucial equation here is $\beta = \varepsilon$, which equates two fragments. (Additional machinery is needed to block unwanted readings, see Sailer 2004.)

This approach is more powerful than resource-sensitive formalisms. The price one has to pay for this additional power is the need to control explicitly whether identical material may coincide or not, e.g., for the analyses of negative concord in Richter & Sailer (2006). (See also article 6 [Semantics: Foundations, History and Methods] (Pagin & Westerståhl) *Compositionality.)*

3.5 Expressivity and compactness

The standard approach to evaluate an underspecification formalisms is to apply it to challenging ambiguous examples, e.g., (67) [= (40)], and to check whether there is an expression of the formalism that expresses *all* and *only* the attested readings of the example:

(67) Every researcher of a company saw most samples.

However, what if these readings are contextually restricted, or, if the sentence has only four readings, as claimed by Kallmeyer & Romero (2008) and others, lacking the reading (45b) with the scope ordering $\exists > \textbf{most}' > \forall$?

Underspecification approaches that model scope in terms of partial order between fragments of semantic representations run into problems already with the second of these possibilities: Any constraint set that encompasses the four readings in which **most**' has highest or lowest scope also covers the fifth reading (45b) (Ebert 2005). This means that such underspecification formalisms are not expressive in the sense of König & Reyle (1999) or Ebert (2005), since they cannot represent *any* subset of readings of an ambiguous expression.

The formalisms are of different expressivity, e.g., approaches that model quantifier scope by lists (such as Alshawi 1992) are less expressive than those that use dominance relations, or scope lists together with an explicit ordering of list elements as in Fox & Lappin's (2005) *Property Theory with Curry Typing*.

Fully expressive is the approach of Koller, Regneri & Thater (2008), which uses *Regular Tree Grammars* for scope underspecification. Rules of these grammars expand nonterminals into tree fragments. For instance, the rule $S \rightarrow f(A, B)$ expands S into a tree whose mother is labelled by f, and whose children are the subtrees to be derived by expanding the nonterminals A and B.

Koller, Regneri & Thater (2008) show that dominance constraints can be translated into RTGs, e.g., the constraint (68) [= (41)] for the semantics of (40) is translated into (69).

(68)

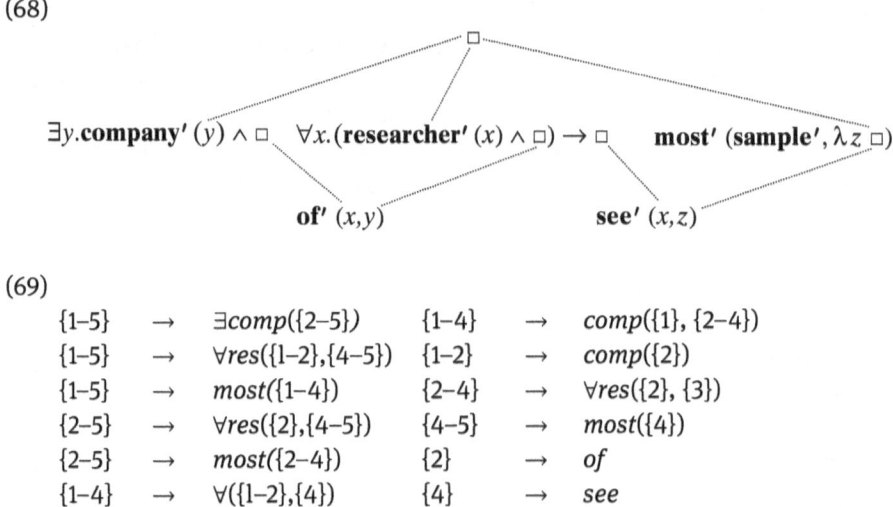

(69)

{1–5}	→	∃*comp*({2–5})	{1–4}	→	*comp*({1}, {2–4})
{1–5}	→	∀*res*({1–2},{4–5})	{1–2}	→	*comp*({2})
{1–5}	→	*most*({1–4})	{2–4}	→	∀*res*({2}, {3})
{2–5}	→	∀*res*({2},{4–5})	{4–5}	→	*most*({4})
{2–5}	→	*most*({2–4})	{2}	→	*of*
{1–4}	→	∀({1–2},{4})	{4}	→	*see*

In (69), the fragments of (68) are addressed by numbers, 1, 3, and 5 are the fragments for the existential, universal, and *most*-DP, respectively, and 2 and 4 are the fragments for *of* and *see*. All nonterminals correspond to parts of constraints; they are abbreviated as sequences of fragments. For instance, {2–5} corresponds to the whole constraint except the existential fragment.

Rules of the RTG specify on the right hand side the root of the partial constraint introduced on the left hand side, for instance, the first rule expresses wide scope of *a company* over the whole sentence. The RTG (69) yields the same five solutions as (68).

In (69), the reading ∃ > **most'** > ∀ can be excluded easily, by removing the production rule {2–5} → *most*({2–4}): This leaves only one expansion rule for

{2–5}. Since {2–5} emerges only as child of ∃*comp* with widest scope, only ∀*res* can be the root of the tree below widest-scope ∃*comp*. This shows that RTGs are more expressive than dominance constraints. (In more involved cases, restricting the set of solutions can be less simple, however, which means that RTGs can get larger if specific solutions are to be excluded.)

This last observation points to another property of underspecification formalisms that is interdependent with expressivity, viz., *compactness*: A (sometimes tacit) assumption is that underspecification formalisms should be able to characterise a set of readings of an ambiguous expression in terms of a representation that is shorter or more efficient than an enumeration (or disjunction) of all the readings (König & Reyle 1999). Ebert (2005) defines this intuitive notion of compactness in the following way: An underspecification formalism is compact iff the maximal length of the representations is at most polynomial (with respect to the number of scope-bearing elements).

Ebert shows that there is a trade-off between expressivity and compactness, and that no underspecification formalism can be both expressive and compact in his sense at the same time.

4 Motivation

This section outlines a number of motivations for the introduction and use of semantic underspecification formalisms.

4.1 Functionality of the syntax-semantics interface

The first motivation for semantic underspecification formalisms lies in the syntax- semantics interface: Semantic underspecification is one way of keeping the mapping from syntax to semantics *functional* in spite of semantically and syntactically homogeneous ambiguities like (26). These expressions can be analysed in terms of a single syntactic structure even though they have several readings. This seems in conflict with the functional nature of semantic interpretation, which associates one specific syntactic structure with only one single semantic structure (see Westerståhl 1998 and Hodges 2001).

Competing approaches to the syntax-semantics interface multiply syntactic structures for semantically and syntactically homogeneous ambiguities (one for each reading) of relinquish the functionality of the syntax-semantics interface altogether to cover these ambiguities. (See article 6 [Semantics: Interfaces] (von Stechow) *Syntax and semantics.)*

4.1.1 Multiplying syntactic structures

Syntactic structures can be multiplied in two ways. First, one can postulate the functional relation between syntactic *derivation trees* (a syntactic structure and its derivation history) and semantic structures rather than between syntactic and semantic structures. This strategy shows up in Montague's (1974) account of quantifier scope ambiguity and in Hoeksema (1985). It is motivated by the definition of semantic interpretation as a homomorphism from the syntactic to the semantic algebra (every syntactic operation is translated into a semantic one), but demotes the semantic structure that results from this derivation by giving the pride of place to the derivation itself.

Second, one can model the ambiguous expressions as syntactically *heterogeneous*. This means that each reading corresponds to a unique syntactic structure (on a semantically relevant syntactic level). Syntactic heterogeneity can then emerge either through different ways of combining the parts of the expression (which themselves need not be ambiguous) or through systematic lexical ambiguity of specific parts of the expression, which enforces different ways of combining them syntactically.

The first way of making the relevant expressions syntactically heterogeneous is implemented in *Generative Grammar*. Here syntactic structures unique to specific readings show up on the level of *Logical Form* (LF). For instance, quantifier scope is be determined by (covert) DP movement and adjunction (mostly, to a suitable S node); relative scope between quantifiers can then be put down to relations of c-command between the respective DPs on LF (Heim & Kratzer 1998). (The standard definition of c-command is that a constituent A c-commands another constituent B if A does not dominate B and vice versa and the lowest branching node that dominates A also dominates B.)

This strategy is also used for scope ambiguities below the word level, which are reconstructed in terms of different syntactic constellations of constituents below the word level. These constituents can correspond to morphemes (as in the case of *dancer* or the Anglo-Saxon genitive), but need not (e.g., for the change-of-state operator in the semantics of *die*).

The second way of inducing syntactic heterogeneity is to assume that specific lexical items are ambiguous because they occur in different syntactic categories. This means that depending on their reading they combine with other constituents in different ways syntactically. For instance, *Combinatory Categorial Grammar* (CCG) incorporates rules of *type raising*, which change the syntactic category and hence also the combinatory potential of lexical items. For instance, an expression of category X can become one of type $T/(T \setminus X)$, i.e., a T which lacks to its right a T lacking an X to its left. If $X = DP$ and $T = S$, a DP becomes a sentence without a following VP, since the VP is a sentence without a preceding DP ($S \backslash DP$).

Hendriks (1993) and Steedman (2000) point out that these rules could be used for modelling quantifier scope ambiguities in terms of syntactically heterogeneous ambiguity: Syntactic type raising changes the syntactic combinatory potential of the involved expressions, which may change the order in which the expressions are combined in the syntactic construction. This in turn affects the order of combining elements in semantic construction. In particular, if a DP is integrated later than another one (DP'), then DP gets wide scope over DP': The semantics of DP is applied to a semantic representation that already comprises the semantic contribution of DP'.

In an example such as (26), the two readings could thus emerge by either first forming a VP and then combining it with the subject (wide scope for the subject), or by forming a constituent out of subject and verb, which is then combined with the object (which consequently gets widest scope).

4.1.2 Giving up the functionality of the syntax-semantics interface

Other researchers give up the functionality of the syntax-semantics interface to handle syntactically and semantically homogeneous ambiguities. One syntactic structure may thus correspond to several readings, which is due to a less strict coupling of syntactic and semantic construction rules.

This strategy is implemented in *Cooper store* approaches (Cooper 1983), in which specific syntactic operations are coupled to more than one corresponding semantic operation in the syntax-semantics interface. In particular, the syntactic combination of a DP with a syntactic structure *S* may lead to the immediate combination of the semantic contributions of both DP and *S* or to appending the DP semantics to a list of DP interpretations (the 'store'). Subsequently, material can be retrieved from the store for any sentence constituent, this material is then combined with the semantic representation of the sentence constituent. This gives the desired flexibility to derive scopally different semantic representations like in (27) from uniform syntactic structures like (2).

The approach of Woods (1967, 1978) works similarly: Semantic contributions of DPs are collected separately from the main semantic representation; they can be integrated into this main representation immediately or later.

Another approach of this kind is Steedman (2007). Here non-universal quantifiers and their scope with respect to universal quantifiers are modelled in terms of Skolem functions. (See Kallmeyer & Romero 2008 for further discussion of this strategy.) These functions can have arguments for variables bound by universal quantifiers to express the fact that they are outscoped by these quantifiers. Consider e.g. the two readings of (26) in Skolem notation:

(70) a. $\forall x.\textbf{woman}'(x) \rightarrow \textbf{man}'(sk_1) \wedge \textbf{love}'(x, sk_1)$ ('one man for all women')
b. $\forall x.\textbf{woman}'(x) \rightarrow \textbf{man}'(sk_2(x)) \wedge \textbf{love}'(x,sk_2(x))$ ('a possibly different man per woman')

For the derivation of the different readings of a scopally underspecified expression, Steedman uses underspecified Skolem functions, which can be specified at any point in the derivation w.r.t. their *environment*, viz., the n-tuple of variables bound by universal quantifiers so far. For (26), the semantics of *a man* would be represented by $\lambda Q.Q(\textbf{skolem}'(\textbf{man}'))$, where **skolem**' is a function from properties P and environments E to generalised skolem terms like $f(E)$, where P holds of $f(E)$.

The term $\lambda Q.Q(\textbf{skolem}'(\textbf{man}'))$ can be specified at different steps in the derivation, with different results: Immediately after the DP has been formed specification returns a Skolem constant like sk_1 in (70a), since the environment is still empty. After combining the semantics of the DPs and the verb, the environment is the 1-tuple with the variable x bound by the universal quantifier of the subject DP, and specification at that point yields a skolem term like $sk_2(x)$.

This sketch of competing approaches to the syntax-semantics interface shows that the functionality of this interface (or, an attempt to uphold it in spite of semantically and syntactically homogeneous ambiguous expressions) can be a motivation for underspecification: Functionality is preserved for such an expression directly in that there is a function from its syntactic structure to its underspecified semantic representation that encompasses all its readings.

4.2 Ambiguity and negation

Semantic underspecification also helps avoiding problems with disjunctive representations of the meaning of ambiguous expressions that show up under *negation*: Negating an ambiguous expression is intuitively interpreted as the disjunction of the negated expressions, i.e., one of the readings of the expressions is denied. However, if the meaning of the expression itself is modelled as the disjunction of its readings, the negated expression emerges as the negation of the disjunctions, which is equivalent to the *conjunction* of the negated readings, i.e., every reading of the expression is denied, which runs counter to intuitions.

For instance, for (26) such a semantic representation can be abbreviated as (71), which turns into (72) after negation:

(71) ∀∃ ∨ ∃∀

(72) ¬(∀∃ ∨ ∃∀) = ¬∀∃ ∧ ¬∃∀

However, if we model the meaning of the ambiguous expression as the set of its fully specified readings, and assume that understanding such an expression proceeds by forming the disjunction of this set, these interpretations follow directly. For (26), the meaning is {∀∃, ∃∀}. Asserting (26) is understood as the disjunction of its readings {∀∃, ∃∀}; its denial, as the disjunction of its readings {¬∀∃, ¬∃∀}, which yields the desired interpretation (van Eijck & Pinkal 1996).

For examples more involved than (26), the most efficient strategy of describing these set of readings would then be to describe their elements rather than to enumerate them, which then calls for underspecification.

4.3 Underspecification in Natural Langugage Processing

One of the strongest motivations for semantic underspecification was its usefulness for Natural Language Processing (NLP). (See also article 14 [Semantics: Typology, Diachrony and Processing] (Pinkal & Koller) *Semantics in computational linguistics.*)

The first issue for which underspecification is very useful is the fact that scope ambiguity resolution can be really hard. For instance, in a small corpus study on quantifier scope in the CHORUS project at the University of the Saarland (using the NEGRA corpus; Brants, Skut & Uszkoreit 2003), roughly 10% of the sentences with several scope-bearing elements were problematic, e.g., the slightly simplified (73):

(73) Alle Teilnehmer erhalten ein Handbuch
      all participants receive a handbook
      'All participants receive a handbook'

The interpretation of (73) is that the same kind of handbook is given to every participant, but that everyone gets his own copy. That is, the scope between the DPs interacts with a type-token ambiguity: an existential quantification over handbook types outscopes the universal quantification over participants, which in turn gets scope over an existential quantification over handbook tokens.

For those examples, underspecification is useful to allow a semantic representation for NLP systems at all, because it does not force the system to make arbitrary choices and nevertheless returns a semantic analysis of the examples.

But the utility of underspecification for NLP is usually discussed with reference to *efficiency*, because this technique allows one to evade the problem of *combinatorial explosion* (Poesio 1990; Ebert 2005). The problem is that in many cases, the number of readings of an ambiguous expression gets too large to be generated and enumerated, let alone to be handled efficiently in further modules of an NLP system (e.g., for Machine Translation).

Deriving an underspecified representation of an ambiguous expression that captures only the common ground between its readings and fully deriving a reading only by need is less costly than generating all possible interpretations and then selecting the relevant one.

What is more, a complete disambiguation may be not even *necessary*. In these cases, postponing ambiguity resolution, and resolving ambiguity only on demand makes NLP systems more efficient. For instance, scope ambiguities are often irrelevant for translation, therefore it would be useless to identify the intended reading of such an expression: Its translation into the target language would be ambiguous in the same way again. Therefore e.g. the Verbmobil project (machine translation of spontaneous spoken dialogue; Wahlster 2000) used a scopally underspecified semantic representation (Schiehlen 2000).

The analyses of concrete NLP systems show clearly that combinatorial explosion is a problem for NLP that suggests the use of underspecification (pace Player 2004). The large number of readings that are attributed to linguistic expressions are due to the fact that, first, the number of scope-bearing constituents per expression is underestimated (there are many more such constituents besides DPs, e.g., negation, modal verbs, quantifying adverbials like *three times* or *again*), and, second and much worse, *spurious ambiguities* come in during syntactic and semantic processing of the expressions.

For instance, Koller, Regneri & Thater (2008) found that 5% of the representations in the Rondane Treebank (underspecified MRS representations of sentences from the domain of Norwegian tourist information, distributed as part of the English Resource Grammar, Copestake & Flickinger 2000) have more than 650 000 solutions, record holder is the rather innocuous looking (74) with about 4.5×10^{12} scope readings:

(74) Myrdal is the mountain terminus of the Flåm rail line (or Flåmsbana) which makes its way down the lovely Flåm Valley (Flåmsdalen) to its sea-level terminus at Flåm.

The median number of scope readings per sentence is 56 (Koller, Regneri & Thater 2008), so, short of applying specific measures to eliminate spurious ambiguities (see section 6.2), combinatorial explosion definitely is a problem for semantic analysis in NLP.

In recent years, underspecification has turned out very useful for NLP in another way, viz., in that underspecified semantics provides an *interface* bridging the gap between deep and shallow processing. To combine the advantages of both kinds of processing (accuracy vs. robustness and speed), both can be combined in NLP applications *(hybrid processing)*. The results of deep and shallow syntactic processing can straightforwardly be integrated on the semantic level (instead of combining the results of deep and shallow syntactic analyses). An example for an architecture for hybrid processing is the 'Heart of Gold' developed in the project 'DeepThought' (Callmeier et al. 2004).

Since shallow syntactic analyses provide only a part of the information to be gained from deep analysis, the semantic information derivable from the results of a shallow parse (e.g., by a part-of-speech tagger or an NP chunker) can only be a part of the one derived from the results of a deep parse. Underspecification formalisms can be used to model this kind of partial information as well.

For instance, deep and shallow processing may yield different results with respect to argument linking: NP chunkers (as opposed to systems of deep processing) do not relate verbs and their syntactic arguments, e.g., experiencer and patient in (75). Any semantic analysis based on such a chunker will thus fail to identify individuals in NP and verb semantics as in (76):

(75) Max saw Mary

(76) named(x_1, Max), see(x_2, x_3), named(x_4, Mary)

Semantic representations of different depths must be compatible in order to combine results from parallel deep and shallow processing or to transform shallow into deep semantic analyses by adding further pieces of information. Thus, the semantic representation formalism must be capable of separating the semantic information from different sources appropriately. For instance, information on argument linking should be listed separately, thus, a full semantic analysis of (75) should look like (77) rather than (78). Robust MRS (Copestake 2003) is an underspecification formalism that was designed to fulfill this demand:

(77) named(x_1, Max), see(x_2, x_3), named(x_4, Mary), $x_1 = x_2$, $x_3 = x_4$

(78) named(x_1, Max), see(x_1, x_4), named(x_4, Mary)

4.4 Semantic construction

Finally, underspecification formalisms turn out to be interesting from the perspective of semantic construction in general, independently of the issue of ambiguity. This interest is based on two properties of these formalisms, viz., their *portability* and their *flexibility*.

First, underspecification formalisms do not presuppose a specific syntactic analysis (which would do a certain amount of preprocessing for the mapping from syntax to semantics, like the mapping from surface structure to Logical Form in Generative Grammar). Therefore the syntax-semantics interface can be defined in a very transparent fashion, which makes the formalisms very *portable* in that they can be coupled with different syntactic formalisms. Tab. 9.1 lists some of the realised combinations of syntactic and semantic formalisms.

Second, the flexibility of the interfaces that are needed to derive underspecified representations of ambiguous expressions is also available for unambiguous cases that pose a challenge for any syntax-semantics interface. For instance, semantic construction for the modification of modifiers and indefinite pronouns like *everyone* is a problem, because the types of functor (semantics of the modifier) and argument (semantics of the modified expression) do not fit: For instance, in (79) the PP semantics is a function from properties to properties, the semantics of the pronoun as well as the one of the whole modification structure are sets of properties.

Tab. 9.1: Realised couplings of underspecification formalisms and syntax formalisms

	HPSG	LFG	(L)TAG
MRS	Copestake et al. (2005)	Oepen et al. (2004)	Kallmeyer & Joshi (1999)
GLS	Asudeh & Crouch (2001)	Dalrymple (2001)	Frank & van Genabith (2001)
UDRT	Frank & Reyle (1995)	van Genabith & Crouch (1999)	Cimiano & Reyle (2005)
HS	Chaves (2002)		Kallmeyer & Joshi (2003)

(79) everyone in this room

Interfaces for the derivation of underspecified semantic representations for examples like (26) can be reused to perform the semantic construction of (79) and of many more examples of that kind, see Egg (2004, 2006). Similarly, Richter & Sailer (2006) use their underspecification formalism to handle semantic construction for unambiguous cases of negative concord. For these unambiguous expressions, the use of underspecification formalisms requires a careful control of the solutions of the resulting constraints: These constraints must have a single solution only (since the expressions are unambiguous), but underspecification constraints were designed primarily for the representation of ambiguous expressions, whose constraints have several solutions.

5 Semantic underspecification and the syntax-semantics interface

In this section, I will sketch the basic interface strategy to derive underspecified semantic structures from (surface-oriented) syntactic structures. The strategy consists in deliberately not specifying scope relations between potentially scopally ambiguous constituents of an expression, e.g., in the syntax-semantics interfaces described for UDRT (Frank & Reyle 1995), MRS (Copestake et al. 2005), CLLS (Egg, Koller & Niehren 2001) or Hole Semantics (Bos 2004).

To derive underspecified semantic structures, explicit bookkeeping of specific parts of these structures is necessary. These parts have 'addresses' (e.g., the labels of UDRT or the handles of MRS) that are visible to the interface rules. This allows interface rules to address these parts in the subconstituents when they specify how the constraints of the subconstituents are to be combined in the constraint of the emerging new constituent. (The rules also specify these parts for the constraint of the new constituent.) Therefore, these interfaces are more powerful than interfaces that only combine the semantic contributions of the subconstituents as a whole.

As an example, consider the (greatly simplified) derivation of the under-specified representation (28) of example (26) by means of the syntax-semantics interface rules (80)–(82). In the interface, each atomic or complex constituent C is associated with a constraint and has two special fragments, a top fragment $[[C_{top}]]$ (which handles scope issues) and a main fragment $[[C]]$. These two fragments are addressed in the interface rules as 'glue points' where the constraints of the involved constituents are put together; each interface rule determines these fragments anew for the emerging constituent. Furthermore, all fragments of the subconstituents are inherited by the emerging constituent.

The first rule builds the DP semantics out of the semantic contributions of determiner and NP:

(80) $[_{DP}$ Det NP$]$ $\overset{(SSI)}{\Rightarrow}$ $⟦\text{Det}⟧(⟦\text{NP}⟧)(\lambda z.\,\square)$; $⟦\text{DP}_{top}⟧ = ⟦\text{Det}_{top}⟧ = ⟦\text{NP}_{top}⟧$

$⟦\text{DP}⟧ : z$

In prose: Apply the main determiner fragment to the main NP fragment and a hole with a λ-abstraction over a variable that is dominated by the hole and constitutes by itself the main DP fragment. The top fragments (holes that determine the scope of the DP, because the top fragment of a constituent always dominates all its other fragments) of DP, determiner, and NP are identical. ('SSI' indicates that it is a rule of the syntax-semantics interface.)

The main fragment of a VP (of a sentence) emerges by applying the main verb (VP) fragment to the main fragment of the object (subject) DP. The top fragments of the verb (VP) and its DP argument are identical to the one of the emerging VP (S):

(81) $[_{VP}$ V DP$]$ $\overset{(SSI)}{\Rightarrow}$ $⟦\text{VP}⟧: ⟦\text{V}⟧(⟦\text{DP}⟧)$; $⟦\text{VP}_{top}⟧ = ⟦\text{V}_{top}⟧ = ⟦\text{DP}_{top}⟧$

(82) $[_{S}$ DP VP$]$ $\overset{(SSI)}{\Rightarrow}$ $⟦\text{S}⟧: ⟦\text{VP}⟧(⟦\text{DP}⟧)$; $⟦\text{S}_{top}⟧ = ⟦\text{DP}_{top}⟧ = ⟦\text{VP}_{top}⟧$

We assume that for all lexical entries, the main fragments are identical to the standard semantic representation (e.g., for *every*, we get [[Det]]: $\lambda Q \lambda P \forall x.Q(x) \rightarrow P(x)$), and the top fragments are holes dominating the main fragments. If in unary projections like the one of *man* from N to N̄ and NP main and top fragments are merely inherited, the semantics of *a man* emerges as (83):

(83) $⟦\text{DP}_{top}⟧$: $\square$

$\exists y.\,\textbf{man}'(y) \wedge \square$

$⟦\text{DP}⟧$: y

The crucial point is the decision to let the bound variable be the main fragment in the DP semantics. The intermediate DP fragment between top and main fragment is ignored in further processes of semantic construction. Combining (83) with the semantics of the verb yields (84):

(84)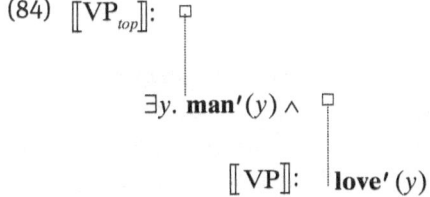

Finally, the semantics of *every woman*, which is derived in analogy to (83), is combined with (84) through rule (82). According to this rule, the two top fragments are identified and the two main fragments are combined by functional application into the main S fragment, but the two intermediate fragments, which comprise the two quantifiers, are not addressed at all, and hence remain dangling in between. The result is the desired dominance diamond:

(85)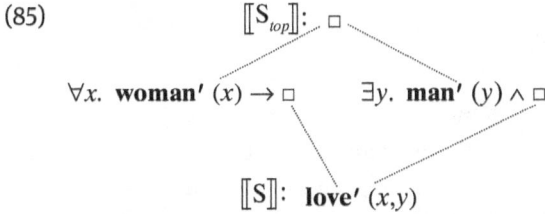

The technique of splitting the semantic contribution of a quantifying DP resurfaces in many underspecification approaches, among them CLLS, Muskens' Logical Description Grammar, and LTAG (Cimiano & Reyle 2005).

6 Further processing of underspecified representations

Topic of this section is the further processing of underspecified representations. One can *enumerate* the set of solutions of a constraint, which has been the topic of much work in computational approaches to underspecification. Related to the enumeration of solutions is work on *redundancy elimination*, which tries to identify set of equivalent readings. The third line of approach is the attempt to derive (fully specified) information from underspecified representations by *reasoning* with these representations. Finally, one can derive a solution (or a small set of solutions) in terms of *preferences*. This enterprise has been pursued both in computational linguistics and in psycholinguistics.

6.1 Resolution of underspecified representations

The first way of deriving fully specified semantic representations from underspecified representations is to enumerate the readings by *resolving* the constraints. For a worked out example of such a resolution, reconsider the derivation of fully specified interpretations from the set of meaning constructors in Glue Language Semantics as expounded in section 3.1. or the detailed account of resolving USDL representations in Pinkal (1996).

For a number of formalisms, specific systems, so-called *solvers*, are available for this derivation. For MRS representations, there is a solver in the LKB (Linguistic Knowledge Builder) system (Copestake & Flickinger 2000). Blackburn & Bos (2005) present a solver for Hole Semantics. For the language of dominance constraints, a number of solvers have been developed (see Koller, Regneri & Thater 2008 and Koller & Thater 2005 for an overview).

6.2 Redundancy elimination

In NLP applications that use underspecification, *spurious ambiguities* (which do not correspond to attested readings) are an additional complication, because they drastically enlarge the number of readings assigned to an ambiguous expression. For instance, Koller, Regneri & Thater (2008) found high numbers of spurious ambiguities in the Rondane Treebank (see section 4.3).

Hurum's (1988) algorithm, the CLE resolution algorithm (Moran 1988; Alshawi 1992), and Chaves' (2003) extension of Hole Semantics detect specific cases of equivalent solutions (e.g., when one existential quantifier immediately dominates another one) and block all but one of them. The blocking is only effective once the solutions are enumerated. In contrast, Koller & Thater (2006) and Koller, Regneri & Thater (2008) present algorithms to reduce spurious ambiguities that map underspecified representations on (more restricted) underspecified representations.

6.3 Reasoning with underspecified representations

Sometimes fully specified information can be deduced from an underspecified semantic representation. For instance, if Amélie is a woman, then (26) allows us to conclude that she loves a man, because this conclusion is valid no matter which reading of (26) is chosen. For UDRT (König & Reyle 1999; Reyle 1992; Reyle 1993; Reyle 1996) and APL (Jaspars & van Eijck 1996), there are calculi for such reasoning with underspecified representations. Van Deemter (1996) discusses different kinds of consequence relations for this reasoning.

6.4 Integration of preferences

In many cases of scope ambiguity, the readings are not on a par in that some are more preferred than others. Consider e.g. a slight variation of (26), here the ∃∀-reading is preferred over the ∀∃-reading:

(86) A woman loves every man.

One could integrate these preferences into underspecified representations of scopally ambiguous expressions to narrow down the number of its readings or to order the generation of solutions (Alshawi 1992).

6.4.1 Kinds of preferences

The preferences discussed in the literature can roughly be divided into three groups. The first group are based on *syntactic structure,* starting with Johnson-Laird (1969) and Lakoff's (1971) claim that surface linear order or precedence introduces a preference for wide scope of the preceding scope-bearing item (but see e.g.Villalta 2003 for experimental counterevidence). Precedence can be interpreted in terms of a syntactic configuration such as c-command (e.g., VanLehn 1978), since in a right-branching binary phrase-marker preceding constituents c-command the following ones.

However, these preferences are not universally valid: Kurtzman & MacDonald (1993) report a clear preference for wide scope of the embedded DP in the case of nested quantification as in (87). Here the indefinite article precedes (and c-commands) the embedded DP, but the ∀∃-reading is nevertheless preferred:

(87) I met a researcher from every university.

Hurum (1988) and VanLehn (1978) make the preference of scope-bearing items to take scope outside the constituent they are directly embedded in also dependent on the category of that constituent (e.g., much stronger for items inside PPs than items inside infinite clauses).

The scope preference algorithm of Gambäck & Bos (1998) gives scope-bearing non-heads (complements and adjuncts) in binary-branching syntactic structures immediate scope over the respective head.

The second group of preferences focus on grammatical functions and thematic roles. Functional hierarchies have been proposed that indicate preference to take wide scope in Ioup (1975) (88a) and VanLehn (1978) (88b):

(88) a. topic > deep and surface subject > deep subject or surface subject > indirect object > prepositional object > direct object
b. preposed PP, topic NP > subject > (complement in) sentential or adverbial PP > (complement in) verb phrase PP > object

While Ioup combines thematic and functional properties in her hierarchy (by including the notion of 'deep subject'), Pafel (2005) distinguishes grammatical functions (only subject and sentenctial adverb) and thematic roles (strong and weak patienthood) explicitly.

There is a certain amount of overlap between structural preferences and the functional hierarchies, at least in a language like English: Here DPs higher on the functional hierarchy also tend to c-command DPs lower on the hierarchy, because they are more likely to surface as subjects.

The third group of preferences addresses the quantifiers (or, the determiners expressing them) themselves. Ioup (1975) and VanLehn (1978) introduce a hierarchy of determiners:

(89) each > every > all > most > many > several > some (plural) > a few

CLE incorporates such preference rules, too (Moran 1988; Alshawi 1992), e.g., the rule that *each* outscopes other determiners, and that negation is outscoped by *some* and outscopes *every*.

Some of these preferences can be put down to a more general preference for logically weaker interpretations, in particular, the tendency of universal quantifiers to outscope existential ones (recall that the $\forall\exists$-reading of sentences like (26) is weaker than the $\exists\forall$-reading; VanLehn 1978; Moran 1988; Alshawi 1992). Similarly, scope of the negation above *every* and below *some* returns existential statements, which are weaker than the (unpreferred) alternative scopings (universal statements) in that they do not make a claim about the whole domain.

Pafel (2005) lists further properties, among them focus and discourse binding (whether a DP refers to an already established set of entities, as e.g. in *few of the books* as opposed to *few books*).

6.4.2 Interaction of preferences

It has been argued that the whole range of quantifier scope effects can only be accounted for in terms of an interaction of different principles.

Fodor (1982) and Hurum (1988) assume an interaction between linear precedence and the determiner hierarchy, which is corroborated by experimental results of Filik, Paterson & Liversedge (2004). They show that a conflict of these principles leads to longer reading times.

The results of Filik, Paterson & Liversedge (2004) are also compatible with the predictions of Ioup (1975), who puts down scoping preferences to an interaction of the functional and quantifier hierarchy. To get wider scope than another quantifier, a quantifier must score high on both hierarchies.

Kurtzman & MacDonald (1993) present further empirical evidence for the interaction of preferences. They point to a clear contrast between sentences like (90a) [=(26)] and their passive version (90b), where the clear preference of (90a) for the ∀∃-reading is no longer there:

(90) a. Every woman loves a man.
  b. A man is loved by every woman.

If preferences were determined by a single principle, one would expect a preference for the passive version, too, either one for its (new) subject, or for the *by*-PP (the former demoted subject).

Kurtzman & MacDonald (1993) argue that the interaction of syntax-oriented principles with the thematic role principle can account for these findings. Since most subjects have higher thematic roles, the principles agree on the scope preference for the subject in the active sentence, but conflict in the case of the passive sentence, which consequently exhibits no clear-cut scope preference.

The interaction between surface ordering and the position of the indefinite article below the universally quantifying *every* and *each* on the quantifier hierarchy is explained by Fodor (1982) and Kurtzman & MacDonald (1993) in that it is easier to interpret indefinite DPs in terms of a single referent than in terms of several ones. The second interpretation must be motivated, e.g., in the context of an already processed universal quantifier, which suggests several entities, one for each of the entities over which the universal quantifier ranges.

The most involved model of interacting preferences for quantifier scope is the one of Pafel (2005). He introduces no less than eight properties of quantifiers that are relevant for scope preferences, among them syntactic position, grammatical function, thematic role, discourse binding and focus. The scores for the different properties are added up for each quantifier, the properties carry weights that were determined empirically.

7 References

Alshawi, Hiyan (ed.) 1992. *The Core Language Engine*. Cambridge, MA: The MIT Press.
Alshawi, Hiyan & Richard Crouch 1992. Monotonic semantic interpretation. In: *Proceedings of the 30th Annual Meeting of the Association for Computational Linguistics (= ACL)*. Newark, DE: Association for Computational Linguistics, 32–39.
Althaus, Ernst, Denys Duchier, Alexander Koller, Kurt Mehlhorn, Joachim Niehren & Sven Thiel 2001. An efficient algorithm for the configuration problem of dominance graphs. In: *Proceedings of the 12th ACM-SIAM Symposium on Discrete Algorithms*. New York: Association for Computing Machinery, 815–824.
Asher, Nicholas & Tim Fernando 1999. Labeled representations, underspecification and disambiguation. In: H. Bunt & R. Muskens (eds.). *Computing Meaning, vol. 1*. Dordrecht: Kluwer, 73–95.
Asher, Nicholas & Alex Lascarides 2003. *Logics of Conversation*. Cambridge: Cambridge University Press.
Asudeh, Ash & Richard Crouch 2002. Glue semantics for HPSG. In: F. van Eynde, L. Hellan & D. Beermann (eds.). *Proceedings of the 8th International Conference on Head-Driven Phrase Structure Grammar*. Stanford, CA: CSLI Publications, 1–19.
Babko-Malaya, Olga 2004. LTAG semantics of NP-coordination. In: *Proceedings of the 7th International Workshop on Tree Adjoining Grammars and Related Formalisms*. Vancouver, 111–117.
Bierwisch, Manfred 1983. Semantische und konzeptionelle Repräsentation lexikalischer Einheiten. In: R. Růžička & W. Motsch (eds.). *Untersuchungen zur Semantik*. Berlin: Akademie Verlag, 61–99.
Bierwisch, Manfred 1988. On the grammar of local prepositions. In: M. Bierwisch, W. Motsch & I. Zimmermann (eds.). *Syntax, Semantik und das Lexikon*. Berlin: Akademie Verlag, 1–65.
Bierwisch, Manfred & Ewald Lang (eds.) 1987. *Grammatische und konzeptuelle Aspekte von Dimensionsadjektiven*. Berlin: Akademie Verlag.
Blackburn, Patrick & Johan Bos 2005. *Representation and Inference for Natural Language. A First Course in Computational Semantics*. Stanford, CA: CSLI Publications.
Bos, Johan 1996. Predicate logic unplugged. In: P. Dekker & M. Stokhof (eds.). *Proceedings of the 10th Amsterdam Colloquium*. Amsterdam: ILLC, 133–142.
Bos, Johan 2004. Computational semantics in discourse. Underspecification, resolution, and inference. *Journal of Logic, Language and Information* 13, 139–157.
Brants, Thorsten, Wojciech Skut & Hans Uszkoreit 2003. Syntactic annotation of a German newspaper corpus. In: A. Abeillé (ed.). *Treebanks. Building and Using Parsed Corpora*. Dordrecht: Kluwer, 73–88.
Bronnenberg, Wim, Harry Bunt, Jan Landsbergen, Remko Scha, Wijnand Schoenmakers & Eric van Utteren 1979. The question answering system PHLIQA1. In: L. Bolc (ed.). *Natural Language Question Answering Systems*. London: Macmillan, 217–305.

Bunt, Harry 2007. Underspecification in semantic representations. Which technique for what purpose? In: H. Bunt & R. Muskens (eds.). *Computing Meaning, vol. 3*. Amsterdam: Springer, 55–85.
Callmeier, Ulrich, Andreas Eisele, Ulrich Schäfer & Melanie Siegel 2004. The DeepThought core architecture framework. In: M.T. Lino et al. (eds.). *Proceedings of the 4th International Conference on Language Resources and Evaluation (= LREC)*. Lisbon: European Language Resources Association, 1205–1208.
Chaves, Rui 2002. Principle-based DRTU for HSPG. A case study. In: *Proceedings of the 1st International Workshop on Scalable Natural Language Understanding (= ScaNaLu)*. Heidelberg: EML.
Chaves, Rui 2003. Non-Redundant scope disambiguation in underspecified semantics. In: B. ten Cate (ed.). *Proceedings of the 8th EESLLI Student Session*. Vienna, 47–58.
Chaves, Rui 2005a. DRT and underspecification of plural ambiguities. In: *Proceedings of the 6th International Workshop in Computational Semantics*. Tilburg University, 78–89.
Chaves, Rui 2005b. Underspecification and NP coordination in constraint-based grammar. In: F. Richter & M. Sailer (eds.). *Proceedings of the ESSLLI'05 Workshop on Empirical Challenges and Analytical Alternatives to Strict Compositionality*. Edinburgh: Heriot-Watt University, 38–58.
Cimiano, Philipp & Uwe Reyle 2005. Talking about trees, scope and concepts. In: H. Bunt, J. Geertzen & E. Thijse (eds.). *Proceedings of the 6th International Workshop in Computational Semantics*. Tilburg: Tilburg University, 90–102.
Cooper, Robin 1983. *Quantification and Syntactic Theory*. Dordrecht: Reidel.
Copestake, Ann & Dan Flickinger 2000. An open-source grammar development environment and broad-coverage English grammar using HPSG. In: *Proceedings of the 2nd International Conference on Language, Resources and Evaluation (= LREC)*. Athens: European Language Resources Association, 591–600.
Copestake, Ann, Dan Flickinger, Carl Pollard & Ivan Sag 2005. Minimal recursion semantics. An introduction. *Research on Language and Computation* 3, 281–332.
Crouch, Richard 1995. Ellipsis and quantification. A substitutional approach. In: *Proceedings of the 7th Conference of the European Chapter of the Association for Computational Linguistics (= EACL)*. Dublin: Association for Computational Linguistics, 229–236.
Crouch, Richard & Josef van Genabith 1999. Context change, underspecification and the structure of Glue Language derivations. In: M. Dalrymple (ed.). *Semantics and Syntax in Lexical Functional Grammar. The Resource Logic Approach*. Cambridge, MA: The MIT Press, 117–189.
Dalrymple, Mary 2001. *Lexical Functional Grammar*. New York: Academic Press.
Dalrymple, Mary, John Lamping, Fernando Pereira & Vijay Saraswat 1997. Quantifiers, anaphora, and intensionality. *Journal of Logic, Language and Information* 6, 219–273.
Dalrymple, Mary, Stuart Shieber & Fernando Pereira 1991. Ellipsis and higherorder unification. *Linguistics & Philosophy* 14, 399–452.
van Deemter, Kees 1996. Towards a logic of ambiguous expressions. In: K. van Deemter & S. Peters (eds.). *Semantic Ambiguity and Underspecification*. Stanford, CA: CSLI Publications, 203–237.
Dölling, Johannes 1995. Ontological domains, semantic sorts and systematic ambiguity. *International Journal of Human-Computer Studies* 43, 785–807.
Duchier, Denys & Claire Gardent 2001. Tree descriptions, constraints and incrementality. In: H. Bunt, R. Muskens & E. Thijsse (eds.). *Computing Meaning, vol. 2*. Dordrecht: Kluwer, 205–227.

Ebert, Christian 2005. *Formal Investigations of Underspecified Representations*. Ph.D. dissertation. King's College, London.
Egg, Markus 2004. Mismatches at the syntax-semantics interface. In: S. Müller (ed.). *Proceedings of the 11th International Conference on Head-Driven Phrase Structure Grammar*. Stanford, CA: CSLI Publications, 119–139.
Egg, Markus 2005. *Flexible Semantics for Reinterpretation Phenomena*. Stanford, CA: CSLI Publications.
Egg, Markus 2006. Anti-Ikonizität an der Syntax-Semantik-Schnittstelle. *Zeitschrift für Sprachwissenschaft* 25, 1–38.
Egg, Markus 2007. Against opacity. *Research on Language and Computation* 5, 435–455.
Egg, Markus & Michael Kohlhase 1997. Dynamic control of quantifier scope. In: P. Dekker, M. Stokhof & Y. Venema (eds.). *Proceedings of the 11th Amsterdam Colloquium*. Amsterdam: ILLC, 109–114.
Egg, Markus, Alexander Koller & Joachim Niehren 2001. The constraint language for lambda-structures. *Journal of Logic, Language and Information* 10, 457–485.
Egg, Markus & Gisela Redeker 2008. Underspecified discourse representation. In: A. Benz & P. Kühnlein (eds.). *Constraints in Discourse*. Amsterdam: Benjamins, 117–138.
van Eijck, Jan & Manfred Pinkal 1996. What do underspecified expressions mean? In: R. Cooper et al. (eds.). *Building the Framework. FraCaS Deliverable D 15, section 10.1*. Edinburgh: University of Edinburgh, 264–266.
Filik, Ruth, Kevin Paterson & Simon Liversedge 2004. Processing doubly quantified sentences. Evidence from eye movements. *Psychonomic Bulletin and Review* 11, 953–959.
Fodor, Janet 1982. The mental representation of quantifiers. In: S. Peters & E. Saarinen (eds.). *Processes, Beliefs, and Questions*. Dordrecht: Reidel, 129–164.
Fox, Chris & Shalom Lappin 2005. Underspecified interpretations in a Curry-typed representation language. *Journal of Logic and Computation* 15, 131–143.
Frank, Annette & Josef van Genabith 2001. GlueTag. Linear logic based semantics for LTAG – and what it teaches us about LFG and LTAG. In: M. Butt & T. Holloway King (eds.). *Proceedings of the LFG '01 Conference*. Stanford, CA: CSLI Publications, 104–126.
Frank, Annette & Uwe Reyle 1995. Principle-based semantics for HPSG. In: *Proceedings of the 7th Conference of the European Chapter of the Association for Computational Linguistics (= EACL)*. Dublin: Association for Computational Linguistics, 9–16.
Fuchss, Ruth, Alexander Koller, Joachim Niehren & Stefan Thater 2004. Minimal recursion semantics as dominance constraints. Translation, evaluation, and analysis. In: *Proceedings of the 42nd Annual Meeting of the Association for Computational Linguistics (= ACL)*. Barcelona: Association for Computational Linguistics, 247–254.
Gambäck, Björn & Johan Bos 1998. Semantic-head based resolutions of scopal ambiguities. In: *Proceedings of the 17th International Conference on Computational Linguistics and the 36th Annual Meeting of the Association for Computational Linguistics (= ACL)*. Montreal: Association for Computational Linguistics, 433–437.
Gawron, Jean Mark & Stanley Peters 1990. *Anaphora and Quantification in Situation Semantics*. Menlo Park, CA: CSLI Publications.
van Genabith, Josef & Richard Crouch 1999. Dynamic and underspecified semantics for LFG. In: M. Dalrymple (ed.). *Semantics and Syntax in Lexical Functional Grammar. The Resource Logic Approach*. Cambridge, MA: The MIT Press, 209–260.
Harris, John 2007. Representation. In: P. de Lacy (ed.). *The Cambridge Handbook of Phonology*. Cambridge: Cambridge University Press, 119–137.

Heim, Irene & Angelika Kratzer 1998. *Semantics in Generative Grammar*. Oxford: Blackwell.
Hendriks, Herman 1993. *Studied Flexibility. Categories and Types in Syntax and Semantics.* Amsterdam: ILLC.
Hirschbühler, Paul 1982. VP deletion and across the board quantifier scope. In: J. Pustejovsky & P. Sells (eds.). *Proceedings of the North Eastern Linguistics Society (= NELS) 12*. Amherst, MA: GLSA. 132–139.
Hobbs, Jerry & Stuart Shieber 1987. An algorithm for generating quantifier scoping. *Computational Linguistics* 13, 47–63.
Hobbs, Jerry, Mark Stickel, Douglas Appelt & Paul Martin 1993. Interpretation as abduction. *Artificial Intelligence* 63, 69–142.
Hodges, Wilfrid 2001. Formal features of compositionality. *Journal of Logic, Language and Information* 10, 7–28.
Hoeksema, Jack 1985. *Categorial Morphology*. New York: Garland.
Huet, Gérard P. 1975. A unification algorithm for typed λ-calculus. *Theoretical Computer Science* 1, 27–57.
Hurum, Sven 1988. Handling scope ambiguities in English. In: *Proceedings of the 2nd Conference on Applied Natural Language Processing (= ANLP)*. Morristown, NJ: Association for Computational Linguistics, 58–65.
Ioup, Georgette 1975. Some universals for quantifier scope. In: J. Kimball (ed.). *Syntax and Semantics 4*. New York: Academic Press, 37–58.
Jaspars, Jan & Jan van Eijck 1996. Underspecification and reasoning. In: R. Cooper et al. (eds.). *Building the Framework. FraCaS Deliverable D 15*, section 10.2, 266–287.
Johnson-Laird, Philip 1969. On understanding logically complex sentences. *Quarterly Journal of Experimental Psychology* 21, 1–13.
Kallmeyer, Laura & Aravind K. Joshi 1999. Factoring predicate argument and scope semantics. Underspecified semantics with LTAG. In: P. Dekker (ed.). *Proceedings of the 12th Amsterdam Colloquium*. Amsterdam: ILLC, 169–174.
Kallmeyer, Laura & Aravind K. Joshi 2003. Factoring predicate argument and scope semantics. Underspecified semantics with LTAG. *Research on Language and Computation* 1, 3–58.
Kallmeyer, Laura & Frank Richter 2006. Constraint-based computational semantics. A comparison between LTAG and LRS. In: *Proceedings of the 8th International Workshop on Tree-Adjoining Grammar and Related Formalisms*. Sydney: Association for Computational Linguistics, 109–114.
Kallmeyer, Laura & Maribel Romero 2008. Scope and situation binding in LTAG using semantic unification. *Research on Language and Computation* 6, 3–52.
Keller, William 1988. Nested Cooper storage. The proper treatment of quantification in ordinary noun phrases. In: U. Reyle & Ch. Rohrer (eds.). *Natural Language Parsing and Linguistic Theories*. Dordrecht: Reidel, 432–447.
Kempson, Ruth & Annabel Cormack 1981. Ambiguity and quantification. *Linguistics & Philosophy* 4, 259–309.
Koller, Alexander, Joachim Niehren & Stefan Thater 2003. Bridging the gap between underspecification formalisms. Hole semantics as dominance constraints. In: *Proceedings of the 11th Conference of the European Chapter of the Association for Computational Linguistics (= EACL)*. Budapest: Association for Computational Linguistics, 195–202.
Koller, Alexander, Michaela Regneri & Stefan Thater 2008. Regular tree grammars as a formalism for scope underspecification. In: *Proceedings of the 46th Annual Meeting of the Association*

for *Computational Linguistics (= ACL)*. Columbus, OH: Association for Computational Linguistics, 218–226.

Koller, Alexander & Stefan Thater 2005. The evolution of dominance constraint solvers. In: *Proceedings of the ACL Workshop on Software*. Ann Arbor, MI: Association for Computational Linguistics, 65–76.

Koller, Alexander & Stefan Thater 2006. An improved redundancy elimination algorithm for underspecified descriptions. In: *Proceedings of the 21st International Conference on Computational Linguistics and the 44th Annual Meeting of the Association for Computational Linguistics (= ACL)*. Sydney: Association for Computational Linguistics, 409–416.

König, Esther & Uwe Reyle 1999. A general reasoning scheme for underspecified representations. In: H.J. Ohlbach & U. Reyle (eds.). *Logic, Language and Reasoning. Essays in Honour of Dov Gabbay*. Dordrecht: Kluwer, 1–28.

Kratzer, Angelika 1998. Scope or pseudoscope? Are there wide-scope indefinites? In: S. Rothstein (ed.). *Events and Grammar*. Dordrecht: Kluwer, 163–196.

Kurtzman, Howard & Maryellen MacDonald 1993. Resolution of quantifier scope ambiguities. *Cognition* 48, 243–279.

Lakoff, George 1971. On generative semantics. In: D. Steinberg & L. Jakobovits (eds.). *Semantics. An Interdisciplinary Reader in Philosophy, Linguistics and Psychology*. Cambridge: Cambridge University Press, 232–296.

Larson, Richard 1998. Events and modification in nominals. In: D. Strolovitch & A. Lawson (eds.). *Proceedings of Semantics and Linguistic Theory (= SALT) VIII*. Ithaca, NY: CLC Publications, 145–168.

Larson, Richard & Sungeon Cho 2003. Temporal adjectives and the structure of possessive DPs. *Natural Language Semantics* 11, 217–247.

Lev, Iddo 2005. Decoupling scope resolution from semantic composition. In: H. Bunt, J. Geertzen & E. Thijse (eds.). *Proceedings of the 6th International Workshop on Computational Semantics*. Tilburg: Tilburg University, 139–150.

Link, Godehard 1983. The logical analysis of plurals and mass terms. A lattice-theoretic approach. In: R. Bäuerle, Ch. Schwarze & A. von Stechow (eds.). *Meaning, Use, and the Interpretation of Language*. Berlin: Mouton de Gruyter, 303–323.

Marcus, Mitchell, Donald Hindle & Margaret Fleck 1983. D-theory. Talking about talking about trees. In: *Proceedings of the 21st Annual Meeting of the Association for Computational Linguistics (= ACL)*. Cambridge, MA: Association for Computational Linguistics, 129–136.

Montague, Richard 1974. *Formal Philosophy. Selected Papers of Richard Montague*. Edited and with an introduction by Richmond H. Thomason. New Haven, CT: Yale University.

Moran, Douglas 1988. Quantifier scoping in the SRI core language engine. In: *Proceedings of the 26th Annual Meeting of the Association for Computational Linguistics (= ACL)*. Buffalo, NY: Association for Computational Linguistics, 33–40.

Muskens, Reinhard 2001. Talking about trees and truth-conditions. *Journal of Logic, Language and Information* 10, 417–455.

Nerbonne, John 1993. A feature-based syntax/semantics interface. *Annals of Mathematics and Artificial Intelligence* 8, 107–132.

Niehren, Joachim, Manfred Pinkal & Peter Ruhrberg 1997. A uniform approach to underspecification and parallelism. In: *Proceedings of the 35th Annual Meeting of the Association for Computational Linguistics (= ACL)*. Madrid: Association for Computational Linguistics, 410–417.

Oepen, Stephan, Helge Dyvik, Jan Tore Lønning, Erik Velldal, Dorothee Beermann, John Carroll, Dan Flickinger, Lars Hellan, Janni Bonde Johannessen, Paul Meurer, Torbjørn Nordgård & Victoria Rosén 2004. Som å kapp-ete med trollet? Towards MRS-based Norwegian-English machine translation. In: *Proceedings of the 10th International Conference on Theoretical and Methodological Issues in Machine Translation (= TMI)*. Baltimore, MD, 11–20.
Pafel, Jürgen 2005. *Quantifier Scope in German*. Amsterdam: Benjamins.
Park, Jong 1995. Quantifier scope and constituency. In: *Proceedings of the 33rd Annual Meeting of the Association for Computational Linguistics (= ACL)*. Cambridge, MA: Association for Computational Linguistics, 205–212.
Pinkal, Manfred 1995. *Logic and Lexicon: The Semantics of the Indefinite*. Dordrecht: Kluwer.
Pinkal, Manfred 1996. Radical underspecification. In: P. Dekker & M. Stokhof (eds.). *Proceedings of the 10th Amsterdam Colloquium*. Amsterdam: ILLC, 587–606.
Pinkal, Manfred 1999. On semantic underspecification. In: H. Bunt & R. Muskens (eds.). *Computing Meaning, vol. 1*. Dordrecht: Kluwer, 33–55.
Player, Nickie 2004. *Logics of Ambiguity*. Ph.D. dissertation. University of Manchester.
Poesio, Massimo 1996. Semantic ambiguity and perceived ambiguity. In: K. van Deemter & S. Peters (eds.). *Semantic Ambiguity and Underspecification*. Stanford, CA: CSLI Publications, 159–201.
Poesio, Massimo, Patrick Sturt, Ron Artstein & Ruth Filik 2006. Underspecification and anaphora. Theoretical issues and preliminary evidence. *Discourse Processes* 42, 157–175.
Pulman, Stephen G. 1997. Aspectual shift as type coercion. *Transactions of the Philological Society* 95, 279–317.
Rambow, Owen, David Weir & Vijay K. Shanker 2001. D-tree substitution grammars. *Computational Linguistics* 27, 89–121.
Rapp, Irene & Arnim von Stechow 1999. Fast 'almost' and the visibility parameter for functional adverbs. *Journal of Semantics* 16, 149–204.
Regneri, Michaela, Markus Egg & Alexander Koller 2008. Efficient processing of underspecified discourse representations. In: *Proceedings of the 46th Annual Meeting of the Association for Computational Linguistics (= ACL), Short Papers*. Columbus, OH: Association for Computational Linguistics, 245–248.
Reyle, Uwe 1992. Dealing with ambiguities by underspecification. A first order calculus for unscoped representations. In: M. Stokhof & P. Dekker (eds.). *Proceedings of the 8th Amsterdam Colloquium*. Amsterdam: ILLC, 493–512.
Reyle, Uwe 1996. Co-indexing labeled DRSs to represent and reason with ambiguities. In: K. van Deemter & S. Peters (eds.). *Semantic Ambiguity and Underspecification*. Stanford, CA: CSLI Publications, 239–268.
Richter, Frank & Manfred Sailer 1996. Syntax für eine unterspezifizierte Semantik. PP-Anbindung in einem deutschen HPSG-Fragment. In: S. Mehl, A. Mertens & M. Schulz (eds.). *Präpositionalsemantik und PP-Anbindung*. Duisburg: Institut für Informatik, 39–47.
Richter, Frank & Manfred Sailer 2006. Modeling typological markedness in semantics. The case of negative concord. In: S. Müller (ed.). *Proceedings of the HPSG 06 Conference*. Stanford, CA: CSLI Publications, 305–325.
Robaldo, Livio 2007. *Dependency Tree Semantics*. Ph.D. disseration. University of Torino.
Sag, Ivan 1976. *Deletion and Logical Form*. Ph.D. dissertation. MIT, Cambridge, MA.
Sailer, Manfred 2000. *Combinatorial Semantics and Idiomatic Expressions in Head-Driven Phrase Structure Grammar*. Doctoral dissertation. University of Tübingen.

Sailer, Manfred 2004. Past tense marking in Afrikaans. In: C. Meier & M. Weisgerber (eds.). *Proceedings of Sinn und Bedeutung* 8. Konstanz: University of Konstanz, 233–248.

Sailer, Manfred 2006. Don't believe in underspecified semantics. In: O. Bonami & P. Cabredo Hofherr (eds.). *Empirical Issues in Formal Syntax and Semantics, vol. 6*. Paris: CSSP, 375–403.

Schiehlen, Michael 2000. Semantic construction. In: W. Wahlster (ed.). *Verbmobil. Foundations of Speech-to-Speech Translation*. Berlin: Springer, 200–216.

Schilder, Frank 2002. Robust discourse parsing via discourse markers, topicality and position. *Natural Language Engineering* 8, 235–255.

Schubert, Lenhart & Francis Pelletier 1982. From English to logic. Context-free computation of 'conventional' logical translation. *American Journal of Computational Linguistics* 8, 26–44.

Shieber, Stuart, Fernando Pereira & Mary Dalrymple 1996. Interaction of scope and ellipsis. *Linguistics & Philosophy* 19, 527–552.

Steedman, Mark 2000. *The Syntactic Process*. Cambridge, MA: The MIT Press.

Steedman, Mark 2007. *Surface-Compositional Scope-Alternation without Existential Quantifiers*. Draft 5.2., September 2007. Ms. Edinburgh, ilcc/University of Edinburgh. http://www.iccs.informatics.ed.ac.uk/~steedman/papers.html, August 25, 2009.

Steriade, Donka 1995. Underspecification and markedness. In: J. Goldsmith (ed.). *The Handbook of Phonological Theory*. Oxford: Blackwell, 114–174.

de Swart, Henriëtte 1998. Aspect shift and coercion. *Natural Language and Linguistic Theory* 16, 347–385.

VanLehn, Kurt 1978. *Determining the Scope of English Quantifiers*. MA thesis. MIT, Cambridge, MA. MIT Technical Report AI-TR-483.

Villalta, Elisabeth 2003. The role of context in the resolution of quantifier scope ambiguities. *Journal of Semantics* 20, 115–162.

Wahlster, Wolfgang (ed.) 2000. *Verbmobil. Foundations of Speech-to-Speech Translation*. Berlin: Springer.

Westerståhl, Dag 1998. On mathematical proofs of the vacuity of compositionality. *Linguistics & Philosophy* 21, 635–643.

Woods, William 1967. *Semantics for a Question-Answering System*. Ph.D. dissertation. Harvard University, Cambridge, MA.

Woods, William 1978. Semantics and quantification in natural language question answering. In: M. Yovits (ed.). *Advances in Computers, vol. 17*. New York: Academic Press, 2–87.

Henriëtte de Swart
10 Mismatches and coercion

1 Enriched type theories —— 321
2 Type coercion —— 323
3 Aspect shift and coercion —— 330
4 Cross-linguistic implications —— 340
5 Conclusion —— 345
6 References —— 346

Abstract: The principle of compositionality of meaning is the foundation of semantic theory. With function application as the main rule of combination, compositionality requires complex expressions to be interpreted in terms of function-argument structure. Type theory lends itself to an insightful representation of many combinations of a functor and its argument. But not all well-formed linguistic combinations are accounted for within classical type theory as adopted by Montague Grammar. Conflicts between the requirements of a functor and the properties of its arguments are described as type mismatches. Three solutions to type mismatches have been proposed within enriched type theories, namely type raising, type shifting, and type coercion. This article focusses on instances of type coercion. We provide examples, propose lexical and contextual restrictions on type coercion, and discuss the status of coercion as a semantic enrichment operation. The paper includes a special application of the notion of coercion in the domain of tense and aspect. Aspectual coercion affects the relationship between predicative and grammatical aspect. We treat examples from English and Romance languages in a cross-linguistic perspective.

1 Enriched type theories

1.1 Type mismatches

According to the principle of compositionality of meaning, the meaning of a complex whole is a function of the meaning of its composing parts and the way these parts are put together. With function application as the main rule for combining linguistic expressions, compositionality requires that complex expressions be interpreted

Henriëtte de Swart, Utrecht, The Netherlands

in terms of function-argument structure. Functors do not combine with just any argument. They look for arguments with particular syntactic and semantic properties. A type mismatch arises when the properties of the argument do not match the requirements of the functor. Such a type mismatch can lead to ungrammaticalities. Consider the ill-formed combination *eat laugh*, where the transitive verb *eat* wants to take an object of category NP, and does not combine with the intransitive verb *laugh* of category VP. In type-theoretical terms, *eat* is an expression of type (e, (e,t)), which requires an expression of type e as its argument. Given that *laugh* is of type (e,t), there is a mismatch between the two expressions, so they do not combine by function application, and the combination *eat laugh* is ungrammatical.

In this article we do not focus on syntactic incompatibilities, but on semantic type mismatches and ways to resolve conflicts between the requirements of a functor and the properties of its argument. Sections 1.2 and 1.3 briefly refer to type raising and type shifting as operations defined within an enriched type theoretical framework. Section 2 addresses type coercion, as introduced by Pustejovsky (1995). Section 3 treats aspectual coercion within a semantic theory of tense and aspect.

1.2 Type raising

As we saw with the ill-formed combination *eat laugh*, a type mismatch can lead to ungrammaticalities. Not all type mismatches have such drastic consequences. Within extended versions of type theory, mechanisms of type-raising have been formulated, that deal with certain type mismatches (cf. Hendriks 1993). Consider the VPs *kiss Bill* and *kiss every boy*, which are both well-formed expressions of type (e,t). The transitive verb *kiss* is an expression of type (e,(e,t)). In the VP *kiss Bill*, the transitive verb directly combines with the object of type e. However, the object *every boy* is not of type e, but of type ((e,t),t). The mismatch is resolved by raising the type of the argument of the transitive verb. If we assume that a transitive verb like *kiss* can take either proper names or generalized quantifiers as its argument, we interpret *kiss* as an expression of type (e, (e,t)), or type (((e,t),t), (e,t)). Argument raising allows the transitive verb *kiss* to combine with the object *every boy* by function application.

1.3 Type shifting

Type raising affects the domain in which the expression is interpreted, but maintains function application as the rule of combination, so it preserves compositionality. For other type mismatches, rules of type-shifting have been proposed, in particular in the interpretation of indefinites (Partee 1987). In standard Montague Grammar, NPs have a denotation in the domain of type e (e.g. proper names) and/or type ((e,t),t) (generalized quantifiers). In certain environments, the indefinite seems to behave more like a predicate (type e,t) than like an argument. We find the predicative use of indefinites in predicative constructions (*Sue is a lawyer, She considers him a fool*), in measurement constructions (*This baby weighs seven pounds*), with certain 'light' verbs (*This house has many windows*), and in existential constructions (*There is a book on the table*, (see article 8 [Semantics: Sentence and Information Structure] (McNally) *Existential sentences*). An interpretation of indefinites as denoting properties makes it possible to treat predicative and existential constructions as functors taking arguments of type (e,t) (see article 8 [Semantics: Interfaces] (de Hoop) *Type shifting*, and references therein). The type-shifting approach raises problems for the role of indefinites in the object position of regular transitive verbs, though. Assuming that we interpret the verb *eat* as an expression of type (e,(e,t)), and the indefinite *an apple* as an expression of type (e,t), we would not know how to combine the two in *eat an apple*. Argument raising does not help in this case, for a functor of type (((e,t),t), (e,t)) does not combine with an argument of type (e,t) either. Two solutions present themselves. If we assign transitive verbs two types, the type (e,(e,t)) and the type ((e,t),(e,t)), we accept a lexical ambiguity of all verbs (Van Geenhoven 1998). If widespread lexical ambiguities are not viewed as an attractive solution, the alternative is to develop combinatory rules other than function application. File Change Semantics and Discourse Representation theory (Heim 1982, Kamp 1981, Kamp & Reyle 1993) follow this route, but not in a strictly type-theoretical setting. The indefinite introduces a variable, that is existentially closed at the discourse level if it is not embedded under a quantificational binder. De Swart (2001) shows that we can reinterpret the DRT rule of existential closure in type-theoretical terms. The price we pay is a fairly complex system of closure rules in order to account for monotone increasing, decreasing and non-monotone quantifiers. These complexities favor a restriction of the property type denotation of indefinites to special contexts where specific construction rules can be motivated by the particularities of the construction at hand.

2 Type coercion

In Section 1, we saw that enriched type theories have formulated rules of type raising and type shifting to account for well-formed natural language examples that present mismatches in stricter type theories. A third way of resolving type mismatches in natural language has been defined in terms of type coercion, and this route constitutes the focus of this article.

2.1 Type coercion as a strategy to resolve type mismatches

The use of coercion to resolve type mismatches goes back to the work on polysemy by James Pustejovsky (Pustejovsky 1995). Pustejosvky points out that the regular rules of type theoretic combinatorics are unable to describe sentences such as (1):

(1) a. Mary finished the novel in January 2007. A week later, she started a new book.
    b. John wants a car until next week.

Verbs like *start* and *finish* in (1a) do not directly take expressions of type e or ((e,t),t), such as *the novel* or *a new book*, for they operate on processes or actions rather than on objects, as we see in *start reading*, *finish writing*. As Dowty (1979) points out, the temporal adverbial *until next week* modifies a hidden or understood predicate in (1b), as in *John wants to have a car until next week*. The type mismatch in (1) does not lead to ungrammaticalities, but triggers a reinterpretation of the combination of the object of the verb. The hearer fills in the missing process denoting expression, and interprets *finish the novel* as 'finish reading the novel' or 'finish writing the novel', and *wants a car* as 'wants to have a car'. This process of reinterpretation of the argument, triggered by the type mismatch between a functor (here: the verb *finish* or *start*) and its argument (here the object *the novel* or *a new book*) is dubbed type coercion by Pustejovsky. Type coercion is a semantic operation that converts an argument to the type expected by the function, where it would otherwise result in a type error. Formally, function application with coercion is defined as in (2) (Pustejovsky 1995: 111), with α the argument and β the functor:

(2) Function application with coercion. If α is of type c, β of type (a,b), then:
    (i) if type c = a, then β(α) is of type b.
    (ii) if there is a σ ∈ Σ_α such that σ(α) results in an expression of type a, then β(σ(α)) is of type b.
    (iii) otherwise a type error is produced.

If the argument is of the right type to be the input of the functor, function application applies as usual (i). If the argument can be reinterpreted in such a way that it satisfies the input requirements of the function, function application with coercion applies (ii). Σ_α represents the set of well-defined reinterpretations of α, leading to the type *a* for σ(α) that is required as the input of the functor β. If such a reinterpretation is not available, the sentence is ungrammatical (iii).

Type coercion is an extremely powerful process. If we assume that any type mismatch between an operator and its argument can be repaired by the hearer simply filling in the understood meaning, we would run the risk of inserting hidden meaningful expressions anywhere, thus admitting random combinations of expressions, and loosing any ground for explaining ungrammaticalities. So the process of type coercion must be severely restricted.

2.2 Restrictions on type coercion

There are three important restrictions Pustejovsky (1995) imposes upon type coercion in order to avoid overgeneralization. First, coercion does not occur freely, but must always be triggered as part of the process of function application (clause (ii) of definition 2). In (1), the operators triggering type coercion are the verbs *finish, start* and *want*. Outside of the context of such a trigger, the nominal expressions *the novel, a new book* and *a car* do not get reinterpreted as processes involving the objects described by these noun phrases (clause (i) of definition 2). Second, type coercion always affects the argument, never the functor. In example (1), this means that the interpretation of *finish, start* and *want* is as usual, and only the interpretation of the nominal expressions *the novel, a new book* and *a car* is enriched by type coercion. Third, the interpretation process involved in type coercion requires a set of well-defined reinterpretations for any expression α (Σ_α in clause ii of definition 2). Pustejovsky (1995) emphasizes the role of the lexicon in the reinterpretation process. He develops a generative lexicon, in which not only the referential interpretation of lexical items is spelled out, but an extended interpretation is developed in terms of argument structure, extended event structure and qualia structure (involving roles). In (1), the relevant qualia of the lexical items *novel* and *book* include the fact that these nouns denote artifacts which are produced in particular ways (agentive role: process of *writing*), and which are used for particular purposes (telic role: process of *reading*). The hearer uses these extended lexical functions to fill in the understood meaning in examples like (1). The qualia structure is claimed to be part of our linguistic knowledge, so Pustejovsky maintains a strict distinction between lexical and world knowledge. See article 6 [Semantics: Theories] (Hobbs) *Word meaning and world knowledge* for more on the relation between word meaning and world knowledge.

Type coercion with verbs like *begin, start, finish,* is quite productive in everyday language use. Google provided many examples involving home construction as in (3a,b), building or producing things more in general (3c-f), and, by extension, organizing (3g, h):

(3) a. When I became convalescent, father urged Mr. X to begin the house.
   b. We will begin the roof on the pavilion on December 1.
   c. Today was another day full of hard work as our team stays late hours to finish the car.
   d. (about a bird) She uses moss, bits of vegetation, spider webs, bark flakes, and pine needles to finish the cup-shaped nest.
   e. Susan's dress is not at any picture, but the lady in the shop gave very good instructions how to finish the dress.
   f. Once I finish an album, I'll hit the road and tour. I got a good band together and I really feel pleased.
   g. The second step was to begin the House Church. (context: a ministry page)
   h. This is not the most helpful way to begin a student-centered classroom.

Examples with food preparation (4a) and consumption (4b) are also easy to find, even though we sometimes need some context to arrive at the desired interpretation (4c).

(4) a. An insomniac, she used to get up at four am and start the soup for dinner, while rising dough for breakfast, and steaming rice for lunch.
   b. The portions were absolutely rediculusly huge, even my boyfriend the human garbage disposal couldn't finish his plate.
   c. A pirate Jeremy is able to drink up a rum barrel in 10 days. A pirate Amelie needs 2 weeks for that. How much time do they need together to finish the barrel?

Finally, we find a wide range of other constructions, involving exercices, tables, exams, etc. to complete (5a), technical equipment or computer programs to run (5b), lectures to teach (by lecturers) (5c), school programs to attend (by students) (5d), etc.

(5) a. Read the instructions carefully before you begin the exam.
   b. Press play to begin the video.
   c. Begin the lesson by asking what students have seen in the sky.
   d. These students should begin the ancient Greek or Latin sequence now if they have not already done so.

These reinterpretations are clearly driven by Pustejovsky's qualia structure, and are thus firmly embedded in a generative lexicon. But type coercion can also apply in creative language use, where the context rather than the lexicon drives the reinterpretation process. If the context indicates that Mary is a goat that eats anything she is fed, we could end up with an interpretation of (1a) in which Mary finished eating the novel, and started eating a new book a week later (cf. Lascarides & Copestake 1998). One might be skeptical about the force of contextual pressure. Indeed, a quick google search revealed no naturally occurring examples of 'begin/finish the book' (as in: a goat beginning/ finishing to eat the book). However, there are other examples that suggest a strongly context-dependent application of type coercion:

(6) a. Is it too late to start geranium plants from cuttings?
(context: a Q&A page on geraniums, meaning: begin growing geranium plants).
b. (After briefly looking at spin as an angular momentum property, we will begin discussing rotational spectroscopy.) We finish the particle on a sphere, and begin to apply those ideas to rotational spectography.
(context: chemistry class schedule; meaning: finish discussing).

The numbers of such examples of creative language use are fairly low, but in the right context, their meaning is easy to grasp. All in all, type coercion is a quite productive process, and the limits on this process reside in a combination of lexical and contextual information.

2.3 Putting type coercion to work

The contexts in (7) offer another prominent example of type coercion discussed by Pustejovsky (1995):

(7) a. We will need a fast boat to get back in time.
b. John put on a long album during dinner.

Although *fast* is an adjective modifying the noun *boat* in (7a), it semantically operates on the action involving the boat, rather than the boat itself. Similarly, the adjective *long* in (7b) has an interpretation as an event modifier, so it selects the telic role of playing the record.

Pustejovsky's notion of type coercion has been put to good use in other contexts as well. One application involves the interpretation of associative ('bridging') definite descriptions (Clark 1975):

(8) Sara brought an interesting book home from the library. A photo of the author was on the cover.

The author and *the cover* are new definites, for their referents have not been introduced in previous discourse. The process of accommodation is facilitated by an extended argument structure, which is based on the qualia structure of the noun (Bos, Buitelaar & Mineur 1995), and the rhetorical structure of the discourse (Asher & Lascarides 1998). Accordingly, the most coherent interpretation of (8) is to interpret *the author* and *the cover* as referring to the author and the cover of the book introduced in the first sentence.

Kluck (2007) applies type coercion to metonymic reinterpretations as in (9), merging Pustejovsky's generative lexicon with insights concerning conceptual blending:

(9) a toy truck, a stone lion.

The metonymic interpretation is triggered by a conflict between the semantics of the noun and that of the modifying adjective. In all these examples, we find a shift to an 'image' of the object, rather than an instance of the object itself.

The metonymic type coercion in (9) comes close to instances of polysemy like those in (10) that Nunberg (1995) has labelled 'predicate transfer'.

(10) The ham sandwich from table three wants to pay.

This sentence is naturally used in a restaurant setting, where one waiter informs another one that the client seated at table three, who had a ham sandwich for lunch is ready to pay. Nunberg analyzes this as a mapping from one property onto a new one that is functionally related to it; in this case the mapping from the ham sandwich to the person who had the ham sandwich for lunch. Note that the process of predicate transfer in (10) is not driven by a type mismatch, but by other conflicts in meaning (often driven by selection restrictions on the predicate). This supports the view that reinterpretation must be contextually triggered in general.

Asher & Pustejovsky (2005) use Rhetorical Discourse Representation Theory to describe the influence of context more precisely (see article 11 [Semantics: Theories] (Kamp & Reyle) *Discourse Representation Theory* for more on discourse theories). They point out that in the context of a fairy tale, we have no difficulty ascribing human-like properties to goats that allow us to interpret examples like (11):

(11) The goat hated the film but enjoyed the book.

In a more realistic setting, we might interpret (11) as the goat eating the book, and rejecting the film (cf. section 2.2 above), but in a fictional interpretation, goats can become talking, thinking and reading agents, thereby assuming characteristics that their sortal typing would not normally allow. Thus discourse may override lexical preferences.

Type coercion, metonymic type coercion and predicate transfer can be included in the set of mechanisms that Nunberg (1995) subsumes under the label 'transfer of meaning', and that come into play in creative language use as well as systematic polysemy. Function application with coercion is a versatile notion, which is applied in a wide range of cases where mismatches between a functor and its argument are repaired by reinterpretation of the argument. Coercion restores compositionality in the sense that reinterpretation involves inserting hidden meaningful material that enriches the semantics of the argument, and enables function application. Lexical theories such as those developed by Pustejovsky (1995), Nunberg (1995), Asher & Pustejovsky (2005), highlighting not only denotational and selective properties, but also functional connections and discourse characteristics are best suited to capture the systematic relations of polysemy we find in these cases.

2.4 The status of type coercion in comprehension

Given the complexity of the enriched interpretation process underlying coercion, we might expect it to encur a processing cost. The status of type coercion in comprehension is subject to debate in the literature. McElree et al. (2001) and Traxler et al. (2002) found evidence from self-paced reading and eye-tracking experiments that sentences such as *the secretary began the memo* involving coercion cause processing difficulties evidenced by longer reading times for relevant parts of the sentence. De Almeida (2004) reports two self-paced reading experiments that failed to replicate crucial aspects of previous studies. He uses these results to argue that type-shifting operations are pragmatic inferences computed over underspecified semantic representations. Pickering et al. (2005) report a new eye-tracking experiment based on de Almeida's stimuli, and claim evidence of coercion cost with these items, also involving verbs of *begin/finish*. According to Pickering et al. (2005) and Traxler et al. (2005), the evidence from eye movement strongly suggests that interpretation is costly when composition requires the on-line construction of a sense not lexically stored or available in the immediate discourse.

The debate between De Almeida on the one hand and McElree et al., Pickering et al. and Traxler et al. on the other suggests that there are two ways we can look at the meaning effects in contexts like *begin the book*. De Almeida does not find online comprehension effects of coercion, which leads him to propose an underspecified semantic representation and treat reinterpretation in the pragmatics. McElree et al. and Traxler et al. do find online comprehension effects of coercion, so they include reinterpretation in the compositional semantics. In the remainder of this paper, we will adopt a semantic approach to coercion, while leaving open the possibility of rephrasing the analysis in an underspecification analysis.

3 Aspect shift and coercion

We find a special application of the notion of coercion in the domain of tense and aspect, which is discussed in this section. Aspectual coercion relies on a conflict between predicative and grammatical aspect, which is resolved by adapting the characteristics of the eventuality description to the requirements of the aspectual operator. The analysis is spelled out in Discourse Representation Theory (DRT), building on insights from de Swart (1998). We will give an informal, more empirical description in sections 3.1–3.5, and specify the construction rules in section 3.6. Working knowledge of DRT is presupposed in this presentation.

3.1 Predicative and grammatical aspect

The appeal to aspectual coercion dates back to work by Moens (1987), Moens & Steedman (1988), and Parsons (1991). Pulman (1997), Jackendoff (1996), de Swart (1998), Zucchi (1998) and subsequent literature work out these ideas along the lines of Pustejovsky (1995), and embed aspectual coercion in the semantics of tense and aspect. Aspectual coercion affects predicative aspect (also called Aktionsart, aspectual class, situation aspect) as well as grammatical aspect. In languages like English, predicative aspect is determined at the predicate-argument level, following insights by Verkuyl (1972, 1993) and Krifka (1989, 1992). The predicate-argument structure provides a description of a situation or an action, referred to as eventuality description. Eventuality descriptions come in various subtypes (Vendler 1957). For instance, *love Susan* describes a state, *walk in the woods* a process, *eat a fish* an event, and *reach the summit* a punctual event or achievement. States are characterized by a lack of anything going on, whereas processes and events are both dynamic eventualities. Non-stative verbs that affect their arguments in a gradual and incremental way refer to a process when they combine with a bare plural or a mass noun (*drink milk*), and to an event when they combine with a quantized NP (*drink a glass of* milk). Events have an inherent endpoint, and have quantized reference (Bach 1986, Krifka 1989).

States and processes lack an inherent endpoint; they are unbounded, and have homogeneous reference. Processes and events require an evaluation over time intervals, whereas states and achievements involve instants (Vendler 1957). In Discourse Representation theory (DRT), the ontological nature of the discourse referents is reflected in the use of designated variables s for states, p for processes and e for events; h is used for homogeneous eventualities (states or processes), and d for dynamic eventualities (processes or events).

According to Comrie (1976: 1–3), "aspects are different ways of viewing the internal temporal constituency of a situation." Grammatical aspect bears on the eventuality description introduced by the predicate-argument structure. In English, the Progressive and the Perfect are examples of grammatical aspect. In the literature, there is a debate about the status of the Perfect as a temporal operator (building on Reichenbach's 1947 ideas), or as an aspectual operator (Comrie 1976 and others). In de Swart (2007), the temporal and aspectual contribution of the perfect is integrated with its discourse properties.

Here we adopt an interpretation of aspectual operators in terms of a mapping relation from one domain of eventualities to another (Bach 1986). Predicative and grammatical aspect are defined in terms of the same kinds of ontological entities: states, processes and events. The mapping approach underlies the DRT approach developed in Kamp & Reyle (1993), de Swart (1998), Schmitt (2001), and others. In *she is eating the fish*, the Progressive takes an event predicate as input, and produces the state of being in the process of eating the fish as its output. In *she has written the letter*, the perfect maps the event onto its consequent state. A tense operator introduces existential closure of the set of eventualities, and locates the eventuality on the time axis. Tense operators thus take scope over predicative and grammatical aspect. Under these assumptions, the syntactic structure of the sentence is as follows:

(12) [Tense [Aspect* [eventuality description]]]

The Kleene star indicates that we can have 0, 1, 2, ... instances of grammatical aspect in a sentence. Tense is obligatory in languages like English, and the eventuality description is fully specified by predicate-argument structure. Grammatical aspect is optional, and aspectual operators apply recursively.

(13) a. Julie was eating a fish.
 [Past [Prog [Julie eat a fish]]]

 b. Julie has been writing a book.
 [Pres [Perfect [Prog [Julie write a book]]]]

The aspectual operator applies (recursively if necessary) on the eventuality description provided by the predicate-argument structure, so in (13b), the perfect maps the ongoing process of writing a book onto its consequent state. Aspectual restrictions and implications for a cross-linguistic semantics of the perfect are discussed in Schmitt (2001) and de Swart (2003, 2007). Article 10 [Semantics: Noun Phrases and Verb Phrases] (Portner) *Perfect and progressive* offers a general treatment of the semantics and pragmatics of the perfect.

Tense operates on the output of the aspectual operator (if present), so in (13a), the state of the ongoing process of eating is located in the past, and no assertion about the event reaching its inherent endpoint in the real world is made. The structure in (13a) gives rise to the semantic representation in DRT format in Fig. 10.1.

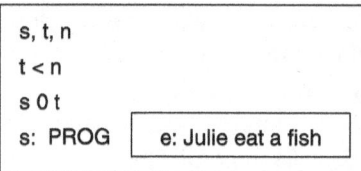

Fig. 10.1: *Julie was eating a fish*

According to Fig. 10.1, there is a state of Julie eating a fish in progress, that is located at some time t preceding the speech time n ('now'). The intensional semantics of the Progressive (Dowty 1979, Landman 1992, and others) is hidden in the truth conditions of the Prog operator, and is not our concern in this article (see article 10 [Semantics: Noun Phrases and Verb Phrases] (Portner) *Perfect and progressive* for more discussion).

3.2 Aspectual mismatches and coercion

It is well known that the English Progressive does not take just any eventuality description as its argument. The Progressive describes processes and events in their development, and the combination with a state verb frequently leads to ungrammaticalities (14a,b).

(14) a. *?Bill is being sick/in the garden.
 b. *?Julie is having blue eyes.
 c. I'm feeding him a line, and he is believing every word.
 d. Bill is being obnoxious.

However, the Progressive felicitously combines with a state verb in (14c) (from Michaelis 2003) and (14d). A process of aspectual reinterpretation takes place in such examples, and the verb is conceived as dynamic, and describing an active involvement of the agent. The dynamic reinterpretation arises out of the conflict between the aspectual requirements of the Progressive, and the aspectual features of the state description. De Swart (1998) and Zucchi (1998) use the notion of aspectual coercion to explain the meaning effects arising from such mismatches. In an extended use of the structure in (12), aspectual reinterpretation triggers the insertion of a hidden coercion operator C_{sd} mapping a stative description onto a dynamic one:

(15)   a. He is believing every word.
           [Pres [Prog [C_{sd} [he believe every word]]]]

       b. Bill is being obnoxious.
           [Pres [Prog [C_{sd} [Bill be obnoxious]]]]

The hidden coercion operator is inserted in the slot for grammatical aspect. In (15), C_{sd} adapts the properties of the state description to the needs of the Progressive. More precisely, the operator C_{sd} reinterprets the state description as a dynamic description, which has the aspectual features that allow it to be an argument of the Progressive operator. In this way, the insertion of a hidden coercion operator resolves the aspectual mismatch between the eventuality description and the aspectual operator in contexts like (15). (15b) gives rise to the semantic representation in DRT in Fig. 10.2:

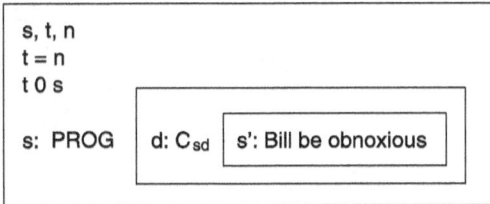

Fig. 10.2: *Bill is being obnoxious*

The dynamic variable *d*, obtained by coercion of the state *s'* is the input for the Progressive operator. The output of the progressive is again a state, but the state of an event or process being in progress is more dynamic than the underlying lexical state. The DRT representation contains the coercion operator C_{sd}, with the subscripts indicating the aspectual characterization of the input and output description. The actual interpretation of the coercion operator is pushed into the truth conditions of C, because it is partly dependent on lexical and contextual information (compare also Section 2). The relevant interpretation of C_{sd} in Fig. 10.2 is DYNAMIC:

(16)   DYNAMIC is a function from sets of state eventualities onto sets of dynamic eventualities in such a way that the state is presented as a process or event that the agent is actively involved in.

Note that (14a) and (14b) cannot easily be reinterpreted along the lines of (16), because of lack of agentivity in the predicate.

Following Moens & Steedman (1988), we assume that all mappings between sets of eventualities that are not labelled by overt aspectual operators are free. This implies that all semantically possible mappings that the language allows between sets of eventualities, but that are not the denotation of an overt grammatical aspect operator like the Progressive, the Perfect, etc. are possible values of the hidden coercion operator. Of course, the value of the coercion operator is constrained by the aspectual characteristics of the input eventuality description and the aspectual requirements of the aspectual operator. Thus, the coercion operator in Fig. 10.1 is restricted to being a mapping from sets of states to sets of events.

3.3 Extension to aspectual adverbials

Grammatical operators like the Progressive or the Perfect are not the only expressions overtly residing in the Aspect slot in the structure proposed in (12). Consider the sentences in (17)–(19), which illustrate that *in* adverbials combine with event descriptions, and *for* and *until* adverbials with processes or states:

(17) *in* adverbials
    a. Jennifer drew a spider in five minutes.   (event)
    b. #Jennifer ran in five minutes.   (process)
    c. #Jennifer was sick in five minutes.   (state)

(18) *for* adverbials
    a. Jennifer was sick for two weeks.   (state)
    b. Jennifer ran for five minutes.   (process)
    c. #Jennifer drew a spider for five minutes.   (event)

(19) *until* adverbials
    a. Jennifer was sick until today.   (state)
    b. Jennifer slept until midnight.   (process)
    c. #Jennifer drew a spider until midnight.   (event)

The aspectual restrictions on *in* and *for* adverbials have been noted since Vendler (1957), see article 9 [Semantics: Noun Phrases and Verb Phrases] (Filip) *Aspectual class and Aktionsart* and references therein. For *until* adverbials, see de Swart (1996), and references therein. A *for* adverbial measures the temporal duration of a state or a process, whereas an *in* adverbial measures the time it takes for an event to culminate. *Until* imposes a right boundary upon a state or a process. Their different semantics is responsible for the aspectual requirements *in*, *for* and *until* adverbials impose upon the eventuality description with which they combine, as illustrated in (17)–(19). We focus here on *for* and *in* adverbials. Both have been treated as measurement expressions that yield a quantized eventuality (Krifka 1989). Thus *to run* denotes a set of processes, but *to run for five minutes* denotes a set of quantized eventualities. Aspectual adverbials can then be treated as operators mapping one set of eventualities onto another (cf. Moens & Steedman 1988). *For* adverbials map a set of states or processes onto a set of events; *in* adverbials a set of events onto a set of events.

The mapping approach provides a natural semantics of sentences (17a) and (18a, b). However, the mismatches in (17b, c) and (18c) are marked as pragmatically infelicitous (#), rather than ungrammatical (*). This raises the question whether the aspectual restrictions on *in* and *for* adverbials are strictly semantic, or rather loosely pragmatic, in which case an underspecification account might be equally successful (cf. Dölling 2003 for a proposal, and article 9 [this volume] (Egg) *Semantic underspecification* for a general discussion on the topic). We can maintain the semantic treatment of aspectual adverbials as two different kinds of measurement expressions, if we treat the well-formed examples that combine *in* with states/processes or *for* with event descriptions as instances of aspectual coercion, as illustrated in (20) and (21):

(20) a. Sally read a book for two hours.   (process reading of event)
    [Past [for two hours [C_{eh} [Sally read a book]]]]
 b. Jim hit a golf ball into the lake for an hour.   (frequentative reading of event)
 c. The train arrived late for several months.   (habitual reading of event)
    [Past [for several months [C_{eh} [the train arrived late]]]]

(21) a. We took the train under the English Channel and were in Paris in 3 hours.   (inchoative reading of state)
    [Past [in three hours [C_{he} [we were in Paris]]]]
 b. Jim broke his leg in a car accident last year. Fortunately, it healed well, and in six months he was walking again.   (inchoative reading of progressive process)
    [Past [in six months [C_{he} [Prog [Jim walk]]]]

The process reading of the event in (20a) reflects that Sally did not necessarily read the whole book, but was involved in reading for two hours. The event description with a *for* adverbial in (20b) implies that there is a golf ball that Jim hit into the lake repeatedly for an hour (Van Geenhoven 2005: 119). In (20a-c), the hidden coercion operator C_{eh} represents the reinterpretation of the event description provided by the predicate-argument structure as an eventuality with homogeneous reference. Depending on the context, a process (20a), a frequentative (20b) or a habitual reading (20c) is the value of C_{eh}.

Examples (21a) and (21b) get an inchoative reading: (21a) picks up on the transition from not being in Paris to being in Paris. The inchoative reading of (21a) and (21b) arises as the reinterpretation of the homogeneous input as a non-homogeneous event by the hidden coercion operator C_{he}. Fig. 10.3 spells out the semantics of (21a) in DRT:

```
e, e', t, n
t < n
e' ⊆ t
dur(t) = three hours
e' = e

e: C_he  | s: we be in Paris
```

Fig. 10.3: *We were in Paris in three hours*

The value of C_{he} in Fig. 10.3 is inchoativity defined as in (22a). Relevant values of the operator C_{eh}, relevant for the examples in (20) are the process reading and the frequentative/habituality reading, defined in (22b,c).

(22) a. INCHO is a function from sets of homogeneous eventualities onto sets of event descriptions in such a way that the event describes the onset of the state or process. This interpretation generates the entailment that the state/process holds after the inchoative event.
   b. PROC is a function from sets of eventualities to sets of processes, in such a way that we obtain the process underlying the event predicate without reference to an inherent culmination point.
   c. FREQ/HAB is a function from sets of eventualities of any aspectual class onto a set of states. Its interpretation involves a generic or quantificational operator over eventualities such that the frequentative/habitual state describes a stable property over time of an agent.

Note that habitual readings are constrained to iterable events, which imposes constraints upon the predicate-argument structure, as analyzed in de Swart (2006).

The advantage of a coercion analysis over an underspecification approach in the treatment of the aspectual sensitivity of *in* and *for* adverbials is that we get a systematic explanation of the meaning effects that arise in the unusual combinations exemplified in (17b, c), (18c), (20) and (21), but not in (17a) and (18a, b). Effects of aspectual coercion have been observed in semantic processing (Piñango et al. 2006 and references therein). Brennan & Pylkkänen (2008) hypothesize that the online effects of aspectual coercion are milder than in type coercion, because it is easier to shift into another kind of event than to shift an object into an event. Nevertheless, they find an effect with magnetoencephalography, which they take to support the view that aspectual coercion is part of compositional semantics, rather than a context-driven pragmatic enrichment of an underspecified semantic representation, as proposed by Dölling (2003) (cf. also the discussion in section 2.4 above).

3.4 Aspectually sensitive tenses

Aspectual mismatches can arise at all levels in the structure proposed in (12). De Swart (1998) takes the English simple past tense to be aspectually transparent, in the sense that it lets the aspectual characteristics of the eventuality description shine through. Thus, both *he was sick* and *he ate an apple* get an episodic reading, and the sentences locate a state and an event in the past respectively. Not all English tenses are aspectually transparent. The habitual interpretation of *he drinks* or *she washes the car* (Schmitt 2001, Michaelis 2003) arises out of the interaction of the process/event description and the present tense, but cannot be taken to be the meaning of either, for *he drank* and *she washed the car* have an episodic besides a habitual interpretation, and *he is sick* has just an episodic interpretation. We can explain the special meaning effects if we treat the English simple present as an aspectually restricted tense. It is a present tense in the sense that it describes the eventuality as overlapping in time with the speech time. It is aspectually restricted in the sense that it exclusively operates on states (Schmitt 2001, Michaelis 2003). This restriction is the result of two features of the simple present, namely its characterization as an imperfective tense, which requires a homogenous eventuality description as its input (cf. also the French Imparfait in section 4.4 below), and the fact that it posits an overlap of the eventuality with the speech time, which requires an evaluation in terms of instants, rather than intervals. States are the only eventualities that combine these two properties. As a result, the interpretation of (23a) is standard, and the sentence gets an episodic interpretation, but the aspectual mismatch in (23b) and (23c) triggers the insertion of a coercion operator C_{ds}, reinterpreting the dynamic description as a stative one (see Fig. 10.4).

(23) a. Bill is sick.
       [Present [Bill be sick]]

   b. Bill drinks.
       [Present [C_{ds} [Bill drink]]]

   c. Julie washes the car.
       [Present [C_{ds} [Julie wash the car]]]

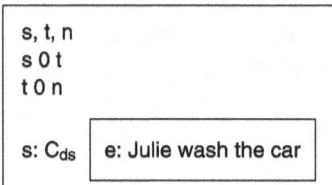

s, t, n
s 0 t
t 0 n

s: C_{ds} e: Julie wash the car

Fig. 10.4: *Julie washes the car*

In (23b) and (23c), the value of C_{ds} is a habitual interpretation. A habitual reading is stative, because it describes a regularly recurring action as a stable property over time (Smith 2005). The contrast between (23a) and (23b, c) confirms the general feature of coercion, namely that reinterpretation only arises if coercion is forced by an aspectual mismatch. If there is no conflict between the aspectual requirements of the functor, and the input, no reinterpretation takes place, and we get a straightforward episodic interpretation (23a). Examples (23b) and (23c) illustrate that the reinterpretations that are available through coercion are limited to those that are not grammaticalized by the language (Moens 1987). The overt Progressive blocks the progressive interpretation of sentences like (23b, c) as the result of a diachronic development in English (Bybee, Perkins & Pagliucca 1994: 144).

3.5 Aspectual coercion and rhetorical structure

At first sight, the fact that an episodic as well as a habitual interpretation is available for *he drank* and *she washed the car* might be a counterexample to the general claim that aspectual coercion is not freely available:

(24) Bill drank.
   a. [Past [Bill drink]]   (episodic interpretation)
   b. [Past [C_{ds} [Bill drink]]]   (habitual intepretation)

(25) Julie washed the car.
   a. [Past [Julie washed the car]]   (episodic interpretation)
   b. [Past [C_{ds} [Julie washed the car]]]   (habitual interpretation)

Given that the episodic interpretation spelled out in (24a) and (25a) does not show an aspectual mismatch, we might not expect to find habitual interpretations involving a stative reinterpretation of the dynamic description, as represented in (24b) and (25b), but we do. Such aspectual reinterpretations are not triggered by a sentence internal aspectual conflict, but by rhetorical requirements of the discourse. Habitual interpretations can be triggered if the sentence is presented as part of a list of stable properties of Bill over time, as in (26):

(26) a. In high school, Julie made a little pocket money by helping out the neighbours. She washed the car, and mowed the lawn.
b. In college, Bill led a wild life. He drank, smoked, and played in a rock band, rather than going to class.

Aspectual coercion may be governed by discourse requirements as in (26), but even then, the shifted interpretation is not free, but must be triggered by the larger context, and more specifically the rhetorical structure of the discourse. An intermediate case is provided by examples in which an adverb in the sentence indicates the rhetorical function of the eventuality description, and triggers aspectual coercion, as in (27):

(27) Suddenly, Jennifer knew the answer.   (inchoative reading of state)
[Past [C_{sd} [Jennifer know the answer]]]

Suddenly only applies to happenings, but *know the answer* is a state description, so (27) illustrates an aspectual mismatch. The insertion of a hidden coercion operator solves the conflict, so we read the sentence in such a way that the adverb *suddenly* brings out the inception of the state as the relevant happening in the discourse.

3.6 Key features of aspectual coercion

In this section, we defined aspectual mapping operations with coercion in DRT. Formally, the proposal can be summed up as follows:

(28) *Aspectual mappings with coercion in DRT*
(i) When a predicate-argument structure S_1 is modified by an aspectual operator Asp denoting a mapping from a set of eventualities of aspectual class a to a set of eventualities of aspectual class a', introduce in the universe of discourse of the DRS a new dr a' and introduce in the set of conditions a new condition a': Asp K_1.

(ii) If S_1 denotes an eventuality description of aspectual class a, introduce in the universe of discourse of K_1 a new discourse referent a', and introduce in the set of conditions of K_1 a new condition a': γ, where γ is the denotation of S_1.

(iii) If S_1 denotes an eventuality description of aspectual class a'' ($a'' \neq a$), and there is a coercion operator $C_{a''a}$ such that $C_{a''a}(γ)$ denotes a set of eventualities of aspectual class a, introduce in the universe of K_1 a new discourse referent a', and introduce in the set of conditions of K_1 a new condition a': $C_{a''a}(γ)$, where γ is the denotation of S_1.

(iv) If S_1 denotes an eventuality description of aspectual class a'' ($a'' \neq a$), and there is no coercion operator $C_{a''a}$ such that $C_{a''a}(γ)$ denotes a set of eventualities of aspectual class a, modification of S_1 by the aspectual operator Asp is semantically ill-formed.

According to this definition, aspectual coercion only arises when aspectual features of an argument do not meet the requirements of the functor (typically an adverbial expression, an aspectual operator, or a tense operator) (compare clauses ii and iii). As a result, we never find coercion operators that map a set of states onto a set of states, or a set of events onto a set of events, but we always find mappings from one aspectual domain onto another one. Reinterpretation requires an enriched interpretation of the argument that meets the aspectual requirements of the functor (clause iii). The functor itself does not shift, but maintains its normal interpretation. The range of possible interpretations of a hidden coercion operator excludes the ones that are the denotation of an overt aspectual operator. Coercion operators generally have a range of possible meanings, which are hidden in the truth conditions, so that the actual interpretation of the coercion operator in a sentence depends on lexical and contextual information. Several possible values for aspectual transitions have been listed in the course of this section.

4 Cross-linguistic implications

Whether we find instances of aspectual coercion in a language, and which meaning effects are created depends on the aspectuo-temporal system of the language. Therefore, it is useful to extend the discussion to languages other than English. We restrict ourselves to some observations concerning Romance languages, the aspectual systems of which are well studied.

4.1 The Romance simple present

The semantic value of coercion operators is limited to those aspect shifts that are not the denotation of overt grammatical operators. In section 3.4 above, we observed that the English Simple Present tense is an aspectually sensitive tense operator, which exclusively locates a state as overlapping with the speech time. The Simple Present gets a habitual reading when it combines with an event predicate (14b, c). There is a clear contrast between English and Romance languages like French, where the simple present tense is also an aspectually sensitive tense operator, but allows both habitual and progressive interpretations, as illustrated in (29) (from Michaelis 2003):

(29) a. Faites pas attention, Mademoiselle. Il vous taquine!
'Don't pay any attention to him, miss. He's teasing you.'

b. La pratique régulière du jogging prolonge la vie de deux à huit ans.
'Regular jogging prolongs life from two to eight years.'

French lacks a grammaticalized progressive. As a result, a progressive or a habitual interpretation is possible as the value of the coercion operator C_{ed}, which is inserted to repair the mismatch between the event description and the aspectually sensitive tense operator. The habitual reading of the coercion operator has been defined in (22d) above; its progressive interpretation is defined in (30):

(30) PROG is a function from sets of eventualities to sets of processes, in such a way that we obtain the process underlying the event predicate without referent to an inherent culmination point.

The Italian and Spanish simple presents are similar to French, but the Portuguese simple present tense behaves like its English counterpart, and a periphrastic progressive is required to refer to an ongoing event (Schmitt 2001).

4.2 The perfective/imperfective contrast in Romance

De Swart (1998) focuses on the contrast between the perfective and imperfective past tenses in French, called the Passé Simple (PS) and the Imparfait (Imp). She adopts Kamp & Rohrer's (1983) insight that Passé Simple sentences introduce events into the discourse representation, and Imparfait sentences introduce states. Given that events typically happen in sequence, and move the narrative time forward, whereas states introduce background information valid at the current reference time, Kamp & Rohrer's characterization of the Passé Simple and the Imparfait provides an insightful account of (31) and (32):

(31) Le lendemain, elle se leva, but un café, et partit tôt.
 The next-day, she REFL got-up.PS, drank.PS a coffee, and left.PS early.
 'The next day, she got up, drank a cup of coffee, and left early.'

(32) Il alla ouvrir les volets. Il faisait un grand soleil.
 He went.PS open.INF the blinds. It made.IMP a large sun.
 'He went to open the blinds. The sun was shining.'

In order to describe the role of the Passé Simple and the Imparfait in narrative discourse, a characterization in terms of events and states/processes is quite useful, so we would like to maintain this insight. However, Kamp & Rohrer (1983) do not work out the relation between the discourse functioning of the sentence, and its internal structure. What is of particular interest to us is the combination of predicative aspect with the different tense forms. (31) and (32) exemplify state descriptions in the Imparfait, and event descriptions in the Passé Simple. Although this seems to be the default, a wider range of possibilities is available in the language. (33) combines a state description with the Passé Simple, and (34) and (35) an event description with the Imparfait:

(33) Il désira voir l'Imprimerie, il la vit et fut content.
 He desired.PS see.INF the Press, he her saw.PS and was.PS content
 'He desired to see the Press, saw it, and was satisfied.'

(34) Chaque jour, Henri écrivait une lettre qu'il envoyait à Florence.
 Every day, Henri wrote.IMP a letter that he sent.IMP to Florence
 'Every day, Henri wrote a letter that he sent to Florence.'

(35) Il faisait ses devoirs quand on sonna à la porte.
 He made.IMP his homework when one rang.PS at the door.
 'He was doing his homework when the doorbell rang.'

The combination of a state description with an Imparfait describes the state in its duration (32), but the combination with the Passé Simple triggers an inchoative reading (33). An event description in the Passé Simple introduces a culminated event (31), but the Imparfait gets a habitual (34) or a progressive interpretation

(35). These meaning effects are well described in French grammars, and a compositional theory of aspect should capture them in a systematic way. In one line of work, the Passé Simple and the Imparfait are described as fused tense forms that combine a past tense with a perfective or an imperfective operator (Smith 1991/1997, Vet 1994, Verkuyl 1993). Given that the contribution of tense and aspect cannot be morphologically separated in the French past tenses, and the semantic contribution of the perfective/imperfective contrast correlates in a systematic way with predicative aspect, de Swart (1998) proposes to treat the Passé Simple and the Imparfait as aspectually sensitive tense operators. The Passé Simple and the Imparfait are both past tense operators, but differ in that the Passé Simple locates quantized events in the past, whereas the Imparfait locates homogeneous states/processes in the past. The eventuality descriptions in (31) and (32) satisfy the aspectual requirements of the tense operator, so their semantic representation does not involve a grammatical aspect operator:

(36) a. Elle but (PS) un café.
    [Past [she drink a coffee]]

   b. Il faisait (IMP) un grand soleil.
    [Past [the sun shine]]

(33)–(35) exemplify a mismatch between the aspectual requirements of the tense form, and the properties of the eventuality description. The insertion of a hidden coercion operator restores compositionality, but requires a reinterpretation of the argument:

(37) a. Il fut (PS) content.
    [Past [C_{he} [he be content]]]

   b. Il faisait (IMP) ses devoirs.
    [Past [C_{eh} [he do his homework]]]

The inchoative reading of (37a) is the result of the reinterpretation of the state description as an event by the coercion operator C_{he} that also played a role in example (21) (definition of INCHO in 22a) above. The process reading of (37b) arises out of the reinterpretation of the event description as an eventuality with homogeneous reference by the coercion operator C_{eh} that also played a role in example (20a) (definition of PROC in 22b) above. The insertion of the coercion operators C_{he} and C_{eh} enriches the semantics of the eventuality description in such a way that it meets the aspectual requirements of the tense operator. The structures in (36) give rise to the following semantic representations in DRT:

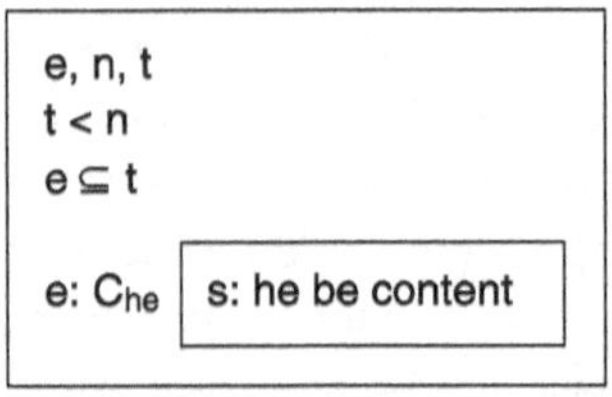

```
┌─────────────────────────────┐
│ e, n, t                     │
│ t < n                       │
│ e ⊆ t                       │
│                             │
│ e: C_he │ s: he be content  │
└─────────────────────────────┘
```
Fig. 10.5: *Il fut content*

The value of the coercion operator depends on lexical and contextual information, so the range of meanings in (33)–(35) is accounted for by the various possible reinterpretations introduced in section 3 above. The coercion operators emphasize that the meaning effects are not part of the semantics of the Passé Simple and Imparfait per se, but arise out of the conflict between the aspectual requirements of the tense operator, and the input eventuality description. The outcome of the coercion process is that state/process descriptions reported in the Passé Simple are event denoting, and fit into a sequence of ordered events, whereas event descriptions reported in the Imparfait are state denoting, and do not move the reference time forward.

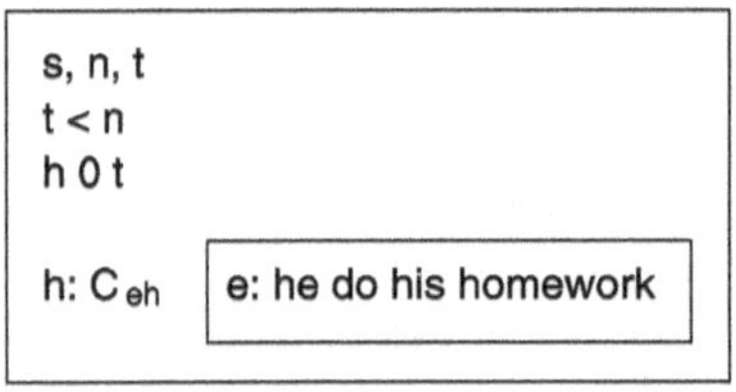

```
┌─────────────────────────────────┐
│ s, n, t                         │
│ t < n                           │
│ h O t                           │
│                                 │
│ h: C_eh │ e: he do his homework │
└─────────────────────────────────┘
```
Fig. 10.6: *Il faisait ses devoirs*

(38) a. Ils   s'   aperçurent   de l'ennemi. Jacques eut   grand peur.
        They REFL noticed.PS   of the ennemi. Jacques had.PS great fear.'
        'They noticed the ennemi. Jacques became very fearful.'

   b. Il   se   noyait   quand l'agent   le   sauva
      He   REFL   drowned.IMP   when the officer him   saved.PS
      en le   retirant   de   l'eau.
      by him   withdraw.   PART from the water.
      'He was drowning when the officer saved him by dragging him out of the water.'

The examples in (38) are to be compared to those in (30) and (31), where no coercion takes place, but the discourse structures induced by the Passé Simple and the Imparfait are similar. We conclude that the coercion approach maintains Kamp & Rohrer's (1983) insights about the temporal structure of narrative discourse in French, while offering a compositional analysis of the internal structure of the sentence.

Versions of a treatment of the perfective/imperfective contrast in terms of aspectually sensitive tense operators have been proposed for other Romance languages, cf. Schmitt (2001). If we embed the analysis of the perfective and imperfective past tenses in the hierarchical structure proposed in (12), we predict that they always take wide scope over overt aspectual operators, including aspectual adverbials, negation, and quantificational adverbs (iterative adverbs like *twice* and frequentative adverbs like *often*). If these expressions are interpreted as mappings between sets of eventualities, we predict that the distribution of perfective/imperfective tenses is sensitive to the output of the aspectual operator. De Swart (1998) argues that eventuality descriptions modified by *in* and *for* adverbials are quantized (cf. section 3.3 above), and are thus of the right aspectual class to serve as the input to the Passé Simple in French. She shows that coercion effects arise in the combination of these adverbials with the Imparfait. De Swart & Molendijk (1999) extend the analysis to negation, iteration and frequency in French. Lenci & Bertinetto (2000) treat the perfective/imperfective past tense distribution in sentences expressing iteration and frequency in Italian, and Pérez-Leroux et al. (2007) show that similar meaning effects arise in Spanish. Coercion effects also play a role in first and second language acquisition, cf. Montrul & Slabakova (2002), Pérez-Leroux et al. (2007), and references therein for aspectuality.

5 Conclusion

This article outlined the role that type coercion and aspectual reinterpretation play in the discussion on type mismatches in the semantic literature. This does not mean that the coercion approach has not been under attack, though. Three issues stand out.

The question whether coercion is a semantic enrichment mechanism or a pragmatic inference based on an underspecified semantics has led to an interesting debate in the semantic processing literature. The question is not entirely resolved at this point, but there are strong indications that type coercion and aspectual coercion lead to delays in online processing, supporting a semantic treatment.

As far as aspectual coercion is concerned, the question whether predicative aspect and grammatical aspect are to be analyzed with the same ontological notions (as in the mapping approach discussed here), or require two different sets of tools (as in Smith 1991/1997) is part of an ongoing discussion in the literature. It has been argued that the lexical component of the mapping approach is not fine-grained enough to account for more subtle differences in predicative aspect (Caudal 2005). In English, there is a class of verbs (including *read, wash, combe,* ...) that easily allow the process reading, whereas others (*eat, build,* ...) do not (Kratzer 2004). Event decomposition approaches (as in Kempchinsky & Slabakova 2005) support the view that some aspectual operators apply at a lower level than the full predicate-argument structure, which affects the view on predicative aspect developed by Verkuyl (1972/1993). The contrast between English-type languages, where aspectual operators apply at the VP level, and Slavic languages, where aspectual prefixes are interpreted at the V-level is highly relevant here (Filip & Rothstein 2006).

The sensitivity of coercion operators to lexical and contextual operators implies that the semantic representations developed in this article are not complete without a mechanism that resolves the interpretation of the coercion operator in the context of the sentence and the discourse. So far, we only have a sketch of how this would have to run (Pulman 1997, de Swart 1998, Hamm & van Lambalgen 2005, Asher & Pustejovsky 2005). There is also a more fundamental problem. Most operators we discussed in the aspectual section are sensitive to the stative/dynamic distinction, or the homogeneous/quantized distinction. This implies that the relation established by coercion is not strictly functional, for it leaves us with several possible outputs (Verkuyl 1999). The same issue arises with type coercion. However, spelling out the different readings semantically would bring us back to a treatment in terms of ambiguities or underspecification, and we would lose our grip on the systematicity of the operator-argument relation.

Notwithstanding the differences in framework, and various problems with the implementation of the notion of coercion, the idea that reinterpretation effects are real, and require a compositional analysis seems to have found its way into the literature.

6 References

de Almeida, Roberto 2004. The effect of context on the processing of type-shifting verbs. *Brain & Language* 90, 249–261.

Asher, Nicholas & Alex Lascarides 1998. Briding. *Journal of Semantics* 15, 83–113.

Asher, Nicholas & James Pustejovsky 2005. Word Meaning and Commonsense Metaphysics. Ms. Austin, TX, University of Texas/Waltham/Boston, MA, Brandeis University.

Bach, Emmon 1986. The algebra of events. *Linguistics & Philosophy* 9, 5–16.

Bos, Johan, Paul Buitelaar & Anne-Marie Mineur 1995. Bridging as coercive accomodation. In: S. Manandhar (ed.). *Proceedings of the Workshop on Computational Logic for Natural Language Processing*. Edinburgh.

Brennan, Jonathan & Liina Pylkkänen 2008. Processing events. Behavioural and neuromagnetic correlates of aspectual coercion. *Brain & Language* 106, 132–143.

Bybee, Joan, Revere Perkins & William Pagliuca 1994. *The Evolution of Grammar. Tense, Aspect and Modality in the Languages of the World*. Chicago, IL: The University of Chicago Press.
Caudal, Patrick 2005. Stage structure and stage salience for event semantics. In: P. Kempchinsky & R. Slabakova (eds.). *Aspectual Inquiries*. Dordrecht: Springer, 239–264.
Clark, Herbert H. 1975. Bridging. In: R. C. Schank & B. L. Nash-Webber (eds.). *Theoretical Issues in Natural Language Processing*. New York: Association for Computing Machinery, 169–174.
Comrie, Bernard 1976. *Aspect. An Introduction to the Study of Verbal Aspect and Related Problems*. Cambridge: Cambridge University Press.
Dölling, Johannes 2003. Aspectual (re)interpretation. Structural representation and processing. In: H. Härtl & H. Tappe (eds.). *Mediating between Concepts and Grammar*. Berlin: Mouton de Gruyter, 303–322.
Dowty, David R. 1979. *Word Meaning and Montague Grammar. The Semantics of Verbs and Times in Generative Semantics and Montague's PTQ*. Dordrecht: Reidel.
Filip, Hana & Susan Rothstein 2006. Telicity as a semantic parameter. In: J. Lavine et al. (eds.). *Formal Approaches to Slavic Linguistics (= FASL) 14*. Ann Arbor, MI: University of Michigan Slavic Publications, 139–156.
Van Geenhoven, Veerle 1998. *Semantic Incorporation and Indefinite Descriptions. Semantic and Syntactic Aspects of Noun Incorporation in West Greenlandic*. Stanford, CA: CSLI Publications.
Van Geenhoven, Veerle 2005. Atelicity, pluractionality and adverbial quantification. In: H. J. Verkuyl, H. de Swart & A. van Hout (eds.). *Perspectives on Aspect*. Dordrecht: Springer, 107–124.
Hamm, Fritz & Michiel van Lambalgen 2005. *The Proper Treatment of Events*. Oxford: Blackwell.
Heim, Irene 1982. *The Semantics of Definite and Indefinite Noun Phrases*. Ph.D. dissertation. University of Massachusetts, Amherst, MA. Reprinted: Ann Arbor, MI: University Microfilms.
Hendriks, Herman 1993. *Studied Flexibility. Categories and Types in Syntax and Semantics*. Doctoral dissertation. University of Amsterdam.
Jackendoff, Ray 1996. The proper treatment of measuring out, telicity and perhaps even quantification in English. *Natural Language and Linguistic Theory* 14, 305–354.
Kamp, Hans 1981. A theory of truth and semantic representation. In: J. Groenendijk, T. Janssen & M. Stokhof (eds.). *Formal Methods in the Study of Language*. Amsterdam: Mathematical Centre, 277–321.
Kamp, Hans & Christian Rohrer 1983. Tense in texts. In: R. Bäuerle, Ch. Schwarze & A. von Stechow (eds.). *Meaning, Use, and Interpretation of Language*. Berlin: Mouton de Gruyter, 250–269.
Kamp, Hans & Uwe Reyle 1993. *From Discourse to Logic*. Dordrecht: Kluwer.
Kempchinsky, Paula & Roumyana Slabakova (eds.) 2005. *Aspectual Inquiries*. Dordrecht: Springer.
Kluck, Marlies 2007. Optimizing interpretation from a generative lexicon. A case study of metonymic type coercion in modified nouns. In: K. Kanzaki, P. Bouillon & L. Danlos (eds.). *Proceedings of the 4th International Workshop on Generative Approaches to the Lexicon*. Paris.
Kratzer, Angelika 2004. Telicity and the meaning of objective case. In: J. Guéron & J. Lecarme (eds.). *The Syntax of Time*. Cambridge, MA: The MIT Press, 75–115.
Krifka, Manfred 1989. Nominal reference, temporal constitution and quantification in event semantics. In: R. Bartsch, J. van Benthem & P. van Emde Boas (eds.). *Semantics and Contextual Expression*. Dordrecht: Foris, 75–115.

Krifka, Manfred 1992. Thematic relations as links between nominal reference and temporal constitution. In: I. Sag & A. Szabolcsi (eds.). *Lexical Matters*. Stanford, CA: CSLI Publications, 29–53.
Landman, Fred 1992. The progressive. *Natural Language Semantics* 1, 1–32.
Lascarides, Alex & Ann Copestake 1998. Pragmatics and word meaning. *Journal of Linguistics* 34, 387–414.
Lenci, Allessandro & Pier M. Bertinetto 2000. Aspect, adverbs and events. Habituality vs. perfectivity. In: J. Higginbotham, F. Pianesi & A. C. Varzi (eds.). *Speaking of Events*. Oxford: Oxford University Press, 245–287.
McElree, Brian, Matthew Traxler, Martin Pickering, Rachel E. Seely & Ray Jackendoff 2001. Reading time evidence for enriched semantic composition. *Cognition* 78, B17–B25.
Michaelis, Laura A. 2003. Headless constructions and coercion by construction. In: E. J. Francis & L. A. Michaelis (eds.). *Mismatch. Form-Function Incongruity and the Architecture of Grammar*. Stanford, CA: CSLI Publications, 259–310.
Moens, Marc 1987. *Tense, Aspect and Temporal Reference*. Ph.D. dissertation. University of Edinburgh.
Moens, Marc & Mark Steedman 1988. Temporal ontology and temporal reference. *Computational Linguistics* 14, 15–28.
Montrul, Silvina A. & Roumyana Slabakova 2002. The L2 acquisition of morphosyntactic and semantic properties of the aspectual tenses preterite and imperfect. In: A. T. Pérez-Leroux & J. M. Liceras (eds.). *The Acquisition of Spanish Morphosyntax. The L1/L2 Connection*. Dordrecht: Kluwer, 113–149.
Nunberg, Geoffrey 1995. Transfers of meaning. *Journal of Semantics* 12, 109–132.
Parsons, Terence 1991. *Events in the Semantics of English. A Study in Subatomic Semantics*. Cambridge, MA: The MIT Press.
Partee, Barbara H. 1987. Noun phrase interpretation and type-shifting principles. In: J. Groenendijk, D. de Jongh & M. Stokhof (eds.). *Studies in Discourse Representation Theory and the Theory of Generalized Quantifiers*. Dordrecht: Foris, 115–143.
Pérez-Leroux, Ana T., Alejandro Cuza, Monica Majzlanova & Jeanette Sánchez-Naranjo 2007. Non-native recognition of the iterative and habitual meanings of Spanish preterite and imperfect tenses. In: J. M. Liceras, H. Zobl & H. Goodluck (eds.). *The Role of Formal Features in Second Language Acquisition*. Mahwah, NJ: Lawrence Erlbaum, 432–451.
Pickering, Martin, Brian McElree & Matthew Traxler 2005. The difficulty of coercion. A response to de Almeida. *Brain & Language* 93, 1–9.
Piñango, Maria M., Aaron Winnick, Rashad Ullah & Edgar Zurif 2006. Time-course of semantic composition. The Case of aspectual coercion. *Journal of Psycholinguistic Research* 35, 233–244.
Pulman, Stephen 1997. Aspectual shift as type coercion. *Transactions of the Philological Society* 95, 279–317.
Pustejovsky, James 1995. *The Generative Lexicon*. Cambridge, MA: The MIT Press.
Reichenbach, Hans 1947. *Elements of Symbolic Logic*. New York: Free Press, paperback edn. 1966.
Schmitt, Cristina 2001. Cross-linguistic variation and the present perfect. The case of Portuguese. *Natural Language and Linguistic Theory* 19, 403–453.
Smith, Carlota S. 1991. *The Parameter of Aspect*. Dordrecht: Kluwer, revised 2nd version 1997.
Smith, Carlota S. 2005. Aspectual entities and tense in discourse. In: P. Kempchinsky & R. Slabakova (eds.). *Aspectual Inquiries*. Dordrecht: Springer, 223–237.

de Swart, Henriëtte 1996. Meaning and use of 'not ... until'. *Journal of Semantics* 13, 221–263.
de Swart, Henriëtte 1998. Aspect shift and coercion. *Natural Language and Linguistic Theory* 16, 347–385.
de Swart, Henriëtte 2001. Weak readings of indefinites. Type-shifting and closure. *The Linguistics Review* 18, 69–96.
de Swart, Henriëtte 2003. Coercion in a cross-linguistic theory of aspect. In: E. J. Francis & L. A. Michaelis (eds.). *Mismatch. Form-Function Incongruity and the Architecture of Grammar.* Stanford, CA: CSLI Publications, 231–258.
de Swart, Henriëtte 2006. Aspectual implications of the semantics of plural indefinites. In: S. Vogeleer & L. Tasmowski (eds.). *Non-definiteness and Plurality.* Amsterdam: Benjamins, 169–189.
de Swart, Henriëtte 2007. A cross-linguistic discourse analysis of the perfect. *Journal of Pragmatics* 39, 2273–2307.
de Swart, Henriëtte & Arie Molendijk 1999. Negation and the temporal structure of narrative discourse. *Journal of Semantics* 16, 1–42.
Traxler, Matthew, Martin Pickering & Brian McElree 2002. Coercion in sentence processing. Evidence from eye-movements and self-paced reading. *Journal of Memory and Language* 4, 530–547.
Traxler, Matthew, Brian McElree, Rihana S. Williams & Martin Pickering 2005. Context effects in coercion. Evidence from eye movements. *Journal of Memory and Language* 53, 1–25.
Vendler, Zeno 1957. Verbs and times. *Philosophical Review* 66, 143–160. Reprinted in: Z. Vendler, *Linguistics in Philosophy.* Ithaca, NY: Cornell University Press, 1967, 97–121.
Verkuyl, Henk J. 1972. *On the Compositional Nature of the Aspects.* Dordrecht: Reidel.
Verkuyl, Henk J. 1993. *A Theory of Aspectuality. The Interaction between Temporal and Atemporal Structure.* Cambridge: Cambridge University Press.
Verkuyl, Henk J. 1999. *Aspectual Issues. Studies on Time and Quantity.* Stanford, CA: CSLI Publications.
Vet, Co 1994. Petite grammaire de l'Aktionsart et de l'aspect. *Cahiers de Grammaire* 19, 1–17.
Zucchi, Sandro 1998. Aspect shift. In: S. Rothstein (ed.). *Events and Grammar.* Dordrecht: Kluwer, 349–370.

Andrea Tyler and Hiroshi Takahashi
11 Metaphors and metonymies

1   Introduction —— 350
2   Traditional approaches to metaphor —— 353
3   Pragmatic accounts of metaphor —— 354
4   Psycholinguistic approaches to figurative language —— 361
5   Cognitive and conceptual accounts —— 363
6   Metonymy —— 373
7   References —— 376

Abstract: For centuries, the study of metaphor and metonymy was primarily the province of rhetoricians. Although scholars developed a number of variations on the theme, the prevailing perspectives, i.e. that these tropes are stylistic devices used primarily for literary purposes and result from some kind of transfer of meaning between similar entities, remained largely unchanged from Aristotle until the mid twentieth century. Aspects of this long tradition still exist in current accounts that continue to argue that metaphoric meaning is in some way deviant, involves transference, and should be analyzed on a word by word basis. In the last 50 years linguists, such as Lakoff and Sperber & Wilson, have joined philosophers, such as Black and Grice, in the debate. The result has been a sharp increase in interest in non-literal language and a number of major innovations in metaphor theory. Metaphor and metonymy are now understood to be ubiquitous aspects of language, not simply fringe elements. The study of metaphor and metonymy have provided a major source of evidence for Cognitive Linguists to argue against the position that a sharp divide exists between semantics and pragmatics. Mounting empirical data from psychology, especially work by Gibbs, has led many to question the sharp boundary between literal and metaphorical meaning. While distinct perspectives remain among contemporary metaphor theorists, very recent developments in relevance theory and cognitive semantics also show intriguing areas of convergence.

1 Introduction

It is an exaggeration to say that metaphor and metonymy are the tropes that launched 1,000 theories. Still, they are long recognized uses of language that

---
Andrea Tyler and Hiroshi Takahashi, Washington, DC, USA

https://doi.org/10.1515/9783110626391-011

have stimulated considerable debate among language scholars and most recently served as a major impetus for Cognitive Linguistics, a theory of language which challenges the modularity hypothesis and postulates such as a strict divide between semantics and pragmatics (cf. article 11 [Semantics: Interfaces] (Jaszczolt) *Semantics and pragmatics*). From Aristotle to the 1930's, the study of metaphor and metonymy was primarily seen as part of the tradition of rhetoric. Metaphor in particular was seen as a highly specialized, non-literal, 'deviant' use of language, used primarily for literary or poetic effect. Although scholars developed a number of variations on the theme, the basic analysis that metaphor involved using one term to stand for another, remained largely unchanged. Beginning with Richards (1936) and his insight that the two elements in a metaphor (the tenor and vehicle) are both active contributors to the interpretation, the debate has shifted away from understanding metaphor as simply substituting one term for another or setting up a simple comparison (although this definition is still found in reference books such as the Encyclopedia Britannica). In the main, contemporary metaphor scholars now believe that the interpretations and inferences generated by metaphors are too complex to be explained in terms of simple comparisons. (However, see discussion of resemblance metaphors, below.)

Richards' insights stirred debate among philosophers such as Black and Grice. Subsequently, linguists (for example, Grady, Johnson, Lakoff, Reddy, Sperber & Wilson, and Giora) and psychologists (for example, Coulson, Gibbs, and Keysar & Bly) have joined in the discussion. The result has been a sharp increase in interest in metaphor and metonymy. Debate has revolved around issues such as the challenges such non-literal language poses for truth conditional semantics and pragmatics, for determining the division between literal and non-literal language, and the insights metaphor and metonymy potentially offer to our understanding of the connections between language and cognition. The upshot has been a number of major innovations which include, but are not limited to, a deeper understanding of the relations between the terms in linguistic metaphor, that is, tenor (or target) and vehicle (or source); exploration of the type of knowledge, 'dictionary' versus 'encyclopedic', necessary to account for interpreting metaphor; and development of a typology of metaphors, that is, primary, complex, and resemblance metaphor.

Given the recent diversity of scholarly activity, universally accepted definitions of either metaphor or metonymy are difficult to come by. All metaphor scholars recognize certain examples of metaphor, such as 'Ted is the lion of the Senate', and agree that such examples of metaphor represent, in some sense, non-literal use of language. Scholars holding a more traditional, truth-conditional perspective might offer a definition along the lines of 'use of a word to create a novel class inclusion relationship'. In contrast, conceptual metaphor theorists hold that metaphor is "a pattern of conceptual association" (Grady 2007) resulting in "understanding and experiencing one kind of thing in terms of another" (Lakoff & Johnson 1980: 5). A key difference between perspectives is that the truth-conditional semanticists represent metaphor as a largely word-level phenomenon, while cognitive semanticists view metaphor as reflective of cognitive patterns of organization and processing more generally. Importantly, even though exemplars of metaphor such as 'Ted is a lion' are readily agreed upon, the prototypicality of such a metaphor is controversial. More traditional approaches tend to treat 'Ted is a lion' as a central example of metaphor; in contrast, conceptual metaphor theory sees it as one of three types of metaphor (a resemblance metaphor) and not necessarily the most prototypical.

According to Evans & Green (2006) and Grady (2008), resemblance metaphors represent the less prototypical type of metaphors and reflect a comparison involving cultural norms and stereotypes. A subset of resemblance metaphors, termed image metaphors, are discussed by Lakoff & Turner (1989) as more clearly involving physical comparisons, as in 'My wife's waist is an hourglass'. For cognitive semanticists, uses such as *'heavy'* in *Stewart's brother is heavy*, meaning Stewart's brother is a serious, deep thinker, represent the most prevalent, basic type of metaphor, termed primary metaphor. In contrast, a truth conditional semanticist (cf. articles 8 [this volume] (Kennedy) *Ambiguity and vagueness* and 9 [this volume] (Egg) *Semantic underspecification*) would likely classify this use of 'heavy' as a case of literal language use (sometimes referred to as a dead metaphor) involving polysemy and ambiguity.

Not surprisingly, analogous divisions are found in the analyses of metonymy. All semanticists recognize a statement such as *'Brad is just another pretty face'* or *'The ham sandwich is ready for the check'* as central examples of metonymy. Moreover, there is general agreement that a metonymic relationship involves referring to one entity in terms of a closely associated or conceptually contiguous entity. Nevertheless, as with analyses of metaphor, differences exists in terms of whether metonymy is considered solely a linguistic phenomenon in which one linguistic entity refers to another or whether it is reflective of more general cognition. Cognitive semanticists argue "metonymy is a cognitive process in which one conceptual entity [...] provides mental access to another conceptual entity within the same [cognitive] domain [...]" (Kövesces & Radden 1998: 39).

The chapter is organized as follows: Section 2 will present an overview of the traditional approaches to metaphor which include Aristotle's classic representation as well as Richards', Black's and Davidson's contributions. Section 3 addresses pragmatic accounts of metaphor with particular attention to recent discussions within Relevance theory. Section 4 presents psycholinguistic approaches, particularly Gentner's 'metaphor-as-career' account and Glucksberg's metaphor

-as- category account and the more recent "dual reference" hypothesis. Section 5 focuses on cognitive and conceptual accounts. It provides an overview of Lakoff & Johnson's (1980) original work on conceptual metaphor, later refinements of that work, especially development of the theory of experiential correlation and Grady's typology of metaphors, and conceptual blending theory. Section 6 addresses metonymy.

2 Traditional approaches to metaphor

Metaphor and metonymy have traditionally been considered stylistic devices employed to embellish literal interpretations of words and sentences for literary and poetic effects, with their meaning involving special deviations from the encoded content of language. Of the two tropes, metaphor has been given far more attention and our discussion here will primarily focus on it. The metaphor/metonymy-as-deviance view goes back at least as far as Aristotle, who defined metaphor (and metonymy) as "giving the thing a name that belongs to something else" (*Poetics* 1457, cited in Gibbs 1994: 210). Aristotle speculated that metaphor involved "transference" of the meaning of one word to another. Thus, his analysis was confined to the word level with a focus on similarities between two things as the basis for metaphors. Aristotle's views engendered two major modes of thought in metaphor research that have continued to the present, one based on the "comparison" of two apparently dissimilar items, and the other based on the "substitution" of one item for another.

These traditional conceptions of metaphor were disputed by I. A. Richards (1936), who claimed that in metaphor, two entities or thoughts are equally "active" and copresent and interactive with each other (Taverniers 2002: 21). In *John is a rat*, for instance, we know that a person ("tenor") and a rat ("vehicle") are obviously distinct but they still can share certain traits, such as being furtive and filthy, and such recognition gives rise to the conceptualization of John as a vile person ("ground" or new meaning). Richards' work represents an important innovation which metaphor scholars continue to draw on; most current analyses recognize the two terms in a metaphor as playing the roles of 'source' and 'target'.

Black (1962, 1979) expanded on Richards' theory and propounded his own version of the interaction model of metaphor in an explicit attempt to overcome the oversimplified view of metaphor as lexical comparison or substitution. For Black, metaphor comprehension in fact "creates" new similarities, rather than simply highlighting certain unnoticed similarities. In *Man is a wolf*, for example, the term *wolf* calls up a system of "associated commonplaces" of the word (such as "fierce", "predatory", "hunting prey in packs", etc.), and that system serves as a "filter" through which *man* is understood, highlighting only those traits that fit the notion of *man*. This leads to a new conceptualization of *man* as a "wolf-like" creature, which constitutes the "cognitive content" of the metaphor that cannot be captured by literal paraphrasing. Interesting echoes of this analysis are found in Sperber and Wilson's recent work involving accessing encyclopedic knowledge when interpreting metaphor and cognitive semanticists' work on blending theory.

Davidson (1978) critiqued Black's interaction model from the perspective of truth-conditional semantics. Sharply distinguishing between what words mean (semantics) and what words are used to do (pragmatics), Davidson argued that metaphor squarely belongs to the realm of language use and itself has no "meaning" or truth-conditional propositional content. To him, "metaphor means what the words mean and nothing more" (Davidson 1978: 30). Davidson thus claims that metaphor is a special use of this literal meaning to evoke some new, unnoticed insight, and that the content of this insight is external to the meaning of the metaphor, thus denying any "cognitive content" in metaphor. Davidson (1981) further argued that, when juxtaposed in an X is Y frame, any two things can be understood as bearing a metaphorical relation, claiming, "There are no unsuccessful metaphors" (Davidson 1981: 201). In other words, there are no constraints on metaphor, and hence no systematic patterns of metaphor. Like Black, and in keeping with the long standing tradition, Davidson believed that metaphor is a lexical phenomenon. Gibbs (1994: 220–221) points out that Davidson's "metaphors-without-meaning" view reflects the centuries-old belief in the importance of an ideal scientific-type language and that Davidson's denial of meaning or cognitive content in metaphor is motivated by a theory-internal need to restrict the study of meaning to truth conditional sentences.

3 Pragmatic accounts of metaphor

Since their inception in the 1960's, most pragmatic theories have preserved or reinforced this sharp line of demarcation between semantic meanings and pragmatic interpretations in their models of metaphor understanding.

In his theory of conversational implicature, Grice (1969/1989, 1975) argued that the non-literal meaning of utterances is derived inferentially from a set of conversational maxims (e.g. be truthful and be relevant). Given the underlying assumption that talk participants are rational and cooperative, an apparent violation of any of those maxims triggers a search for an appropriate conversational implicature that the speaker intended to convey in context (cf. articles 15 [Semantics:

Interfaces] (Simons) *Implicature* and 17 [Semantics: Interfaces] (Potts) *Conventional implicature and expressive content*). In this conception of non-literal language understanding, known as the "standard pragmatic model", metaphor comprehension involves a series of inferential steps – analyze the literal meaning of an utterance first, then reject it due to its literal falsity, and then derive an alternative interpretation that fits the context. In *Robert is a bulldozer*, for instance, the literal interpretation is patently false (i.e. violates the maxim of quality) and this recognition urges the listener to infer that the speaker must have meant something non-literal (e.g., "persistent and does not let obstacles stand in his way in getting things done"). In his speech act theory, Searle (1979) also espoused this standard model and posited an even more elaborate set of principles and steps to be followed in deriving non-literal meanings.

One significant implication of the standard pragmatic view is that metaphors, whose interpretation is indirect and requires conversational implicatures, should take additional time to comprehend over that needed to interpret equivalent literal speech, which is interpreted directly (Gibbs 1994, 2006b). The results of numerous psycholinguistic experiments, however, have shown this result to be highly questionable. In the majority of experiments, listeners/readers were found to take no longer to understand the figurative interpretations of metaphor, metonymy, sarcasm, idioms, proverbs, and indirect speech acts than to understand equivalent literal expressions, particularly if these are seen in realistic linguistic and social contexts (see Gibbs 1994, 2002 for reviews; see also the discussion below of psycholinguistic analyses of metaphor understanding for findings on processing time for conventional versus novel figurative expressions).

Within their increasingly influential framework of relevance theory, Sperber & Wilson (1995; Wilson & Sperber 2002a, 2002b) present an alternative model of figurative language understanding that does not presuppose an initial literal interpretation and its rejection. Instead, metaphors are processed similarly to literal speech in that interpretive hypotheses are considered in their order of accessibility with the process stopping once the expectation of "optimal relevance" has been fulfilled. A communicative input is optimally relevant when it connects with available contextual assumptions to yield maximal cognitive effects (such as strengthening, revising, and negating such contextual assumptions) without requiring any gratuitous processing effort. At the heart of this "fully inferential" model is the idea that "human cognition tends to be geared to the maximization of relevance" (i.e. the Cognitive Principle of Relevance) and that "every ostensive stimulus conveys a presumption of its own optimal relevance" (i.e. the Communicative Principle of Relevance) (Wilson & Sperber 2002a: 254–256). With respect to non-literal meanings, relevance theorists embrace a "continuity view, on which there is no clear cut-off point between 'literal' utterances, approximations, hyperboles and metaphors, and they are all considered to be interpreted in the same way" (Wilson & Carston 2006: 406), a position very similar to that of Conceptual Metaphor theorists and Cognitive Linguistics (see below). In their latest articulation of relevance theory, Sperber & Wilson (2008: 84) call their approach to figurative language a "deflationary" account in which they posit no mechanism specific to metaphor, making abundantly clear their position that there is "no interesting generalization" applicable only to metaphors, distinct from literal and other non-literal types of language use. On this view, metaphor comprehension simply calls for finding an interpretation that satisfies the presumption of optimal relevance, as with any other ostensive stimuli (i.e. stimuli, verbal or nonverbal, that are designed to attract an audience's attention to home in on the meaning intended by the communicator, who conveys this very intention to the audience in what Sperber & Wilson 2004 call "ostensive-inferential communication"). To achieve this, the listener needs to enrich the decoded sentence meaning at the explicit level to derive its "explicature" (through disambiguation, reference assignment, and other enrichment processes) and complement it at the implicit level by supplying contextual assumptions which combine with the adjusted explicit meaning to yield enough contextual implications (which vary in degrees of strength) or other cognitive effects to make the utterance relevant in the expected way (Sperber & Wilson 2004: 408). In *Caroline is a princess*, for instance, the adjusted explicit content may contain not just the encoded concept PRINCESS (daughter of royalty) but a related "ad hoc" concept PRINCESS* in the context in which the assigned referent of *Caroline* is manifestly not royal. This ad hoc concept matches particular contextual assumptions or "implicated premises" (such as "spoiled" and "indulged") made accessible through the encyclopedic knowledge about the concept *princess*. The combination of the explicit content (CAROLINE IS A PRINCESS*) and the encyclopedic assumptions (A PRINCESS IS SPOILED, INDULGED, etc.) yields some strong contextual implications or "implicated conclusions" (CAROLINE IS SPOILED, INDULGED, etc.). Notice that this online process of constructing an ad hoc concept at the explicit level involves what Carston (2002a, 2002b) and Wilson & Carston (2006) call "broadening", or category extension where the ad hoc concept (in this case PRINCESS*) comes to cover a broader scope of meaning than the linguistically encoded concept (PRINCESS). Lexical broadening is held to be pervasive in everyday language use, particularly in the form of approximation (using *flat* to mean "flattish" in a sentence like *Holland is flat*), and it does not preserve literalness, unlike "narrowing", the other variety of loose use of language in which the constructed meaning is narrower or more specific than the linguistically encoded meaning, as in the use of *temperature* in a sentence like *I have a temperature* (Sperber & Wilson 2008: 91), in which *temperature* is taken to mean an internal body temperature above 98.7 degrees. While some cases of non-literal use of language, such as hyperbole, involve only broadening of the encoded concept, most metaphors involve both broadening and narrowing and thus cannot be treated as cases of simple category extension (Sperber & Wilson 2008: 95; see also the discussion of the "class inclusion" view of metaphor below). In the case of *Caroline is a princess*, the contextually derived ad hoc concept PRINCESS* is narrowed, in a particular context, from the full extension of the encoded concept PRINCESS to cover only a certain type of princess ("spoiled" and "indulged"), excluding other kinds (e.g. "well-bred", "well-educated", "altruistic", etc.). It is also at the same time a case of broadening in that the ad hoc concept covers a wider category of people who behave in self-centered, spoiled manners, but are non-royalty, and whose prototypical members are coddled girls and young women.

The relevance theoretic account of figurative language understanding thus pivots on the "literal-loose-metaphorical continuum", whereby no criterion can be found for distinguishing literal, loose, and metaphorical utterances, at least in terms of inferential steps taken to arrive at an interpretation that satisfies the expectation of optimal relevance. What is crucial here is the claim that the fully inferential process of language understanding unfolds equally for all types of utterances and that the linguistically encoded content of an utterance (hence, the "decoded" content of the utterance for the addressee) merely serves as a starting point for inferring the communicator's intended meaning, even when it is a "literal" interpretation. In other words, strictly literal interpretations that involve neither broadening nor narrowing of lexical concepts are derived through the same process of mutually adjusting explicit content (i.e. explicature, as distinct from the decoded content) with implicit content (i.e. implicature), as in loose and metaphorical interpretations of utterances (Sperber & Wilson 2008: 93). As seen above, this constitutes a radical departure from the standard pragmatic model of language understanding, which gives precedence to the literal over the non-literal in the online construction of the speaker's intended meaning. Relevance theory assumes, instead, that literal interpretations are neither default interpretations to be considered first, nor are they equivalent to the linguistically encoded (and decoded) content of given utterances. The linguistically denoted meaning recovered by decoding is therefore "just one of the inputs to an inferential process which yields an interpretation of the speaker's meaning" (Wilson & Sperber 2002b: 600) and has "no useful theoretical role" in the study of verbal communication (Wilson & Sperber 2002b: 583). Under this genuinely inferential model, "interpretive hypotheses about explicit content and implicatures are developed partly in parallel rather than in sequence and stabilize when they are mutually adjusted so as to jointly confirm the hearer's expectations of optimal relevance" (Sperber & Wilson 2008: 96; see also Wilson & Sperber 2002b). As an illustration of how the inferential process may proceed in literal and figurative use of language, let us look at two examples from Sperber & Wilson (2008).

(1) *Peter:* For Billy's birthday, it would be nice to have some kind of show.
    Mary: Archie is a magician. Let's ask him. (Sperber & Wilson 2008: 90)

In this verbal exchange, the word *magician* can be assumed to be ambiguous in its linguistic denotation, between (a) someone with supernatural powers who performs magic (MAGICIAN$_1$), and (b) someone who does magic tricks to amuse an audience (MAGICIAN$_2$). In the minimal context given, where two people are talking about a show for a child's birthday party, the second encoded sense is likely to be activated first, under the assumption that Mary's utterance will achieve optimal relevance by addressing Peter's suggestion that they have a show for Billy's birthday party. Since magicians in the sense of MAGICIAN$_2$ put on magic shows that children enjoy, this assumption, combined with Peter's wish to have a show for Billy's birthday, yields an implicit conclusion that Archie could put on a magic show for Billy's birthday party, which in turn helps to stabilize the explicit content of Mary's utterance as denoting that Archie is a MAGICIAN$_2$. The overall interpretation that emerges in the end to satisfy the expectation of optimal relevance would thus be something along the lines of "Archie is a MAGICIAN$_2$ who could put on a magic show for Billy's birthday party that the children would enjoy". This inferential process for the literal interpretation of the word *magician*, which involves neither broadening nor narrowing, also holds for its metaphorical interpretation, such as the one in (2) below.

(2) *Peter:* I've had this bad back for a while now, but nobody has been able to help.
    Mary: My chiropractor is a magician. You should go and see her. (Sperber & Wilson 2008: 96)

If we assume that Mary's utterance will achieve optimal relevance by addressing Peter's expressed concern about his back pain, the use of the word *magician*, combined with Peter's worry that no ordinary treatments work for him, is likely to activate the first sense MAGICIAN$_1$ to invite the assumption that magicians can achieve extraordinary things. This assumption, together with the information that chiropractors are those who specialize in healing back pain, then yields an implicit conclusion that Mary's chiropractor is capable of achieving extraordinary things and would thus be able to help Peter better than others. This conclusion in turn helps to stabilize the explicit content of Mary's utterance as involving a metaphorical MAGICIAN*, an ad hoc concept contextually constructed on the fly, through broadening, to mean someone who is capable of achieving extraordinary things in certain situations. The overall interpretation that congeals in the end would thus be something along the lines of "Mary's chiropractor is a MAGICIAN*, who would be able to help Peter better than others by achieving extraordinary things". These two examples indicate that literal and metaphorical interpretations are derived through essentially equivalent inferential steps (see Sperber & Wilson 2008: 95–96 for a more detailed explication of the inferential steps putatively involved in the interpretation of these two examples).

Given these observations, relevance theorists argue that their account of metaphor is psychologically and cognitively plausible and escapes the psycholinguistic criticism leveled against the standard pragmatic model. Since the relevance theoretic heuristic for utterance understanding, as was seen above, is to take a path of least effort and stop once the expectation of relevance is fulfilled, understanding metaphorical expressions does not presuppose the primacy of literal interpretations and their rejection, but can go straight to non-literal interpretations from the minimal decoding of linguistically coded stimuli. Furthermore, hypotheses about explicatures, implicated premises, and implicated conclusions should not be taken to be sequentially ordered but they are rather developed online in parallel against a background of expectations (Wilson & Sperber 2002a: 261–262). Nevertheless, it still remains unclear how the notions of narrowing and broadening can account for "category-crossing" cases like *Robert is a bulldozer*, where its supposed ad hoc concept BULLDOZER* (with psychological properties such as "aggressive" and "obstinate") cannot be drawn from the lexical entry of *bulldozer* or its encyclopedic entry because such properties simply do not exist in these entries stored in long-term memory, a gap in the relevance-theoretic explanation of metaphor as a kind of loose talk, as acknowledged by Carston (2002a). This problem pertains most centrally to the issue of "emergent meaning" to be discussed below in the review of cognitive linguistic approaches to metaphor, particularly in connection with the theory of conceptual blending.

Another theoretical issue recently raised by some philosophers of language (Stern 2006; Camp 2006a) with regard to relevance-theoretic and other "contextualist" accounts of metaphor (Sperber & Wilson 1995; Wilson & Sperber 2002a, 2002b; Wilson & Carston 2006; Carston 2002a, 2002b; Recanati 2004) is whether or how much contextual factors "intrude" into the realm of semantics to affect "what is said", as opposed to "what is merely communicated", in figurative language understanding (see the June 2006 special issue of *Mind and Language*, for a recent overview of this issue). In the traditional or Gricean view, "what is said" is equated with what is linguistically encoded, or a minimal propositional form supplied by the semantics of an utterance, plus the "saturation" of variables (such as indexicals) present in linguistic structure. This minimal literal proposition (i.e. "sentence meaning") in turn serves as the basis for further pragmatic inferencing to yield "what is implicated" or meant by the speaker (i.e. "speaker's meaning"). On this view, metaphor does not impinge upon "what is said", but simply remains a matter of communicating something by saying something else (hence, a "violation" of maxims).

Those in the contextualist camp challenge this conception as an oversimplification, and argue that metaphorical language prompts the addressee to create ad hoc concepts through the kind of narrowing and broadening discussed above, which contributes to the explicit content of the utterance (Carston 2002a: 85). From the contextualist viewpoint, therefore, metaphor does affect what is overtly communicated (or "explicature" in relevance-theoretic terms) in determining the full explicit proposition of an utterance, as opposed to its minimal literal proposition, which is criticized as being too fragmentary to provide the basis for further pragmatic inferencing.

Contra Davidson (1978) and Rorty (1989), few present-day "literalists", in fact, dispute that metaphors "express truths" and concern truth-evaluable semantic content (Stern 2006: 245). Neither do they accept the traditional view, which stipulates that "what is said" is simply conventionally encoded semantic meaning (Camp 2006a: 300). What current literalists are objecting to, instead, is the way contextualists are treating "what is said" as a notion "radically disconnected from conventional meaning" (Camp 2006a: 300). Literalists contend that the contextualist accounts of metaphor fail to explain how the metaphorical depends on the literal, or how literal meanings are somehow "active" in metaphorical interpretations of utterances (Stern 2006: 250; also see Giora's discussion of the role of salient meaning in metaphor understanding). It is worth noting that this contextualist-literalist controversy on how metaphor affects "what is said" arises only when one maintains a highly modular view of linguistic meaning and communication, in which a rather strict division of labor is presupposed between semantics and pragmatics, as well as a divide between encoded word meaning and encyclopedic knowledge.

One final sticky point of contention surrounding the relevance theoretic account of metaphor concerns the role of context in the time course of figurative language processing, an issue raised by Rachel Giora, who puts forth an alternative model of language understanding dubbed the graded salience hypothesis (Giora 1997, 1998, 1999, 2002, 2008, inter alia). Citing a large body of empirical research attesting to the primacy of context-independent "salient" lexical meanings, including her own experimental work, Giora argues that relevance theory fails to explain cases in which contextually incompatible lexical meanings are in fact activated (or fail to be "suppressed") in the initial stage of metaphor understanding. Under her hypothesis, the meaning that is obligatorily accessed in the initial phase of comprehension is the most salient meaning coded in the mental lexicon, rather than the contextually sanctioned meaning, regardless of its literal or non-literal status, a position that runs counter to the "direct access" model assumed in relevance theory, where only contextually compatible meanings are activated to satisfy the expectation of optimal relevance. According to Giora, the degree of salience of a word or an expression is modulated by its conventionality, familiarity, frequency, or prototypicality (e.g. the meaning that one has just learned, the meaning activated by previous context, the meaning frequently used in a particular discourse community, etc.), rather than its contextual compatibility. In this theory, textual context is thus assigned a limited role in the initial stage of comprehension and, most importantly, it is ineffective in blocking the activation of highly salient meanings even when they are contextually incompatible since "it does not interact with lexical processes but runs in parallel" (Giora 2002: 490). Context does come into play in the later stage to prompt sequential processing whereby the salient meaning, when contextually inappropriate, is rejected in favor of a meaning that matches the context. Therefore, measures that tap online processing show that processing novel metaphors, for instance, activates the salient literal meaning initially, long before the metaphoric meaning becomes available (Giora 1999: 923). Giora argues that this calls for the revision of the relevance theoretic account of metaphor that incorporates the graded salience hypothesis to capture the psychologically real online process of metaphor understanding (Giora 1998).

4 Psycholinguistic approaches to figurative language

In metaphor research, there is a long genealogy of psycholinguistic studies conducted to examine how people produce and understand figurative language and a number of theories have been proposed in this tradition to explain possible psychological processes behind metaphor production and comprehension. Among those psycholinguistic approaches to metaphor, two influential perspectives, among others, have emerged in recent years, largely independently from the traditional and pragmatic accounts of figurative language discussed above, to capture aspects of online metaphor processing: the "career of metaphor" theory developed by Gentner and colleagues (e.g. Bowdle & Gentner 2005; Gentner & Bowdle 2001; Gentner & Wolff 1997), and the "metaphor-as-categorization" theory proposed by Glucksberg and associates (Glucksberg 2001; Glucksberg & Keysar 1990). Focusing mostly on nominal metaphors of the "X is Y" type such as *My lawyer is a shark*, these two approaches differ most saliently in how they explain such nominal metaphorical statements are processed online. In the career-of-metaphor theory, any metaphorical expressions are understood in either of two distinct processing modes, namely, either as a simile (i.e. a comparison assertion) or as a categorization (i.e. a class inclusion assertion), and the processing mode of each metaphorical expression hinges on its degree of familiarity. Under this model, therefore, novel metaphors are invariably processed as comparisons at first but after repeated use become gradually conventionalized and then eventually become familiar enough to be processed as categorization assertions. In other words, a metaphor "undergoes a process of gradual abstraction and conventionalization as it evolves from its novel use to becoming a conventional 'stock' metaphor" (Gentner & Bowdle 2008: 116). What underlies this theory is the assumption that metaphors are essentially comparisons in their origin. By contrast, metaphor-as-categorization theorists argue that metaphors are fundamentally different from comparisons and are rather intended and understood as categorical, class-inclusion statements. On this view, the sentence *My lawyer is a shark* is thus understood by seeking the closest superordinate category that encompasses the two concepts, *lawyer* and *shark* (in this case, the category of predators, or any creatures that are vicious, aggressive and merciless), rather than by comparing the properties of *lawyer* and *shark* to find common features. Despite these differences, on the other hand, the metaphor-as-categorization theory shares with the career-of-metaphor theory the basic assumption that metaphors and similes are fundamentally equivalent and are thus essentially interchangeable: while the latter argues that metaphors are implicit similes, in which features are extracted from the two given concepts and matched with one another, the former contends that metaphors can be expressed as similes to make implicit categorization assertions.

More recent evidence, however, paints a different picture, according to Glucksberg (2008), suggesting that both the comparison view and the categorization view are wrong in their view of metaphors and similes. In order to test the finding by Bowdle & Gentner (2005) that novel metaphors were preferred in simile/comparison form (X is like Y), while conventional ones were preferred in metaphor/categorization form (X is Y), Haught & Glucksberg (2004) selected a set of apt and comprehensible conventional metaphors (e.g. *My lawyer was (like) a shark* and *Some ideas are (like) diamonds*) and then made them novel by using adjectives that are applicable to the metaphor topic, but not to the literal metaphor term (e.g. *My lawyer was (like) a well-paid shark*). Participants in this study rated these modified novel metaphors as apt as their original conventional counterparts when they were presented in metaphor/categorization form, but much less apt in simile/comparison form, offering a counterexample to the career of metaphor hypothesis. Based on the finding of this study, Glucksberg (2008: 77) proposes the "dual reference" hypothesis, that "the metaphor vehicle in similes refers at the literal level, but in metaphors at the superordinate metaphorical level", saying that a metaphorical shark can plausibly be well paid but the literal marine creature is not readily characterizable in terms of monetary income. This new hypothesis does seem to reconcile the discrepancy between the two positions (career-of-metaphor vs. metaphor-as-categorization) in their attempts to unravel the online mechanism of metaphor understanding, especially for noun-based metaphors intensely studied in this strand of research on figurative language processing. Yet it still fails to offer much in the way of illuminating insights into what actually motivates and constraints particular uses of metaphor in the first place. This brings us to more cognitively and conceptually oriented approaches to metaphor.

5 Cognitive and conceptual accounts

Conceptual metaphor (and metonymy) theory, as first articulated by George Lakoff and Mark Johnson (1980), represents a radical departure from theories discussed thus far and is clearly embedded in a larger theory of language (Cognitive Linguistics) which holds that language is a reflection of human cognition and general cognitive processes (cf. articles 1 [Semantics: Theories] (Talmy) *Cognitive Semantics*, 2 [Semantics: Theories] (Taylor) *Prototype theory*, 3 [Semantics: Theories] (Gawron) *Frame Semantics*, and 9 [Semantics: Interfaces] (Kay & Michaelis) *Constructional meaning* for broader perspectives on language and cognition within the framework of Cognitive Linguistics). Moving away from the deviance tradition, Lakoff & Johnson focused on the ubiquity of, often highly conventionalized, metaphor in everyday speech and what this reveals about general human cognition. Rather than placing metaphor on the periphery of language, Lakoff & Johnson argue that it is central to human thought processes and hence central to language. They defined metaphor as thinking about a concept (the target) from one knowledge domain in terms of another domain (the source). In particular, they articulated the notion of embodied meaning, i.e., that human conceptualization is crucially structured by bodily experience with the physical-spatial world; much of metaphor is a reflection of this structuring by which concepts from abstract, internal or less familiar domains are structured by concepts from the physical/spatial domains. This structuring is held to be asymmetrical. The argument is that many of these abstract or internal domains have not developed language in their own terms, for instance, English has few domain specific temporal terms and generally represents time in terms of the spatial domain. Thus language from the familiar, accessible, intersubjective domains of the social-spatial-physical is recruited to communicate about the abstract and internal.

This overarching vision is illustrated in Lakoff & Johnson's well known analysis of the many non-spatial, metaphoric meanings of *up* and *down*. They note that *up* and *down* demonstrate a wide range of meanings in everyday English, a few of which are illustrated below:

(3) a. *The price of gas is **up/down**.* AMOUNT
 b. *Jane is further **up/down** in the corporation than most men.* POWER, STATUS
 c. *Scooter is feeling **up/down** these days.* MOOD

Their argument is that all these uses of *up* and *down* reflect a coherent pattern of human bodily experience with verticality. The importance of up and down to human thinking is centrally tied to the particularities of the human body; humans have a unique physical asymmetry stemming from the fact that we walk on our hind legs and that our most important organs of perception are located in our heads, as opposed to our feet. Moreover, the up/down pattern cannot be attributed simply to these two words undergoing semantic extension, as the conceptual metaphor is found with most words expressing a vertical orientation:

(4) a. *The price of gas is **rising/declining**.*
 b. *She's in **high/low** spirits today.*
 c. *She's **over/under** most men in the corporation.*

This analysis explains a consistent asymmetry found in such metaphors; language does not express concepts from social/physical/spatial domains in terms of concepts from abstract or internal domains. For example, concepts such as physical verticality are not expressed in terms of emotions or amount; a sentence such as *He seems particularly confident* cannot be interpreted to mean something like *He seems particularly tall*, whereas *He's standing tall now* does have the interpretation of a feeling of confidence and well being for Conceptual Metaphor Theorists, the asymmetry of mappings represents a key, universal constraint on the vast majority metaphors.

In contrast to other approaches, conceptual metaphor theory tends not to consider metaphoric use of words and phrases on a case-by-case, word-by-word basis, but rather points out broader patterns of use. Thus, a distinction is made between conceptual metaphors, which represent underlying conceptual structure, and metaphoric expressions, which are understood as linguistic reflections of the underlying conceptual structure organized by systematic cross-domain mappings. The correspondences are understood to be mappings across domains of conceptual structure. Cognitive semanticists hold that words do not refer directly to entities or events in the world, but rather they act as access points to conceptual structure. They also advocate an encyclopedic view of word meaning and argue that a lexical item serves as an access point to richly patterned memory (Langacker 1987, 1991, 1999, 2008; also see the discussion of Conceptual Blending below).

Lakoff & Johnson argue that such coherent patterns of bodily experience are represented in memory in what they term 'image schemas', which are multi-modal, multi-faceted, systematically patterned conceptualizations. Some of the best explored image schemas include BALANCE, RESISTANCE, BEGINNING-PATH-END POINT, and MOMENTUM (Gibbs 2006a). Conceptual metaphors draw on these image-schemas and can form entrenched, multiple mappings from a source domain to a target domain. *Her problems are weighing her down* is a metaphorical expression of the underlying conceptual metaphor DIFFICULTIES ARE PHYSICAL BURDENS, which draws on the image schematic structure representing physical resistance to gravity and momentum. The metaphor maps concepts from the external domain of carrying physical burdens onto the internal domain of mental states. Such underlying conceptual metaphors are believed to be directly accessible without necessarily involving any separate processing of a literal meaning and subsequent inferential processes to determine the metaphorical meaning (Gibbs 1994, 2002). Hence, Conceptual Metaphor Theory questions a sharp division between semantics and pragmatics, rejecting the traditional stance that metaphoric expressions are first processed as literal language and only when no appropriate interpretation can be found, are then processed using pragmatic principles. The same underlying conceptual metaphor is found in numerous metaphorical expressions, such as *He was crushed by his wife's illness* and *Her heart felt heavy with sorrow*. Recognition of the centrality of mappings is a hallmark of Conceptual Metaphor Theory; Grady (2007: 190), in fact, argues that the construct of cross-domain mapping is "the most fundamental notion of CMT". Additionally, since what is being mapped across domains is cognitive models, the theory holds that the mappings allow systematic access to inferential structure of the source domain, as well as images and lexicon (Coulson 2006). So, the mapping from the domain of physical weight to the domain of mental states includes the information that the effect of the carrying the burden increases and decreases with its size or weight, as expressed in the domain of emotional state in phrases such as *Facing sure financial ruin, George felt the weight of the world settling on him,* and *Teaching one class is a light work load,* and *Everyone's spirits lightened as more volunteers joined the organization and the number of all night work sessions were reduced.* Conceptual metaphor theorists argue that while the conceptual metaphor is entrenched, the linguistic expression is often novel.

Coulson (2006) further notes that viewing metaphorical language as a manifestation of the underlying conceptual system offers an explanation for why we consistently find limited but systematic mappings between the source domain and target domain (often termed 'partial projection'). The systematicity stems from the access to higher order inferential structures within the conceptual domains which allows mappings across abstract similarities, rather than just at the level of objective features of the two domains, which may in fact be quite different.

Mapping from the domain of physical weight to the domain of mental states would include the following correspondences (Fig. 11.1):

PHYSICAL WEIGHT	MENTAL STATE
Carrier	Experiencer
Object carried	Difficult situation
Physical stress of carrying	Mental/emotional reaction to situation
Size, weight of object	Degree of difficulty

Fig. 11.1: Cross-domain mapping from physical weight to mental states

In their original work, Lakoff & Johnson also investigated metaphors that were less clearly tied to essential human bodily experiences, such as ARGUMENT IS WAR. Critiques of a Lakoffian approach tend to focus on these metaphors and idioms (e.g., Camp 2006b; Keysar & Bly 1995; Wilson & Carston 2006; cf. article 5 [this volume] (Fellbaum) *Idioms and collocations*). They point out that such metaphors can violate the argument that familiar, bodily experiences are used to understand more abstract, less familiar concepts (here in their daily lives, many more people are likely to experience verbal disagreements than open warfare). Moreover, these critics argue that if metaphors are anchored in basic bodily experience, we should expect them to be found universally. In addition, they question why only some of the information from the domain of war is projected onto argument. Although Lakoff & Johnson clearly state that projections from source to target domains are partial, their early work offers no systematic principles for constraint (see below for further discussion; also see Gibbs & Perlman 2006 and Gibbs 2006c for detailed discussion of some of the potential methodological problems with the cognitive linguistic approach to metaphor and their suggestions about how best to address such concerns).

However, even the early conceptual metaphor work contains the beginnings of differentiation between metaphor closely related to embodied meaning (image schema and primary metaphors) and other types of conceptual metaphor. Joseph

Grady and his colleagues (e.g., Grady 1997, 2008; Oakley & Coulson 1999) have deepened the original insights concerning embodied experience through analyzing metaphors such as THEORIES ARE BUILDINGS as complex metaphors made up of several 'primary metaphors'. Grady (1999a) posits a typology of metaphors at the center of which is primary metaphor (or experiential correlation). He argues that THEORIES ARE BUILDINGS is a complex metaphor composed of two primary metaphors ORGANIZATION IS COMPLEX PHYSICAL STRUCTURE and FUNCTIONING/PERSISTING IS REMAINING ERECT/WHOLE. Thus, any entity that we understand as involving organization, such as foreign policy or social customs, as well as theories, can exploit conceptual structure from the domain of complex physical structure, buildings being a prime, humanly salient example. Together with the general commitment to mapping between conceptual domains, the model of experiential correlation goes a long way towards accounting for partial projection, since the domain of buildings is not being mapped, but rather the more generic domain of complex physical structure (see more below). It also accounts for the multiple mappings between sources and targets, since things understood as organization can be mapped to multiple examples of complex physical structure. Moreover, the analysis suggests that while primary metaphors, such as ORGANIZATION IS COMPLEX PHYSICAL STRUCTURE and FUNCTIONING/PERSISTING IS REMAINING ERECT/WHOLE will be found in most languages, the precise cross-domain mappings or complex metaphors which occur will differ from language to language.

Grady points out that humans regularly observe or experience the co-occurrence of two separable phenomena, such that the two phenomena become closely associated in memory. Grady identifies scores of experiential correlations, of which MORE IS UP is probably the most frequently cited. The argument is that humans frequently observe liquids being poured into containers or objects added to piles of one sort or another. These seemingly simple acts actually involve two discrete aspects which tend to go unrecognized–the addition of some substance and an increase in vertical elevation. Notice that it is possible to differentiate these two phenomena; for instance, one could pour the liquid on the floor, thus adding more liquid to a puddle, without causing an increase in elevation. However, humans are likely to use containers and piles because they offer important affordances involving control and organization which humans find particularly useful. The correlation between increases in amount and increases in elevation are ubiquitous and important for humans and thus form a well entrenched experiential correlation or mapping between two domains. Another important experiential correlation Grady identifies is AFFECTION IS WARMTH. He argues that many of the most fundamental experiences during the first few months of life involve the infant experiencing the warmth of a caretaker's body when being held, nursed and comforted. Thus, from the first moments of life, the infant begins to form an experiential correlation between the domain of temperature and the domain of affection. This experiential correlation (or primary metaphor) is reflected in expressions such as *warm smile* and *warm welcome*. Conversely, lack of warmth is associated with discomfort and physical distance from the caretaker, as reflected in the expressions *cold stare* or *frigid reception*.

The theory of experiential correlation has begun to gain support from a number of related fields. Psycholinguistic evidence comes from work by Zhong & Leonardelli (2008) who investigated the AFFECTION IS WARMTH metaphor and found that subjects report experiencing a sense of physical coldness when interpreting phrases such as 'icy glare'. From the area of child language learning, Chris Johnson (1999) has argued that caretaker speech often reflects experiential correlations such as KNOWING IS SEEING and that children may have no basis for distinguishing between literal and metaphorical uses of a word like *see*. If caretakers regularly use *see* in contexts where it can mean either the literal 'perceive visually', as in "Let's see what is in the bag" or the metaphorical 'learn; find out', as in "Let's see what this tastes like", children may develop a sense of the word which conflates literal and metaphorical meanings. Only at some later stage of development, they come to understand there are two separate uses and go through a process Johnson terms *deconflation*. Thus, Johnson argues that the conceptual mappings between experiential correlates are reinforced in the child's earliest exposure to language.

Experiential correlation and the theory of primary metaphors was also a major impetus for the "Neural Theory of Language" (Lakoff & Johnson 1999; Narayanan 1999). This is a computational theory which has successfully modeled inferences arising from metaphoric interpretation of language. Experiential correlations are represented in terms of computational 'neural nets'; correlation mappings are treated as neural circuits linking representations of source and target concepts. Consistent with a usage-based, frequency driven model of language, the neural net model assumes that neural circuits are automatically established when a perceptual and a nonperceptual concept are repeatedly co-activated.

The theory of experiential correlation moves our understanding of metaphor past explanations based only on comparison or similarity or ad hoc categories. It addresses the conundrum of how it is that much metaphoric expression, such as 'warm smile', involves two domains that have no immediately recognizable similarities.

Grady does not claim that all metaphor is based on experiential correlation. In addition to primary metaphors and their related complex metaphors, he posits another type, resemblance metaphor, to account for expressions such as *Achilles is a lion*. These are considered one-shot metaphors that tend to have limited extensions. They involve mappings based on conventionalized stereotypes, here the western European stereotype that lions are fierce, physically powerful and fearless. Key to this account is Grady's adherence to the tenets of lexical meaning being encyclopedic in nature (thus *lion* acts as an access point to the conventional stereotypes) and mappings across conceptual domains. Clearly, resemblance metaphors with their direct link to conventional stereotypes are expected to be culturally-specific, in contrast to primary metaphors which are predicted to be more universal. Grady (1999b) has analyzed over 15 languages, representing a wide range of historically unrelated languages, for the occurrence of several primary metaphors such as BIG IS IMPORTANT. He found near universal expression of these metaphors in the languages examined.

The work by Grady and his colleagues addresses many of the criticisms of Lakoff & Johnson (1980). By setting up a typology of metaphors, conceptual metaphor theory can account for the occurrence of both universal and language specific metaphors. Within a specific language, the notion of complex metaphors, based on multiple primary metaphors, offers an explanation for systematic, recurring metaphorical patterns, including a compelling account of partial projection from source to target. The construct of experiential correlation also provides a methodology for distinguishing between the three proposed types of metaphor. Primary metaphors and their related complex metaphors are strictly asymmetrical in their mappings and ultimately grounded in ubiquitous, fundamental human experiences with the world. In contrast, resemblance metaphors are not strictly asymmetrical. So we find not only *Achilles is a lion* but also *The lion is the king of beasts*. Moreover, metaphor theorists have not been able to find a basic bodily experience that would link lions (or any fierce animals) with people. Finally, identifying the three categories allows an coherent account of embodied metaphor without having to entirely abandon the insight that certain metaphors, such as 'My wife's waist is an hourglass' or 'Achilles is a lion', are based on some sort of comparison.

Lakoff & Johnson (1980) also hypothesized that certain idioms, such as 'spill the beans' were transparent (or made sense) to native speakers because they are linked to underlying conceptual structures, such as the CONTAINER image schema. Keysar & Bly (1995, 1999) question the claim that such transparent idioms can offer insights into cognition. They argue that the native speakers' perception of the relative transparency of an idiom's meaning is primarily a function of what native speakers believe the meaning of the idiom to be. This is essentially a claim for a language based, rather than conceptually based meaning of idioms and metaphors. Keysar & Bly carried out a set of experiments in which they presented subjects with attested English idioms which could be analyzed as transparent, but which had fallen out of use. Examples included 'the goose hangs high' and 'to play the bird with the long neck'. They argued that an idiom such as 'the goose hangs high' can be considered transparent because 'high' potentially links to physical verticality and the conceptual metaphor GOOD IS UP. Subjects were taught either the actual meaning of the idiom or its opposite. For 'the goose hangs high' the actual meaning was 'things look good' and the opposite meaning was 'things look bad'. For subjects learning the 'opposite or non-transparent' meaning, the instruction included the information that the meaning of the idiom was not analyzable, on parallel to 'kick the bucket'. Essentially they found that, under these circumstances, subjects were able to learn the nontransparent meanings and that learning the nontransparent meaning suppressed inferences which might arise from the more transparent meaning. Conversely, for subjects learning the transparent meanings, inferences which might arise from the opposite interpretation were suppressed. They concluded that once a particular meaning is assigned to an idiom, native speakers do their best to mine possible additional meaning from it; simultaneously, learned meanings suppress possible alternative interpretations and inferences. They take this as evidence that transparent idioms, which Conceptual Metaphor Theory holds are related to established conceptual structure, at best provide potential insight into processing strategies.

However, a careful look at the target idioms suggests that they are not particularly transparent, nor based in everyday experience. For instance, although 'the goose hangs high' contains a reference to vertical elevation, the rest of the content must also be taken into consideration. College students in late 20th century USA are hardly likely to have had much experience with hanging geese and what they might signify. Others, such as 'to play the bird with the long neck' whose actual meaning is 'be on the look out for', hardly appears to be based in everyday bodily experience.

Such accounts overlook the fact that "certain conceptual pairings tend to recur and to motivate a great percentage of the actual metaphors that continue to exist in the language" (Grady 2007: 197). Moreover, transparent idioms such as 'spill the beans' often do not occur as isolated set phrases. Related idioms include 'spill one's guts' and 'spill it!' While Keysar & Bly may be right in claiming there is no such thing as an 'impossible metaphor' and that humans tend to draw inferences appropriate to the meaning their discourse community assigns to an idiom regardless of its potential opposite interpretations, conceptual metaphor scholars have been able to identify numerous sets of patterned pairings, along with persuasive accounts of their embodied motivations. Moreover, these pairings persist in the language, rather than going out of fashion. To date, theories that hold that metaphors are only linguistic in nature and have no ties to conceptual structure have yet to offer an explanation for the occurrence of these enduring, frequently encountered mappings.

Conceptual Blending and Integration Theory (Fauconnier & Turner 1998, 2002) developed out of conceptual metaphor theory and Mental Space Theory (Fauconnier 1994, 1997) to account for certain on-line, novel conceptualizations that involve emergent meaning, or additional, non-literal meaning, that cannot be accounted for solely from the information contained in the target and source spaces. The basic notion is that mappings occur across two or more temporary mental input spaces, which draw select, structured information from distinct domains. Simultaneously, select information from each of the input spaces is projected into a third, blended space; it is the integration of these select projections in blended space that gives rise to emergent meaning.

This framework holds that words do not refer directly to entities in the world, but rather they act as prompts to access conceptual structure and to set up short term, local conceptual structures called mental spaces. Mental spaces can be understood as 'temporary containers for relevant, partial information about a particular domain' "(Coulson 2006: 35). The key architecture of the theory is the conceptual integration network which is 'an array of mental spaces in which the processes of conceptual blending unfold' " (Coulson 2006: 35). A conceptual integration network is made up of two or more input spaces structured by information from distinct domains, a generic space that contains 'skeletal' conceptual structure that is common to both input spaces, and a blended space. Mappings occur across the input spaces as well as selectively projecting to the blended space.

One of the most often cited examples of a conceptual blend is *That surgeon is a butcher,* which is interpreted to mean that the surgeon is incompetent and careless. Neither the surgeon space nor the butcher space contains the notion of incompetence. The key issue is how to account for this emergent meaning. Both spaces contain common structure such as an agent, an entity acted upon (human versus animal), goals (healing the patient versus severing flesh), means for achieving the goals (precise incisions followed by repair of the wound versus slashing flesh, hacking bones), etc. Analogy mappings project across the two input spaces linking the shared structure. The notion of incompetence arises in the blended space from the conflict between the goal of healing the patient, which projects from the surgeon space, and the means for achieving the goal, slashing flesh and hacking, which projects from the butcher space. Sweetser (1999) has also analyzed noun-noun compounds such as *land yacht* (large, showy, luxury car) and *couch potato* (person who spends a great deal of time sitting and watching TV) as blends. Such noun-noun compounds are particularly interesting as the entities being referred to are not yachts or potatoes of any kind. Conceptual blending theory subsumes conceptual metaphor, with its commitment to embodied meaning. Its adherents also argue that the processes occurring in non-literal language and a variety of other phenomenon, such as conditionals and diachronic meaning extension, are essentially the same as those needed to explain the interpretation of literal language.

Over the past decade, there has been a growing convergence between cognitive semanticists and relevance theorists in the area of metaphor analysis (see Gibbs & Tendahl 2006). For instance, as we saw above, the latest versions of relevance theory (e.g., Wilson & Sperber 2002a, 2002b; Wilson & Carston 2006; Sperber & Wilson 2008) now posit entries for lexical items which include direct access to 'encyclopedic assumptions' which are exploited in the formation and processing of metaphors and metonymies, a position which is quite similar to Langacker's (1987) analysis of words being prompts to encyclopedic knowledge.

Wilson & Carston (2006: 425) also accept the analysis that physical descriptions such as 'hard, rigid, inflexible, cold', etc apply to human psychological properties through inferential routes such as 'broadening' to create superordinate concepts (HARD*, RIGID*, COLD*, etc) which have both physical and psychological instances. They further argue that ad hoc, on the fly categories can be constructed through the same process of broadening. For instance, they posit that the process of broadening provides an inferential route to the interpretation of *Robert is a bulldozer,* where the encoded concept *bulldozer* has the logical feature, i.e. encoded meaning, MACHINE OF A CERTAIN KIND and the following encyclopedic assumptions:

(5) a. large, powerful, crushing, dangerous to bystanders, etc.
 b. looks like this (xxx); moves like this (yyy), etc.
 c. goes straight ahead regardless of obstacles.
 d. pushes aside obstructions; destroys everything in its path.
 e. hard to stop or resist from outside; drowns out human voices, etc.

They continue, "Some of these encyclopedic features also apply straightforwardly to humans. Others, (powerful, goes straight ahead …) have both a basic, physical sense and a further psychological sense, which is frequently encountered and therefore often lexicalized" (Wilson & Carston 2006: 425).

However, the "inferential" theory of metaphor skirts the issue of how the very process of creating "ad hoc" concepts (such as 'hard to stop') and extended lexicalized concepts (such as COLD* or RIGID*) may be motivated in the first place. The qualities and consequences of physical coldness manifested by ice are not the same as the affectations of lack of caring or standoffishness which are evoked in the interpretation of an expression such as *Sally is a block of ice*. The physical actions and entities involved in a scenario of a bulldozer moving straight ahead crushing physical obstacles such as mounds of dirt and buildings is manifestly different than the actions of a person and the entities involved in a situation in which a person ignores the wishes of others and acts in an aggressive and obstinate manner. As noted above, it remains unclear how the notions of narrowing and broadening are 'straight forward inferences' in cases like *Robert is a bulldozer*, where the key psychological properties such as "aggressive" and "obstinate" cannot be drawn from the lexical entry of "bulldozer" or its encyclopedic entry because such properties simply are not part of our understanding of earth moving machines.

Another gap in the relevance theory approach, and indeed all approaches that treat metaphor on a word-by-word basis, is the failure to recognize that most metaphors are part of very productive, systematic patterns of conceptualization based on embodied experience. For instance, Wilson & Carston argue that *block of ice* has a particular set of encyclopedic assumptions, such as solid, hard, cold, rigid, inflexible, and unpleasant to touch or interact with, associated with it. This treatment fails to systematically account for the fact that the words *icy*, *frigid*, *frosty*, *chilly*, even *cool*, are all used to express the same emotional state. In contrast, conceptual metaphor theory accounts for these pervasive patterns through the construct of experiential correlation and embodied meaning. Similarly, the account of *Robert is a bulldozer* outlined above fails to recognize the underlying image schemas relating to force dynamics, such as momentum and movement along a path, that give rise to any number of conceptually related metaphoric expressions to describe a person as obstinate, powerful and aggressive. Robert could have also been described as behaving like a *run away freight train* or as *bowling over* or *mowing down his opponents* to the same effect, even though the dictionary entries (and their related encyclopedic entries) for freight trains, bowling balls, and scythes or lawn movers would have very little overlap with that of a bulldozer.

6 Metonymy

Over the centuries, metonymy has received less attention than metaphor. Indeed, Aristotle made no clear distinction between the two. Traditionally, metonymy was defined as a trope in which the name of one entity is used to refer to another entity. Thus, it was seen as a referring process involving meaning transfer. In particular, it was represented as a word that takes its expression from things that are 'near and close' (Nerlich 2006). Nunberg (1978) characterized metonymic 'transfer' as having a 'referring function', so that, for instance, the producer can be used to refer to the produced, as in *There are several copies of Stoppard on the shelf* or the part-whole relation (synecdoche) as in *Many hands make light work*.

Some of the most common patterns in English include container for contents, cause for effect, possessor for possessed, type for token (*This wine is one of our best sellers*).

Not surprisingly, cognitive semanticists have provided a strikingly different perspective on metonymy. Consistent with their analysis of metaphor, cognitive semanticists represent metonymy as a fundamental cognitive process which is reflected in linguistic expressions. As with metaphor, the linguistic expression used in a metonymy is understood as an access point to some other larger conceptual structure. The key aspect which distinguishes metonymy from metaphor is that metonymy establishes connections between conceptual entities which co-occur within a single conceptual domain, whereas metaphor establishes connections across two different conceptual domains. In contrast to traditional views that explain the connections between the two entities involved in a metonymy in terms of spatial or physical contiguity or closeness, cognitive semantics understands the entities to be conceptually 'close'.

Cognitive semanticists have pointed out that metonymy is not limited to the type of referring functions illustrated above. Langacker (1984) argues that a ubiquitous aspect of talk involves highlighting certain aspects of a scene or entities within a scene. He refers to the highlighted facets as 'the active zone', that which is more conceptually 'active' or salient in the particular conceptualization. He notes that in talking about our interaction with objects an active zone is usually invoked. So in the sentence *Lucy used a hammer to pry the nail out of the wall* the standard interpretation is that the claw of the hammer was applied to the head of the nail; this is in contrast to *Lucy used her father's new hammer to pound the steak* in which the active zones are the face of the hammer which is applied to the entire surface of the steak. While such use of language certainly involves a part-whole relation, it is so ubiquitous within the contextualized interpretation of language that it has generally gone unrecognized and so treated as literal interpretation. Relevance theorists have recently addressed it as a straightforward contextual inference (Wilson & Carston 2006). Cognitive linguists point to such metonymic uses as support for the assertion of no strict divide between semantics and pragmatics, a point with which the current version of Relevance Theory concurs (Wilson & Carston 2006). Within the cognitive linguistic framework, this omnipresence of metonymic language use in everyday talk is ascribed to what is known as the "reference point" mechanism, or the fundamental human cognitive ability to "invoke the conception of one entity for purposes of establishing mental contact with another, i.e. to single it out for individual conscious awareness" (Langacker 1999: 173). Metonymy thus essentially reflects a pervasive reference point organization wherein the entity linguistically designated by a metonymic expression serves as a salient point of reference that affords mental access to a conceptually close but distinct entity actually intended by the speaker. This reference point ability has manifold linguistic ramifications and is reflected not only in metonymic expressions but also in various grammatical and discourse phenomena, most notably possessives, anaphoric relationships and topicality.

In his detailed exposition of metonymy from the cognitive linguistic perspective, Barcelona (e.g., 2002, 2003, 2005a, 2005b) defines metonymy as a mapping of a cognitive domain (the source) onto another domain (the target), wherein the source and target are in the same functional domain and are linked by a pragmatic function that provides mental access to the target. In this definition, metonymy (which is fundamentally "conceptual" in nature as seen above) is thus a mapping between two (sub)domains that are interrelated within a broader, functionally motivated domain essentially equivalent to what Lakoff (1987) calls an "idealized cognitive model (ICM)" or what Fillmore (1982) calls "frames". The source maps onto (i.e. imposes a particular perspective on) and activates the target in virtue of a pragmatic (i.e. experientially based) link. Under this model, any semantic shift that satisfies these requirements is at least a "schematic" metonymy, which is one of the three types of metonymy posited by Barcelona on the basis of their different degrees of "metonymicity" as measured by the relative conceptual distinction between the source domain (i.e. the reference point) and the target domain. The other two types of metonymy are "typical" metonymies (i.e. schematic metonymies whose target is clearly distinct from the source, either because it is a relatively secondary or peripheral subdomain of the source, or because it is a functionally distinct subdomain within a larger overall domain) and "prototypical" metonymies (i.e. typical "referential" metonymies with individual entities as targets). These three classes of metonymy thus constitute a continuum of metonymicity, with each exemplified in the following instances (Barcelona 2005b: 314):

(6) a. *Belgrade* did not sign the Paris agreement.
 b. She's just a pretty *face*.
 c. He walked *with drooping shoulders*. He had lost his wife.
 d. This book weighs two kilograms.
 e. This book is highly instructive.

According to Barcelona, (6a) is an instance of prototypical metonymy as it is referential and has an individual (the Yugoslavian government) as the target, while (6b) and (6c) are examples of typical metonymy as they are not referential in nature but the targets are clearly distinct from the sources (BODY FOR PERSON and BODY POSTURE FOR EMOTION, respectively). On the other hand, (6d) and (6e) are instances of "purely schematic" metonymies as the whole domain BOOK is mapped onto its subdomains PHYSICAL OBJECT and SEMANTIC CONTENT, respectively, thereby activating those aspects of the overall domain BOOK. Notice here that these examples would not qualify as instances of metonymy under more restrictive models, such as the one presented by Croft (2002), who defines metonymy as domain "highlighting", a cognitive operation which highlights a secondary or noncentral subdomain within the overall domain matrix constituted by the speaker's encyclopedic knowledge of the source concept. Since PHYSICAL OBJECT and SEMANTIC CONTENT would be highly intrinsic subdomains of the BOOK domain matrix (hence primary rather than secondary), (6d) and (6e) would not represent any salient highlighting in Croft's sense. This noncentrality requirement, also shared by Ruiz de Mendoza (2000), is not a necessary condition in Barcelona's definition because he fully embraces the notion of prototype effects in the category of metonymy and believes that his model has the advantage of presenting a more unified analysis where the fundamental similarity can be captured between undisputed examples of metonymy like (6a) and more controversial cases like (6d) and (6e) (Barcelona 2002: 226–229). While most semanticists would argue that this approach is too inclusive, as most linguistic expressions used in context would be considered metonymic in one way or another, it may well be the sheer reflection of the fact that metonymic relationships in language use are "the rule rather than the exception" as testified by the ubiquity of active zone phenomena pointed out by Langacker (Bercelona 2002: 229).

7 References

Barcelona, Antonio 2002. Clarifying and applying the notions of metaphor and metonymy within cognitive linguistics: An update. In: R. Dirven & R. Porings (eds.). *Metaphor and Metonymy in Comparison and Contrast*. Berlin: Mouton de Gruyter, 207–277.

Barcelona, Antonio 2003. Metonymy in cognitive linguistics: An analysis and a few modest proposals. In: H. Cuyckens et al. (eds.). *Motivation in Language: Studies in Honor of Günter Radden*. Amsterdam: Benjamins, 223–255.

Barcelona, Antonio 2005a. The fundamental role of metonymy in cognition, meaning, communication and form. In: A. Baicchi, C. Broccias & A. Sanso (eds.). *Modeling Thought and Constructing Meaning: Cognitive Models in Interaction*. Milano: Franco Angeli, 109–124.

Barcelona, Antonio 2005b. The multilevel operation of metonymy in grammar and discourse, with particular attention to metonymic chains. In: F.J.I. Ruiz de Mendoza & M. Sandra Peña (eds.). *Cognitive Linguistics: Internal Dynamics and Interdisciplinary Interaction*. Berlin: Mouton de Gruyter, 313–352.

Black, Max 1962. Metaphor. In: M. Black (ed.). *Models and Metaphors*. Ithaca, NY: Cornell University Press, 25–47.

Black, Max 1979. More on metaphor. In: A. Ortony (ed.). *Metaphor and Thought*. Cambridge: Cambridge University Press, 19–45.

Bowdle, Brian & Dedre Gentner 2005. The career of metaphor. *Psychological Review* 112, 193–216.
Camp, Elisabeth 2006a. Contextualism, metaphor, and what is said. *Mind & Language* 21, 280–309.
Camp, Elisabeth 2006b. Metaphor in the mind. The cognition of metaphor. *Philosophy Compass* 1, 154–170.
Carston, Robyn 2002a. Metaphor, ad hoc concepts and word meaning – more questions than answers. *UCL Working Papers in Linguistics* 14, 83–105.
Carston, Robyn 2002b. *Thoughts and Utterances: The Pragmatics of Explicit Communication.* Oxford: Blackwell.
Coulson, Seana 2006. Metaphor and conceptual blending. In: K. Brown (ed.). *The Encyclopedia of Language and Linguistics.* 2nd edn. Amsterdam: Elsevier, 32–39.
Croft, William 2002. The role of domains in the interpretation of metaphors and metonymies. In: R. Dirven & R. Porings (eds.). *Metaphor and Metonymy in Comparison and Contrast.* Berlin: Mouton de Gruyter, 161–205.
Davidson, Donald 1978. What metaphors mean. *Critical Inquiry* 5, 31–47.
Davidson, Donald 1981. What metaphors mean. In: M. Johnson (ed.). *Philosophical Perspectives on Metaphor.* Minneapolis, MN: University of Minnesota Press, 200–219.
Evans, Vyvyan & Melanie Green 2006. *Cognitive Linguistics: An Introduction.* Mahwah, NJ: Lawrence Erlbaum Associates.
Fauconnier, Gilles 1994. *Mental Spaces: Aspects of Meaning Construction in Natural Language.* Cambridge: Cambridge University Press.
Fauconnier, Gilles 1997. *Mappings in Thought and Language.* Cambridge: Cambridge University Press.
Fauconnier, Gilles & Mark Turner 1998. Conceptual integration networks. *Cognitive Science* 22, 133–187.
Fauconnier, Gilles & Mark Turner 2002. *The Way We Think: Conceptual Blending and the Mind's Hidden Complexities.* New York: Basic Books.
Fillmore, Charles 1982. Frame semantics. In: Linguistic Society of Korea (ed.). *Linguistics in the Morning Calm.* Seoul: Hanshin, 111–138.
Gentner, Dedre & Brian Bowdle 2001. Convention, form, and figurative language processing. *Metaphor and Symbol* 16, 223–247.
Gentner, Dedre & Brian Bowdle 2008. Metaphor as structure mapping. In: R.W. Gibbs (ed.). *The Cambridge Handbook of Metaphor and Thought.* Cambridge: Cambridge University Press, 109–128.
Gentner, Dedre & Phillip Wolff 1997. Alignment in the processing of metaphor. *Journal of Memory and Language* 37, 331–355.
Gibbs, Raymond W. 1994. *The Poetics of Mind: Figurative Thought, Language, and Understanding.* Cambridge: Cambridge University Press
Gibbs, Raymond W. 2002. A new look at literal meaning in understanding what is said and implicated. *Journal of Pragmatics* 34, 457–486.
Gibbs, Raymond W. 2006a. *Embodiment and Cognitive Science.* Cambridge: Cambridge University Press.
Gibbs, Raymond W. 2006b. Metaphor: Psychological aspects. In: K. Brown (ed.). *The Encyclopedia of Language and Linguistics.* 2nd edn. Amsterdam: Elsevier, 43–50.
Gibbs, Raymond W. 2006c. Introspection and cognitive linguistics: Should we trust our own intuitions? *Annual Review of Cognitive Linguistics* 4, 135–151.

Gibbs, Raymond W. (ed.) 2008. *The Cambridge Handbook of Metaphor and Thought*. Cambridge: Cambridge University Press.

Gibbs, Raymond W. & Marcus Perlman 2006. The contested impact of cognitive linguistic research on the psycholinguistics of metaphor understanding. In: G. Kristiansen et al. (eds.). *Cognitive Linguistics: Current Applications and Future Perspectives*. Berlin: Mouton de Gruyter, 211–228.

Gibbs, Raymond W. & Markus Tendahl 2006. Cognitive effort and effects in metaphor comprehension: Relevance theory and psycholinguistics. *Mind & Language* 21, 379–403.

Giora, Rachel 1997. Understanding figurative and literal language: The graded salience hypothesis. *Cognitive Linguistics* 8, 183–206.

Giora, Rachel 1998. When is relevance? On the role of salience in utterance interpretation. *Revista Alicantina de Estudios Ingleses* 11, 85–94.

Giora, Rachel 1999. On the priority of salient meanings: Studies of literal and figurative language. *Journal of Pragmatics* 31, 919–929.

Giora, Rachel 2002. Literal vs. figurative language: Different or equal? *Journal of Pragmatics* 34, 487–506.

Giora, Rachel 2008. Is metaphor unique? In: R.W. Gibbs (ed.). *The Cambridge Handbook of Metaphor and Thought*. Cambridge: Cambridge University Press, 143–160.

Glucksberg, Sam 2001. *Understanding Figurative Language: From Metaphors to Idioms*. Oxford: Oxford University Press.

Glucksberg, Sam 2008. How metaphors create categories – quickly. In: R.W. Gibbs (ed.). *The Cambridge Handbook of Metaphor and Thought*. Cambridge: Cambridge University Press, 67–83.

Glucksberg, Sam & Boaz Keysar 1990. Understanding metaphorical comparisons: Beyond similarity. *Psychological Review* 97, 3–18.

Grady, Joseph 1997. Theories are buildings revisited. *Cognitive Linguistics* 8, 267–290.

Grady, Joseph 1999a. A typology of motivation for conceptual metaphor: Correlation vs. resemblance. In: R.W. Gibbs & G.J. Steen (eds.). *Metaphor in Cognitive Linguistics*. Amsterdam: Benjamins, 79–100.

Grady, Joseph 1999b. Crosslinguistic regularities in metaphorical extension. Paper presented at *The Annual Meeting of the Linguistics Society of America (LSA)*. Los Angeles, CA, January 6–9.

Grady, Joseph 2007. Metaphor. In: D. Geeraerts & H. Cuyckens (eds.). *The Oxford Handbook of Cognitive Linguistics*. Oxford: Oxford University Press, 188–213.

Grady, Joseph 2008. 'Superschemas' and the grammar of metaphorical mappings. In: A. Tyler, Y. Kim & M. Takada (eds.). *Language in the Context of Use: Discourse and Cognitive Approaches to Language*. Berlin: Mouton de Gruyter, 339–360.

Grady, Joseph, Todd Oakley & Seana Coulson 1999. Blending and metaphor. In: R.W. Gibbs & G.J. Steen (eds.). *Metaphor in Cognitive Linguistics*. Amsterdam: Benjamins, 101–124.

Grice, H. Paul 1969. Utterer's meaning and intentions. *Philosophical Review* 78, 147–177. Reprinted in: H. P. Grice. *Studies in the Way of Words*. Cambridge, MA: Harvard University Press, 1989, 86–116.

Grice, H. Paul 1975. Logic and conversation. In: P. Cole (ed.). *Syntax and Semantics 3: Speech Acts*. New York: Academic Press, 41–58.

Haught, Catrinel & Sam Glucksberg 2004. When old sharks are not old pros: Metaphors are not similes. Paper presented at *The annual meeting of the Psychonomic Society (PS)*, Minneapolis, MN.

Johnson, Christopher 1999. Metaphor vs. conflation in the acquisition of polysemy: The case of *see*. In: M.K. Hiraga, C. Sinha & S. Wilcox (eds.). *Cultural, Typological, and Psychological Perspectives in Cognitive Linguistics*. Amsterdam: Benjamins, 155–169.

Keysar, Boaz & Bridget M. Bly 1995. Intuitions of the transparency of idioms: Can one keep a secret by spilling the beans? *Journal of Memory and Language* 34, 89–109.

Keysar, Boaz & Bridget M. Bly 1999. Swimming against the current: Do idioms reflect conceptual structure? *Journal of Pragmatics* 31, 1559–1578.

Kövecses, Zoltán & Günter Radden 1998. Metonymy: Developing a cognitive linguistic view. *Cognitive Linguistics* 9, 37–77.

Lakoff, George 1987. *Women, Fire, and Dangerous Things: What Categories Reveal about the Mind*. Chicago, IL: The University of Chicago Press.

Lakoff, George & Mark Johnson 1980. *Metaphors We Live by*. Chicago, IL: The University of Chicago Press.

Lakoff, George & Mark Johnson 1999. *Philosophy in the Flesh: The Embodied Mind and its Challenge to Western Thought*. New York: Basic Books.

Lakoff, George & Mark Turner 1989. *More Than Cool Reason: A Field Guide to Poetic Metaphor*. Chicago, IL: The University of Chicago Press.

Langacker, Ronald W. 1984. Active zones. In: C. Brugman et al. (eds.). *Proceedings of the Annual Meeting of the Berkeley Linguistics Society (BLS) 10*. Berkeley, CA: Berkeley Lingiustics Society, 172–188.

Langacker, Ronald W. 1987. *Foundations of Cognitive Grammar, vol. 1. Theoretical Prerequisites*. Stanford, CA: Stanford University Press.

Langacker, Ronald W. 1991. *Concept, Image, and Symbol: The Cognitive Basis of Grammar*. Berlin: Mouton de Gruyter.

Langacker, Ronald W. 1999. *Grammar and Conceptualization*. Berlin: Mouton de Gruyter.

Langacker, Ronald W. 2008. *Cognitive Grammar: A Basic Introduction*. Oxford: Oxford University Press.

Narayanan, Srini 1999. Moving right along: A computational model of metaphoric reasoning about events. In: *Proceedings of the National Conference on Artificial Intelligence (AAAI-99)*. Menlo Park, CA: AAAI Press, 121–128.

Nerlich, Brigitte 2006. Metonymy. In: K. Brown (ed.). *The Encyclopedia of Language and Linguistics*. 2nd edn. Amsterdam: Elsevier, 109–113.

Nunberg, Geoffrey 1978. *The Pragmatics of Reference*. Bloomington, IN: Indiana University Linguistics Club.

Recanati, François 2004. *Literal Meaning*. Cambridge: Cambridge University Press.

Richards, Ivar A. 1936. *The Philosophy of Rhetoric*. New York: Oxford University Press.

Rorty, Richard 1989. *Contingency, Irony, and Solidarity*. Cambridge: Cambridge University Press.

Ruiz de Mendoza, Francisco J. 2000. The role of mappings and domains in understanding metonymy. In: A. Barcelona (ed.). *Metaphor and Metonymy at the Crossroads: A Cognitive Perspective*. Berlin, New York: Mouton de Gruyter, 109–132.

Searle, John R. 1979. Metaphor. In: A. Ortony (ed.). *Metaphor and Thought*. Cambridge: Cambridge University Press, 92–123.

Sperber, Dan & Deirdre Wilson 1995. *Relevance. Communication and Cognition*, 2nd edition. Oxford: Blackwell.

Sperber, Dan & Deirdre Wilson 2004. Relevance theory. In: L.R. Horn & G.L. Ward (eds.). *The Handbook of Pragmatics*. Oxford: Blackwell, 607–632.

Sperber, Dan & Deirdre Wilson 2008. A deflationary account of metaphors. In: R.W. Gibbs (ed.). *The Cambridge Handbook of Metaphor and Thought*. Cambridge: Cambridge University Press, 84–105.
Stern, Josef 2006. Metaphor, literal, literalism. *Mind & Language* 21, 243–279.
Sweetser, Eve 1999. Compositionality and blending. Semantic composition in a cognitively realistic framework. In: T. Janssen & G. Redeker (eds.). *Cognitive Linguistics: Foundations, Scope, and Methodology*. Berlin: Mouton de Gruyter, 129–162.
Taverniers, Miriam 2002. *Metaphor and Metaphorology. A Selective Genealogy of Philosophical and Linguistic Conceptions of Metaphor from Aristotle to the 1990s*. Ghent: Academic Press.
Wilson, Deirdre & Robyn Carston 2006. Metaphor, relevance and the 'emergent property' issue. *Mind & Language* 21, 404–433.
Wilson, Deirdre & Dan Sperber 2002a. Relevance theory. *UCL Working Papers in Linguistics* 14, 249–287.
Wilson, Deirdre & Dan Sperber 2002b. Truthfulness and relevance. *Mind* 111, 583–632.
Zhong, Chen-Bo & Geoffrey J. Leonardelli 2008. Cold and lonely: Does social exclusion literally feel cold? *Psychological Science* 19, 838–842.

Violeta Demonte
12 Adjectives

1   The semantic category adjective —— 381
2   Main characteristics of adjectives —— 382
3   Attributive and predicative adjectives and classifications of adjectives in formal semantics —— 386
4   A new look at semantic classes of adjectives. The role of scales, measures, degree and vagueness in the semantics of adjectives —— 393
5   References —— 411

Abstract: This chapter focuses on the main characteristics of the semantic category adjective. It presents basic classifications of adjectives in formal semantics and current lines of debate regarding classes of adjectives and their semantic analysis.

In section 1 the standard definition of adjectives as predicates, functions from entities to truth values (type < e,t >), is introduced. Section 2 addresses the morphosyntactic and semantic properties characterising adjectives: they are modifiers, they are gradable, and show independence of the object. In section 3 the distinction between predicative and attributive adjectives is established and qualified in terms of syntactic position, semantic type (S/N vs. CN/CN) and rules for interpretation (predicate conjunction vs. function analysis). The distinction intersective / non-intersective adjective is explained. Section 4 provides a new analysis of the semantics of adjectives in terms of scales, degrees, standards/ norms and boundedness. Adjectives are taken to be type < e,d > and they can be relative or absolute. Relative adjectives have an extension that depends on a standard and a comparison class, they give rise to vagueness. Absolute adjectives do not depend on an external norm, they have closed scales which can be lower closed or upper closed. Colour and relational adjectives as well as non-gradable modal and frequency adjectives are finally described.

1 The semantic category adjective

In a common sense ontology of things in the world adjectives can be defined as the class of words that express properties, while verbs and nouns represent, respectively, events and entities (Croft 1991). In more strict terms it could be

Violeta Demonte, Madrid, Spain

https://doi.org/10.1515/9783110626391-012

said that adjectives denote qualities, verbs encode activities / processes, accomplishments, achievements and states (Vendler 1967) and nouns denote 'natural classes' (Carlson 1980).

It is not easy to give a simple semantic definition for adjectives. In categorial grammar the three classes of words function as predicates since they express in the majority of cases one-place properties. More strictly, if we take the definition of categories as based on a system of semantic types derived from entities and truth values, adjectives ought to be considered (in an extensional semantics) as functions from entities to truth values, (1c). The same characterization will hold for the intransitive verb in (1a) and the non-relational noun in (1b):

(1) a. Irene works—λx (works (x))
    b. Irene is a primatologist—λx (primatologist (x))
    c. Irene is happy—λx (happy (x))

Consequently, the characterization of adjectives as type < e,t >, (1c), cuts across the syntactic categories adjective, intransitive verb and noun such as *primatologist*. This semantic definition of adjectives as one-place properties is coherent with the fact that many languages do not have a part of speech class of adjectives, and nouns and verbs are then used to cover its prototypical functions (Dixon 1977; Croft 1991). However, the argument for the necessity to represent common sense ontology in formal semantics is strong since in languages with a productive, open class of adjectives there are very clear general syntactic, morphological and semantic criteria distinguishing adjectives from verbs and nouns.

2 Main characteristics of adjectives

The purpose of this section is to briefly determine which are the specific morphosyntactic and semantic properties that characterize the class of adjectives. There are at least two ways to give support to the assertion that adjectives are a semantic and syntactic category with specific properties distinct from nouns and verbs. One way is to discuss the differences between adjectives and intransitive verbs and adjectives and nouns (see Hamann 1991: §1.2, §1.3 and Baker 2003 for this discussion). The other is to present what could be called prototypical syntactic and semantic features of the category adjective (Larson & Segal 1995; Demonte 1999). Both approaches will be combined in the following short discussion about the main characteristics of adjectives.

2.1 Adjectives are modifiers

The definition of adjectives as functions from entities to truth values captures adequately the predicative use of adjectives (*This person is intelligent*). However, all authors agree that the primary function of adjectives is to modify nouns directly in structures like *an intelligent person*. As a consequence, adjectives have often been assigned to the category CN/CN. If CN is a primitive both for N and A, the complex category CN/CN defines adjectives as the category able to combine with common nouns to form new common nouns. This definition is standard among researchers working on categorial grammars (Cresswell 1991). In descriptive terms we could say that modifiers are expressions optionally added to other expressions; modifiers are therefore not required by the argument structure of the modified term, in this case, by the semantics of the nominal.

2.2 Adjectives are gradable and they are a locus for vagueness

Degrees and scales. Most adjectives can take degree modifiers like *very, terribly, too, enough, rather*, (2a), they can be used in comparative constructions, (2b), and in certain languages they accept measure phrases, (2c). *Very* is a typical adjectival modifier, and so are polarity intensifiers such as *terribly* or *lightly*.

(2) a. A very tall man - *A very man
    b. The more happy person - *A more person
    c. Mary is two feet tall.

Most degree modifiers, though, are cross categorial. Some verbs (i.e. verbs with incremental themes, Kennedy & McNally 2005) have scales similar to adjectives and share many modifiers with them (see Doetjes 2008 on this regard). Nouns are different from verbs and adjectives (see the right side of (2a) and (2b)) in that they have restrictions in the use of scalar modifiers. In many languages, for example Spanish, only plural and mass nouns accept modifiers such as *mucho/a* 'many' and partitive-like expressions like *un montón de tomates* 'a bunch of tomatoes'. These expressions do not have a clear degree interpretation even if they calculate quantity.

Semantically speaking, then, most adjectives can be described as being intrinsically gradable predicates (Kamp 1975; Croft 1991; Larson & Segal 1995). In simple terms, the constructions in (2) mean that the properties described by the adjectives hold of their respective modified constituent (or of their subjects) 'to a certain degree'. According to Bierwisch (1989: 78) in *Hans ist groß* 'Hans is big' the gradable adjective has a contrastive interpretation, its truth conditions depend "on a contextually determined comparison class". In terms of Larson & Segal (1995: 130) it can be asserted that adjectives are in fact two place predicates one argument being a thing for which they hold true and the other an extra parameter for "delineations" (Lewis 1970), where a delineation is "a standard according to which something is judged to fall under the predicate".

In a thorough more recent treatment of gradable adjectives (in the line of Bartsch & Vennemann 1972, 1973; Bierwisch 1989; Cresswell 1976; Heim 1985, 2000; Hellan 1981; Kennedy 1997; Kennedy & McNally 2005; Klein 1991; Seuren 1973 or von Stechow 1984), Kennedy (2007) defines gradable adjectives as elements that "map their arguments onto abstract representations of measurements, OF DEGREES". He also assumes a formal notion of SCALE as a totally ordered set of degrees (formalized either as points or intervals) relative to specific dimensions (for instance cost, length and so forth) (Kennedy 2007: 4). This line of research analyzes gradable adjectives either as measure functions (type $< e,d >$) or as relations between individuals and degrees. Below, in §4, I will expand more on this important issue of how to provide a semantic analysis of gradable adjectives.

For the time being it has to be noted that gradability does not hold in the same way for all adjectives. Empirically, only dimensional / measure adjectives (*tall, big, long, round, heavy*), evaluative adjectives (*beautiful, industrious, good, intelligent*)--the two previous terms are due to Bierwisch (1989)-- and participial adjectives derived from certain aspectual verbs (*dry, closed, empty*) can be considered strictly speaking gradable. However, these adjectives differ among themselves in the way they structure the *scale* according to which the quality is used to order the objects. They also differ as to whether they do or do not describe a relation to a context dependent *comparison class* (the standard of comparison) that sets the norm for gradability (we will develop these issues in §4.1 below). However, various lexical classes of adjectives do not fit straightforwardly into this characterization. One example is colour adjectives like *red* or *blue*. Even if they have to be considered gradable since they accept degree modifiers and can be conceived as regions on a continuous spectrum (Sapir 1944, *apud* Barker 2002: 7), nevertheless, they differ from other gradable adjectives, on the one hand, with respect to the content of their scale and, on the other, in that they serve to capture quantity relations. Relational adjectives like *wooden* or *medical* are ambiguous as to gradability (see below §4.3). Privative adjectives like *fake* or *alleged* are not gradable at all.

Vagueness and ambiguity. Adjectives denote qualities and qualities are intrinsically gradable. In certain cases the lexical meaning of the adjective requires its argument to have a given degree (e.g. *empty*); in other cases, although the predicate adjective also measures some gradable concept, a 'standard of comparison' is necessary in order to apply a property to an individual. This standard plays a role in semantic interpretation introducing variation in truth conditions related to vagueness, imprecision or ambiguity. An expression containing an adjective can be said to be vague when truth conditions are undetermined (cf. article 8 [this volume] (Kennedy) *Ambiguity and vagueness* for a thorough treatment of the topic of vagueness). The meaning of a vague expression depends both on the lexical meaning and on context. A sentence like (3) is a typical example of vagueness:

(3) This is a cold cup of coffee.

The variability of meaning in (3) depends on whether we are talking about the coffee we want to drink with a croissant for breakfast or if we talk about a black coffee that is to be drunk with ice; that is, the standard for coldness varies from context to context (Kennedy & McNally 2005; Kennedy 2007).

Vagueness is different from other forms of meaning variability. In fact, in certain cases adjectives have different readings depending on the variable on which the property is predicated, and on its location. In Larson's (1995) well known example:

(4) Olga is a beautiful dancer.

we do not find vagueness but ambiguity, (4) can mean 'Olga dances beautifully' or 'Olga is a beautiful person and she dances'. In other words, the ambiguity of (4) seems to depend both on the gradable nature of the adjective and on the argument structure of the N *dancer*, where the presence of an event argument can be hypothesized. Observe that such an ambiguity disappears in *Olga is a beautiful French woman* since *French woman* does not contain an event argument (see below §3.2).

2.3 Independence of the object

The ability to be a modifier and the nature of gradable predicates exhibited by adjectives are strongly related to another semantic characteristic of this class of words that, following Dixon (1977) as well as Larson & Segal (1995), we will refer to as 'independence of the object'. In expressions like *the yellow flower* or *This flower is yellow* the semantic contribution of the adjective is to assert that a given feature applies to a given object; it is used to describe and/or distinguish objects that are referred to by a single common noun. In other words, semantically adjectives apply to terms able to identify objects, to expressions bearing referential indices (Baker 2003: 112, 191). They do not identify objects, they ascribe properties to entities. In a similar sense, Hamann (1991: 660), based on Dixon (1977), notes that the properties referred to by adjectives are not 'non-criterial' ones but only 'additional' ones. Among the most important properties expressed by adjectives are size, colour, value, age, etc.

3 Attributive and predicative adjectives and classifications of adjectives in formal semantics

The previous section has assumed without further qualification that there is a distinction between predicative and attributive adjectives. This distinction will now be qualified in terms of syntactic position, type (or meaning) and rules used for adjective interpretation.

Syntactically, adjectives are predicative in copular sentences (*The man is clever*) and attributive inside NP's (*the clever man*). Predicative adjectives are S/N (semantic type < e,t >), that is, they denote functions from entities to truth values. The simplest interpretation of adjectives in predicate position is that they are extensional and denote set intersection. In this use two set denoting expressions, N and A, are combined to form a complex set-denoting expression. In other words, *The man is healthy* is interpreted using predicate conjunction, that is, the intersection between the set of beings which are *healthy* and the set of men.

Typically, attributive adjectives, like in *bright moon*, are CN/CN, they are functions from CN denotations to CN denotations; sometimes, they are 'intensional', namely, they do not express properties but behave like operators that modify the properties expressed by the noun as in *alleged murderer*; thus the noun phrase describes new properties. In more general terms, they take a noun to make a complex noun and are interpreted as functions mapping the meaning (intension) of a noun with which the adjective combines to that of A+N combination, the meaning of *moon* to that of *bright moon*.

In the line of Partee (1995) we will name the predicative analysis 'the conjunction analysis', and the attributive analysis 'the function analysis'. Bolinger (1967) sets up the distinction between the conjunction (or set intersection) and the function analyses in terms of referent modification vs. reference modification, respectively. We will see immediately that other semantic classifications serve better to distinguish classes of adjectives and semantic interpretations.

Actually, it is evident that the two just mentioned rules serve for the interpretation of A + N combinations. It is also evident that the double distinction just reviewed does not match one to one specific semantic classes of adjectives. There is a reduced set of adjectives that can be used only predicatively (*asleep, flush, awake, ready*) and another reduced set of adjectives that cannot be predicative (*mere, main, former*— *the mere fact* vs. **The fact is mere*). Most adjectives admit both uses, as is well known.

To account for this situation, there have been two approaches (making in fact three lines of analysis) to the basic semantic classification of adjectives. A few authors, focusing on those languages where the distinction attribution vs. predication is morphologically marked, argue for syntactic-semantic categorial distinction between the two classes of adjectives (Siegel 1976/1980). However, most other authors propose reductionist analyses. This second type of analysis allows for two approaches: one of the two types, sometimes predicative adjectives (Bierwisch 1967, 1989; Kamp 1975), most frequently attributive ones (Cresswell 1976; Montague 1970; Heim & Kratzer 1998), is considered as basic and the other as derived. The derived type can be obtained either through meaning postulates, lexical rules of type shifting (Partee 1995; Heim & Kratzer 1998), derivation of attributive adjectives (second-order functions) from first-order properties by means of context-dependent models which sharpen the vagueness of the predicates (Kamp 1975), or through specific *attr* or *pred* operators (Hamann 1991), among other mechanisms.

In the following subsections the advantages as well as the weaknesses of each of the three approaches will be briefly discussed. Throughout the discussion, we will introduce and try to schematize the most common classifications of adjectives in formal semantics.

A word of caution is necessary before we go any further. It is simply impossible to discuss all the nuances and technical details elaborated in the large literature on these matters. In order to simplify things and for the sake of understanding, in this chapter formal details will not be developed unless unavoidable. The reader should consult Hamann (1991) where the author traces the lengthy debates on these issues and provides interesting examples. Partee (1995) is also an illuminating, exhaustive discussion of classes of adjectives.

3.1 Two classes of adjectives

In certain languages (e.g. the West African languages of Vata and Ghadi) adjectives are used only in attributive environments. Other languages (e.g. Slave or Ika) use adjectives only in predicative constructions (see Baker 2003: 206–207 for examples of both cases). Based on similar facts and on the morphological distinction made in Russian between short-form adjectives (which are used only predicatively) and long-form adjectives (which occur both in predicate position and prenominally) Siegel (1976/1980) argues that there are two distinct adjectival categories which are each assigned one of the two basic semantic types CN/CN and S/N; in addition, some adjectives will have both versions (Siegel 1976/1980: 54):

(5) a. Studentka umna [Short Form]
    '(The) student (is) intelligent (in general, absolute terms)'

   b. Studentka umnaja [Long Form]
    '(The) student (is) intelligent (in her role as student)' [Siegel 1976/1980: 11]

As noted by Baker (2003: 207), the cases that motivate Siegel's solution are the exception and not the rule. The main argument against Siegel's approach is the fact that most adjectives, without any external sign, can be both predicates and attributes in languages typologically very diverse: Romance languages, Celtic languages, Australian languages, Semitic languages, Bantu languages, etc. Moreover, adjectives with a single use have common semantic properties: exclusively predicative adjectives (*sorry, ready*) denote very transitory properties; exclusively attributive adjectives (*main, former*) rather than contributing descriptive content provide information about when and how the context of the noun might apply to its argument.

In contrast with Siegel's approach most semanticists have sought for a unified class of adjectives taking either one or the other meaning depending on factors like presence of the copula, positioning, features of the head noun, and, crucially, their internal lexical properties. In fact, the existence of a single basic class of adjectives should not be seen as an advantage or disadvantage of a theory. However, the strategy of looking for one basic type of adjectives, and for mechanisms to derive from it the alternative interpretation, has been very useful to set the limits of compositionality, to discuss different aspects of lexical rules, and to compare alternative semantic models. There is not enough space here to discuss these questions carefully but let us sketch the main elements of the two approaches which seek to unify adjectives under a single category.

3.2 The conjunction or predicative approach. Intersective and non-intersective adjectives

This approach, in principle the simplest one, asserts that all adjectives modifying nouns are basically one-place predicates. Being predicative they will all adjust to the set intersection analysis. This analysis can be applied to constructions like (6):

(6) x is a red table = x is a table and x is red.

Adjectives like *red* are for this reason named 'intersective adjectives'. It is a fact that clear cases of intersective adjectives are not the most frequent ones. Colour adjectives and technical and scientific terms like *endocrine* (Kamp 1975: 124) are the typical examples of this use.

It is well known that most adjectives are not intersective. Let us consider in (7), (8) and (9) the most conspicuous cases of 'non-intersective adjectives':

(7) A tall kid.

(8) A skilful carpenter.

(9) A former student / The alleged murderer.

Before explaining the cases in (7), (8) and (9), a brief note on the terminology is in order. Dimension adjectives like *tall* have been classified as '(non)-intersective', as well as 'subsective' and 'relative' depending on the authors. Value adjectives like *skilful* have been called 'non-intersective', 'relative' and 'special subsective'. Intensional adjectives like *former* have been classified as 'non-intersective', 'non-subsective', 'privative' and 'non-standard'. The triple distinction 'absolute (no example in the series in (7) to (9), but see (6)),—relative—non-standard' is due to Bartsch & Vennemann (1972). The naming 'subsective-intersective—subsective-non intersective—privative' comes from Kamp (1975) and Partee (1995). Let us go now to the examples.

If *tall* in (7) were a truly intersective adjective the following should be a valid inference, which is not the case:

(10) x is a (tall) kid ⇒ x belongs to the set of tall things

However, vague, context-dependent adjectives like *tall*, *heavy* (*a heavy book*), *hot* (*hot wine*), *new* (*a new cook*) do not mark intersection *stricto sensu* rather they designate only a subset of the set of individuals picked up by N. A *tall kid* can be short as a representative of human females, for example. We can paraphrase *a tall kid* through a '*for*' expression:

(11) 'x is tall for a kid'.

This view is controversial, however. Heim & Kratzer (1998) argue that these adjectives are intersective when the context is taken into account (but see Portner 2005 for an argument against this view). A more common assumption is that these adjectives are subsective (non-intersective) because they are gradable. In §4 it will be seen that the subsective meaning derives from the denotation of adjectives like *tall*; such a denotation involves a relation to a contextually determined standard of comparison.

Skilful carpenter, (8), and most value or evaluative adjectives (*clever* (*clever musician*), *experienced* (*experienced magician*)), have a behaviour similar to *tall* regarding inferences, namely, a *skilful carpenter* can perfectly well be a *clumsy gardener* or *writer*. Nevertheless, in the interpretation relevant to the present discussion, they do not exactly designate a subset of the individuals covered by N. More strictly, even if we could say that they pick up a subset of the individuals designated by N they do so based on some of the properties associated to the N (those that allow somebody to be a carpenter), rather than on a contextual standard. They thus admit an *as* paraphrase:

(12) 'x is skilful as a carpenter'.

In subsection 3.4 it will be shown that this special subsective denotation (which is parallel to a regular subsectiveness derived from gradability) can be best accounted for if a Davidsonian semantics is assumed.

Finally, in (9) we find an adjective whose effect is "to produce a complex noun phrase AN that is satisfied only by things that do not satisfy N" (Kamp 1975: 125: *former president, fake gun*, etc.). These adjectives are called privative or non-standard.

If we want to have a single semantic type for all adjectives, intersective and non-intersective, the crucial question for a unified analysis under the conjunction approach or the 'predicative-first analysis' (Hamann 1991: 664) is whether attributive denotations can be considered 'secondary' and derived through specific rules which boost the category change of the adjective. A general modifier rule of this type could be, for example, the one proposed by Bierwisch (1989: 98) according to which the external theta role of the adjective is 'absorbed' by the external theta role of the modified head. Hamann (1991) proposes an 'attr' operator that "changes an α ∈ s///n into a noun modifier of category (s/n)/(s/n) or CN/CN" (Hamann 1991: 664); material realizations of this operator would be the inflectional affixes appearing on attributive adjectives in German or Russian; recall the examples in (5) and consider the pair *Devuška umna* (short form) 'The girl is smart' vs. *umnaja devuška* (long form) 'the smart girl', where in the long attributive adjective the demonstrative *ja*, which acts as a suffix, is added. In the classical first generation Generative Grammar analysis a similar idea was proposed, namely that all adjectives originate in deep structure relative clauses and there is a rule of 'relative clause reduction' giving rise to constructions with attributive adjectives.

However, there are many reasons to reject the proposal that attributive uses are secondary. The most important one is that some adjectives (privative ones) do not have a predicative counterpart. In addition, attributive adjectives have a reference modification function (Bolinger 1967) that cannot be captured if they are given a predicative origin. Lastly, this analysis does not distinguish adjectives from verbs and nouns in terms of their semantic type. Consequently, a unified analysis appears to be more tenable if all adjectives are treated as functions from intensions to intensions.

3.3 The function or attributive approach

According to this approach all adjectives are of category CN/CN, that is, they map properties onto properties. With this approach there are no problems with possible entailments (recall (10)). As Hamann states, "as we know nothing about the resulting property, all entailments are a priori blocked" (Hamann 1991: 665). In analyses where the attributive denotation is primary the different entailments coming out from the semantic relations adjectives establish in (7), (8) and (9) are specified through meaning postulates (Montague 1970; Partee 1995) or in the lexical entry of the adjective (Kamp 1995).

The problem with this solution is that many value adjectives like *beautiful* are ambiguous in structures such as *Olga is a beautiful dancer* and, more importantly, they are only intersective if the common noun designates a general class. *Olga is a beautiful woman* lacks the 'as a' reading and it designates the intersection between the set of women and the set of beautiful things. A comparison class provided by the context, though, is necessary to assert the truth of the sentence, as we will see in §4.

Additionally, the function or attributive solution works only partially for adjectives like the one in *former teacher* since the function account does not provide an explanation for the fact that even if the *teacher* is equivalent, say, to *the man with green glasses, former teacher* is not exactly *former man with green glasses*. An explanation for this case needs an account of the way time parameters are encoded in predicates, as observed by Heim & Kratzer (1998).

3.4 The event account of certain non-intersective adjectives

In the following section of this chapter it will be argued that an important part of the discussion about differences between intersective and non-intersective readings of adjectives can be properly recast and illuminated if a degree analysis is assumed establishing that adjectives project the individuals to which they apply onto scales or ordered sets of degrees. Before introducing this view it is interesting to isolate a well known set of adjective constructions ambiguous between intersective and non-intersective interpretations such as the one in (4). To recall, a sentence like *My daughter is an intelligent student* can mean that 'she is student and an intelligent person' (intersective reading) or that 'when she studies she acts intelligently' (non-intersective reading). In standard analyses, the ambiguity of the mentioned sentence is traced back to the semantics of the adjective. However, in a series of works, Larson (1983, 1995, 1998 and Larson & Segal 1995) claims that the source of the ambiguity must be linked not to the adjective but to the noun properties. In a nutshell, adopting a Davidsonian event analysis for adjectival modification in which the semantics of the noun is relativized to events, Larson states that "when an adjective combines with a noun denoting an event-individual pair, the adjective can be predicated of either the x parameter or the e parameter" (Larson 1998: 89). It is in this double possibility where the ambiguity of these sentences is rooted. For a sentence like *Olga is a beautiful dancer*, when the adjective is predicated of Olga, (13a), it is this person who is considered to be beautiful, when it is predicated of the event variable, (13b), it is the dancing what is beautiful, see Larson (1998: 8):

(13) a. Qe [dancing (e, Olga)... beautiful (Olga, C)]
      b. Qe [dancing (e, Olga)... beautiful (e,C)]

A claim that Larson's analysis makes is that, aside from the fact that adjectives such as *beautiful*, *intelligent* or *industrious* indicate the degree to which the property expressed by the adjective holds of its subject, in their second reading (available only with certain N's) they express eventive properties of N, perhaps manner or time. A consequence of this analysis is that "there are no truly non-intersective adjectives" (Larson 1998: 11), the question being with which set the adjective intersects.

There are, moreover, empirical reasons for the proposal. A central argument for it — although we will not reproduce it in detail here— according to Larson (1998: §2.2), is the parallel behaviour of Adj+N and Adv+V constructions in the phenomenon of 'substitution failure' with non intersective adjectives (Siegel 1976/1980; McConnell-Ginet 1982). Substitution fails from the sentence *Olga dances beautifully* to *Olga sings beautifully*, as well as from *Olga is a beautiful dancer* to *Olga is a beautiful singer*, and vice versa; that is, even if *dancer* and *singer* are coextensive, it will not follow that if Olga is beautiful as a dancer she will also be beautiful as a singer. The inference from *Olga is a beautiful dancer* to *Olga is a beautiful singer* fails because in the two predicates (*dances* vs. *sings—dancer* vs. *singer*) there is an additional semantic element, the event argument, to which the adverb *beautifully* and the adjective *beautiful* refer separately. The event approach also provides some hints as to the nature of strictly non-intersective adjectives that apply mainly to events, such as *fast,* and on the restrictions on their coordination with adjectives that would apply exclusively to individuals such as *blonde*: **She is a blonde and fast dancer* (Larson 1998: §3).

We will come back in §4.3 to other types of A+N combinations where the adjective has an adverbial interpretation (*an occasional sailor, a sporadic shot,* etc.)

4 A new look at semantic classes of adjectives. The role of scales, measures, degree and vagueness in the semantics of adjectives

The category adjective is not the only gradable category, some verbs and nouns also accept degree modifiers (Bolinger 1972; Doetjes 1997, 2008; Neeleman, van de Koot & Doetjes 2004). Furthermore, as noted by Bolinger (1972), among others, it is not the case that all adjectives accept degree modification. However, as said above, gradability is more general among adjectives, it takes different nuances across different classes of them and it appears to be a prototypical characteristic of this class of words. In this section, after general considerations concerning approaches to the semantics of gradable adjectives, three classes of gradable adjectives will be described: a) relative-absolute adjectives, §4.1, b) colour and relational adjectives, §4.2, and c) modal, manner and frequency adjectives, §4.3. (Incidentally, considerably more space will be devoted to the first set since they have received a more extended treatment in the literature.) In the course of this description the main features of adjectival scales will be characterized. Since adjectival modifiers have a crucial role in the identification of subclasses of adjectives, some aspects of the semantics of adjectival modifiers will also be discussed.

4.1 Relative and absolute adjectives

Two approaches to scales, norms or standards and boundedness. The aim of this section is to analyze the distinction between 'relative' and 'absolute' adjectives. However, before addressing this analysis it will be convenient to provide a basic frame of reference. We have noted, in effect, that the main distinctions among adjectives involve not only the dichotomy attribution-predication but also gradability. It is therefore important to recall that there are two basic approaches to the semantics of gradable adjectives.

The first basic approach is developed in Klein (1980). On this approach the semantic type of the adjective is always < e,t > and denotes the set of individuals in the positive extension of the adjective—those which are "A". A negative extension can also be defined—those individuals which are not "A", as can a set of individuals which is neither in the positive nor the negative extension, those that belong to the 'extension gap'. The immediate problem for this approach is how to introduce an ordering among the individuals in these extensions. Klein does this by appealing to 'comparison classes'. Comparison classes can be arbitrarily small on his analysis and for any well-defined comparison class for an adjective A it has to be possible to say that at least one member is A and the other is not A. By taking all possible comparison class pairs into consideration it is possible to develop a semantics for comparatives and other degree expressions.

A second approach, the one that could now be considered standard, assumes that the semantic type of gradable adjectives includes a degree argument. In this view, also called the relational view, gradable adjectives either denote 'measure functions' (type < e,d >, Kennedy 2007), or relations between degrees and individuals (type < d,(e,t) >, Creswell 1976; Hellan 1981, a.o.). This analysis is the one assumed in what follows in this section even though one criticism which has been made of it by Klein and others is that it effectively entails the comparative relation 'is X-*er* than x' as an unanalyzed primitive of the semantics of any positive gradable adjective, making it mysterious that the syntax of the comparative should consistently be more complex than that of the positive form crosslinguistically (cf. article 13 [this volume] (Beck) *Comparison constructions* for discussion of comparatives).

Both approaches just schematized reappear in the discussion of the two subclasses of gradable predicates: 'relative' and 'absolute' adjectives. In descriptive terms, relative adjectives, independent of its predicative or attributive use, are those whose extension depends on a norm or standard and a comparison class (*large*, *big*, *short*); vagueness is a consequence of the truth conditions imposed by the unmarked form of the adjective. Absolute adjectives (*empty*, *dry*, *wet*) do not depend on an external norm, they contain, so to say, an internal obligatory scale, they intrinsically relate objects to maximum or minimum degrees of a property and do not give rise to vagueness.

Two analyses of these two classes of adjectives will be summarized below: the first one relies on the 'comparison class' and the second one on the 'measure function' frame of reference.

In the first one, which will be exemplified through Hamann (1991), scales are used which express a context dependent partitioning of a domain into inverse positive and negative extensions. Hamann (1991) distinguishes two subclasses of relative adjectives: dimension adjectives (*tall*) and value adjectives (*good*), which differ in the way they build up their 'norm': dimension adjectives take the average as norm, while value adjectives have a context dependent norm of expectation. This is the reason, according to this author, why measure phrases can accompany the positive element of a pair of dimension adjectives, (14a). This modification is not possible either with the negative element of the pair or with value adjectives, (14b and c). The examples in (14) are taken from Hamann (1991: 668) (in §4.1 we will provide a more theoretically founded explanation for (14b)):

(14)   a. The board is two meters long.
       b. ???The board is two meters short.
       c. ???Belinda is hundred units beautiful (ugly).

According to Hamann, dimension adjectives give rise to antonym pairs (*tall-short*) whose elements share a common property. In contrast value adjectives occur in clusters with related meanings (*dumb, stupid* vs. *clever, intelligent, wise*). Both classes of adjectives build a 'scale', now, in the scale of dimension adjectives there is a zero point and "isomorphism to an order with a smallest element" applies. In the scale of value adjectives there is no origin and there appear two areas separated by different orientations (Hamann 1991: 670, her Fig. 13.1):

Fig. 12.1: Section of Hamann's (1991) scale for value adjectives

(It has to be noted that in Hamann's view scales are not the same as in degree based semantics). The common property of both subtypes of relative adjectives is that they have a systematic 'extension gap' in between the positive and the negative pole extension of the adjective; in other words, there exists a set of individuals for whom decision about whether they are in the positive or the negative extension of the adjective is not possible.

In contrast to this class, Hamann proposes that 'absolute adjectives' include forms like *dead-alive* or *single-married*, namely, those which are extensional and intersective. Unlike relative adjectives, according to this author and against the common view, they do not give rise to antonym pairs but they are complementary or have many counterparts. Absolute adjectives do not have an extension gap, a condition for gradability according to Hamann (1991: 668); thus, they are not gradable. This author includes colour, nationality and relational adjectives within this class.

There are various shortcomings of this approach that will only briefly be mentioned. First, since this analysis assumes that there are two domains for members of antonymous pairs, each of them taking an opposite direction, it can correctly explain 'indirect comparison' in cases where adjectives have the same polarity, (15). However it has problems to account for the semantic oddness of a sentence like (16), an example of 'cross polar anomaly':

(15) Mary is more intelligent than she is beautiful.

(16) ??*El Quijote* is longer than *Pedro Páramo* is short.

Briefly, (16) shows that comparative constructions where positive and negative forms of antonymous pairs co-occur are anomalous; this suggests that antonymous adjectives map their arguments onto complementary and not inverse regions of the same scale (see Kennedy 2001 for a detailed exposition of this argument). In other words, if distance is measured from the mid-point of a scale and a concept of positive and negative degree has not been assumed it will be difficult to explain why adjectives cannot be compared in cases such as those in (16).

A second weakness of this analysis comes from the fact that it does not explicitly account for vagueness. Vagueness, strictly speaking, appears only with relative adjectives (Kennedy 2007) although both classes are gradable since both relate objects to abstract representation of measurement. Finally, Hamann's approach does not make distinctions within the complex class of absolute adjectives.

A second approach to absolute and relative gradable adjectives starts in Seuren (1978, 1984) and von Stechow (1984) and it has received its most recent formalization in the works by Kennedy (1997/1999, 2001 and 2007), Kennedy & McNally (2005) and Rotstein & Winter (2004). This approach shares some aspects with the previous one but it has a broader empirical coverage and it provides a more conspicuous account of the truth conditional variability of gradable adjectives.

It has been stated above that Bartsch & Vennemann (1972, 1973) and Kennedy (1997/1999, 2007) analyze gradable adjectives as measure functions of type < e,d >. Consequently, they define an adjective like *tall* as a function from the domain of individuals to some positive degree of the dimension 'height' ordered in a scale. Recall that a set of 'degrees' ordered with respect to some dimension (height, cost) constitute a scale; a scale may have a maximum and a minimum value.

The main claims which comprise this general view are roughly the following:

a) Relative adjectives (*tall, expensive, big - short, cheap, small*) do not have standard values by default; in contrast, absolute adjectives have constant

standards (*wet / dry, clean / dirty, healthy / sick*) although they are the same type < e,d >. This difference derives from the fact that they project onto different types of scales: 'unbounded' (or open) and 'bounded' (or closed), respectively. *Tall* is unbounded because there is not a maximum height, while *dry* is bounded because there is a maximum degree of dryness, i.e. when there is no water at all. Moreover, boundedness of a scale determines a distinction between what Rotstein & Winter (2004) call 'total' and 'partial' adjectives or, better, what Kennedy & McNally (2005) call 'maximum standard' and 'minimum standard' adjectives. We will come back to this distinction in §4.1.
b) Relative and absolute adjectives also differ in that the former have, and the latter lack, a context dependent standard of comparison.
c) This theory makes fruitful claims for the treatment of comparatives and for 'degree specification' –*two meters tall*. See below in this section for some observations regarding these two questions.

Let us consider now examples of relative and absolute adjectives and let us try to extend on the previous claims and elaborate on the semantic properties of each class.

In relative adjectives the positive form contains the comparison class as a constituent of its semantic representation. In fact, Bartsch & Vennemann (1972) assume a denotation for the positive form of adjectives like *tall* similar to (17) (taken from Kennnedy 2007: 8):

(17) $[[_{\text{Deg}} pos]] = \lambda g \lambda k \in D_{\langle e,t \rangle} \lambda x.g(x) > \textbf{norm}(k)(g)$

In this formulation of *pos* denotation "k is a property and *norm* is a function that returns the average degree to which the objects in the set defined by k (the comparison class) measure g" (Kennedy 2007: 8).

Given (17), sentence (18a) means that the house has a greater price than the norm for another comparable house, where the relevant similarity (area, type of construction, size, etc.) is contextually determined. In (18b) the comparative term defines an ordering relation between degrees, namely, the average price of houses in London and the average price of houses in Madrid. Now, in both cases the delimiting point between *expensive* and *non-expensive* objects is fixed: it is the average degree to which the objects in the comparison class have the property denoted by the adjective:

(18) a. This house is expensive.
      b. Houses in London are more expensive than in Madrid.

Kennedy notes that this way of fixing the comparison class faces problems regarding the truth conditions of the positive form, since it predicts that borderline cases should not exist. Suppose that the average price of apartments in the most expensive area of Madrid is 900.000€; does this mean that an apartment whose price is 880.000€ is not expensive? The analysis of the positive form of relative adjectives should account for the fact that (19) is not a contradiction:

(19) The price of this apartment is lower than the average price of apartments in this area, but it is still expensive.

In other words, the denotation of *pos* would be better if it is assumed that the comparison class is something else (apartments in Europe overall, things an average person buys in his/her lifetime, etc.) contributing to the meaning of the positive form. Kennedy (2007) claims that (20) (identical to his (27)) provides the appropriate formalization:

(20) $[[_{Deg} pos]] = \lambda g \lambda x. g(x) \geq \mathbf{s}(g)$

In (20) **s** "is a context sensitive function that chooses a standard of comparison in such a way as to ensure that the objects that the positive form is true of 'stand out' in the context of utterance relative to the kind of measurement that the adjective encodes" (Kennedy 2007: 17). Given (20), sentence (18a) could be true if the difference between its price and that of less expensive houses in the comparison class is sufficiently big, even if the price of the house is below the average price. A relevant aspect of a proposal in which scale structure and a comparison class are introduced is that it makes a clear distinction between positive and negative adjectives in terms of positive and negative degrees. The reason why negative adjectives cannot be associated with measure phrases (**Bartleby is 40 pages short* vs. *Bartleby is 40 pages long*) would be that negative degrees refer to infinite open intervals while numerals refer to degrees that start at a zero point (see Kennedy 2001: §3.3).

Let us now consider the semantics of 'absolute adjectives' starting with the examples in (21) and (22):

(21) a. The towel is wet.
b. The towel is wetter that the dress.

(22) a. The table is dry.
b. The table is dryer than the floor.

The two examples introduce absolute adjectives. The explanation for their meaning is, in general terms, similar to the one just developed but there are also clear differences between the two classes. We will now examine three cases illustrating the aspects in which absolute adjectives diverge from relative ones.

First, since Cruse's (1980) seminal work it has been noted that absolute adjectives have a scale different from that of relative ones. He proposes the scale structure shown in Fig. 13.2 (taken from Rotstein & Winter 2004). In his terms, scale 'a' is for non-complementary adjectives and scale 'b' is for complementary ones:

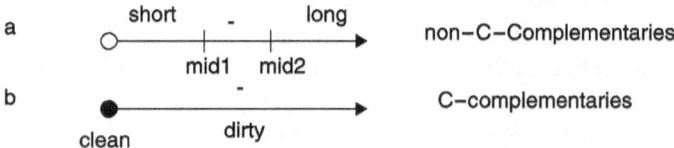

Fig. 12.2: Cruse's (1980) scales for (non-) complementary adjectives

(Incidentally, from now on resource to the distinction complementary / non-complementary will be obviated. The reason is simply that there is no strict correspondence between the complementary / non-complementary distinction and the scale structure facts considered as basic for establishing truth conditions (see Unger 1975; Kennedy & McNally 2005 and also Rotstein & Winter 2004 for a discussion of this issue).)

According to these scales, the points delimiting the denotation of adjectives like *tall* or *long* (the standard value) are located in the middle of the scale (we have critically analyzed above a similar conceptualization). Adjectives like *clean* or *wet* have a scale that is bounded on one end and the standard value of both adjectives is situated at this end. Following work by Kennedy & McNally (2005), to which we will return below in the second subsection of §4.1, it will be assumed here that adjectives in 'a' (absolute ones) have closed scales and adjectives in 'b' (relative ones) have open scales. This distinction serves to account for the different distribution of the modifiers *almost* and *completely* with both classes of adjectives:

(23) a. The house is almost clean.
     b. (#)John is almost tall.

(24) a. The house is completely clean.
     b. *John is completely tall.

Regarding the modifier *almost*, the generalization describing (23)–(24) is that *almost* modifies absolute adjectives or, more explicitly, it "requires a scale that is at least partially closed (contains an end point)" (Amaral 2006). A possible definition of this modifier is that it denotes a short interval in the scale of the adjective "which is disjoint to the denotation of A but adjacent to it from below" (Rotstein & Winter 2004: 277). Another possible definition is that it selects for the maximum value on the scale: "it denotes closeness to the standard (maximum value) in the relevant scale" (Amaral 2006). If the standard value of an adjective like *clean* (an absolute total adjective in Rotstein & Winter's terms, a maximum standard adjective in other) corresponds to the possession of a minimal amount of the relevant property (in their view, the lower bound on the scale of the property associated with the antonymous adjective) then *almost clean* denotes an object that is less clean than anything else in the positive denotation of *clean* and more clean than anything representing lack of cleanness.

The oddness of (23b) (with a relative adjective), on the other hand, indicates that it is not only satisfaction of a 'mid-point' standard value that guarantees the truth of sentences with relative adjectives, otherwise *almost tall* should be acceptable since there is space enough to include an interval before the standard. Note, incidentally, that data are more complicated than it could appear; the acceptability of (25), related to (23b), suggests that the formalization in (20) is stronger than the one in (17); it is the 'significant' height what sets the standard:

(25) It is common knowledge that a 14 year old teenager is tall if his height is 1.75m. Your son is 1.73, so he is almost tall.

Regarding *completely* and the contrast it introduces let us recall that this 'modifier of maximality' refers to the end of a scale (at least in one of its readings). (24a) indicates that absolute adjectives make reference to (maximal) bounds. The extreme oddness of (24b) shows that maximum and (minimum) values are not relevant in the scale for relative adjectives. Tests with 'proportional modifiers' such as *half* provide similar results; a glass can be *half empty / half full* contrasting with the impossibility for an object to be **half tall* or **half short*. If the scale of the adjective does not contain a maximum or a minimum it is not possible to calculate the distance from a mid point to a given limit.

A second factor distinguishing the two classes of adjectives is context dependency. We have said that relative adjectives are gradable and vague; what about absolute adjectives on this regard? Of course there is ample evidence that absolute adjectives are gradable. Recall (21b) and (22b), where *wet* and *dry* appear in comparative constructions; truly non-gradable adjectives like *hepatic* or *senatorial* are impossible in such contexts. In this sense, adjectives like *dry/*

wet, complete/incomplete, open/closed denote functions from objects to ordered sets of degrees of dryness, completeness or closeness. However, as reasoned by Kennedy (2007), absolute adjectives do not fit into the interpretive scheme in (17), which asserts that the standard value for the objects to which the property applies is fixed contextually.

Observe on this regard the sentences in (26). They show that both relative, (26a), and absolute adjectives, (26b), accept measure phrases. Additionally, the negative forms of each pair reject such phrases:

(26) a. The 14 year old boy is 1.50m tall / *1.50m short.
 b. The door is 5cm open / *5cm closed.

However, the meaning of the grammatical sentences is quite different. Sentence (26a) does not entail that the boy is tall. In contrast (26b) does entail that the door is open. (27) shows a similar contrast: (27a) does not entail that the flea is big (compared to other animals), while *full* in (27b) entails that there is no room for anybody else:

(27) a. The flea is big.
 b. The concert hall is full.

This meaning contrast gives support to the idea that absolute adjectives have fixed standards as opposed to the context dependent standard of comparison associated with relative adjectives.

Third, relative and absolute adjectives differ as to the entailment patterns they give rise to. Cruse (1980) and also Rotstein & Winter (2004) correctly describe the entailment relations induced by pairs of antonymous absolute adjectives. In (28) assertion of one form implies negation of the other and vice versa:

(28) a. The towel is wet. $\Rightarrow$ The towel is not dry.
 b. The towel is dry. $\Rightarrow$ The towel is not wet.

Rotstein & Winter attribute this pattern to the fact that the intervals denoted by absolute adjectives are always disjoint, that is, on the scale for these adjectives the minimal positive degree of an adjective touches, so to say, a maximal negative degree of the same scale. Now, relative adjectives do not have this entailment pattern as shown in (29):

(29) This boy is not tall $\not\Rightarrow$ This boy is short (he could well be at the normal height for his group of age).

The contrast between (28) and (29) follows from the fact that relative adjectives permit borderline cases because they have an extension gap. The standards in this case need not be disjoint or, in other words, they do not partition the set; on the contrary there must be some relation among them if borderline cases exist.

Another difference involving entailments is that comparisons with relative adjectives do not give rise to positive or negative entailments, (30a), compared to the clear positive and negative entailments of comparatives with absolute adjectives, (30b) and (30c), respectively (remind also (21) and (22)):

(30) a. Table 1 is bigger than table 2 $\not\Rightarrow$ Table 1/2 are (not) big.
 b. Towel 1 is wetter than towel 2 $\Rightarrow$ Towel 2 is wet.
 c. Cup 1 is fuller than cup 2 $\Rightarrow$ Cup 2 is not full.

Summarizing, the internal structure of scales, context dependency base of standards vs. restrictions imposed by the meaning of the adjective, and entailment patterns are among the phenomena that clearly distinguish between gradable relative and gradable absolute adjectives. Let us now extend on these distinctions.

Defining classes of adjectives in terms of the structure of scales: open and closed scales; total / partial or minimum / maximum standard absolute adjectives. In order to characterize these differences it is important to begin by recalling Cruse's (1980) observation that certain adjectives have closed scales while others have open scales. Namely, adjectives like *clean / dirty, healthy / sick, full / empty, open / closed, perfect / imperfect, safe / dangerous* describe properties that can have maximum and minimum values; adjectives like *expensive, long, tall* do not. Since Yoon (1996) and Rotstein & Winter (2004) it has been shown that there are crucial differences among absolute adjectives. In Yoon's terms some of them are 'total predicates', the other are 'partial predicates'. Briefly, total adjectives (the first members of the previous pairs) describe lack of dirt, malady, closeness, imperfection, etc., while partial ones (the second member of the pairs) describe the existence of such property. More explicitly, Yoon notes that total adjectives like *clean* or *safe* get a universal reading in certain contexts, their basic meaning being that they imply 'no degree of the relevant property'. Their antonyms *dirty* and *dangerous*, partial adjectives, imply possession of 'some degree of the relevant property'. For something to be clean it has to be totally clean, while something is dirty if it simply has some dirtiness on it. In the rest of this section, though, the distinctions between scales that lack maximal and minimal elements (open) and scales with either one of these elements or both (closed)—instead of the total / partial opposition—will be taken as a cue to set up subclasses of absolute adjectives.

Kennedy & McNally (2005) establish four types of scales taking into consideration the just mentioned logical possibilities. The typology in (31), and some of the examples of the adjectives selecting such a scale, is taken from Kennedy (2007: 59); see also Kennedy & McNally (2005: 23):

(31) a. totally open: o————o
 Tall/short, big/small, long/short, sad/happy, wise/ignorant

 b. lower closed: ●————o
 Worried/unworried, dirty/clean, bent/straight, famous/unknown

 c. upper closed: o————●
 Willing/unwilling, safe/dangerous, healthy/sick, naked/dressed,

 d. (totally) closed: ●————●
 Full/empty, hard/soft, transparent/opaque, sad/happy, dry/wet, open/closed), conscious/unconscious, satiated/hungry,

Evidence for this typology comes from the restrictions on adjective cooccurrence with 'end-point oriented modifiers'. As is known, a crucial property of adjectives entering into polar oppositions is that if a positive member of this opposition uses a scale with a minimal degree then its negative counterpart will use one with the maximal degree. Polar modifiers of maximal and minimal degree (*completely*, *perfectly* or *slightly*) will be compatible with the positive or negative members of antonym pairs in a systematic way: those that pick up maximal degrees will appear with positive adjectives only if they use an upper bound scale, as can be seen in the contrast in (32), where *known* uses a lower bound scale; namely, these modifiers will give rise to unacceptability with the positive form of such adjectives, (32a), and to acceptability with the negative one, (32b):

(32) a. This song is {??completely / ??fully known}.
 b. This song is completely unknown.

Inversely, and in the same line, if something is maximally *safe* it cannot then be minimally *dangerous*:

(33) a. Something is perfectly safe.
 b. Something is ??slightly dangerous.

The polar modifiers that can be used to test the existence of the classes b), c) and d) in (31) are the following (incidentally, we will skip here reference to modifiers like *very* (simply) boosting the standard of the adjective. The main function of this modifier appears to be to identify adjectives taking a comparison class, i.e. relative adjectives):

a. End-point oriented maximality modifiers: *completely, totally, fully, and perfectly*. These are only compatible with adjectives that map their arguments onto scales with maximal elements.
b. End-point oriented minimality modifiers: *slightly*. These modifiers restrict the degree argument of a gradable adjective to be a minimum (small degree) on the scale of the adjective. In effect, Rotstein & Winter (2004: 281) say that "slightly A entails not completely A."
c. Proportional modifiers: *half, rather, quite*. They are compatible with adjectives that select both maximal and minimal elements.

Taking this rough classification as a framework we obtain the following generalizations that provide positive evidence for the typology in (31):

a. Open scale adjectives: both members of the antonyms pair are unacceptable with the two types of end point-oriented modifiers:

(34) ??completely / ??slightly {tall/short, expensive/cheap}.

b. Lower closed scale adjectives in their positive forms are unacceptable with upper end point-oriented modifiers and compatible with lower end point-oriented ones. The reverse holds for their negative forms (see also (32)):

(35) a. ??perfectly / slightly worried.
    b. perfectly / ??slightly unworried.

c. Upper closed scale adjectives, in their positive forms are acceptable with upper end point-oriented modifiers and not compatible with lower end-point ones. The reverse holds for their negative forms (see also (33)):

(36) a. perfectly, totally / ??slightly healthy.
    b. ??perfectly / slightly sick.

d. Closed scale adjectives: the two members of the antonymous pair are acceptable with both upper and lower end point-oriented modifiers. Proportional modifiers that indicate mid or partial points in the scale of the adjective in relation to a given end-point are also markers of closed scales:

(37) completely / perfectly / slightly / half / quite {full/empty, hard/soft}

A descriptive generalization can be made to conclude this section. If we review Dixon's (1982) set of universal classes of adjectives: 1) 'dimension' (*tall/short, thin/thick, deep/shallow, big/small, wide/narrow*), 2) 'speed' (*fast/slow*), 3) 'age' (*old/new, recent/past*), 4) 'physical property' (*light/heavy, sweet/sour, liquid/solid, wet/dry, hot/cold, pure/impure, full/empty, tasty/insipid*) 4) 'value' (*ugly/beautiful, perfect/imperfect, good/bad*), 5) 'human propensity' (*greedy/generous, sad/happy, sensible/insensible, wise/dumb, aggressive/calm*), and 6) 'colour', we see that there is no strict correspondence between these classes and the ones established above; that is, members of all Dixon's classes fall into the four classes defined in terms of scales.

4.2 Other types of standards and other classes of adjectives: colour, form and relational adjectives

As we have suggested above 'colour adjectives' are typical examples of intersective predicates: the expression *a yellow sweater* refers to something that is a member of both the set of sweaters and the set of yellow things. In this regard, they are similar to certain 'form adjectives': *square, round, oval*, and so on. All these adjectives fail to give rise to pairs of forms where one describes lack of a property and the other existence of such property, as well as to 'relative' antonymous.

At first sight most colour adjectives appear to be gradable since they accept various types of degree modifiers:

(38) This chair is very / too / totally red.

All the combinations in (38) are acceptable but the meanings of *very / too red* and *totally red* are not identical to the ones we have just analyzed. Although we can assert that gradation is always involved, *very* projects the argument of *red* not onto a scale containing an asymmetrically ordered set of degrees of redness but rather onto a scale containing prototypes and shades of redness. This reading that we could call the prototypicality reading can be obtained, for instance, if we are comparing the *red chair* mentioned in (39) with another one in the same environment and the second one is closer in certain features (brightness, proximity in the spectrum, etc.) to the colour that defines what we might call a 'neutral' red:

(39) This chair is very red; I like better the other one, which is less red.

In a similar but not identical sense, when we say: *Oh, your dress is very yellow!* we are confronting the object with our subjective expectations regarding the colour. For this reason it is impossible to describe a dress we saw at a store saying simply: *?The dress I saw was very yellow*, some qualifications should follow, for instance: *... compared {to others I prefer / to the type of yellow suitable to my age}*. Observe that, in contrast, it is perfectly possible to describe a person we just met by asserting: *The professor was very tall* ('standing out regarding a context dependent standard'). But there is also a second possibility different from the interpretations we have been describing up to now. If we are describing a complex object such as the interior of a house with many rooms, and we say: *God, this house is very red!* the reading by default is that in which we are talking about the extension of red things in the house: lamps, walls, carpets, that is, about 'quantity of red'. In summary, degree, prototypicality / subjective expectation and quantity are the concepts we need to describe how modifiers interact with nouns in expressions with colour adjectives. From here, various readings there can be suggested, a standard scalar one with two flavours: prototypicality and subjective expectation, and a quantity one.

As to the possible scalar readings, here we will not discuss their precise scale structure or the formalization necessary to account for the suggested semantic interpretations. Intuitively, it is plausible to say that such a scale might be closer to the scale of relative adjectives and not to that of absolute ones. A piece of evidence that the scale associated with colour adjectives in their prototypicality reading is not that of absolute adjectives is that maximality modifiers only pick up the quantity reading:

(40) a. The sky is totally blue.   (that is, 'Without clouds').
　　 b. The house is totally green.   ('It has been painted all green').

As for the quantity reading, it is possible that the scale structure associated with it would have to specify part-whole relations as is the case for certain nouns.

For a better understanding of the previous observations regarding colour adjectives a final comparison with so called 'relational adjectives' might perhaps be useful. Relational, denominal forms, 'classifying adjectives' (Warren 1984; Demonte 1999 for Spanish) like *digital, musical, republican, artistic* or *French* are typical examples of adjectives that are subject to restrictions on being used predicatively: we cannot say **The scientist is nuclear*, or **The archaeology is medieval*, etc., although there are data contradicting this view. For example, it is possible to say: 'The journal is monthly', 'The decision was international' or 'This area is industrial'. The reason for this double behaviour is that relational adjectives belong into two different syntactic-semantic classes (Bosque & Picallo 1996; Demonte 1999): some of them are 'argumental' or 'thematic' (*constitutional* *reform* in the sense of 'reform of the Constitution'), other are 'classificative'. Only classificative ones appear in predicative position. Additionally, in general terms, relational adjectives are not used with intensifiers or in comparatives (**very hormonal*, **very molecular*, etc. or **This offer is more financial than that one*); and they do not build antonym pairs. However, some of these adjectives, mainly classificative ones, appear to be gradable. Observe the sentences in (41):

(41) a. The singing of canaries is very musical.
 b. This person is very French.
 c. This soil is very sandy.

The semantic interpretation that relational adjectives receive in these sentences suggests a connection with colour adjectives. In effect, (41a) and (41b) show what we may call the reading of prototypicality; (41c) exhibits the quantity reading. The corresponding paraphrases appear in (42):

(42) a. The singing of this bird has properties that remind us central features of music.
 b. If French are, prototypically, well behaved, have good taste for food and have a strong sense of their country, then x can be considered very French (to be above the prototypical standard).
 c. The quantity of sand in this soil is much above what {we need to have / considered good for certain purposes / more than average, etc.}

There are still many questions open as to the possible syntactic and semantic properties of relational adjectives (see McNally & Boleda 2004 and Fábregas 2007 on this regard); however I will not pursue this matter any further here since it falls far away the purposes of this chapter.

4.3 (Non-gradable) modal, manner and (in)frequency adjectives and the adverbial behaviour of certain adjectives

In §3.1 and §3.2 the distinction between predicative and attributive adjectives was presented. In §3.3 it was seen that predicative adjectives are amenable to an intersective or conjunctive analysis and that there are also various classes of non-intersective adjectives the latter having a predicative modifier analysis. In §3.4 a proposal was presented that reanalyzes a subset of non intersective modifiers by using an event based approach. In §4, we focused on different approaches to gradability.

In this last subsection a schematic approach to the characteristics of the adjectives illustrated in (43) through (45), that is: (non-gradable) intensional modal, manner and frequency adjectives, will be provided:

(43) Mary interviewed a *possible candidate*. (Modal) [from Larson 2000]

(44) The *brutal aggression* against Albania. (Manner) [from Cinque 1994]

(45) The / An *occasional sailor* strolled by. (Frequency) [from Bolinger 1967 and Stump 1981]

All the previous sentences have adverbial counterparts; all of them are ambiguous and the ambiguity can be traced back to the adjective. Generally speaking, we can say that they have an 'external' (outside of NP) reading and an 'internal' (closer to the N) reading, although aside from this generalization there is no uniform analysis for the three cases. To be more specific, in the example in (43) there is both an 'implicit relative reading' (the adjective modifies the noun through an implicit relative clause) and a 'direct modification reading' (the adjective directly modifies the noun, Larson 1999, 2000), see (46). In (44) we find a subject-oriented reading as well as a manner reading of the adjective, see (47). In (45) the adjective can have both the 'external' reading corresponding to a sentential adverb and an attributive reading (Zimmermann 2003), see (48). More explicitly, let us consider in (46) to (48) the suggested paraphrases, corresponding, respectively, to the examples in (43) to (45):

(46) Mary interviewed every possible candidate.
    a. Mary interviewed everyone that was a *possible candidate*. [Direct modification reading]
    b. Mary interviewed every (actual) candidate that it was *possible* for her to interview. [Implicit relative reading] [Larson 2000]

(47) The *brutal* aggression against Albania.
    a. It was *brutal* of them to invade Albania. [Subject oriented reading]
    b. The aggression against Albania was *brutal*. [Manner reading]

(48) The / An *occasional* sailor strolled by.
    a. *Occasionally*, a sailor strolled by. [External reading]
    b. Someone who sails *occasionally* strolled by. [Internal / attributive reading] [Zimmermann 2003]

Stump (1981) refers to (48a) as the 'adverbial usage of frequency adjectives' and also distinguishes a 'generic usage of frequency adjectives' such as in (49):

(49) An *occasional* cup of coffee helps keep John awake.

In the remainder of this section we will discuss separately the case of *possible* and that of *occasional*. Manner adjectives will not be further addressed; they have been introduced simply to emphasize a common property of these three types of adjectives that can be characterized by saying that all of them can be interpreted outside the DP in which they occur. Another common characteristic of these cases is that their semantic ambiguity might be due to a structural ambiguity that we cannot observe directly. If the appropriate structural analysis is established, the basis for semantic composition is straightforward.

'Possible' and Implicit Relative Reading. Larson (2000) notes that the ambiguity found in (43), gloss (46), is restricted to *possible* and is not attested with other adjectives close in meaning to it, (50a). Moreover, the determiner plays a crucial role in the phenomenon: only universal quantifiers and superlatives induce the 'Implicit Relative Reading', (50b):

(50) a. Mary sampled every potential / probable food.
   'Mary sampled everything that was potentially / probably a food'.
   *'Mary sampled every food that it was possible / probable to sample'.
   b. Mary interviewed a/no/three/more/ taller possible candidate.
   *'Mary interviewed a / no / three / more / taller candidate(s) that it was possible to interview'.

Related to these restrictions is the fact that ambiguity disappears when *possible* appears postnominally; in (51) only the Implicit Relative Reading is available:

(51) Mary interviewed every candidate possible.
   'Mary interviewed every candidate that it was possible for her to interview'.

It is interesting to notice that in languages like Spanish where adjectives can appear pre and postnominally a clear correlation shows between position and reading, only 'Direct Modification Reading' is found in prenominal position, only Implicit relative reading shows when the adjective is postnominal (Demonte 2008):

(52) a. Atendió a todos los *posibles* visitantes.
   'He attended all the (people that were) possible visitors'. [Direct Modification Reading]
   b. Atendió a todos los visitantes *posibles*.
   'He received all the visitors it was possible for him to attend'. [Implicit Relative Reading]

Now, recall that in English postnominal adjectives are permitted by universal determiners but not by the rest of them. Based on these facts and correlations, Larson (2000) claims that a sentence like (43), gloss (46), "in its Implicit Relative Reading might actually derive from a source equivalent to (9) [our (53)] where the A originates postnominally and is subsequently fronted, and where the adjective takes an infinitival complement that remains elliptical":

(53) Mary interviewed every possible$_i$ candidate [t$_i$ [for her to interview t].

We will not develop here the derivation of (43) and (51) (through 'Antecedent Contained Deletion') that follows from (53); the reader is referred to Larson (2000) for its details. It is evident, moreover, that prenominal adjectives with Direct Modification Reading will have a different structural source, one in which they have a position closer to the noun. A fact suggesting this double generation is that sentences like (54) with two instances of the same adjective with different readings (marked in the examples) are possible in English:

(54) Mary interviewed every possible [IRR] possible [DMR] candidate.

To close this subsection it could be interesting to simply witness another construction with an adverbial adjective that is possibly amenable to a similar analysis with an implicit event; see (55) where *quick* can well refer to an (implicit) event of drinking a cup of coffee quickly, even if it appears as a nominal modifier:

(55) A quick cup of coffee helps keep John awake.

The 'occasional' construction. Another case of mismatch between overt syntactic structure and semantic structure is the one instantiated by so called '*occasional* constructions' like the one in (45), to which the two readings annotated in (48) are associated. Let us provide another relevant example:

(56) A sporadic shot was heard.
   'Sporadically, a shot was heard'.

The mismatch that the reading in (56) represents is a puzzle for compositional semantics. As noted by Larson (1999, 2000) and Zimmermann (2003), the problem is how to account for the DP external reading of these 'infrequency' adjectives (the label is such because the phenomenon shows only with forms like *sporadic, occasional, infrequent* but not with *frequent* and similar ones).

The external reading in (56) is sanctioned by specific conditions: a) the presence of articles (definite or indefinites) is required: *Two / most sporadic shots...* has only the attributive reading; b) the infrequency adjective must be adjacent to the determiner: in *A sporadic loud shot was heard* the intermediate adjective blocks the external reading; c) coordination with another adjective also blocks the intended reading: in *An occasional and clear shot was heard* the adjective cannot be interpreted as having scope over the entire sentence. If we interpret a sentence like (56) as a fact of adverbial quantification over events, it is evident that a syntactic configuration in which the adjective is inside the DP does not provide an appropriate structure for semantic interpretation, if we take for granted, as is standard, that syntactic binding is the basis for semantic binding. There are various options to derive the appropriate structure with the adjective in a position from which it can bind an event. Among them, there appear to be stronger arguments to choose the one defended by Larson (2000) and Stump (1981), namely, that of movement and incorporation of the adjective to the Determiner in order to form a complex quantifier able to bind the event, as in (57) (corresponding to (45)), from Zimmermann (2003: 254):

(57) $[_{IP} [_{QP} [_Q \text{the/an+occasional}_1] [_{NP} t_1 \text{ sailor}]] [_{VP} \text{e(vent) strolled by}]]$

The arguments for this option as opposed to that of LF extraction of the adjective, or LF movement to Spec of DP, the other logical options, will not be reproduced here; but see Zimmermann (2003) for a detailed discussion of these matters.

Research for this work has been partially supported by the Ministerio de Ciencia e Innovación Grant HUM2007-30541-E. Special thanks go to Louise McNally and Paul Portner for their invaluable help in organizing and clarifying the main issues of this paper. I also thank Héctor Fernández-Alcalde and Olga Fernández-Soriano for comments, suggestions and assistance for editing. All errors remain mine.

5 References

Amaral, Patrícia 2006. On the semantics of almost. Paper presented at the *Annual Meeting of the Linguistic Society of America (= LSA)*. Albuquerque, NM, January 5–8.
Baker, Mark 2003. *Lexical Categories. Verbs, Nouns and Adjectives*. Cambridge: Cambridge University Press.
Barker, Chris 2002. The dynamics of vagueness. *Linguistics & Philosophy* 25, 1–36.
Bartsch, Renate & Theo Vennemann 1972. The grammar of relative adjectives and comparison. *Linguistische Berichte* 20, 19–32.

Bartsch, Renate & Theo Vennemann 1973. *Semantic Structures. A Study in the Relation between Syntax and Semantics*. Frankfurt/M.: Athenäum Verlag.
Bierwisch, Manfred 1967. Some semantic universals of German adjectivals. *Foundations of Language* 3, 1–36.
Bierwisch, Manfred 1989. The semantics of gradation. In: M. Bierwisch & E. Lang (eds.). *Dimensional Adjectives. Grammatical Structure and Conceptual Interpretation*. Berlin: Springer, 71–262.
Bolinger, Dwight 1967. Adjectives in English. Attribution and predication. *Lingua* 18, 1–34.
Bolinger, Dwight 1972. *Degree Words*. The Hague: Mouton.
Bosque, Ignacio & Carme Picallo 1996. Postnominal adjectives in Spanish. *Journal of Linguistics* 32, 349–385.
Carlson, Gregory 1980. *Reference to Kinds in English*. New York: Garland Press.
Cinque, Guglielmo 1994. On the evidence for partial N-movement in the Romance DP. In: G. Cinque et al. (eds.). *Paths towards Universal Grammar*. Washington DC: Georgetown University Press, 85–110.
Cresswell, Maxwell John 1976. The semantics of degree. In: B. H. Partee (ed.). *Montague Grammar*. New York: Academic Press, 261–292.
Cresswell, Maxwell John 1991. Syntax and semantics of categorial languages. In: A. von Stechow & D. Wunderlich (eds.). *Semantik – Semantics. Ein internationales Handbuch der zeitgenössischen Forschung – An International Handbook of Contemporary Research* (HSK 6). Berlin: de Gruyter, 148–155.
Croft, William 1991. *Syntactic Categories and Grammatical Relations*. Chicago, IL: The University of Chicago Press.
Cruse, Alan D. 1980. Antonyms and gradable complementaries. In: D. Kastovsky (ed.). *Perspektiven der Lexikalischen Semantik: Beitrage zum Wuppertaler Semantikkolloquium vom 2.–3. Dez. 1977*. Bonn: Bouvier Verlag, 14–25.
Demonte, Violeta 1999. El adjetivo. Clases y usos. La posición del adjetivo en el sintagma nominal. In: I. Bosque & V. Demonte (eds.). *Gramática descriptiva de la lengua española*, Chapter 3, Vol I. Madrid: Espasa Calpe / RAE, 129–215.
Demonte, Violeta 2008. Meaning-form correlations and the order of adjectives in Spanish. In: C. Kennedy & L. McNally (eds.). *The Semantics of Adjectives and Adverbs*. Oxford: Oxford University Press, 71–100.
Dixon, Robert M. W. 1977. *Grammar of Yidin*. Cambridge: Cambridge University Press.
Dixon, Robert M. W. 1982. Where have all the adjectives gone? In: R.M.W. Dixon. *Where Have all the Adjectives Gone? And Other Essays in Semantics and Syntax*. Berlin: de Gruyter, 1–26. First published in: *Studies in Language* 1, 1977, 19–80.
Doetjes, Jenny 1997. *Quantifiers and Selection. On the Distribution of Quantifying Expressions in French, Dutch and English*. Ph.D. dissertation. Leiden University.
Doetjes, Jenny 2008. Adjectives and degree modification. In: Ch. Kennedy & L. McNally (eds.). *The Semantics of Adjectives and Adverbs*. Oxford: Oxford University Press.
Fábregas, Antonio 2007. The internal syntactic structure of relational adjectives. *Probus* 19, 1–36.
Hamann, Cornelia 1991. Adjectival semantics. In: A. von Stechow & D. Wunderlich (eds.). *Semantik – Semantics. Ein internationales Handbuch der zeitgenössischen Forschung – An International Handbook of Contemporary Research* (HSK 6). Berlin: de Gruyter, 657–673.
Heim, Irene 1985. *Notes on Comparatives and Related Matters*. Ms. Austin, TX, University of Texas.

Heim, Irene 2000. Degree operators and scope. In: B. Jackson & T. Matthews (eds.). *Proceedings of Semantic and Linguistic Theory* X. Ithaca, NY: CLC Publications, 40–46.
Heim, Irene & Angelika Kratzer 1998. *Semantics in Generative Grammar*. Oxford: Blackwell.
Hellan, Lars 1981. *Towards an Integrated Analysis of Comparatives*. Tübingen: Narr.
Kamp, Hans 1975. Two theories of adjectives. In: E. Keenan (ed.). *Formal Semantics of Natural Languages*. Cambridge: Cambridge University Press, 123–155.
Kennedy, Christopher 1997. *Projecting the Adjective. The Syntax and Semantics of Gradability and Comparison*. Ph.D. dissertation. University of California, Santa Cruz, CA. Reprinted: New York: Garland, 1999.
Kennedy, Christopher 2001. Polar opposition and the ontology of degrees. *Linguistics & Philosophy* 24, 31–70.
Kennedy, Christopher 2007. Vagueness and grammar: The semantics of relative and absolute gradable adjectives. *Linguistics & Philosophy* 30, 1–45.
Kennedy, Christopher & Louise McNally 2005. Scale structure and the semantic typology of gradable predicates. *Language* 81, 345–381.
Klein, Ewan 1980. A semantics for positive and comparative adjectives. *Linguistics & Philosophy* 4, 1–45.
Klein, Ewan 1991. Comparatives. In: A. von Stechow & D. Wunderlich (eds.). *Semantik – Semantics. Ein internationales Handbuch der zeitgenössischen Forschung – An International Handbook of Contemporary Research* (HSK 6). Berlin: de Gruyter, 673–691.
Larson, Richard 1983. *Restrictive Modification*. Ph.D. dissertation. University of Wisconsin, Madison, WI.
Larson, Richard 1995. Olga is a beautiful dancer. Paper presented at the *Winter Meeting of the Linguistic Society of America (= LSA)*. New Orleans, LA, January 6–8.
Larson, Richard 1998. Events and modification in nominals. In: D. Strolovich & A. Lawson (eds.). *Proceedings of Semantics and Linguistic Theory (= SALT) VIII*. Ithaca, NY: CLC Publications, 145–168
Larson, Richard 1999. Semantics of adjectival modification. Paper presented at the *Landelijke Onderzoekschool Taalwetenschap Winter School (= LOT)*, Amsterdam.
Larson, Richard 2000. ACD in AP? Paper presented at the *19th West Coast Conference on Formal Linguistics (= WCCFL)*. UCLA, Los Angeles, CA.
Larson, Richard & Gabriel Segal 1995. *Knowledge of Meaning*. Cambridge, MA: The MIT Press.
Lewis, David 1970. General semantics. *Synthese* 22, 18–67.
McConnell-Ginet, Sally. 1982. Adverbs and logical form. *Language* 58, 144–184.
McNally, Louise & Gemma Boleda 2004. Relational adjectives as properties of kinds. In: O. Bonami & P. Cabredo Hofherr (eds.). *Empirical Issues in Formal Syntax and Semantics* 5, 179–196, http://www.cssp.cnrs.fr/eiss5/mcnally-boleda/index_en.html, August 9, 2011.
Montague, Richard 1970. Universal Grammar. *Theoria* 36, 373–398. Reprinted in: R. H. Thomason (ed.). *Formal Philosphy. Selected Papers of Richard Montague*. New Haven, CT: Yale University Press, 1974, 222–246.
Neeleman, Ad, Hans van de Koot & Jenny Doetjes 2004. Degree expressions. *The Linguistic Review* 21, 1–66.
Partee, Barbara 1995. Lexical semantics and compositionality. In: L. R. Gleitman & M. Lieberman (eds.). *Language. An Invitation to Cognitive Science*. Cambridge, MA: The MIT Press, 311–360.
Portner, Paul 2005. *What is Meaning? Fundamentals of Formal Semantics*. Oxford: Blackwell.

Rotstein, Carmen & Yoad Winter 2004. Total adjectives vs. partial adjectives: Scale structure and higher-order modifiers. *Natural Language Semantics* 12, 259–288.
Sapir, Edward 1944. Grading. A study in Semantics. *Philosophy of Science* 11, 91–116.
Seuren, Pieter A. 1973. The comparative. In: F. Kiefer & N. Ruwet (eds.). *Generative Grammar in Europe*. Dordrecht: Reidel, 528–564.
Seuren, Pieter A. 1978. The structure and selection of positive and negative gradable adjectives. In: D. Farkas et al. (eds.). *Papers from the Parasession on the Lexicon*, Chicago Linguistic Society (= CLS) 14. Chicago IL: Chicago Linguistic Society, 336–346.
Seuren, Pieter A. 1984. The comparative revisited. *Journal of Semantics* 3, 109–141.
Siegel, Muffy 1976. *Capturing the Adjective*. Ph.D. dissertation. University of Massachusetts, Amherst. Reprinted: New York: Garland, 1980.
von Stechow, Arnim 1984. Comparing semantic theories of comparison. *Journal of Semantics* 3, 1–77.
von Stechow, Arnim & Dieter Wunderlich (eds.) 1991. *Semantik – Semantics. Ein internationales Handbuch der zeitgenössischen Forschung – An International Handbook of Contemporary Research* (HSK 6). Berlin: de Gruyter.
Stump, Gregory 1981. The interpretation of frequency adjectives. *Linguistics & Philosophy* 5, 221–256.
Unger, Peter 1975. *Ignorance*. Oxford: Clarendon Press.
Vendler, Zeno 1967. *Linguistics in Philosophy*. Ithaca, NY: Cornell University Press.
Warren, Beatrice 1984. *Classifying Adjectives*. Gothenburg: Acta Universitatis Gothoburgensis.
Yoon, Youngeun 1996. Total and partial predicates and the weak and strong interpretations. *Natural Language Semantics* 4, 217–236.
Zimmermann, Malte 2003. Pluractionality and complex quantifier formation. *Natural Language Semantics* 11, 249–287.

Sigrid Beck
13 Comparison constructions

1 Introduction —— 415
2 The standard theory: von Stechow (1984) —— 416
3 Open questions for the standard theory and new developments —— 439
4 Summary and conclusions —— 472
5 References —— 473

Abstract: The article introduces a version of von Stechow's (1984) theory of comparatives as the most far-reaching and widely adopted foundation of semantic analyses of comparison constructions. It illustrates the range covered by this theory by applying it to other constructions like superlatives, equatives and so on. Various kinds of negation are pointed out as an area for further research. The theory serves as the starting point of two research projects that the field is currently engaged in: on the one hand, the interaction of comparison with quantification, and on the other hand, the range of crosslinguistic variation that comparison constructions are subject to. The present state of affairs is sketched for both domains.

1 Introduction

The goal of this article is to answer the following question: what is the semantics of comparatives and how is it compositionally derived? There are some desiderata for that answer, beyond the obvious ones of getting the semantics right, covering a decent range of data on comparatives, and providing a theoretically plausible syntax/semantics interface. They include in particular extendability of the analysis to other comparison constructions like superlatives, equatives and so on, and extendability of the analysis from the standard application to English to comparison constructions in other languages.

My starting point for this enterprise will be von Stechow (1984). The paper discusses and incorporates the earlier literature on the subject to such an extent that I will only make very specific reference to older papers where necessary. I present a modernized version of this influential work in section 2, including comments on obvious extensions and problems solved. I then turn to questions left

Sigrid Beck, Tübingen, Germany

https://doi.org/10.1515/9783110626391-013

unanswered by this theory in section 3. That section serves to present much of the subsequent literature on comparison constructions, and the important issues that occupy the discussion. Section 4 summarizes the main results as well as the remaining problems in the theory of comparison today.

The discussion is presented in the general framework of the Heim & Kratzer (1998) textbook. I assume that syntactic structures of the level of Logical Form are compositionally interpreted by a few general principles of composition: function application, predicate abstraction and predicate modification. Truth conditions are presented in a semi-formal metalanguage using among other things Heim & Kratzer's version of the Lambda-notation.

2 The standard theory: von Stechow (1984)

Section 2.1 introduces the standard degree semantics and compositional analysis of the comparative construction. The analysis is designed to be extended to other comparison constructions, which is demonstrated in section 2.2. Its generality is one of the strengths of the standard analysis, as are some other properties concerning interaction with scope bearing elements and negative polarity; this is discussed in section 2.3. We will note at certain points in the discussion that the theory, though highly successful, leaves particular questions unaddressed. This motivates the research presented in section 3.

2.1 Comparatives

2.1.1 The basic idea

The apparently simplest types of comparative construction are data like (1). It is tempting to view the comparative form of the adjective in (1a) as an expression denoting a relation between two individuals, cf. (2) (e.g. Larson 1988).

(1) a. Caroline is taller than Georgiana.
    b. Caroline is taller than 6′.

(2) [[taller]] = $\lambda x.\lambda y.$ y's height > x's height

(1b) on the other hand suggests that a comparison is made to a height, i.e. a degree of tallness (see e.g. Klein 1991 for a thorough definition of degrees and measurement). Cases of so-called comparative subdeletion, also known as subcomparatives, like (3) (Bresnan 1973) show that this must be so: through changing the adjective, we compare Caroline and the sofa according to different dimensions. Each dimension must provide a degree. The degrees are what is ultimately related by the 'larger than' relation '>'.

(3) Caroline is taller than the sofa is long.
'Caroline's height exceeds the length of the sofa.'

It seems natural therefore to suppose that the comparative is a relation between two degrees—the '>' relation; it acts separately semantically from the adjective it morphologically combines with. The subcomparative shows us furthermore that both the main clause and the *than*-clause must make available those degrees. Degrees are introduced by adjectives. This subsection develops this idea.

(4) a. [[-er]] : the degree matrix clause > the degree *than*-clause
    b. [[tall]] : x is tall to degree d

Before we proceed, I should note that these proposals (while widespread and influential) are not uncontested in the literature on comparatives. Some authors reject the idea that the comparative operator acts separately semantically from the adjective it combines with morphologically (e.g. Pinkal 1989a,b. Similar suggestions can be found in Kennedy 1997; see also section 3). Klein (1980) among others takes the unmarked, positive form of the adjective as basic, not the abstract underlying entry in (4b). The precise semantics of the comparative operator is of course the object of much debate (see e.g. Seuren 1978, Heim 2007, Schwarzschild 2008 for a different view). In recent work, Moltmann (2005) doubts that comparatives necessarily use a degree semantics (compare section 3.2). A careful discussion of a number of choices that go into the theory introduced here can be found in Klein (1991). My own discussion begins with these choices made.

2.1.2 Degrees, scales and adjective meanings

We introduce a new semantic type for degrees, <d>. The set D_d, the denotation domain for d, consists of mutually disjoint sets (heights, distances, weights...) each of which comes with an ordering relation. For example (from von Stechow 2005):

(5) SD := the set of all spatial distances
    >SD := {<x,y> ∈ SD x SD: x is a greater spatial distance than y}

(6) TD := the set of all temporal distances
>TD := {<x,y> ∈ TD x TD: x is a greater temporal distance than y}

(7) Call each such pair (X, $>_x$) a scale.
Properties of orders: $>_x$ is total on X, asymmetric, transitive, irreflexive.

The denotation domain of degrees D_d is the union of all of these sets. The members of SD are things like *15cm* or *3 miles*, the members of TD are *3 minutes*, *2 hours* and the like. Note that the degree *3 minutes* is not ordered relative to *15cm*.

Measure functions are partial functions that assign a unique degree to individuals. Height(x) is the maximal degree to which x is tall etc.

(8) Measure functions (type <e,d>):
Height = λx: x ∈D_e.x's height
Intelligence = λx: x ∈D_e.x's intelligence
Weight = λx: x ∈D_e.x's weight

Kennedy (1997) takes this to be the adjective meaning. We follow von Stechow, in whose framework gradable adjectives are relations between individuals and degrees (compare also article 12 [this volume] (Demonte) *Adjectives* for discussion). Adjectives relate individuals with *sets* of degrees, for example the degrees of height that they reach. We use the monotonicity property in (10).

(9) Gradable adjectives (type <d,<e,t>>; von Stechow):
[[tall]] = λd: d ∈D_d.λx: x ∈D_e. Height(x) ≥ d
[[intelligent]] = λd: d ∈D_d.λx: x ∈D_e. Intelligence(x) ≥ d

(10) ∀x∀d∀d'[f(d)(x)=1 & d'<d → f(d')(x)=1]

More accurately, the degree arguments of adjectives must be restricted to particular sorts: [[tall]] is restricted to spatial distances measured in the vertical dimension, (11a). We will mostly assume this tacitly and not represent it, cf. (11b). We also frequently write (11c) for (11b).

(11) a. [[tall]] = λd:d∈D_d & d is a vertical distance in SD.λx:x∈D_e.Height(x) ≥ d
b. [[tall]] = λd: d ∈D_d.λx: x ∈D_e. Height (x) ≥ d
c. [[tall]] = λd.λx. x is d-tall

We proceed with the simplest imaginable semantics for measure constructions (more discussion is to follow below, in sections 2.2 and 3.2): the measure phrase refers to a degree and occupies the degree argument slot of the adjective. The measure construction will be true if the individual reaches the degree measured. While there is usually an implicature to the effect that this is the maximal degree reached, (13) shows that she can exceed that degree without contradiction in a context in which the implicature does not arise.

(12) a. Caroline is 6′ tall.
b. Caroline is [$_{AP}$ 6′ [A′ tall]]
c. [[tall]] (6′)(C)=1 iff Height(C) ≥6′

(13) a. Context: There is a discussion about whether Caroline can join the school basketball team. The rules state that one has to be at least 6′ tall in order to do so.
b. Caroline is 6′ tall. In fact I think she is even 6′2″.

2.1.3 Comparison with a degree - composition in the main clause

This understanding of adjective meaning equips us to consider the composition of the comparative construction. We concentrate on the main clause and compare with a degree as in (14). The semantics of (14a) adopted in Heim (2001) is (14b). The maximality operator used in (14b) is defined in (15). An appropriate meaning for the comparative morpheme is (16). The comparative relates a degree and a property of degrees - the degree being 6′ in our example and the property being the degrees of height that Caroline reaches. Remember (17) in order to connect the semantic representation in (14) with the intuitive paraphrase.

(14) a. Caroline is taller than 6′.
b. max(λd.C is d-tall)>6′
'Caroline's height exceeds 6′.'

(15) max(P) = ιd:P(d)=1 & ∀d′[P(d′)=1 → d′≤d]

(16) comparative morpheme (comparison to a degree, type <d,<<d,t>,t>):
[[-er]] = λd.λP.max(P)>d

(17) a. λd.C is d-tall = λd. Height(C)≥d
b. max(λd.C is d-tall) = max(λd. Height(C)≥d) = C's height

The underlying syntactic structure of our example (14a) is taken to be (18a), where the degree expression 'more/-er than 6"' occupies the specifier position of AP (Heim 2001; she calls this constituent a DegP). In order to derive the surface (14a) above, one assumes movement of the adjectival head to join the comparative morpheme (Bresnan 1973); alternatively, insertion of dummy 'much' would yield 'Caroline is more than 6' tall'. (This is a sketch of a 'classical' derivation; see Bhatt & Pancheva 2004 for a modern analysis.)

Of more interest to us is the Logical Form, the input to compositional interpretation, given in (18b). The DegP is not of a suitable type to fill the degree argument slot of the adjective and is raised (QRed) to a sentence adjoined position. (18b) is straightforwardly interpretable to yield (14b), with the intermediate step in (19) and predicate abstraction in (20) (following Heim & Kratzer 1998). Note that the DegP is of type <<d,t>,t>, a quantifier over degrees, and thus an excellent candidate to undergo QR (as Heim 2001 points out).

(18) a. Caroline is [$_{AP}$ [$_{DegP}$ more/-er than 6'] tall]   (underlying structure)
b. [$_{DegP}$ more/-er than 6'] [1 [Caroline is [t1 tall]]] (Logical Form)

(19) [[[-er than 6']]] = $\lambda P. \max(P) > 6'$

(20) [[[1 [Caroline is [t1 tall]]]] = $\lambda d. C$ is d-tall

Next, we consider difference degrees and example (21a). An accurate description of the example's truth conditions is (21b), which says that Caroline's height is at least the degree denoted by the *than*-phrase plus the difference degree.

(21) a. (Georgiana is 6' tall.) Caroline is 2" taller than that.
b. $\max(\lambda d. C$ is d-tall$) \geq 6'+2''$
'Caroline's height is at least 6'2".'

We must integrate the difference degree into the semantics. (22) gives the comparative another argument position for the difference degree and (23) interprets our example. If there is no difference degree given, as in (24), we assume that the difference degree slot is existentially quantified over, as indicated in (25a), (26a); (25a) is the same as (25b) and (26a) is the same as (26b), our original semantics from (16).

(22) comparison to a degree with difference degree (type <d,<d,<<d,t>,t>>>):
[[-er$_{diff}$]] = $[\lambda d.\lambda d'.\lambda P.\max(P) \geq d+d']$

(23) a. [2″ [-er$_{diff}$ than 6′]] [1 [Caroline is t1 tall]]
 b. [[-er$_{diff}$]] (6′)(2″)(λd.C is d-tall) = 1 iff
 max(λd.C is d-tall)≥6′+2″ iff
 C's height is at least 6′2″.

(24) Caroline is taller than 6′.

(25) a. ∃d′[d′>0 & max(λd.C is d-tall)≥6′+d′]
 b. max(λd.C is d-tall)>6′

(26) simple comparison to a degree (type <d,<<d,t>,t>):
 a. [[-er$_{simple}$]] = λd.λP. ∃d′[d′>0 & max(P)≥d+d′]
 b. [[-er$_{simple}$]] = λd.λP. max(P)>d

2.1.4 Descriptions of the item of comparison – the than-clause

We now consider data in which the item of comparison is not in an obvious way a degree. It has been assumed since Bresnan (1973) that the semantically most transparent case is the subcomparative. Note: in order to get an acceptable subcomparative, choose your example in such a way that the two adjectives operate on the same scale. As we saw above, IQ points stand in no ordering relation to spatial distances, for instance. The desired semantics for example (27b) is given in (28).

(27) a. Caroline is taller than the sofa is long.
   'Caroline's height exceeds the length of the sofa.'
 b. The desk is higher than the door is wide.
   'The height of the desk exceeds the width of the door.'

(28) max(λd.the desk is d-high) > max(λd′.the door is d′-wide)

We are led to assume that the subordinate clause, just like the main clause, provides us with a set of degrees. The comparative operator uses the maximum of the degrees described to make the comparison. Thus we use a meaning for the comparative morpheme (simple version) given in (29). A Logical Form like (30) will serve as an appropriate input to derive the meaning described.

(29) comparative morpheme for clausal comparatives (type <<d,t>,<<d,t>,t>>):
 [[-er$_{simple}$]] = λD1.λD2. max(D2)>max(D1)

(30) [-er$_{simple}$ than [2 [the door is t2 wide]]] [1 [the desk is t1 high]]

[[[2 [the door is t2 wide]]]] = λd'.the door is d'-wide

[[[1 [the desk is t1 high]]] = λd.the desk is d-high

Note that if we suppose that we can derive particular degrees from sets of degrees by some other method (like maximality in free relatives, Jacobson 1995), the contribution of *-er* is simply the 'larger than' relation in (31). The contribution of the max operator is represented in the LF (30'). This would achieve uniformity with the 'comparison to a degree' examples in the last subsection. We will work with (29) (the most common semantics for the comparative morpheme) and come back to (31) later.

(31) possible generalization - comparative morpheme of type <d,<d,t>>:
[[-er$_{simple}$]] = λd.λd'.d'>d

(30') [-er$_{simple}$ than [max [2[the door is t2 wide]]]] [max [1[the desk is t1 high]]]

These are the important features of the analysis: The *than*-clause is a wh-clause with a degree gap. The degree-gap is the trace of a wh-moved operator interpreted via predicate abstraction. The comparative morpheme and the *than*-clause form a constituent at LF - a quantifier over degrees according to the semantics in (29). LF movement of this quantifier creates another predicate abstraction over a degree variable in the matrix clause. At the surface structure, the *than*-clause must be extraposed, and once more we have either movement of the adjective to support *-er* or we insert dummy *much*. An argument for predicate abstraction over degree variables can be drawn from degree questions: As the LF in (32b) shows, *how* spells out the wh-operator that creates abstraction over the degree argument (compare e.g. Beck 1996 for this kind of compositional semantics of degree questions).

(32) a. How high is the desk?
 b. [Q [how1 [the desk is t1 high]]]
 c. [[Q]] (λd.the desk is d-high)
 d. For which d: the desk is d-high

The interpretation of examples with difference degrees once more requires us to use a version of *-er* with an extra argument slot for the difference degree:

(33) Caroline is 3" taller than the sofa is long.
 'Caroline's height exceeds the length of the sofa by at least three inches.'

(34) [[3" [-er [than [2[the sofa is t2 long]]]]] [1[Caroline is t1 tall]]]

(35) a. [[-er$_{diff}$]]   = λD1.λd.λD2.max(D2)≥max(D1)+d
    b. [[-er$_{simple}$]]   = λD1.λD2.∃d[d>0 & max(D2)≥max(D1)+d
                    = λD1.λD2. max(D2)>max(D1)

The subcomparative is special in that there is no genuine deletion process. Most comparatives are less obvious in that various parts of the degree description we need semantically in the *than*-clause have been elided. Below is a simple example involving comparative deletion (an elided AP; Bresnan 1973). Ellipsis is indicated by strikethrough. We assume that there is no semantic difference to the cases discussed.

(36) a. Caroline is taller than Georgiana is.
    b. [[-er [than [2[Georgiana is [~~AP~~ t2 tall]]]] [2[Caroline is [AP t2 tall]]]]

We have concentrated so far on examples in which the adjective is used predicatively. The analysis can be straightforwardly extended to the data below (with the comparative adjective used attributively, and an adverbial comparative). What distinguishes such examples from the one discussed is a matter of syntax: the size, kind and position of the ellipsis. See in particular Lechner (2004) for comprehensive discussion of the syntax of comparison, as well as further references.

(37) a. Mr Bingley keeps more servants than Mr Bennet does.
    b. [[-er   [than [2[Mr Bennet does [~~VP~~ keep t2 many servants]]]]
         [2[Mr Bingley keeps t2 many servants]]]

(38) a. Colonel Fitzwilliam behaved more amiably than his cousin did.
    b. [[-er   [than [2[his cousin did [~~VP~~ behave t2 amiably]]]]
         [2[Colonel Fitzwilliam behaved t2 amiably]]]

(39) a. Colonel Fitzwilliam behaved more amiably than Lizzy had expected.
    b. [[-er   [than [2[Lizzy had expected [~~XP~~ C.F. behave t2 amiably]]]]
         [2[Colonel Fitzwilliam behaved t2 amiably]]]

We will return to (1a) - the phrasal comparative - below. This concludes the description of the basic theory. The important aspects of the theory of comparatives introduced here are:
- comparison is between degrees;
- matrix and *than*-clause provide sets of degrees via abstraction over a degree variable;

- the comparative morpheme relates their maxima;
- adjectives denote relations between degrees and individuals.

With these features of the theory in place, it is straightforward to extend data coverage in many ways.

2.2 Extensions

2.2.1 Phrasal comparatives

Heim (1985) spells out a semantic analysis of phrasal comparatives that does not take them to be elliptical clausal comparatives - a 'direct' analysis. A semantic interpretation is proposed for the comparative as in (41). The Logical Form of (40a)=(1a) is as in (42a). This is interpreted to yield the same semantics as the clausal equivalent, as demonstrated in (42b).

(40) a. Caroline is taller than Georgiana.
 b. $max(\lambda d.C\text{ is }d\text{-tall}) > max(\lambda d'.G\text{ is }d'\text{-tall})$

(41) phrasal comparative morpheme (type <e,<<d,<e,t>>,<e,t>>>):
 $[[\text{-er}_{phrasal}]] = \lambda y.\lambda R.\lambda x.max(\lambda d.R(d)(x)) > max(\lambda d'.R(d')(y))$

(42) a. [Caroline [[-er$_{phrasal}$ than Georgiana] [1[2[t2 is t1 tall]]]
 b. $[[\text{-er}_{phrasal}]]$ (G) ($\lambda d.\lambda x.x$ is d-tall) (C) = 1 iff
  $max(\lambda d.C\text{ is }d\text{-tall}) > max(\lambda d'.G\text{ is }d'\text{-tall})$

In contrast to the clausal comparative, there is no syntactic ellipsis in phrasal comparatives on this analysis. A conceivable alternative would be to reduce the phrasal comparative to the elliptical clausal comparative (42').

(42') [-er$_{simple}$ than [2[Georgiana [~~XP~~ is t2 tall]]]] [2[Caroline is t2 tall]]

Heim also argues that it is unclear whether this analysis is to be preferred to an ellipsis analysis. Phrasal and clausal comparatives in English show a very similar behaviour. A recent analysis that reduces the phrasal comparative to the clausal one, and much interesting discussion, is found in Lechner (2004). Thus, while a direct semantic analysis is possible, it is not certain that this is desirable for English phrasal comparatives. One ought to keep in mind that the discussion has been largely based on English (and German; but see Pancheva 2006, Merchant

2006), and be open to the idea that a given language might or might not have a phrasal comparative. Turkish, for example, appears to have only *than*-phrases, not *than*-clauses (Hofstetter 2009), and so does Hindi-Urdu (Bhatt & Takahashi 2008). This makes an analysis along the lines of (42′) unappealing and one along the lines of (42) rather appealing for this language. The crosslinguistic variation regarding phrasal vs. clausal comparatives is the subject of Bhatt & Takahashi (2008) and Kennedy (2009).

2.2.2 Other comparison operators: equatives, superlatives and intensional comparisons

2.2.2.1 Equatives

Von Stechow (1984) observes that the equative seems to be a close relative to the comparative; just the relation expressed is slightly different. Examples and an analysis are given below. The semantics derived corresponds to 'at least as Adj as'.

(43) a. Mary is as tall as Kitty is.
b. Mr Darcy is as rich as Mr Bingley is, if not richer.

(44) $[[as]] = \lambda D1.\lambda D2.\ max(D2) \geq max(D1)$

(45) [[as [1[Kitty is t1 tall]]] [1[Mary is t1 tall]]]
'The height degree reached by Mary is at least as big as the one reached by Kitty.'

Equatives permit differentials that express multiplication. The meaning of (46b) is given in (47). A semantics for equatives that provides a slot for the differential is given in (48) and a compositional analysis of the example is sketched in (49).

(46) a. "He could not help seeing that you were about five times as pretty as every other woman in the room." ('Pride and Prejudice', Jane Austen; available at Gutenberg archives: http://www.gutenberg.org)
b. The curtain is twice as wide as the window.
c. Das Pflanzloch muss   doppelt so tief   sein, wie die Zwiebel dick ist.
   the hole   should doubly as deep be   as the bulb   thick is
   'The hole should be twice as deep as the body of the bulb is thick.'
   (from DasErste.de - Ratgeber - Heim+Garten - Gärtnertipps für den Monat September at www.wdr.de/tv/ardheim/sendungen/2007/september/070916-5phtml)

(47) The curtain's width ≥ 2* the window's width

(48) $[[as_{diff}]] = \lambda d.\lambda D1.\lambda D2.\ max(D2) \geq d * max(D1)$

(49) a. [[twice as][1[the window is t1 wide]][1[the curtain is t1 wide]]]
     b. max (λd.the curtain is d-wide) ≥ 2 * max(λd.the window is d-wide)

See Bhatt & Pancheva (2004) and Rett (2007) for some recent discussion of the equative.

2.2.2.2 Superlatives

There is an intuitively obvious connection between comparative and superlative in that (50a) means (50b):

(50) a. Caroline is the tallest.
     b. Caroline is taller than anyone else.

The superlative differs from the comparative in its surface appearance—it does not necessarily come with an indication of the intended item of comparison. Heim (1985, 2001) spells out the following semantics (meaning of -*est* in (51), example, Logical Form and truth conditions in (52)):

(51) $[[-est]] = \lambda R_{<d,<e,t>>}.\lambda x.max(\lambda d.R(d)(x)) > max(\lambda d.\exists y[y \neq x\ \&\ R(d)(y)])$

(52) a. Caroline is the tallest.
     b. Caroline [-est [tall]]
     c. $[[-est]]\ (\lambda d.\lambda z.z\ is\ d\text{-}tall)(C) = 1$ iff
        C's height > max(λd.∃y[y≠C & y is d-tall])

(53) is an example of the well-known absolute vs. relative ambiguity (Ross 1964, Szabolcsi 1986). It has been suggested that the readings correspond to two different possible syntactic scopes of the superlative morpheme, as spelled out below.

(53) a. Sally climbed the highest mountain.
     b. Sally climbed a higher mountain than anyone else did.   (relative)
     c. Sally climbed a mountain higher than any other mountain. (absolute)

(54) a. Sally [-est [1[climbed a t1 high mountain]]]   (relative)
     b. [[-est]] (λd.λz.z climbed a d-high mountain)(Sally)

(55) a. Sally [climbed the [-est [1[t1 high mountain]]]] (absolute)
   b. Sally climbed the (λx. [[-est]] (λd.λz.z is a d-high mountain)(x))

But, one ought to relativize the superlative to a set of contextually relevant entities one is comparing with. Reading (53b) for instance must be about other relevant mountain climbers. We give the superlative a resource domain variable for the quantification in the item of comparison:

(56) [[-est]] =λC.λR<d,<e,t>>.λx.max(λd.R(d)(x))>max(λd.∃y[y≠x & C(y) & R(d)(y)])

It has been argued (Heim 1999) that this step makes the first LF (54) superfluous, because C could be the set of mountains total, or the mountains climbed by some relevant person. See Stateva (2002) for more discussion of this and further issues relating to the status and scope possibilities of the superlative operator, as well as for further references.

2.2.2.3 Intensional comparisons

In most examples considered so far, one individual was compared to another (or several others) according to some dimension. The following intensional comparisons are different in that we must consider one and the same individual under different circumstances—in the actual situation vs. in other hypothetical situations. The examples can be paraphrased by more familiar comparison constructions employing intensional verbs (*have to, require*).

(57) a. Caroline is too tall to sleep on the sofa.
   'Caroline would have to be less tall than she is to sleep on the sofa.'
   b. "[…] I have had the pleasure of your acquaintance long enough to know, that you find great enjoyment in occasionally professing opinions which in fact are not your own." ('Pride and Prejudice', Jane Austen)
   'I have had the pleasure of your acquaintance as long as is required to know that you find great enjoyment in occasionally professing opinions which in fact are not your own.'
   c. "[…] they both of them frequently staid so long, that even Bingley's good humour was overcome, […]"('Pride and Prejudice', Jane Austen)
   '… they would have had to stay less long than they did for Bingley's good humour not to be overcome, …'

That means that they relate the here and now to other conceivable situations. We see from the paraphrases that the comparison made by the *too, enough* and *so that* constructions relate e.g. Caroline's actual height to her height in hypothetical situations/worlds. As a first step towards a semantics of these constructions, consider Heim (2001) on *too* below. In the presentation of the example, I write '@' for the actual world and 'R' for the accessibility relation (compare e.g. Kratzer 1991 for a standard semantics of modality; see also article 14 [Semantics: Noun Phrases and Verb Phrases] (Hacquard) *Modality*).

(58) [[too]] = λw.λP<d,<s,t>>.max(λd.P(d)(w)) > max(λd.∃w'[R(w,w') & P(d)(w')])

(59) a. Caroline is too tall.
   b. max(λd.Height(C)(@)≥d) > max(λd.∃w'[R(@,w') & Height(C)(w')≥d])
   c. Caroline's actual height exceeds the maximal height she reaches in any relevant alternative world (where relevant other worlds are ones where C sleeps on the sofa).
   d. [too [1[Caroline is t1 tall]]]
   e. [[tall]] = λd:d∈D_d.λx:x∈D_e.λw.Height(x)(w) ≥ d

See in particular Meier (2003) for a discussion of intensional comparison operators. Note that we need to change from the extensional semantics used so far for simplicity to an intensional semantics. As an example, the proper intensional lexical entry for 'tall' is given in (59e). We will use an intensional semantics in this article where it is relevant and an extensional one where it is not.

2.2.3 Positive, antonyms and less

2.2.3.1 Positive and antonyms

The gradable predicates that we are investigating do not always occur in an explicit comparison. Rather, a frequent use of adjectives is one that does not immediately suggest that a comparison is made at all—the positive form of the adjective.

(60) a. Caroline is tall.
   b. Mr Darcy is rich.

The positive will make us aware of antonyms, or scalar opposites. The pertinent points are: the positive polar and the negative polar adjective in the antonym pair operate on the same scale (cf. (61)). There is a neutral area on the scale of things that have the property expressed by neither of the antonyms; the positive says that an individual is beyond the neutral area on the scale (in the right direction)—cf. (62) (see Bierwisch 1989, Kennedy 2001 and von Stechow 1984, 2006 for discussion).

(61) Mr Darcy is taller than Mr Bingley.
⇔ Mr Bingley is shorter than Mr Darcy.

(62) a. Mr Darcy is tall. =⇒ Mr Darcy is not short.
b. Mr Bingley is not tall. =/⇒ Mr Bingley is short.
c. Mr Bingley is neither tall nor short.

We adopt here the negation theory of antonymy (e.g. Heim 2007), illustrated below. The negative polar adjective is a lexically negated version of the positive polar one.

(63) a. [[tall]] = $\lambda d.\lambda x.\text{Height}(x) \geq d$
b. [[short]] = $\lambda d.\lambda x.\sim\text{Height}(x) \geq d$
 = $\lambda d.\lambda x.\text{Height}(x) < d$

(64) -- > SD
/////////////////////////////////\\\\\\\\\\\\\\\\\\\
Darcy is d-tall   Darcy is not d-tall = Darcy is d-short

Here is von Stechow's (2006) proposal on the semantics of the positive. He assumes a contextually given delineation interval L_c between polar opposites; L_c is a dense interval of degrees with s_c- as lower bound and approaching s_c+ as an upper bound, i.e., $L_c = [s_c\text{-}, s_c\text{+})$. The positive can be defined as a universal quantifier stating that the degree predicate is true of every d in L_c, as in (65) below. Some examples from von Stechow's paper follow.

(65) [[Pos_c <<d,t>,t>]] = $\lambda D.\forall d[d \in L_c \to D(d)]$

(66) a. Ede is tall.
b. Pos ($\lambda d.\text{Ede is d-tall}$) iff $\forall d[d \in L_c \to \text{Height}(E) \geq d]$
c. |..........)s-.................(s+......Height(E)....................> ∞

(67) a. Ede is not tall.
b. $\sim$Pos ($\lambda d.\text{Ede is d-tall}$) iff $\sim\forall d[d \in L_c \to \text{Height}(E) \geq d]$
c. |..........)s-......Height(E).........(s+............................> ∞
or
|.........Height(E).......)s-.........(s+............................> ∞

(68) a. Ede is short.
    b. Pos (λd.Ede is d-short) iff $\forall d[d \in L_c \rightarrow$ Height(E) < d]
    c. |.......Height(E).......)s–..........(s+..............................> ∞

(69) a. Ede is not short.
    b. ~Pos (λd.Ede is d-short) iff ~$\forall d[d \in L_c \rightarrow$ Height(E) < d]
    c. |.....................)s–.......Height(E)...........(s+.............> ∞
    or
    |.....................)s–...............(s+.......Height(E)..........> ∞

Von Stechow's positive operator provides a unified semantics for the positive, i.e. it combines with both pairs of a polar opposition, and is compatible with the negation theory of antonymy. The interpretation of the positive is context dependent. In contrast to earlier analyses of the positive (e.g. Lewis 1970, Kamp 1975, Klein 1980), this semantics takes the relational adjective meaning of type <d,<e,t>> we need for comparative semantics as its starting point and derives the positive from that. Rett (2007) presents a further development of such a view; she decomposes the contribution of the positive into a modifier and a quantifier part (the modifier relating the degree argument of the adjective to the contextual standard). The quantifier occurs in the positive, but the modifier occurs in other constructions that imply comparison to a contextual standard (e.g. John is as short as Mary is $\Rightarrow$ John is short). Also, see Kennedy (2007), Rett (2007) and article 12 [this volume] (Demonte) *Adjectives* for further interesting issues regarding the distinction between relative and absolute gradable adjectives and the positive.

We ought to reconsider the contribution of the comparative morpheme when we take into account comparatives with antonyms. The degrees of which the *than*-clause is true does not have a maximum, see (70d). We would get the right result if we compared the minima of the two sets that syntax allows us to derive - as can be brought about by the alternative lexical entry for the comparative morpheme in (71). While this works as an immediate remedy of the problem at hand, it is unattractive to have to assume a second meaning for the comparative when it combines with negative polar adjectives.

(70) a. Mr Bingley is shorter than Mr Darcy is.
    b. [[-er [than [2 [Mr Darcy is t2 short] [2 [Mr Bingley is t2 short]]
    c. [[short]] = λd.λx.Height(x)<d
    d. [[2 than Mr Darcy is t2 short]] = λd.Height(D)<d   no max!
    e. [[2 Mr Bingley is t2 short]] = λd.Height(B)<d

(71) a. clausal comparative morpheme for negative polar adjectives:
$[\![\text{-er}_{anto}]\!] = \lambda D1.\lambda D2.\min(D2) < \min(D1)$
b. $\min(\lambda d.\text{Height}(B)<d) < \min(\lambda d.\text{Height}(D)<d)$

Heim proposes instead a subset semantics (e.g. in Heim 2007) for *-er* given in (72) below. This subset semantics is applied to (70) in (73), and to a regular positive polar adjective in (74). We see that the truth conditions of (74) are the same as before - the sentence is true iff Mr Darcy's height is above Mr Bingley's height on the Height scale.

(72) $[\![\text{-er}]\!] = \lambda D1.\lambda D2.D1 \subset D2$

(73) a. Mr Bingley is shorter than Mr Darcy is.
b. $[\lambda d.\text{Height}(D)<d] \subset [\lambda d.\text{Height}(B)<d]$
c. The degrees of height that lie above Darcy's height are a subset of the degrees of height that lie above Bingley's height.

(74) a. Mr Darcy is taller than Mr Bingley is.
b. $[\lambda d.\text{Height}(B)\geq d] \subset [\lambda d.\text{Height}(D)\geq d]$
c. The degrees of height that lie below Bingley's height are a subset of the degrees of height that lie below Darcy's height.

The subset semantics has the advantage that it works for the antonym case as well. We will keep it in mind as a viable alternative to the max interpretation of the comparative (see also subsection 2.3). Note, however, that since the *than*-clause no longer refers to a degree, the standard theory's analysis of differentials (e.g. *Mr Darcy is 2" taller/shorter than Mr Bingley is*) is lost. (See Schwarzschild 2008, and informally already Klein 1991, for a semantics for differentials within this analysis of the comparative, which however becomes rather more complex.)

2.2.3.2 Less

It is tempting to analyse *less* as making a parallel but reversed contribution to *-er*:

(75) a. "Wickham's a fool, if he takes her with a farthing less than ten thousand pounds." ('Pride and Prejudice', Jane Austen)
b. Mr Bingley has five thousand a year. Mr Bennet has less than that.

(76) a. $[\![\text{less}_{diff}]\!] = \lambda D1.\lambda d.\lambda D2.\max(D1) \geq \max(D2)+d$
b. $[\![\text{less}_{simple}]\!] = \lambda D1.\lambda D2.\max(D2) < \max(D1)$

On the other hand, one could be guided by the idea that "less tall" means "shorter", and "short" in turn means "not tall", and try to compose "less tall" out of the meaningful components *-er* plus negation plus *tall*. An important motivation for the researchers that have contemplated this step is the ambiguity in (78) (Seuren 1973, Rullmann 1995, Heim 2007).

(77) a. less tall = -er + little + tall
 b. little is degree predicate negation (type <d,<<d,t>,t>>):
 [[little]] = λd.λP.P(d)=0

(78) a. Lucinda was driving less fast than was allowed.
 b. Lucinda was driving (legally) below the speed limit.
 c. Lucinda was driving (illegally) below the minimum speed permitted.

Below is a derivation of the unproblematic 'legal' reading (in the max version, using (79b) as an assumption about the context: the legal speed is between 30mph and 50mph).

(79) a. [[[than [2[was allowed [Lucinda drive t2 fast]]] =
 λd.Lucinda was allowed to drive d-fast =
 b. [30mph , 50mph]
 c. L's actual speed < max(λd.Lucinda was allowed to drive d-fast)
 = L's actual speed < 50mph

But what about the second 'illegal' reading? There seems to be no principled derivation of it using (76) (but see Meier 2002 for a different view and an analysis based on a more elaborate semantics for modals). One could employ a minimum operator instead of a maximum operator for the embedded clause, but what would be the motivation? On the other hand, (77) can help here. Heim's (2007) analysis of the ambiguity is given in (80)–(82). The underlying structure in (80), which decomposes *less fast* into *-er* + *little* + *fast*, can lead to two different LFs, (81a) and (81b). They differ with respect to the scope of *little*=negation in the *than*-clause.

(80) Lucinda drive [[-er than allowed Lucinda drive t little fast] little] fast

(81) a. [[-er than   [1[allowed [t1 little] [2[L drive t2 fast]]]
                      [1[L drive t1 little fast]]]
    b. [[-er than   [1[[t1 little] [2[allowed L drive t2 fast]]]
                      [1[L drive t1 little fast]]]

(82) [[[1[L drive t1 little fast]]]]] = λd.Lucinda drove d-slow
= degrees of speed that Lucinda did not reach

The two LFs provide us with two different intervals for the meaning of the *than*-clause, (83) and (84) respectively. This allows us to account for the ambiguity, as demonstrated in (85a) and (85b) (with Heim's subset semantics), and (85a'), (85b') (with the min semantics from (71)). Crucially, decomposition is used in both versions.

(83) [[[1[allowed [t1 little] [2[L drive t2 fast]]]]]] =
λd.Lucinda was allowed to drive d-slow =
[30mph, ∞)

(84) [[[1[[t1 little] [2[allowed L drive t2 fast]]]]]] =
λd.Lucinda was not allowed to drive d-fast =
[50mph, ∞)

(85) a. [λd.Lu was allowed to drive d-slow] ⊂ [λd.Lu drove d-slow]
= Lucinda was illegally slow

    a'. min(λd.Lu drove d-slow)<min(λd.Lu was allowed to drive d-slow)
= Lucinda was illegally slow

    b. [λd.Lu was not allowed to drive d-fast] ⊂ [λd.Lu drove d-slow]
= Lucinda was below the speed limit

    b'. min(λd.Lu drove d-slow)<min(λd.Lu was not allowed to drive d-fast)
= Lucinda was below the speed limit

See Heim (2007, 2008) and Büring (2007a,b) for a thorough discussion of the consequences of such an approach to *little* and *less*, and once more subsection 2.3 for a related remark. It seems to me that the outcome of this lively debate is yet to be fully determined.

2.2.4 Measure phrases

Analysing adjectives as denoting a relation between a degree and an individual leads us to expect that they can combine directly with a degree denoting expression (see also once more article 12 [this volume] (Demonte) *Adjectives*). This appears to be verified by measure constructions like (86), and this is how we sketched the contribution of measure phrases at the beginning of section 2.

(86) "I hope you saw her petticoat, six inches deep in mud."
('Pride and Prejudice', Jane Austen)

(87) a. [[deep]] = $\lambda d.\lambda x.$ Depth(x) $\geq d$
b. [[six inches deep]]   = [[deep]] (6")
    = $\lambda x.$ Depth(x) $\geq 6"$

The property in (87b) will be true of objects whose depth is greater than or equal to six inches (e.g. the mud covering of Lizzy's petticoat). This corresponds to an interpretation 'at least six inches deep'. We can make explicit whether we have an 'at least' or an 'exactly' interpretation in mind:

(88) Caroline is at least/exactly/at most 6' tall.

This suggests that a more precise analysis of measure phrases should take them to be quantifiers over degrees, type <<d,t>,t>, as in von Stechow (2005). The three versions of the LF in (90) below mean: Height(C) $\geq$ 6'; Height(C) = 6' and Height(C) $\leq$ 6'.

(89) a. [[at least]] = $\lambda d.\lambda D.max(D) \geq d$
b. [[exactly]] = $\lambda d.\lambda D.max(D) = d$
c. [[at most]] = $\lambda d.\lambda D.max(D) \leq d$

(90) [[at least/exactly/at most 6'] [1[Caroline is t1 tall]]] =
[[at least/exactly/at most]] (6') ($\lambda d.C$ is d-tall)

(91) max($\lambda d.C$ is d-tall) = max($\lambda d.$Height(C) $\geq$ d) = Height(C)

The same slightly refined understanding of measures as quantified measure phrases should go into difference degrees - an example is given in (92).

(92) a. Caroline is 6' tall.
    Mr Darcy is exactly 3" taller than that.
b. max($\lambda d.$ max($\lambda d'.D$ is d'-tall) $\geq$ d+6') = 3"
c. [exactly 3"] [2 [[t2 -er than that] [1 [Mr Darcy is t1 tall]]]]
    The largest degree d such that Darcy is d-much taller than 6' is exactly 3".

It is odd under this analysis, however, that not all adjectives in English permit such measure phrases to fill their degree argument slot, as seen e.g. in (93). See section 3.2 below for a discussion of Schwarzschild's (2005) objections.

(93) *five dollars expensive

2.3 Issues addressed

The generality of this theory of comparison speaks for itself; but let us make some of its strengths more explicit.

2.3.1 Inference relations among comparison constructions

The extendability of the standard analysis of comparatives to other constructions that we observed in the last subsection is a desideratum of a successful theory of comparison, as demonstrated by some sample inferences between the various comparison constructions. It should be clear from the analyses discussed in this section that the theory predicts all of these facts.

(94) a. Mr Darcy is taller than 6'.
Caroline is exactly 6' tall.
$\Longrightarrow$ Mr Darcy is taller than Caroline is.

b. Georgiana is not as tall as Caroline is.
$\Longrightarrow$ Caroline is taller than Georgiana is.

c. Mary is not taller than Kitty.
$\Longrightarrow$ Kitty is at least as tall as Mary.

d. Kitty is the tallest (among the younger Miss Bennets).
The younger Miss Bennets are Mary, Kitty and Lydia.
$\Longrightarrow$ Kitty is taller than Mary and Kitty is taller than Lydia.

e. The rules require that nobody taller than 1.5m enter the bouncy castle.
Joe is 1.6m tall.
$\Longrightarrow$ Joe is too tall (to enter the bouncy castle).

f. Mary is taller than (as tall as) Kitty is
$=\!/\!\!\Rightarrow$ Mary is tall.

2.3.2 NPIs and disjunctions: Semantics, inferences, licensing

The combination of predicate abstraction and subsequent maximalization gives the comparison scope in a non-trivial sense. This can be seen in the interaction with other operators. Let us first consider disjunction and NPIs. The data in (95a) and (96a) intuitively have the readings paraphrased in (95b) and (96b), which can be derived by giving the comparison scope over the disjunction and the existential quantifier associated with NPI *any*.

(95) a. Caroline is taller than Elizabeth or Georgiana is.
b. Caroline is taller than Elizabeth is and Caroline is taller than Georgiana is.
c. Height(C)>max(λd.E is d-tall or G is d-tall)

(96) a. Caroline is taller than anyone in Derbyshire.
b. Everybody in Derbyshire is shorter than Caroline.
c. Height(C)>max(λd.$\exists$x[person_in_Derby(x) & x is d-tall])

It is interesting that NPI *any* is licensed in *than*-clauses. Adopting Ladusaw's (1979) analysis of NPI distribution as licensing in downward monotonic contexts, this follows from von Stechow's (1984) analysis. Examples (97) and (98) illustrate inferences from supersets to subsets in *than*-clauses, and (99) provides a few more examples of acceptable NPIs.

(97) Caroline is taller than anyone in Derbyshire.
Lambton is in Derbyshire.
=⇒ Caroline is taller than anyone in Lambton.
λd.$\exists$x[person_in_Lam(x) & x is d-tall] $\subseteq$ λd.$\exists$x[person_in_Derby(x) & x is d-tall]

(98) Thilo ran faster than I skied or biked.
=⇒ Thilo ran faster than I skied.
λd.I skied d-fast $\subseteq$ λd.I skied d-fast or I biked d-fast

(99) a. Thilo ran faster than I <u>ever</u> could.
b. Es waren mehr Leute da, als da zu sein <u>brauchten</u>.
It were more people there than there to be needed
'There were more people there than needed to be.'

The meaning that the standard theory provides can thus explain the interpretation and acceptability of NPIs in these *than*-clauses.

2.3.3 Scope

The motivation for von Stechow's proposals comes to a considerable extent from the interaction of the comparative with other operators. The scope bearing maximality operator is argued for with an example involving modal possibility.

(100) a. A polar bear can be larger than a grizzly bear can be.
 b. The largest possible height for a polar bear exceeds the largest possible height for a grizzly.
 c. max(λd.∃w'[R(@,w') & a polar bear is d-large in w']) > max(λd.∃w'[R(@,w') & a grizzly bear is d-large in w'])

(101) a. I can write this paragraph faster than someone else could.
 b. The largest possible speed with which I write this paragraph exceeds the largest possible speed with which some other relevant person writes this paragraph.

Von Stechow discusses other intensional operators (propositional attitude verbs and counterfactuals), with respect to which comparative degrees can be described de re or de dicto. I will not enter into this discussion because it seems to me that today one would favour a different solution for plain de re/de dicto readings, namely choice of world variable (Heim 2001, Percus 2000). But it is instructive to recapitulate von Stechow's discussion of the comparative's interaction with nominal quantifiers. The following concerns nominal scope bearing elements in the *than*-clause. Consider first (102) which is unacceptable. Giving the nominal quantifier in the *than*-clause narrow scope relative to the comparison (like we did with the disjunction, NPIs, modals and indefinites above) allows us to predict this. The set of degrees denoted by the *than*-clause can be argued not to have a maximum, making the meaning of the whole undefined and hence unacceptable (von Stechow 1984, Rullmann 1995). This phenomenon has been termed the Negative Island effect in comparatives - perhaps somewhat misleadingly, since syntactic islands are not the issue here, but I will follow the terminology.

(102) a. *Lydia is taller than none of her sisters is.
 b. #max(λd.~∃x[x is a sister of Lydia's and x is d-tall])

However, quantifiers do not appear to always take narrow scope relative to the comparison. The only reading intuitively available for (103) is one in which the nominal appears to outscope the comparison. A narrow scope reading of 'everyone else' seems to be unavailable.

(103) Caroline is taller than everyone else is.
'Everyone else is shorter than Caroline.'

(103') a. For every x, x≠C: C is taller than x
b. #C's height > max(λd.∀x[x≠C → x is d-tall])
= C's height exceeds the height of the shortest other person

The puzzle that emerges here is this: what scope possibilities does a quantificational element in the *than*-clause have? When does it take narrow scope relative to the comparative, and when does it take wide scope? That is: Why doesn't (102) have an acceptable wide scope negation reading (amounting to: 'No one is shorter than Lydia'), and why doesn't (103) have an additional narrow scope universal reading? And what happens with operators in the main clause? These questions will be discussed in section 3 below.

2.3.4 Negation

Example (102) poses a second problem (besides illustrating the scope question). There seems to be a difference between the negation that features as part of a negative polar adjective ('lexical' negation, if you will), and 'syntactic' negation as it shows up in (102) (terminology inspired by Heim 2008): lexical negation in a *than*-clause seems to yield a well-formed and interpretable sentence while syntactic negation yields a negative island effect (according to the explanation above, an uninterpretable structure). The contrast is illustrated by (104) and (105).

(104) a. ... than Mr Darcy is short.
b. ... than Mr Darcy isn't tall.

(105) a. Mr Bingley is shorter than Mr Darcy is (short).
b. *Mr Bingley is shorter/taller than Mr Darcy isn't (tall).

This difference does not emerge from the semantics set up here. The maxima of the two *than*-clauses in (104) are equally undefined. We have seen in section 2.2 two ways of providing a well-defined semantics for comparatives containing (104a): the min-semantics in (71) and the subset semantics in (72). Both would be able to apply to (104b) in the same way. As far as I can see, we expect in particular that (106a) can have the interpretation in (106b/c). Examples (107a) as well as (102) above are less problematic since they could be ruled out as a case of cross-polar anomaly (Kennedy 2001, Heim 2007); but (107b) could also be expected to be OK.

(106) a. *Mr Bingley is shorter than Mr Darcy isn't tall.
  b. min(λd.Height(B)<d) < min(λd.~D is d-tall])
     = min((λd.Height(B)<d) < min(λdHeight(D)<d])
  c. (λdHeight(D)<d) ⊂ (λd.Height(B)<d)

(107) a. *Mr Bingley is taller than Mr Darcy isn't (tall).
  b. *Mr Bingley is taller than Mr Darcy isn't short.

While (104), (105) distinguish lexical from syntactic negation, there is, perhaps, some reason to regard lexical negation as related to structural negation from the ambiguity in (107′a), which is analogous to the ambiguity in (78). To see this, take *few* to be the antonym of *many*; the lexical negation contained in *few* seems to be able to take variable scope within the *than*-clause, just like *little*. But at the same time (as Heim 2008 observes) (107′b) with *fast*'s antonym *slow* does not share the ambiguity we get with *less*.

(107′) a. There are fewer employees in the room than is allowed.
       'The number of employees is below the permitted minimum.'
       'The number of employees is below the permitted maximum.'

  b. Lucinda was slower than is allowed.
     'Lucinda was illegally slow.'
     #'Lucinda stayed below the speed limit.'

It is not clear to me how best to account for the different effects of lexically vs. syntactically negated degree predicates, and where within this spectrum we have to locate the negation with *little* and *less*, which might be called 'morphological'. While I consider this an important topic, I have nothing more to say about it and must leave this issue unresolved.

3 Open questions for the standard theory and new developments

Two important questions arose above: in section 2.2 we noted that measure phrases are not as universally acceptable as one would expect under the present analysis. And in section 2.3 we observed that the interaction of the comparison operator with other scope bearing elements is unclear. I will discuss these issues below. In doing so, I extend the measure phrase question to a larger issue:

the substantial crosslinguistic variation that the expression of comparison is subject to. These topics are grouped together here because unlike the facts discussed above, which lead to natural extensions of the standard theory, they have the potential to substantially enrich or change our picture of the semantics of comparison, as will become clear shortly.

3.1 Scope: Quantifiers in the matrix clause and in the than-clause

A substantial body of literature on comparison in the 1990s and the first decade of this century has been concerned with the behaviour of scope bearing elements in comparison constructions (e.g. Heim 2001, 2006; Kennedy 1997; Schwarzschild & Wilkinson 2002; Sharvit & Stateva 2002; Stateva 2000). This subsection provides an overview of its main results.

3.1.1 Degree operators and the matrix clause

When one considers scope bearing elements in the matrix clause, the impression can arise that there is no scope interaction at all. This is indeed Kennedy's (1997) position. For illustration, consider (108) (Heim 2001).

(108) John is 6′ tall.
Every girl is exactly 1″ taller than that.

Example (108) has the reading in (108'a), which I abbreviate as in (108'a'), simplifying the semantics of the *exactly*-differential. (I will use this simplification frequently in this section.)

(108') a. For every girl x: max(λd.Height(x)$\geq$6′+d)=1
 a'. For every girl x: x's height = 6′+1″
 b. #max(λd.for every girl x: x's height $\geq$d)=6′+1″
 'The height of the shortest girl is 6′1″.'

If the sentence could have the reading in (108'b), it would express that the largest degree of height reached by every girl exceeds John's height by one inch - i.e. the height of the shortest girl is one inch above John's height. The sentence would then truthfully describe the situation depicted below, where x marks the height of the shortest girl and J marks John's height on the height scale. Intuitively, the sentence cannot be used to describe this situation. Thus it appears that the quantifier 'every girl' must take scope over the comparison. (110) below is parallel.

(109)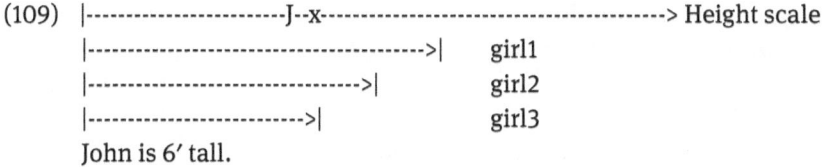
|------------------------>| girl1
|------------------------>| girl2
|------------------------>| girl3
John is 6′ tall.

(110) Every girl is at most 1″ taller than that.
 a. For every girl x: x's height ≤ 6′1″
 b. #the height of the shortest girl ≤ 6′1″

The only available reading is the one in which the quantifier takes scope over the comparison. Note that the differential is added to truth conditionally distinguish the two readings; the plain 'every girl is taller than that' would not allow one to distinguish them, because if the shortest girl is taller than 6′, they all are.

Other types of data that show this pattern of scopal behaviour, identified by Heim (2001), are exemplified by (111) and (112) below.

(111) John is 6′ tall.
Every girl is less tall than that.

(112) a. For every girl x: x's height < 6′
 b. #max(λd.for every girl x: x's height =d)<6′
   'The height of the shortest girl is less than ≥6′.'

(113) John is 6′ tall.
Exactly three girls are taller than that.

(114) a. For exactly 3 girls x: x is taller than 6′
 b. #max(λd.for exactly 3 girls x: x's height≥d)>6′
   'At least 3 girls are taller than 6′.'

Given such observations, Kennedy (1997) proposes that comparison operators do not take scope—say: DegPs do not cross quantified DPs at LF.

On the other hand, Heim (2001) claims that contrary to first impressions, DegPs do take scope. This is visible truthconditionally with some intensional verbs (for example *need, allow, require*) in interaction with *less than* and differential comparatives. It is also visible in some cases of syntactic or semantic ellipsis (where a property of degrees shows up as the argument of a comparison operator that includes an intensional verb) with ordinary comparatives, superlatives and *too*-comparisons. We begin with the truth conditional argument, which is inspired by Stateva (2000). Note first that von Stechow already used a variant of (115) to support an analysis in which the comparative takes non-trivial scope.

(115) John is 6′ tall.
A panda bear can be at most 1″ taller than that.

(116) max(λd.∃w′[R(@,w′) & a panda bear is d-tall in w′]) ≤ 6′+1″
= the largest possible height for a panda bear is 6′1″

Below are the relevant data from Heim's paper. The relevant reading of (117a) is (118a), in which the comparison takes scope over the modal verb. Similarly for (117b). The reader may verify that the same point could have been made with the data in (120).

(117) This draft is 10 pages long.
  a. The paper is required to be exactly 5 pages longer than that.
  b. The paper is allowed to be exactly 5 pages longer than that.

(118) a. max(λd.∀w′[R(@,w′) → the paper is d-long in w′]) = 10pp + 5pp
     = the minimum length required for the paper is 15 pages
  b. ∀w′[R(@,w′) → max(λd.the paper is d-long in w′) = 10pp + 5pp]
     = the paper must have the length of 15 pages

(119) a. max(λd.∃w′[R(@,w′) & the paper is d-long in w′]) = 10pp + 5pp
     = the maximum length allowed for the paper is 15 pages
  b. ∃w′[R(@,w′) & max(λd.the paper is d-long in w′) = 10pp + 5pp]
     = the paper is permitted to have the length of 15 pages

(120) a. The paper is required to be less long than that.
  b. The paper is allowed to be less long than that.

Not all intensional verbs pattern with *allowed* and *required*, though. For example, *might* does not like to take narrow scope relative to comparison. Compare Heim (2001) for more discussion. The question raised by these data for the standard theory is: why are there so few quantifiers that the comparison can outscope? Given that the comparison is an operator that can be (indeed, must be) raised at LF, we would expect it to be able to outscope other quantifiers besides the *required/allowed* type. Heim (2001) considers a syntactic explanation for this that would rule out LF configurations such as (121) (termed 'Kennedy's generalization'). (121) in effect rules out raising of a DegP across a problematic intervener, the QP. What counts as a problematic intervener can be diagnosed independently by looking at intervention effects in wh-constructions (Beck 1996) and distinguishes modals like *require* from quantifiers like *every girl*. The question remains why such a constraint should be operative in the domain of comparison constructions (compare the generalization in Beck 2007 on intervention effects).

(121) *[DegP <<d,t>,t> ... [QP[... tDegP ...]] ...]

Oda (2008) offers a reinterpretation of some of the facts discussed in Heim (2001). She observes that for the cases with *exactly*-differentials, the truth conditions of the minimum requirement reading can be derived by giving only the differential scope over the modal, not the comparative. This would leave the *less*-comparatives as the sole evidence for the comparative being a syntactically mobile quantifier.

(118') a. max(λd.$\forall$w'[R(@,w') $\rightarrow$ the length of the paper in w' $\geq$ d+10pp]) = 5pp
           = the minimum length required for the paper is 15 pages
        b. [exactly 5pp [1[required [[t1 -er than that] [2[the paper be t2 long]]]]

It should be stressed that the data in (115), (117) and (120) and their interpretation in Heim (2001) support crucial aspects of the standard theory of comparison. That theory analyses the comparative as a quantificational element taking independent scope at the level of LF. Heim's scope data lend some support to this view, provided that we reach a comfortable understanding of the limitations on scope interaction that (121) describes. Oda's observation weakens that point, however. We should therefore consider the second kind of evidence that Heim provides, ellipsis. Example (122) is an instance of VP ellipsis in the *than*-clause. Importantly, the ellipsis includes the subordinate intensional verb *want*. In order to derive (122)'s interpretation, we need to create (for syntactic as well as interpretive purposes) a constituent that includes *want*, but not *5cm -er*. The LF (122'b) provides such a constituent; it does so by QRing the DegP to a position above *want*.

(122) John wants to be (exactly) 5cm taller than Bill does.
       'The height John wants to reach is 5cm above the height that Bill wants to reach.'

(122′) a. max(λd.∀w'[R(@,w') → John is d-tall in w]) =
5cm + max(λd.∀w'[R(@,w') → John is d-tall in w])
b. [5cm -er than   [1 Bill does ~~want to be t1 tall~~]]
[1[John -s want to be t1 tall]]

Ellipsis thus provides a second kind of evidence in favour of a quantifier analysis of the comparative. Compare Heim (2001) for further considerations and more discussion. See Sharvit & Stateva (2002) for a different view of the semantic side.

3.1.2 Degree operators and the than-clause: Facts

We have already come across the problem of quantifiers in *than*-clauses in section 2.3. Remember the data below, where we observed that the quantifier, surprisingly, seemed to take obligatory wide scope over the comparison.

(124)   Caroline is taller than everyone else is.
'Everyone else is shorter than Caroline.'

(124′) a. ∀x[x≠C → C is taller than x]
b. #C's height > max(λd.∀x[x≠C → x is d-tall])
= C's height exceeds the height of the shortest other person

When we consider the Logical Forms that would correspond to the two potential readings, it becomes obvious why the facts are unexpected. Constraints on QR (i.e. its clauseboundedness) would lead one to expect that LF (124a) is impossible while LF (124b) is fine. The facts appear to indicate the opposite. Many other quantifiers (below: 'exactly n') are parallel.

(124) a. [everyone else [1[[DegP -er [CP than [2[t1 is t2 tall]] [2[C is t2 tall]]]]]
b. [[-er [CP than [2[everyone else is t2 tall]]]] [2[C is t2 tall]]]

(125)   John is taller than exactly three girls are.
'There are exactly three girls who are shorter than John is.'

The puzzle here is in a sense larger than our question about quantifiers in the matrix clause. A normal expectation would be that a quantifier in a *than*-clause is contained inside a scope island, and must take scope there. That we get only an apparent wide scope reading of quantifiers like nominal 'every N' is very surprising. Even worse, Schwarzschild & Wilkinson (2002) observe that intensional verbs and other expressions, which cannot undergo QR, also give rise to readings that look like wide scope:

(126) John is taller than I had predicted (that he would be).
    a. $\forall w[R(w,@) \rightarrow max(\lambda d.\text{John is d-tall in }@) > max(\lambda d.\text{John is d-tall in }w)$
       For every world compatible with my predictions:
       John's actual height exceeds John's height in that world.
    b. #John's height exceeds the height that he reaches in all worlds compatible with my predictions.
       = John's actual height exceeds the minimum I predicted.

For the standard theory, these facts raise the question of why so many quantifiers take scope out of the embedded clause, and for some of them, how this is possible at all.

Once more, it depends on the choice of quantificational element what scope effects we observe. Our modals of the *required/allowed* type can take narrow scope relative to the comparison here as well as in the matrix clause.

(127) The paper is longer than is required.
    a. The paper's length $> max(\lambda d.\forall w'[R(w',@) \rightarrow$ the paper is d-long in w'])
       The length of the paper exceeds the required minimum.
    b. #$\forall w'[R(w',@) \rightarrow$ the paper is longer in @ than in w']
       The paper is illegally long.

(128) The paper is longer than is allowed.
    a. The paper's length $> max(\lambda d.\exists w'[R(@,w')$ & the paper is d-long in w'])
       The paper is illegally long.
    b. #$\exists w'[R(@,w')$ & the paper is longer in @ than in w']
       It is possible for the paper to be shorter than it actually is.

Remember from section 2.3 that some indefinites (for example NPIs) in the embedded clause can also take narrow scope relative to the comparison.

(129) a. Caroline is taller than anyone in Derbyshire.
    b. Height(C) $> max(\lambda d.\exists x[\text{person\_in\_Derby}(x)$ & x is d-tall])

Regarding negative quantifiers, they certainly lack a wide scope reading of the quantifier, and are claimed to be ungrammatical because the narrow scope reading makes no sense (cf. section 2.3).

(130) *Lydia is taller than none of her sisters is.

(131) a. *Lydia's height > max(λd.~∃x[x is a sister of Lydia's and x is d-tall])
       max undefined!
    b. #no sister of Lydia's is such that Lydia is taller than she is.

In sum, the standard theory of comparison offers the following perspective on the facts: some scope bearing elements favour a wide scope reading relative to the comparison (many nominal quantifiers (*every*, *most*, numerals), adverbial quantifiers, and many intensional verbs). Other scope bearing elements favour a narrow scope reading relative to the comparison (negative quantifiers, NPIs, some indefinites, disjunction, some intensional verbs). Scope behaviour seems not to be guided by syntactic structure. Why?

3.1.3 Degree operators and the than-clause: Analyses

Schwarzschild & Wilkinson (2002) are inspired by the puzzle outlined above to develop a complete revision of the semantics of comparison. According to them, the quantifier data show that the *than*-clause provides us with an interval on the degree scale—in (132) below an interval into which the height of everyone other than Caroline falls.

(132) Caroline is taller than everyone else is.
    'Everyone else is shorter than Caroline.'

    ----------|---------------|-----------------x-------------->
              x_1 x_2 x_3 C
    interval on the height scale that covers everyone else's height
    (that interval is related to Caroline's height by the comparative)

(133) [[than everyone else is]] = λD. everyone else's height falls within D
    (where D is of type <d,t>)

To simplify, I will suppose that it is somehow ensured that we pick the right matrix clause interval (Joe's height in the example below). (135) is a rough sketch of Schwarzschild & Wilkinson's analysis of this example.

(134) Joe is taller than exactly 5 people are.

(135) Subord: [λD'. exactly 5 people's height falls within D']
      Matrix + Comp: MAX D':[Joe's height - D']≠0
                      the largest interval some distance below Joe's height

whole clause: the largest interval some distance below Joe's height is an interval into which exactly 5 people's height falls.

Note that the quantifiers *everyone else* and *exactly 5 people* are not given wide scope over the comparison at all under this analysis. The interval idea allows us to interpret them within the *than*-clause. While solving the puzzle of apparent wide scope operators, the analysis makes wrong predictions for apparently narrow scope quantifiers. The available reading cannot be accounted for.

(136) Caroline is taller than anyone else is.

(137) a. Caroline's height > max(λd. ∃x[x≠Caroline & x is d-tall])
 b. #the largest interval some distance below Caroline's height is an interval into which someone else's height falls.
 = Someone is shorter than Caroline.

Heim (2006) therefore adopts the interval analysis, but combines it with a scope mechanism that derives ultimately a wide and a narrow scope reading of a quantifier relative to a comparison. I will give a summary of her analysis here.

Let us begin with apparent wide scope of quantifier data, like (138). Heim's LF for the sentence is given in (139). She employs an operator Pi (Point to Interval, credited to Schwarzschild 2004). Compositional interpretation (somewhat simplified for the matrix clause) is given in (141).

(138) John is taller than every girl is.

(139) [IP [CP than [1[every girl [2[[Pi t1] [3[t2 is t3 tall]]]]]]
 [IP 4 [[-er t4] [5[John is t5 tall]]]]

(140) [[Pi]] = λD.λP.max(P)∈D

(141) [[[4[[-er t4] [5[John is t5 tall]]]]] = λd. John is taller than d
 [[[3[t2 is t3 tall]]]] = λd.x is d-tall
 [[[2[[Pi t1] [3[t2 is t3 tall]]]]] = λx.[λD.λP.max(P)∈D](D')(λd.x is d-tall)
 = λx. max(λd.x is d-tall)∈D'
 = λx. Height(x) ∈D'
 [[[than [1[every girl [2[[Pi t1] [3[t2 is t3 tall]]]]]]]] =
 λD'.∀x[girl(x) → Height(x)∈D']
 intervals into which the height of every girl falls

[[(138)]] =
λD′.∀x[girl(x) → Height(x) ∈D′] (λd. John is taller than d) =
∀x[girl(x) → Height(x) ∈(λd. John is taller than d)] =
∀x[girl(x) → John is taller than x]

The *than*-clause provides intervals into which the height of every girl falls. The whole sentence says that the degrees exceeded by John's height is such an interval. Lambda conversion simplifies the whole to the claim intuitively made, that every girl is shorter than John.

The analysis is a way of interpreting the quantifier inside the *than*-clause and deriving the apparently wide scope reading over comparison by giving the quantifier scope over the shift from degrees to intervals (the Pi operator). This strategy is applicable to other kinds of quantificational elements, such as intensional verbs, in the same way. A differential makes no difference to the derivation, as is demonstrated below.

(142) John is 2″ taller than every girl is.

(143) [[[than [1[every girl [2[[Pi t1] [3[t2 is t3 tall]]]]]]] =
λD′. ∀x[girl(x) → max(λd.x is d-tall) ∈D′]
intervals into which the height of every girl falls
[[(142)]] = [λD′.∀x[girl(x) → max(λd.x is d-tall) ∈D′]] (λd. John is 2″ taller than d)
= ∀x[girl(x) → John is 2″ taller than x]

(144) a. John is taller than I had predicted (that he would be).
b. ∀w[R(w,@) → max(λd.John is d-tall in @)>max(λd.John is d-tall in w)]
For every world compatible with my predictions:
John's actual height exceeds John's height in that world.

(145) [IP   [CP than [1[I had predicted [CP [Pi t1] [2[AP John t2 tall]]]]]
       [IP 3   [John is taller than t3]]]

(146) [[[3[John is taller than t3]]]] = (λd.John is taller than d in @)
[[[2[$_{AP}$ John t2 tall]]]] = λd. John is d-tall in w
[[[CP [Pi t1] [2[$_{AP}$ John t2 tall]]]]] = λw. max(λd. John is d-tall in w) ∈ D′
[[[than [1[I had predicted [$_{CP}$ [Pi t1] [2[AP John t2 tall]]]]]]] =
    [λD′. ∀w[R(w,@) → max(λd. John is d-tall in w) ∈D′]]
    intervals into which John's height falls in all my predictions
[[(144a)]] = [λD′. ∀w[R(w,@) → max(λd. John is d-tall in w) ∈D′]]
    (λd.J is taller than d in @) =

for every w compatible with my predictions:
J's actual height exceeds J's height in w.

(147) Pi shifts from properties of degrees to properties of intervals:
$\lambda d.\text{Height}(x) \geq d$ ==> $\lambda D.\text{Height}(x) \in D$

In contrast to Schwarzschild & Wilkinson's original interval analysis, Heim is able to derive apparently narrow scope readings of an operator relative to the comparison as well. The sentence in (148) is associated with the LF in (149). Note that here the shifter takes scope over the operator *required*. This makes *required* combine with the degree semantics in the original, desired way, giving us the minimum compliance length (just like it did before, without the intervals). The shift with Pi is essentially harmless.

(148) a. The paper is longer than is required.
 b. The paper's length > max($\lambda d.\forall w[R(w,@) \rightarrow$ the paper is d-long in w'])
 The length of the paper exceeds the required minimum.

(149) [IP   [CP   than   [1[[[Pi t1] [2[required [the paper t2 long]]]]]
           [IP   3   [the paper is longer than t3]]]

(150) [[[3[the paper is longer than t3]]]]] = ($\lambda d.$the paper is longer than d in @)
 [[[2[required [the paper t2 long]]]] =
  ($\lambda d.\ \forall w[R(w,@) \rightarrow$ the paper is d-long in w])
 [[[than [1[[[Pi t1] [2[required [the paper t2 long]]]]]]] =
 [$\lambda D'.$ max($\lambda d.\ \forall w[R(w,@) \rightarrow$ the paper is d-long in w]) $\in D'$]
 intervals into which the required minimum falls
 [[(148a)]] =
 [$\lambda D'.$ max($\lambda d.\ \forall w[R(w,@) \rightarrow$ paper is d-long in w]) $\in D'$]
  ($\lambda d.$the paper is longer than d in @) =
 The paper is longer than the required minimum.

Pi-phrase scope interaction is summarized below:

(151) Pi takes narrow scope relative to quantifier.
 ==> apparent wide scope reading of quantifier over comparison.
 Pi takes wide scope relative to quantifier.
 ==> apparent narrow scope reading of quantifier relative to comparison.

The idea behind this analysis, to sum up, is that *than*-clauses include a shift from degrees to intervals, which allows us to give one denotation for the *than*-clause with the quantifier on both types of readings. The shift itself can take narrow or wide scope relative to a *than*-clause quantifier. The shift amounts to a form of type raising. Through semantic reconstruction, the matrix clause is interpreted in the scope of a *than*-clause operator when that operator has scope over the shifter. Comparison is ultimately between points/degrees, not intervals.

Heim's analysis is able to derive both wide and narrow scope readings of operators in *than*-clauses. It does so without violating syntactic constraints. There is, however, an unresolved question: when do we get which reading? How could one constrain Pi-phrase/operator interaction in the desired way? One place where this problem surfaces is once more negation, where we expect an LF that would generate an acceptable wide scope of negation reading—e.g. (152b) for (152a). The reading predicted, derived in (153), is not available.

(152) a. *John is taller than no girl is.
     b. [IP   [CP   than   [1[no girl [2[[Pi t1] [3[t2 is t3 tall]]]]]
              [IP   4   [[-er t4] [5[John is t5 tall]]]]

(153) [[[4[[-er t4] [5[John is t5 tall]]]]] = λd. John is taller than d
      [[[than [1[no girl [2[[Pi t1] [3[t2 is t3 tall]]]]]]]] =
          λD'. for no girl x: max(λd.x is d-tall) ∈D'
          intervals into which the height of no girl falls
      [[(152)]] = [λD'. for no girl x: max(λd.x is d-tall) ∈D'] (λd. John is taller than d)
          = for no girl x: John is taller than x

The interval idea brings a substantial new feature to the analysis of comparison. It seems well motivated by the quantifer data. But one must ask whether a genuine scope analysis of the shift to intervals is what is needed.

Two recent lines of research take Heim (2006) as their point of departure. The first, represented by Gajewski (2008), Schwarzschild (2008), and loosely speaking also van Rooij (2008), maintains that there is a scope bearing element in the *than*-clause whose position relative to a quantifier determines which reading we get. But the semantics of comparison is changed back to a Seuren-type semantics (Seuren 1978), so that the scope bearing element is not Pi, but negation. An example analysis is given below. Like Pi, negation needs to be able to take flexible scope (to distinguish e.g. the reading that *required* as opposed to *every girl* gives rise to), and so this type of analysis runs into the same overgeneration problem as the Pi analysis. See Beck (2010) for discussion.

(138) John is taller than every girl is.

(138') a. $\exists d[\text{Height}(J) \geq d \ \& \ \forall x[\text{girl}(x) \rightarrow \text{Height}(x) < d]]$
'every girl is shorter than John.'
b. [[than every girl is]] =
[[than λd [every girl [1[NOT [t1 is d tall]]]]]] =
than $\lambda d. \forall x[\text{girl}(x) \rightarrow \text{Height}(x) < d]]$

The second line of research rejects a scope interaction view of the readings that quantifiers in *than*-clauses give rise to. I summarize its main features in the next subsection.

3.1.4 A selection analysis

The problem diagnosed above regarding an analysis in terms of the scope of the Pi operator concerns the fact that we do not observe a genuine scope ambiguity. Which reading we get depends on which quantifier interacts with the comparison operator; it seems fixed in each case. An alternative account not based on scope would not face this problem of overgeneration, provided we can find an alternative analysis. One possibility, sketched below, takes the following perspective: The quantifiers show us that we must use intervals in the semantic composition. Comparison is ultimately between points, i.e. degrees. We maintain the simple semantics for the comparative operator repeated below:

(154) comparative morpheme of type <d,<d,t>>:
 $[[\text{-er}_{\text{simple}}]] = \lambda d. \lambda d'. d' > d$

Therefore we must have a strategy to reduce the interval back to a point— the selection of a particular point from the interval. This idea may be behind Schwarzschild & Wilkinson's proposal originally, although it is not what they end up doing. I illustrate it here with a strategy from Beck (2010).

3.1.4.1 Selection of point from interval: Unproblematic cases

Let us suppose that it is in principle possible to relate individuals and sets of degrees - 'intervals' by an adjective meaning (see Beck 2010 for a suggestion of how this may come about). In the example in (155), this would give rise to the meaning for the *than*-clause in (155') - a set of intervals, just like in the Heim (2006) analysis. In many examples, it suffices to simply choose the end point of the interval denoted by the *than*-clause for comparison with the main clause. The strategy is to find the shortest (minimal) *than*-clause interval(s) and choose from it the end point (maximum) on the relevant scale. The end point will be the item of comparison. This is demonstrated below for universal and existential quantifiers.

(155) a. John is taller than every girl is.
b. For every girl x: John's height exceeds x's height.

(155') a. [[[than [1[every girl [2[t2 is t1 tall]]]]]]] =
$\lambda D'. \forall x[girl(x) \to max(\lambda d.x \text{ is d-tall}) \in D']$
intervals into which the height of every girl falls
b. tall: Height(x)∈D

(156) choosing the smallest such interval(s):
$min(S<<d,t>,t>) = \lambda D.S(D) \& \sim\exists D'[D' \subset D \& S(D')]$

(157) identifying the end point:
a. ordering of intervals: $I>J$ iff $\exists d[d \in I \& \forall d'[d' \in J \to d>d']]$
I extends beyond J
b. $max(S<<d,t>,t>)$ = the max relative to the ≥ relation on intervals
= the interval that extends highest on the scale
c. Max(S)   := max (max(S))
= the maximal degree in the interval that extends highest

(158) John is taller than Max (min ([[*than*-clause]])
= John is taller than the height of the tallest girl.

(159)   Max (min ([[*than*-clause]])
          min ([[*than*-clause]])
----------|-------------------------|------------------x-------------->
         x1   x2   x3   J

(160) a. John is taller than I had predicted (that he would be).
b. For every world compatible with my predictions:
John's actual height exceeds John's height in that world.

(161) [[[than [1[I had predicted [$_{CP}$ John t1 tall]]]]]]] =
[$\lambda D'. \forall w[R(w,@) \to$ John's height in w $\in D']$]
intervals into which John's height falls in all my predictions

(162) John is taller than Max (min ([[*than*-clause]]))
= John is taller than the height according to the tallest prediction.

(163) a. Caroline is taller than anyone else is.
b. C's height exceeds the largest degree of height reached by one of the others.

(164) [[[than [1[any one else [2[t2 is t1 tall]]]]]]] =
λD'. ∃x[x≠Caroline & max(λd.x is d-tall)∈ D']
intervals into which the height of someone other than Caroline falls

(165) Caroline is taller than Max (min ([[*than*-clause]]))
= Caroline is taller than the height of the tallest other person.

(166)
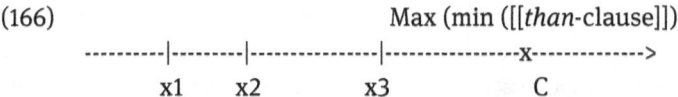
```
----------|---------|----------------|-----------------x-------------->
      x1      x2          x3                  C
```

Note that there is no scope interaction between Pi and the quantifier according to this strategy: with the NPI example as well as with the universal NP, the shift to intervals occurs locally within the AP, i.e. it always 'takes narrow scope'.

A problem this strategy appears to face concerns *have to/require*, (167a). Remember that these intensional verbs give rise to a different interpretation than the *predict* - type, treated above, namely (167b). But their LF would be parallel, (168). It looks as if we have to choose the beginning point of the minimal *than*-clause interval instead of the end point (cf. (169)). We would have to ask ourselves why the strategy for point selection changes.

(167) a. The paper is longer than is required.
b. The paper's length > max(λd.∀w[R(w,@) → the paper is d-long in w'])
= The length of the paper exceeds the required minimum.

(168) [[[CP   than [1[[required [XP the paper t1 long]]]]]]] =
[λD'. ∀w[R(w,@) → the paper's length in w ∈ D']
intervals into which the paper's length falls in all worlds compatible with the rules

(169) The paper is longer than Max$_<$ (min ([[*than*-clause]]))
(where < is the "smaller than" ordering of points and intervals on the height scale)
= the paper is longer than the minimum compatible with the requirements

However, Krasikova (2008) provides a solution to this problem. She proposes that a strengthening operation reduces the *than*-clause interval to a point internally—

exhaustification from Fox (2006), which I represent here as a covert scalar 'only' (cf. (170)). This strengthening operation is not available with other universal quantifiers, thus accounting for the difference between *require* and *predict*.

(170) [[[CP   than [1[[onlyC,< required [XP the paper t1 long]]]]]]]
= [λD'. it is onlyC,< required that the paper's length fall within D']

Suppose that the domain of quantification of *only* is as in (171a), propositions that vary in the place of the interval containing the paper's length. Suppose furthermore that the scale that *only* is sensitive to in this case amounts to a difficulty scale. A typical context for our example is one in which the difficulty is in reaching a certain length; that is, the problem is with reaching a certain length. Then the meaning of the *than*-clause described in (171b) will give us intervals containing the minimum requirement length. The shortest such interval is the minimum requirement length itself. Selection with Max is trivial, and we get the correct truth conditions in (172).

(171) a. C={that the paper's length fall in D1, that the paper's length fall in D2, ..., that the paper's length fall within Dn}
b. [λD'. it is onlyC,< required that the paper's length fall within D'] =
[λD'. for all p∈C such that the paper's length falls within D' $<_{difficult}$ p: it is not required that p] =
[λD'. nothing more difficult is required than that the paper's length fall within D']
c. If D1>D2>...>Dn:
min([λD'. it is onlyC,< required that the paper's length fall within D']) = min([λD'. nothing more difficult is required than that the paper's length fall in D'])
= {Dn}
= {the minimum compliance length}

(172) The paper is longer than Max. ({Dn})
= the paper is longer than the minimum compatible with the requirements.

The plot is thus to blame semantic properties of the specific modals that give rise to this reading for their difference from other universal quantifiers; see Krasikova (2008) and also Beck (2010) for details.

Note that the negation facts follow straightforwardly from the selection strategy. The only LF of (173a) is (173b), which leads to an undefined interpretation as before, cf. (174).

(173) a. *John is taller than no girl is.
   b. [IP   [CP   than   [1[no girl [2[t2 is t1 tall]]]]]
          [IP   4[[-er t4] [5[John is t5 tall]]]]

(174) [[[4[[-er t4] [5[John is t5 tall]]]]] = λd. John is taller than d
   [[[than [1[no girl [2[t2 is t1 tall]]]]]]] =
   λD'. for no girl x: max(λd.x is d-tall) ∈D'
   intervals into which the height of no girl falls
   Max is undefined ==> negation in the *than*-clause leads to undefinedness

Here is a summary of our easy preliminary success: We keep the idea of a shift to intervals, but the shift always occurs locally. The resulting meaning of the *than*-clause, a set of intervals, is reduced to a degree by selection of the relevant maximum element. Ungrammaticality of the negation data is predicted. So is lack of ambiguity, since selection always yields one unambiguously determined comparison. The difference between *predict*-type verbs and *required*-type verbs is traced to independent factors (unrelated to scope). For the comparative itself, a classical analysis is maintained.

3.1.4.2 More problematic data

Schwarzschild & Wilkinson's semantics is rather more complicated than the simple-minded approach described above, and for good reason. They take into account two types of data that are especially problematic: differentials and numeral NP quantifiers. We will consider both in turn. Below is an example that combines a universal quantifier in the *than*-clause with a differential comparative. We have already observed that the sentence claims that the girls all have the same height, which is 2" below John's.

(175) John is (exactly) 2" taller than every girl is.

Compared to Heim and Schwarzschild & Wilkinson, we have a problem. They predict the correct interpretation (177) (illustrated below for Heim's analysis) while we predict (178).

(176) [[[than [1[every girl [2[[Pi t1] [3[t2 is t3 tall]]]]]]]] =
   λD'. ∀x[girl(x) → max(λd.x is d-tall) ∈D']
   intervals into which the height of every girl falls

(177) [[(175)]] = [λD'.∀x[girl(x) → max(λd.x is d-tall) ∈D']](λd. John is 2" taller than d)
   = ∀x[girl(x) → John is 2" taller than x]

(178) John is 2″ taller than Max (min([[*than*-clause]]))
= John is 2″ taller than the tallest girl.

It looks as if universal NPs in *than*-clauses, when combined with difference degrees, led to an assumption that the *than*-clause interval is actually a point, i.e. that the girls all have the same height in the example. I will call this an equality assumption, EQ. This seems to speak in favour of a scope solution. However, consider the example below, which is formally parallel. The sentence can be used to describe the situation depicted, where my colleagues' incomes cover a wide span. We compare with the beginning point of the interval. This is exactly what the selection strategy leads us to expect (the beginning point being the maximum relative to the 'less' relation). (180) and (181) are further examples taken from the web.

(179) Ich verdiene ziemlich genau 500 Euro weniger als alle meine Kollegen.
I make just about 500 Euros less than everyone else in my department.
(Some even earn 1000 Euros more than I do.)
```
-----------------SB---------| /////////////////////////\------------------------>
                |- 500----|---    1100    -------|
```

(180) Aden had the camera for 100 $ less than everyone else in town was charging.

(181) WOW! almost 4 seconds faster than everyone else, and a 9 second gap on Lance.

Note that while data like (175) are a problem for the selection strategy (in that I haven't specified how to derive the additional EQ meaning component), the data above are a problem for the scope strategy (in that the predicted equality interpretation is clearly not what is intended). I refer the reader to Beck (2010) for an analysis of these data, in particular the contrast between (175) and (179)–(181). There I argue that the data ultimately speak in favour of selection. For present purposes, it seems enough to note that (179)–(181) make selection a viable alternative.

Finally, we consider a last problematic case, which has so far been unreconcilable with the simple minded selection strategy, namely numeral NPs. An example is given in (182), together with an illustration of how the selection strategy makes the wrong prediction.

(182) John is taller than exactly five of his classmates are.
= exactly 5 of John's classmates are shorter than he is.
≠ John is taller than the tallest of his 5 or more classmates.

(183) λD'. for exactly 5 x: max(λd.x is d-tall) ∈D'
intervals into which the height of exactly 5 classmates falls
Max (min([λD'. for exactly 5 x: max(λd.x is d-tall) ∈D'])) =
the height of John's tallest classmate, as long as there are at least 5

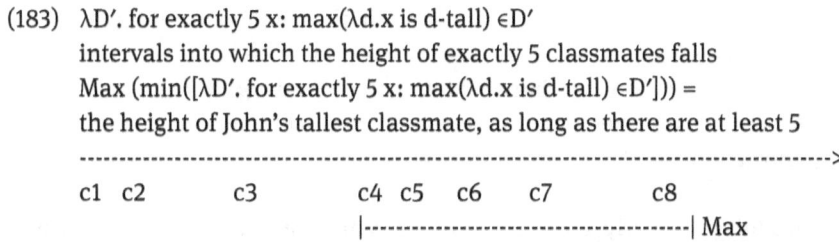

It is possible to avoid this problem. Let us first be more precise in our semantic analysis of 'exactly 5' (compare Hackl 2000, 2009; Krifka 1999 on the semantics of such NPs). A simple example is discussed in (184); '*' is Link's star operator which pluralizes predicates.

(184) a. Exactly three girls weigh 50lbs.
b. max(λn . ∃X[*girl(X) & card(X)=n & *weigh_50lbs(X)])=3
'the largest number of girls each of which weighs 50 lbs is three.'

If we accordingly give the *than*-clause in (182) the semantics in (183'), nothing changes: we still compare with the tallest of at least five classmates. What we have achieved is simply to make the composition of 'exactly five classmates' more transparent. It consists of an indefinite plural plus a quantificational 'exactly' binding a cardinality variable.

(183') λD'.max(λn.∃X[*classmate(X) & card(X)=n & *Height(X) ∈D'])=5
Intervals into which the height of exactly five of John's classmantes falls
(≈(183))

The reading we want to derive is one in which both of these meaning components appear to be interpreted with wide scope outside the *than*-clause. It is not actually surprising that an indefinite should appear to be able to scope outside the *than*-clause: we know that indefinites can take exceptionally wide scope, and whatever mechanisms bring this about ordinarily can do so in comparatives as well. I choose to demonstrate this point with a choice function analysis of (185) (compare e.g. Reinhart 1997, Kratzer 1998).

(186) a. Mr Bingley is richer than some of his neighbours are.
b. There are some neighbours of Mr Bingley's that are poorer than he is.

(186') [[[than [1[[some of his7 neighbours] [*[2[t2 be t1 rich]]]]]]] =
[λD'. f(*neighbour_of_B)∈[*λx.Wealth(x)∈D']]

intervals into which the wealth of each of the neighbours of Bingley's chosen by f falls
∃f[Mr Bingley is richer than Max(min([[*than*-clause]])) =
Mr Bingley is richer than the richest of the neighbours chosen by some choice function f

Now if in addition 'exactly' is evaluated in the matrix clause, we derive the desired interpretation for (182), as demonstrated in (186).

(186) [[[than [1[[n of his7 classmates] [*[2[t2 be t1 tall]]]]]]]] =
[λD'. f(λX.card(X)=n & *classmate(X)) ∈ [*λx.Height(x) ∈D']]
intervals into which the height of each of the n classmates picked by f falls
max(λn. ∃f[John is taller than Max (min ([[*than*-clause]])))=5
'the largest number n such that John is taller than the tallest of the n classmates of his chosen by some choice function f is 5.'

(186') [exactly 5 [λn. John is taller [than[n of his classmates are ~~tall~~]]]]

This means that we can interpret the nominal quantifier in the *than*-clause, but have to evaluate the contribution of 'exactly' in the matrix. This would suggest an LF like (186'), which may still seem unsatisfactory (how does 'exactly n' end up where it occurs in (186')?). However, we follow Krifka's (1999) arguments that expressions like 'exactly', 'at least' and 'at most' are interpreted via an alternative semantics. The evaluating operator, moreover, is not the word 'exactly' itself, but a higher proposition level operator, called EXACT here. A more proper LF representing a version of Krifka's analysis for example (184) is given below. The semantics of EXACT uses alternatives to the asserted proposition (which vary according to the numeral), as well as the asserted numeral (5 in the example).

(184') a. Exactly three girls weigh 50lbs.
b. [EXACT [XP (exactly) three$_F$ girls weigh 50lbs]]

(184") [[three$_F$ girls weigh 50lbs]]$_O$ = ∃X[*girl(X) & card(X)=3 & *weigh_50lbs(X)]
[[three$_F$ girls weigh 50lbs]]$_F$ =
{∃X[*girl(X) & card(X)=n & *weigh_50lbs(X)]:n∈N}

(187) [[EXACT]] ([[XP]]$_f$) ([[XP]]$_O$) = 1
iff [[XP]]$_O$ =1 & ∀q ∈ [[XP]]$_F$: ~([[XP]]$_O$->q) -> ~q
'Out of all the alternatives of XP, the most informative true one is the ordinary semantics of XP.'

(184''') [[(184'b)]] =1 iff
∃X[*girl(X) & card(X)=3 & *weigh_50lbs(X)] &
∀n[n>3 -> ~∃X[*girl(X) & card(X)=n & *weigh_50lbs(X)]] iff
max(λn.∃X[*girl(X) & card(X)=n & *weigh_50lbs(X)])=3

We are now in a position to provide an LF for example (182) that derives the desired interpretation, (188); the truth conditions are made explicit in (188').

(188) a. [EXACT [John is taller
        [than Max min [(exactly) n_f of his classmates are ~~tall~~]]]]
    b. Out of all the alternatives 'John is taller than n of his classmates are', the most informative true one is 'John is taller than 5 of his classmates are'.

(188') max(λn. ∃f[CH(f) & John is taller than
        Max(min (λD'. ∀x∈f((λX.*classmate(X) & card(X)=n):Height(x) ∈D'])=5
        'the largest number n such that John is taller than the tallest of the
        n classmates of his selected by some choice function f is 5.'

Thus I suggest that a proper semantic analysis of numeral NPs makes the facts compatible with a simple selection analysis of *than*-clauses after all. No scope strategies specific to comparatives need to be employed; the mechanisms we have used have been argued for independently, and the complications they bring with them are orthogonal to comparative semantics. What has not been demonstrated here is that the above proposals account precisely for the range of readings that the various quantifiers in *than*-clauses give rise to. This must be left for another occasion (compare Beck 2010 for more discussion).

The interval+selection approach seems rather successful. It captures the negation data, lack of genuine scope interaction, it is reconcilable with numeral NP facts under the right assumptions about their semantics, and even differentials have shown us that scope cannot be the whole story. I propose to enrich the standard theory with intervals, but in the actual comparison to reduce the interval back to a point with a selection strategy, and compare degrees as before. The simple lexical entry for the comparative morpheme in (189) provides the required semantics.

(189) [[-er$_{simple}$]] = λd.λd'.d'>d

Compared to von Stechow's (1984) original proposals, the addition of the shift to an interval meaning for adjectives/APs makes a genuine difference. Another change concerns the way that maximality enters into semantic composition.

It is not part of the semantics of the comparative here, but rather an interpretational strategy operating on the *than*-clause independently. This, however, seems very minor.

3.1.5 Subsection summary

This subsection has taken a closer look at the interaction of comparison operators with other quantifiers. Following work by Schwarzschild & Wilkinson and Heim, I have departed from von Stechow's original analysis by incorporating intervals of degrees into the semantics of comparison. This makes it possible to interpret the quantifier uniformly inside the *than*-clause, i.e. it takes narrow scope relative to the comparison. Furthermore, in contrast to Heim and her successors, I propose that despite appearances, there is no scope interaction between quantifier and shifter. Instead, there is uniformly selection of a point from the subordinate clause interval. Apparent scope effects like the interpretation of *have to*-type modals and *exactly n* NPs have been explained away via recourse to alternative interpretational strategies, which have been argued for independently of *than*-clauses. My perspective is motivated by the lack of clear scope interaction in *than*-clauses. This is in line with what we would expect from the point of view of syntactic theory, where a quantifier inside an embedded clause would not normally interact with a matrix clause operator.

By contrast, we might expect a comparison operator to interact with a clausemate quantifier, and hence expect scope interaction with another matrix clause operator. The empirical picture that we find is such that comparative operators tend to take narrow scope, and can only outscope a limited set of other quantifiers. Heim's (2001) interpretation of this state of affairs, which we follow here, is that an independent constraint prevents comparison operators from taking scope over quantifiers in most cases, but that the crucial data in which a comparison operator does outscope another quantifier support the quantificational analysis of comparison operators by the standard theory.

3.2 Crosslinguistic variation in the expression of comparison

The question addressed in this subsection is essentially how general the proposed theory of comparison is. The theory was developed largely on the basis of comparison constructions in English. We will now examine other languages, taking as our starting point the observation from section 2 that the behaviour of measure phrases is not entirely expected from our theoretical point of view.

3.2.1 Measure phrases

Schwarzschild (2005) observes that a measure phrase addition to an adjective in the unmarked form is not so widely acceptable as one might suppose from the semantics introduced in section 2. In English, many adjectives do not permit MPs (let us refer here with MP to the plain expression 'five inches', '10 degrees' without the quantifier part 'exactly', 'at least' etc.).

(190) a. *5 dollars expensive.
 b. *80 lbs heavy.
 c. *minus 5 degrees cold.

(191) $[[\text{heavy}]] = \lambda d.\lambda x.\text{Weight}(x) \geq d$

Under the standard analysis, we believe that MPs saturate an argument slot of adjectives; according to the version in section 2.2 they do not saturate the argument slot directly, but indirectly through quantifying over it. Either way this is a standard way of composition that should always be available. Why aren't measure additions to adjectives more systematically possible then?

Crosslinguistically, Schwarzschild notes, there is considerable variation regarding MPs. Languages seem to tend to allow MPs as the difference degree argument in comparatives, while sometimes not allowing them with unmarked adjectives (so called 'direct MPs') at all. Japanese, Russian, Spanish are like that; (192) is an example from Japanese. When languages allow direct MPs, there is still variation with respect to lexical items, cf. the difference in (193a) between German and English, both of which do allow direct MPs. To our question above about English MPs we must add the question why languages vary so much with respect to the possibility of direct MPs. And finally, Schwarzschild observes that (193b) is impossible, where we try to use 'John's weight' as an argument of the adjective. This is puzzling if we take 'John's weight', like '80 pounds', to denote a degree. (193c) illustrates that a difference MP is possible even where a direct MP is not in English.

(192) a. Sally-wa   5 cm   se-ga   takai.
       Sally-Top   5 cm   back-Nom   tall
       'Sally is 5cm taller/*Sally is 5cm tall.'
    b. Sally-wa   Joe-yori   5 cm   se-ga   takai.
       Sally-Top   Joe-YORI   5 cm   back-Nom   tall
       'Sally is 5cm taller than Joe.'

(193) a. 40 kg schwer [German]
 *80 lbs heavy [English]
 b. *Sally is John's weight heavy.
 c. Sally is 4 lbs heavier than Bill.

Schwarzschild proposes that MPs do not refer to a degree. They are true or false of intervals, i.e. sets of degrees, cf. (194). MPs are thus of type <<d,t>,t> (i.e. plain MPs already are quantifiers), and it is not expected that they be able to combine directly with an adjective of type <d<e,t>>. Schwarzschild proposes that there is a lexical rule that shifts adjectives from expressions with a degree argument position to expressions with an interval argument position. We can then combine intersectively with the MP (although a short movement is still needed to resolve the type mismatch, under the standard assumptions about composition adopted here). The result in (196) can then be existentially closed as in (197).

(194) a. [[two inches]] = $\lambda D<d,t>$. D can be partitioned into a two-membered set of whose elements the predicate 'inch' is true.
 b. A set X is a partition of a set Y iff
  (i) for all $Z \in X$: $Z \subseteq Y$
  (ii) $\cup X = Y$
  (iii) For any two $Z1, Z2 \in X$: $Z1 \cap Z2 = \{\}$

(195) [[long2]] = [$\lambda D<d,t>$. λx. $D = \lambda d.$[[long1]](d)(x)]

(196) [<<d,t>,t> two inches] [<<d,t>,t> 1[this pen is t1 long2]] =
 $\lambda D_{<d,t>}$. $D = \lambda d.$[[long1]](d)(this_pen)] & D can be partitioned into 2 inches =
 $\lambda D_{<d,t>}$. $D = [\lambda d.$this pen is d-long] & D can be partitioned into 2 inches

(197) $\exists D[D = [\lambda d.$this pen is d-long] & D can be partitioned into 2 inches]

Schwarzschild proposes that a particular adjective may or may not be able to undergo the relevant type shifting rule, thus allowing him to describe the variation within a language like English. Also, a language may lack this type shifting altogether and not permit direct measure phrases. It is a property of the comparative, however, that it may measure the difference between the two degrees described, thus differential measure phrases are generally possible. We can capture this insight of Schwarzschild's with a slight modification of the meaning of the comparative morpheme we proposed earlier:

(198) a. differential comparative (classical version with interval differential):
 $[[\text{-er}_{diff}]] = \lambda D1.\lambda D_{diff}.\lambda D2.D_{diff}(\max(D2)-\max(D1))$
 b. differential comparative (version section 3.1 with interval differential):
 $[[\text{-er}_{diff}]] = \lambda d.\lambda D_{diff}.\lambda d'.D_{diff}(d'-d)$
 'The difference between max Matrix and max *than*-clause is D_{diff}.'

An MP like 'two inches' can combine with the differential comparative directly, but not with an unmarked adjective.

I feel convinced by Schwarzschild's reasoning that 'two inches' and the like do not refer to a degree. In the theoretical framework of this article, a slightly different version of his proposals suggests itself. One could QR the MP, as in von Stechow's approach above, to make them combine with the rest of the clause.

(199) a. This pen is two inches long.
 b. [two inches <<d,t>,t>] [<d,t>1[this pen is t1 long]]
 c. $[[\text{long}]] = \lambda d.\lambda x.\text{Length}(x) \geq d$

(200) [$\lambda d.$ Length(this_pen) $\geq d$] can be partitioned into a two-membered set of whose elements the predicate 'inch' is true.
 'The degrees of length reached by this pen can be partitioned into two inch-long intervals.'

With regard to the English facts, it seems to me that nothing is gained by the type shift (195) compared to the Stechow-like analysis (199), together with the lexical stipulation that a given adjective can vs. cannot take a specifier that would host the measure phrase. Note that the type shifting of the adjective is practically vacuous. I would also like to point out the contrast between degree questions like (201a) and pronominals (201b) versus measure constructions like (201c), which I think is quite systematic.

(201) a. How cold is it?
 b. Today's temperature is minus 5 degrees.
  When I was in New Hampshire, it was that cold, too.
 c. *minus 5 degrees cold

The question word *how* should range over the same type of object that is the denotation of the MP; even more transparently pronominal *that* picks up the meaning of 'minus 5 degrees'. Thus whatever excludes the MP must be something very superficial that does not exclude the question or the degree pronoun. I don't really see how the type shift could make the distinction and would lean towards a syntactic explanation. I therefore tentatively endorse the analysis (199), (200). This can be combined with Krifka's theory of 'exactly', 'at least' and 'at most' from the previous subsection to derive the data discussed in section 2.2 ('at most 6′ tall' and the like). I am not sure what to say about the interesting observation in (193b). If 'John's weight' indeed refers to a degree, this is a very puzzling fact. Moltmann (2005) would not analyse it as such, however, but as a particularized property (let's say in the present framework not an expression of type <d> but one of type <e>)—which could well be unsuitable for combination with an adjective.

In the next subsections, we will try to connect the crosslinguistic variation observed here with other points of crosslinguistic variation in the expression of comparison. We will have something more to say about the crosslinguistic observations on MPs that Schwarzschild makes.

3.2.2 Parameters of variation in the expression of comparison

There is considerable crosslinguistic variation in how comparisons are expressed. This is best understood in the case of comparatives. The seminal typological work here is Stassen (1985). He observes that there are languages that appear to use different strategies altogether from the English comparatives we have seen. Two such types of comparison are given in (202) and (203); (202) exemplifies Stassen's 'exceed' strategy and (203) exemplifies the conjunctive strategy (Stassen identifies three more types of comparison which differ according to the interpretation of the counterpart of *than*; they will not concern us here.).

(202) *exceed-Strategy* (Stassen 1985):
Naja   ga   mdia   -da   de   dzegam-kur.   [Margi]
he   Subj   exceed -me   with   tall-Abstr.Noun
He is taller than me / he exceeds me in height.

(203) *conjunctive Strategy* (Villalta 2007):
Mary na   lata   to   Frank na   kwadogi.   [Motu]
Mary   tall   but   Frank   short
'Mary is taller than Frank.'

Beck et al. (2009) (referred to in the following as B17, after the joint DFG-funded project that supported the work reported there) have conducted a systematic investigation into crosslinguistic variation in comparative constructions, which is theoretically guided by the theory introduced in this article. They propose that there are clusters of empirical properties that identify the settings of grammatical parameters; three such parameters are suggested. I summarize their main results below.

3.2.2.1 Degree semantics

The basis of the grammar of comparison in English is the degree ontology used in the semantics. Adjectives (more precisely, gradable predicates) have an argument position for degrees. Those argument positions must be saturated in the syntax. Degree operators have a semantics that does that, indirectly, through quantifying over degrees. In order to determine whether the language under investigation is like English in this respect, B17 evaluate the comparison data from that language with respect to:

(i) whether the language has a family of expressions that plausibly manipulate degree arguments: comparative, superlative, equative morphemes, items parallel to *too*, *enough* and *so that*.
(ii) whether the language has expressions that plausibly refer to degrees and combine with degree operators: comparison with a degree (CompDeg) like (108b) in section 2, difference comparative (DiffC) like (129a) in section 2.

Motu, B17's representative of a conjunctive language, gives a clear negative answer to both of these questions. Other types of data that would be indicative of a degree semantics, like measure phrases or degree questions, are unavailable as well. Thus we see no evidence for an underlying degree semantics, and B17 accordingly speculate that there is the following parameter of language variation:

(204) Degree Semantics Parameter (DSP):
A language {does/does not} have gradable predicates (type <d,<e,t>> and related), i.e. lexical items that introduce degree arguments.

The DSP is a point of systematic variation in the lexicon (similar in spirit to proposals in Chierchia 1998 regarding crosslinguistic variation in nominal semantics). Motu would, of course, have the negative setting [−DSP]. This leaves us with the task of finding a semantic analysis for Motu adjectives. They occur only in one form, which seems similar to the English positive form in its context dependency. Our task is, thus, to come up with an adjective meaning for Motu adjectives that is similar to the English positive form, but does not introduce a type <d> argument (cf. the negative DSP setting hypothesised above). Context dependency, i.e. apparent vagueness, can come in through different means than the English positive, though. Vague predicates in whose semantics degrees and a positive operator are unlikely to be involved are the English examples (205) with *success* and, even more clearly, *behind the sofa*, as pointed out by B17 (I discuss *success* in the following for simplicity).

(205) a. The meeting was a success.
   b. The meeting was, to some extent, a success.
   c. The picture is behind the sofa.
   d. The picture is roughly/in a sense behind the sofa.

An analysis of *success* in terms of context dependency could look as in (206′). This follows Klein's (1980) analysis of the English positive, which B17 do not adopt for English positive adjectives, but find plausible for other examples of context dependency like this one.

(205′) [[success]] = λc.λx.x counts as a success in c   (c a context)

B17's suggestion is that Motu adjectives have this kind of context dependent semantics. I.e. *tall*$_{Motu}$ ≠ *tall*$_{English}$, but *tall*$_{Motu}$ is similar to English *success*. The Motu example in (203) is analysed in (206).

(206) a. [[tall$_{Motu}$]] = [λc.λx.x counts as tall in c]
   b. [[short$_{Motu}$]] = [λc.λx.x counts as short in c]
      [[short$_{Motu}$]]^c must be a subset of [λx. x does not count as tall in c]
   c. [[Mary na lata, to Frank na kwadogi]]^c = 1 iff
      Mary counts as tall in c and Frank counts as short in c

The sentence is predicted to be true in the context it is uttered in as long as the context can be construed as ranking Mary and Frank on the height scale with Mary on the tall side and Frank on the short. The point is that Motu has no degree operators, not even the positive. Perhaps degrees and scales are a level of abstraction above context dependency that a language may or may not choose to develop.

3.2.2.2 Degree operators

A more subtle variation between English and Japanese is already observed in Beck, Oda & Sugisaki (2004). While Japanese (207) looks superficially similar to English (208a), several important empirical differences between the two languages lead Beck, Oda & Sugisaki to propose a different semantics, closer to that of English (208b,c).

(207) *Japanese* (Beck, Oda & Sugisaki):
   Sally-wa   Joe-yori   se-ga   takai.
   Sally-Top   Joe-YORI   back-Nom   tall

(208) a. Sally is taller than Joe.
　　　b. Compared to Joe, Sally is tall.
　　　c. Compared to Joe, Sally is taller.

In contrast to English, Japanese does not permit direct measure phrases (cf. section 3.2, datum repeated in (209) below), subcomparatives (cf. (210)), or degree questions (cf. (211)). Moreover, the negative island effect we observed in English comparatives does not arise; the example in (212) has a different, sensible interpretation, as the paraphrase indicates. Beck, Oda & Sugisaki also note that in contrast to English, a matrix clause modal verb in a Japanese comparison construction does not permit the wide scope reading of the comparative operator (example given in (213)). The acceptability of a differential comparative (209b), however, indicates that the semantics underlying the *yori*-construction is a degree semantics.

(209) a. Sally-wa　　5 cm　　se-ga　　　takai.
　　　　　Sally-Top　5 cm　　back-Nom　tall
　　　　　Sally is 5cm taller/*Sally is 5cm tall.
　　　b. Sally-wa　　Joe-yori　　5 cm　　se-ga　　　takai.
　　　　　Sally-Top　Joe-YORI　　5 cm　　back-Nom　tall
　　　　　Sally is 5cm taller than Joe.

(210) a. *Kono　　tana-wa　　　[ano　　doa-ga　　　hiroi　　yori　(mo)]
　　　　　this　　shelf-Top　　[that　door-Nom　　wide　　YORI　(mo)]
　　　　　(motto)　takai.
　　　　　(more)　 tall
　　　b. This shelf is taller than that door is wide.

(211) a. John-wa　　dore-kurai　　　　kasikoi　　no?
　　　　　John-Top　which degree　　smart　　　Q
　　　　　'To which degree is John smart?'
　　　b. How smart is John?

(212) a. John-wa　　　　[dare-mo　　kawa-naka-tta　no　　　yori]
　　　　　John-Top　　　anyone　　　buy-Neg-Past　NO　　　YORI
　　　　　takai　　　　 hon-o　　　　katta.
　　　　　expensive　　book-Acc　　bought
　　　　　'John bought a book more expensive than the book that nobody bought.'
　　　b. *John bought a more expensive book than nobody did.

(213) Sono   ronbun   wa   sore   yori(mo)   tyoodo   5_peeji
       that   paper   Top   that   YORI(MO)   exactly   5_page
       nagaku-nakerebanaranai.
       long-be_required
       'The paper is required to be exactly 5 pages longer than that.'

These basic facts as B17 would cluster them are summarized in (214):

(214) Japn: *subcomparative (SubC), *measure phrase (MP),
               *degree question (DegQ), NegI-Effect (NegIs) and Scope not like
               English but: Differential comparative (DiffC) ok!

Thus B17 take Japanese to have the positive setting of the DSP. Some other parameter must be responsible for the differences to English that we observe. B17 follow Beck, Oda & Sugisaki in suggesting that Japanese does not permit quantification over degree arguments. This is expressed in the following parameter:

(215) Degree Abstraction Parameter (DAP) (Beck, Oda & Sugisaki):
       A language {does/does not} have binding of degree variables in the syntax.

If there is no binding of degree variables, a language cannot have degree operators like the English comparative. This explains the properties Scope (for a degree operator to take wide scope, binding of degree variables is necessary), NegIs (since the *yori*-clause does not denote a set of degrees but a set of individuals, it is fine), DegQ (which again needs binding of degree variables, as seen above in section 2), SubC (comparing two sets of degrees requires degree variable binding) and MP (since measure constructions involve quantification over degrees). But of course once more we face the question of what the semantics of the normal comparison construction then is.

Beck, Oda & Sugisaki consider English *compared to* and Japanese *yori* to be context setters not compositionally integrated with the main clause. They provide us with an individual (type <e>) that is used to infer the intended comparison indirectly. Thus we would be concerned in (216) with a comparative adjective without an overt item of comparison, such as English (217a) (without context) or (217b) (where the intended context is given explicitly). I present Beck, Oda & Sugisaki's semantics for Japanese *kasikoi* in the version developed in Oda (2008) in (216'). The analysis implies that Japanese adjectives are inherently comparative and context dependent. Unlike in English, there is no separable comparative operator.

(216) Sally wa Joe yori kasikoi.
Sally Top Joe YORI smart
'Sally is smarter than Joe.'

(217) a. Mr Darcy is smarter.
b. Compared to Mr Bennet, Mr Darcy is smarter.

(216′) a. $[[\text{kasikoi c}]]^g = \lambda x.\max(\lambda d.\ x \text{ is d-smart}) > g(c)$
b. $[[\text{Sally wa kasikoi}]]^g = 1$ iff $\max(\lambda d.\ S \text{ is d-smart}) > g(c)$
c. c := the standard of intelligence made salient by comparison to Joe
:= Joe's degree of intelligence

Thus even when there is evidence that the language under investigation employs a degree semantics, it may still lack English-type quantifiers over degrees. For a given language and comparison construction, we need to ask whether the constituent seemingly corresponding to the English *than*-constituent is really a compositional item of comparison denoting degrees, and whether there is a genuine comparison operator. B17 suggest that the parameter setting [+DSP], [−DAP] is also exemplified by Mandarin Chinese, Samoan, and the *exceed*-type languages that they investigate, Moore and Yoruba. See also Oda (2008), Krasikova (2007) and Kennedy (2009) for more discussion of the DAP.

3.2.2.3 Degree phrase arguments

Another group of languages appears to be closer to English than Japanese, but still not completely parallel. Russian, Turkish and Guarani belong to this group and show the behaviour summarized in (218) (cf. the B17 paper).

(218) Russian, Turkish, Guarani: *SubC, *MP, *DegQ
but: DiffC ok, English-like NegIs- and Scope-Effects

I use Guarani data from Fleischer (2007) (documented in the B17 paper) to illustrate.

(219) Pe   arahaku   haku- ve   5 grado   che aimo'a- vãe'kuri gui
this   temperature warm- more 5 degrees I   think   past-m   than
'The temperature is 5 C° warmer than I thought.'

(220) *Maria   ojogua   petei   aranduka   hepy-   ve-
Maria   bought   a   book   expensive   more

         va   avave   nd- ojogua i-   vaekue- gui
         mode nobody not buy   neg past   than
         Maria bought a more expensive book than nobody.

(221)   Maria ojogua   va'era mbovy -ve   apytimby ka'ay Pedro -gui.
         Maria buy   must   little COMP   packet   tea   Pedro than
         Maria had to buy fewer packets of tea than Pedro.
         (ok: the minimal requirement imposed on Maria is lower than the minimal requirement imposed on Pedro.)

(222)   *Pe   juguatakuri potei ára   ipuku
         this   journey   past   six   days   long
         This journey was six days long.

(223)   *Mba'eita   itujá   Pedro
         How   old   Pedro
         How old is Pedro?

(224)   *Pe   mesa   i-   jyvate- ve   pe   oke   i-   pe-   gui.
         This   table   cop   high-   more   this   door   cop   wide   than
         This table is higher than this door is wide.

(219), (220) and (221) indicate that Guarani (like Russian and Turkish) has an English-like degree semantics for main clause and subordinate clause - i.e. has the parameter setting [+DSP], [+DAP]. But we must ask how the differences to English degree constructions (222)-(224) arise. B17 propose that the following parameter creates the cluster SubC, MP, DegQ:

(225)   Degree Phrase Parameter (DegPP):
         The degree argument position of a gradable predicate {may/may not} be overtly filled.

The degree argument position (SpecAP in the presentation in this article) is filled by the MP at the surface in measure constructions, and by overt or non-overt *how* in DegQ and SubC. The difference between SubC and ordinary comparatives can be tied to ellipsis, in that comparatives with ellipsis only have a filled SpecAP at the level of LF. Thus the languages with *DegQ, *SubC, *MP are identified by the parameter setting [–DegPP], while at the same time being [+DSP] and [+DAP].

A language like English would, according to B17's analysis, have the parameter setting [+DSP], [+DAP], [+DegPP]. Besides English, the properties identified by these settings are documented in German, Bulgarian, Hindi, Hungarian and Thai (cf. B17). It seems likely that there is some connection between the effects characterised with the DegPP here and the language internal restrictions on MPs observed in subsection 3.2; we need to investigate in more detail the circumstances under which the degree argument position of an adjective may be overtly filled (cf. the contrast in (201) above).

3.2.3 Subsection summary

The table below provides a summary of the predictions that B17's three parameters are designed to make (n/a means that the relevant data cannot be constructed—e.g. Scope, a judgement on wide scope degree operators, makes no sense in a language without degrees).

Tab. 13.1: Parametric Variation

	DiffC	NegIs	Scope	SubC	MP	DegQ	Language Ex.
−DSP	no	n/a	n/a	n/a	no	no	Motu
+DSP, −DAP	yes	no	no	no	no	no	Japanese
+DSP, +DAP, −DegPP	yes	yes	yes	no	no	no	Guarani
+DSP, +DAP, +DegPP	yes	yes	yes	yes	yes	yes	English

The table lists all possibilities opened by the parameters: If a language is [−DSP], it must be [-DAP] as well, because there can be no abstraction over degree variables without degree semantics. Similarly, if a language is [−DAP] it is also [−DegPP] because the DegPs are all operators over degree arguments and can only be interpreted with the help of binding of the degree argument slot.

The interest in such parameters lies in the fact that they make predictions about a range of phenomena. Each parameter is responsible for a set of effects, a cluster of empirical properties. Taken together, the settings of the proposed parameters group languages together that share a bunch of key properties in the realm of comparison constructions.

In sum, this subsection has not unearthed problems for our analysis of English comparison constructions. But it has demonstrated the need to identify ways in which other types of languages differ from English with respect to the grammar of comparison. Such differences, according to B17's results, may concern systematic properties of the lexicon (DSP), or the means of compositional interpretation available (DAP), or the mapping of lexical items into the syntax (DegPP).

Of course, these three parameters do not exhaust the potential for crosslinguistic variation in the domain of comparison constructions. Bhatt & Takahashi (2008) for example discuss more fine-grained differences between English, Hindi and Japanese, concerning the kind of comparative morpheme a language makes available. They propose that Hindi only has the phrasal comparative from section 2.2, not the clausal comparative morpheme from English. See also once more Kennedy (2009) on this issue.

4 Summary and conclusions

The theory of comparison introduced in section 2, which originates with von Stechow (1984), is highly successful. It uses a degree ontology, according to which degrees are introduced into natural language semantics by gradable predicates. Various comparison operators bind the degree arguments of gradable predicates. Comparison is abstract in that it compares for instance the maxima of such derived degree predicates. The theory is extendable from the comparative to various other comparison constructions in English and similar languages. We arrive by and large at a very coherent picture of the syntax and semantics of degree.

The quantifier data examined above require us to modify our perspective somewhat, taking into consideration a shift within the adjective phrase from degrees to intervals. They may not require a more radical change in the semantic analysis of comparison.

For languages that differ with regard to the grammar of comparison substantially from English, semantic theory has yet to provide complete alternative analyses which capture those differences. These analyses will shed some light on parametric variation in semantics and at the syntax/semantics interface.

I would like to thank Remus Gergel, Stefan Hofstetter, Svetlana Krasikova, Doris Penka, Paul Portner, John Vanderelst and Elisabeth Villalta for comments on an earlier version of this article. My understanding of the grammar of comparison has benefited greatly from discussions with Rajesh Bhatt, Irene Heim, Chris Kennedy and Arnim von Stechow. I am also very grateful to Uli Sauerland and the Semantics Network for opportunities to present parts of the work contained in this paper, and to the DFG for financial support of the Semantics Network and the crosslinguistic project on comparison B17 in the SFB 441.

5 References

Beck, Sigrid 1996. *Wh-constructions and Transparent Logical Form*. Ph.D. dissertation. University of Tübingen.
Beck, Sigrid 2007. The grammar of focus evaluation. In: U. Sauerland & H-M. Gärtner (eds.). *'Interfaces + Recursion = Language'? Chomsky's Minimalism and the View from Syntax and Semantics*. Berlin: Mouton de Gruyter, 255–280.
Beck, Sigrid 2010. Quantifiers in *than*-clauses. *Semantics and Pragmatics* 3, 1–72.
Beck, Sigrid, Toshiko Oda & Koji Sugisaki 2004. Parametric variation in the semantics of comparison: Japanese vs. English. *Journal of East Asian Linguistics* 13, 289–344.
Beck, Sigrid, Svetlana Krasikova, Daniel Fleischer, Remus Gergel, Stefan Hofstetter, Christiane Savelsberg, John Vanderelst & Elisabeth Villalta 2009. Crosslinguistic variation in comparison constructions. In: J. van Craenenbroeck (ed.). *Linguistic Variation Yearbook 2009*. Amsterdam: Benjaemins, 1–66.
Bhatt, Rajesh & Roumyana Pancheva 2004. Late merger of degree clauses. *Linguistic Inquiry* 35, 1–45.
Bhatt, Rajesh & Shoichi Takahashi 2008. When to reduce and when not to: crosslinguistic variation in phrasal comparatives. Paper presented at *The 31th GLOW Colloquium 2008*, Newcastle University.
Bierwisch, Manfred 1989. The semantics of gradation. In: M. Bierwisch & E. Lang (eds.). *Dimensional Adjectives*. Berlin: Springer, 71–261.
Bresnan, Joan 1972. *Theory of Complementation in English Syntax*. Ph.D. dissertation. MIT, Cambridge, MA.
Bresnan, Joan 1973. Syntax of the comparative clause in English. *Linguistic Inquiry* 4, 275–343.
Büring, Daniel 2007a. Cross-polar nomalies. In: T. Friedman & M. Gibson (eds.). *Proceedings of Semantics and Linguistic Theory (= SALT)* 17. Ithaca, NY: CLC Publications, 37–52
Büring, Daniel 2007b. When *less* is *more* (and when it isn't). Paper presented at the *39th Regional Meeting of the Chicago Linguistic Society (CLS)*.
Chierchia, Gennaro 1998. Reference to kinds across languages. *Natural Language Semantics* 6, 339–405.
Fleischer, Daniel 2007. *Comparison Constructions in Guarani*. Ms. Tübingen, University of Tübingen.
Fox, Danny 2006. *Free Choice and the Theory of Scalar Implicatures*. Ms. Cambridge, MA, MIT.
Gajewski, Jon 2008. More on quantifiers in comparative clauses. In: Jon Gajewski. T. Friedman and S. Ito (eds.). *Proceedings of Semantics and Linguistic Theory (= SALT)* 18, 340–357.
Hackl, Martin 2000. *Comparative Quantifiers*. Ph.D. Dissertation. MIT, Cambridge, MA.
Hackl, Martin 2009. On the grammar and processing of proportional quantifiers: *most* versus *more than a half*. *Natural Language Semantics* 17, 63–98.
Heim, Irene 1985. *Notes on Comparatives and Related Matters*. Ms. Austin, TX, University of Texas.
Heim, Irene 1999. *Notes on Superlatives*. Ms. Cambridge, MA, MIT.
Heim, Irene 2000. Degree operators and scope. In: B. Jackson & T. Matthews (eds.). *Proceedings of Semantics and Linguistic Theory (SALT)* 10. Ithaca, NY: CLC Publications, 40–64.

Heim, Irene 2001. Degree operators and scope. In: C. Féry & W. Sternefeld (eds.). *Audiatur Vox Sapientiae. A Festschrift for Arnim von Stechow*. Berlin: Akademie Verlag, 214–239.
Heim, Irene 2006. *Remarks on Comparative Clauses as Generalized Quantifiers*. Ms. Cambridge, MA, MIT. http://semanticsarchive.net/, August 9, 2011.
Heim, Irene 2007. Little. In: M. Gibson & J. Howell (eds.). *Proceedings of Semantics und Linguistic Theory (= SALT)* 16. Ithaca, NY: CLC Publications, 35–58.
Heim, Irene 2008. Decomposing antonyms? In: A. Grønn (ed.). *Proceedings of Sinn und Bedeutung* 12. Oslo: Department of Literature, Area Studies and European Languages, 212–225.
Heim, Irene & Angelika Kratzer 1998. *Semantics in Generative Grammar*. Malden, MA: Blackwell.
Hofstetter, Stefan 2009. Comparison constructions in Turkish. In: A. Riester & T. Solstad: *Proceedings of Sinn und Bedeutung* 13. Stuttgart: University of Stuttgart, 187–201.
Jacobson, Pauline 1995. On the quantificational force of English free relatives. In: B. Partee et al. (eds.). *Quantification in Natural Languages*. Dordrecht: Kluwer, 451–486.
Kamp, Hans 1975. Two theories of adjectives. In: E. Keenan (ed.). *Formal Semantics of Natural Language*. Cambridge: Cambridge University Press, 123–155.
Kennedy, Christopher 1997. *Projecting the Adjective: the Syntax and Semantics of Gradability and Comparison*. Ph.D. dissertation. University of California, Santa Cruz, CA.
Kennedy, Christopher 2001. Polar opposition and the ontology of degrees. *Linguistics & Philosophy* 24, 33–70.
Kennedy, Christopher 2007. Vagueness and grammar. The semantics of relative and absolute gradable adjectives. *Linguistics & Philosophy* 30, 1–45.
Kennedy, Christopher 2009. Modes of comparison. M. Elliot et al. (eds.). *Proceedings of Chicago Linguistic Society (CLS)* 43. Chicgo, IL: Chicago Linguistic Society, 141–165.
Klein, Ewan 1980. A semantics for positive and comparative adjectives. *Linguistics & Philosophy* 4, 1–45.
Klein, Ewan 1991. Comparatives. In: A. von Stechow & D. Wunderlich (eds.). *Semantics. An International Handbook on Contemporary Research* (HSK 6). Berlin: de Gruyter, 673–691.
Krasikova, Svetlana 2007. Comparison in Chinese. Paper presented at *CSSP*, Paris.
Krasikova, Svetlana 2008. Quantifiers in comparatives. In: A. Grønn (ed.). *Proceedings of Sinn und Bedeutung* 12. Oslo: Department of Literature, Area Studies and European Languages, 337–352.
Kratzer, Angelika 1991. Modality. In: A. von Stechow & D. Wunderlich (eds.). *Semantics. An International Handbook of Contemporary Research* (HSK 6). Berlin: de Gruyter, 639–650.
Kratzer, Angelika 1998. Scope or pseudoscope? Are there wide scope indefinites? In: S. Rothstein (ed.). *Events and Grammar*. Dordrecht: Kluwer, 163–196.
Krifka, Manfred 1999. At least some determiners aren't determiners. In K. Turner (ed.). *The Semantics/Pragmatics Interface from Different Points of View*. Oxford: Elsevier, 257–291.
Ladusaw, William A. 1979. *Polarity Sensitivity as Inherent Scope Relations*. Ph.D. dissertation. University of Texas, Austin, TX.
Larson, Richard K. 1988. Scope and comparatives. *Linguistics & Philosophy* 11, 1–26.
Lechner, Winfried 2004. *Ellipsis in Comparatives*. Berlin: Mouton de Gruyter.
Lewis, David 1970. General semantics. *Synthese* 22, 18–67.
Meier, Cecile 2002. Maximality and minimality in comparatives. In: G. Katz, S. Reinhard & P. Reuter (eds.). *Proceedings of Sinn und Bedeutung* 6. Osnabrück: University of Osnabrück, 275–287.

Meier, Cecile 2003. The meaning of 'too', 'enough' and 'so that'. *Natural Language Semantics* 11, 69–107.
Merchant, Jason 2006. *Phrasal and Clausal Comparatives in Greek and the Abstractedness of Syntax*. Ms. Chicago, IL, University of Chicago.
Moltmann, Friederike 2005. Comparatives without degrees. A new approach. In: P. Dekker & M. Franke (eds.). *Proceedings of the 15th Amsterdam Colloquium*. Amsterdam: ILLC, 155–160.
Oda, Toshiko 2008. *Degree Constructions in Japanese*. Ph.D. dissertation. University of Connecticut, Storrs, CT.
Pancheva, Roumyana 2006. Phrasal and clausal comparatives in Slavic. In: J. Lavine et al. (eds.). *Proceedings of Formal Approaches to Slavic Linguistics (= FASL) 14*. Ann Arbor, MI: University of Michigan, 236–257.
Percus, Orin 2000. Constraints on some other variables in syntax. *Natural Language Semantics* 8, 173–229.
Pinkal, Manfred 1989a. On the logical structure of comparatives. In: R. Studer (ed.). *Logic and Natural Language*. Berlin: Springer, 146–167.
Pinkal, Manfred 1989b. Die Semantik von Satzkomparativen. *Zeitschrift für Sprachwissenschaft* 8(2), 206–256.
Reinhart, Tanya 1997. Quantifier Scope: How labour is divided between QR and choice functions. *Linguistics & Philosophy* 20, 335–397.
Rett, Jessica 2007. Evaluativity and antonymy. In: T. Friedman & M. Gibson (eds.). *Proceedings of Semantics and Linguistic Theory (= SALT) 17*. Ithaca, NY: CLC Publications, 210–227.
van Rooij, Robert 2008. Comparatives and Quantifiers. In: O. Bonami & P. Cabredo Hofherr (eds). *Empirical Issues in Syntax and Semantics, Vol. 7*. Paris: CSSP, 423–444.
Ross, John R. 1964. *A Partial Grammar of English Superlatives*. M.A. thesis. University of Pennsylvania.
Rullmann, Hotze 1995. *Maximality in the Semantics of Wh-Constructions*. Ph.D. dissertation. University of Massachusetts at Amherst.
Schwarzschild, Roger & Karina Wilkinson 2002. Quantifiers in comparatives: A semantics of degree based on intervals. *Natural Language Semantics* 10, 1–41.
Schwarzschild, Roger 2004. *Scope Splitting in the Comparative*. Handout, MA, MIT Colloquium, October 15, 2004.
Schwarzschild, Roger 2005. Measure phrases as modifiers of adjectives. *Recherches Linguistiques de Vincennes* 35, 207–228.
Schwarzschild, Roger 2008. The semantics of comparatives and other degree constructions. *Language and Linguistics Compass* 2, 308–331.
Seuren, Peter 1973. The comparative. In: F. Kiefer & N. Ruwet (eds.). *Generative Grammar in Europe*. Dordrecht: Reidel, 528–564.
Sharvit, Yael & Penka Stateva 2002. Superlative expressions, context, and focus. *Linguistics & Philosophy* 25, 453–504.
Stassen, Leon 1985. *Comparison and Universal Grammar*. Oxford: Blackwell.
Stateva, Penka 2000. In defense of the movement theory of superlatives. In: R. Daly & A. Riehl (eds.). *Proceedings of ESCOL 1999*. Ithaca, NY: CLC, Publications, 215–226.
Stateva, Penka 2002. *How Different are Different Degree Constructions?* Ph.D. dissertation. University of Connecticut, Storrs, CT.
von Stechow, Arnim 1984. Comparing semantic theories of comparison. *Journal of Semantics* 3, 1–77.

von Stechow, Arnim 2005. *Different Approaches to the Semantics of Comparison*. Ms. Tübingen, University of Tübingen.
von Stechow, Arnim 2006. *Times as Degrees*. Ms. Tübingen, University of Tübingen.
Szabolcsi, Anna 1986. Comparative superlatives. In: N. Fukui, T. Rapoport & E. Sagey (eds.). *MIT Working Papers in Linguistics* 8. Cambridge, MA: MIT, 245–265.
Villalta, Elisabeth 2007. *Comparison Constructions in Motu*. Ms. Tübingen, University of Tübingen.

Claudia Maienborn and Martin Schäfer
14 Adverbs and adverbials

1 Introduction: Towards a definition of adverbs and adverbials —— 477
2 Semantic classification of adverbials —— 481
3 Adverbials at the syntax/semantics interface —— 492
4 Theoretical approaches —— 495
5 Challenges to compositionality and ontology —— 501
6 Conclusion —— 510
7 References —— 510

Abstract: The article offers an overview of the heterogeneous set of lexical and semantic classes and subclasses of adverbs and adverbials with their characteristic inferential and distributional properties. Furthermore, it sketches major theoretical approaches that have been developed to account for adverbial semantics and introduces some current issues of debate concerning the proper combination of lexical, compositional, and conceptual semantics for adverbials.

1 Introduction: Towards a definition of adverbs and adverbials

Adverbs and adverbials are highly adaptive expressions. They arise in a variety of environments from which they take on certain characteristic features. This makes them a very flexible means of natural language expression. Their semantics raises some intriguing puzzles for linguistic theory that have attracted much interest in current semantic research as documented, e.g., by the articles in Lang, Maienborn & Fabricius-Hansen (2003), Austin, Engelberg & Rauh (2004) or McNally & Kennedy (2008). The aim of this article is to provide an overview outlining the major semantic issues involving adverbs and adverbials and sketching some major theoretical approaches that have been developed to account for adverbial semantics, as well as current debates.

Claudia Maienborn, Tübingen, Germany
Martin Schäfer, Jena, Germany

https://doi.org/10.1515/9783110626391-014

The article is organized as follows: The introductory section provides a characterization of adverbs and adverbials that will serve as a working base for the remainder of this article. Section 2 lays out a classification of adverbials based on semantic criteria and includes some remarks on the delineation of adverbials and secondary predicates. Section 3 discusses the syntax/semantics interface addressing the relationship between the position of adverbials and their interpretation. Section 4 presents three major formal semantic approaches that have been developed for adverbials: the operator approach most prominently advocated by Thomason & Stalnaker (1973), McConnell-Ginet's (1982) argument approach, and the nowadays widely adopted Davidsonian predicate approach. On this basis, Section 5 discusses some challenges concerning the compositional semantics and the underlying ontology of adverbials that current theories address. The article ends with a short conclusion in Section 6.

Clear-cut definitions of adverbs and adverbials are difficult to formulate. Since we define the word class *adverb* on the basis of the syntactic function *adverbial*, we will start with the latter. Not all aspects mentioned in this definition hold for all adverbials, but it covers most types of adverbials unambiguously treated as such in the literature.

1.1 Adverbials

The term "adverbial" refers to a specific syntactic function within a sentence and therefore contrasts with other syntactic functions, such as subject, object, and predicate. Adverbials are traditionally conceived of as being those elements that serve to specify further the circumstances of the verbal or sentential referent. They are restricted to a set of semantically limited usages, prototypically specifying time, place, or manner, cf. the italicized strings in (1).

(1) a. Paul laughed *the whole day*.
    b. The children played *in the kindergarten*.
    c. Henriette dances *beautifully*.

The adverbials in (1) pass standard constituency tests: They can be elicited by questions, can be replaced by pronouns, and are movable. The type of *wh*-word used for elicitation varies with the semantics of the adverbial. Temporal adverbials like *the whole day* in (1) answer the question *When/For how long ... ?*, depending on whether they specify the time or length of the laughing. The prepositional phrase *in the kindergarten* in (1) is a locative adverbial, answering the question *Where ... ?* Finally, *beautifully* in (1) is a manner adverbial, answering the question *How ... ?*

As the sample sentences in (1) already show, the function of adverbials may be realized by different kinds of phrasal units, here noun/determiner phrases, prepositional phrases and adverb phrases. Other phrasal units frequently functioning as adverbials are adjective phrases and clauses; for an overview cf. van der Auwera (1998), cf. also article 15 [this volume] (Sæbø) *Adverbial clauses*.

The prototypical adverbial is optional and corresponds syntactically to an adjunct, acting semantically as a modifier. Examples for subcategorized adverbials are given in (2).

(2) a. Norah treated James *(badly).
    b. John behaved *(admirably).
    c. New York lies *(on the Hudson river bank).

The sentences in (2) require the presence of the adverbials –note, though, that *John behaved* is acceptable due to a conventionalized reading of bare *behave* as *behave well* –, contrasting with verbs like *to dress* in (3), which is acceptable without an adverbial when pragmatically licensed as in (3b); cf. Ernst (1984) and Goldberg & Ackerman (2001).

(3) a. Norah dresses #(stylishly).
    b. Norah dresses, but the natives prefer to go naked.

1.2 Adverbs

The term "adverb" refers to a specific word class or lexical category and therefore contrasts with other word classes, such as nouns, adjectives, verbs, or prepositions.

On the one hand, both adverbs and prepositions are uninflected, with adverbs differing from prepositions in having phrasal status. Reductionist approaches have therefore proposed to analyze at least some adverbs as intransitive, i.e. objectless, prepositions; e.g. Jackendoff (1972), Wunderlich (1984). While this might be a viable option for some adverb candidates such as *up, down, away*, there is some consensus that such reductionist attempts are only feasible within certain limits suggesting that a lexical category of adverbs is needed after all; cf. the discussion in Delfitto (2000: 16ff).

On the other hand, adverbs differ from nouns, adjectives, and verbs in that they often do not possess clear markers for category membership and can only be defined via their syntactic function of being prototypically used as adverbials. In English, both cases exist: There is a large class of deadjectival *-ly* adverbs that can be identified through their morphology as adverbs. On the other hand, words like *well* are identified as adverbs because they can only have an adverbial function.

For English, any further attempt to give a positive definition of the word class "adverb" is wrought with difficulties. First of all, a subclass of English adverbs (and adverbs in other Germanic languages) can, besides serving as standard adverbials, be used to modify adjectives or other adverbs, cf., e.g., *extremely* in (4).

(4) a. He drives extremely/too/very fast.
    b. an extremely/very awkward situation.

This kind of usage is not restricted to traditional degree adverbs like *extremely*, *too*, and *very*. A fairly large class of adverbs can be used as modifiers of adjectives, cf. (5).

(5) Joe is provocatively/disappointingly/grotesquely/remarkably stupid.

Notice that these adverbs are not parallel to the degree adverbs in (4). See Morzycki (2008) for a detailed discussion of this point; Rawlins (2008) discusses the pre-adjectival use of *illegally*.

A second difficulty concerns items like *tonight, tomorrow, yesterday* which are usually considered prototypical English adverbs. These items, besides being used adverbially, can also serve as subjects; cf. (6).

(6) a. *Yesterday* was a beautiful day.   [Adv as subject]
    b. Peter worked in his office *yesterday*.   [Adv as adverbial]

This data is problematic insofar as we argued above that the adverbial function is the basis for the category "adverb". If we continue to classify items like *yesterday* as adverbs, we have to accept that some adverbs can serve both as adverbials and as subjects. An elegant solution to this problem is given in Huddleston & Pullum (2002: 564ff), who analyze *yesterday* and similar items as pronouns. This analysis explains their distributional pattern, which they share with standard noun phrases, cf. (7).

(7) a. *The whole year* was a study in failure and disillusion.   [NP as subject]
    b. Peter worked in his office *the whole year*.   [NP as adverbial]

A further characteristic of adverbs in English and German is the fact that they cannot occur as prenominal attributive modifiers of nouns, cf. (8) for English.

(8) a. *the well runner.
    b. *the extremely conditions.

Adverbs are often classified according to their lexical semantics, cf. e.g. (9):

(9) a. now, tomorrow, afterwards   [temporal adverbs]
    b. here, elsewhere, inside   [locative adverbs]
    c. often, seldom, frequently   [frequency adverbs]

Finally, it should be noted that, cross-linguistically, the word class adverb is not frequent; cf. Sasse (1993).

2 Semantic classification of adverbials

Common classifications of adverbials are based on either semantic or syntactic criteria, or both. Here, we will give a classification based on semantic criteria alone and discuss the interaction of adverbial subclasses with syntax in Section 3. Adverbials may be subdivided into three major groups: *predicational adverbials, participant-oriented adverbials*, and *functional adverbials* (these terms are adapted from Ernst 2002), which may be roughly characterized as follows. Predicational adverbials assign a (gradable) property to the verbal or sentential referent they combine with. Participant-oriented adverbials introduce a new entity that takes part in the eventuality described by the verb. "Functional adverbials" is the cover term for the remaining adverbials, including quantificational and discourse-related adverbials. Before embarking on a more detailed discussion of these semantic subclasses, we will briefly introduce the semantic notions of opacity and veridicality, which will turn out to be crucial devices in classifying adverbials.

Opacity

In extensional systems of logic, it is usually assumed that Leibniz' Law holds: Two co-referential expressions can be freely substituted for one another without changing the truth value of the original expression. Expressions for which this law does not hold are *oblique* or *referentially opaque*. As (10) shows, adverbials can give rise to opaque contexts:

(10) a. Necessarily, Sam Peckinpah is Sam Peckinpah.
     b. Necessarily, Sam Peckinpah is the director of The Wild Bunch.

While (10a) is analytically true (in most systems of logic), (10b) is false. Adverbials can be characterized as to whether they create opaque contexts for all positions in a sentence, for just specific positions, or for no positions at all.

Veridicality

An adverbial is *veridical* (or *factive*), if a sentence containing the adverbial entails the sentence without the adverbial. It is *nonveridical*, if there is no such entailment. Some adverbials, e.g. functional adverbials like *never*, are *antiveridical*, that is, they entail that the sentence without the adverbial is not true; cf. Giannakidou (1999) and also Bonami, Godard & Kampers-Manhe (2004).

2.1 Predicational adverbials

Predicational adverbials can typically be characterized as supplying a gradable property on the verbal or sentential base. (By restricting predicational adverbials to those expressing gradable properties we exclude, e.g., form adjectives like *rectangular*, which do not appear in adverbial function.) In Germanic languages, predicational adverbials are typically realized by deadjectival adverbs. They appear in a wide variety of adverbial usages. Typically, a single predicational can have at least two different usages, the exact usage depending on its lexical semantics; cf. Ernst (1984, 2002). One example is given in (11).

(11) a. Rudely, Claire greeted the queen.
　　　b. Claire greeted the queen rudely.

In (11a) it is judged as rude that Claire greeted the queen, regardless of how she greeted her; *rudely* serves as a subject-oriented adverbial here. In (11b), in contrast, what is qualified as rude is not the very fact of greeting the queen, but the specific way in which Claire greeted her; here *rudely* serves as a manner adverbial.

The most basic division in providing a further semantic subclassification for predicational adverbials is that between *sentence adverbials* and *verb-related adverbials* (sometimes also termed "higher" and "lower" adverbials). Sentence adverbials have a hierarchically high attachment site; they stand in a relation to or combine with the overall proposition expressed by the rest of the sentence without the adverbial (= the sentential base). Verb-related adverbials have a lower attachment site within the VP and are more closely connected to the verbal referent.

Some sort of distinction between sentence adverbials vs. verb-related adverbials along the lines sketched above can be found in almost any semantic classification of adverbials, although details and further subdivisions may differ to some extent. The subdivision developed in the following draws on previous classifications, especially by Bartsch (1972/1976), Jackendoff (1972), Bellert (1977), Ernst (1984, 2002), and Parsons (1990). Each subclass will first be introduced on intuitive grounds and, if available, by some characteristic paraphrases that are indicative of their underlying semantics. Afterwards, each subclass will be characterized in terms of opacity, veridicality and further semantic and inferential properties. (For a critical discussion of paraphrases, cf. e.g. Jackendoff (1972: 52) and Ernst (1984), for a very elaborate system of paraphrases, cf. Bartsch (1972).)

2.1.1 Sentence adverbials

Sentence adverbials can be further subdivided into subject-oriented adverbials, speaker-oriented adverbials and domain adverbials.

Subject-oriented adverbials

The term goes back to Jackendoff's (1972) "subject-oriented adverbs". Subject-oriented adverbials assign a specific property to the agent, based on the action as described by the proposition expressed by the sentential base, cf. (12).

(12) Peter arrogantly/idiotically put his love letters on the net.

In (12), the speaker judges Peter to be arrogant/idiotic, basing his judgement on Peter's action of putting his love letters on the net. Sentences containing subject-oriented adverbials allow paraphrases analogous to the one given in (13) for sentence (12).

(13) It was arrogant/idiotic of Peter to put his love letters on the net.

Subject-oriented adverbials are veridical and they have scope over negation: (14a) entails (14b).

(14) a. Peter arrogantly did not answer my phone call.
     b. Peter did not answer my phone call.

Finally, subject-oriented adverbials appear to be anomalous in questions, cf. (15).

(15) ?Did Peter arrogantly not answer my phone call?

Bellert (1977) relates this behavior to the general observation that we cannot ask a question and assert a proposition in one and the same sentence. As Wyner (1994: 28ff) and Geuder (2000: 165ff) point out, subject-oriented adverbials do not create opaque contexts.

Speaker-oriented adverbials

Speaker-oriented adverbials provide a commentary by the speaker on the proposition expressed by the sentential base. They allow further subdivision into *speech-act adverbials*, *epistemic adverbials*, and *evaluative adverbials*.

Speech-act adverbials characterize the speaker's attitude towards the content (16a) or the form (16b) of what s/he is saying; cf. Mittwoch (1977).

(16) a. Honestly/frankly, I have no idea what you're talking about.
  b. Briefly/roughly, Peter did not manage to convince her.

In declaratives, speech-act adverbials allow the addition of the participle *speaking* without change in meaning, i.e. *Honestly speaking, …* Furthermore, they can appear in explicit perfomative utterances, e.g. *I sincerely apologize*.

Epistemic adverbials express the speaker's expectation with regard to the truth of the sentential base; cf. (17a). They can be paraphrased according to the pattern given in (17b). (Note that *maybe* is special in that it is not gradable, but shares the general characteristics of the other predicationals used here.)

(17) a. Maybe/probably/surely Mary is still alive.
  b. It is maybe/probably/surely true that Mary is still alive.

Epistemic adverbials are often referred to as "epistemic modals", contrasting with alethic and deontic modals; cf., e.g., Parsons (1990: 62f) on epistemic vs. alethic modals and Bonami, Godard & Kampers-Manhe (2004) on epistemic vs. alethic and deontic interpretations of modals. An example for an alethic modal is the usage of *necessarily* in, e.g., *Two and two is necessarily four*; deontic modals refer to rule or law based knowledge as, e.g., *In the USA, the president is necessarily the commander in chief*; cf. article 14 [Semantics: Noun Phrases and Verb Phrases] (Hacquard) *Modality*. Epistemic adverbials cannot be directly negated (18a) nor do they have negative counterparts (18b), and they are nonveridical (18c).

(18) a. *Matthew is not probably dead.
     b. *Matthew is improbably dead.
     c. Matthew is probably dead.   ↛ Matthew is dead.

All three types of modals create opaque contexts for both subject and complement positions, cf. the pattern for *necessarily* in (19) and (20).

(19) a. Necessarily, nine is an odd number.
     b. The number of planets is nine.
     c. ↛ Necessarily, the number of planets is an odd number.

(20) a. Necessarily, nine is an odd number.
     b. Nine is a lucky number.
     c. ↛ Necessarily, nine is a lucky number.

Evaluative adverbials express the opinion of the speaker with regard to the state of affairs expressed by the rest of the sentence, cf. (21).

(21) Fortunately/surprisingly, Peter is back in Australia.

Paraphrases for evaluative adverbials follow the pattern of (23) for sentence (22).

(22) Fortunately/unfortunately, Peter is back in Australia.

(23) It is fortunate/unfortunate that Peter is back in Australia.

As the above example illustrates, evaluatives often come with negative counterparts, although they usually cannot be negated analytically, cf. (24).

(24) a. Peter is fortunately back in Australia.
     b. *Peter is not fortunately back in Australia.

They are veridical, and usually they cannot occur in hypothetical contexts, cf. (25). (See Bellert (1977: 344f) for an explanation of why these two properties cooccur.)

(25) If firemen had (*unfortunately) not been available, my grandpa would maybe/*fortunately have extinguished the fire himself.

Evaluatives are also anomalous in questions, cf. (26).

(26) *Is Peter fortunately back in Australia?

Because of the last two features, evaluative adverbials have recently been linked to positive polarity items; cf. Nilsen (2004) and Ernst (2007, 2009). With regard to opaque contexts, evaluatives behave similarly to subject-oriented adverbials, cf. Bonami, Godard & Kampers-Manhe (2004).

Domain adverbials

Domain adverbials restrict the domain in which the proposition expressed by the rest of the sentence is claimed to hold true; cf. Bellert (1977), McConnell-Ginet (1982), Bartsch (1987), Ernst (2004).

(27) a. Emotionally Zardock is cold as ice.
 b. Politically he is as good as dead.
 c. Botanically, a tomato is a fruit.

Thus, (27a) says that the proposition expressed by *Zardock is cold as ice* is true when the viewpoint on this proposition is restricted to the domain of emotions, but remains neutral wrt. Zardock's body temperature.

Domain adverbials do not appear to be veridical, cf. the pattern in (28).

(28) Deixis-wise, this sentence is intriguing.
 ↛ This sentence is intriguing.

The entailment failure in (28) is of a different nature than that with epistemic adverbials, though. When dropping the domain adverbial, the sentence will still be evaluated from a certain viewpoint. In this case the domain will be restricted to some default or contextually salient value. That is, domain adverbials support an inferential pattern along the lines of (28'). It is only because we cannot be sure that omitting the domain adverbial will keep the implicitly involved domain constant that the inferential pattern in (28) does not go through.

(28') Deixis-wise, this sentence is intriguing.
 → Wrt. some domain, this sentence is intriguing.

2.1.2 Verb-related adverbials

Verb-related adverbials have a lower attachment site within the VP and are more closely connected to the verbal referent. Usually, at least mental-attitude adverbials, manner adverbials, and degree adverbials are distinguished.

Mental-attitude adverbials

Mental-attitude adverbials describe the attitude of the agent with regard to the activity described by the verbal predicate, cf. (29).

(29) Claire reluctantly/gladly went to school.

The adverbial *reluctantly* in (29) does not primarily describe the manner of going to school, but Claire's attitude towards going to school. It is only secondarily that this attitude might also have an impact on Claire's manner of going to school. Mental-attitude adverbials can take scope over sentence negation, cf. (30).

(30) Martha gladly did not go to school.

However, in this case the agent does not have a certain attitude wrt. a negated proposition but wrt. the *omission* of a certain action, which is in turn an action. For instance, in (30) Martha is glad about staying at home.

The mental-attitude adverbials in the above examples do not create opaque contexts. This is not a general property of mental-attitude adverbials, though. The mental-attitude adverbial *intentionally*, for example, creates opaque contexts for the complement position but not for the subject position; cf. (31), a classic example from Thomason & Stalnaker (1973).

(31) Oedipus intentionally married Jocasta.
    a. Oedipus is the son of Laius. → The son of Laius intentionally married Jocasta.
    b. Jocasta is Oedipus' mother. ↛ Oedipus intentionally married his mother.

Bonami, Godard & Kampers-Manhe (2004) label *intentionally* and similar items, like *by chance*, "adverbs of attitude towards a state of affairs".

Manner adverbials

Manner adverbials are used to specify the manner in which an eventuality or an action unfolds; prototypical examples are given in (32).

(32) Klogman defended himself skillfully/intelligently/hectically.

Manner adverbials cannot take scope over sentence negation, cf. (33).

(33) Frankie does not run fast. ≠ Frankie does not run and he does so fast.

There is a straightforward semantic explanation for this behavior: Sentence negation tells us that there is no eventuality of V-ing. Consequently there is no target available for a potential manner modifier. Apparent counterexamples such as (34) are based on event coercion. They require the interpolation of an event that can be plausibly associated with the negated proposition; cf. articles 10 [this volume] (de Swart) *Mismatches and coercion* and 8 [Semantics: Theories] (Maienborn) *Event semantics*.

(34) Klogman skillfully didn't answer the question.

On a manner reading of *skillfully* in (34), what is skillful is some activity of Klogman which allows him to uphold the state of not-answering the question, that is, he skillfully dodged the question; cf. (Schäfer 2005: 161).

We will return to a more detailed discussion of manner adverbials in Section 5.2.

Degree adverbials

Degree adverbials indicate the extent or intensity to which somebody does something; cf. (35).

(35) Lochnan loves her very much/deeply.

Similarly to manner adverbials, degree adverbials cannot take scope over sentence negation:

(36) Frankie does not love her very much. ≠ Frankie does not love her and he does so very much.

Besides these three major subtypes there are further instances of verb-related adverbials with a low attachment site such as the verb-related counterparts of domain adverbials, the so-called *method-oriented adverbials* (cf. Schäfer 2005), which describe certain means or methods of doing something, cf. (37).

(37) a. United Stated destroyed Switzerland economically.
b. The scientist classified the plants genetically.
c. They analyzed the data linguistically.

Some verb-related predicational adverbials may deviate from the standard behavior of predicationals in non-trivial ways. Thus, *halfway* in (38) is neither veridical nor gradable.

(38) The door is halfway closed. ↛ The door is closed.

2.2 Participant-oriented adverbials

Participant-oriented adverbials—or *circumstantials*, as they are also called—are predominantly realized through prepositional phrases. They introduce a new participant that takes part in the eventuality described by the verb. On a Neo-Davidsonian view, they are linked to the verb's eventuality argument through a thematic role just like standard agent or patient arguments; cf. articles 3 [this volume] (Davis) *Thematic roles* and 8 [Semantics: Theories] (Maienborn) *Event semantics*. Sentence (39a), e.g., has two participant-oriented adverbials *in the garage* and *with a knife*, which specify the place and the instrument role of the event. A standard Neo-Davidsonian logical form is given in (39b); cf. Section 4.3. for details.

(39) a. Peter opened the box with a knife in the garage.
    b. ∃e [OPEN (e) & AGENT (e, peter) & PATIENT (e, the box) & LOCATION (e, the garage) & INSTR (e, a knife)]

Just as predicationals, participant-oriented adverbials can have different uses. Following the terminology in Maienborn (2001), we distinguish between *event-related adverbials*, which restrict the verb's eventuality argument, and *frame adverbials*, which set a frame for the overall proposition; cf. the different meaning contributions of the locative, temporal, and instrumental phrase in (40) vs. (41):

(40) a. We met Jürgen Klinsmann in the USA.
    b. The Queen visited Jamestown in 1957.
    c. Siri examined the diamond with a loupe.

(41) a. In the USA, resigned military officials are not frowned upon.
    b. In 1957, moral integrity still had some value.
    c. With a loupe, small fissures of a diamond become visible.

We will discuss the different uses of participant-related adverbials in more detail in Section 5.1.

2.3 Functional adverbials

Ernst's (2002) last class, the so-called "functional adverbials" comprise a rather heterogeneous set of adverbials including adverbial quantifiers as in (42a) as well as discourse-anaphoric adverbials as in (42b).

(42) a. They often/never/usually carried out his orders.
b. They therefore/thus/notwithstanding became congenial companions.

We won't discuss these adverbials any further here but refer the reader to articles 4 [Semantics: Noun Phrases and Verb Phrases] (Keenan) *Quantifiers* and 15 [Semantics: Sentence and Information Structure] (Zimmermann) *Discourse particles*.

2.4 Adverbials and secondary predicates

Having laid out a semantic classification for adverbials we want to close this overview with some remarks on the delineation of adverbials on the one hand and resultative and depictive secondary predicates on the other hand; cf. also article 16 [this volume] (Rothstein) *Secondary predicates*.

Both resultatives and depictives introduce a secondary predicate into the sentence that in a sense "lives on" the primary verbal predicate. This secondary predicate holds of one of the verb's arguments. That is, unlike verb-related adverbials, secondary predicates do not qualify the verbal referent but one of its arguments. More specifically, depictives, as in (43), express a secondary property of the subject or the object referent that holds at least for the temporal duration of the verbal referent; cf. Rothstein's (2003) notion of *time-participant-connectedness*.

(43) Peter eats meat nude/raw.

Whenever a psychological adjective, i.e., an adjective denoting a particular state of mind, is used, the distinction between mental-attitude adverbials and subject depictives is blurred, especially in languages which do not use use different morphological forms to differentiate between the adverbial use and the adjectival use as secondary predicate, cf. the German example in (44).

(44) Gudrun ist traurig nach Hause gegangen.
Gudrun has sad/sadly to home gone.
'Gudrun went home sad/sadly.'

Geuder (2000) attempts to tease these different usages apart and contains a detailed discussion of the English data. Himmelmann & Schultze-Berndt (2005) take a wide range of typological data into account, showing that across languages there is considerable variation in how depictives are encoded.

As for resultatives, they introduce a secondary predicate into the sentence that holds true of one of the verb's arguments as a result of the event expressed by the main predicate; cf. e.g. (45), which expresses that the tulips became flat as a result of the gardener watering them.

(45) The gardener watered the tulips flat.

There is a vast literature on resultatives; cf. the references in article 16 [this volume] (Rothstein) *Secondary predicates*. One particular topic of interest relating to adverbials are manner-resultative ambiguities such as the one in (46); *elegantly* may have a manner reading as in (46a) as well as a resultative reading as in (46b); cf., e.g., the discussion in Eckardt (1998, 2003), Geuder (2000), Dölling (2003). (Note that the resultative interpretation of (46) involves a so-called "implicit resultative" (Schäfer 2005): Rather than predicating over one of the verb's overtly expressed arguments the secondary predicate holds for an implicit argument, viz. Judith's dress.)

(46) Judith dresses elegantly.
    a. The way in which Judith dresses is elegant.
    b. Judith dresses, so that as a result, her dress is elegant.

The manner and the resultative reading in (46) are conceptually easily distinguishable, because there isn't any connection between the way one dresses and the result of dressing. Yet, such a clear-cut distinction between manner and resultative readings is not always possible; cf. the sentences in (47).

(47) a. Arndt fixed the chair perfectly.
    b. Sarah grows roses marvelously.

The manner of fixing a chair or growing roses can only be qualified as perfect or marvelous if the result is of a comparably high quality and vice versa. If the result of, e.g., Arndt's fixing the chair is perfect, then the way he did it must have been perfect, too. So, manner and resultative readings cannot be completely disentangled in these cases; cf. Quirk et al.'s (1985: 560) notion of *blends*.

2.5 Summary

The following Fig. 15.1 provides an overview of the adverbial subclasses that were introduced in this section.

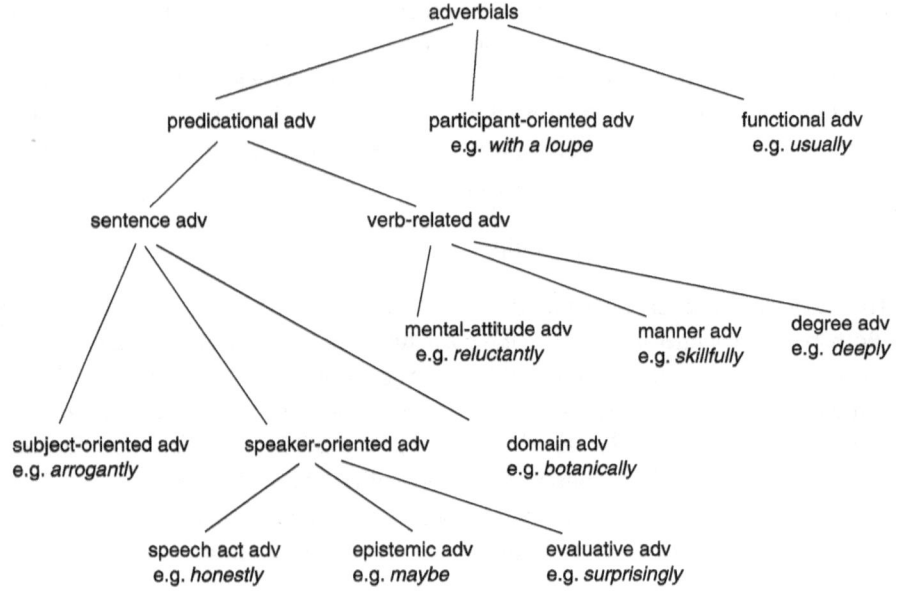

Fig. 15.1: Semantic classification of adverbials

3 Adverbials at the syntax/semantics interface

The semantic interpretation of an adverbial correlates to some degree with its syntactic position. Jackendoff (1972) was the first to discuss this point in some detail; he distinguished three basic positions for adverbials in English: initial position, final position without an intervening pause, and auxiliary position (i.e. between the subject and the main verb). For illustration, consider English *-ly* adverbs. Some *-ly* adverbs can occur in all three positions. But English also has *-ly* adverbs which can occur only in the initial and aux positions along with *-ly* adverbs that occur only in the aux and final positions; cf. (48).

(48) a. (Frequently) Horatio has (frequently) lost his mind (frequently).
    b. (Evidently/probably) Horatio (evidently/probably) lost his mind*
       (evidently/probably).
    c. *(Completely/easily) Stanly (completely/easily) ate his wheaties
       (completely/easily).

Jackendoff argues that the different distributional patterns can also be distinguished on semantic grounds, e.g. the adverbials showing the pattern in (48b) are speaker- or subject-oriented, whereas manner adverbials show the pattern in (48c).

In the last decade, the correlation between syntactic position and semantic interpretation of adverbials has received considerable attention. Two main strands of thought can be distinguished: an entirely syntax-driven one (represented by Cinque 1999), and one based on semantic scope (represented by Ernst 1998, 1999, 2002 and Haider 1998, 2000).

Cinque (1999) has made an influential proposal to explain the order of adverb(ial)s in purely syntactic terms, by assuming a universal hierarchy of functional heads that encodes the hierarchy of adverbials. Adverbials are integrated as specifiers, each one having a designated specifier position; cf. Alexiadou (1997) and Laenzlinger (1998) for similar proposals and see also Alexiadou (2004a, b) for a recent overview. (Note that Cinque (1999: 28ff) excludes participant-oriented adverbials—"circumstantials" in his terms—from his adverb hierarchy because he considers them to lack a rigid ordering, suggesting that they should be treated completely separately. Alexiadou (1997) and Laenzlinger (1998) conceive of the universal adverb hierarchy as also including specifier positions for circumstantials.)

Cinque's purely syntactic account has been criticized by, e.g., Ernst (1998, 1999, 2002) and Haider (1998, 2000) for leading to an unnecessary proliferation of functional heads which duplicate underlying semantically motivated distinctions; see also Shaer (2003). Ernst and Haider argue instead that the ordering restrictions on adverbials have no genuine syntactic sources but can be derived from independent semantic properties. According to this view, the syntax does not specify explicit attachment sites for (non-subcategorized) adverbials but allows them to be adjoined wherever this is not explicitly forbidden. The distribution of adverbials is accounted for by an interface condition mapping syntactic c-command domains onto semantic domains. Haider (1998, 2000) distinguishes three semantic domains: PROPOSITION > EVENT > PROCESS/STATE. Ernst (1998, 2002) assumes a richer hierarchy: SPEECH ACT > FACT > PROPOSITION > EVENT > SPECIFIED EVENT. Once the mapping procedure reaches a higher semantic domain, modifiers that address the lower domain are ruled out.

The difference between the two approaches can be seen when looking at the sentence pair in (49).

(49) a. Marie probably cleverly found a good solution.
     b. *Marie cleverly probably found a good solution.

On Cinque's account the ordering in (49a) is syntactically well-formed because this reflects the assumed order of the relevant functional heads, whereas (49b) does not. Ernst and Haider, on the other hand, argue that (49a) is fine, because *cleverly* selects for EVENTS first, and *probably*, which requires an object of the higher semantic domain PROPOSITION, is applied afterwards. When *probably* is applied first, as in (49b), the result is of type PROPOSITION, which does not fit with *cleverly* anymore. Thus, on Ernst's and Haider's account (49b) is semantically ill-formed.

While Ernst's and Haider's outline of a semantic explanation of the distributional facts can be considered a promising alternative to Cinque's hard-wired syntactic codification, many of its details remain to be worked out. For instance, as Frey (2003: 201ff) points out, in Haider's approach ordering restrictions are only assumed to hold between adverbials. The placement of adverbials is not expected to be sensitive to the position of arguments. Yet, as Frey (2003) shows, adverbials are not only ordered with respect to each other but also with respect to the arguments of the verb. Furthermore, Frey (2003) argues that on Ernst's and Haider's account adverbials shouldn't be able to move around but only appear in base-generated positions, otherwise they would be uninterpretable. This doesn't fit with the facts either in a scrambling language like German or in English; cf. the discussion in Frey (2003) and see also the argumentation in Maienborn (2001) for different base positions for locative adverbials.

With these observations in mind, Frey (2003) develops a compromise between a rigid syntactic solution and a semantic scope approach by assuming five broader classes of adverbials, each of which is assigned a syntactic base region defined by characteristic structural requirements. Adverbials are freely base generated within the limits of their characteristic region and they are allowed to move. (50) lists Frey's five adverbial classes and their syntactic positioning restrictions wrt. each other and wrt. the verb's arguments in terms of c-command ('>'); cf. Frey (2003: 202f).

(50) *Adverbial classes and base positions according to Frey (2003):*
sentence adverbials > frame and domain adverbials > event-external adverbials (e.g. causals) > highest ranked argument > event-internal adverbials (e.g. locatives, instrumentals) > (internal arguments) > process-related adverbials (e.g. manner) > verb

Frey's proposal has been taken up, further elaborated and/or challenged by numerous authors; cf. e.g. the articles in Lang, Maienborn & Fabricius-Hansen (2003).

A last complication at the syntax/semantics interface that should be mentioned here involves parenthetical adverbials, that is, adverbials that are prosodically marked as standing outside the regular syntactic structure. In English and German, these occurrences of adverbials appear with so-called comma-intonation, reflecting the corresponding use of commata in writing. When adverbials are not integrated into a sentence, they can appear in many more positions than when they are integrated, cf. (51a) vs. (51b).

(51) a. Peter obviously never came back home.
 b. (Obviously,) Peter (, obviously,) never came back home (, obviously).

How these parentheticals are treated syntactically is not entirely clear. Their semantic contribution often corresponds to at least one of the regular, integrated, usages, and there tend to be preferences for a particular use specific to a given parenthetical position; see Bonami, Godard & Kampers-Manhe (2004), Haegeman, Shaer & Frey (2009) for more discussion and Shaer (2003, 2009) for a semantic analysis based on Haegeman's (1991/2009) orphans-approach.

4 Theoretical approaches

The foremost problem in dealing with adverbials in formal semantics is that there is no natural place for them in the standard functor/argument set up. Neither do (non-subcategorized) adverbials behave syntactically or semantically as "passive" arguments, that are required by other categories and assigned to fixed positions, nor are they "active" functors, opening up specific argument requirements and assigning structural positions. We have to accept that standard formal semantics was not invented with adverbials in mind. This makes them a particularly challenging subject for formal semantic accounts.

This section discusses three classical formal semantic treatments of adverbials, all of which propose different ways of accounting for and reconciling the semantics of adverbials with some basic functor/argument account. These are (a) the operator approach most prominently advocated by Thomason & Stalnaker (1973), (b) McConnell-Ginet's (1982) argument approach, and (c) the predicate approach, whose breakthrough came with the spread of Davidsonian event semantics (Davidson 1967). (The order here does not so much reflect the original publication history but rather the order of influence on the linguistic community.)

4.1 The operator approach

The most influential text on adverbials as operators is Thomason & Stalnaker (1973), but cf. also Montague (1970), Clark (1970), Parsons (1972), Cresswell (1973), and Kamp (1975). Within this framework, adverbials are analyzed as endotypical functors. That is, they are functors that, when applied to some argument of a certain logical type, yield a result of the same type. This accounts for the typical iterability of adverbials: Since they do not change the logical type of their environment they may be iterated.

Within this framework, Thomason & Stalnaker (1973) strive to account for the differences between adverbials like *slowly* and *intentionally* on the one hand and *necessarily* on the other hand. They analyze the former as predicate modifiers and the latter as a sentence modifier. One important difference between the two types of modifiers lies in their behavior with regard to opaque contexts. The epistemic adverbial *necessarily* gives rise to opaque contexts everywhere in a sentence, whereas *intentionally* only creates opaque contexts for the object position; see Section 2.1.1.

Thomason & Stalnaker (1973) account for this difference by analyzing sentence modifiers as functions from sentence intensions to sentence intensions, that is, *necessarily* is of type <<s,t>,<s,t>>, and sentence (52a) can be represented as (52b), where the caret is used to indicate the intension.

(52) a. Necessarily, nine is odd.
 b. NECESSARILY ^[ODD (nine)]

Under this analysis the opaqueness effects are accounted for straightforwardly, because sentence modifiers apply to sentence intensions.

In contrast, predicate modifiers map the intensions of one-place predicates into intensions of one-place predicates. The restriction to one-place predicates means that, in the case of transitive verbs, predicate modifiers are applied after the direct object has combined with the verb, but before the verb combines with the subject, cf. (53).

(53) a. Oedipus intentionally married Jocasta.
 b. INTENTIONALLY ^[λx [MARRY (x, jocasta)]](oedipus)

This account correctly predicts that opacity arises with regard to the object position but not with regard to the subject position. (Note that λ-conversion into an intension is not possible here.) The opacity pattern exhibited by *intentionally* is thus elegantly accounted for. Other adverbs like, e.g., *slowly* are treated in a similar way as *intentionally*, although here we do not find parallel opacity effects, cf. (54).

(54) a. Renate slowly repaired the broken toy.
 b. Renate is the director of the German Department.

→ The director of the German Department slowly repaired the broken toy.
c. The broken toy is my puppet. → Renate slowly repaired my puppet.

No theory-internal explanation is available for these patterns. Note, however, that *slowly* cannot operate on predicate extensions, either, because this would lead to yet other unwanted consequences; cf. e.g. McConnell-Ginet (1982: 162f): Given a scenario with co-extensional dancers and singers, that is, all individuals who are singing are also dancing and vice versa, there would be no way of distinguishing, say, the slow dancers from the slow singers (due to Leibniz' Law).

One of the major motivations for the operator approach, besides accounting for the opacity effects, was a proper treatment of scope effects. A classical problem concerning the scope of adverbials is illustrated by the sentence in (55) taken from Parsons (1972).

(55) John painstakingly wrote illegibly.

Parsons (1972: 131) argues that the correct interpretation of (55) requires that "the illegibility of the writing was at least one of the things John was taking pains to do". That is, *painstakingly* clearly has scope over *illegibly*. In the operator approach, this is predicted, because in the course of forming the complex predicate, the syntactically higher adverbial is applied last, yielding (56).

(56) PAINSTAKINGLY [ILLEGIBLY ^[λx [WRITE (x)]]](john)

The second classical scope problem is discussed by Thomason & Stalnaker (1973) and concerns the different readings available for (56a/b).

(57) a. Sam carefully sliced all the bagels.
b. Sam sliced all the bagels carefully.

While the exact reading differences for (57a/b) are somewhat subtle (cf. the discussion in Eckardt 1998: 8f), they become more obvious if *carefully* is replaced, e.g., with *quickly*, where *quickly sliced all the bagels* is preferably interpreted as meaning that the overall time it took Sam to slice all the bagels was short, while *sliced all the bagels quickly* does not tell us anything about the overall amount of time, but only gives the time span for each individual slicing. Thomason & Stalnaker formalize this difference by having the quantifier within the complex predicate for (57a), but letting it have widest scope for (57b), see the formalizations in (58), where x is taken to range over bagels.

(58) a. CAREFULLY ^[λy ∀x [SLICE (y, x)]](sam)
    b. ∀x [CAREFULLY ^[λy SLICE (y, x)](sam)]

The operator approach is usually also chosen to treat non-intersective adjectives in attributive modification as, e.g., *former* in *the former alcoholic*.

4.2 The argument approach

An alternative to the operator approach is presented in McConnell-Ginet (1982). McConnell-Ginet's article discusses sentence adverbials as well as verb-related adverbials (her *Ad-Verbs*). Here, we will only focus on the latter. As mentioned above, McConnell-Ginet shows that an extensional operator approach will not work for adverbs like *slowly*. Furthermore, she argues that an intensional solution lacks psychological plausibility and therefore isn't adequate, either. Her own account draws on the observation that some manner adverbials are obligatory in a similar way as direct objects; see the discussion of the sample sentences (2) in section 1.1. McConnell-Ginet goes on to argue that verb-related adverbials in general should be treated as arguments of the verb. According to this view, verbs have a latent potential of being further specified wrt. certain dimensions. What adverbials do is activate this potential and fill in a corresponding value. For instance, the verb *to run* has a latent argument slot for speed, which may be activated and filled in by an adverbial such as *quickly*. A simplified representation of (59a) along these lines is given in (59b).

(59) a. Fritz runs quickly.
    b. RUN (fritz, quickly)

In order to derive this representation, McConnell-Ginet introduces the operation of *verb-augmentation*, by which additional argument slots can be made available whenever needed. Treating adverbials as arguments is particularly appealing in the case of non-optional adverbials, e.g. for verbs like *behave* in (60).

(60) The kids behaved admirably.

McConell-Ginet's approach distinguishes subcategorized and optional adverbials only by the mode of integration. While subcategorized adverbials already have an argument slot available in the lexical entry of the verb, optional adverbials trigger verb-augmentation. After this operation has taken place, the two types of adverbials are no longer distinguishable. In addition, verb-augmentation does not distinguish different types of Ad-Verbal modifiers. See Landman (2000) and Marten (2002) for further discussions of McConnell-Ginet's original approach and possible extensions.

4.3 The predicate approach

In his seminal paper "The logical form of action sentences" published in 1967 the language philosopher Donald Davidson argues for a new ontological category of events. This proposal has proven to be exceptionally fruitful for linguistics paving the way for simpler and more adequate analyses of a multitude of linguistic phenomena; cf. article 8 [Semantics: Theories] (Maienborn) *Event semantics*. Davidson (1967) argues that a sentence such as (61a) does not express a mere relation between Jones and the toast but introduces a hidden event argument, which stands for the proper event of buttering, thus yielding (61b) as a formal representation for (61a).

(61) a. Jones buttered the toast.
 b. ∃e [BUTTER (jones, the toast, e)]

One of the main motivations of Davidson's proposal was to provide a straightforward analysis of adverbial modification. If verbs introduce a hidden event argument, then (intersective) adverbial modifiers can be analyzed as simple first order predicates that add information about this event. Thus, Davidsons's famous sentence (62a) receives a formal representation as in (62b), or—adopting the so-called Neo-Davidsonian framework of, e.g. Higginbotham (1985, 2000) and Parsons (1990)—as in (62c).

(62) a. Jones buttered the toast in the bathroom with the knife at midnight.
 b. ∃e [BUTTER (jones, the toast, e) & IN (e, the bathroom) & INSTR (e, the knife) & AT (e, midnight)]
 c. ∃e [BUTTER (e) & AGENT (e, jones) & PATIENT (e, the toast) & IN (e, the bathroom) & INSTR (e, the knife) & AT (e, midnight)]

While Davidson's original proposal was confined to participant-oriented adverbials, Parsons (1990) extends the scope of the Davidsonian approach to manner adverbials like *slowly*. Event-based treatments of mental-attitude adverbials are discussed in Eckardt (1998), Wyner (1998), and Geuder (2000).

Davidson's analysis of adverbials has two major merits. First, it accounts for the typical entailment patterns that characterize (intersective) adverbials directly on the basis of their semantic representation. That is, the entailments in (63a–d) follow from (63) simply by virtue of the logical rule of simplification. (Due to this feature, Davidson's approach cannot (easily) handle non-veridical adverbials.)

(63) Jones buttered the toast in the bathroom at midnight.
    a. Jones buttered the toast in the bathroom and Jones buttered the toast at midnight.
    b. Jones buttered the toast in the bathroom.
    c. Jones buttered the toast at midnight.
    d. Jones buttered the toast.

Furthermore, Davidson's approach does not allow us to infer (63) from (63b) and (63c), since the latter sentences might relate to different events—a feature dubbed *non-entailment* by Katz (2008). Again, this captures the data correctly.

The second major merit of Davidson's account is that it treats adverbial modifiers on a par with adnominal modifiers, thereby acknowledging their fundamental similarities. Both adverbial and standard attributive modifiers provide one-place predicates, the only difference being whether these predicates are applied to a noun's referential argument or to the verbal event argument. More generally speaking, the Davidsonian predicate approach makes a considerable step forward towards a truly compositional semantics for adverbials by teasing apart lexical and combinatorial ingredients of their meaning contribution. The lexical meaning of a manner expression such as *loud* or a locative such as *in the garden* simply denotes a certain property as in (64), irrespective of whether these expressions happen to be used as adnominal (65) or adverbial (66) modifiers (or as subcategorized arguments or main predicates together with the copula); cf., e.g., Bierwisch (1988), Wunderlich (1991), Maienborn (2001). (But see Section 5.2. for some qualifications concerning an adequate representation for manner expressions.)

(64) a. *loud:* $\qquad$ $\lambda x\,[\text{LOUD}\,(x)]$
     b. *in the garden:* $\quad$ $\lambda x\,[\text{IN}\,(x,\,\text{the garden})]$

(65) a. *loud girl:* $\qquad$ $\lambda y\,[\text{GIRL}\,(y)\,\&\,\text{LOUD}\,(y)]$
     b. *girl in the garden:* $\quad$ $\lambda y\,[\text{GIRL}\,(y)\,\&\,\text{IN}\,(y,\,\text{the garden})]$

(66) a. *sing loudly:* $\qquad$ $\lambda e\,[\text{SING}\,(e)\,\&\,\text{LOUD}\,(e)]$
     b. *sing in the garden:* $\quad$ $\lambda e\,[\text{SING}\,(e)\,\&\,\text{IN}\,(e,\,\text{the garden})]$

Given their common lexical roots it comes as no surprise that adverbials such as *fast* and *slowly* in (67) display the same kind of context-dependency as their adjectival counterparts, requiring the inclusion of comparison classes; cf., e.g., the degree-based analyses of these adjectives in Bierwisch (1989) and Kennedy (2007).

(67) Compared to other swimmers, Sarah crossed the channel fast, but compared to Hovercrafts, she crossed it slowly.

In summing up we should note that the three classical accounts of the semantics of adverbials were originally proposed as alternatives to each other, although they differ considerably in scope. For instance, a Davidsonian predicate approach is not particularly well-suited for adverbials that create opaque contexts, whereas McConnell-Ginet's (1982) argument approach seems especially attractive for subcategorized adverbials. Moreover, there is no principled incompatibility between using events on the one hand and analyzing at least some adverbials as operators on predicates; cf. Eckardt (1998: 12f). Given the wide acceptance of events and their multifaceted use in present-day semantic theory, current accounts of adverbial semantics mostly rely on the use of events as formal semantic objects in one way or another. On this basis more sophisticated and differentiated analyses of adverbial classes are being developed that strive to account, e.g., for the particular behavior of adverbials wrt. information structure (see especially Eckardt 2003 on this point) as well as to deal with the further challenges that adverbials still pose. Two of them concerning compositionality and ontological issues will be discussed in the next section.

5 Challenges to compositionality and ontology

5.1 Uncovering the compositional machinery

In the previous section we pointed out that a Davidsonian predicate approach to adverbials makes a considerable step forward in separating the lexical and the combinatorial meaning components that interact in yielding the characteristic semantics of adverbials. (68) repeated from (64b) above specifies the lexical meaning of a locative adverbial for illustration. The standard combinatorics may be spelled out by a modification template MOD as in (69). MOD takes a modifier and an expression to be modified and yields a conjunction of predicates thus accounting for the fundamental insight of the Davidsonian predicate approach; cf. also Heim & Kratzer (1998) for an alternative solution.

(68) *in the garden*: λx [IN (x, the garden)]

(69) MOD: λQ λP λx [P(x) & Q(x)]

Leaving details aside, the application of MOD to an adverbial and a verbal eventuality predicate will guarantee that the adverbial is predicated of the verb's event argument as in (70).

(70) *sing in the garden*: λe [SING (e) & IN (e, the garden)]

This gives us the desired result—at least for the standard conception of intersective adverbials. Unfortunately, matters turn out to be more intricate upon closer inspection. Using locatives as a test case, Maienborn (1996, 2001, 2003) shows that, in addition to supplying a holistic predicate of the verb's event argument, circumstantial adverbials may take various further interpretations. More specifically, Maienborn distinguishes three different usages of locative adverbials: as *frame adverbial*, as *event-external adverbial*, or as *event-internal adverbial*; cf. (71a–c), respectively. Only the event-external variant in (71b) follows the standard MOD pattern in (69) whereas the frame and the event-internal variants appear to behave differently. Since it would be both implausible and theoretically unattractive to trace these meaning differences back to a lexical ambiguity of the respective locatives, they must emerge somehow in the course of composition.

(71) a. In Argentina, Maradona is still very popular.
      b. Maradona signed the contract in Argentina.
      c. Maradona signed the contract on the last page.

The first noticeable difference is that frame adverbials (which we already mentioned in Section 2.2, see the discussion of (40)–(41)) pattern with domain adverbials in being non-veridical. Frame adverbials are not part of what is properly asserted but restrict the speaker's claim. Therefore, their omission does not preserve truth if the domain restrictions expressed through the frame adverbial do not pattern with the default domain restrictions; cf. the discussion of (28) in Section 2.1.1. By contrast, both event-external and event-internal locatives are veridical:

(72) a. In Argentina, Maradona is still very popular.
      ↛ Maradona is still very popular.

b. Maradona signed the contract in Argentina.
→ Maradona signed the contract.
c. Maradona signed the contract on the last page.
→ Maradona signed the contract.

Secondly, frame and event-internal adverbials differ from event-external adverbials in being semantically underspecified in crucial respects. A frame adverbial such as (73) may receive several interpretations along the dimensions spelled out, e.g., in (73a–c).

(73) In Italy, Maradona was married.
a. When he was in Italy, Maradona was married.
b. According to the laws in Italy, Maradona was married.
c. According to the belief of the people in Italy, Maradona was married.

That is, one can only say that frame adverbials restrict the speaker's claim, but which dimension exactly is being restricted is left semantically underspecified. Basically the same holds true for event-internal adverbials. Their common semantic contribution consists in specifying some internal aspect of the verb's event argument, whose exact role is left semantically implicit and can only be determined when taking into account conceptual knowledge about the respective event type. Take, e.g., (71c): The locative (in its preferred, event-internal, reading) does not express a location for the overall event of Maradona signing the contract—this would be the event-external reading—but only for one of its parts, viz. Maradona's signature (which, by the way, isn't referred to overtly in the sentence).

A particularly puzzling feature of frame and event-internal locatives that is related to their semantic indeterminacy is that they may take on non-locative interpretations. More specifically, frame adverbials may have a temporal reading (cf. the paraphrase (73a)), whereas event-internal adverbials tend to allow additional instrumental or manner readings; cf. (74).

(74) a. The cook prepared the chicken in a Marihuana sauce.
b. The bank robbers escaped on bicycles.
c. Paul is standing on his head.

The adverbial in (74a) specifies a particular mode of preparing the food. Thus, it makes some sort of manner contribution. The adverbial in (74b) supplies information about the means of transport that was used by the bank robbers. It could be replaced by an instrumental phrase like *with the cab*. In the case of (74c), one might even doubt whether the original locative meaning of the preposition is still present at all. In this case, there should be an entity that is located on Paul's head. What could that sensibly be? (Note that it can't be the regular subject referent Paul, which would include the head as a proper part. Maienborn (2003: 498ff) proposes a possible answer to this puzzle that is based on the locative's regular meaning. According to this solution it is Paul's remaining body (modulo his head) that is located on—and thus supported by—Paul's head.)

Note that these supplementary, non-locative readings of frame and event-internal ad-verbials are most appropriately queried by using the respective non-locative interrogatives:

(73′) a. When was Maradona married?

(74′) a. How did the cook prepare the chicken?
b. How / With what did the bank robbers escape?
c. How is Paul standing?

Standard event-external adverbials, on the other hand, always refer to the overall location of the verb's event argument. They do not share the ability of event-internal and frame modifiers to convey additional non-locative information, and they can only be questioned by a locative interrogative.

The challenge that circumstantial adverbials such as locatives pose to a formal semantics of adverbs is, on the one hand, that there is good reason to assume that expressions such as *in Argentina* or *on the last page* have a unique lexical meaning, i.e. they express the property of some entity being located in a particular spatial location. On the other hand, we have to account for the different readings of locatives and their characteristic properties in terms of inferential behavior, semantic indeterminacy and the emergence of supplementary non-locative interpretations.

In a nutshell, the solution proposed in Maienborn (1996, 2001, 2003) takes the following track. First, it is shown that there is a strict correlation between the position of a locative adverbial and its interpretation. More specifically, the three types of locatives are argued to have distinctive syntactic base positions, each corresponding to one of Frey's (2003) adverbial positions; see (50). Event-internal adverbials are base-generated at the V-periphery, event-external adverbials are base-generated at the VP-periphery, and frame adverbials have a high base-adjunction site within the C-Domain. These distinct structural positions provide the key for a compositional account, since an adverbial will be linked up with different target referents depending on its structural position. While event-external adverbials are linked up to the verb's event argument, event-internal and frame adverbials are semantically underspecified in this respect. Event-internal adverbials are linked up to a referent that is related to the verb's event argument, and frame adverbials are linked up to a referent that is related to the topic of the sentence. The identification of these target referents is shown to depend on discourse and world knowledge. The non-locative readings of event-internal and frame adverbials are reconstructed as a side effect of the pragmatic resolution of semantic indeterminacy; cf. also articles 9 [this volume] (Egg) *Semantic underspecification* and 5 [Semantics: Theories] (Lang & Maienborn) *Two-level Semantics*. Maienborn proposes a compositional account for these adverbials that is sensitive to the observed structural and pragmatic influences while still preserving the basic insights of the classical Davidsonian approach. To this end, the template MOD in (69) is replaced by a more general variant MOD* in (75), whose application is regulated by the interface condition in (76); cf. Maienborn (2003: 489).

(75) MOD*: $\lambda Q\, \lambda P\, \lambda x\, [P(x)\ \&\ R(x, v)\ \&\ Q(v)]$

(76) Condition on the application of MOD*:
If MOD* is applied in a structural environment of categorial type X, then R = PART-OF, otherwise (i.e. in an XP-environment) R is the identity function.

MOD* introduces a free variable v and a relational variable R. If applied in an XP-environment, R is instantiated as identity, i.e. v is identified with the referential argument of the modified expression, thus yielding the standard variant MOD. This is the case with event-external adverbials. If MOD* is applied in an X-environment, R is instantiated as PART-OF; cf. also Dölling (2003) for a formal account of the flexibility of adverbial modification that is similar in spirit.

The relation PART-OF pairs entities with their integral constituents. In the case of events, among these are the event's participants. The result of applying MOD* to a sentence with an event-internal adverbial such as (77a) is given in (77b).

(77) a. The bank robber escaped on the bicycle.
b. $\exists e\, [\text{ESCAPE}\,(e)\ \&\ \text{THEME}\,(e, \text{bank robber})\ \&\ \text{PART-OF}\,(e, v)\ \&\ \text{ON}\,(v, \text{bike})]$

According to the semantic representation in (77b), an entity v which is involved in the escaping event is located on the bicycle. This is as far as the compositional semantics of event-internal adverbials takes us. The identification of v and its exact role in e can only be spelled out at the conceptual level taking into account world knowledge, e.g., about extrinsic and intrinsic movement, the use of vehicles for extrinsic movement, spatial prerequisites that need to be fulfilled in order for a vehicle to function properly, etc. A simplified conceptual spell-out for (77b) is given in (77c); cf. Maienborn (2003: 490ff) for details; see also article 5 [Semantics: Theories] (Lang & Maienborn) *Two-level Semantics*.

(77) c. ∃e [ESCAPE (e) & EXTRINSIC-MOVE (e) & THEME (e, bank robber)
  & INSTR (e, bike) & VEHICLE (bike) & SUPPORT (bike, bank robber)
  & ON (bank robber, bike)]

This conceptual spell-out provides a plausible utterance meaning for sentence (77a). It goes beyond the compositionally determined meaning in the following respects: (a) it specifies that the escape was taken by extrinsic means (EXTRINSIC-MOVE). As a consequence, (b) the bike is identified as the instrument of locomotion in the given event. This in turn leads (c) to an instantiation of the free variable v by the discourse referent representing the bank robber and an identification of the PART-OF relation with the THEME-role. For other cases, as, e.g., (78) more conceptual inferencing will be required in order to identify a suitable referent to which the event-internal locative applies.

(78) Paul tickled Maria on her neck.

That is, what turns out to be located on Maria's neck in (78) could be, e.g., Paul's hand or maybe some feather he used for tickling Maria. Although not manifest at the linguistic surface, such conceptually inferred units qualify as potential instantiations of the compositionally introduced free variable v.

Maienborn (2001: §6) sketches how MOD* may also account for the semantics of frame adverbials. Generalizing Klein's (1994) notion of *topic time*, frame adverbials can be seen as providing an underspecified restriction on an integral part of a *topic situation*.

All in all Maienborn's proposal suggests that the flexibility of adverbial modification is the result of adverbials (a) having several potential structural integration sites in combination with (b) being subject to a particular kind of semantic indeterminacy.

5.2 What are manners?

In Section 2 above, we distinguished, among other things, between manner adverbials, degree adverbials, and other adverbials, *half-way* being one of them. But already the notion of manner adverbials is not very clearly defined, and is usually taken to comprise a rather large group of adverbials. Thus, all adverbs in (79) are typically considered manner adverbials.

(79) a. Peter runs fast/slowly.
 b. Marie sings loudly/quietly.
 c. Kim dances beautifully/woodenly.
 d. Claire solved the problem skillfully/intelligently.

All these adverbials can be questioned by *How ...?* They are all veridical, and they cannot take scope over sentence negation nor do they create opaque contexts. Nevertheless, their meaning contributions to the sentence are very different. This can be easily seen by looking at the behavior of the adverbials in (79) with regard to standard paraphrases for manner adverbials. Standard paraphrases like *... in a ADJ manner* or *The way X VERBs is ADJ* are not appropriate for all these items. They are perfectly applicable to (79c): *Kim dances beautifully/in a beautiful manner* and *The way Kim dances is beautiful* are synonymous. However, they do not fit for (79a/b): *to run fast* means that the speed of the running was fast, not the manner. Similarly, *to sing loudly* means that the sound-volume of the singing was loud, not the manner. Finally, (79d) seems to correspond to these paraphrases only on one reading, according to which Claire reached the solution by a series of intelligent steps. On a reading of (79d) according to which the solution arrived at is an intelligent one, the paraphrases turn out to be inappropriate, and a classification of this reading as an resultative or a blend might be more fitting. A further difference between (79d) and the other adverbials in (79a–c) is that it involves a direct relation to the subject: Roughly, the subject appears as intelligent through the way of solving the problem or the kind of the solution s/he provided. Obviously, assuming a plain analysis as one-place predicates over events for the adverbials in (79) won't suffice to account properly for all these peculiarities.

(80) a. Peter talked loudly.
 b. $\exists e\, [\text{AGENT}\,(e, peter)\,\&\,\text{TALK}\,(e)\,\&\,\text{LOUD}\,(e)]$

An analysis of (80a) along the lines of (80b) does not make explicit that the adverbial specifies the sound-volume of the talking, i.e., that it is specifying one particular aspect of the talking event. Another strange effect of a plain Neo-Davidsonian representation is that the verb and the manner adverbial appear to be semantically on a par (both providing one-place predicates over events) while intuitively and syntactically, they are not.

One possible way toward a more elaborate theory of manner adverbials that helps overcome some of these shortcomings consists in introducing manners as a further ontological category in our formal language. This idea has recently been brought back into the discussion by Piñón (2007, 2008). Its first, dismissive, discussion can be found in Fodor (1972), whereas Dik (1975) was the first champion of this approach. The main idea is simple enough: we need to be able to access the conceptual properties of the events introduced by the verb in order to gain an adequate understanding of manner modification. Thus, in order to capture the fact that *loudly* assigns the property LOUD to the sound-volume of the talking, we need to retrieve the corresponding conceptual coordinate of the talking event. Similarly, for *fast*, we need the conceptual coordinate for speed. What kind of coordinate do we need for adverbs like *beautifully* and *intelligently*? The availability of the manner paraphrase for these adverbs shows us that we need a coordinate that is more complex than those needed for *loudly* and *fast* and that it cannot be reduced to what are essentially quite straightforward, monodimensional scales of the intuitively clear concepts speed and sound-volume. For the sake of simplicity, we will assume that in both cases the required coordinate is in fact a manner of the events in question, so that, consequently, *beautifully* is predicated of the manner of dancing, and *intelligently* of the manner of answering the question. A simplified illustration of a semantic representation for (79c) is given below, where the conceptual coordinate manner is linked to the event argument via an underspecified relation R; cf. (81). (This corresponds to one of the versions considered in Fodor 1972.)

(81) a. Peter danced beautifully.
b. $\exists e\ [\text{AGENT}\ (e, \text{peter})\ \&\ \text{DANCE}\ (e)\ \&\ \exists m\ [R\ (e, m)\ \&\ \text{BEAUTIFUL}\ (m)]]$

While clearly pointing in the right direction, this approach obviously also raises many intricate questions. While we cannot do justice to all of them here, it is helpful to briefly consider the pros and cons of this approach.

As Piñón (2007) points out, one argument in favor of assuming manner as an ontological entity is that it can be perceived, as evidenced by expressions such as (82); cf. the discussion on perception reports as one of the main criteria for assuming the ontological category of events in article 8 [Semantics: Theories] (Maienborn) *Event semantics*.

(82) I saw how Linda danced.

Furthermore, as Piñón (2007) argues, assuming manners also allows us to systematically relate the *in an X manner* paraphrase to manner adverbials, since in both cases we have predicates of manners. The head noun of the paraphrasing prepositional phrase refers to a manner, and the attributive adjective predicates of this manner. In the very same way, its adverbial counterpart predicates of the manner made available as a conceptual coordinate of the event referred to by the verb.

Finally, this fine-grained analysis of manner modification can also be used to account for otherwise unexplainable patterns, e.g., the different behavior of the adverb *audibly* in (83a/b) discussed in Cresswell (1985: 186ff).

(83) a. Isolde audibly precedes/follows Jeremy.
     b. Kiri sings/dances audibly.

As Cresswell points out, in the case of (83a), it can be some activity other than the preceding/following itself that causes the audibility, whereas in the case of (83b), what is audible is the sound of the singing/dancing. This observation can be accounted for by assuming that the conceptual structure of dancing/singing events differs from the conceptual structure of preceding/following events in that only the former but not the latter readily provide the corresponding sound-coordinate. The scope-taking usages of manner adverbials discussed in Section 4.1 can also be accounted for by resorting to an analysis based on manners, cf. Piñón (2007) and Schäfer (2008) for two formal accounts.

Obvious objections to this approach concern matters of ontology: What exactly are manners supposed to be, and what do we mean when we speak of coordinates of events? Manners, speeds, and sound volumes are all ontologically dependent on the events introduced by the verbs in the respective sentences, that is, they do not and cannot exist by themselves. These ontologically dependent entities can be viewed as coordinates in the conceptual structure of their host events. The exact nature and internal structure of these coordinates is still an unanswered question, but Geuder's (2006) discussion of manner adverbs and their relation to conceptual dimensions is a promising starting point; cf. also the notion of *dossiers* in article 1 [this volume] (Bierwisch) *Semantic features and primes*.

Note that this analysis has some striking resemblance to the semantics for event-internal adverbials proposed in the previous section; cf. the discussion of MOD* in (75). That is, conceptually dependent units such as speed, sound-volume, or manner may be made accessible for further specification via a semantically underspecified event relation.

Event-internal circumstantials and manner adverbials thus both enable and enforce a closer look into the internal structure of events. Obviously, much remains to be done in this area. Manner adverbials, despite their innocent appearance as being the paradigmatic case for a textbook Davidsonian analysis, still turn out to pose many riddles that a formal semantics for adverbials will have to solve.

6 Conclusion

Adverbials and their dedicated word class, the adverbs, comprise a heterogeneous set of lexical and semantic classes and subclasses with very specific inferential and distributional properties. They are only loosely tied to the surrounding syntactic and semantic structure, leaving much space for variation and adaptation. What the vast majority of adverbs has in common is that they are non-subcategorized linguistic parasites: Wherever they find a suitable integration site, they attach to it and supply additional and uncalled-for information. Precisely because of this parasitic nature and their frappant flexibility, adverbials constitute a challenge for linguistic theory, which, in turn, must account for this flexible means of natural language expression in terms of a sufficiently rigid account of their lexical, compositional, and conceptual semantics.

7 References

Alexiadou, Artemis 1997. *Adverb Placement: A Case Study in Antisymmetric Syntax*. Amsterdam: Benjamins.
Alexiadou, Artemis 2004a. Adverbs across frameworks. *Lingua* 114, 677–682.
Alexiadou, Artemis (ed.) 2004b. *Taking up the Gauntlet. Adverbs across Frameworks. Lingua* 114, 677–682.
Austin, Jennifer, Stefan Engelberg & Gesa Rauh (eds.) 2004. *Adverbials. The Interplay between Meaning, Context, and Syntactic Structure*. Amsterdam: Benjamins.
van der Auwera, Johan (ed.) 1998. *Adverbial Constructions in the Languages of Europe*. Berlin: Mouton de Gruyter.
Bartsch, Renate 1972/1976. *Adverbialsemantik. Die Konstitution logisch-semantischer Repräsentationen von Adverbialkonstruktionen*. Frankfurt/M. Athenäum. English Translation: *The Grammar of Adverbials. A Study in the Semantics and Syntax of Adverbial Constructions*. Amsterdam: North-Holland, 1976.
Bartsch, Renate 1987. The construction of properties under perspectives. *Journal of Semantics* 5, 293–320.
Bellert, Irena 1977. On semantic and distributional properties of sentential adverbs. *Linguistic Inquiry* 8, 337–351.
Bierwisch, Manfred 1988. On the grammar of local prepositions. In: M. Bierwisch, W. Motsch & I. Zimmermann (eds.). *Syntax, Semantik und Lexikon*. Berlin: Akademie Verlag, 1–65.
Bierwisch, Manfred 1989. The semantics of gradation. In: M. Bierwisch & E. Lang (eds.). *Dimensional Adjectives*. Berlin: Springer, 71–261.
Bonami, Olivier, Danièle Godard & Brigitte Kampers-Manhe 2004. Adverb classification. In: F. Corblin & H. de Swart (eds.). *Handbook of French Semantics*. Stanford, CA: CSLI Publications, 143–184.
Cinque, Guglielmo 1999. *Adverbs and Functional Heads. A Cross-Linguistic Perspective*. Oxford: Oxford University Press.

Clark, Romane 1970. Concerning the logic of predicate modifiers. *Noûs* 4, 311–335.
Cresswell, Max J. 1973. *Logics and Languages*. London: Methuen.
Cresswell, Max J. 1985. *Adverbial Modification. Interval Semantics and Its Rivals*. Dordrecht: Reidel.
Davidson, Donald 1967. The logical form of action sentences. In: N. Rescher (ed.). *The Logic of Decision and Action*. Pittsburgh, PA: University of Pittsburgh Press, 81–95. Reprinted in: D. Davidson (ed.). *Essays on Actions and Events*. Oxford: Oxford University Press, 1980, 105–122.
Delfitto, Denis 2000. Adverbs and the syntax/semantics interface. *Italian Journal of Linguistics* 12, 13–53.
Dik, Simon C. 1975. The semantic representation of manner adverbials. In: A. Kraak (ed.). *Linguistics in the Netherlands 1972–1973*. Assen: Van Gorcum, 96–121.
Dölling, Johannes 2003. Flexibility in adverbal modification: Reinterpretation as contextual enrichment. In: E. Lang, C. Maienborn & C. Fabricius-Hansen (eds.). *Modifying Adjuncts*. Berlin: de Gruyter, 511–552.
Eckardt, Regine 1998. *Events, Adverbs, and Other Things. Issues in the Semantics of Manner Adverbs*. Tübingen: Niemeyer.
Eckardt, Regine 2003. Manner adverbs and information structure. Evidence from the adverbial modification of verbs of creation. In: E. Lang, C. Maienborn & C. Fabricius-Hansen (eds.). *Modifying Adjuncts*. Berlin: de Gruyter, 261–305.
Egg, Markus 2006. Anti-Ikonizität an der Syntax-Semantik-Schnittstelle. *Zeitschrift für Sprachwissenschaft* 25, 1–38.
Ernst, Thomas 1984. *Towards an Integrated Theory of Adverb Position in English*. Bloomington, IN: Indiana University Linguistics Club.
Ernst, Thomas 1998. Scope based adjunct licensing. In: P. Tamanji & K. Kusumoto (eds.). *Proceedings of the Annual Meeting of the North East Linguistic Society (= NELS)* 28. Amherst, MA: GLSA, 127–142.
Ernst, Thomas 1999. Adjuncts, the universal base, and word order typology. In: P. Tamanji, M. Hirotami & N. Hall (eds.). *Proceedings of the Annual Meeting of the North East Linguistic Society (= NELS)* 29. Amherst, MA: GLSA, 209–223.
Ernst, Thomas 2002. *The Syntax of Adjuncts*. Cambridge: Cambridge University Press.
Ernst, Thomas 2004. Domain adverbs and the syntax of adjuncts. In: J. Austin, S. Engelberg & G. Rauh (eds.). *Adverbials. The Interplay between Meaning, Context, and Syntactic Structure*. Amsterdam: Benjamins, 103–129.
Ernst, Thomas 2007. On the role of semantics in a theory of adverb syntax. *Lingua* 117, 1008–1033.
Ernst, Thomas 2009. Speaker-oriented adverbs. *Natural Language and Linguistic Theory* 27, 497–544.
Fodor, Jerry A. 1972. Troubles about actions. In: D. Davidson & G. Harman (eds.). *Semantics of Natural Language*. Dordrecht: Reidel, 48–69.
Frey, Werner 2003. Syntactic conditions on adjunct classes. In: E. Lang, C. Maienborn & C. Fabricius-Hansen (eds.). *Modifying Adjuncts*. Berlin: de Gruyter, 163–209.
Geuder, Wilhelm 2000. *Oriented Adverbs. Issues in the Lexical Semantics of Event Adverbs*. Doctoral dissertation. University of Tübingen.
Geuder, Wilhelm 2006. Manner modification of states. In: Ch. Ebert & C. Endriss (eds.). *Proceedings of Sinn und Bedeutung (= SuB)* 10. Berlin: ZAS, 111–124.
Giannakidou, Anastasia 1999. Affective dependencies. *Linguistics & Philosophy* 22, 367–421.

Goldberg, Adele & Farrell Ackerman 2001. The pragmatics of obligatory adjuncts. *Language* 77, 798–814.
Haegeman, Liliane 1991/2009. Parenthetical adverbials: The radical orphanage approach. In: S. Chiba et al. (eds.). *Aspects of Modern English Linguistics: Papers presented to Masatomo Ukaji on his 60th Birthday*. Tokio: Kaitakusha, 232–254. Reprinted in: B. Shaer et al. (eds.). *Dislocated Elements in Discourse. Syntactic, Semantic, and Pragmatic Perspectives*. New York: Routledge, 2009, 331–347.
Haegeman, Liliane, Benjamin Shaer & Werner Frey 2009. Postscript: Problems and solutions for orphan analyses. In: B. Shaer et el. (eds.). *Dislocated Elements in Discourse. Syntactic, Semantic, and Pragmatic Perspectives*. New York: Routledge, 348–365.
Haider, Hubert 1998. Adverbials at the syntax-semantics interface. In: H. Kamp & U. Reyle (eds.). *Tense and Aspect Now. Perspectives on Problems in the Theory of Tense and Aspect*. Tübingen: Niemeyer, 51–67.
Haider, Hubert 2000. Adverb placement: Convergence of structure and licensing. *Theoretical Linguistics* 26, 95–134.
Heim, Irene & Angelika Kratzer 1998. *Semantics in Generative Grammar*. Oxford: Blackwell.
Higginbotham, James 1985. On semantics. *Linguistic Inquiry* 16, 547–593.
Higginbotham, James 2000. On events in linguistic semantics. In: J. Higginbotham, F. Pianesi & A. Varzi (eds.). *Speaking of Events*. Oxford: Oxford University Press, 49–79.
Himmelmann, Nikolaus P. & Eva Schultze-Berndt 2005. Issues in the syntax and semantics of participant-oriented adjuncts: An introduction. In: N. P. Himmelmann & E. Schultze-Berndt (eds.). *Secondary Predication and Adverbial Modification. The Typology of Depictives*. Oxford: Oxford University Press, 1–67.
Huddleston, Rodney & Geoffrey K. Pullum 2002. *The Cambridge Grammar of the English Language*. Cambridge: Cambridge University Press.
Jackendoff, Ray 1972. *Semantic Interpretation in Generative Grammar*. Cambridge, MA: The MIT Press.
Kamp, Hans 1975. Two theories about adjectives. In: E. L. Keenan (ed.). *Formal Semantics of Natural Language*. Cambridge: Cambridge University Press, 123–155.
Katz, Graham 2008. Manner modification of state verbs. In: L. McNally & Ch. Kennedy (eds.). *Adjectives and Adverbs. Syntax, Semantics, and Discourse*. Oxford: Oxford University Press, 220–248.
Kennedy, Christopher 2007. Vagueness and grammar: The semantics of relative and absolute gradable predicates. *Linguistics & Philosophy* 30, 1–45.
Klein, Wolfgang 1994. *Time in Language*. London: Routledge.
Krifka, Manfred 1992. A compositional semantics for multiple focus construction. In: J. Jacobs (ed.). *Informationsstruktur und Grammatik*. Opladen: Westdeutscher Verlag, 17–53.
Laenzlinger, Christopher 1998. *Comparative Studies in Word Order Variation: Adverbs, Pronouns and Clause Structure in Romance and Germanic*. Amsterdam: Benjamins.
Landman, Fred 2000. *Events and Plurality. The Jerusalem Lectures*. Dordrecht: Kluwer.
Lang, Ewald, Claudia Maienborn & Cathrine Fabricius-Hansen (eds.) 2003. *Modifying Adjuncts*. Berlin: de Gruyter.
Larson, Richard K. 1998. Events and modification in nominals. In: D. Strolovitch & A. Lawson (eds.). *Proceedings from Semantics and Linguistic Theory (= SALT) VIII*. Ithaca, NY: Cornell University Press, 145–168.
Maienborn, Claudia 1996. *Situation und Lokation. Die Bedeutung lokaler Adjunkte von Verbalprojektionen*. Tübingen: Stauffenburg.

Maienborn, Claudia 2001. On the position and interpretation of locative modifiers. *Natural Language Semantics* 9, 191–240.
Maienborn, Claudia 2003. Event-internal adverbials: Semantic underspecification and conceptual interpretation. In: E. Lang, C. Maienborn & C. Fabricius-Hansen (eds.). *Modifying Adjuncts*. Berlin: de Gruyter, 475–509.
Marten, Lutz 2002. *At the Syntax-pragmatics Interface: Verbal Underspecification and Concept Formation in Dynamic Syntax*. Oxford: Oxford University Press.
McConnell-Ginet, Sally 1982. Adverbs and logical form. A linguistically realistic theory. *Language* 58, 144–184.
McNally, Louise & Christopher Kennedy (eds.) 2008. *Adjectives and Adverbs. Syntax, Semantics, and Discourse*. Oxford: Oxford University Press.
Mittwoch, Anita 1977. How to refer to one's own words: Speech-act modifying adverbials and the performative analysis. *Journal of Linguistics* 13, 177–189.
Montague, Richard 1970. English as a formal language. In: B. Visentini (ed.). *Linguaggi nella Società e nella Tecnica*. Milan: Edizioni di Comunità, 189–223. Reprinted in: R. H. Thomason (ed.). *Formal Philosophy. Selected Papers of Richard Montague*. New Haven, CT: Yale University Press, 188–221.
Morzycki, Marcin 2008. Adverbial modification of adjectives: Evaluatives and a little beyond. In: J. Dölling, T. Heyde-Zybatow & M. Schäfer (eds.). *Event Structures in Linguistic Form and Interpretation*. Berlin: de Gruyter, 103–126.
Nilsen, Øystein 2004. Domains for adverbs. *Lingua* 114, 809–847.
Parsons, Terence 1972. Some problems concerning the logic of grammatical modifiers. In: D. Davidson & G. Harman (eds.). *Semantics of Natural Language*. Dordrecht: Reidel, 127–141.
Parsons, Terence 1990. *Events in the Semantics of English. A Study in Subatomic Semantics*. Cambridge, MA: The MIT Press.
Piñón, Christopher 2007. Manner adverbs and manners. Handout, *7. Ereignissemantik-Konferenz*, Tübingen, December 20, 2007. http://pinon.sdf-eu.org/covers/mam.html, August 9, 2011.
Piñón, Christopher 2008. From properties to manners: A historical line of thought about manner adverbs. In: A. Lobke et al. (eds.). *Papers of the Linguistic Society of Belgium*, vol. 3, 2008. http://pinon.sdf-en.org/covers/pm.html, August 9, 2011.
Quirk, Randolph, Sidney Greenbaum, Geoffrey Leech & Jan Svartvik 1985. *A Comprehensive Grammar of the English Language*. Harlow: Longman.
Rawlins, Kyle 2008. Unifying *illegally*. In: J. Dölling, T. Heyde-Zybatow & M. Schäfer (eds.). *Event Structures in Linguistic Form and Interpretation*. Berlin: de Gruyter, 81–102.
Rothstein, Susan 2003. Secondary predication and aspectual structure. In: E. Lang, C. Maienborn & C. Fabricius-Hansen (eds.). *Modifying Adjuncts*. Berlin: de Gruyter, 553–590.
Sasse, Hans-Jürgen 1993. Syntactic categories and subcategories. In: J. Jacobs, A. v. Stechow, W. Sternefeld & T. Vennemann (eds.). *Syntax– Ein internationales Handbuch zeitgenössischer Forschung* (HSK 9). Berlin: de Gruyter, 646–686.
Schäfer, Martin 2005. *German Adverbial Adjectives: Syntactic Position and Semantic Interpretation*. Doctoral dissertation. University of Leipzig.
Schäfer, Martin 2008. Resolving scope in manner modification. In: O. Bonami & P. Cabredo Hofherr (eds.). *Empirical Issues in Syntax and Semantics 7*. Paris: CSSP, 351–372.
Shaer, Benjamin 2003. "Manner" adverbs and the association theory: Some problems and solutions. In: E. Lang, C. Maienborn & C. Fabricius-Hansen (eds.). *Modifying Adjuncts*. Berlin: de Gruyter, 211–259.

Shaer, Benjamin 2009. German and English left-peripheral elements and the "orphan" analysis. In: B. Shaer et al. (eds.). *Dislocated Elements in Discourse. Syntactic, Semantic, and Pragmatic Perspectives*. New York: Routledge, 366–397.
Thomason, Richard H. & Robert C. Stalnaker 1973. A semantic theory of adverbs. *Linguistic Inquiry* 4, 195–220.
Wunderlich, Dieter 1984. Zur Syntax der Präpositionalphrasen im Deutschen. *Zeitschrift für Sprachwissenschaft* 3, 65–99.
Wunderlich, Dieter 1991. How do prepositional phrases fit into compositional syntax and semantics? *Linguistics* 29, 591–621.
Wyner, Adam Zachary 1994. *Boolean Event Lattices and Thematic Roles in the Syntax and Semantics of Adverbial Modification*. Ph.D. dissertation. Cornell University, Ithaca, NY.
Wyner, Adam Zachary 1998. Subject-oriented adverbs are thematically dependent. In: S. Rothstein (ed.). *Events in Grammar*. Dordrecht: Kluwer, 333–348.

Kjell Johan Sæbø
15 Adverbial clauses

1   Introduction —— 515
2   Temporal clauses —— 516
3   Modal clauses —— 524
4   Instrumental and free adjunct clauses —— 533
5   Conclusions —— 538
6   References —— 540

Abstract: Adverbial clauses are subordinate clauses that modify their superordinate clauses. This modification can occur at various levels (such as verb phrase, tense phrase, mood phrase) and in various dimensions (such as times and worlds) and ways. These variations give rise to a categorization of adverbial clauses (temporal, modal, ...) and a subcategorization according to a range of relations within these dimensions, depending on the subjunction. Thus within the modal category it is customary to distinguish between causal, conditional, purpose, result, and concessive clauses. Sometimes the subjunction does not seem to encode much meaning of its own and the clause acts more like a relative clause, modifying a quantificational adverb or a modal, or specifying an underspecified predicate; sometimes, when there is no subjunction ("free" adjunct clauses), the contribution of the clause is underspecified.

1 Introduction

Adverbial clauses are a proper subclass of the class of all adverbials. To a considerable extent, this subclass relation distributes over the major semantic categories of adverbials commonly identified (see article 14 [this volume] (Maienborn & Schäfer) *Adverbs and adverbials*). Thus in the temporal category, there are closely comparable clausal and nonclausal adverbials, e.g.: "since Benitez arrived at Anfield" - "since June 2004". Locative adverbials and manner adverbials tend to be nonclausal, but instrumental adverbials can be both: "by hammering it" - "with a hammer". In the modal category, clausal adverbials predominate; there are no close counterparts to conditional or causal clauses in the form of (nonanaphoric) adverbs or prepositional phrases.

Kjell Johan Sæbø, Oslo, Norway

In the typical case, the clause consists of a subjunction S and a tensed sentence T. If S is temporal, T can be assumed to denote a set of times, and S can be ascribed the type ((it) ((it)t)), where i is the type of times. If S is modal, its argument will be a proposition and its type will be ((st) ((st)t)). Modal and temporal subjunctions can thus be thought of as determiners over worlds and times, respectively. Instrumental and "free" adjunct clauses, on the other hand, tend to be untensed; this is to be expected if the operator (which is often covert) is taken to operate on sets of events and to act as a determiner over events.

This simple general picture is variously enriched and complicated by variations in the specific world, time, and event determiner meanings that specific subjunctions encode. These meanings range from the quite simple - existential (indefinite), definite, universal - to the quite complex (though there is no stable correlation between complexity of form and complexity of content), and the complexities go in several directions: some temporal subjunctions impose constraints concerning maximality ("while"), posteriority ("after"), or both ("since"), while some ("before") encode both temporal and modal information; some modal subjunctions make implicit reference to negation ("because") or intention ("in order that"). Sometimes there is reason to believe that the subjunction ("when") depends on a possibly covert adverb of quantification which the clause serves to restrict; sometimes the conveyed relation is very vague - especially when the clause is untensed and there is no subjunction or preposition encoding anything, the intended relation is grossly underspecified and must be inferred from the context; then a variety of fairly specific meanings may result - temporal, causal, conditional - or we may be left with a loose "accompanying circumstance" interpretation.

Temporal clauses are treated first, as they present relatively simple and clear-cut cases. Next, modal clauses are addressed, starting with conditional clauses, which are similar to temporal clauses and a key to the meaning of all modal clauses. Instrumental and "free", "absolute" clauses are treated last.

2 Temporal clauses

Temporal clauses are a subclass of temporal adverbials; like non-clausal temporal adverbials, they help situate events or states temporally. But in contrast to most non-clausal temporal adverbials, they do so indirectly, through other events or states. Thus in (1a), the event described by the verb is placed within the frame of a calendrical year, while in (1b), it is placed within a frame of a year's duration through the state described by the verb of the "when" clause:

(1) a. My dad left in 1963.
 b. My dad left when I was 7.

Similarly, in (2a), the events described by the verbs are placed in the immediate vicinity of a certain time of the clock, while in (2b), they are placed in the immediate vicinity of a time identified through the event described by the verb of the "when" clause:

(2) a. At six in the morning, she got up and started on the long way home from Ramallah to Jenin.
 b. When day broke, she gathered her children and grandchildren together and hotfooted it the 20 km to safety in Benin.

There are a number of variations on the theme thus exemplified by "when", corresponding to a variety of different temporal subjunctions, some relatively simple, like "when", others with a more complicated semantics.

2.1 Existential "when" and "while" clauses

When the eventuality described by the verb of the existential "when" clause or the verb of the root clause is a state, there is a symmetry between the two clauses in the sense that the temporal interpretation is preserved if they change roles, as in (1b) and (1c).

(1) a. My dad left in 1963.
 b. My dad left when I was 7.
 c. I was 7 when my dad left.

The same applies when one of the two clauses has imperfective aspect, as observed for English by Partee (1984), cf. (3a/b), and for French by Kamp & Rohrer (1983); cf. the Italian sentence pair (4a/b) (Bonomi 1997) and the Russian sentence pair (5a/b).

(3) a. Nureyev revisited Russia when his mother was dying.
 b. When Nureyev revisited Russia his mother was dying.

(4) a. Ahmad Jamal fu   notato   da Miles Davis quando suonava in un trio.
Ahmad Jamal was noted   by Miles Davis when   played   in a   trio
'Ahmad Jamal was noticed by Miles Davis when he was playing in a trio.'

b. Quando fu notato da Miles Davis, Ahmad Jamal suonava in un trio.

(5) a. My   s   Iroj   gotovili   dokumenty,   kogda   pozvonil   Borja.
we   with   Ira   prepared   documents   when   called   Boris
'Irina and I were preparing the documents when Boris called.'

b. Kogda my s Iroj gotovili dokumenty, pozvonil Borja.

The two versions may differ with regard to information structure (background or presupposition versus focus) and discourse relations, but hardly as far as the temporal relation is concerned.

This symmetry can be accounted for on natural assumptions about aspect, tense, time adverbials, and their interaction. Consider (1b). Assume that the phrase "I be 7" denotes a set of states, that it merges with a covert imperfective aspect to denote the set of times included in the runtime of one of those states, and that this merge merges with the past tense to denote the set coming from that set by filtering out the non-past times. Assume that the phrase "my dad leave" denotes a set of events, that it merges with a covert perfective aspect to denote the set of times including the runtime of one of those events, and that this merge merges with the past tense to denote the set coming from that set by filtering out the non-past times. An intuitively correct interpretation results if we treat the subjunction "when" as an existential determiner over times: There is a nonempty intersection between the set of past times included in the runtime of some "I be 7" state on the one hand and the set of past times including the runtime of some "my dad leave" event on the other hand. Due to the symmetry of intersection, the interpretation of (1c) is the same. Similarly for (3a) and (3b), where both verb phrases denote sets of events but "his mother die" merges with an overt imperfective aspect. Similarly also for cases of mixed tenses (e.g. past - past perfect).

We can thus use the term "existential" for "when" clauses when they serve to relate single eventualities temporally. In (1) and (3), there is effectively just one maximal eventuality of the described type. In the general case, however, the set of past times included in or including the runtime of some eventuality of the described type must be assumed to be restricted to a contextually determined time interval (a topic time in the sense of Klein 1994, 2009), with room only for one eventuality, as in (2b). It has often been noted that the eventuality described in a temporal clause tends to be presupposed, as if there were a definite description; this way, attention is limited to one maximal eventuality. Although English "when" is indifferent to the number of relevant maximal eventualities (see 1.2 on universal "when" clauses), a subjunction may well come with the constraint that there is only one to be considered - e.g., German "als".

In English, "when" can be used for both past and future times, cf. (6), but it is not uncommon to use two distinct subjunctions; thus in German, "als" is reserved for past times while "wenn" is used for future times (and in universal temporal and in conditional clauses).

(6) a. When I am 18 I will volunteer to serve in the armed forces.
    b. I will be 18 when we get married.

Recall that when the eventuality described by the verb of the existential "when" clause or the verb of the root clause is a state, there is a symmetry between the two clauses in the sense that the temporal interpretation is preserved if they change roles. However, as has often been noted, once both verbs describe events and have perfective aspect, the symmetry breaks down. Scholars from Heinämäki (1978) via Partee (1984), Hinrichs (1986), Sandström (1993) and Bonomi (1997) to Glasbey (2004) have observed that eventive "when" clauses typically 'move time forward', introducing a new reference time (topic time in the sense of Klein 1994, 2009) located 'just after' the event; "the event described by [the "when" clause] *precedes* (possibly as a cause) the event described by [the main clause]" (Bonomi 1997: 496); in the face of counterexamples, however, this is only "a pragmatic implicature".

(7) When she died she left a massive doll collection.

(8) Labonte broke his shoulder when he wrecked at Darlington in March of 1999.

(9) When she died she was buried somewhere along the Ho Chi Minh Trail.

(10) I will marry him when he gets a divorce.

In (7) and (8), the "when" clause event and the main clause event plausibly coincide temporally, or the runtime of the former includes that of the latter, while in (9) and (10), the former is likely to precede the latter. The reverse is not possible; the former cannot be taken to succeed the latter. Sandström (1993) and Glasbey (2004) appeal to discourse relations like 'consequentiality' or 'reaction' to predict the forward-movement use of "when". It remains an open question, though, whether and, in the event, how the semantics of "when" should be constrained to capture this asymmetry. Some scholars prefer to formulate detailed meaning rules, others would rather appeal to more general pragmatic principles.

"While" clauses are similar to "when" clauses but seem to require that their predicates are atelic or supplied with progressive aspect (if not, as in (11), they are still interpreted as atelic), so the temporal relation conveyed will always be simultaneity, as in (11) and (12), or inclusion, as in (13).

(11) I sat with him while he regained consciousness.

(12) While she worked he was vomiting.

(13) While he slept she glued his chesspieces to the board.

This will follow if we assume that "while" operates on the set of time intervals provided by the tense phrase to yield the set of maximal elements (intervals not properly included in another interval), quantifying existentially over this set and the set supplied by the tense phrase of the main clause; then the content of the construction will be analytic if the "while" clause is perfective: We would claim that there is a maximal time interval including, instead of included in, the runtime of an event of the given type. This is contradictory, unless the context provides a finite frame time; but then, the "while" clause will not serve to restrict that frame. This is one way of predicting that "while" only tolerates sets of intervals included in, not including, the runtime of an eventuality of a given type; there may be alternative ways.

2.2 Universal "when" clauses

When the eventuality type described by the predicate can have several maximal instantiations, the "when" clause can be interpreted as a universal quantifier over times. This is the natural reading of sentences like (14a) and (15a).

(14) a. When the customers were rude, I was annoyed and wanted to cry.

(15) a. When the Moon is rising, it seems larger than when it is high in the sky.

This can be modelled by saying that the clause serves to restrict a covert habituality operator. Two facts support this view. First, a habituality operator (or adverb of quantification) can be overt, as in (14b) and (15b). (As Bonomi (1997) points out, while overt adverbs of quantification can have different forces, the covert adverb is always universal or generic.) Second, habituality can be observed in connection with non-clausal temporal adverbials as well, cf. (15c).

(14) b. Sometimes when I am alone, I google myself.

(15) b. When the Moon is rising, it often seems larger than when it is high in the sky.
c. In the evening, the Moon often seems larger than in the night.

Such an analysis is not quite simple, though. First, as discussed by de Swart (1991), different temporal subjunctions, including "after" and "before", interact with overt or covert-universal adverbs, hence they convey distinctive temporal information of their own which must be taken account of. Second, as discussed by Johnston (1994), it is not invariably the case that the temporal clause is the restrictor and the main clause is the nuclear scope of the adverb; it can be the other way around. This variation can be modelled with the help of focus, but Johnston derives it from a distinction between IP and VP adjunction: If the temporal clause is adjoined at IP level, it serves as the restrictor; if it is adjoined at the level of the VP, it serves as the nuclear scope.

2.3 "Since" (and "until") clauses

"Since" clauses are a subset of "since" adverbials, as the word "since" can be used as a subjunction and as a preposition (the same goes for "until"). Unlike (existential) "when" and "while" clauses, "since" (and "until") clauses are not directly about times including or included in the runtime of a salient eventuality of the described type; rather, such times serve to delimit a relevant interval to the left (these adverbials are accordingly sometimes called boundary adverbials; cf. e.g. Fabricius-Hansen 1986: 201). The right boundary of the relevant interval - the interval interacting with the intervals coming from the main clause - is an evaluation time, the utterance time if the main clause is in the present perfect (and the "since" clause in the simple past) tense; cf. (16a) and (17a). If the tense of the main (and "since") clause is past perfect, as in (16b) and (17b), the evaluation time, the right boundary of the relevant time span, is a (here) contextually fixed past time.

(16) a. Her life has changed since she had her baby.
b. Her life had changed since she had had her baby.

(17) a. She has been weepy since she had her baby.
  b. She had been weepy since she had had her baby.

Intuitively, in (16) the relevant time span is claimed to include the runtime of the main clause eventuality, while in (17) it is the other way around; the time between her having her baby and now (then) is claimed to be included in the runtime of her being weepy. This follows from simple considerations of the interplay between aspect, tense, and time adverbials once it is observed that in (16), the aspect of the main clause is perfective while in (17) it is imperfective: The main clause of (16a) can be taken to denote the set of past times abutting the utterance time (due to the present perfect) and including the runtime of a her life changing event, while that of (17a) can be taken to denote the set of past times abutting the utterance time and included in the runtime of a she being weepy state. If now the "since" clause denotes the time span stretching from the left boundary (the past runtime of the salient she having her baby event) to the right boundary (the utterance time), then on the most basic of composition rules this time is to be a member of the set of times denoted by the main clause, and the result is in accordance with our intuitions.

We encounter a slightly different usage of e.g. German "seit" in sentences like (18) or (19), where the tense in the subordinate clause is the present (or past), not the past (or past perfect).

(18) a. Seit sie Mutter ist, hat sie Angst vorm Fliegen.
  since she mother is has she fear of flying
  'Since she became a mother she has had fear of flying.'

  b. Seit sie Mutter war, hatte sie Angst vorm Fliegen.
  since she mother was had she fear of flying
  'Since she had become a mother she had had fear of flying.'

(19) Seit sie alleine lebt, hat sie enorme Fortschritte gemacht.
  since she alone lives has she enormous forwardsteps made
  'She has made enormous progress since she started living alone.'

Here the subordinate clause does not contribute a left boundary to the time span relevant for the superordinate clause, it contributes the relevant time span directly, through the runtime of the state described - though the constraint remains that this time abut the utterance, or, in the general case, evaluation time. Iatridou & von Fintel (2005) strive to reconcile this reading, where the two eventualities may seem to be presented as simultaneous, with the 'boundary' reading discussed above.

"Since" is restricted to past times; when talking about the future, we use the subjunction "until" instead; the use of German "seit" in (18) or (19), however, is mirrored in the future not by "bis" (≈ until) but by "solange" (≈ as long as). This lexical split might be taken to indicate that "seit" is really ambiguous.

2.4 "Before" and "after" clauses

(20a) is very similar in meaning to (16a). (20b) is a bit less similar:

(20) a. Her life has changed after she had her baby.
b. Her life changed after she had her baby.

Here the simple past in the superordinate clause shows that what corresponds to the right boundary in the "since" case can be properly prior to the utterance time. It would seem that "after" just expresses a subsequence relation; say, the runtime of an event of the type described in the main clause succeeds the runtime of the salient event of the type described in the "after" clause. And we would expect the subjunction "before" to express the converse relation: that the runtime of an event of the type described in the main clause *precedes* the runtime of the salient event of the type described in the "before" clause.

(21) She had her baby before her life changed.

As observed in connection with "when" clauses, the information structure, in terms of what is given and what is new, may well be different, but purely semantically, it is difficult to detect a difference between (20b) and (21). We tend to think of "after" and "before" as logical converses, differing only in the direction of the temporal relation. However, closer scrutiny casts doubt on this view. Anscombe (1964) provided evidence which led her to conclude that while "after" involves existential quantification, "before" involves universal quantification. Heinämäki (1978) also proposed truth conditions on which "before" is not only opposite to, but also stronger than "after". In one sense, however, "before" appears to be *weaker* than "after": the latter, but not the former, is veridical, i.e. the temporal clause is entailed. Thus (22a) means something quite different from (22b).

(22) a. Spermicides destroy sperm before they penetrate the egg.
b. Sperm penetrate the egg after spermicides destroy them.

Beaver & Condoravdi (2003) propose a uniform analysis of "after" and "before" differing only in the temporal relation, tracing the other differences to this asymmetry as it relates to initial parts of main clause eventuality runtimes and branching possible worlds. On this analysis, since worlds are identical in the backward but not in the forward direction, the reversal of the temporal order has a modal significance.

3 Modal clauses

In their analysis of "before" clauses, Beaver & Condoravdi (2003) (see 2.4) utilize possible worlds, similar to but possibly different from the actual world, to explain the non-veridicality of "before" and the ensuing non- or even counterfactual interpretations. This makes "before" clauses partway modal. Modal clauses relate the superordinate clause proposition to the subordinate clause proposition through some accessibility relation between possible worlds. This intensional, mood phrase modification can take various forms.

3.1 Conditional clauses

Intuitively, the only difference between (10), with a temporal "when" clause, and (23), with a conditional "if" clause, is that in (23), the event of him getting a divorce is not entailed or presupposed; the temporal relation between his getting a divorce and my marrying him seems to be the same.

(10) I will marry him when he gets a divorce.

(23) I will marry him if he gets a divorce.

So one might think that (23) only makes a prediction about the case where he in fact gets a divorce; in case he doesn't, the sentence is trivially true. However, this notion of conditionals as material implications has by most scholars been considered too weak; (23) does seem to make a claim even if the antecedent is actually false, the same claim, mutatis mutandis, as the counterfactual (24).

(24) I would have married him if he had gotten a divorce.

Here, the "subjunctive" past tense forms presuppose that the antecedent is false, so for the sentence to be true or false, one has to look beyond the actual world to see whether the consequent is true together with the antecedent.

The possible-world analysis of "if" clauses originated with Stalnaker (1968) and was refined and variously modified by Lewis (1973a) and Kratzer (1981), i.a. (see article 15 [Semantics: Noun Phrases and Verb Phrases] (von Fintel) *Conditionals* for recent developments and alternative treatments). On Stalnaker's original simple analysis, for (23) to be true in a world w, the consequent (that I marry him) must be true in the world closest to w (possibly w itself) where the antecedent (that he gets a divorce) is true; similarly for (24) (though here the closest world must be different from w and the events are in the past). This analysis, treating the "if" clause as a definite description over worlds, has recently been revived by Schlenker (2004).

To account for the temporal parallel between the "when" construction (10) and the "if" construction (23), one must say that in the closest world to w where there is a future time including the runtime of an event of him getting a divorce, one such time includes the runtime of an event of me marrying him, or something more restricted. This amounts to analysing "if" as (modal) "if" + "when" (Fabricius-Hansen & Sæbø 1983).

There is a vast literature on conditional clauses (see article 15 [Semantics: Noun Phrases and Verb Phrases] (von Fintel) *Conditionals)*; they have probably been the subject of more discussion than all the other kinds of adverbial clauses taken together. This is not accidental: in some way or other, they are at the base of the meaning of all the other modal clause types.

3.2 Result clauses

What is commonly referred to as result clauses (or consecutive clauses) come in two varieties: Clauses introduced by "so (that)", as in (25) or (26), and clauses apparently introduced by "that", correlated with "so" modifying a gradable adjective in the main clause, as in (27) and (28).

(25) The walls tumbled down so that the Israelites could enter the city.

(26) Villages have been sealed off so that residents must enter or leave through control points.

(27) The wall is so high (that) I cannot get over it.

(28) In some places the rock face is so steep that you have to use a ladder.

Traditionally, result clauses have been considered to convey a causal relation and be closely related to causal clauses (see 2.3). Meier (2000) offers evidence against this view, arguing instead that the subordinate clause is overtly or covertly modalized (in (25)–(28) it is overtly modalized) and interpreted as a hidden, incomplete conditional for which the main clause provides the antecedent - in Kratzer's theory (e.g. 1991), a proposition added to the modal base for the modal. In addition, the main clause is entailed. On this analysis, the (26) "that" clause is interpreted as the set of propositions p such that (if p) must (residents enter through control points); "so" denotes a relation between a set of propositions and a proposition to the effect that the latter is true and in the former. The result is an interpretation corresponding to the following paraphrase: Villages have been sealed off, and if they have, residents must enter through control posts.

The analysis of the variant involving adjectives (cf. (27) and (28)) is more complicated (see also Meier 2001); simplifying a little, the main clause still supplies a conditional antecedent for an essentially binary modal overtly or covertly present in the result clause, but now, this proposition involves a degree in the actual world; a paraphrase of (27) could be: The wall is as high as it is (a tautology of course) and if it is as high as it actually is, I cannot get over it.

Meier's work (2000, 2001) is the only formal semantic treatment of result clauses so far. It makes crucial use of the theory of modality developed by Kratzer (e.g. 1981) and the notion of a hidden conditional and even in many cases a hidden modal. Kratzer's own theory extended to "if" clauses, and Meier takes it further; ahead might lie a conception of other kinds of modal clauses, say, causal clauses, as serving the purpose of supplying overt or covert modals with conversational background propositions. As yet, however, there is scarce evidence as to whether this is a feasible course, as the main focus of recent research on causal clauses has been on necessary conditionship and counterfactual dependence, as detailed in the next subsection.

3.3 Causal clauses

Causal clauses are clauses introduced by subjunctions like "because", German "weil", French "parce que", or Russian "потому что", clauses which can be used for answering "why" questions. The basic piece of meaning conveyed by these words is that the proposition expressed (or the event described) in the subordinate clause is the cause of, or reason for, the proposition expressed (or the event described) in the main clause, the effect, or consequence.

(29) They cannot return to their homes because the village has been destroyed.

For Meier (2000), one argument against ascribing a causal semantics to result clauses (see 3.2.) is that a paraphrase with a causal term does not make sense when the sentence represents a symptom relation, as in (30):

(30) The light on it is on so (that) it is getting power.

One would not say that the reason that the machine or motor is getting power is that the light on it is on. A more appropriate paraphrase, and one on which Meier (2000), as we have seen, bases her analysis, is in terms of conditionals:

(31) If the light on it is on it is getting power.

The same is true of causal clauses too: They can convey a symptom relation, in which case a paraphrase in terms of "if" is appropriate:

(32) It is getting power because the light on it is on.

And in fact, the dominant theory of causality and causal clauses was long based on, essentially, an implication from the cause to the effect: Between 1748, when Hume, as Lewis (1973b) put it, defined causation twice over, and 1973, when Lewis revived the second definition (see below), the first one, according to which the cause is, given a set of premises, a sufficient condition for the effect, ruled the ground (see Sæbø 1991 for a more thorough discussion of this tradition).

One may be reluctant to call the regularity instantiated by (32) a causal regularity; the properly causal relation runs in the other direction, cf. (33):

(33) The light on it is on because it is getting power.

Still, a regularity analysis in terms of sufficient conditions and circumstances might be appropriate for causal clauses; what is in the word "because" might be wider than what is in the word "cause". But the mainstream of "because" analysis has assumed a distinction between normal and abnormal cases (to put it bluntly): (29) and (33) instantiate the standard case while (32) instantiates one (the evidential use) of a range of derived cases, where causal clauses are used to provide reasons for speech acts (cf. e.g. Rutherford 1970); representatives, as in (32), or different kinds of directives, expressed by imperatives or interrogatives (see Sæbø 1991: 629f. for details).

However, in regard to what has been considered standard causal clauses, it will often seem inadequate to say that the cause, together with certain facts and rules, is sufficient for the effect. (34) might just lend itself to such an analysis, along the lines of a paraphrase like: always, if Constantine, or any emperor, embraces Christianity, or any novel religion, and relevant laws obtain and the circumstances resemble those obtaining in the case at hand, that religion is victorious; but a corresponding paraphrase of (35) is either implausible or rather vacuous.

(34) Christianity was victorious because Constantine embraced it.

(35) Christianity was victorious because Constantine defeated Maxentius in 312.

On the other hand, the counterfactual analysis, the seminal paper of which is Lewis (1973b), is well equipped to cope with this kind of examples, where laws are less relevant than our particular beliefs about possible worlds. This is Hume's (1748) second definition: If the cause were not, nor would the effect be. As applied to (35), this analysis predicts the paraphrase (36):

(36) Christianity would not have been victorious if Constantine had not defeated Maxentius in 312.

This is a plausible paraphrase, and it has been widely embraced as an adequate basis for the semantics of "because" and other causal and causative expressions. Essentially, "q because p" is reduced to the counterfactual "not q if not p", and this counterfactual is, in turn, given a ceteris-paribus analysis; the consequent is to hold in such possible worlds where the antecedent holds but where ideally all other facts about the world remain. To be explicit, "because" is assigned the following denotation in a world w: That relation between two propositions p and q such that (i) both are true in w and (ii) in the closest world to w where p is false, q is false as well. (This is the semantics for conditionals according to Stalnaker 1968 and a simplification of the semantics for conditionals according to Lewis 1973a.)

There are ways in which this analysis can be refined so as to explain further facts about causal clauses: First, they should not refer to a time posterior to the time referred to by the main clause, cf. (37), and this can be made to follow from the counterfactual analysis if the similarity relation between worlds is explicated in terms of branching time (in a similar way as the nonveridicality of "before" as opposed to "after" could be explained by Beaver & Condoravdi 2003; see 2.4) (cf. Sæbø 1980).

(37) #The settlements perished around 1400 because the supply ships stopped coming around 1420.

It is reasonable to assume that the world closest to the actual world w where the supply ships went on coming around 1420 was identical to w around 1400, so that there is a contradiction: the settlements are to have perished and not to have perished around 1400.

Second, causal clauses seem stronger than corresponding counterfactuals, in particular concerning *causal selection*: A fact may depend counterfactually on many other facts, yet only some of them are likely to count as causes. Thus (38) seems to be contradicted by (39), although the two corresponding counterfactuals are compatible:

(38) She got the job because she applied for it.

(39) She got the job because she was qualified for it.

One solution to this problem, proposed by Dowty (1979: 106ff.), citing Abbott (1974), is to say that for a causal factor to be a (the) cause, it must be false in a relatively close world: "It does seem that often, if not always, we select as the "cause" of an event that one of the various causal conditions that we can most easily imagine to have been otherwise, that is, one whose "deletion" from the actual course of events would result in the least departure from the actual world." (Dowty 1979: 107) This idea might also be used to account for the differences between causes expressed by causal clause modifiers like "partly" and "mainly":

(40) She is an A student partly because she has private tutors, but mostly because she studies diligently.

It is not obviously plausible, however, that the "mostly because" fact is in this case a more labile fact than the "partly because" fact. Rather, it would seem that the main clause fact depends more heavily on the "mostly" cause, in the sense that if the "partly" cause were false and the "mostly" cause true, she would be, say, a B student, whereas if the "mostly" cause were false but the "partly" cause true, she would be, say, a C student. Let us say that "a partly because b but mostly because c" entails "a because b and because c" and, in addition, "if not b (but still c), almost a" and "if not c (but still b), far from a", where "almost" and "far from" have a modal meaning along the lines of Rapp & von Stechow (1999), i.e. in terms of world similarities. Assume that f assigns to the world w and the proposition p the closest world to w where p is true; the different status between b and c could be captured by stating that the distance between $f(w, \sim b)$ and $f(f(w, \sim b), a)$ (where w is the actual world) is significantly shorter than that between $f(w, \sim c)$ and $f(f(w, \sim c), a)$.

This may not be the final answer to how constructions like (40) should be treated, but the suggestion illustrates how the framework of counterfactual dependence and possible world similarity can be exploited to express such subtle distinctions as causal clauses in natural languages appear to call for.

As for the non-standard cases referred to above, where causal clauses are used for giving reasons for speech acts, and not necessarily assertives, there have been several attempts at assimilating them to the standard case, ranging from the performative hypothesis (Ross 1970) to pragmatically oriented approaches (cf. Sæbø 1991: 629f. for a more thorough discussion). One may note that while English "because" clauses can be used for giving reasons for directives or interrogatives, in other languages this is mainly done with subjunctions corresponding to "since", where the causal relation is arguably presupposed, or with causal conjunctions like French "car" or German "denn" (cf. Scheffler 2005 for a recent treatment of "denn").

3.4 Purpose clauses

As observed by Aristotle (Metaphysics, Book 5, Chapter 2), causal clauses are not the only ones that can answer "why" questions; purpose clauses can too. Purposes, or ends, figure as his fourth type of cause:

"'Cause' means [...] (4) The end, i.e. that for the sake of which a thing is; e.g. health is the cause of walking. For 'Why does one walk?' we say; 'that one may be healthy'; and in speaking thus we think we have given the cause."

Now clearly, a purpose clause does not answer a "why" question in the same way as a causal clause; (41) and (42) (in Classical Greek) are far from synonymous:

(41) Peripatei hina hugiainêi.
 'I walk in order to be healthy.'

(42) Peripatei epeidê hugiainei.
 'I walk because I am healthy.'

Both clauses may serve to give a cause, but not the same type of cause. Causal ("epeidê") clauses give a source-of-motion cause, a causa efficiens, while purpose ("hina") clauses give a cause-as-end, a causa finalis:

"[...] as [causes] are spoken of in several senses it follows [...] that things can be causes of one another (e.g. exercise of good condition, and the latter of exercise; not, however, in the same way, but the one as end and the other as source of movement)."

This seems to imply that (41) is closely related to the reversal of (42), (43):

(43) Hugiainei epeidê peripatei.
 'I am healthy because I walk.'

One analysis of purpose clauses has been based on this relation: von Wright (1971) proposed that a sentence like (44) entails that the agent believes (45):

(44) Viegan vai bivan. (North Sami)
 'I run in-order-that I keep warm.'

(45) Bivan dainna go viegan.
 'I keep warm because I run.'

"If...I say that he ran in order to catch the train, I intimate that he thought it... necessary, and maybe sufficient, to run, if he was going to reach the station before the departure of the train." (von Wright 1971: 84)

"We ask 'Why?' The answer often is simply: 'In order to bring about p.' It is then taken for granted that the agent considers the behavior which we are trying to explain causally relevant to the bringing about of p..." (von Wright 1971: 96f.)

Consider the following paraphrase of "a does m in order to e": "a wants to e and a does m and a believes that doing m is the best way to e". It seems convincing, but unfortunately, it is too weak: It fails to distinguish between two ends where one counts as the purpose and the other is just a pleasant side-effect:

(46) MS sponsors us to spur development.

(47) MS sponsors us to save taxes.

Both (46) and (47) could come out true on the analysis inspired by von Wright, even if one might be inclined to reject either (46) or (47).

But there is another way of relating purpose clauses to causal clauses, suggested by von Wright (1971: 192): (48) might "depend on the truth of a nomic connection between his 'anxiety to catch the train' ... and his running." This analysis, which has been subscribed to by many linguists (e.g. von Stechow, Krasikova & Penka 2006: 153), predicts that (48) and (49) are synonymous:

(48) He ran in order to catch the train.

(49) He ran because he wanted to catch the train.

More generally, it seems possible to equate "q in order that p" with "q because the agent wants that p", - which, in turn, would be evaluated via the counterfactual "not q if the agent did not want that p".

This will distinguish between (46) and (47) if MS wants to spur development and to save taxes and considers it necessary for both ends to sponsor us but only one end is such that MS would not sponsor us if it did not want that end.

Note that one cannot assume that "the agent" is the agent of the eventuality described in q - this eventuality is not invariably an action, or even an event:

(50) From time to time, the bridge goes up in order that a ship may pass beneath it.

(51) The bridge is so high in order that ships may pass beneath it.

Here the agent must be the causer of the event or state described in q. The next pair of examples show that in addition, (s)he must be required to deliberately cause that event or state: (52) only has a reading on which the main clause event is agentive, but (53) also has a reading on which the main clause event is non-agentive.

(52) We started an avalanche to reach the summit.

(53) We started an avalanche because we wanted to reach the summit.

3.5 Concessive clauses

Concessive clauses, introduced by subjunctions like English "although", are like causal clauses in that they are factive with respect to the subordinate clause and the main clause, but unlike causal clauses in that they cannot have narrow scope vis-à-vis other operators; negation, say, will unambiguously affect the main clause, not the concessive relation, in a sentence like (54):

(54) The burglars were not monitored although there were cameras around them.

(55) The burglars were not caught because they were monitored (but because...).

As observed by König (1988) and by Haspelmath & König (1998), concessive subjunctions are often related to conditional subjunctions in combination with scalar particles ("even though", "even if"), and this is suggestive of their meaning: They seem to imply that the main clause proposition would *a fortiori* be true if the concessive clause proposition were not true, that is to say, "q although p" seems to entail p and q and, moreover, to imply that q would surely hold were p not to hold; cp. (56) and (57):

(56) The burglars were caught although they were not monitored.

(57) The burglars were caught; they were not monitored; and if they had been monitored, they would have been caught.

This analysis, advocated by i.a. König (1991) and by König & Siemund (2000), means that the concessive "q although p" implies the same counterfactual as that entailed by the causal "~q because p". As observed by König & Siemund (2000), a sentence like (56) can be paraphrased by a sentence like (58), where negation has wide scope but is taken to affect the main clause ('it is not the case that the burglars were not caught because they were not monitored'):

(58) The burglars did not escape because they were not monitored.

In this case, it is reasonable to assume that the causal, counterfactual relation and the causal clause proposition are presupposed, escaping negation. What must evidently be stipulated is that this semantic structure is the only possible semantic structure for concessives: the concessive counterfactual relation, "q if ~p", is systematically out of focus.

4 Instrumental and free adjunct clauses

The types of adverbial clauses treated in 2. and 3. leave a residue of mostly nonfinite adjunct clauses expressing a wide variety of meanings. Often, these meanings are underspecified, depending on contextual factors for specification.

4.1 Instrumental clauses

The common notion of instrumental clauses is that they present one action as an "instrument" of another; they are often formed by a preposition and a gerund phrase, as in (59) and the French translation (60), but they can also be formed by a subjunction and a finite clause, as in the German version (61):

(59) Rosa Parks stood up by remaining seated.

(60) Elle s'est levée en restant assise.

(61) Sie stand auf, indem sie sitzen blieb.

The "instrument" relation is difficult to make precise. The main clause action type tends to be relatively unspecific, the subordinate clause elaborating on it by providing more specific content. The above examples are instructive in this regard: At one level, the instrumental clause contradicts the main clause; but the latter's predicate is to be read not in the literal, concrete sense but in the derived, abstract sense, and the instrumental clause predicate serves to specify what makes the act of Rosa Parks an act of standing up (to injustice) - namely, being a remaining seated act.

There is a strong intuition, going back to Anscombe (1957), that the "by" phrase predicate and the superordinate clause predicate describe one event in two ways. The immediate problem facing an analysis based on this intuition is that it easily predicts a symmetry between the two predicates; crucially, however, the structure is asymmetric:

(62) ? Rosa Parks remained seated by standing up.

According to Bennett (1994), this asymmetry falsifies the "Anscombe thesis". On the other hand, attempts at ascribing an asymmetric relation to the instrumental preposition or subjunction are likely to run into problems as well. It is tempting, for example, to assume a causal relation between two events or propositions; but when the main clause predicate is causative, as it often is, it will not do to give a causal meaning to the preposition or subjunction, since this will result in a duplication of the causal relation already expressed, in (63) by "change the course of history".

(63) By remaining seated, Rosa Parks changed the course of history.

It is useful to note that a verb like "change" is a manner-neutral causative in that it does not specify the way in which the change is brought about, and intuitively, the "by" phrase predicate fills this slot, specifying the causing event type. Similarly, predicates like "stand up (to injustice)" or "defy the bus driver", called *criterion predicates* by Kearns (2003), can be said to open a slot for the event type that meets the relevant - conventional or intentional - criteria. These observations underlie the analysis proposed by Sæbø (2008), where the causative or criterial, abstract predicates are decomposed to lay bare an argument place for a concrete predicate, merging with the "by" phrase predicate by unification. This or a similar analysis would carry over to "en" gerund phrases in French and to corresponding instrumentals in other languages. Another, similar approach is taken by Engelberg (2005), who invokes the notion of supervenience to model the dependence of a verb like "help" on more specific eventuality descriptions.

But, as observed by Fabricius-Hansen & Behrens (2001), German "indem" clauses have a wider field of use than English "by" or French "en" phrases; although "indem" typically establishes a relation of Elaboration between main and subordinate clause, it is not always obvious that the main clause predicate at some level of decomposition involves the subordinate clause predicate as a kind of argument. Translation studies reveal that "indem" clauses are often translated by "free" gerund clauses, without a preposition, into English, and vice versa; a form of adjunct known to cover a wide spectrum of relations, to be treated in the next section.

4.2 Participial clauses

When there is no subjunction or preposition to signal a relation, so that nonfiniteness is the only sign of subordination, an adjunct clause may be expected to modify its main clause in a quite unspecific way. In large measure, this is borne out: Present (gerund) or past participial clauses allow for a wide array of interpretations (cf. Kortmann 1995 and König 1995). However, as shown by e.g. Behrens (1998), a clear tendency can be observed to maximize the interpretational options offered by the lexical content and the context, ranging from mere 'accompanying circumstance' to more 'semantical' discourse relations.

Consider first a few cases similar, but not identical, to the "instrumental" cases considered above: In (64)–(67), it will not do to interpose the preposition "by", yet the relation between the two event types is not very different from the relation between the two event types in (59) or (63).

(64) The trout struggled, wriggling and writhing.

(65) I drove cautiously, looking out for danger on the road.

(66) A fellow traveller was playing guitar, using a knife for a slide.

(67) She did the job with the tools at hand, using a chisel for a pry bar.

The reason that an instrumental "by" is not appropriate here seems to be that the main predicate does not provide a variable for the adjunct predicate; still, the latter is taken to elaborate on the former, and, as argued by Behrens (1998), building on Asher (1993), elaboration here seems to mean that the adjunct event is a subevent of the main event. Thus in (64), the wriggling and the writhing are to be interpreted as subactivities of the struggling. According to König (1995), the two "converbs" and the main verb describe two aspects or dimensions of one event.

Behrens (1998) identifies a distinct form of event unification induced by postposed *-ing* adjuncts with causative verbs, as in (68):

(68) A passenger train carrying Kenyans and hundreds of tourists from abroad to the coastal port of Mombasa derailed at high speed on Wednesday, killing at least 32 people, including five foreigners.

While the subject of an *-ing* adjunct is generally assumed to be coreferent with the subject of the main clause, maybe through a subject controlled PRO, in (68) this is not intuitively correct: The train is not what killed the people; rather, it is the event of the train's derailment. On the analysis proposed by Behrens (1998: 113ff.), the subject PRO is in such cases an event PRO, controlled by the main clause event and equal to the unspecified causing event.

Preposed *-ing* adjuncts provide particular interpretational options. Under given conditions, the adjunct can be intended to convey largely the same relations as a conditional, "if" clause (Stump 1985), cf. (69) and (70), a causal, "because" clause, cf. (71), or a temporal, "when" or "while" clause; cf. (72)–(74):

(69) Driving slowly through Thorpe, you will see signs for Dovedale on the way.

(70) Looking out abeam, we would see a hollow like a tunnel formed as the crest of a big wave toppled over on to the swelling body of water.

(71) Having confessed to having sex with the girl, the man was sentenced to one year on an abandoned island.

(72) Reaching the coast, they sought to prevent departure from their homeland by rising in rebellion.

(73) Reaching the coast, they pick up the scent of their home river.

(74) Investigating a murder, Chief Inspector Maigret has difficulty penetrating the wall of silence maintained by the family involved.

Generally, as argued by Behrens (1998), free -ing adjuncts seem to lend themselves to the strongest relation relevant and plausible in view of the lexical items at hand and the context. This is not to deny that in many cases, the strongest relation there is license to infer is that of an 'accompanying circumstance', or connectedness; the adjunct and the main clause are about the same time, the same place, and the same subject, cf. (75) and (76).

(75) Smiling, she said, "I'll miss you."

(76) He walked out of the woods carrying an axe.

Such a relation is characteristic of yet another underspecified adverbial clause type: Absolute constructions, to be treated in the next section.

4.3 Absolute clauses

While the "converb constructions" (Haspelmath & König 1995) discussed above mostly display participle verbs with empty subjects, this term is also used to cover "absolute" small clauses like those in (77):

(77) Dazed and shaking he pulled himself up, his left arm hurting him.

Such adverbial small clauses can be augmented with a comitative preposition ("with"), without much of a change in meaning (note, however, that these augmented absolute adjuncts can constitute the sole focus domain of the sentence and should probably be classified as depictives; see article 14 [this volume] (Maienborn & Schäfer) *Adverbs and adverbials* on the delineation between adverbials and depictives):

(78) She woke up in the middle of the night with her arm hurting her.

(79) He woke up that Thursday morning with a gun pointing at him.

Furthermore, the absolute small clause can have an adjective or a prepositional phrase as its predicate:

(80) Cécile woke with a start, her neck stiff from having fallen asleep in a straight-backed chair.

(81) Cécile is standing with a gun in her hand and her finger on the trigger.

Semantically, what unites these cases is, unspecified as the relation between the main clause (host) eventuality and the SC (supplement) eventuality may be, the notion of a concomitant eventuality, attended by T(ime)-S(pace)-P(articipant)-connectedness (Rothstein 2003; Fabricius-Hansen 2007): The two eventualities manifest a unity of time and place and thus a "perceptual unity" (König 1995), and, some participant of the host event must bind an explicit or implicit anaphor in the supplement. In (77)–(81), the subject of the host binds an explicit possessive or nonpossessive anaphor in the subject or predicate of the supplement.

TSP-connectedness can hold across sequences of autonomous sentences; what absolute constructions will provide is a guarantee of TSP-connectedness. However, Fabricius-Hansen (2007) argues that in addition to conveying such relations, such constructions serve to build groups of events or states, expressing that the host and supplement eventualities form interesting sums of eventualities, an idea going back to Pusch (1980). According to this analysis, in (77) the core event and the co-eventualities all add up to one super-, group eventuality. Thus, even adverbial clauses without any overt sign of the mode of modification will modify their main, host clauses semantically in a nontrivial way.

5 Conclusions

The range of phenomena bundled together under the label *adverbial clauses* is so diverse as to defy easy generalization. What can safely be said, though, is that any adverbial clause serves to modify some aspect of the main clause meaning: At some level between, from below, the verb phrase, denoting a set of events or states, the tense phrase, denoting a set of times, and the mood phrase, taken to denote a set of worlds, the subordinate clause merges with the main clause to further identify its denotation, whether by functional application, intersection, quantification, or unification.

Generally, this proceeds by way of the meaning of the subordinate clause at the relevant level. Thus a "free", nonfinite clause can be considered to contribute a set of eventualities, a temporal clause contributes a set of times, and a modal clause contributes a set of worlds; the subjunction (or relevant interpretive mechanism) then relates this to the corresponding dimension of the meaning of the main clause, in the lexically (or discourse structurally) determined way. In the simplest cases, the subjunction can be likened to a definite, indefinite, or universal determiner, turning the modal ("if") or temporal ("when") clause set of worlds or times into a definite world or a quantifier over times (a set of sets of times).

Elsewhere, more elaborate relations are involved; some temporal subjunctions define intervals stretching to or from the evaluation time ("since", "until") or convey precedence relations ("after", before"), modal subjunctions may involve negation ("because", "although") or intention ("in order that"). In yet other, notably instrumental, cases, it is less clear what relation between two sets of eventualities is encoded in the subjunction; and in "free", nonfinite adjunct clauses, there is no lexical sign of the relation. Although often, there is ample reason to infer a modal or a temporal relation or a relation of elaboration as event inclusion, often enough all that can be inferred is an "attendant (accompanying) circumstance", where main clause and subordinate clause eventualities can be assumed to add up to a more comprehensive, super-event.

Subjunctions vary in two dimensions: Specificity and complexity (of meaning). One might expect semantic simplicity vs. complexity to correlate with lexical, or morphological, simplicity or complexity; - this, however, is easily falsified: The Ancient Greek ("hina") or North Sami ("vai") purpose subjunctions testify to an advanced level of grammaticalization while expressing one of the most elaborate semantic relations.

Several subjunctions do double duty in the sense that they underspecify the semantic relation they encode - they correspond to two (or more) subjunctions in another language. For example, English "when" can be universal or existential in the past or future; German "wenn" can be conditional or temporal (universal or existential in the future). This attests to (1) the interrelatedness of the temporal and the modal dimension (also indicated by the use of past forms in counterfactual environments, cf. Iatridou 2000), and (2) the role of the context of utterance in clarifying what relation is meant by a certain adverbial clause.

So what are, again, adverbial clauses - is a common characterization so vague as to be vacuous? Probably not; for one thing, they differ from other adverbials in utilizing the same kind of material they serve to modify (basically, things that clauses can express); and second, they differ from other subordinate clauses in carrying a more or less complex and specific semantic relation on their own, - even when the relation is, by itself, highly unspecific, contextual and pragmatic factors conspire to narrow it down.

6 References

Abbott, Barbara 1974. Some problems in giving an adequate model-theoretic account of CAUSE. In: C. Fillmore et al. (eds.). *Berkeley Studies in Syntax and Semantics* 1. Berkeley, CA:, University of California, 1–14.
Anscombe, Gertrude E. M. 1957. *Intention*. Oxford: Blackwell.
Anscombe, Gertrude E. M. 1964. Before and after. *The Philosophical Review* 73, 3–24.
Aristotle. *Metaphysics*. Quoted from The Perseus Digital Library. http://www.perseus.tufts.edu/hopper, August 9, 2011.
Asher, Nicholas 1993. *Reference to Abstract Objects in Discourse*. Dordrecht: Kluwer.
Beaver, David & Cleo Condoravdi 2003. A uniform analysis of before and after. In: R. Young & Y. Zhou (eds.). *Proceedings of Semantics and Linguistic Theory (= SALT) XIII*. Ithaca, NY: Cornell University, 37–54.
Behrens, Bergljot 1998. *Contrastive Discourse. An Interlingual Approach to the Interpretation and Translation of Free -ing Participial Adjuncts*. Doctoral dissertation. University of Oslo.
Bennett, Jonathan 1994. The "namely" analysis of the 'by' locution. *Linguistics & Philosophy* 17, 29–51.
Bonomi, Andrea 1997. Aspect, quantification and *when*-clauses in Italian. *Linguistics & Philosophy* 20, 469–514.
Dowty, David R. 1979. *Word Meaning and Montague Grammar. The Semantics of Verbs and Times in Generative Semantics and in Montague's PTQ*. Dordrecht: Reidel.
Engelberg, Stefan 2005. Stativity, supervenience, and sentential subjects. In: C. Maienborn & A. Wöllstein (eds.). *Event Arguments. Foundations and Applications*. Tübingen: Niemeyer, 45–68.
Fabricius-Hansen, Cathrine 1986. *Tempus fugit. Über die Interpretation temporaler Strukturen im Deutschen*. Düsseldorf: Schwann.
Fabricius-Hansen, Cathrine 2007. On Manners and Circumstances. In: R. Nilsen, N. Amfo & K. Borthen (eds.). *Interpreting Utterances: Pragmatics and its Interfaces*. Oslo: Novus Press, 39–50.
Fabricius-Hansen, Cathrine & Bergljot Behrens 2001. *Elaboration and Related Discourse Relations in an Interlingual Perspective* (SPRIK reports 13): Oslo University of Oslo.
Fabricius-Hansen, Cathrine & Kjell Johan Sæbø 1983. Über das Chamäleon *wenn* und seine Umwelt. *Linguistische Berichte* 83, 1–35.
Glasbey, Sheila 2004. Event structure, punctuality, and *when*. *Natural Language Semantics* 12, 191–211.
Haspelmath, Martin & Ekkehard König (eds.) 1995. *Converbs in Cross-linguistic Perspective. Structure and Meaning of Adverbial Verb Forms. Adverbial Participles, Gerunds*. Berlin: Mouton de Gruyter.
Haspelmath, Martin & Ekkehard König 1998. Concessive conditionals in the languages of Europe. In: J. van der Auwera (ed.). *Adverbial Constructions in the Languages of Europe*. Berlin: Mouton de Gruyter, 563–640.
Heinämäki, Orvokki 1978. *Semantics of English Temporal Connectives*. Bloomington, IN: Indiana University Linguistics Club.
Hinrichs, Erhard 1986. Temporal anaphora in discourse of English. *Linguistics & Philosophy* 9, 63–82.

Hume, David 1748. *An Enquiry concerning Human Understanding*. http://www.gutenberg.org/etext/9662, August 9, 2011.
Iatridou, Sabine 2000. The grammatical ingredients of counterfactuality. *Linguistic Inquiry* 31, 231–270.
Iatridou, Sabine & Kai von Fintel 2005. *Since since*. Ms. Cambridge, MA, MIT.
Johnston, Michael 1994. *The Syntax and Semantics of Adverbial Adjuncts*. Ph.D. dissertation. University of California, Santa Cruz, CA.
Kamp, Hans & Christian Rohrer 1983. Tense in texts. In: R. Bäuerle, Ch. Schwarze & A. von Stechow (eds.). *Meaning, Use and Interpretation of Language*. Berlin: de Gruyter, 250–269.
Kearns, Kate 2003. Durative achievements and individual-level predicates on events. *Linguistics & Philosophy* 26, 595–635.
Klein, Wolfgang 1994. *Time in Language*. London: Routledge.
Klein, Wolfgang 2009. How time is encoded. In: W. Klein & P. Li (eds.). *The Expression of Time*. Berlin: Mouton de Gruyter, 39–82.
König, Ekkehard 1988. Concessive connectives and concessive sentences. Cross-linguistic regularities and pragmatic principles. In: J. A. Hawkins (ed.). *Explaining Language Universals*. Oxford: Blackwell, 145–166.
König, Ekkehard 1991. Concessive relations as the dual of causal relations. In: D. Zaefferer (ed.). *Semantic Universals and Universal Semantics*. Berlin: de Gruyter, 190–209.
König, Ekkehard 1995. The meaning of converb constructions. In: M. Haspelmath & E. König (eds.). *Converbs in Cross-linguistic Perspective. Structure and Meaning of Adverbial Verb Forms. Adverbial Participles, Gerunds*. Berlin: Mouton de Gruyter, 57–96.
König, Ekkehard & Peter Siemund 2000. Causal and concessive clauses. Formal and semantic relations. In: E. Couper-Kuhlen & B. Kortmann (eds.). *Cause, Condition, Concession, Contrast. Cognitive and Discourse Perspectives*. Berlin: Mouton de Gruyter, 341–360.
Kortmann, Bernd 1995. Adverbial participial clauses in English. In: M. Haspelmath & E. König (eds.). *Converbs in Cross-linguistic Perspective. Structure and Meaning of Adverbial Verb Forms. Adverbial Participles, Gerunds*. Berlin: Mouton de Gruyter, 189–238.
Kratzer, Angelika 1981. The notional category of modality. In: H.-J. Eikmeyer & H. Rieser (eds.). *Words, Worlds, and Contexts. New Approaches in Word Semantics*. Berlin: de Gruyter, 38–74.
Kratzer, Angelika 1991. Modality. In: A. von Stechow & D. Wunderlich (eds.). *Semantik – Semantics. Ein internationales Handbuch zeitgenössischer Forschung – An International Handbook of Contemporary Research* (HSK 6). Berlin: de Gruyter, 639–650.
Lewis, David K. 1973a. *Counterfactuals*. Oxford: Blackwell.
Lewis, David K. 1973b. Causation. *Journal of Philosophy* 70, 556–567.
Meier, Cécile 2000. *Konsekutive Konstruktionen und relative Modalität*. Doctoral dissertation. University of Tübingen.
Meier, Cécile 2001. Result Clauses. In: R. Hastings, B. Jackson & Z. Zvolensky (eds.). *Proceedings of Semantics and Linguistic Theory (= SALT) XI*. Ithaca, NY: Cornell University, 268–285.
Partee, Barbara 1984. Nominal and temporal anaphora. *Linguistics & Philosophy* 7, 243–286.
Pusch, Luise 1980. *Kontrastive Untersuchungen zum italienischen Gerundio. Instrumental- und Modalsätze und das Problem der Individuierung von Ereignissen*. Tübingen: Niemeyer.
Rapp, Irene & Arnim von Stechow 1999. Fast 'almost' and the visibility parameter for functional adverbs. *Journal of Semantics* 16, 149–204.

Ross, John R. 1970. On declarative sentences. In: R. A. Jacobs & P. S. Rosenbaum (eds.). *Readings in English Transformational Grammar*. Waltham, MA: Ginn, 222–272.
Rothstein, Susan 2003. Secondary predication and aspectual structure. In: E. Lang, C. Maienborn & C. Fabricius-Hansen (eds.). *Modifying Adjuncts*. Berlin: de Gruyter, 553–590.
Rutherford, William 1970. Some observations concerning subordinate clauses in English. *Language* 46, 97–115.
Sæbø, Kjell Johan 1980. Infinitive perfect and backward causation. *Nordic Journal of Linguistics* 3, 161–173.
Sæbø, Kjell Johan 1991. Causal and purposive clauses. In: A. von Stechow & D. Wunderlich (eds.). *Semantik – Semantics. Ein internationales Handbuch zeitgenössischer Forschung – An International Handbook of Contemporary Research* (HSK 6). Berlin: de Gruyter, 623–631.
Sæbø, Kjell Johan 2008. The structure of criterion predicates. In: J. Dölling, T. Heyde-Zybatow & M. Schäfer (eds.). *Event Structures in Linguistic Form and Interpretation*. Berlin: Mouton de Gruyter, 127–147.
Sandström, Görel 1993. *When-Clauses and the Temporal Interpretation of Narrative Discourse*. University of Umeå: Department of General Linguistics.
Scheffler, Tatjana 2005. Syntax and semantics of causal *denn* in German. In: P. Dekker & M. Franke (eds.). *Proceedings of the 15th Amsterdam Colloquium*. Amsterdam: ILLC, 215–220.
Schlenker, Philippe 2004. Conditionals as definite descriptions. *Research on Language and Computation* 2, 417–462.
Stalnaker, Robert 1968. A theory of conditionals. In: N. Rescher (ed.). *Studies in Logical Theory*. Oxford: Blackwell, 98–112.
von Stechow, Arnim, Sveta Krasikova & Doris Penka 2006. Anankastic conditionals again. In: T. Solstad, A. Grønn & D. Haug (eds.). *A Festschrift for Kjell Johan Sæbø*. Oslo: Unipub, 151–171.
Stump, Gregory T. 1985. *The Semantic Variability of Absolute Constructions*. Dordrecht: Reidel.
de Swart, Henriëtte 1991. *Adverbs of Quantification. A Generalized Quantifier Approach*. Groningen: Grodil.
von Wright, Georg Henrik 1971. *Explanation and Understanding*. London: Routledge.

Susan Rothstein
16 Secondary predicates

1 Introduction: The issues —— 543
2 Resultative predication: the direct predication account —— 548
3 Resultative and depictive predication: the complex predicate account —— 553
4 Depictive predication: circumstantial predication and weak adjuncts —— 560
5 Remaining issues —— 563
6 Conclusion —— 565
7 References —— 566

Abstract: This paper discusses how to give an analysis of secondary predication structures within a compositional semantic theory. There are two basic options for analysing secondary predicates compositionally. One is to treat them as direct predication structures within a small clause and the other is to analyse them as forming complex predicates together with the matrix verb at the VP level. We compare these approaches, showing that depictives and circumstantials (which we analyse as depictives under the scope of a modal operator) have a plausible compositional interpretation only under the complex predicate approach. Resultative secondary predicates can in principle be analysed either way. However, we suggest the complex predicate account is preferable for two reasons: (i) the small clause account assumes a lexical relation between the matrix verb and the small clause, and this lexical relation is elusive and difficult to specify; (ii) the complex predicate account allows an explanation of why depictives and resultatives are the only two kinds of secondary predicates semantically available. We show that on the complex predicate account, the semantic range of available secondary predicates follows from general constraints on event structure.

1 Introduction: The issues

Secondary predicates are one place non-verbal predicate expressions which occur under the scope of a main verb. Crucially, they share an argument with the main verb, the subject of the secondary predicate being either the subject or the direct object of the matrix verb. Secondary predicates are usually grammatically optional, which means that they can in most cases be dropped from the sentence without

Susan Rothstein, Bar-Ilan University, Israel

https://doi.org/10.1515/9783110626391-016

making the sentence ungrammatical. Hence the term "secondary predication", or "adjunct predication". Following Halliday (1967), three kinds of secondary predicates are classically recognised: resultatives, depictives and circumstantials. *Resultatives* are typically predicated of the direct object of the main verb, which is thus simultaneously the direct object of the main verb and the subject of the predicate. A resultative predicate denotes a property which its subject has at the end of the event expressed by the main verb. *Depictives* can be predicates of either subject or object of the main verb and typically express a property that their subject has while the event expressed by the main verb is going on. *Circumstantials* can also be predicated of either subject or object of the main verb and typically express a property that their subject has as a condition of the event expressed by the main verb taking place. These are illustrated in (1)–(3), respectively. (The predicates are in italics and are coindexed with their subjects. Note that (2c) is ambiguous. In fact all depictives and circumstantials are in principle ambiguous, but in the examples other than (2c) context disambiguates the sentences.)

(1) Resultatives:
    a. John painted the house$_i$ *red*$_i$.
    b. Bill watered the tulips$_i$ *flat*$_i$.
    c. Mary sang the child$_i$/herself$_i$ *asleep*$_i$.

(2) Depictives:
    a. Mary ate the carrots$_i$ *raw*$_i$.
    b. John$_i$ drove the car *drunk*$_i$.
    c. John$_i$ kissed Mary$_j$ *drunk*$_{i/j}$.

(3) Circumstantials:
    a. John can carry that bucket$_i$ *empty*$_i$.
    b. John$_i$ can carry that bucket *sober*$_i$.
    c. He eats carrots$_i$ *raw*$_i$.

The questions raised by secondary predicates are what exactly do they mean, and how are they licenced? For each kind of secondary predicate, we must ask what structural properties it has and what lexical restrictions there are on choice of predicate and matrix verb. Secondary predicates and matrix verbs share an argument, and this raises the more general issue of how a compositional theory of interpretation allows secondary predication at all. Third, there is the 'global' question of why there appear to be resultative, depictive and circumstantial secondary predicates, but no others. In this paper, I am going to concentrate largely on structural issues, including compositionality, and the implications of the third question of why there are the kinds of secondary predicates that there are. As we shall see, there are essentially two different kinds of solutions to the compositionality problem, and I shall argue that only one of the solutions permits an answer to the global issues of what the different forms of secondary predication have in common and why they have the constraints that they do.

First, let us look in more depth at the questions to be addressed. We begin by reviewing some of the more obvious properties that resultative and depictive predicates have. (I shall assume for the moment that circumstantial predication is a form of depictive predication and shall argue for this later in the paper.) For *resultatives*, the important points include (i) the observation noted in Simpson (1983) that resultatives are always predicated of direct objects, or subjects that can be analysed as underlying direct objects, that is as subjects of passives and unaccusatives. (Note that Rappaport Hovav & Levin (2001) argue, contra Simpson (1983), that there are subject-oriented resultatives, and that these are semantically distinguished from object-oriented resultatives, since they may occur when the result predicate event and the matrix predicate event are temporally conflated. This issue is discussed briefly in section 5.), (ii) the fact that resultatives can be predicated of a direct object which is not a thematic argument of the main verb, including fake reflexives as illustrated in (1c), and (iii) the observation from Dowty (1979) and others, that the effect of adding a resultative predicate when the main verb is an activity is to derive a VP with accomplishment properties (in the sense of Vendler 1967; cf. article 9 [Semantics: Noun Phrases and Verb Phrases] (Filip) *Aspectual class and Aktionsart*). In (4a/b) we see that the singular direct object of the V+resultative gives a telic VP while the mass and bare plural direct objects of the same predicate give atelic VPs, as is normally the case with accomplishments. When the resultative is not present, the properties of the direct object do not affect the telicity of the VP, as we see in (5). This is characteristic of activity predicates. This data is discussed in some detail in Rothstein (2004):

(4) a. John hammered the nail flat in an hour/#for an hour.
    b. John hammered metal/nails flat for an hour/#in an hour.

(5) a. John hammered metal/nails for an hour/#in an hour.
    b. John hammered the nail for an hour/#in an hour.

Depictive predicates in English have fewer obvious outstanding characteristics. They can be predicated of both subject and object, as shown in (2). The main question that arises is what kinds of predicates can be used as depictives. It is generally agreed that in English, depictive predicates must denote non-inherent and transitory properties, and various different explanations for why this is the case have been proposed (e.g. Rapoport 1991, 1999, Condoravdi 1992). But crosslinguistically, there is quite some variation as to which categories (semantic and syntactic) can be used as depictive predicates. Himmelmann & Schultze-Berndt (2005a) propose a typology which enables some predictive generalisations to be made. *Circumstantials* are the least well studied group of secondary predicates, and as Himmelmann and Schultze-Berndt suggest, can probably be analysed as a subkind of depictives. We will look at the arguments for reducing circumstantial predicates to depictives in section 4.

The general issue that secondary predication of all kinds raises concerns compositional interpretation. A compositional theory of semantic interpretation prima facie makes it impossible for two predicates to share an argument. Once a constituent of type $<\alpha,\beta>$ has applied to a constituent of type α, it yields a constituent of type β, and the α is no longer available to be the argument of any other constituent. If the secondary predicates above apply directly to their arguments, then those arguments are no longer available to be arguments of the verb. If they do not apply directly to their arguments, the question is how they are interpreted.

Let us put the problem more formally. Assume a standard type theory with three basic types: e, the type of event, d, the type of individual entity and t, the type of truth values. Assume that APs denote relations between individuals and eventualities (where states are a subtype of eventuality); they are thus of type $<d,<e,t>>$, and combine with individuals to yield sets of events. Sets of eventualities of type $<e,t>$ are normally expressed by sentence-like constituents, including small clauses (see the discussion in Rothstein 1999). A compositional semantic theory predicts that a (non-attributive) AP constituent will combine directly with an argument to give a constituent of type $<e,t>$. There is no obvious way in which the predicates in the sentences (1–3) can combine directly with their subjects, since these subjects need still to be available as to saturate arguments of the main verb, and the question is therefore, how are these adjectival predicates grammatically licenced and semantically interpreted? There are essentially two possible directions. One is to assume that secondary predicates do apply directly to their arguments and yield a single constituent, although this is not immediately obvious at surface structure. The challenge is then to make the case out for the constituent, and to explain how, if the predicate has applied to its subject directly, the argument requirements of the verb are also met. We will call this the "direct predication" approach. The second direction is to assume that the secondary predicate does not combine directly with its argument, but that it combines first with the verb to form a complex predicate which is then applied to the shared argument, satisfying the complex predicate directly and the verb and the Adjective Phrase indirectly. We will call this the "complex predicate" approach. How the particular properties of resultatives and depictives are to be explained depends of course on which general direction is taken.

A crucial issue concerning research on secondary predication (although this is not always explicitly recognised) is the following: Is secondary predication a unified phenomenon, i.e. are resultatives and depictives interpreted via the same kind of operation? If the assumption is that secondary predication is a unified phenomenon then both depictive and resultative predication will be interpreted via *either* the direct predication *or* the complex predication approach, but whichever solution is used for the one, will be used for the other too. If the different kinds of secondary predication are non-homologous and merely have analogous surface properties, then one can be interpreted via direct predication and the other via a complex predicate formation operation. De facto, most semantic accounts have concentrated on the problems of resultative predication, probably because resultatives interact in particularly interesting ways with issues of aspect and telicity. Representative of the direct predication account of resultatives is Kratzer's (2005) analysis, in which the resultative predicate complement and its subject form a subordinate predication structure which is the complement of an intransitive verb. In my own work (Rothstein 2001, 2004), I have argued for the complex predicate approach, showing that it allows a unified approach to both depictive and resultative predication. I am still convinced of the fruitfulness of this latter approach for reasons which I will try to make clear; however, the purpose of this paper is not to reiterate the analysis that I already presented there, but rather to show what underlying issues semantic accounts of secondary predication need to take account of, and how the two approaches deal with them.

The structure of the paper is as follows. In the next section, I review the direct predication account of secondary predication from a structural and semantic perspective. We see that this approach yields a natural account of the semantics of resultative predication, and discuss one well-worked out account, that of Kratzer (2005), focusing on the implications of her analysis and the questions that her account raises. In section 3, I discuss depictive predication and show that there is no direct predication analysis which is plausible for depictive predication. A direct predication account of resultatives thus commits us to a non-unified account of the semantics of secondary predication. I review the alternative account of secondary predication as complex predicate formation in Bach (1980) and Rothstein (2001, 2004), and compare it with the direct predication account, and I show how the analysis of depictive predication can be extended to account for resultative predication in a straightforward way. We see that this 'single' account of secondary predication explains why depictives and resultatives are just the forms of secondary predication allowed. In section 4, I will address some issues in the semantics of depictive predication, and in particular the relation between depictives, circumstantials, and weak adjuncts. In section 5, I review briefly some cross-linguistic issues.

2 Resultative predication: the direct predication account

The puzzle underlying the structural analysis of secondary predication is whether or not two predicates can be predicated separately of a single argument. For example, in (6a), the DP *the carrots* is both the direct object of *eat* and the subject of the depictive predicate *raw*, and in (6b) *the house* is the direct object of *paint* and the subject of the resultative predicate *red*.

(6) a. John ate the carrots *raw*.
 b. Mary painted the house *red*.

Classical syntactic accounts of these structures in the government binding framework (Chomsky 1981) argued that two predicates could not share an argument, and therefore argued that secondary predicates must be predicated of null pronominal subjects (PRO). (Note that Williams 1980, 1983, Schein 1995, Rothstein 1983, 2001 all argued against a direct predication approach within the Government and Binding framework. An overview of the syntax of these constructions is given in Rothstein 2006.) Chomsky (1981) posited that secondary predicates formed small clauses with null subjects as in (7), where the null pronominal subject is anaphorically dependent on the lexical argument:

(7) a. John [ate the carrots [PRO raw]$_{SC}$]$_{VP}$
 b. Mary [painted the house [PRO red]$_{SC}$]$_{VP}$

As far as I know, no coherent semantic account of how the structures in (7) are to be interpreted has ever been given. However, the idea that the small clause is central to resultative constructions was developed by Hoekstra (1988), based on the following fact. A peculiarity of resultatives, unlike depictives, is that while they must be predicated of direct objects, they can be predicated of direct objects which are not thematic arguments of the matrix verb (sometimes called 'unselected objects'), as in (8) (see discussion in Simpson 1983, Carrier & Randall 1992):

(8) a. John ran the pavement thin.
 b. They clapped the singer off the stage.
 c. He laughed himself sick.

Examples like these suggest that the subject of the resultative predicate and its subject do form a small clause, with (8a), for example, having the structure in (9):

(9) John ran [the pavement thin]$_{SC}$

Rothstein (1983) originally proposed that (9) was the appropriate structure for small clauses with unselected objects. Hoesktra (1988) argued that all resultatives are structured this way and that sentences like (7b), where the direct object is a thematic argument of both the verb and the resultative, should also be analysed as having syntactic structures directly analogous to (9):

(10) John painted [the house red]

Hoekstra thus argued that all resultatives formed small clauses with their subjects. He proposed that the subject of the small clause raised to direct object position in order to be assigned case. There is thus no direct semantic or thematic relation between the matrix verb and its direct object. Hoekstra argues that what looks like a thematic relation between the verb and its direct object is in fact pragmatic. *Paint* does not assign a thematic role to *the house* in (10), and there is thus no lexically based entailment that if John painted the house red, then he painted the house. Since *John ran the pavement thin* clearly does not entail that John ran the pavement, we do not want there to be an entailment in (9) either. However, Hoekstra argued, since resultatives imply a causal relation between the event denoted by the main verb and the result state expressed by the resultative predicate, the semantic relation between verb and direct object follows from the pragmatics of the situation. We normally understand that the house becoming red as a result of the painting event means that the house was directly affected by the painting event, and the entailment that the house was painted is reduced to this implicature.

Kratzer (2005) takes a similar position to Hoekstra with respect to the syntactic structure of resultatives, and puts it together with a semantic analysis which explains where the result meaning comes from. She argues that resultative predicates are concealed causatives in a sense related to that of Bittner (1999). *John ran the pavement thin* means something like "There was an event (or habit) of John running and this event (or habit) directly caused a state of the pavement being thin". *John painted the house red* will mean, analogously, "There was an event of John painting and as a direct result of that painting event, there was a state of the house being red". She shows that to support this analysis, two arguments have to be made. One is that all matrix verbs in resultative constructions can plausibly be analysed as intransitives and the second is that there is a plausible compositional basis for introducing the causative relation. It seems to me that *any* compositional direct predication account of resultatives will be faced with exactly these issues. An account which predicates the resultative directly of its subject will be forced to treat the verb as intransitive and will need to explain where the result reading comes from.

Kratzer's arguments that the matrix verb is intransitive are essentially as follows:

(i) Very many verbs that can appear with resultative predicates have an intransitive form. For example, *John painted* is a very normal sentence in English.
(ii) Even when the verb seems transitive, an intransitive form is possible in reduplicated constructions:

(11) a. They watered the tulips flat.
b. #They watered.
c. They watered and watered (until all the flowers were drenched sufficiently).

(iii) In those cases where the verb seems truly transitive, it is possible to analyse the apparent resultative as an adverb. This is much easier to argue in German, where there is no morphological distinction between adjectives and adverbs. Thus *dünn* in (12a) is ambiguous between an adjectival interpretation *thin* and the adverbial *thinly*. Kratzer argues that in these situations, since the verb seems to be truly transitive as (12b) shows, *dünn* must be given an adverbial interpretation. Support for this comes from the fact that it can be questioned by *Wie* or "how", usually a questioner of adverbs.

(12) a. Sie haben den Teig   dünn ausgerollt.
They have the dough thin out-rolled.

b. Sie   haben *(den Teig) ausgerollt.
They have the dough out-rolled.
"They rolled out the dough."

c. Wie haben sie den Teig   ausgerollt? Dünn.
How have they the dough out-rolled Thin.
"How did they roll the dough? Thin."

It is much harder to make this argument in English. Despite the fact, as Kratzer points out, that some adjectives may have an adverbial usage, these are frequently idiomatic. And while it is difficult to make truth conditional distinctions between *they rolled the dough out thinly* and *they rolled the dough out thin*, there are other cases where the adverbial and adjective seem to have very different interpretations, and where an intransitive form of the verb is unacceptable:

(13) a. They developed the picture fuzzy.
      b. They developed the picture fuzzily.
      c. They developed *(the picture).

In (13a) the result of the developing is a picture in which the subject of the picture is represented in a fuzzy way, but the method which achieved that might have been precise in the extreme. In (13b) the adverbial modifies how the event took place and says nothing about the resulting picture.

(iv) Kratzer's fourth point is that if the matrix verb has to be syntactically intransitive, we have a natural explanation for why unaccusatives do not appear with resultatives. Since unaccusatives are fundamentally transitive (in the sense that they take an underlying direct object), they cannot appear in a construction where the verb must be intransitive.

Having set out the arguments that the matrix verb is intransitive in resultatives and that the structures in (9) and (10) are plausible, Kratzer goes on to address the issue of where the result meaning comes from. The small clause is derived by applying the Adjective Phrase, denoting a set of states, to its subject to give a property of states, so that in *John painted that house red*, the small clause *that house red* denotes the set of states in (14):

(14) $\lambda s.\text{State}(s) \land \text{RED}(\text{THAT HOUSE},s)$

If the syntactic structure consists of a matrix predicate with a small clause denoting a set of states, then where does the result meaning come from? Intuitively there should be a cause relation holding between the matrix event and the set of states denoted by the small clause. Kratzer argues that since there is no lexical item introducing such a causal relation, there are two possible options: (i) the cause relation is introduced by a type shifting operation, or (ii) there is a morphologically null lexical item which introduces the necessary relation. The type shifting operation she envisages would shift the predicate in (14) from a property of states to a property of events such as (15).

(15) $\lambda e.\exists s[\text{State}(s) \land \text{Event}(e) \land \text{RED}(\text{THAT HOUSE},s) \land \text{Cause}(e,s)]$

An operation of event identification would identify the event argument in (15) with the event argument of the matrix predicate and give the following meaning for *John painted the house red* in (16):

(16) $\exists e \exists s[\text{Event}_{\text{action}}(e) \land \text{PAINT}(e) \land \text{Agent}(e) = \text{JOHN} \land \text{State}(s) \land \text{RED}(\text{THAT HOUSE},s) \land \text{Cause}(e,s)]$

The disadvantage of the type shifting operation is that it introduces lexical information, and, as Kratzer writes, "restrictive systems of compositional principles or type shifts shouldn't introduce operations of this kind". The other option is to assume that the causal meaning is introduced by a null morpheme, a zero-derivational affix which attaches to the adjectival head. It would have the denotation in (17):

(17) T([cause]) = $\lambda P_{<st>}\lambda e.\exists s$ [State(s) $\wedge$ Event(e) $\wedge$ P(s) & Cause(e,s)]

Kratzer comes down in favour of this second option, partly so as to keep type shifting operations restrictive and partly because restrictions on the interaction of a derivational affix with other affixes which can apply to adjectives might explain some of the restrictions concerning which classes of adjectives can and cannot occur as resultative predicates. Note that in both the type shifting and the zero-morpheme analyses, the matrix verb is related to the small clause via event identification, a form of complex predicate formation which applies to a pair of event predicates. The precise meaning is that there is an event which is simultaneously a painting event and an event of causing a state of the house being red.

I have spent some time on the details of Kratzer's analysis because it is the best worked out (possibly the only completely worked out) compositional analysis of the semantics of resultatives from the direct predication approach, and thus is an indication of what kind of features such an approach must have, and what the restrictions are on working the details of such a theory out. We have seen that if the resultative is to be predicated of the subject, then the verb must be analysed as intransitive (presumably of the activity type) and that an explicit semantic relation relating the activity expressed by the intransitive in the matrix clause and the denotation of the small clause must be introduced into the derivation. Three central questions can be raised about this analysis described above, and crucially about any direct predication account. (i) Is the matrix verb truly intransitive? (Some potential counterexamples to the claim that it is were cited in (13).) (ii) Is it appropriate to introduce a semantic 'cause' relation? It is clear that some semantic relation has to be introduced to relate the matrix verb and the small clause, but there is evidence that 'cause' is too strong. Rothstein (2001, 2003) argues that 'cause' is too strong because of examples such as (18), where the matrix event does not cause the state given in the resultative, no matter whether the causation is constrained to be direct or indirect. (For discussions of the distinction between direct and indirect causation see Dowty 1979, Kratzer 2005, Bittner 1999.) In each of the cases in (18), the event denoted by the main verb is not the process which causes the result state. Rather, it is an event which *accompanies* the process leading to the result state.

(18) a. The audience clapped the singer off the stage.
   b. In 1945, on Liberation Day, the people of Amsterdam danced and sang the Canadian soldiers to Dam Square.
   c. As the guards slowly pulled the levers, the crowd cheered the gates of the building open/closed.

In (18a), the clapping of the audience does not cause the singer to leave the stage; on the contrary, applause is often intended to prevent the singer leaving the stage for as long as possible. In (18b), the Canadian soldiers who were liberating Amsterdam had orders to go to Dam Square, and were going there independent of what the local population did. In (18c), it is clearly the pulling of the levers which opens (or closes) the gates of the building, and not the cheering of the crowd.

Kratzer (2005) argues that her theory covers only adjectival resultatives, and that the non-causal resultative all involve non-adjectival predicates, which should be analysed separately, but as (18c) shows, there are non-causal adjectival resultative predicates too, and there is no independent reason, as far as I know, for separating adjectival from PP resultatives. The examples in (18) could be taken as evidence that a weaker relation than 'cause' is involved, but an examination of the range of examples shows that it would be difficult to formulate a simple relation which could be introduced either by a type shifting rule or by a null derivational morpheme. (iii) The third issue is that a direct predication analysis of resultatives such as the analysis described here cannot plausibly be extended to depictive predication. In the next section we look more closely at depictive predication and complex predicate formation.

3 Resultative and depictive predication: the complex predicate account

3.1 Depictive predication

Depictive predication raises exactly the same compositional problem as resultatives, since the depictive predicate shares an argument with the matrix verb. However, there are two crucial differences. First, there are no intransitive depictive predicates analogous to *sing the child/herself asleep* in example (1c), and therefore there is no surface evidence for a small clause analysis of depictive predication analogous to the Hoekstra/Kratzer analysis of resultatives. Also, the matrix verb is clearly not inherently intransitive, since depictives can occur with obligatory transitives such as in one reading of (19a), where the predicate *drunk* is coindexed with *Mary*. Second, depictive predicates can straightforwardly be predicated of subjects as in the other reading of (19a) and (19b):

(19) a. John$_i$ met Mary$_j$ drunk$_{i/j}$.
 b. John$_i$ drove the car drunk$_i$.

This means there is no analysis that can be given in which the depictive predicate forms a constituent with its subject either at surface structure or at some other level of representation. The only possible constituent structure allowing interpretation via direct predication is the one suggested in (7), where the depictive is predicated of a null pronominal and some anaphoric relation holds between the null anaphor and the surface subject of the sentence. Chomsky (1981), Franks & Hornstein (1992) and Legendre (1997) argue for a version of the small clause structure for depictives, though none give a semantic interpretation. Giving such a semantic interpretation would be in principle possible; however the relation between the main verbs and the depictive predicates in (19) seems roughly to be one of temporal inclusion between events. (19b) means roughly "John drove the car and he was drunk all the time that the driving event was going on". So representing the semantic interpretation in (19b) in terms of the relation between two clauses would require a relation involving the temporal properties of two independent propositional functions, and this would require equipping the small clause with enough abstract structure for tense and mood to be fully represented. However, there is no explicit, theory-independent, syntactic evidence in favour of a small clause structure and certainly not for assigning a small clause of this kind abstract tense and mood nodes, and there is some evidence against doing so (see e.g. Williams 1980, 1983, McNulty 1988, Rothstein 2001). We assume then, a more restrictive theory of interpretation, where what you interpret is a surface structure free of null pronominal elements, but this means that a direct predication account is impossible and we are committed to a complex predicate analysis.

There are two versions of the complex predicate approach. One is a lexical approach, which assumes that the verb and predicate form a complex predicate in the lexicon via a process of lexical extension. This treats secondary predicate formation as a change in the structure of the verbal predicate analogous to McConnell-Ginet's (1982) analysis of adverbial modification. This approach has been developed especially by Wunderlich (1997), and one of the advantages is that it determines constraints on choices of depictive predicates via lexical restrictions. The second approach is to assume that complex predication formation is a syntactic operation as argued in Bach (1980), and Rothstein (2001, 2004). Prima facie evidence that depictive predication involves a syntactic operation is the fact that subject and object depictive predicates are apparently generated in different syntactic positions, as (20) below shows. On the basis of the syntactic arguments of Andrews (1982), subject and object oriented depictive predicates are argued to be part of the VP, with object oriented depictive predicates as sisters to the V and subject oriented depictives as sisters to the V':

(20)   John$_i$ [[rode the bicycle$_j$ bent out of shape$_j$]$_V$, drunk$_i$]$_{VP}$

The reason for the different positions is that operations applying to V constituents obligatorily include the object oriented predicate, but only optionally include the subject oriented predicate as (21) shows:

(21)   a. What John$_i$ did drunk$_i$ was ride the bicycle$_j$ (bent out of shape$_j$).
       b. What John$_i$ did was ride the bicycle$_j$ (bent out of shape$_j$) drunk$_i$.
       c. #What John did bent out of shape$_j$ was ride the bicycle$_j$.
       d. What John did was ride the bicycle$_j$ bent out of shape$_j$.

This can be taken as evidence against a lexical extension (or any lexical) account of complex predicate formation since we would expect word formation rules to yield strings all parts of which are generated immediately under the same syntactic node. (Note that it is of course possible that there is cross-linguistic variation as to whether complex predicate formation is a syntactic or a lexical operation, although this is more plausible for resultative predication. Thus, Neeleman (1994) and Neeleman & Weerman (1993) argue that the complex predicate formation involved in resultative predication is a lexical process in Dutch. The grammatical operations which indicate lexical complex-predicate formation for Dutch resultatives (movement, passive formation adverb placement and so on) give ungrammatical results in English where the Dutch results are grammatical, indicating that English resultatives are not the result of a lexical operation. We come back to this in section 5.)

The semantic interpretation of depictive predication is relatively straightforward. As we already just noted, *John drove the car drunk* means something like "John drove the car and he was drunk at the time he drove the car". The relation between the two predicates cannot be reduced merely to event conjunction, since the crucial semantic relation is that the two events are temporally cotemporaneous. Furthermore, the absence of "intransitive depictives" such as *#John drove Mary drunk* with the interpretation "John drove while Mary was drunk' indicate that the matrix predicate and the depictive predicate must share a participant.

Rothstein (2004) argues that complex predicate formation applies to the matrix and depictive predicates, and follows Lasersohn (1992), who argues that the semantics of event conjunction are best captured using an operation of event summing. However, Rothstein (2004) argues that in complex predicate formation of this kind the relevant operation sums the pair of eventualities and forms a new singular event out of them. This operation is called S-summing (or singular summing), and it applies to pairs of eventualities under the condition that they share a participant and a run-time. The analysis assumes an event theory in which states as well as actions and changes (activities, accomplishments and achievements in Vendler's framework) are all subtypes of eventualities. Complex predicate formation sums eventualities and forms a singular eventuality out of them under the condition that the eventualities share a run time and a participant. Thus in *John drove the car drunk*, complex predicate formation forms a new singular event out of the two predicates $\lambda x \lambda e.\text{DRIVE}(e) \wedge \text{Th}(e)=\text{THE CAR} \wedge \text{Ag}(e) = x$ and $\lambda x \lambda e.\text{DRUNK}(e) \wedge \text{Arg}(e) = x$, and denotes as set of atomic events which are events of driving the car while drunk. The operation of S-summing is given in (22), where the superscript "S" indicates an operation of forming a singularity, so that '$^S(e_1 \sqcup e_2)$' is the singular entity formed out of the sum of e_1 and e_2 and t is the operation which maps events onto their running times, as defined in Krifka (1998).

(22) $\text{S-SUM}[\alpha(e_1), \beta(e_2)] = \lambda e.\exists e_1 \exists e_2 [e=^S(e_1 \sqcup e_2) \wedge \alpha(e_1) \wedge \beta(e_2) \wedge \tau(e_1) \sqsubseteq \tau(e_2) \wedge \text{Arg}(e_2)=\text{Arg}(e_1)]$

The interpretation of the VP *drive the car drunk* is given in (23a). Predicate abstraction over external argument (the x variable in (23a)) gives the expression in (23b) which can then be applied to the subject argument to give the interpretation *John drove the car drunk* as in (23b). (This is a slightly different formulation of the constraints on S-summing in secondary predication than the formulation given in Rothstein 2003, 2004.):

(23) a. *drive the car drunk*:
$\lambda e.\exists e_1 \exists e_2 [e=^S(e_1 \sqcup e_2) \wedge \text{DRIVE}(e_1) \wedge \text{Th}(e_1)= \text{THE CAR} \wedge \text{Ag}(e_1)=x$
$\wedge \text{DRUNK}(e_2) \wedge \text{Arg}(e_2)= x \wedge \tau(e_1) \sqsubseteq \tau(e_2)]$

b. $\lambda x \lambda e.\exists e_1 \exists e_2 [e=^S(e_1 \sqcup e_2) \wedge \text{DRIVE}(e_1) \wedge \text{Th}(e_1) = \text{THE CAR} \wedge \text{Ag}(e_1) = x$
$\wedge \text{DRUNK}(e_2) \wedge \text{Arg}(e_2)= x \wedge \tau(e_1) \sqsubseteq \tau(e_2)]$

c. *John drove the car drunk*
$\exists e \exists e_1 \exists e_2 [e = ^S(e_1 \sqcup e_2) \wedge \text{DRIVE}(e_1) \wedge \text{Th}(e_1) = \text{THE CAR} \wedge \text{Ag}(e_1) = \text{JOHN}$
$\wedge \text{DRUNK}(e_2) \wedge \text{Arg}(e_2) = \text{JOHN} \wedge \tau(e_1) \sqsubseteq \tau(e_2)]$

A slightly more complex version of the summing operation allows depictive predicates to be predicated of direct objects. The transitive verb is combined with the secondary predicate and the combined predicated applies to the direct object. (24) gives the object oriented interpretation of *John met Mary$_i$ drunk$_i$*.

(24) *John met Mary drunk*
$\exists e \exists e_1 \exists e_2 [e = {}^S(e_1 \sqcup e_2) \land \text{MEET}(e_1) \land \text{Th}(e_1) = \text{MARY} \land \text{Ag}(e_1) = \text{JOHN}$
$\land \text{DRUNK}(e_2) \land \text{Arg}(e_2) = \text{MARY} \land \tau(e_1) \sqsubseteq \tau(e_2)]$

This account of depictive predicate formation reduces the semantic relation between the matrix predicate and the adjunct to temporal coincidence and participant sharing and captures the essential meaning of the construction, namely that it allows an assertion that a property P holds of a participant x of an event e while that event e is taking place.

The other major questions concerning depictive predication concern what predicates can be depictives. This question applies if depictives are taken to be formed at the lexical or the syntactic level. A well-known restriction is that depictives seem to be non-inherent, or transitory or stage level. One semantic explanation of this restriction is given in Rapoport (1991). She proposes that the complex predicate formation involved in secondary predicate formation occurs via an operation of event identification between the matrix and secondary predicate. Assuming, following Kratzer (1995), that individual level predicates have no event argument, the infelicity of individual level predicates as depictive predicates would follow from the fact that they had no event argument to link. However, this makes the constraint restricting depictives to stage level predicates into a structural distinction, and there is good reasons to assume that the restriction is pragmatic and context dependent. Rothstein (1983) shows that individual level predicates can occur as depictives if the context allows them to be interpreted as transitory as in *The artist drew Alice (in Wonderland) tall*, or when modified as in *Emma drew Harriet more elegant than she actually was*. Conversely, Condoravdi (1992) and McNally (1994) have each argued that individual level predicates can be interpreted as depictives in an appropriate context without losing their non-transitory meaning, as in for example *He was born a Republican, he lived a Republican and he died a Republican*. This is a particularly interesting example because the sentence is essentially asserting that *Republican* is to be interpreted as an individual-level predicate. These examples all indicate that the possibility of using an adjective as a depictive predicate is not dependent on the structural properties of the adjective, but rather on the contextual informativeness of asserting that the running time of the event denoted by the verb is temporally contained in the running time of the state denoted by the adjective. If the state denoted by the adjective is not transitory, then special circumstances are required for the assertion not to be trivial.

The second kind of restriction concerns what kinds of expressions can be depictive predicates cross-linguistically, both on a categorical level (in English, depictives are generally restricted to APs, in other languages this is not necessarily the case) and on a semantic level. Himmelmann & Schultze-Berndt (2005a) propose a tentative semantic map for depictive predicates. They show that properties can be grouped in types (physical condition, mental condition, physical configuration, etc.) and structured into a semantic domain. On the basis of a number of languages studied, they show that there are patterns, definable on the basis of their map, for the semantic restrictions on what kinds of predicates can occur as depictives. Importantly, these kinds of restrictions can be formulated at both the syntactic and the lexical level. Thus, if there is cross-linguistic variation as to whether depictive predicate formation is a lexical or a syntactic operation, it remains plausible that the operation is restricted in essentially the same way, no matter at what level it applies.

3.2 Extending this analysis to resultative predication

We have seen that it is possible to give a direct predication account of resultatives but that this approach is not plausible for depictive predication. Thus, if we want to treat secondary predication as a single phenomenon, it is necessary to extend the complex predicate formation account of depictives to account for resultatives too. I will give an outline of how this can be done. Details of the analysis can be found in Rothstein (2004).

Assume a version of the Vendler analysis of verb classes. The precise details are not essential, nor is it essential whether Vendler classes are to be taken as categorising verbs or verb phrases. What is essential is the idea that there are four classes of verbal templates denoting four kinds of eventualities. Three of them, activities, states and achievements are simple predicates, denoting simple eventualities, while the fourth, accomplishments, denotes a complex eventuality which includes a gradual process of change. This can be defined in the framework of Dowty (1979), or Krifka (1992), or Rothstein (2004) as long as the notion of event culmination (i.e., end of the incremental process or process of change) is well defined. Since this notion is required in order to explain when accomplishments are telic, any well-defined theory of accomplishments will meet this constraint. An accomplishment meaning might be represented as in (25), modeled on Dowty's (1979) analysis of accomplishments and recast in Parsons' (1990) representation which represents verbs as denoting sets of events:

(25) $\lambda e.\exists e_1 \exists e_2 [e={}^S(e_1 \sqcup e_2) \land (DO(P))(e_1) \land Cul(e_1) = e_2 \land Arg(e_2) = Th(e_1)]$
"a set of complex eventualities consisting of an activity and a culmination of the activity, where the theme of the activity is the argument of the culmination eventuality"

We then assume complex predicate formation is available as for depictive predication with a single added assumption. In the previous section, complex predicate formation was constrained to apply only when the eventualities in the denotations of the two predicates share a participant and have the same run time. We add the assumption that this constraint can hold between the *subeventuality* of the matrix predicate and the secondary predicate. This means that the secondary predicate can have the same run time and share a participant with the culmination of the matrix event rather than with the matrix event itself. *Paint the house red* will be derived from the complex predicate *paint.... red* being applied to the argument *the house*. The VP will have the denotation in (26):

(26) paint the house red:
$\lambda e.\exists e_1 \exists e_2 [e = {}^S(e_1 \sqcup e_2) \land \text{PAINT}(e_1) \land Th(e_1) = \text{THE HOUSE} \land \text{RED}(e_2)$
$\land Arg(e_2) = \text{THE HOUSE} \land \tau(cul(e_1)) \sqsubseteq \tau(e_2)]$
"The set of painting the house events at the culmination of which the house is red"

This gives an adequate semantics for the resultative. There is no explicit 'cause' operator, which explains why there are non-causal resultatives as in (18). Where there is a causal implication we assume it is derived pragmatically, and where the resultative is in the scope of an activity verb, we assume that the activity shifts into an accomplishment template in order to accommodate the resultative.

This analysis explains several features about resultative constructions, in addition to extending to non-causative resultatives. In particular, it explains why resultative-modified verbs behave as accomplishments with respect to the telic/non-telic distinction, as shown in (4) and (5). Furthermore, it explains why there are only resultative and depictive predicates: since the Vendler templates make available only sets of eventualities denoted by verbs and in some cases also their culminations, the two kinds of possible secondary predicates are depictives, which are related directly to the eventuality denoted by the main verb of the predicate and resultatives, which are related to the culmination of these eventualities. By extending the complex predicate analysis from depictives to resultatives we thus analyse them as instances of the same phenomenon, which a direct predication account of resultatives cannot do.

4 Depictive predication: circumstantial predication and weak adjuncts

Halliday (1967) isolated three different kinds of secondary predicates: depictives, resultatives and circumstantials (although he uses the term 'conditionals'). The predicates included in this third group include the examples in (3) above, repeated here:

(3) a. John can carry that bucket *empty*.
    b. John can carry that bucket *sober*.
    c. John eats carrots *raw*.

Here the predicate intuitively gives a condition or circumstance under which the matrix predicate holds, e.g. "John can carry the bucket when it is empty/when he is sober" or "John eats carrots on condition that they are raw." Halliday also considers sentences such as (27) conditionals since they give the condition Bill was young when he died.

(27) Bill died young.

However, this is a very different, non-modal, sense of conditional and, as Himmelmann & Schultze-Berndt (2005a) argue, whatever evidence there is that the circumstantials in (3) are not true depictives does not apply to (27). (27) is not any different from the depictives in (2), except that, usually, depictive predicates are transitory, and there is an obvious sense in which *young* in (27) cannot be transitory, since after the event of dying, one's age cannot change. But we have already seen in the previous section that the non-permanence of properties denoted by depictives is a contextual issue, and so this should not be taken as a basis for arguing that (27) is an example of some different kind of predication.

The true circumstantials in (3) are very different from (27). In the examples in (3), the semantic 'effect' of the secondary predicate is truly conditional. They can all be paraphrased as explicit conditionals: (3a) can be paraphrased as "If that bucket is empty, John can carry it" , (3b) as "If John is sober, he can carry that bucket". (3c) "If carrots are raw, John eats them (too)". They 'feel' different from the depictive predicates because in the interpretation of depictives, there is no semantically determined relation between the event denoted by the verb and the state denoted by the predicate, except for the temporal containment and shared participant condition, while in the examples in (3), the conditionality implies a stronger semantic relation. Himmelmann & Schultze-Berndt (2005a) argue that there are very few ways to distinguish between depictives and circumstantials, and that circumstantials should be a subkind of 'depictives in the broad sense'. One way that they do suggest for distinguishing true depictives from circumstantials is via negation. They suggest that true depictives are under the scope of negation, while circumstantials are not. According to them, (28a) implies that John was not happy (and that *happy* is thus under the scope of negation) whereas (28b) does not have the same negative implication about the rawness of the carrots.

(28)   a. John didn't leave happy.
       b. John doesn't eat carrots raw.

However, this is not a good argument. Both (28a) and (28b) are prima facie examples of sentential negation. (28a) asserts that there was no event of John leaving happy and (28b) asserts that John does not have the habit of eating carrots raw. Different implicatures as to whether the secondary predicate is true of its subject follow from the interaction of the predicates, the modal (in (28b)) and the focal structure of the sentence. (The role of focus in licensing and interpreting depictives has been discussed insightfully in Winkler 1997.) Furthermore, (29) explicitly indicates that the circumstantial is under the scope of negation since the negative polarity item *any way* is licensed inside the secondary predicate.

(29)   John doesn't eat carrots cooked (in) any way.

There is prima facie evidence then, that circumstantials are generated in the same syntactic position as depictives. If this is the case, then the VPs in the examples in (3) should be interpreted as complex predicates formed from the secondary predicate and the matrix verb via an S-summing (or similar) operation, and the conditional effect (and any other differences between depictives and circumstantials) should be derivable from some other property of the clause.

The most obvious property that clauses containing circumstantials have in common, which distinguishes them from the depictives we have discussed up to now, is that they are all explicitly modal. This does result in differences between depictives and circumstantials. For example, free choice *any* which is licenced in (non-negative) modal contexts is acceptable in circumstantial predicates but not in 'ordinary' depictives. In (30a), *cooked in any way* is acceptable as a modifier of a generic and under the scope of a habitual, but not modifying a specific definite, within an episodic predicate as in (30b). In (30c), which is acceptable, the modifier is in the scope of a possibility operator which licenses free choice *any*, but in the infelicitous (30d), it is in the scope of a modal of necessity which fails to licence free choice *any*.

(30) a. John eats carrots cooked in any way! (He just hates carrots raw).
b. #Last night John ate the carrots cooked in anyway.
c. I can carry that suitcase full of anything.
d. #I must carry that suitcase full of anything.

This raised the possibility that circumstantials are depictives occurring under the scope of modal operators, and that the special properties of circumstantials derive from the modality of the clause. We assume that the ordinary rule of S-summing applies, and that the derived complex V will head a VP predicate which is securely under the scope of the modal. Thus (3c) will be analysed as a generic statement asserting how John eats carrots, as in (31):

(31) $\forall_{GEN} w,x,s\ [ACC(w,w_0) \wedge CARROTS(x) \wedge C(w,x,s) \rightarrow \exists e,e_1,e_2[e=^S(e_1 \sqcup e_2)$
$\wedge EAT(e_1) \wedge Ag(e_1) = JOHN \wedge Th(e_1) = x \wedge RAW(e_2) \wedge Arg(e_2) = x$
$\wedge \tau(e_1) \sqsubseteq \tau(e_2) \wedge e \sqsubseteq s]]$
"For all (non-exceptional) w,x,s, where w is a world accessible to w_0, x is in the denotation of *carrots*, and x is in a contextually relevant situation s in w, John eats x raw in s."

The conditional effects will follow as a result of the interaction of the modal, the depictive and the information structure of the sentence in ways that need to be made precise for each kind of modal.

A separate question is the relation between depictives, circumstantials and weak adjuncts. Stump (1985) draws the distinction between strong and weak adjuncts, illustrated in (32a) and (32b) respectively:

(32) a. Having unusually long arms, John can reach the ceiling.
b. Standing on a chair, John can reach the ceiling.

Stump notes that an individual level predicate in an adjunct position, as in (32a), is entailed as a property of its subject by the truth of the sentence, whereas this is not the case with the stage-level predicate adjunct in (32b). If (32a) is true, then John has unusually long arms, whereas if (32b) is true, John need not be standing on chair. Furthermore, the strong adjunct in (32a) is interpreted causally, while the weak adjunct in (32b) is interpreted conditionally.

The examples in (32) are both participial adjuncts, but the adjectival adjuncts in (33) all clearly pattern like the weak adjunct in (32b) and contrast both with the depictives discussed above, and the strong adjunct illustrated in (32a):

(33) a. Tired, John drove home.
   b. Drunk, John met Mary.
   c. Drunk, John drives dangerously.

In examples (33a–c), the adjuncts are interpreted as "when" clauses. In (33a/b) where the VP is an episodic predicate, the weak adjunct is most naturally interpreted as a fronted secondary predicate (with a tendency to predicate the secondary predicate of the subject if possible - note that by far the most natural reading of (33b) is with *drunk* predicated of the subject rather than the direct object). So (33a) most naturally means "John drove home in a state of being tired" and (33b) asserts that "John met Mary in a state of being drunk." In (33c), as in the weak adjunct in (32b), where the sentence contains a modal operator, the natural reading is to interpret the adjunct as part of the restriction on the operator, rather than as a fronted depictive, with the readings "In all contextually relevant (i.e. driving) situations in which John is drunk, he drives dangerously" and "In all contextually relevant situations in which John is standing on a chair, he can reach the ceiling." We assume that the contrast between (33a/b) and the examples (32b/33c) follows from the tripartite structure of the clause in the latter examples induced by the modal operator. This allows the fronted adjunct to be interpreted as part of the restriction on the modal. All four of these interpretations contrast with the 'strong adjunct' in (32a), which, as noted above, has a causal interpretation and is naturally paraphrased with a 'because' clause: "Because he has unusually long arms, John can reach the ceiling."

5 Remaining issues

There are necessarily a number of issues which have not even been touched on in this overview, and in this section I will mention two central ones.

(i) *subject oriented resultatives*
A number of researchers (Wechsler 1997, Verspoor 1997, Rappaport Hovav & Levin 2001) have pointed out that examples like (34) indicate that resultatives may be subject oriented:

(34) a. The wise men followed the star *out of Bethlehem*. (Wechsler 1997)
   b. John wriggled *free of his bonds*. (Rappaport Hovav & Levin 2001)

Rappaport Hovav & Levin argue that these subject oriented resultatives have a different event structure from object-oriented resultatives, suggesting that the resultative predicate is temporally dependent on the matrix event and positing a relation of 'event-conflation'. Rappaport Hovav and Levin focus on the exact conditions under which examples like (34) are possible and how these differ from the object oriented example in (1), and do not discuss compositional interpretation. Two directions for interpretation are in principle possible. One is to extend the predicate composition operations proposed in section 4 to account for (34). This is difficult because the resultative interpretation should follow from the interaction between the eventuality denoted by the predicate and the culmination of the matrix event, and such a semantic interaction should be possible only to a predicate within the VP. A second, more plausible direction is to assume that the predicates in (34) modify the matrix verb, providing a measure on the extent of the event, and deriving a telic VP, and then to argue that the resultative effect follows from the telicity of the VP.

(ii) *cross-linguistic issues*

The discussion in this overview has focused on compositional issues in the interpretation of secondary predicates in English. Many researchers have pointed out empirical differences between secondary predication in English and in other languages (see e.g. Neeleman 1994, Neeleman & Weerman 1993 for Dutch, Sybesma 1999 for Mandarin Chinese, the papers in Himmelmann & Schultze-Berndt 2005b for various languages, Washio 1997 for Japanese, Soowon & Maling 1997 for Korean, and many others).

As a cross-linguistic phenomenon, differences in secondary predication data can be sorted into approximately three kinds. (i) Essentially the same semantic operations are involved, but the precise constraints on relations between e.g. the matrix and the secondary predicate differ from language to language. This is the position implicitly taken in Himmelmann & Schultze-Berndt (2005a) with respect to cross-linguistic restrictions on what can function as a depictive predicate. (ii) Essentially the same semantic operation is involved, but at a different 'level' of grammar. For example, Neeleman (1994) and Neeleman & Weerman (1993) argue that resultative predication in Dutch is a word-formation operation. Plausibly then, in Dutch the complex-predicate formation operation proposed here in section 4 is a lexical rather than a structural operation. (iii) What look like secondary predicate constructions are actually different kinds of constructions interpreted via different operations. In this case resultatives in different languages might be only analogous to English resultatives, rather than the same kind of phenomenon. Only careful case studies can tell, for a particular language, which is the right direction to go in.

6 Conclusion

I have presented an account of secondary predications which focuses on the problem that secondary predicates cause for a compositional semantic theory. We solved the problem for depictive predicates straightforwardly by analysing them as forming complex predicates together with the matrix verb at the VP level via a semantic operation which relates the eventuality denoted by the matrix verb and the eventuality denoted by the predicate. Circumstantial predicates can be analysed as depictive predicates under the scope of a modal operator. Weak adjuncts are ambiguous between fronted depictives (in episodic sentences) and restrictions on the modal operator (in modal sentences).

Resultatives are open to analysis in one of two ways. One possibility is to analyse them as forming small clauses together with their subjects, and to posit a null lexical head which expresses the resultative relation, and which most plausibly occurs within the small clause. I suggested that there are disadvantages to this approach, namely (i) the difficulty in specifying exactly what the lexical relation is in particular because there are non-causal resultative constructions, (ii) if depictives and resultatives are analysed as non-related constructions, then we leave entirely unexplained the fact that there are precisely these two kinds of secondary predicates. I have proposed a second approach to resultative constructions which treats them as complex predicates on a par with depictive constructions but with the predicate denotation related to the culmination of the matrix event rather than the matrix verb itself. The constraints on what kind of secondary predicates there are then follows from general constraints on event structure.

We have seen that while the problem of specifying the lexical relation involved (and other related problems) may be solved in a direct predication account of resultatives, it does not seem plausible to postulate a direct predication account of depictives. Thus if resultative and depictive predication are to be treated as a unified phenomenon, a complex predicate account of both constructions must be pursued. I have tried to show that this approach seems to be fruitful, but more research is required, especially cross-linguistic research, in order to see whether the approach ultimately is successful.

With respect to cross-linguistic research, I have further noted that cross-linguistic variation occurs particularly in the properties of resultatives constructions, and that this may follow from a number of parametric differences, in particular whether complex predicate formation operates in the syntax or in the lexicon. Clearly the details of such differences and potential explanations are topics for further study.

Finally, an interesting question which has arisen recently in the work of Cormack & Smith (1992, 1999) and Kratzer (2005) is the relationship between secondary predicate formation and serial verb construction. Since both have in common that they are operations which produce a complex predicate from two heads which share an argument, it is very tempting to see parallels between them. However, as Baker (1989) has pointed out, the characterising property of true serial verb constructions is that the verbs share internal arguments, whereas in secondary predication the shared argument is always the external argument of the head of the secondary predicate. Serial verbs thus present a different, though related, problem for compositional theories of interpretation, and should therefore be treated separately.

Thanks to Paul Portner for helpful comments on an earlier version of this article!

7 References

Andrews, Avery 1982. A note on the constituent structure of adverbials and auxiliaries. *Linguistic Inquiry* 13, 313–317.
Bach, Emmon W. 1980. In defense of passive. *Linguistics & Philosophy* 3, 297–341.
Baker, Mark 1989. Object sharing and projection in serial verb constructions. *Linguistic Inquiry* 20, 513–553.
Bittner, Maria 1999. Concealed causatives. *Natural Language Semantics* 7, 1–78.
Carrier, Jill & Janet Randall 1992. The argument structure and syntactic structure of resultatives. *Linguistic Inquiry* 23, 173–234.
Chomsky, Noam 1981. *Lectures on Government and Binding*. Dordrecht: Foris.
Condoravdi, Cleo 1992. *Individual-level Predicates in Conditional Clauses*. Ms. New Haven, CT, Yale University.
Cormack, Annabel & Neil Smith 1994. Serial verbs. In: J. Harris (ed.). *UCL Working Papers in Linguistics* 6, London: University College London, 63–88.
Cormack, Annabel & Neil Smith 1999. Why are depictives different from resultatives? In: C. Iten & A. Neeleman (eds.). *UCL Working Papers in Linguistics* 11, London: University College London, 251–284.
Dowty, David 1979. *Word Meaning and Montague Grammar*. Dordrecht: Kluwer.
Franks, Steven & Norbert Hornstein 1992. Secondary predication in Russian and proper government of PRO. In: R. Larson et al. (eds.). *Control and Grammar*. Dordrecht: Kluwer, 1–50.
Halliday, Michael 1967. Notes on transitivity and theme in English, Part I. *Journal of Linguistics* 3, 37–81.
Himmelmann, Nikolaus P. & Eva Schultze-Berndt 2005a. Issues in the syntax and semantics of participant-oriented adjuncts: an introduction. In: N. Himmelmann & E. Schultze-Berndt (eds.). *Secondary Predication and Adverbial Modification*. Oxford: Oxford University Press, 1–50.
Himmelmann, Nikolaus P. & Eva Schultze-Berndt (eds.) 2005b. *Secondary Predication and Adverbial Modification*. Oxford: Oxford University Press.
Hoekstra, Teun 1988. Small clause results. *Lingua* 74, 101–139.

Kratzer, Angelika 1995. Stage-level and individual-level predicates. In: G. Carlson & F. Pelletier (eds.). *The Generic Book*, Chicago, IL: The University of Chicago Press, 125–175.
Kratzer, Angelika 2005. Building resultatives. In: C. Maienborn & A. Wöllstein (eds.). *Event Arguments. Foundations and Applications*. Tübingen: Niemeyer, 177–212.
Krifka, Manfred 1992. Thematic relations as links between nominal reference and temporal constitution. In: I. Sag & A. Szabolsci (eds.). *Lexical Matters*. Stanford, CA: CSLI Publications, 29–53.
Krifka, Manfred 1998. The origins of telicity. In: S. Rothstein (ed.). *Events and Grammar*. Dordrecht: Kluwer, 197–235.
Lasersohn, Peter 1992. Generalized conjunction and temporal modification. *Linguistics & Philosophy* 15, 381–410.
Lasersohn, Peter 1995. *Plurality, Conjunction and Events*. Dordrecht: Kluwer.
Legendre, Géraldine 1997. Secondary predication and functional projections in French. *Natural Language and Linguistic Theory* 15, 1–45.
McConnell-Ginet, Sally 1982. Adverbs and logical form. *Language* 58, 144–184.
McNally, Louise 1994. Adjunct predicates and the individual/stage level distinction. In: P. Spaelti & E. Duncan (eds.). *Proceedings of the West Coast Conference on Formal Linguistics* 12, 561–576.
McNulty, Elaine 1988. *The Syntax of Adjunct Predicates*. Ph.D. dissertation. University of Connecticut, Storrs, CT.
Neeleman, Ad 1994. *Complex Predicates*. Ph.D. dissertation. Utrecht University.
Neeleman, Ad & Fred Weerman 1993. The balance between syntax and morphology: Dutch particles and resultatives. *Natural Language and Linguistic Theory* 11, 433–475.
Parsons, Terry 1990. *Events in the Semantics of English*. Cambridge, MA: The MIT Press.
Rapoport, Tova R. 1991. Adjunct predicate licensing and D-structure. In: S. Rothstein (ed.). *Perspectives on Phrase Structure: Heads and Licensing*. New York: Academic Press, 159–187.
Rapoport, Tova R. 1999. Structure, aspect and the predicate. *Language* 75, 653–676.
Rappaport Hovav, Malka & Beth Levin 2001. An event-structure account of English resultatives. *Language* 77, 766–797.
Rothstein, Susan 1983. *The Syntactic Forms of Predication*. Ph.D. dissertation. MIT, Cambridge, MA.
Rothstein, Susan 1999. Fine-grained structure in the eventuality domain: The semantics of predicate adjective phrases and 'be'. *Natural Language Semantics* 7, 347–420.
Rothstein, Susan 2001. *Predicates and their Subjects*. Dordrecht: Kluwer.
Rothstein, Susan 2004. *Structuring Events: A Study in the Semantics of Lexical Aspect*. Oxford: Blackwell.
Rothstein, Susan 2006. Secondary predication. In: M. Everaert & H. van Riemsdijk (eds). *The Blackwell Companion to Syntax*. Oxford: Blackwell, 209–233.
Schein, Barry 1995. Predication. In: A. Cardinaletti & T. Guasti (eds.). *Small Clauses*. New York: Academic Press, 49–76.
Simpson, Jane 1983. Resultatives. In: L. Levin, M. Rappaport & A. Zaenen (eds.). *Papers in Lexical-Functional Grammar*. Bloomington, IN: Indiana University Linguistics Club, 143–158.
Soowon, Kim & Joan Maling 1997. A crosslinguistic perspective on resultative formation. In: R. Blight & M. Moosally (eds.). *The Syntax and Semantics of Predication*. Austin, TX: University of Texas, 189–204.

Stump, Gregory 1985. *The Semantic Variability of Absolute Constructions*. Dordrecht: Kluwer.
Sybesma, Rint 1999. *The Mandarin VP.* Dordrecht: Kluwer.
Vendler, Zeno 1967. *Linguistics in Philosophy*. Ithaca, NY: Cornell University.
Verspoor, Cornelia 1997. *Contextually Dependent Lexical Semantics*. Ph.D. dissertation. University of Edinburgh.
Washio, Ryuichi 1997. Resultatives, compositionality and language variation. *Journal of East Asian Linguistics* 6, 1–49.
Wechsler, Stephen 1997. Resultative predicates and control. In: R. Blight & M. Moosally (eds.). *The Syntax and Semantics of Predication*. Austin, TX: University of Texas, 307–321.
Williams, Edwin 1980. Predication. *Linguistic Inquiry* 11, 203–238.
Williams, Edwin 1983. Against small clauses. *Linguistic Inquiry* 14, 287–308.
Winkler, Susanne 1997. *Focus and Secondary Predication*. Berlin: Mouton de Gruyter.
Wunderlich, Dieter 1997. Argument extension by lexical adjunction. *Journal of Semantics* 14, 95–142.

Index

absolute clause 537
adjective 221, 222, 381–411, 417–419
adjunct clause 515, 516, 533, 535, 539
adverbial 54, 218, 334–337, 345, 407–411, 477–510, 515, 516, 521, 550
– behaviour of certain adjectives 407–411
– clauses 479, 515–539
adverb 345, 477–510
ambiguity 236–252, 268, 273–283, 302, 303, 385, 392, 409, 439
– and negation 275, 302, 439
– and semantic theory 236, 240, 243–247, 268
antonymy 172, 174, 179–181, 186, 192, 201, 222, 429, 430
argument
– linking 77, 305
– realization 67, 68, 99, 100, 103–105, 108–113, 117–122, 126, 129, 135, 138–141, 145, 194
– structure 8–11, 19, 20, 30, 61–76, 82–90, 112, 121, 127–134, 142, 143, 194, 321, 332, 336–339, 346, 383, 385
aspect shift 330, 341
aspectual
– adverbials 56–59, 72, 334, 335, 345
– coercion and rhetorical structure 338, 339
– mismatches 332, 333, 337–339
attribution 387, 393
attributive and predicative adjectives 381, 386–393

causal clause 515, 526–533
characteristics of adjectives 381–385, 408, 409
circumstantial predication 543–547, 560–563
coercion 72, 195, 247, 248, 281, 312–346, 488
cognitive and conceptual accounts 353, 363–373
cognitive semantics 199, 350, 351, 354, 363, 374
collocation 152–157, 163, 168, 183–189, 198, 199, 366
– vs. collocations 152–155

comparatives 254, 394, 397, 402, 407, 415–417, 421–425, 430, 435–438, 441–443, 457–461, 464, 467, 470
comparison 180, 251–255, 261–267, 351–353, 362, 368, 384, 394–406, 415–472, 501
complex predicates 141, 194, 543, 561, 565
compositionality 23, 38, 65, 81, 152–167, 197, 241, 283, 296, 297, 321, 322, 329, 343, 388, 501–509, 544
conceptual metaphor 23, 158, 159, 351–356, 363–373
conceptual structure 2, 3, 10, 12, 24–26, 37, 38, 59–67, 70, 74–76, 86, 112, 115, 126–145, 363–374, 509
concessive clause 515, 532, 533
contextualism and interest relativity 256, 262–268
co-occurence 152–154, 168, 367, 403

degree
– adverbial 486, 488, 506
– operators and the than-clause 444–451
– semantics 416, 417, 449, 465–471
degrees, scales and adjective meanings 417–419
denominal verbs 83, 86, 143, 144
depictive predication 543–547, 553–563
diachronic change 165, 191
Distributed Morphology 47, 86–91
dossiers 1, 29, 32–34, 39–42, 509
duality 201–228, 232, 233
– groups 201, 202, 210–228, 232
– square 212, 213, 224, 227, 233
– tests 208, 216

enriched type theories 321–325
epistemic uncertainty 256, 259
equatives 415, 425, 426
event structure 47, 48, 59–60, 66, 69–73, 77, 112–116, 126, 127, 131–136, 139–145, 194, 325, 543, 561–565
expressivity and compactness 283, 297–299

features and types 7–10
figurative language 355–363

Generative Semantics 28, 48–56, 60, 61, 66, 81, 86, 139, 142, 192
gradability 384, 390, 393, 395, 407

homogeneous ambiguities 274, 277–283, 299, 301
homonymy and polysemy 187–190, 247, 280
hyponymy 172–179, 182, 186, 187, 192

idiomaticity 154, 164
idioms 100, 102, 152–168, 183, 355, 366, 369, 370
– as constructions 159, 164, 165
– in the mental lexicon 152, 166–168
idiom-specific lexemes 156
indeterminacy 237, 238, 243, 255, 503–506
inferences 25, 33, 62, 63, 107, 122, 194, 197, 329, 351, 368, 370, 373, 390, 435, 436
instrumental clause 533, 534
internal and external negation 203–205, 215, 217
intersective and non-intersective adjectives 381, 388–393, 407, 498

lexical
– decomposition 26, 28, 31, 42, 47–66, 69, 70, 73–75, 78, 79, 91, 104, 114–117, 193
– entailments 60, 119
– properties of idioms 153–157
– semantics 54, 59, 66, 70, 99, 141, 174, 187, 190, 247, 481, 482
– variation 158, 161–168
Lexical Conceptual Structure 59, 66, 67, 70, 86, 112, 115, 126, 199
Lexical Decomposition Grammar 48, 69, 73–75, 78
Lexical Relational Structures 47, 48, 81–85, 127, 142
locative adverbials 256, 478, 494, 501–504, 515
Logical Form 2, 3, 28, 54, 243, 286, 295, 300–306, 416, 420, 421, 424, 426, 444, 489, 490, 499

manner adverbials 478, 482, 486–488, 493, 498, 499, 506–509, 515
meaning postulates and semantic atomism 196–198

measure phrases 383, 395, 398, 401, 418, 433–435, 439, 460–468
mental-attitude adverbial 486, 487, 490, 499
mental structure 1, 25, 74, 371
metaphor 23, 40–43, 116, 158, 159, 163, 174, 184, 185, 189, 190, 248, 281, 350–374
– traditional approaches to 352–354
metonymy 190, 248, 281, 350–355, 363, 373–376
mismatches 312–346
modifier 61–67, 74, 132, 174, 184, 241, 279–282, 306, 327, 381–385, 390–400, 403–407, 410, 430, 479, 480–488, 496–501, 504, 529, 561
Montague Semantics 4, 47, 48, 56–59, 70, 194
multiplying syntactic structures 299–301
multi-word units 152–155, 168

Natural Semantic Metalanguage 47, 48, 79–81
negation relation 205–210, 222, 233
non-compositionality 152–157, 160

paradigmatic relations (see also *sense relations*) 173–176, 183, 186, 187, 199
participial clause 535–537
part-whole relations 75, 174, 182, 406
perfective/imperfective contrast in Romance 341–345
phase quantification 201, 202, 221, 228–233
Phonetic Form 2, 3
phrasal comparatives 423–425, 472
phrasal lexical items 154
positive and antonyms 180, 222, 230, 396, 403, 428–431
pragmatic accounts of metaphor 352, 354–361
predicate decomposition 47, 48, 63, 126–132, 135, 136, 139–142, 145
predication 66–70, 108, 201–207, 213–217, 221, 223–228, 233, 254, 387, 393, 481–484, 489, 543–549, 552–560, 564–566
primes and universals 38–43
primitive predicates 54, 66, 128, 132, 135–138
primitive thematic roles 64, 109–111
psycholinguistic approaches to figurative language 361–363
purpose clause 121, 530–532

quantification 30, 52, 81, 82, 201–203, 213–223, 226–233, 275, 289–293, 303, 311, 411, 415, 427, 454, 468, 516–523, 538

relative and absolute adjectives 381, 389, 393–406, 430
relevance theory 178, 350, 352, 355–357, 360, 361, 372–374
resultative 54, 58, 78, 113, 140, 141, 165, 490, 491, 507, 543–555, 558–560, 563–565
– predication 547–559, 564
result clause 525–527
Romance simple present 341
root vs. event structure 126, 133–136, 145

secondary predicates 478, 490, 491, 543–548, 554, 557–566
selectional restriction 53, 55, 155, 156, 172
semantic
– classes of adjectives 381–411
– form 1, 3, 10, 36, 74–77, 127, 306
– theory 54–60, 63–69, 99, 100, 173, 192, 206, 236–240, 243, 244, 255, 268, 321, 322, 472, 501, 543, 546, 565
– types 174, 194, 251, 322, 381, 382, 386–391, 394, 417
– underspecification 116, 247, 272–314, 335, 345
sense exclusion/inclusion 174, 175, 181
sense relations 172–174, 177, 186, 187, 190–198, 204, 247
– and word meaning 172–174, 177, 190–192, 198
– basic 173, 174
– paradigmatic 172–176, 179, 182, 183, 186, 187, 192–199
– syntagmatic 174, 183, 195, 196
small clause 113, 537, 538, 543, 546–554, 565
speaker-oriented adverbial 483, 484, 493
Square of Oppositions 202, 223–225, 227, 233
subevents 67, 70–73, 77, 104, 109, 115, 126, 139–141, 536, 559
subeventual analysis 126, 139, 141
subject-oriented adverbial 482–486, 493
subnegation 208–213, 222, 233
superlatives 254, 409, 415, 425–427, 442, 465

supervaluations 256–259, 262
synonymy 172, 174, 177–179, 186, 192
syntagmatic relations (see also *sense relations*) 172, 183, 186, 187, 194, 199
syntax-semantics interface 63, 69, 99, 105, 241, 243, 273, 283, 287, 299–302, 306–309, 415, 472, 478, 492–495
systematic/idiosyncratic features 1, 17, 28–33, 39, 41

temporal clause 516–524, 539
testing for ambiguity 242
thematic hierarchies 64, 73, 99–101, 111–121, 142
thematic relation 100, 114, 118, 135, 137, 549
thematic role(s) 1, 18, 60, 64, 66, 72, 73, 85, 99–122, 135, 142, 312, 313, 489, 549
– and aspectual phenomena 64, 72, 108,
– and plurality 100, 108
– in model-theoretic semantics 60, 101–105, 115, 122
– systems 103, 109–122
– uniqueness 104–110, 113–117
Two-level Semantics 73–79, 86, 280
type coercion 195, 321–329, 337, 345, 346
– in comprehension 329, 330
type mismatch 321–325, 328, 345, 462

underspecification 116, 188, 247, 272–275, 279–286, 289–291, 294–299, 302–310, 330–336, 346, 352, 505
– in Natural Languagage Processing 303–305
underspecified representation 272, 282–284, 287, 289, 292–295, 304, 306, 309–311
universals 38, 69

vagueness 177, 188, 236–240, 252–263, 266–268, 273, 274, 282, 352, 381–387, 393–396, 465
verb phrase idioms 152–154
veridicality 481–483, 524, 528

word sense 173
world knowledge 13, 74, 121, 136, 174, 183, 196, 325, 505

www.ingramcontent.com/pod-product-compliance
Lightning Source LLC
Chambersburg PA
CBHW031538300426
44111CB00006BA/103